THE
DRAFT

THE
DRAFT

• A Year Inside the NFL's Search for Talent •

PETE WILLIAMS

St. Martin's Press ⚑ *New York*

For Lance

www.stmartins.com

Book design by Michael Collica

LIBRARY OF CONGRESS CATALOGING-IN-PUBLICATION DATA

Williams, Pete, 1969–
     The draft : a year inside the NFL's search for talent / Pete Williams.
         p. cm.
     ISBN-13: 978-0-312-35438-1
     ISBN-10: 0-312-35438-X
     1. Football draft—United States. 2. Football players—United States—
Recruiting. 3. National Football League. I. Title.

GV954.32.W55 2006
796.332'64—dc22

                                                                    2005057440

First Edition: March 2006

10 9 8 7 6 5 4 3 2 1

CONTENTS

THE
DRAFT

PROLOGUE

THE 2005 NFL DRAFT
Saturday, April 23, 2005

T he citizens of Waycross, Georgia turned out in force to watch the 2005 NFL Draft. More than three hundred gathered at the city's new community center to honor Fred Gibson, who had gone from Waycross to stardom at the University of Georgia and now was looking at a big payday in the NFL.

Banners were posted, along with blown-up images from Gibson's Bulldogs career. There were wide-screen televisions tuned to ESPN, a giant, bouncy house set up for the kids, and an impressive spread of ribs, barbecue, chicken, potato salad, baked beans, and cake.

Gibson, a skinny six-four wide receiver, arrived at the community center an hour into the first round and couldn't believe the turnout. His immediate family was there, along with uncles, aunts, cousins, former coaches, and seemingly everyone he had known since early childhood.

NFL teams selected three wide receivers among the first picks— Braylon Edwards of Michigan, South Carolina's Troy Williamson, and Mike Williams of Southern Cal—but Gibson was not concerned. He didn't expect to get picked that early.

His agents Doug Hendrickson and Demetro Stephens of Octagon were not on hand but offered encouragement over the phone. They believed Gibson could go as early as the end of the first round, certainly no later than the third.

It was a festive atmosphere at the Waycross community center. The guest of honor played the role of gracious host, all the while keeping an eye on ESPN. The draft proceeded slowly during the first round, with selections trickling out every fifteen minutes.

Gibson grew a little anxious at the end of the round when the Baltimore Ravens chose Oklahoma's Mark Clayton at number twenty-two and the hometown Atlanta Falcons opted for Roddy White of Alabama-Birmingham at number twenty-seven. Gibson had worked out alongside Clayton and White at the Senior Bowl, the late-January all-star game in Mobile, Alabama. He couldn't begrudge the teams for drafting such talented receivers.

The party grew silent early in the second round when the Philadelphia Eagles selected Reggie Brown, who also was a wide receiver out of the University of Georgia. The two Bulldogs were linked together, though for much of their careers Gibson was viewed as the better pro prospect.

Gibson pumped his fist and smiled. "Good for Reggie," he said.

The draft moved more quickly now, just five minutes per pick starting with the second round, and Gibson paid closer attention. "Just sit tight," Hendrickson told him over the phone.

More receivers came off the board. The Chicago Bears selected Oklahoma's Mark Bradley. Roscoe Parrish, a speedy five-ten receiver from Miami, went to the Buffalo Bills. The Green Bay Packers picked up Terrence Murphy from Texas A&M and the San Diego Chargers grabbed Northern Colorado's Vincent Jackson.

Gibson stood in disbelief as the second round ended. He checked his cell phone to make sure he hadn't missed anything. Friends did their best to distract him. Surely he would go soon.

The third round got underway shortly after 9:00 P.M. The Tennessee Titans, with the fourth pick in the round, chose Indiana's Courtney Roby. Teams were drafting quickly now, but it seemed nobody wanted a wide receiver. Fourteen selections passed. Much of the Waycross crowd dispersed, but Gibson remained. Surely the call would come soon.

The Cincinnati Bengals were on the clock now, having already selected two of Gibson's Georgia teammates: defensive end David Pollack in the first and linebacker Odell Thurman in the second. The Bengals chose a wide receiver in the third round, but it was Chris Henry of West Virginia.

Two picks later, the Seattle Seahawks selected Georgia quarterback David Greene. Gibson was happy for "Greeney." Like the rest of his

Bulldogs teammates, Greene was picked at or before where most of the endless mock drafts projected him in the weeks leading up to the draft.

The next ten selections yielded no receivers. It was approaching 11:00 P.M. when Tennessee drafted Brandon Jones. Gibson couldn't believe it. Did the entire NFL really consider *three* wide receivers from Oklahoma better than him?

The crowd had all but departed by the time the Denver Broncos ended the first day of the draft by selecting Maurice Clarett, a controversial figure for his failed attempt to challenge the NFL's draft-eligibility rules and for accusing Ohio State, his former school, of all manner of wrongdoing.

There would be four more rounds tomorrow. Gibson put on a brave face and accepted encouragement from the stragglers. As he drove his white GMC Yukon back to his grandmother's house, he pondered how much money he had lost in the last twelve hours.

A year earlier, the last pick in the second round—defensive end Marquis Hill of Louisiana State University—received a signing bonus of $1.15 million from the New England Patriots. The final draftee in the third round—Purdue linebacker Landon Johnson, taken by the Cincinnati Bengals—received a signing bonus of $441,000. Gibson didn't even want to think about first-round cash.

But it wasn't just the money. Gibson knew that where a player was drafted influenced the direction of his career. Sure, plenty of low draft picks went on to stardom; New England Patriots quarterback Tom Brady, a sixth-round pick, was the NFL's most visible example. Still, the higher a player was drafted, the more slack teams would give him to learn complex schemes and make an impact. Teams found it easier to cut ties with players in which they had invested little.

How, Gibson wondered, did teams forget about him? Had he not done everything he could have since his college career ended on New Year's Day, when Georgia defeated Wisconsin in the Outback Bowl in Tampa?

Gibson excelled at the Senior Bowl and performed decently at the NFL scouting combine in February. Admittedly, his time in the forty-yard dash (4.55 seconds) was nothing to brag about, but he had run faster for scouts during the University of Georgia's "pro day" in March. Over the last four months, he had undergone dozens of interviews with NFL teams and always came across as gregarious, confident yet humble. Everyone loved "Freddy G."

At least that's how it seemed to Gibson. Surely, NFL teams did not view *thirteen* wide receivers in a better light. Did they?

Back home, Gibson broke down in front of his grandmother, Delores Bethea, who had raised him after her daughter, Brenda, gave birth to him at age thirteen. It was the first time he had cried in front of Bethea in years.

"They're telling me I can't play football," he sobbed. "Am I not good enough to play?"

Bethea comforted her grandson. Tomorrow would be another day.

In Charlotte, Chris Canty tried not to watch the draft. It was like passing an automobile accident; he knew it was ugly but had to know what was happening. Unlike Fred Gibson, he kept the day a low-key affair. He wisely did not invite friends over, preferring to watch with family. As the day wore on, his parents, both brothers, and assorted uncles and aunts tried to turn the topic of conversation elsewhere.

The last eight months had been a roller coaster for Canty, a six-seven defensive end who had played at the University of Virginia. Before the 2004 season, many scouts viewed Canty as a potential first-round pick. A month into the year, he shredded three of the four ligaments in his left knee during a game against Syracuse. He underwent grueling rehabilitation to restore the knee and by late January was feeling close to 100 percent.

That's when he walked into a nightclub in Scottsdale and ended up in a scuffle. Words were exchanged. In the darkness, someone smashed a bottle in Canty's face. He suffered a detached left retina. Even now, three months later, there still were bruises.

Some teams worried about the eye. Others had concerns about the knee. Some wondered about both. Still, Canty believed he could go as high as the second round, at least that's what he said agent Ethan Lock had led him to think.

Canty had spent the last month trying to eliminate the concern teams had about his knee and eye. It didn't help that he did not work out at the University of Virginia's pro day in Charlottesville on March 23, taking a few extra weeks to prepare for a private workout at his former high school in Charlotte. Since he missed the first day of the NFL combine, where players are physically examined, tested, and interviewed before all thirty-two teams in Indianapolis, he had to travel back to Indianapolis in early April for a physical. The knee checked out fine, but the eye doctor expressed concern about the retina. Those reservations became part of the official league file.

A dozen teams sent representatives to Canty's workout on April 14. The Baltimore Ravens and Dallas Cowboys also flew him in for interviews. Canty performed all of the familiar combine drills, but concerns lingered.

"There's not much market for a one-legged, one-eyed defensive end," one general manager said before the draft.

So Canty watched as teams selected five defensive ends in the first round. He couldn't argue with the picks, though it still hurt to see guys he once was rated alongside go high. At Virginia, Canty had played a key role in head coach Al Groh's 3-4 defense, an increasingly popular scheme in the NFL that featured three down lineman and four linebackers.

Groh had spent much of his coaching career as an NFL assistant under Bill Parcells, who was remodeling his Dallas Cowboys defense into the 3-4. Parcells wielded two picks in the first round and chose a pair of defensive ends with no major physical ailments, Troy State's Demarcus Ware and Marcus Spears of LSU.

The second round featured just two defensive ends. The Miami Dolphins grabbed Iowa's Matt Roth with the fourteenth pick. Canty figured his best hope was the Ravens, and they did select an end with the twenty-first pick, but it was Oklahoma's Dan Cody.

By the third round, Canty began thinking the wait could go into Sunday. Only two teams took ends. Those players, Notre Dame's Justin Tuck (New York Giants) and Vincent Burns of Kentucky (Indianapolis Colts), were rated below Canty, at least before the eye injury.

Few players had fallen as far as Canty, who sighed as the Broncos picked the ultimate damaged goods, former Ohio State running back Maurice Clarett, to close ESPN's first day of draft coverage.

Shirley Canty tried to console her son. A tall, striking woman, she served as pastor of the Calvary United Methodist Church in Charlotte. "You have to trust God's plan for your life," she said.

Chris nodded. Tomorrow was Sunday, the second day of the NFL Draft. They would pray about it in the morning. Perhaps later that day God's plan would materialize.

For now, Chris stared at the wide-screen television in the corner of the living room. Throughout the room were framed news clippings from his career at the University of Virginia, along with a handsome display of his oversized diploma, and a photo taken from the center of the school's historic grounds, an area designed by school founder Thomas Jefferson

ESPN analysts were recapping the day's events. Canty watched the names scroll along the bottom. There were former University of Virginia teammates, along with opposing players he had outplayed. There were guys he had trained with in Arizona before the NFL scouting combine, and a few names that didn't ring a bell.

All told, one hundred and one players heard from NFL teams on the first day of the NFL Draft. Sixteen months earlier, after Canty's junior season, there were agents and draft experts projecting him as a second-round pick for the 2004 draft if he left school early. Even an NFL advisory committee rated him a potential first-day selection.

Instead, Canty bypassed the draft, hung around to earn the diploma, enrolled in graduate school, and now was staring blankly at Chris Berman, wondering how so much could change so quickly.

Chapter One:

FIRST CONTACTS

E d Hawthorne and Ed Walsh looked at the young football agent sitting across the table from them and chuckled. Jack Scharf seemed right out of central casting. With a lantern jaw, bleached-white teeth, and jelled dark hair, he looked like a taller Tom Cruise. The forty-five-hundred-dollar, custom-tailored Armani suit, cuff links and white monogrammed shirt he wore covered a lean physique, shaved to accentuate the muscles. Scharf's rented Jaguar XJ8 sat outside Walsh's law office in New Haven, Connecticut.

"Say it, Jack," Hawthorne said.

Scharf shook his head. "C'mon guys."

Hawthorne raised an eyebrow. "Jack?"

"All right," Scharf said, taking a deep breath. "Show me the money."

Walsh and Hawthorne laughed. "Not bad," Hawthorne said. "Louder."

"Show Me the Money!" Scharf yelled, channeling Cruise. *"Show . . . Me . . . the . . . Mon-ey!"*

The Eds cackled. It was early September 2004, and Scharf was among the first agents to make a presentation in the hopes of representing Hawthorne's nephew, Anttaj, a 312-pound defensive tackle at the University of Wisconsin, for the 2005 NFL Draft.

There was little resemblance between Ed and Anttaj. Walsh, the family attorney, liked to greet agents in a conference room first and then introduce Ed Hawthorne to gauge the response. Most agents showed little reaction, though the recruiting process did have its amusing moments.

Whenever agents reached Anttaj on his cell phone in Wisconsin, he directed them to Uncle Ed. One agent called Uncle Ed and immediately dealt the race card.

"You know, Ed," the agent said. "All of our brothers are coming out of the NFL today and they're broke. Why? Because of the white agents, that's why; and I'm here to make sure that doesn't happen to 'Taj."

Hawthorne paused. "Do you realize I'm white?"

Ed's sister, Eileen, had raised her biracial son alone.

"Well, you know," the agent said after an awkward pause, "I've got white family, too."

That agent never got a meeting with the Eds, who vetted potential representatives for Anttaj, allowing him to spend his senior season focused on football and not on who might guide him through the NFL Draft in April.

The Eds liked what they saw of Jack Scharf, who beneath the slick, Jerry Maguire veneer had, at thirty-five, established himself as a legitimate player in the brutal world of football agents. He had flown from his office in San Antonio to New Haven armed with binders full of spreadsheets and contract information, showing how his company—Momentum Sports—had skillfully landed contracts for its clients at better than the market rate.

Scharf's presentation included testimonials from clients such as Nick Barnett, a linebacker drafted in the first round out of Oregon State by the Green Bay Packers in 2003. There were DVDs outlining the marketing efforts Momentum would undertake on behalf of Anttaj, and the trainers the company would employ to get Anttaj ready for the February NFL scouting combine in Indianapolis, where draft hopefuls are tested physically and psychologically by NFL teams.

The Eds flipped through Scharf's literature. His clients from the previous year were a mix of third- and fourth-round selections, though the Denver Broncos selected Tatum Bell, a running back from Oklahoma State, in the second round.

"You do all of this for a third-round pick?" Hawthorne asked. Anttaj Hawthorne was considered, at this early stage, a likely first-round choice.

"Absolutely," Scharf said.

The meeting, which had begun late in the afternoon, continued for three hours. At this early juncture, the Eds had met with only a few agents and were still in the information-gathering stage, learning how contracts were negotiated and what the process leading up to the NFL Draft entailed.

In the coming weeks, the Eds would investigate Scharf and the rest of the agents they interviewed. They would start on the Internet, searching through Google, and follow up with calls to the NFL Players Association to determine if any agents had been disciplined or engaged in unethical activity.

For now, they liked what they saw of Jack Scharf—or "Show Me," as they would call him throughout Walsh's firm. The ladies in the office would become fond of Show Me, though the older ones tended to prefer Tom Condon, the former Kansas City Chiefs lineman-turned-lawyer and agent, who, at fifty-two, looked like an older version of Jack Scharf.

NFL playing experience was the least of the advantages Condon held over Scharf, a graduate of UCLA and the Southwestern University School of Law in Los Angeles, who had been a licensed NFL agent for less than three years. As head of the football division for the International Management Group (IMG), the world's largest sports agency, Condon was the most powerful agent in football, with a lengthy list of clients that included Indianapolis Colts quarterback Peyton Manning and his brother Eli, who had been the top pick in the 2004 draft.

Condon also was a New Haven native whose high school, Notre Dame of West Haven, was a rival of Anttaj's Hamden High. Condon had scored a July meeting with the Eds that included Anttaj, who had not yet returned to Wisconsin.

For now, Condon was the leader in the race to secure Anttaj, though the Eds had other agents to interview. There would be more to learn about contracts, marketing, and the NFL draft process.

But as they said good-bye to Jack Scharf, sending him on his way in the Jaguar XJ8, they concluded that "Show Me" definitely was in the running.

On a late afternoon in mid-September, Pat Dye Jr. looked out the window of his sixteenth-floor office overlooking Lenox Square in Atlanta's upscale Buckhead district. Already the city's notorious traffic was beginning to thicken on the surrounding arteries.

Though it was just a week after Labor Day, the recruiting season for the 2005 NFL Draft was well underway, and already Dye knew his Pro-

Files Sports Management firm was in a dogfight for talent in its own backyard.

The son of the former longtime Auburn football coach, Pat Dye Jr. had over the previous seventeen years parlayed a childhood spent around college football and his dad's vast network of connections into a lucrative agent practice.

Now Dye Jr. and his business partner, Bill Johnson, represented forty NFL players, nearly all of which attended college in the southeast. Almost half of their clients had played at Auburn or the University of Georgia, located an hour away in Athens.

Atlanta had become a popular base of operations for sports agents. The NFL Players Association counted forty-seven registered agents from greater Atlanta. Most of the schools in the football-rich Southeastern Conference were within a four-hour drive, along with much of the Atlantic Coast Conference. Three prominent precombine training centers are based in Atlanta, along with the NFL's Falcons, who train out of palatial digs in the northeastern suburb of Flowery Branch.

Auburn and Georgia figured to be the nation's most fertile agent-recruiting grounds for the 2005 NFL Draft. Auburn had three players projected as likely first-rounders—running backs Ronnie Brown and Carnell "Cadillac" Williams, along with defensive back Carlos Rogers. Quarterback Jason Campbell's stock also was rising.

At Georgia, fiery defensive end David Pollack had surprised many people by not turning pro after his junior season. Dye, like other agents, had conceded Pollack to IMG and Tom Condon, who made inroads with the player as a junior. Pollack, under NCAA rules, could not commit to an agent, even orally, but the rest of the field knew better than to waste their time.

Dye was in the hunt for Pollack's roommate, quarterback David Greene, along with Georgia's two wide receivers, Reggie Brown and Fred Gibson. But the player Dye and his competitors lusted after was Thomas Davis, a 220-pound safety who NFL scouts projected as a future All-Pro linebacker in the mold of Ray Lewis, the Baltimore Ravens star. Davis and linebacker Odell Thurman were juniors, but, like Pollack a year earlier, they faced the tantalizing prospect of turning pro early.

Dye organized his recruiting by starting with a list of thirty to forty prospects in May. Some, such as Greene, Brown, Rogers, and Williams, he had recruited for more than two years. From there, he contacted twenty players via phone or mail, figuring he would have a serious shot with a dozen and sign five or six.

At forty-two, Dye came across as younger, with a thick mane of light brown hair, a slight Southern drawl, and a perpetual smile. "If agent recruiting was a beauty contest," said agent Ken Harris, a friendly rival based in Tampa, "Pat Dye would win every time."

Dye didn't fit the profile of a football agent, at least not in the Jerry Maguire or Jack Scharf sense, but his route was not an unfamiliar one. After graduating from Auburn in 1984 and Samford University's law school in 1987, he went to work at the Birmingham firm of Burr and Forman, serving as an attorney while building a football representation business on the side.

Two months after receiving his agent certification by the NFL Players Association, Dye traveled to Mobile, Alabama, for the Senior Bowl, the annual postseason meat market of draft-eligible talent. He arrived at the hotel lobby conservatively dressed in a pinstripe suit and wingtips, and encountered every sleazy stereotype he'd feared. There were agents dressed like pimps, openly paying players. There were agent "runners" promising women and even drugs to potential clients. It was everything Pat Dye Sr. had warned him about and more.

"There's nothing a college football coach hates more than dealing with agents," Dye Jr. says. "They distract the player, potentially jeopardize eligibility. And, I told my father, for those reasons I wanted to go into it. The industry needed more honest, reputable people, and I know that sounds self-righteous. He warned me. 'If you did it the right way, and I know you will, it's going to be a long uphill battle getting players, because I know the kind of things that go on in this business.' And he was right."

Dye almost got back in the car and returned to Birmingham. Instead, he stayed, vowing to build his business aboveboard. His name helped, along with his father's network of contacts. Within eighteen months, Dye Jr. had built a practice of about a dozen clients. Recognizing that the process of recruiting NFL clients was akin to solicitation in the law field, Dye took his clients to Atlanta and the sports entertainment division of Robinson-Humphrey, a major financial services firm.

There Dye worked under Richard Howell, who represented just one NFL player, former Georgia Tech linebacker Pat Swilling of the New Orleans Saints. Howell was better known for his NBA clients, and over the next four years Dye helped Howell land Tech point guard Kenny Anderson, Clemson center Elden Campbell, and Tom Gugliotta, a forward from North Carolina State.

The football practice also thrived. Dye and Howell signed running backs Emmitt Smith and Garrison Hearst, defensive end Tony Bennett, and defensive tackle Kelvin Pritchett. Soon the entrepreneurial bug bit Dye, and in January of 1994 he and an assistant left Howell, setting up shop on Dye's dining room table before dividing his basement into two offices.

Dye signed everything away to get a bank line of credit. Within two months he had negotiated nearly $20 million in new contracts, including a $12 million deal for Bennett with the Colts that included a $3 million signing bonus. That enabled Dye to lease office space in Buckhead.

It was an amicable departure; Dye had, after all, brought a football business to Robinson-Humphrey. Swilling stayed with Howell. So did Smith, who was in the midst of a long-term deal with Dallas. Hearst joined Dye two years later after his contract expired.

Now, nearly a decade later, Dye's client list included few superstars, but plenty of solid veterans such as Atlanta Falcons linebacker Keith Brooking and defensive tackle Rod Coleman, Minnesota Vikings running back Michael Bennett, and Dexter Coakley, the Dallas Cowboys linebacker. Dye represented Jon and Matt Stinchcomb, offensive tackles out of the University of Georgia who, during the 2004 season, played for the New Orleans Saints and Tampa Bay Buccaneers respectively.

Dye loved his work, though it was a brutal business, especially for a father of two children under the age of four. Many of his competitors were single or had a staff of young agents to handle the bulk of the recruiting. Dye still was struggling with the transition to fatherhood while working in a business where clients demand round-the-clock attention.

"I had my first meeting with a recruit and his family this past weekend," Dye said. "I can always be called slow out of the gate. May and June are the only months to catch your breath. I have two young kids, and obviously we're here for existing clients, but I try not to beat the bushes in those months. Then July comes and we have rookie negotiations. In August, you're just monitoring players and hoping they make their teams. Yeah, you're assessing your recruiting list, but I don't get out personally until September."

Dye knew better than to take any business for granted. Larger agencies such as Octagon and SFX had increased their presence in the southeast in recent years. Condon and IMG would swoop in for a high-profile client such as Pollack or Eli Manning, the Ole Miss quarterback taken first the previous year.

But as Dye mapped out his intense fall calendar of recruiting, a more low-profile opponent was taking aim at Dye's home turf of Auburn and Georgia.

Across Lenox Square, Todd France was looking to take his one-year-old sports agency to the next level.

Far beyond the Pat Dye Jr. level.

It had been quiet a year for France and his young agency, FAME (France Athlete Management Enterprises). On August 24, 2003, France resigned from Career Sports Management, the Atlanta agency where he had spent four years building the football division under CSM founder Lonnie Cooper, who represented numerous NBA head coaches, along with Atlanta Braves pitcher John Smoltz.

On September 3, 2003, France's most prominent client, running back Priest Holmes, signed a four-year contract extension with the Kansas City Chiefs worth potentially thirty-six million dollars. The following day, sixteen Career Sports clients faxed termination letters to Cooper's office, hiring France.

Cooper did not let France go quietly. Five weeks later, Career Sports filed suit against France and FAME in Fulton County, Georgia, Superior Court, seeking a judgment that CSM was entitled to all fees from player contracts consummated before September 9, 2003, and unspecified damages against France and FAME.

The saga was a familiar one in the football agent business. A young, aspiring agent goes to work for an established firm to learn the industry. He soon finds he's doing much of the grunt work of recruiting and babysitting clients. Frustrated that the managing partner gets all of the credit, to say nothing of some, if not all, of the commissions, he decides to bolt and start his own agency. The clients, who have grown close to the younger agent, follow.

In 2001, David Dunn left veteran agent Leigh Steinberg, taking fifty clients with him. Steinberg filed suit, and in November of 2002 a jury awarded Steinberg $44.6 million in damages. The NFL Players Association's disciplinary committee voted to suspend Dunn for two years, but Dunn filed for personal bankruptcy, which halted all administrative actions against him. (A federal appeals court overturned the $44.6 million verdict in March of 2005, ruling that mistakes were made by the trial court judge.)

Dunn continued to operate, landing prominent clients for the 2003 and 2004 drafts.

Darrell Wills took a similar route.

Wills worked for IMG, serving as a lead recruiter and agent in the southeast. Shortly before the 2004 draft, he left to form his own agency, taking six clients with him. The NFLPA revoked the agent certification of Wills on the grounds that he violated a non-compete clause in his IMG contract.

Wills reinvented himself as an athlete manager, in the mold of a Hollywood agency. He founded Imagine Sports, partnered with a certified agent and a financial advisor, and began recruiting players for the 2005 NFL Draft.

France's situation was not entirely analogous. Dunn and Wills had joined established football agencies led by two of the NFL's most prominent agents, Steinberg and Tom Condon, respectively. Cooper's background was in representing NBA head coaches and a handful of baseball players. His primary business was creating sports sponsorship deals for companies such as Bell South, the Home Depot, and Keebler.

France, who came to work for Cooper as a marketing employee less than a year out of college, in April of 1994, created the football division virtually from scratch in 1999. Prior to that, the company's only football clients were former University of Georgia quarterback Eric Zeier and another ex-Bulldog, Brandon Tolbert, a linebacker drafted in the seventh round by Jacksonville in 1998.

While Cooper's lawsuit meandered through the courts, France pushed ahead. For the 2004 draft, he landed Georgia Tech linebacker Daryl Smith and Darius Watts, a wide receiver from Marshall University. Both were chosen in the second round.

Now, just a year after leaving Cooper, France had a well-appointed suite of offices not far from Dye, in the shadow of the Ritz-Carlton Buckhead and Emeril's restaurant. There were plenty of blond-wood furnishings and a marketing room full of posters and point-of-sale advertising pieces featuring clients such as Holmes and linebackers Takeo Spikes (Buffalo Bills) and Kendrell Bell (Pittsburgh Steelers).

At thirty-three, France looked younger, despite a few flecks of gray. He kept his otherwise dark hair short, which accentuated protruding ears, and though he possessed a wry, self-deprecating sense of humor, he wore a perpetual look of suspicion. France, who was single, spent much of his time on the road. There were clients to recruit and NFL veterans to service. He often pulled into rest areas to avoid falling asleep at the wheel. On this morning in mid-September, France had made an appearance in the office, though it would be brief. It was Rosh Hashanah.

Tomorrow, it would be back to recruiting. He was lobbying hard for Georgia safety Thomas Davis, Auburn defensive back Carlos Rogers, and Roddy White, a wide receiver from the University of Alabama-Birmingham. France also was on the hunt for Auburn running back Ronnie Brown. Unlike Dye, who was recruiting both Brown and Cadillac Williams, France had decided it best to recruit just one Auburn back.

It was a bold wish list for a young agency, albeit one with established clients such as Holmes, Spikes, and Bell. Already France had heard stories of other agents telling potential clients about the Cooper lawsuit. Besides, his competitors told recruits, France never had represented a first-round pick.

"Can it be that hard?" France asks, sitting at a conference table. "I have eighteen clients. It's not like I just started last year. I did a $36-million contract for Priest Holmes, a $32 million deal for Takeo Spikes. This is all about sales, selling your capabilities, and selling yourself to parents that you can take care of their son and do whatever it is you need to do. And that's not just the contract, that's everything. Someone is going to want the huge agency. You can't win everyone. But you get your foot in the game and you battle away.

"I don't care what you tell me, I'm going to go for it. I know what my capabilities are and what I can deliver, and I'm going to preach it, communicate it, and hope that they agree. There's no exact recipe for any of this, but nobody is going to stop me. I will be relentless."

Jack Scharf was running on adrenaline. His meeting with Ed Hawthorne and Ed Walsh was part of a four-day stint crisscrossing the country, trying to convince the parents that he was the man to represent their sons for the 2005 NFL Draft.

Though it was still mid-September, the draft eight months away, recruiting season was in full swing for "Show Me" Scharf and the rest of the more than 1,300 football agents competing for just 400 or so players who stood any chance at becoming one of the 255 players selected by one of the NFL's thirty-two teams in late April.

At this point, many players with any shot of a pro career had been dealing with agents for at least four months. Many top stars, as freshman and sophomores, begin hearing from agents just hoping to lay the groundwork for when they become draft eligible.

Starting in May of their draft-eligible year, when the NFL's scouting combines release their evaluations of rising seniors, agents begin an all-out blitz on the nation's top talent.

There is a constant barrage of overnight packages, with binders, CD-ROMs, DVDs, and other media from agents touting their skills and experience. Former college teammates, now in the pros, call of on behalf of their reps to recruit. The agents themselves phone players and their parents relentlessly.

Though NCAA regulations prohibit players from committing to agents, even orally, some players make up their minds early, if only to clear the phone lines and make time for girlfriends, parties, and perhaps even a little studying.

To stay within the guidelines, players often do not reveal their choice of agent, sometimes not even to the winning party, until after their final game. Other players deal with the hard sales pitches, spending their fall semesters meeting with agents after classes and practices. Some, like Wisconsin's Anttaj Hawthorne and Georgia's David Pollack, enlisted family members to narrow the field.

That's where Scharf believed he held an advantage. He was not afraid to embark on a grueling travel schedule, like the one this week that took him from his office in San Antonio on Monday to New Haven to visit the Hawthorne camp.

Scharf woke up on Tuesday to fly to Cleveland and meet the family of Justin Geisinger, a left tackle from Vanderbilt, moved on to Fort Lauderdale on Wednesday to charm the family of another Vanderbilt player, defensive end Jovan Haye, before arriving in Tampa to visit with the parents of Louisville wide receiver J. R. Russell.

Now, sitting in the Champions sports bar at Tampa's Westshore Marriott shortly after midnight on Friday, Scharf felt good about the week.

Scharf believed that if he could just get into the home, he could make a successful pitch, using his professional presentation, charm, and even his looks to make a lasting impression. In this way, he was like Tom Cruise's Jerry Maguire, who fancied himself "The Lord of the Living Room."

Jerry Maguire pulled up to the homes of prospective clients in a rented Pontiac Grand Prix or Ford Taurus. Not Scharf, who insisted on a four-door Jaguar XJ8, or even the tan convertible version that Hertz has provided in Tampa at a cost of $129 a day, a bargain compared to rates in many cities.

"It's for that ten-minute period when the player walks you out to the car at the end of a meeting," Scharf said. "Do you want to be seen in a convertible Jag or a Toyota Camry? Obviously, you've got to sell yourself as a skilled negotiator and someone who can market the player to NFL teams and get him ready for the draft. But sometimes it's that ten minutes that makes the difference. Perception is reality.

"I spent six thousand dollars on this trip. Hotel rooms, airfare, four Jaguars that I barely drove. It's crazy that you do all this to visit twenty-one- or twenty-two-year-old kids or parents that sometimes barely have enough money to pay the electric bill. But that's what motivates them, the idea of making their lives better."

Scharf looked at his watch. He had a 7:00 A.M. flight, and his sights were set on about fifteen players, all of whom would require his best efforts. With any luck, he would land five or six, but he knew better than to take anyone for granted. Not after last season, when a cornerback named Dunta Robinson from the University of South Carolina signed at the last moment with Jason Chayut and Brian Mackler of Manhattan-based Sportstars.

The Houston Texans took Robinson with the tenth overall pick and signed him to a deal that included bonuses of $8 million. For Scharf, working on the NFL's standard 3 percent commission, the deal represented a $240,000 loss.

Still, he had five players drafted in the first four rounds in 2004, following a 2003 haul that included Barnett, the linebacker from Oregon State taken in the first round by the Green Bay Packers. In just three years, Scharf and Jeff Griffin, his colleague at Momentum Sports, had become players in the piranha tank of sports agents.

The field still was dominated by major agencies such as International Management Group (IMG) and its football division, run by former NFL players Tom Condon and Ken Kremer, along with SFX and Octagon, which in the late 1990s consolidated several boutique agencies. There were successful, self-promoting individual agents such as Leigh Steinberg and Drew Rosenhaus, who each touted themselves as the inspiration for Jerry Maguire and wrote autobiographies focusing mostly on their negotiating skills.

It was a vicious competition, Scharf knew. Agents often undercut one another on commissions. Stealing clients was commonplace. The business was rampant with reports of agents providing cash and other inducements to college players. Though illegal, the practice rarely was investigated by the NCAA, colleges, or individual states that require agent licensing. The NFL Players Association, which certifies agents and in theory polices them, paid little attention.

Scharf, who says he plays by the rules, never knows quite what he's up against. Still, after departing the bar at the Westshore Marriott, he felt comfortable about his prospects for the 2005 draft, at least the four players whose families he just met.

He even felt confident about Hawthorne, who potentially could become the first blue-chip, consensus first-rounder he ever signed.

"I'm not going to jinx myself and say which guys I'm going to sign," Scharf said. "But there's no way I'm not going to get at least two of the four."

Chapter Two:

THE PRO DEPOT

T im Ruskell hunched over a laptop computer and pondered how Ronnie Brown could help the Atlanta Falcons. A file provided dozens of details about the running back from Auburn University, from his physical skills to work ethic to intelligence.

The scouting report was one of hundreds that Ruskell, forty-seven, would read over the next seven months. On this afternoon, September 28, 2004, the Falcons were off to a surprising 3-0 start, but Ruskell kept one eye on the distant NFL Draft.

As an assistant general manager in the National Football League, Ruskell's days were spent searching for replacements for injured players and fielding frequent calls from agents and reporters. The day-to-day operation of a NFL franchise is all-consuming, but like his colleagues throughout the league, Ruskell never took his eyes off the next generation of talent. Though he no longer wore the title of scout or director of scouting, he still spent much of his time jetting around the country to watch college football practices, interview coaches, and sometimes hang around for games on Saturdays.

"I don't know how else to do it," Ruskell said. "I can't just look at tape and tell you how this guy is going to be. I have to have the whole package to put together."

During a seventeen-year stint with the Tampa Bay Buccaneers that ended with the 2003 season, Ruskell, along with general manager Rich McKay and player personnel director Jerry Angelo, developed an uncanny knack for discovering guys who were the complete package, even in cases where other teams saw weaknesses. Where some teams focused on a lack of size and speed, the McKay regime noticed leadership and drive. Where other teams noted a lack of raw football talent, they recognized extra doses of heart and hustle.

In 1993, the Buccaneers followed Ruskell's recommendation and took a flyer late in the third round on a safety from Stanford University who was slow, undersized, and playing baseball in the Florida Marlins organization. Ten years later, John Lynch left the Bucs with Hall of Fame credentials and a reputation as one of the game's hardest hitters and one of its most civic-minded players off the field.

In 1995, Tampa Bay used the second of its first-round picks on Derrick Brooks, a promising, if undersized, linebacker from Florida State. Brooks, like Lynch, became a perennial Pro Bowler and Hall of Fame candidate.

In 1997, the Bucs risked the twelfth overall pick on Warrick Dunn, a five-nine Florida State running back who many teams thought was too small to be anything more than a third-down back in the NFL. McKay and his staff viewed Dunn differently, believing he possessed unusual confidence and determination.

Dunn, like Brooks, became a Pro Bowl player and one of the league's most charity-minded players. Brooks took groups of underprivileged children on international vacations. Dunn purchased homes for single mothers, taking care of the down payment and furnishings.

In the third round of the 1997 draft, the Buccaneers thought a slow, skinny cornerback from the University of Virginia possessed the intelligence and leadership intangibles to become an NFL star. Most NFL scouts thought Tiki Barber's twin brother, Ronde, was a midlevel prospect at best.

Tiki, a running back selected in the second round by the New York Giants, became a star in New York. But Ronde, a third-round pick by the Buccaneers, also emerged as a Pro Bowl talent and a key contributor to the team that won the Super Bowl after the 2002 season.

McKay, Ruskell, and Angelo, who became general manager of the Chicago Bears before the 2001 season, quickly realized that a college player's character was as important a variable in predicting future performance as size, speed, and talent. They were willing to overlook a few transgressions only in the case of a phenomenal talent like Warren

Sapp. Even then they made it a point to thoroughly investigate predraft reports of Sapp's drug use themselves.

Character was an umbrella term that the McKay regime divided into "football character" and "personal character." Within each category was a range of traits, but the common denominators were heart, hustle, integrity, citizenship, work ethic, intelligence, leadership, and overachieving on the football field.

The character-first philosophy was not born out of a desire to lead the league in community service. Instead, McKay and Ruskell believed it was simply sound business. So-called "character guys" were less likely to squander their talent, end up on the police blotter, or become troublemakers in the locker room.

In baseball, the Oakland A's and general manager Billy Beane had gained notoriety by using statistical analysis to make draft decisions, dismissing conventional scouting measurements of physiques, potential, and "tools" to assemble low-budget teams that thrived against more well-heeled opponents. The unconventional approach had drawn raves from business leaders, who believed it had applications beyond sports.

Beane's philosophies were chronicled in the best-selling book *Moneyball* by Michael Lewis. McKay enjoyed the work of Lewis, a fellow Princeton graduate, and admired Beane for going against the grain of the rest of the league. At the same time, McKay saw no application to football, and not just because the NFL's economic system created more of a level playing field.

Beane and his disciples placed a huge emphasis on on-base percentage, slugging, and other stats, generally ignoring how a player's personality would affect team chemistry. In baseball, chemistry often was irrelevant. Barry Bonds could cordon himself off from teammates and clash with the media, and nobody cared so long as he kept producing. Teams were forever lining up to acquire high-maintenance, well-traveled players such as Kevin Brown and Gary Sheffield, no matter the baggage they carried.

In the NFL, a problem child such as Keyshawn Johnson or Terrell Owens, no matter how talented, could upset the delicate chemistry of a locker room. The difference, McKay believed, was that NFL schemes were far more interwoven than the game of baseball, where it was easier to isolate a talented malcontent.

Baseball, though a team sport, is essentially a series of isolated matchups. Players were traded in midseason and didn't miss a beat. In football, skills were not always transferable. A player that thrived in one team's offensive or defensive schemes might not fit on a different roster.

"Taking a *Moneyball* concept and trying to apply it to us doesn't work, because there are too many factors," McKay said. "This isn't just about a guy who is going to play left field. The left fielder for the A's is called upon to do the same thing as the left fielders for the Cardinals, Yankees, or Devil Rays. We ask our left corner[back] to do a lot of different things than what the Rams ask of their left corner. The difference with football is that a drafted player has to come in and grow within our schemes."

Just as some baseball people criticized Beane and his moneyballers for looking at players as a collection of stats, McKay believed some NFL teams put too much weight on scouting "measurables" such as size, speed in the forty-yard dash, and the vertical leap. They were important variables, and players needed to reach certain standards across the board, but it was dangerous, McKay felt, to underemphasize the character element.

McKay believed the football scouting process, with its exhaustive background checks and interviews, was analogous to the corporate hiring process.

"It's the reference side of the business taken as far as you can take it. When you hire an employee, you can do the background check, the interview, and call all the references. But until that employee comes on site and works for six months, you really don't know. You can feel better about some than others, but you don't know. What you've got to do is try and eliminate as many of the nonpredicting factors as you can and minimize the risk."

These days, McKay and Ruskell are hardly the only executives that factor character into their evaluation. Speak with a team official at any point in the months leading up to the draft and he's just as likely to reference character as he is a player's physical skills or performance. But no team places such a premium on the intangible as the Falcons do.

"We think character is a pretty good indication of whether you'll live up to your ability," Ruskell said. "It's all about potential. Do you want the guy that has the ability but isn't going to reach that potential? No, because you don't know what you're going to get from day to day. If he's feeling good, he'll give it his all. But if he's not, then you're not going to get that premium player."

Ruskell turned back to the laptop and the Ronnie Brown file. It's what the Falcons call a "College II" report. Falcon scouts visit schools rich with draft talent, like Auburn, three times during the college football season and once during the summer before, when college coaches have more time to chat. During this downtime, scouts build relationships for later in the season. They also file a preliminary "College I" report, which includes physique, medical reports, and basic biographical information.

The College II is more extensive and includes ratings on athletic ability, toughness, instincts, production—all things scouts can glean by watching practice and interviewing. Players are rated 1 to 5 in each category, and Brown, projected as an early first-round pick, had a lot of 4s and 5s.

Ruskell had no idea where the Falcons would be picking. The team was 3-0, but that could mean anything at this point. "I like Ronnie Brown a lot," he said. "You can't eliminate anyone from consideration."

The College II report is mostly complete after a school has played two or three games, though the character report is a work in progress, constantly updated as scouts conduct interviews.

"Nobody wants to tell you flat out if a guy has character issues," Ruskell said. "That's where you have to read between the lines. You pick up hints. Once you've gotten even the hint of a red flag, even if you're not told directly, then you start up the machine."

The Falcons employ a former U.S. Secret Service agent to conduct such investigations, which is hardly unusual. Every team has ex-law-enforcement personnel in similar roles. Then there's the NFL itself, which employs former FBI assistant director Milt Ahlerich as the head of its security. "Not much gets by thirty-two teams looking for information," Ruskell said.

"They dug all the way back to things I did in the eighth grade," said Sapp, now with the Oakland Raiders. "I heard about some of the stuff they found and I thought, 'Damn, how deep can they dig on me?'"

There's no common path to the executive suites of an NFL front office. There are plenty of ex-players, scouts, and coaches. Some have shifted from the college ranks. Ernie Accorsi and Marty Hurney, the general managers of the New York Giants and Carolina Panthers, respectively, began their careers as sportswriters.

Ruskell also logged time in the media business, working as an on-air radio personality in Tampa and Sarasota for five years after graduating in 1978 with a degree in journalism from the University of South Florida. Ruskell played football in high school, but USF did not field a team until two decades later.

He was working at Budget Tapes & Records in Tampa his freshman year when John Herrera, the first scout hired by the expansion Buccaneers, walked in and discovered that the kid behind the register knew a lot about music and football.

Because of that chance meeting, Ruskell worked in 1976 as ball boy for the inaugural Buccaneers team for $1.25 an hour. It wasn't easy duty, shuttling balls from station to station in Tampa's oppressive humidity. During the first practice in franchise history, Ruskell discovered an errant football that was in danger of interrupting a drill. With his hands already full of balls, he kicked it to the sidelines.

Coach John McKay, a stickler for detail and order, decided to send a message to the team by kicking the ball boy out of practice. Ruskell was rehired that night, fired on at least one other occasion, and eventually adapted McKay's attention to detail as his own philosophy. As a ball boy, Ruskell worked alongside McKay's son Rich, then seventeen. Sometimes Ruskell would catch passes from a veteran quarterback named Steve Spurrier.

"I don't know what to say when people ask me how to get into football," Ruskell says. "Don't do it my way. Don't wait for someone to walk through the door and strike up a friendship."

John McKay, who had won four national championships at Southern Cal, proved to be the best man to guide the hapless Bucs, who lost their first twenty-six games and posted just three winning seasons in his nine years in Tampa. The cigar-chomping, floppy-hat-wearing coach always provided the proper perspective with gallows humor and an endless stream of one-liners. In response to a reporter's question about his team's execution following an especially lopsided loss, McKay replied, "I'm in favor of it."

The Buccaneers, undermanned and clad in garish creamsicle orange uniforms, set the standard for personnel mismanagement and poor on-field performance. Owner Hugh Culverhouse, a tax attorney, alienated fans by taking his NFL profits and plowing them into other investments instead of back into the team. The "Yucks" squandered draft choices, despite perennially picking near the top of the first round.

At least McKay had family around. John "J. K." McKay, a former USC Trojan and the older of the two McKay boys, played wide receiver for the Bucs during the first three seasons. Rich's career as a quarterback ended after a freshman season at Princeton—he played four years on the golf team—but he was no less passionate about football.

During the 1979 season, Rich was home from college and suffering from mononucleosis when he stood on the sideline, against doctors' orders, to watch the Buccaneers defeat Kansas City 3–0, to clinch the NFC Central Division title. Two weeks later, the team, led by quarterback Doug Williams, upset Philadelphia in the first round of the playoffs before losing to the Los Angeles Rams in the NFC championship, the highlight of his father's tenure in Tampa.

During those early years, Rich McKay would travel from Princeton into New York in April to sit at the Buccaneers draft table, and he would relay the picks to the podium. He sometimes listened to games in his dorm by telephone by having someone in Tampa prop a radio next to the receiver.

After Princeton, McKay graduated in 1984 from Stetson University law school near St. Petersburg, clerked two years for a Tampa judge, and spent six years serving as the Buccaneers legal counsel, while working at the law firm of Hill, Ward, and Henderson.

Ruskell, meanwhile, got his first scouting gig in 1983 when he was hired by Herrera, who had become the general manager of the Saskatchewan Roughriders of the Canadian Football League (CFL). After two years in Canada, Ruskell scouted for the Tampa Bay Bandits of the United States Football League (USFL) before Angelo hired him in 1987 to be a regional scout for the Buccaneers. Four years later, Ruskell became the director of college scouting.

In 1992, McKay took a paycut and went to work full time for the Buccaneers as vice president of football administration. Unlike Ruskell, who toiled in scouting for second-tier football leagues, McKay's football experience was on the legal side. As general counsel, he had renegotiated the Buccaneers lease at Tampa Stadium in 1990 and put together leases for the teams in the fledgling World League of American Football. At one point, he spent four days at the NFL's New York headquarters sifting through the leases for every NFL franchise.

Culverhouse, who died of lung cancer at age seventy-five on August 25, 1994, taught McKay a lasting lesson in the importance of exhaustive research. With the team for sale following Culverhouse's death, the trustees of the estate, on November 8, 1994, appointed the thirty-five-year-old McKay general manager.

The move generated little media coverage, though Bucs beat writers noted that McKay, and not head coach Sam Wyche, now would have final say on the draft and personnel decisions. It was the first time the Bucs would have a GM with such authority.

Not that it seemed like much of a promotion at the time. With a pending ownership change, McKay had no guarantee of long-term employment. John McKay, now retired, all but discouraged him from taking the gig. Rich told his wife, Terrin, that he might only be GM for seven games, since new owners likely would clean house.

Still, McKay threw himself into the job, knowing full well he needed to overcome the advantages of nepotism and those who viewed him as "John's kid" or "Hugh's boy." While trying his best to assure employees that there was some hope of retaining their jobs under a new regime, he spent two weeks meeting daily with Angelo and Ruskell to figure out why the Buccaneers, in less than two decades, had become what McKay called the "worst franchise in the history of sport." They determined it was because, from the top down, there was no commitment to winning. Secondly, the personnel decisions were horrendous, especially in the first round of the NFL Draft.

After selecting future Hall of Famer Lee Roy Selmon with their first overall pick in 1976, the Bucs in 1977 chose powerful USC running back and McKay family favorite Ricky Bell over Tony Dorsett, the Heisman Trophy–winning back from Pittsburgh. Dorsett became a Dallas Cowboys legend, rushing for more than 12,000 yards. Bell rushed for 1,263 yards in 1979, but his career was derailed by a rare heart disease that killed him in 1984 at age twenty-nine.

In 1986, Auburn running back Bo Jackson turned down Tampa Bay's offer and decided to play baseball, eventually joining the NFL as a Raider. In 1990, the Bucs drafted Alabama linebacker Keith McCants with the fourth overall pick, bypassing the likes of Junior Seau and Emmitt Smith. McCants was a bust, as were other first-round, top-ten picks such as Broderick Thomas (1989), offensive tackle Charles McRae (1991), and defensive end Eric Curry (1993).

In 1987, the Bucs dealt a young quarterback to San Francisco for cash and a pair of draft picks. The players chosen made little impact. Steve Young ended up in the Hall of Fame.

Then there was the time the Bucs literally drafted the wrong guy. In 1982, the team's contingent in New York—McKay notes that it was the one year in his college and law school tenure he did not attend the draft—turned in the wrong card to the podium as a result of a malfunctioning speaker phone back in Tampa. Instead of spending their first-round pick (the number-seventeen choice) on Booker Reese, a defensive end from Bethune-Cookman, they turned in the card for Sean Farrell, a guard from Penn State.

Fortunately for the Buccaneers, the rest of the teams in the first round did not share their high opinion of Reese, and they were able to trade up and draft him in the second round.

"There was too much emphasis put on potential, and not on production," McKay said. "When the word character was used, it was really talking about 'characters,' not character. And so we said we're going to change the way we approach this and go with overachievers. The idea was that, even if we miss on that player and they may not be Pro Bowlers, they're still going to be good players. We need players. We keep having these drafts and you looked at them, and in the first five rounds not one guy was even a starter. That can't happen. You've got to have more than that."

During the 1992 draft, with McKay sitting in as an observer, the Buccaneers had no first-round pick, because former head coach Ray Perkins, acting as personnel director, had traded it nearly two years earlier to the Indianapolis Colts for quarterback Chris Chandler, who had since been cut. Because the Bucs finished 3-13 in 1991, that pick became the number-two choice in the 1992 draft.

"The second pick in the draft was traded for a quarterback who'd been there two years, not played, and was cut," McKay says. "The idea was, 'We're going to have a great year; by then we'll be a great team. This will be a low pick and we'll be happy we did it.' But you just don't know what can happen."

It didn't help that the Buccaneers were forever changing coaching staffs, shifting offensive and defensive schemes, and enduring constant roster turnover. Players drafted to fit one scheme became far less valuable, if not worthless, under a new coordinator.

"We cannot continue to have turnover," McKay told Ruskell and Angelo. "We need to have the same coaches and the same staff, and we need to grow with them because it'll help us from a personnel standpoint."

That sounded good to Malcolm Glazer, who in January of 1995 purchased the Buccaneers from the Culverhouse estate for $192 million, a record price at the time for a sports franchise. In his introductory press conference, Glazer addressed concerns that he would move the team.

"The Bucs stop here," he said. "Tampa is going to have this team forever, as far as the Glazers are concerned."

The community quickly learned the pledge was conditional. Glazer wanted a new stadium to replace the "Big Sombrero," the Bucs antiquated concrete home, which featured aluminum bench seats, no modern amenities, and suites that were quite literally skyboxes, perched high above the top row of seats.

Glazer, a red-bearded, bespectacled Palm Beach resident, originally from Rochester, who made his fortune in trailer parks, nursing homes, restaurants, and TV stations, initially offered to pay for half the new facility. Instead, he spent the first year of his ownership entertaining offers from Baltimore, Los Angeles, Hartford, Connecticut, and Orlando. That gave him the leverage to extract a half-cent sales tax from Hillsborough County that would provide $168 million in financing. Though pitched as a "community investment tax" to finance a wide range of public projects, voters were not fooled. Still, they passed it by a narrow margin rather than risk losing the Buccaneers.

In the end, Glazer did not need to contribute a penny to a state-of-the-art stadium that helped the Buccaneers produce a $40 million profit in 1999. McKay, the league's resident expert on stadium leases, helped negotiate a deal that allowed the Glazers to keep all luxury suite revenue, along with almost all income from tickets, concessions, parking, and advertising. They even received a healthy slice of non-Bucs event revenue. The team did have to pay rent of $3.5 million, along with ticket surcharges of about $1.5 million annually, but that did not even cover the Tampa Stadium Authority's annual operations costs.

While McKay was laying the financial groundwork for Glazer's investment to more than quadruple by 2004, according to *Forbes* magazine, he ensured the football side of the operation measured up.

With a reputation as an administrative guy, McKay hit the road as a general manager in the midnineties, joining Ruskell and Angelo to learn the business of NFL scouting.

"To this day, I don't know what a football guy is, but I knew there were people who thought I wasn't one," McKay says. "I knew I didn't know how area scouts worked, and that's what I wanted to learn. I'd take three-day visits to scout parts of the country and see how scouts did things, what their hours were, how they wrote their reports. I did it from their perspective so I could understand what they do. Going on the road for three weeks, and dealing with the volume of reports that must be written by an area scout, it's not an easy task at all."

McKay, Ruskell, and Angelo looked back on a decade of Buccaneer drafting and saw some common denominators. For starters, the Bucs traded away first-round picks three times, hindering the rebuilding process. As for the players that did not pan out, all of them were college stars that projected as productive NFL players.

Or did they? McKay, with his legal background and lack of NFL scouting experience, wondered if too much emphasis was placed on football skills and potential, and not enough on character, intangibles, and performance. Would they not be better off placing more weight on the nonfootball side of scouting? Wouldn't it make sense to select proven overachievers, albeit ones with perhaps lesser skills, than high-upside guys with raw talent? Were they as thorough as they needed to be when interviewing players? Were they ignoring obvious character red flags?

McKay, Angelo, and Ruskell vowed to avoid players with histories of making bad personal choices off the field. There was no way to completely predict how a player would respond to the dangerous combination of fame, money, and lots of free time. But McKay figured they could increase the odds of avoiding trouble through more extensive character research.

The new philosophy was put to an immediate test for the 1995 draft, McKay's first as general manager. Like the rest of the league, the Bucs were impressed with Sapp, the defensive tackle from the University of Miami. But they figured he would be long gone by the time Tampa Bay picked at number-seven. Instead, the staff wondered how they might grab Derrick Brooks, a promising if undersized linebacker from Florida State who, though of first-round caliber, did not warrant the seventh selection.

The Bucs thoroughly investigated both players, venturing to their colleges and, in the case of Sapp, his hometown of Apopka, Florida, to interview high school coaches, family members, friends—anyone that could provide insight. They believed Brooks made the most of his talents—a mature young man that commanded respect from teammates and opponents. Sapp, though a bit of a handful, was a true talent and a student of the game. He could talk at length about teams that thrived before he entered grade school, especially such dominating defenses as the Pittsburgh Steelers "Steel Curtain," the Minnesota Vikings "Purple People Eaters," or the "Doomsday Defense" of the Dallas Cowboys.

In the weeks before the draft, Sapp's stock began to fall. He acknowledged testing positive for marijuana as a University of Miami freshman and again at the NFL scouting combine. But the *New York Times* reported that Sapp also tested positive for cocaine at the combine. Sapp denied the cocaine charge and the NFL said the report was inaccurate.

Still, the damage was done. McKay and Ruskell flew to Miami to have lunch with Sapp. Having investigated Sapp thoroughly, they were well aware of the drug issues and knew that other teams, with lesser background work, might pass automatically.

"Whatever other issues you may have had, you knew Warren was not going to be unsuccessful," McKay said. "He would not allow it. Some teams weren't paying attention to those issues beforehand. So when they came up, they had to pass since they had not researched them. So he slipped accordingly."

Still, the priority for the Buccaneers was Brooks. McKay dealt his number-seven pick to Philadelphia for the number-twelve choice and two second-round selections. Then he traded two second-round picks to Dallas for the number-twenty-eight pick in the first round. That left Tampa Bay with the number-twelve and number-twenty-eight picks. If Sapp was gone at number-twelve, the Bucs felt they still might get Hugh Douglas, a promising defensive end from Central State in Ohio.

The first ten teams passed on Sapp. That left the Minnesota Vikings. The Bucs knew that head coach Dennis Green and defensive coordinator Tony Dungy liked Sapp.

With the Vikings on the clock, McKay, Ruskell, Angelo, and Bucs head coach Sam Wyche took a stroll on the practice field at One Buc Place.

"Is there any reason we shouldn't take this guy?" Wyche asked. "Do these teams know something we don't?"

The Tampa Bay brass felt comfortable with Sapp. Then they caught a break. Just a few months earlier, the *Minneapolis Star Tribune* had reported that a former employee at Stanford University, where Green previously coached, had threatened to add sexual harassment charges against Green to an employment discrimination suit she had filed against the university. (The suit was settled before any further charges were filed.)

Against this back drop, the Vikings decided they could not afford another public relations crisis, and selected Derrick Alexander, a defensive end from Florida State. The Bucs grabbed Sapp and, sixteen picks later, took Brooks.

When the first day of the 1995 draft ended, McKay and Ruskell rolled a video machine onto the back porch at One Buc Place, the team's cramped, antiquated headquarters. They lit cigars, opened a couple of beers, and watched tapes of the first two players drafted during McKay's tenure as general manager.

"If we were ever going to turn around the fortunes of this franchise," McKay said, "these were going to be the two guys to help us do it."

After twelve straight losing seasons, the turnaround was not immediate. Wyche was fired after a 7-9 season in 1995, replaced with Dungy, the Vikings defensive coordinator. A soft-spoken, deeply religious man who was an undersized defensive back for the Pittsburgh Steelers in the 1970s, Dungy had an affinity for solid citizens who managed to perform beyond their physical capabilities.

"Coach [Chuck] Noll always evaluated the player and the person," Dungy says. "There are a lot of talented football players around, but not everybody is going to make your team better. It's important to have guys who are good teammates, that fit in well, that are going to impact you positively, and character is a big part of that."

Not only was Dungy on the same page, he shared McKay's view of the coach's role in the draft. Around the league, head coaches such as New England's Bill Parcells and Jimmy Johnson, the former Dallas Cowboys coach who had just taken over in Miami, were exerting more control over the draft, seeing themselves as de facto general managers, even at a time when the league's young economic system of free agency and a salary cap made the role of the general manager more complex.

McKay viewed the draft as the domain of the GM and the scouting department. Input from the coaching staff was crucial, solicited at times, but the vast majority of the evaluations needed to come from the scouts. It was impractical to think that coaches could spend eighteen hours a day preparing their teams, from late July through December, if not January, and then take a leading role in evaluating college players.

The Buccaneers had spent much of their first two decades without a strong presence in the personnel department, letting the head coach make draft day decisions. Often, as was the case with Wyche, the head coach also was director of operations.

"With Sam, it was like, 'Let's watch a few plays. Okay, he's our guy,'" Ruskell said. "Rich saw the flaws in the system."

McKay told scouts to think of themselves as writing the draft equivalent of Cliff Notes for the coaching staff.

"We've synthesized this material," McKay would tell the coaching staff. "Now you have to read it and go out and be a cross-checker. This is what we saw, and you tell us we're right or wrong if you see it differently."

The important thing, McKay knew, was that the entire organization had a clear picture of where it wanted to go personnelwise, from the on-field schemes to character issues, and how each new player would add to the chemistry.

"It's no different than when you and your wife bring home the baby," McKay said. "You still have to motivate the player, work him into your schemes. You may find that he can't do this or that, but that's okay. Let him do something else. It's your job as an organization to make him successful. It's too easy to say, 'We may have missed.'"

The Bucs produced a solid draft class in 1996, the first year of the Dungy era, selecting defensive linemen Regan Upshaw (California) and Marcus Jones (North Carolina) in the first round. In the second round, they grabbed Mike Alstott, a bruising fullback from Purdue, and in the third picked up Donnie Abraham, a cornerback out of East Tennessee State, a Division 1-AA program.

Upshaw, Alstott, and Abraham started immediately. Alstott and Abraham would go on to play in Pro Bowls. Alstott, nicknamed the "A Train," became one of the most popular Buccaneers in team history. Jones was slower to develop, but recorded twenty sacks over the 1999 and 2000 seasons.

In 1997, the Bucs hit the jackpot with Dunn and Ronde Barber. They also grabbed offensive linemen Jerry Wunsch (Wisconsin) in the second round and Frank Middleton (Arizona) in the third. Both were starters during the Bucs' late-nineties resurgence. Dunn, Wunsch, and Barber, like Alstott and Brooks, became active in the community.

There were setbacks, to be sure, especially at wide receiver. The Bucs squandered picks on two of Spurrier's Florida wide receivers. Years before Spurrier himself bombed as head coach of the Washington Redskins, Reidel Anthony (a first-round pick after Dunn in 1997) and Jacquez Green (a second-rounder, and the Bucs' first pick in 1998) failed to make an impact. Ditto for Marquise Walker, a Michigan wide receiver taken in the third round in 2002, the Bucs' first overall selection.

Still, unlike previous regimes, the new Buccaneer front office stayed the course with players and philosophy. During training camp before the 1997 season, Barber looked overmatched and struggled to pick up the Buccaneers defensive schemes.

Angelo and Ruskell had lobbied hard to draft Barber, even though Dungy and Herman Edwards, who coached the defensive backs, had reservations. The coaches were impressed with Ronde Barber the person, but not as a potential NFL defensive back.

"He came to camp and was one of the worst players I've ever seen," Ruskell said. "We should have cut him. Jerry and I were backtracking saying, 'You liked him. No, *you* liked him.' He looked like a total bust. You have to give Tony Dungy and Herm Edwards all the credit. They told us, 'You drafted him. You liked him, and we're going to hang in there with him.' And now the guy is one of the best cornerbacks in the league."

Between Dungy's coaching and an influx of players from the draft, the Buccaneers engineered a complete turnaround. After posting a 6-10 record and a fourteenth straight losing season in 1996, the team went 10-6 in 1997. The Bucs finished 8-8 in 1998 before reaching the NFC title game following the 1999 season.

By now, most of the starting lineup on both sides of the ball had come out of McKay drafts. With a strong pipeline of talent, the Bucs were able to release veteran nose tackle Brad Culpepper before the 2000 season and replace him with Anthony McFarland, the first-round pick in 1999. Aging linebacker Hardy Nickerson was let go in favor of Jamie Duncan, a third-round choice in 1998.

In 1999, the *Fort Worth Star-Telegram*, using a complicated draft evaluation formula that included Pro Bowl appearances and player ranking among statistical leaders in various offensive and defensive categories, determined that Tampa Bay had been the best drafting team since 1995.

McKay was quickly reaching his goal of using the draft much like a Major League Baseball team does to stock its farm system. Instead of developing in the minor leagues, they could ease their way into the NFL on special teams or in backup roles.

Not only did the process make the team younger, McKay was better able to allocate valuable money under the salary cap. Instead of re-signing expensive veterans or signing even pricier free agents, he could move second- and third-year players into more prominent roles. With half the roster playing under their relatively modest rookie contracts, it created payroll flexibility.

With a team so close to Super Bowl caliber before the 2000 season, McKay addressed the club's few pressing needs by signing free agent offensive linemen Jeff Christy and Randall McDaniel. For the final piece, McKay dealt the team's two first-round picks in the 2000 draft to the New York Jets for Keyshawn Johnson, the talented but problem child wide receiver. A year later, the Bucs signed quarterback Brad Johnson.

The moves did not push the Bucs over the edge. Instead, the team needed late-season rallies to reach the playoffs in 2000 and 2001, both times losing to the Eagles in Philadelphia. Bryan and Joel Glazer, who oversaw their father's investment, ordered McKay to fire Dungy.

A long, meandering search for Dungy's replacement followed, with unsuccessful flirtations with Parcells and Steve Mariucci. The Glazers rejected McKay's recommendation to hire Marvin Lewis and then traded a pair of first-round picks and two second-round picks to the Oakland Raiders for the right to negotiate with Jon Gruden. During the process, McKay received permission to pursue other employment.

McKay interviewed with Arthur Blank, cofounder of the Home Depot, who had just purchased the Falcons for $545 million. Like the pre-McKay Buccaneers, the Falcons were perennial bottom feeders. Though they reached the Super Bowl after the 1998 season, the Falcons never had posted back-to-back winning seasons.

Blank and McKay clicked immediately, with Blank sharing McKay's vision for building a perennial contender by shrewd use of the NFL draft. Blank, who stressed community service to his Home Depot employees, liked how McKay emphasized character when acquiring players. The men also discovered they shared a passion for long-distance running.

In the end, McKay's ties to Tampa ran too deep. A press conference served as a public reconciliation between McKay and the Glazers, with McKay signing a six-year, $12 million contract extension with Tampa Bay.

Gruden, meanwhile, proved to be just what the Buccaneers needed. Unlike the low-key Dungy, Gruden was not afraid to play the role of fiery motivator. With Dungy's groundwork and a few free agents, Gruden led the Bucs to a 12-4 record and a stunning rout of his former employer, the Raiders, in Super Bowl XXXVII.

The honeymoon didn't last. Two months after the Super Bowl, during owners' meetings in Phoenix, Gruden voiced his feelings that McKay, cochairman of the NFL's competition committee, spent too much time on league issues and not enough on the Bucs. Not only that, Gruden was unimpressed with McKay's recent drafts.

It was inevitable that Gruden's philosophies were going to clash with the McKay regime. Gruden, upon taking the job, planned to overhaul the roster. McKay intervened and added a few pieces to what would become a Super Bowl champion.

Gruden preferred veteran players, though he liked to take an active role in the draft process, too. As for salary cap implications and waiting for draft picks to develop, he'd worry about those matters later. Gruden slept just four hours a night. Patience and long-term planning were not his strong suits.

McKay, with Dungy's backing, avoided players who had run-ins with the law. Gruden lobbied successfully for the Bucs to sign running back Michael Pittman, who was convicted in 2001 for domestic abuse. McKay, unable to match Atlanta's lucrative offer to model citizen Warrick Dunn, went along.

After winning the Super Bowl, Gruden pushed for more control. Every time an aging former star like Junior Seau or Emmitt Smith became available, Gruden expressed interest. He couldn't understand why the Bucs didn't acquire Kyle Turley, a high-maintenance player who didn't fit McKay's character-based system.

McKay, meanwhile, preached building through youth and the draft, and keeping an eye on the long-term salary cap picture—where storm clouds were gathering because of his pre–Super Bowl free agent signings.

Gruden could overlook off-the-field transgressions, even lobbying during the 2003 season for the Bucs to sign Darrell Russell, whose rap sheet included a suspension for violating the league's substance abuse policy and rape charges that were dismissed.

As the 2003 season came to a close, McKay had had enough. He again asked for and received permission to be released from his contract. This time, he and the Falcons' Blank struck a deal. McKay took the high road, thanking everyone in Tampa, including Gruden. Still, even in his opening remarks upon taking the Falcons job, he made it clear where their differences lie.

"We're not in this business to do anything other than win, and I'm one who wants to win the right way. I want to have the right players. I want to have guys that get out in the community. We always said there was a 'Buc player.' And we used to have pictures of Warrick Dunn and Derrick Brooks and John Lynch and we said those are 'Buc players.'"

Now McKay and Ruskell tried to find players to fit the same mold in Atlanta. It's an ambitious formula, to be sure. Rarely does a month pass where an NFL player is not arrested for some crime. In the 1998 book *Pros and Cons: The Criminals Who Play in the NFL,* authors Jeff Benedict and Don Yaeger investigated the criminal records of NFL players and concluded that at least 21 percent of players in the league had been charged with a serious crime.

Many of those players were top stars in the NFL. By eliminating players with criminal backgrounds or character issues from draft consideration, the Falcons could neglect a valuable source of talent.

McKay doesn't think so. "This isn't just a business decision of wanting reliable players. You need to have good guys. It helps fans identify with the football team and it sends the right message in the locker room. When you draft guys, just like when you sign free agents, they have to walk into your locker room. The guys there are thinking, 'Why did they get this guy?' When you bring in the right guys, they'll feel better about it."

McKay believes it's not a stretch to say that the character-first philosophy helped the Buccaneers overcome the fallout from the passing of the unpopular community investment tax that kept the Glazers from moving the team out of Tampa.

"Having good guys was gigantic for us," McKay said. "We had a franchise that not only was disliked but close to hated. People were angered when our players got into trouble with the law. Nobody had a good feel for the franchise from a winning or character standpoint. As we started to win, people began to like the team and wanted to go to games, but also to support the team by wearing shirts and putting flags on cars. That's not just winning, but also having guys that were winning off the field by getting involved in the community."

Not every player turns out to be a choir boy. Dwight Smith, a third-round pick by the Buccaneers under McKay in 2001, pleaded guilty two years later to a misdemeanor charge of brandishing a handgun in an apparent case of road rage. Kenyatta Walker, the team's first-round pick in 2001, was arrested and charged with disorderly conduct in 2003 when he refused to leave a nightclub in the Ybor City section of Tampa. Police needed to use pepper spray to subdue the 300-pound Walker, a chronic underachiever on the field.

"Can you ever be 100 percent right on a guy? Of course not," McKay said. "Some guys will start to hang out with the wrong people. They've never had money and now they're in trouble. That's going to happen. My concern is that we don't go looking for those guys."

McKay and Ruskell, like most NFL executives, do not spend much time grading their draft performances. They try to project where a player is going to be in three years, since by then he will have likely pushed out a veteran and reached his NFL potential. Occasionally they'll look back at a three-year-old draft and grade their thought processes. They find that when they're wrong it's more often because they misjudged a player's football potential, more so than his character.

"What I tell coaches is not to blame the player because we drafted him and he wasn't what we thought he was," McKay says. "Let's blame ourselves and try and make it work. It's like if your child calls from the police station because he's been arrested for DUI. I assume you're going to go down and get them out. You're going to help them out and get them better. It's the same with a player. If a player doesn't work at middle linebacker, move him to outside linebacker, or special teams where he can make you better. Don't just get mad at the player. What happens to all of us is that you get so mad at the player. Why isn't he better than this? He isn't. Sometimes you miss in that regard."

McKay has an additional member of his investigative team. Blank, the Falcons sixty-two-year-old owner, takes an active role in sizing up players the team is considering acquiring, though unlike owners such as Jerry Jones in Dallas and Daniel Snyder of the Washington Redskins, he does not try to be the de facto general manager.

Whether it's joining coaches to meet with free agents over dinner, or sitting in on interviews at the combine, Blank sells the players on Atlanta and his commitment to winning. He also outlines the organization's vast philanthropic endeavors.

Blank, who retired as cochairman of the Home Depot in 2001, believes the same philosophies of customer service and community involvement that built the company into a home improvement juggernaut, translate to the NFL. He cites the 2003 season, when Falcons fans continued to pack the Georgia Dome, even after quarterback Michael Vick broke his leg and the team lost seven straight games.

"At Home Depot, we had tens of thousands of our associates that would spend time in the field doing community work," Blank says. "We created an atmosphere that said giving back is our responsibility, and we made it easy for employees to do so. We got very positive feedback throughout these communities. People felt an alliance, an allegiance with us. That's why, even in 2003, fans still filled up the dome. Fans are going to be loyal to an organization, not just because of wins and losses, but for what it stands for in the community.

"I'm not suggesting every guy on the team is a priest or rabbi. There are degrees of character issues, but you don't want to cross that line because you run a lot of risks. One of the terms I've learned to be sensitive to is risk and reward. Now when I hear it in a character context, I don't want those players on the team."

McKay knows that the character philosophy can come across as holier-than-thou. After all, he tabbed Sapp as the cornerstone in Tampa, and Sapp is in no danger of winning a NFL Man of the Year award. The Falcons have thrived behind Vick, who though not drafted by McKay, has endured a couple of embarrassing off-the-field episodes.

"Nobody says that they're all going to be perfect," McKay said. "You have to bring in guys that come from all different walks of life and backgrounds. You're going to have guys that don't exactly fit the mold as far as being team players and treating others with respect. You can't draft all As in character, and if you did you'd probably lose every game."

On the afternoon of September 28, 2004, McKay was sitting on bleachers overlooking the practice fields at the Falcons training center in Flowery Branch, a rural but growing suburb forty miles northeast of Atlanta. It's the Taj Mahal of NFL facilities, with a seventy-five thousand-square-foot corporate headquarters, an indoor turf field, a massive locker room, palatial executive offices—even an interactive Falcons museum and gift shop. Soon construction will begin on luxury garden apartments for players to live in during training camp in 2005, a first in the NFL.

At forty-five, McKay's age finally has caught up with him. With thinning, prematurely gray hair, he never quite looked the part of boy wonder, even as a thin thirty-five-year-old general manager who often could be found around the Buccaneers training complex wearing workout clothes following a lunchtime run. Recent laser surgery has allowed him to discard eyeglasses he wore for years.

It also could be that McKay always seemed older because of a long football background, from a childhood spent around championship teams at Southern Cal, to high school years as a Buccaneers ball boy, to nearly two decades in NFL front offices. He's served on several league committees, most notably the competition committee, which he's cochaired since 1998.

Throw in a Princeton diploma, a law degree, stadium lease experience, and public relations savvy, and it's the type of resume that would seem perfect for the role of NFL commissioner. McKay long has been mentioned as a successor to Paul Tagliabue, though the topic is perhaps the only question that can make the usually unflappable general manager squirm.

"It makes me very uncomfortable. You're taking about an existing guy that has done a fantastic job and has been very nice to me. If he said tomorrow, 'Okay, I want out,' then I wouldn't mind anybody asking me—although there are a lot of people in the line way ahead of me."

First, McKay wants to put together back-to-back winning seasons for the first time in Atlanta Falcons history. Like the dozens of agents that work out of Atlanta because it provides for easy access to many of the schools in the football-rich ACC and SEC, McKay is able to see a lot of college football during the busy NFL season. It helps that the University of Georgia, which does not have an indoor practice field, occasionally buses the team an hour, from Athens to Flowery Branch, to use the Falcons' facilities during bad weather. On those days, McKay and his staff got an exclusive look at the Bulldogs.

Athens had been a popular destination for NFL scouts and agents this fall. Defensive end David Pollack was projected as an early first-round pick. Quarterback David Greene, wide receivers Reggie Brown and Fred Gibson, and free safety Thomas Davis, a junior leaning toward going pro, also figured to be early draft selections.

Not that the Falcons president, once dubbed a "nonfootball guy," was going to wait for the talent to come to him. He would take an annual trip to the West Coast, where his father once coached at the University of Southern California and played at the University of Oregon. He would fit in as many scouting trips as possible around the Falcons' season and make sure to interview his younger players about former college teammates eligible for this year's draft.

"The thing I learned from law and trial work is that those that are the most prepared win," McKay said. "Not the most talented lawyer. You don't have to give the best closing argument or have the prettiest exhibits or the most impressive witnesses. It's the most prepared that tends to win. Same thing with the draft. Draft day itself should be easy, a nice fun day that unfolds the way you thought it should. Do we have the most talented staff? I think we have one of the best, but that's open to debate. I do know that nobody is going to outwork us."

McKay and his staff, like those of other NFL teams, generally have little trouble getting access to college football departments. College coaches recognize that the higher their players are drafted, the easier it will be to recruit high school kids dreaming of NFL careers.

Some coaches limit access, fearing that the presence of NFL scouts might influence their underclassmen to leave school early, or at the very least distract them from preparations for the upcoming game. Either way, there's a sometimes uneasy alliance between college football programs and the NFL that goes back nearly a century. It was this very conflict that led to the creation of the NFL Draft.

Chapter Three:

THE DRAFT— THEN AND NOW

As early as 1920, professional football faced the problems of rapidly escalating salaries, players leaving teams for better financial offers, and the use of college players still enrolled in school.

On January 28, 1922, five months before the American Professional Football Association changed its name to the National Football League, John Clair of the Acme Packing Company admitted to using players who had college eligibility remaining during the 1921 season for the Green Bay Packers. Clair and the Green Bay management withdrew from the league.

Curly Lambeau promised to obey league rules and bought back the Packers franchise, but the issue of using college players did not go away. In 1925, Red Grange took off his University of Illinois uniform on a Saturday in late November and made his professional debut for the Chicago Bears the following Thursday, Thanksgiving Day.

George Halas, the player-coach-owner of the Bears, decided to put a stop to the practice, or at least keep others from following his lead. During a league meeting in 1926, he proposed a rule prohibiting teams from acquiring players whose classes had not yet graduated.

Halas violated his own rule in 1930, signing Notre Dame running back Joe Savoldi. In 1931, league president Joe Carr fined the Bears,

Packers, and Portsmouth (Ohio) Spartans one thousand dollars each for using college players whose classes had not graduated, and over the next few years more tension arose between the league and college coaches.

During a meeting of the nine league owners on May 19, 1935, Bert Bell, the owner of the struggling Philadelphia Eagles, proposed a draft. Teams would pick, in reverse order of finish, from among the players whose college eligibility was ending.

It was a simple concept, one not yet employed by any other professional sports league, and one that would become a cornerstone of the NFL's competitive balance.

Bell, whose Eagles had finished the 1934 season 2-9 and had not posted a winning record in their first three years in the league, had a vested interest in the draft. Teams such as the Bears and New York Giants, which dominated the league in its early years, had little to gain.

Still, Halas and Giants owner Tim Mara embraced the plan, recognizing that competitive balance was essential to draw fans to games during the Depression. Others would suggest the draft had less to do with leveling the playing field than it did with holding down salaries. After all, a drafted player could negotiate with just one team.

"There is some truth to that argument," Halas said in his autobiography. "But time proved that by leveling the clubs, the draft system heightened the attractiveness of the sport. It created bigger audiences, which brought bigger revenue, which brought higher salaries for all players."

When NFL owners met at the Ritz Carlton Hotel in Philadelphia for the inaugural NFL Draft on February 8, 1936, the setting was less formal than that of a modern-day fantasy football gathering.

The group included league pioneers Halas, Mara, Art Rooney of the Pittsburgh Pirates, George Preston Marshall of the Boston Redskins, Curly Lambeau of the Green Bay Packers, Charles Bidwill of the Chicago Cardinals, Dan Topping of the Brooklyn Dodgers, George Richards of the Detroit Lions and, of course, Bell, representing the Philadelphia Eagles.

None of the owners arrived wielding scouting reports, three-ring binders, or anything that could constitute formal research. On a wall was posted a list of ninety players whose eligibility had expired, culled from various All-America and all-conference teams.

Bell, a onetime University of Pennsylvania quarterback, who in 1946 would become the NFL's second commissioner, kicked off the draft by selecting Jay Berwanger, a halfback from the University of Chicago who had captured the inaugural Heisman Trophy.

Berwanger greeted the news of his historic selection with indifference. At a time when star players such as Bronco Nagurski of the Bears made just four hundred dollars a game, Berwanger didn't view professional football as an attractive career path. He planned to become a sports writer, of all things, and covered football for the *Chicago Daily News* before moving on to a more lucrative business career.

Bell, who would sign none of his nine draft picks, dealt Berwanger to Halas, who would have no better luck signing him. The low salaries scared off all but thirty-one of the eighty-one players from the 1936 draft. Among those not to sign were Notre Dame halfback Bill Shakespeare, selected third overall by the Pittsburgh Pirates; and an end from Alabama, taken in the fourth round by the Brooklyn Dodgers, by the name of Paul "Bear" Bryant.

The draft generated no media coverage, just a three-paragraph mention buried in the *New York Times* sports section several days later.

In 1937, with the addition of the Cleveland Rams, the draft grew from nine rounds to ten. The process expanded several more times until it reached thirty rounds in 1943. Most players drafted that year reported for military service, not the NFL.

There were other wrinkles, all in the name of promoting parity. From 1938–1948, the NFL allowed only the teams with the five worst records to draft in the second and fourth rounds.

In 1947, the NFL introduced the "bonus selection." One randomly selected team received an extra pick, a predraft choice. Once a team was selected, it was disqualified from future lotteries, a system that lasted through 1958. The bonus selections included future Hall of Famers Chuck Bednarik (Philadelphia, 1949) and Paul Hornung (Green Bay, 1957).

The early drafts were jovial, free-flowing affairs. Cigarette smoke hung over the room. Bell served as master of ceremonies, establishing a precedent for future commissioners throughout sports on draft day, announcing the picks himself and mangling difficult surnames.

After World War II, NFL teams continued to struggle to convince many of their draft picks to play in the league. The draft had effectively stopped the escalation of salaries by restricting players to one potential employer.

The All-American Football Conference changed that in 1946. Unlike a pair of short-lived operations both known as the American Football League, the AAFC represented a legitimate threat. The inaugural AAFC included the Cleveland Browns, San Francisco 49ers, and Miami Seahawks, who were replaced the following year by the Baltimore Colts.

The Browns were especially adept at acquiring talent, including quarterback Otto Graham, fullback Marion Motley, guard Bill Willis, center Frank Gatski, tackle/kicker Lou Groza, and end Dante Lavelli—all future members of the Pro Football Hall of Fame.

The AAFC didn't bother with a draft its first year. With so much talent coming home from the war and only ten NFL teams, there was no need. The NFL, taking no chances on revealing its players, held its draft in secret.

In a harbinger of the AFL–NFL conflict to come in the 1960s, separate leagues caused salaries to escalate. Dan Topping, who owned the baseball and NFL Yankees, offered two-sport Georgia star Charley Trippi a two-year baseball deal for $200,000, along with a football contract. Charles Bidwill, owner of the AAFC's Chicago Cardinals, countered with a four-year deal for $100,000 and a tryout with the Cubs. Trippi, who had spoken to Bidwill first, signed with Chicago.

The Trippi signing accelerated talks for a common draft, if not a merger. With teams in both leagues struggling financially, especially in the AAFC, the leagues merged on December 9, 1949. Only the Browns, 49ers, and Colts entered the NFL intact.

Competition from the AAFC did not inspire NFL teams to assemble scouting staffs and devote significant resources to scouting. Throughout the 1940s, some team executives would prepare for their next pick by perusing the pages of Street & Smith's Football Year Book or other college football magazines.

A few teams set up informal scouting networks of college coaches and former players, but the Los Angeles Rams, under owner Dan Reeves, were the first to assemble what could be called a scouting department.

Reeves, who purchased the Cleveland Rams in 1941 and moved them to Los Angeles in 1946, believed the key to football success was finding overlooked talent. Among his first hires was Eddie Kotal, a former Green Bay Packers player and small-college coach.

The scouting lifestyle Kotal created remains pretty much intact today. He spent two hundred days a year on the road, traveling from campus to campus to watch players and interview coaches. He'd start by hitting most of the major schools in the spring and then crisscross the country from the beginning of August practices through the final games. Kotal would visit as many as ten schools a week, following a familiar pattern of watching game films and interviewing coaches. After dinner, he'd retire to his hotel room to write reports.

Kotal also timed players in the forty-yard dash. Paul Brown, who began his professional coaching career in Cleveland in 1946, figured it was an accurate measure of football speed, since it was the approximate distance a player would cover on a punt. (Brown also measured the cognitive abilities of his players by giving them a twelve-minute, fifty-question test similar to the Wonderlic, the fifty-question aptitude test players now take during the NFL Scouting combine.)

Kotal built vast networks of contacts throughout the country and filed his reports in dozens of notebooks. Reeves and Kotal assembled files on every senior in the country, rolling into the drafts throughout the 1950s with trunks full of information. Other teams shook their heads in amazement, many still drafting out of *Street & Smith's* or by phoning college contacts between selections.

There were no phones in the draft room back then, and team officials sometimes disappeared for a half hour or more, there being no time limits on picks. The Rams were ahead of the game in this area, too. Under the direction of a savvy public relations director and future general manager named Pete Rozelle, they set up shop at the 1956 draft with a phone at their table.

The Rams, with a huge advantage in scouting, posted winning records in nine of their first ten seasons in Los Angeles, reaching the championship game three straight years (1949–51) and winning in 1951.

In scouting, the Rams left no stone unturned. In 1946, they broke the league's color barrier by signing UCLA halfback Kenny Washington and end Woody Strode, who became the first African Americans to play in the NFL in the modern era. In 1949, the Rams acquired Paul "Tank" Younger out of Grambling as a free agent, making the running back the first player in the NFL to come from an all-black college.

Reeves and Kotal specialized in the overlooked small-school player, believing other teams placed too much emphasis on level of competition. In 1951, they spent a nineteenth-round choice on a defensive end from tiny Arnold College. Andy Robustelli ended up in the Pro Football Hall of Fame.

Some small college players were not even in school when the Rams discovered them. Future Hall of Famer Dick "Night Train" Lane, who had played at Scottsbluff Junior College, wandered into the Rams office after a four-year stint in the army and was given a tryout. In 1953, the Rams discovered defensive tackle Gene "Big Daddy" Lipscomb, who did not play college ball, playing football in the military.

The Rams did not limit their college scouting to football. Before the 1950 season, the Rams signed Bob Boyd, a track star from Loyola of Los

Angeles who played seven years at wide receiver. In 1955, they spent a thirtieth-round pick on K. C. Jones, a member of the San Francisco University national championship basketball team. Jones reported to training camp before opting for a career with the Boston Celtics.

The Rams were the first team to understand the value of hoarding draft picks. Six times between 1952 and 1959 they had two first-round picks. In 1955, they drafted four times in the second round.

Sid Gillman, the Rams head coach from 1955 to 1959, inspired future generations of NFL scouts by separating game film into offensive and defensive reels, cutting the film further to isolate specific plays and situations.

Still, it's not as though the Rams or any other team had a crystal ball. In 1955, the Pittsburgh Steelers spent a ninth-round draft pick on a former walk-on quarterback from Louisville. The Steelers cut the kid, who had gone to high school in Pittsburgh, and Johnny Unitas signed with the Baltimore Colts, becoming one of the best quarterbacks ever.

The 1957 draft, held on November 27, 1956, featured another accidental find. The Cleveland Browns were desperate for a quarterback, but Notre Dame's Paul Hornung, Stanford's John Brodie, and Purdue's Len Dawson were gone by the time the Browns picked sixth. So the Browns "settled" for Jim Brown, the All-America running back from Syracuse.

The Green Bay Packers, meanwhile, were laying the groundwork for their success in the 1960s. Jack Vainisi began scouting for the Packers in 1950, and, like Eddie Kotal, developed a network of high school and college coaches around the country. Vainisi traveled constantly, even spending much of his honeymoon in 1952 driving through Texas and Oklahoma looking at players.

Vainisi scouted and recommended seven future Hall of Famers, including Hornung and Alabama quarterback Bart Starr (nineteenth round, 1956). In 1958, he drafted a pair of future Canton enshrinees, taking Louisiana State fullback Jim Taylor in the second round and Illinois linebacker Ray Nitschke in the fourth.

Vainisi worked like a man with little time; he suffered from a heart condition that killed him in 1960 at the age of thirty-three, but not before he convinced the Packers board to hire a New York Giants assistant coach named Vince Lombardi as head coach.

The draft still remained a low-key affair, held late in the year and staged at various points in hotels in Chicago, Milwaukee, and Philadelphia. Many players learned of their selections in the newspapers, receiving calls days later from team officials. By the time they reported to a postseason all-star game such as the Senior Bowl or East–West Shrine Game, they already were drafted.

"I got the call at my fraternity house maybe a week later," says Boyd Dowler, the Packers third-round pick out of Colorado in 1959, who would become a standout wide receiver. "It's not like anyone was calling a press conference."

Still, there were signs that scouting and the draft process were becoming more formalized. In the late 1950s, Austin Gunsel, a former FBI agent, joined the NFL's finance department, eventually working as treasurer and unofficial director of security. Gunsel implemented a policy of hiring an ex-FBI agent in each NFL city, a role that would evolve to include background screening of NFL draft picks.

The defining year that transformed the NFL Draft from a backroom gathering into a high-stakes, competitive affair was 1960, the year the American Football League and the NFL's Dallas Cowboys began play and Rozelle was elected NFL commissioner.

Unlike the AAFC and previous incarnations of the AFL, the new American Football League appeared to have financial staying power. Its ringleader was twenty-seven-year-old Lamar Hunt, the son of oil millionaire H. L. Hunt. The younger Hunt, unable to land a stake in an NFL team, formed a new AFL, with franchises in eight cities: Boston, Buffalo, New York, Houston, Dallas, Denver, Oakland, and Los Angeles.

The AFL held its first draft on November 23, 1959, and it quickly became apparent that the new league was willing to battle the NFL for every top college star. The fight reached a crescendo after the 1964 college football season when the AFL's New York Jets signed Joe Namath, the promising quarterback from the University of Alabama, to a three-year deal for more than four hundred thousand dollars.

The NFL, suffering defections among veteran players as well, hoped to put an end to its pesky competitor, or at least banish it to minor league status. Using levels of secrecy and scope that would have made the CIA proud, the NFL essentially kidnapped the draft class in November of 1965.

Commissioner Rozelle had been inspired more than a year earlier by his former boss, Rams owner Dan Reeves, to put together "Operation Hand-holding," more commonly known as the NFL's baby-sitting program. Reeves believed that the key to preventing college players from signing with the AFL was to establish relationships early on in the process. By employing businessmen skilled in the art of sales to serve as recruiters of sorts, they could get a head up on the AFL.

Reeves intended to implement his plan in Los Angeles, but Rozelle realized it could be done leaguewide. He borrowed Bert Rose, the former Rams public relations director, who was to direct the Los Angeles babysitting operation, and assigned him the entire league.

The operation was unveiled on a limited scale for the draft in November of 1964. By the following year, after the Namath signing, it was a well-oiled machine.

The NFL assigned 125 babysitters, officially called "representatives," to fan out across the country and attach themselves to top prospects in the two weeks leading up to the draft. Some babysitters were scouts, but many were selected from the front offices of various teams. Others were local salesmen. It was the babysitter's job to sell the NFL. On draft day, a call center was set up in New York and teams were patched through to players and their supervisors, who helped negotiate terms. Armed with a partial list of selections from the AFL's draft three weeks earlier, the NFL quickly was able to sign the vast majority of draft talent.

By January, 75 percent of the 232 players drafted by the fourteen NFL teams had signed contracts. Only 40 were lost to the AFL. The AFL signed 46 percent of its 181 draftees. Of the 111 players drafted in both leagues, 79 signed with the NFL, 28 with the AFL, and 4 went unsigned.

With the leagues spending a combined $7 million to sign their 1966 draft choices, it was becoming clear that neither side was winning. Following a series of secret merger meetings between the AFL's Hunt and Tex Schramm of the Dallas Cowboys, Rozelle announced a merger on June 8, 1966.

By then the Cowboys had taken the lead in scouting and dominating the draft. Schramm, the former Rams general manager who had taken a similar role with the Cowboys, longed for a way to streamline and organize the mountains of data collected on college seniors. While working for CBS Sports during a brief interlude between NFL jobs, Schramm covered the 1960 winter Olympics in Squaw Valley, California, and was impressed by the power of an IBM computer used to calculate stats and times.

Since the cost of a computer was too much for one team to bear, Schramm enlisted the Rams and 49ers, both friendly competitors, to share the investment. Over the next four years, the teams created a computer model to evaluate players. They called their three-team combine "Troika."

It took more than four years to develop a computer system that could quantify the subjective elements of scouting. The result was a standard scouting form that graded players in five areas: character, quickness, competitiveness, strength, and mental alertness. Each player was ranked in each category from one to nine, with nine being the highest.

The first computer rankings, produced before the 1965 draft, listed Namath, the Alabama quarterback, at the top of the list. Even cynics could not argue with the computer's results.

The Cowboys' pioneering use of computers fostered a stereotype of the team relying on technology to draft. Fans envisioned Tom Landry, the team's stoic head coach, waiting as a massive machine beeped and chirped, finally belching out a slip with a name.

In reality, the computer was just a tool for the Cowboys' thorough scouting system led by Schramm and Gil Brandt, a former hospital baby photographer and part-time Rams employee who became the Cowboys' first personnel director.

Brandt attended the University of Wisconsin, but instead of playing football he became one of the first self-taught draft experts or "draft-niks," writing to college athletic departments to borrow game films. By reuniting in Dallas, Schramm and Brandt continued the pioneering scouting legacy of the Rams.

The Cowboys drafted wisely with their first-ever pick, selecting defensive tackle and future Hall of Famer Bob Lilly from Texas Christian with the thirteenth overall pick in 1961. But the Cowboys would become better known for mining the ranks of undiscovered talent.

Brandt, like Eddie Kotal, was a tireless worker, building a deep network of contacts in college football offices, right down to secretaries and trainers. He sent gifts to sources and peppered prospects with Cowboys information. In Brandt's first months on the job, he signed two dozen free agents, a trend he would continue throughout his career, even when the Cowboys were well stocked.

Like the 1950s Rams, the Cowboys focused on small schools, going where other teams did not. Brandt wrote college coaches in other sports for recommendations on athletes that might make good football players, and gambled on them with low draft picks or free agent contracts.

Basketball players Cornell Green (Utah State) and Pete Gent (Michigan State) became productive NFL players at cornerback and wide receiver, respectively. (Kentucky's Pat Riley and Ohio State's John Havlicek stuck with the NBA route.) Bob Hayes, best known as a gold medal sprinter at the 1964 Olympics, became a star wide receiver, though Carl Lewis never took the Cowboys up on their offer.

Then there was Naval Academy quarterback Roger Staubach, whom the Cowboys drafted in the tenth round in 1964 and waited for while he fulfilled a five-year service commitment.

The Cowboys were the first team to scout for "character" in terms of citizenship. Landry, the no-nonsense coach, wanted clean-cut, God-fearing, family men. He figured hard-partying players were less likely to make the most of their talents and more likely to embarrass the franchise. It was an ambitious goal, though the Cowboys benefited from players in both categories.

Brandt began interviewing players whenever possible. He asked them what they thought of the Dallas Cowboys, to gauge their passion for playing for the franchise. Not that it was a tough sell. In 1966, the Cowboys began a stretch of twenty consecutive winning seasons.

"We'd ask a lot of stupid questions," Brandt said. "We'd say, 'Just out of curiosity, did you play Little League baseball? Yeah? What position did you play?' If the kid said second base, you'd think, 'Uh-oh. He must not have been a very good athlete. Otherwise he would have been playing shortstop.'"

By the early 1970s, Schramm and Brandt feared the rest of the league had caught up with the Dallas scouting juggernaut. No longer were teams ignoring small schools and other popular Cowboys' fishing holes.

"Our scouts have seen it coming," Schramm told the *Fort Worth Press* in 1973. "They say it's like a jungle out there. Every place they go to look at a player they run over half a dozen scouts from other teams."

The gap between the Cowboys and everyone else closed in part because of the creation of combines, like the early Troika, where teams pooled scouting resources and shared basic information to save time and money. In 1963, three teams formed LESTO (Lions-Eagles-Steelers Talent Organization). The Bears came on board the following year to make it BLESTO. CEPO (Central Eastern Personnel Organization), formed in 1964, was made up of the Colts, Browns, Packers, and St. Louis Cardinals.

The Dallas run wasn't quite over, in part because the Cowboys, like the earlier Rams, believed in stockpiling draft picks. With selections obtained from other teams, they drafted defensive end Ed "Too Tall" Jones with the first overall pick in 1974. The following year, Dallas selected defensive tackle Randy White with the second pick, obtained from the New York Giants in exchange for quarterback Craig Morton.

Then there was Tony Dorsett. The Tampa Bay Buccaneers, who drafted future Hall of Famer Lee Roy Selmon with their first-ever pick in 1976, kicked off the 1977 draft by taking running back Ricky Bell, who had played for Bucs head coach John McKay at Southern Cal.

Dallas then traded four picks to Seattle for the rights to the number-two selection, which they used on Dorsett, the Heisman Trophy winner at Pittsburgh and the first college running back to rush for more than 6,000 yards. Dorsett would rush for 12,739 yards in the NFL, nearly 10,000 more than Bell.

Still, Schramm's prediction of a more level scouting playing field was coming true. From 1971 through the 1981 season, four teams won all of the Super Bowls, and the common denominator between Dallas, the Pittsburgh Steelers, Miami Dolphins, and Oakland Raiders was an ability to take advantage of scouting and the draft.

The Steelers drafted at least one Hall of Famer each year between 1969 and 1972. After a forgettable 1973 draft, they put together the best class of all time in 1974. Despite picking late each round because of a 10-4 record in 1973, the Steelers chose future Hall of Famers with four of their first five picks: wide receiver Lynn Swann in the first, linebacker Jack Lambert in the second, wide receiver John Stallworth in the fourth, and center Mike Webster in the fifth. No other team ever has selected more than two future Canton enshrinees in one draft.

By the late 1970s, the draft had been moved ahead from November to January to April, allowing teams a full four months from the end of the college bowl schedule to further analyze players.

In 1971, Dallas, San Francisco, and Buffalo, descendants of the original "Troika" combine, staged the first scouting combine event. Fifty players showed up to be measured, poked, and physically tested. Over the next twelve years, as many as three combines were staged over separate weekends following the Super Bowl. BLESTO brought its players to the Pontiac Silverdome for a few years. The National Football Scouting combine, a descendant of CEPO, held its event in Tampa, while a third group, which included Dallas and Seattle, used the Seattle Kingdome.

In 1984, the NFL brought some sanity to the process, establishing one leaguewide combine, held at the New Orleans Superdome. Only five teams did not participate. All twenty-eight clubs showed up in 1985, when the combine took place in Tempe, Arizona, and was marred by rain. The combine returned indoors to New Orleans for a year before finding a permanent home in Indianapolis and the Hoosier Dome (now the RCA Dome).

The crumbling of the Schramm-Brandt-Landry dynasty in Dallas began with a series of bad drafts in the late '70s and early '80s. With Staubach's career winding down, Dallas passed on Notre Dame quarterback Joe Montana, selected by the 49ers in the third round in 1979. With Montana at the helm, the 49ers won four Super Bowls. His favorite target, wide receiver Jerry Rice, came out of tiny Mississippi Valley State in 1985, and became the scouting poster child for small-school players.

A new wave of talent became available in 1990 when underclassmen became eligible for the draft. A year earlier, Oklahoma State running back Barry Sanders challenged the NFL's rule that a player needed to be four seasons removed from high school to be draft eligible. The NFL made an exception for Sanders, and a year later the rule was rewritten to require the passage of just three college seasons after the player's high school graduation for eligibility.

Dallas, coming off a 1-15 season and under the new management of owner Jerry Jones and head coach Jimmy Johnson, spent the first pick of the new underclassman era in 1990 on Emmitt Smith, a junior running back from the University of Florida. Along with Troy Aikman, the team's number-one pick from the year before, Smith would build a new Cowboys powerhouse.

After the 1992 season, players with four years of experience were granted unrestricted free agency in a settlement of a lawsuit filed in 1987 by the NFL Players Association. In 1993, a new collective bargaining agreement between the union and the NFL created a salary cap. Free agency seemed, on the surface, to lessen the importance of the draft. Teams now could plug gaps with free agents.

In reality, the draft became more important. A good draft, especially at the lower rounds, could provide talent at a bargain price, locked in for years. On the flip side, a high-priced bust selected in the first round could wreck a team's salary cap flexibility to sign talent in the years to come. Now more than ever, a team's scouting efforts needed to focus on whether a player had the physical skills, mental makeup, and character to cut it in the NFL.

The Indianapolis Colts and San Diego Chargers came to know this better than anyone. In 1998, the Colts held the first pick in the draft and were torn between two quarterbacks: Peyton Manning of Tennessee and Ryan Leaf of Washington State.

Both were big, strong-armed passers with undeniable talent. Manning, the son of former Saints quarterback Archie, lived in the film room and grew up with the idea of following his dad into the NFL. Leaf was less polished, but many scouts believed he had a higher "upside."

With millions of dollars on the line, the Colts and Chargers spent the months leading up to the draft getting inside the heads of both. The Chargers turned to Jonathan Niednagel, a researcher at the Brain Type Institute in Missouri, who believed there were sixteen distinct "brain types." That explained why some people are better suited to be quarterbacks or CEOs than others.

A year earlier, Niednagel's stock rose when he gave the Orlando Magic a glowing review on prep star Tracy McGrady before the NBA Draft. He warned the Chargers that Leaf did not have the brain type to handle the pressures of leading a rebuilding team. Manning, Niednagel believed, would be a star.

The Chargers didn't listen and handed Leaf a bonus of $11.25 million. From the beginning, Leaf established a pattern of poor play and immature behavior. The Chargers released him after three horrific seasons and he was out of football two years after that, arguably the biggest bust in draft history.

With the dawn of the new millennium, scouting and success in the draft continued to separate the most successful franchises from everyone else. The New England Patriots, under head coach Bill Belichick and general manager Scott Pioli, built a dynasty through the draft, led by quarterback Tom Brady, a sixth-round pick in 2000.

By the time the Manning–Leaf debate heated up in the spring of 1998, the NFL Draft had become a multimedia extravaganza. Sports radio, which exploded in the 1990s, became a twenty-four hour barroom for endless speculation. Draft talk could be found every day of the year. It was the perfect never-ending debate, since nobody, with the possible exception of Niednagel, could truly predict the success or failure of a player.

The emergence of the Internet in the late 1990s created an additional outlet for draft discussion. Suddenly every self-proclaimed draft expert needed to have a Web site, complete with player information and a regularly updated mock draft.

Then there was ESPN, which turned a smoky backroom business meeting into must-see TV.

When ESPN asked the NFL to broadcast its annual "selection meeting" in 1980, it was not because network officials envisioned millions of viewers or a cult following for year-round draft coverage. The year-old, fledgling cable sports station in Bristol, Connecticut, merely was looking for some much needed programming. Anything featuring the NFL shield seemed like a good bet.

The future "worldwide leader of sports" was in just seven million homes at the time, and had not yet landed contracts to televise major sports leagues. When ESPN's president Chet Simmons approached Rozelle about televising the draft, the commissioner all but laughed.

Even a marketing visionary like Rozelle found it difficult to see the allure of watching a bunch of guys sitting around tables shouting out names. That didn't sound like riveting television, especially not on Tuesday and Wednesday afternoons, which was when the draft was held until 1988.

The move to weekends that year was not one of Rozelle's shrewd marketing decisions, but merely a concession to New York's Marriott Marquis hotel, which began hosting the draft in 1985 to boost business. Three years later, Marriott needed the space to handle the lucrative midweek banquet circuit.

Instead of paying more for the weekday space, Rozelle shifted the draft to Saturday and Sunday, much to the chagrin of team officials, who didn't want to give up a weekend in the off-season.

They would never get it back. The league and the network quickly discovered that there were millions of football-starved fans across the nation just like the crazy young men who showed up at the draft site to boo the New York Jets' selections in person. The Marriott Marquis would be the last of a long series of hotels to host the event, giving way to a theater at Madison Square Garden.

ESPN drew nearly 1.7 million viewers in 1988 to view the draft. By 1993, the audience had grown to 2.5 million. In 2004, a staggering 31 million viewers tuned in over what had become a marathon, two-day affair to hear that their team was "on the clock."

ESPN is now in more than ninety million homes and is the only network to have broadcast the four major team sports during the same year. But even with multiple channels and thousands of hours of live coverage, the draft arguably is its signature event—or rather pseudo-event.

For all of ESPN's multiple sets, prepackaged features, and glitzy introductions, the draft, at its essence, is nothing more than a business meeting conducted in painfully slow fashion, at least in the first round. Still, each spring the network manages to grab attention away from athletes competing in actual contests.

Nothing is more suited to ESPN, its army of analysts, and its self-promotional engine, than the NFL Draft. There's a five-month calendar of preliminary events, beginning with college bowl games, many of which appear on ESPN. There's the Senior Bowl, held in late January and heavily covered by ESPN, and the late-February NFL combine, which is broadcast exclusively on the NFL's own network, but is covered extensively by ESPN. That leaves two months for ESPN to scrutinize the volatile draft "stocks" of every position and player, which it does to some degree all year.

The draft has become the NFL's off-season marketing platform, stealing attention from the first month of the Major League Baseball schedule and the end of the NBA and NHL regular seasons, and keeping the NFL in the forefront.

That's significant because the NFL, among the four major sports leagues, has the longest stretch between its championship game and first regular season contest. The draft, held in late April, falls almost in the middle of the hiatus. Unlike baseball, with its unknown cast of high school and college draftees, or the NBA's increasingly European contingent of draft picks, NFL selections are college stars and familiar faces to fans, especially in the early rounds.

Because of parity in the NFL, fans believe their teams are just one young player away from the Super Bowl, even though few NFL draft picks make an impact as rookies. Still, most at least play special teams and contribute in backup roles. They certainly don't disappear for years in the minor leagues like their counterparts in baseball and hockey.

Then there's the unbridled popularity of the NFL itself, fueled by lasting labor peace and competitive balance, to say nothing of undertones of sex (cheerleaders) and violence, along with a weekly episode format that's ideal for television and the short attention spans of the technological age. Most teams compete in new, publicly funded stadiums, and have waiting lists of thousands of fans willing to purchase tickets.

The NFL has become a runaway cash machine. In September of 2004, *Forbes* Magazine, in its annual listing of franchise values, valued nineteen NFL clubs at $700 million or more. The only sports team ranked ahead of the lowest-valued NFL franchise (Arizona Cardinals,

$552 million and climbing, with a new stadium under construction) was the New York Yankees.

No sport, with the possible exception of NASCAR, approaches the NFL's popularity.

"Baseball is America's pastime," Howie Long said during his Pro Football Hall of Fame induction speech in 2000. "But football is truly America's passion."

That passion is channeled by thousands of draftniks, who, through the Internet, follow the ups and downs of a player in the months leading up to the draft with the intensity of day traders. The draftniks mock-draft endlessly and collect information obsessively.

No draftnik rivals the legendary Joel Buchsbaum, a reclusive, self-taught football analyst who for more than two decades watched film and worked a network of sources as vast as any NFL scout or executive, almost exclusively by phone from his Brooklyn apartment. His *Pro Football Weekly* columns and draft books were considered must-reading for fans and NFL executives, many of whom turned to *him* for information. New England Patriots head coach Bill Belichick and Ernie Accorsi, the general manager of the New York Giants, were among those that attended Buchsbaum's funeral in 2002.

Buchsbaum, with a gaunt physique and nasal voice, never was a good fit for television, though he appeared regularly on radio. The TV void was filled by Mel Kiper Jr., who, as an eighteen-year-old in 1979, assembled his own draft guide and distributed it to NFL executives and media.

Accorsi, then the general manager of the Colts, was among those that sent words of encouragement. By 1984, Kiper was on ESPN and becoming the face of the draft, with his signature pompadour hair and endless stream of player information.

In his early ESPN days, Kiper was more likely to take teams to task for what he viewed as bad selections, famously calling out the Jets in 1989 for drafting linebacker Jeff Lageman from the University of Virginia in the first round.

"It's obvious to me the Jets don't know what the draft's all about," Kiper said.

Kiper knew exactly what the draft was about, and what it was becoming, a year-round process that blurred college and professional football and channeled the passions of fans of both. From one draft report in 1979, he built an empire of draft publications. He parlayed a one-weekend ESPN gig into yearlong employment that included regular draft projections online and on television and a college football–themed radio show in the fall.

"When you say Mel Kiper you think of the NFL draft," Kiper has said. "That's something I've always been very proud of."

As for Lageman, he enjoyed a productive, decade-long career with the Jets and Jacksonville Jaguars. Perhaps Kiper could be forgiven for undervaluing the linebacker. After 1942, when Pittsburgh drafted halfback Bill Dudley first overall, the University of Virginia generated just three first-round picks in the next forty-six years.

After Lageman, the Cavaliers produced five first-round selections in the next decade, most notably Herman Moore of the Detroit Lions in 1991. But entering the 2004 season, no Cavalier had been selected before the third round since the 2000 draft.

That was bad for recruiting, since it did not speak highly of Virginia's ability to prepare players for the NFL. Nobody knew that better than Al Groh, the longtime former NFL assistant now at the helm of his alma mater, who ran his ship like a pro franchise and was determined to make Virginia the top NFL prep school.

Chapter Four:

PRO COLLEGE
FOOTBALL

The Virginia Cavaliers were 4-0 and ranked tenth in the country when they took the field at home against Clemson on October 7, 2004. Al Groh, the longtime Bill Parcells disciple who had resigned as head coach of the New York Jets after a one-year stint four years earlier, had transformed a Virginia program with a recent history of good, but not great squads into a national title contender.

Across the sideline, Tommy Bowden paced anxiously. Son of Bobby Bowden, the veteran Florida State head coach, Tommy saved his job at Clemson with a strong finish in 2003. That mattered little now, what with the Tigers off to a 1-3 start and fans again calling for his head.

Clemson defeated Virginia twenty-nine straight times before the Cavaliers stopped the streak in 1990. The teams had split the series since, with Virginia holding a slight advantage, but the Cavaliers fans still remembered the streak and took great joy in Clemson's downfall.

With so many subplots, ESPN officials were thrilled with their decision months earlier to schedule the upstart Cavaliers and struggling Tigers as one of their two Thursday night matchups. The national media had not converged on Charlottesville, though Virginia's spacious press box had a larger-than-average crowd on hand.

For a group of eleven National Football League scouts and executives patrolling the sidelines before the game, the contest was meaningless;

they planned to depart long before the finish to beat traffic. They were on hand to get a close look at about a dozen of Groh's players with serious NFL potential, along with a lesser number of Clemson standouts.

The Cavaliers stormed out of a tunnel pumped full of smoke by a fog machine, to the delight of a sellout crowd of 61,833. Groh jogged over to the sidelines and greeted three friends from his NFL days.

There was Tom Donahoe, the president and general manager of the Buffalo Bills, whom Groh met when Donahoe was an area scout with the Pittsburgh Steelers and Groh was head coach at Wake Forest in the early 1980s. There was Terry Bradway, who took over as general manager of the New York Jets after Groh departed, and Charlie Casserly, the Houston Texans general manager, who never worked with Groh but shares a mutual respect based on their years of NFL experience.

The NFL officials, or at least their scouting staffs, had watched videotapes of Groh's players and were impressed with their size, speed, and playing ability. The executives had spent the previous hour roaming the sidelines as players warmed up, analyzing "body types." They took notes on whether bodies were chiseled or soft, whether arms were long or short, and whether calves were skinny or tight.

Now they turned to Groh to help fill in the gaps that videotape or medical evaluations could not provide. Were there any discipline problems? Did a particular player lack heart or motivation? How passionate was a certain player about football? The line of questioning was not nearly as deep as it might be back at the Virginia football facility, without a game on the line, but it was valuable nonetheless.

They expressed interest in Elton Brown, the massive, six-six, 338-pound offensive guard considered among the best in the country at his position. They asked about Alvin Pearman, who technically was the backup tailback, but saw significant playing time, thrived on special teams, and showed flashes of NFL potential. The scouts were curious about defensive end Chris Canty, who was projected as a first-round pick in the 2005 draft as recently as two weeks ago, before a devastating knee injury against Syracuse sidelined him for the rest of the season.

Brown, Pearman, and Canty were seniors, along with a half dozen other players with lesser NFL prospects. They were hardly the only Virginia players eligible for the 2005 NFL Draft, though the scouts knew better than to ask Groh—or any other college coach—about underclassmen.

Players that are at least three seasons removed from high school are eligible for the draft. Juniors can leave early. So can a sophomore, if he spent a year in prep school following high school graduation or was "redshirted," not playing as a college freshman in order to develop further.

Groh, like most college coaches, believes there is almost never a reason for a player to leave school for the NFL with eligibility remaining. After all, he could benefit from another year of development at the college level.

That's usually true—less than half of underclassmen who declare early for the draft are selected in the first three rounds—but it's *definitely* true that college football coaches win more games when their best players complete their college eligibility, rather than leaving early for the NFL.

It's a sometimes uneasy alliance between the NFL and the colleges. The college coaches stress that they're serving student-athletes, and don't want players looking beyond the next game, let alone to the next level. At the same time, they realize the best way to recruit high school kids to their school is to produce a steady parade of players to the NFL.

So the college coaches throw open their office doors during the season, allowing NFL scouts to arrive early on weekday mornings and watch videotape of players. The scouts, always clad in golf shirts or jackets bearing their NFL team logos, can spend much of the morning chatting with trainers, assistant coaches, tutors, and the head coach himself about players. After lunch they can watch practice.

On game days, they receive press-box credentials and can wander the field before the game. In exchange for such carte blanche access, they agree not to ask about or express interest in underclassmen, even those widely considered to be leaving early.

Sometimes college coaches will let NFL friends know if players are coming out early, if only to give them a head start on scouting. Like character evaluation, it's one area where scouts must have a strong network of sources to provide them with inside information.

"It's imperative that scouts dig deeper," says Donahoe, the Bills president. "You need guys you can trust that will tell you if someone is a good character guy or not. If you have developed those right relationships, you'll get an honest evaluation."

By now, many scouts had been clued in about Heath Miller, who was in his fourth season at Virgina but was just a junior because of a redshirt season in 2001. As a sophomore, Miller led all tight ends in the nation with seventy receptions for 835 yards. Like many draft prospects, he already was dealing with agents, which was allowed under the guidelines of the National Collegiate Athletic Association (NCAA), so long as the player receives nothing of value, not even a can of soda.

Scouts viewed Miller as the prototype tight end for the increasingly popular West Coast offense, which emphasizes short passes and places a premium on catching over blocking when it comes to tight ends.

Miller kept in close contact with Matt Schaub, the Virginia quarterback the previous season, who now was a rookie with the Atlanta Falcons, for advice about choosing an agent. David Dunn, Schaub's representative, was lobbying hard through Schaub and directly to represent Miller for the NFL Draft.

As a student, Miller was a senior. But he was a junior by NCAA guidelines, which technically made him off limits to NFL scouts, though most knew to treat him like a senior and scout accordingly.

Three other players were *definitely* off limits. Ahmad Brooks and Darryl Blackstock were NFL prototype linebackers and represented Groh's finest work as a talent developer since returning to the college ranks. D'Brickashaw Ferguson quietly had emerged as one of the nation's top left tackles.

Brooks and Blackstock, standing six-four and weighing between 240 and 260 pounds, delivered bone-crunching tackles and ran much faster than other players their size. Nobody knew that better than Groh, who as a linebackers coach under Parcells for the Jets, New York Giants, and New England Patriots had worked closely with the likes of Hall of Famer Lawrence Taylor and Pro Bowlers Carl Banks, Mo Lewis, Chris Slade, and Willie McGinest.

Blackstock and Ferguson were juniors, Brooks a sophomore, but all three were eligible for the draft, Brooks by virtue of a season spent in prep school.

Few players in college football in 2004 had as much upside as Brooks, named by *USA Today* the 2001 High School Defensive Player of the Year. Ahmad ran so fast, hit with so much force, and possessed so much raw athletic ability that Groh had at times lined him up as a kickoff returner, wide receiver, and safety.

Brooks, like every other college football player with pro potential, was getting bombarded with letters and phone calls from many of the one thousand three hundred agents registered by the NFL Players Association, all hoping to earn a 3 percent commission on the career earnings of the next Lawrence Taylor.

The agents had their work cut out for them, and not just because Brooks was so coveted and unsure of whether he was coming out. His father, Perry, played eight seasons at defensive tackle for the Washington Redskins and knew all about dealing with agents. Having grown up in a two-parent household with the financial comfort that comes from an NFL career, Brooks did not need to leave early for pro football riches.

Blackstock was a different story. When he was a freshman, his then-girlfriend became pregnant, and he now had a thirteen-month-old son, Savion, to support.

The agents would try their best to get close to Blackstock, Brooks, and Ferguson. As for the scouts and NFL executives, they knew to keep their distance.

Chris Canty tried to get comfortable as he watched ESPN's coverage of the Virginia–Clemson game. Lying in a hospital bed in Birmingham, Alabama, amid a fog of painkillers, he surveyed the wreckage of his left knee and, he feared, his football career.

Al Groh, ever wary of the media, had refused to disclose much about Canty's injury, even though there was no chance of the senior defensive end returning to play college football. The only thing Groh told the press was that Canty had suffered a season-ending, "severe left knee injury."

Severe? Canty's lower leg had essentially been ripped from his body at the knee. It was still in one piece, but the posterior cruciate ligament (PCL), lateral collateral ligament (LCL), and anterior cruciate ligaments (ACL) were shredded. Only the medial collateral ligament (MCL) remained intact.

The first thought Canty had upon being helped from the football field in agony twelve days earlier was not when he'd play football again, but whether he would ever *walk* again.

It was a routine play. Canty chased down Syracuse tailback Damien Rhodes from behind. Two players—one from each team—converged and Canty's left knee buckled from the weight of the pile.

Canty, like the rest of his teammates, knew the story of Anthony Poindexter, the team's running backs coach who, as a hard-hitting safety for the Cavaliers in 1998, saw a once-promising NFL career crumble amid a similar pile of bodies. Poindexter had returned for a senior season, turning down an early entrance to the NFL.

After the 2003 season, Canty requested a rating from an NFL advisory committee that evaluates the draft prospects of juniors and other players three years removed from high school. It's a notoriously conservative bunch, and the information it provides to juniors all but discourages players from going pro early. The letter begins with, "Since 1990, when the National Football League reluctantly concluded that a change in its eligibility standards was necessary . . ." as if the NFL made the decision unilaterally, not in the face of litigation.

The committee, which is made up of twelve NFL scouts and executives, along with representatives from BLESTO and National Football Scouting, "serves in a limited advisory capacity for players faced with the decision of whether to make such a declaration" for the NFL Draft. The committee provides one of five assessments. The player either:

- will be drafted in round one
- will not be drafted higher than the second round
- will not be drafted higher than the fourth round
- will not be drafted higher than the sixth round
- will not be drafted

The committee stresses that the rating is merely a "good faith opinion" and is "in no way a commitment or guarantee of any player's selection." Despite the explicit instructions and qualified language of the rating, players often interpret the rating of "will not be drafted higher than the second round" as "will likely be drafted in the second round."

That's sufficient reason for many players to go pro. But not for Canty, who did not play football until his junior year of high school in Charlotte, North Carolina, and received only two Division 1 scholarship offers, from Virginia and Boston College.

He arrived in Charlottesville in the fall of 2000, a gangly six-seven, 215 pounds, with decent potential. A "project," in coach-speak. Canty immediately set up shop in the weight room and steadily put on weight. By 2002, he was a well-chiseled 280 pounds and led ACC defensive linemen in tackles. On pace to graduate after the 2003 season, there seemed little reason to return.

Instead, Canty purchased disability insurance, enrolled in graduate school and, like Poindexter six years earlier, shredded three of the four ligaments in a knee on a similar play.

As Canty underwent an examination in the training room the morning after the injury, Groh was among his first visitors.

"You can't control what happened, but you can control how you react to it," Groh said. "Now you just have to be the fastest guy to come off this kind of injury."

Canty nodded and forced a smile, even as he winced in pain. Virginia players marveled at how Groh could compartmentalize any setback, no matter how serious. Just another minor obstacle to overcome, he made it seem.

There was precedent. Running back Willis McGahee endured the same injury at the University of Miami and now was thriving for the Buffalo Bills.

I can do this, Canty told himself.

The next visitor was Poindexter. Unlike Groh, his expression was not one of compassion or encouragement, but urgency.

"Listen to me, you've got to get out of here as fast as you can and have the surgery," Poindexter said. "I waited three weeks to get it done. Scar tissue sets in. You want to give this the best shot possible."

Within days, Canty was stretched out uncomfortably on a plane to Birmingham, where James Andrews, the orthopedist who had put hundreds of pro athletes back together, operated on the knee.

Now Canty watched from the hospital bed as the Cavaliers moved on without him. Faith, he reminded himself, would be his guide. Shirley Canty, the pastor of the Calvary United Methodist Church in Charlotte, and her congregation were praying hard on behalf of her injured son.

Yes, Chris Canty told himself, he would make it back in time for the NFL Draft, now just six and a half months away. He would become the fastest guy to return from the surgery and would have the pro career NFL scouts had envisioned nine months earlier. That much, he knew, was certain.

First, he had to figure out how to walk again.

As Canty settled in to watch the second half, the NFL scouts and executives quietly observed the game from the press box. They were assigned seats in two rows on the far end of the box, far away from the media, and with plenty of space between one another.

It's not that scouts worry about competitors peeking at their notes; given the grueling travel and marathon hours, many of them become good friends. Besides, they glean most of their information from watching film, practice, and interviewing coaches, and they take few notes during games. Virginia's media relations department, following Groh's lead, just wanted to make sure the NFL representatives felt comfortable.

It was an impressive gathering of NFL brass, who were on hand not only because of the volume of draft-eligible talent in the game, but because Thursday night is a good time for a general manager or personnel director to duck out and see a game.

During the season, a NFL general manager is immersed in the day-to-day running of a team. There are injured players to replace, constant meetings with team owners, coaches, and agents, and a daily barrage of interview requests from reporters.

The bulk of scouting is handled by a staff of "area scouts" spread out across the country, like the ones on hand that evening representing the Carolina Panthers and Dallas Cowboys. Over the course of the college football season, they file hundreds of reports, which in January become the basis for a more thorough evaluation that includes the general manager and coaching staff.

Still, most GMs try to find the time during the season to see at least three college games a month, usually not far from home. When the team is playing on the road on Sunday, the executives will visit a nearby school on Friday and Saturday. The idea is to build a working knowledge of college players in the fall so they'll be up to speed when draft meetings begin in earnest in December and January.

For Vinny Cerrato, the vice president of football operations for the Washington Redskins, attending the Virginia–Clemson game was a no-brainer. He made the two-hour drive from his northern Virginia home and would be back in the office early the following morning.

Like other NFL executives, Cerrato relies heavily on a vast network of college coaches he knows from previous jobs, first as recruiting coordinator at Notre Dame from 1986–1990 and from nine seasons spent in scouting with the San Francisco 49ers.

Before the game, while his competitors from other teams chatted up Al Groh, Cerrato checked in with Clemson offensive line coach Brad Scott and Mark D'Onofrio, Virginia's tight ends and special teams coach.

Cerrato had never worked with either, though he sometimes recruited head-to-head against Scott when Scott was Florida State's recruiting coordinator in the late '80s. Cerrato also tried unsuccessfully to recruit D'Onofrio to Notre Dame (D'Onofrio chose Penn State). Still, those are significant enough connections, so that Cerrato feels comfortable turning to the two assistants for insight into players.

Then again, Cerrato is blessed with the ability to build lasting relationships, even with unlikely people. He was among the first employees hired when Daniel Snyder purchased the Redskins in 1999, and aside from spending the 2001 season as an analyst for ESPN, he has stayed in the good graces of the notorious taskmaster. Cerrato counts sports agent Gary Wichard among his closest friends, even serving in his wedding party.

Building a network of people for draft scouting purposes was no different.

"When you want to know about a player, you start with the friends you have on the coaching staff," Cerrato says. "From there, you go to the strength coach, trainer, graduate assistants—regardless of whether you have previous relationships or not. You learn in this business how to build relationships quickly."

Cerrato had a national championship ring from his stint under Lou Holtz at Notre Dame and a Super Bowl ring from the 49ers from 1994. But the Redskins had struggled under Snyder's ownership. Even Joe Gibbs, the Hall of Fame coach who came out of retirement nine months earlier, had made little difference over the first month of the 2004 NFL season.

The 2005 draft would be the second since Gibbs's return. Gibbs always has been a fan of using multiple tight ends, retaining as many as five on the roster, and Cerrato was keeping an eye on Heath Miller, Virginia's All-American.

Early in the second half, with Virginia just ten yards from the end zone, Miller ran a perfect pattern to his left and reached over his shoulder for the ball. But quarterback Marcus Hagans overthrew him.

"We ran that same play against Dallas last week," Cerrato says.

NFL rules prohibit team employees from commenting on underclassmen. Cerrato did not speak directly about Miller, though he almost certainly knew the tight end was likely to go pro.

"A lot of times, the school will tell you if a guy is coming out," Cerrato said, not referring to Miller specifically.

At halftime, Cerrato departed to beat the traffic. Most of his colleagues followed shortly. For NFL scouts, the game is far less important than information gleaned beforehand.

Two seats over from Cerrato's empty chair, Tom Donahoe scribbled down notes and chatted with Bill Rees, the director of player personnel for the San Francisco 49ers. Donahoe shuffled scouting reports on Clemson and Virginia players provided by BLESTO, one of the two scouting services most NFL teams subscribe to.

For Donahoe, the president and general manager of the Buffalo Bills, the trip to Charlottesville was a welcome respite from the day-to-day running of a struggling franchise.

A former high school football and basketball coach, Donahoe rose through the ranks of the Pittsburgh Steelers scouting department and spent most of the 1990s running one of the decade's most successful teams. After losing a power struggle with head coach Bill Cowher and getting fired, Donahoe spent a year working for ESPN before being hired by the Buffalo Bills, another team of the '90s.

Unfortunately for Donahoe, the Bills were light years removed from the team that appeared in four consecutive Super Bowls (losing all four) under head coach Marv Levy and quarterback Jim Kelly. Though the Bills finished 11-5 as recently as 1999, and 8-8 the season before his hiring, Donahoe inherited an aging roster with contracts that provided him little flexibility under the salary cap. Some twenty-three million dollars of cap money already had been spent on players long gone.

Donahoe did what he could, shipping a first-round pick to New England for Drew Bledsoe, who resurrected his career in Buffalo. Before the 2003 season, Donahoe carved enough room under the salary cap to sign star safety Lawyer Milloy, a victim of the cap in New England.

Still, the turnaround had been slow. Under Donahoe, the Bills went 3-13 in 2001, 8-8 in 2002, and 6-10 in 2003. They were 0-3 when Donahoe boarded team owner Ralph Wilson Jr.'s private jet to Charlottesville.

"We've had so many problems the first couple of years in Buffalo because of cap problems and a roster that badly needed to be turned over," Donahoe said. "Our roster was terrible three years ago, just pathetic."

Like his colleagues around the league, Donahoe faced the challenge of managing the salary cap. Successful franchises create a pipeline of young, relatively inexpensive players through the draft. As established players grow older and gain the leverage to demand more lucrative contracts, teams can release them, confident that the younger players can step into expanded roles.

The problem occurs when draft picks don't pan out, forcing teams to re-sign the veteran or acquire a comparable free agent to fill in the gap. That results in a bigger hit to the salary cap, especially if the veteran player gets hurt or his skills deteriorate quickly.

"You always have to be looking ahead with the cap and contracts," Donahoe says. "Sometimes you're forced with the cap to make decisions, and some guys you just can't keep. Ideally, you want to have a roster where you have guys from the draft you can plug in. But we've got so many holes right now, we're just trying to get players anywhere we can get them."

With a five-year contract through 2005, Donahoe's future in Buffalo hinged in part on having a successful draft in 2005. That was what made out-of-the-way trips to places like Charlottesville so important. Of course, as his NFL competitors in the press box reminded him as he packed up to leave, it's a lot easier with a private jet at your disposal.

"My travel isn't nearly as tough as what these guys face," said Donahoe, who logged thousands of hard scouting miles working for the Steelers. "Plus, this is the best part of the job. You can take a lot of the other stuff and you can have it, but going out and evaluating players, that's the fun aspect of what I do."

Anthony Poindexter huddled on the sidelines with Virginia's running backs, barking instructions and imploring his troops to raise their level of play even higher. It was late in the third quarter and the Cavaliers were well on their way to rushing for 257 yards against Clemson.

Poindexter never figured on working as a college football assistant coach, at least not at the age of twenty-eight. With a shaved head, confident swagger, and a powerful six-one build, he looked like he belonged in the NFL. Most figured the former All-American safety, known as one of the game's most ferocious hitters during his college years, would spend at least a decade in the league.

Instead, Poindexter lasted just parts of three seasons with the Baltimore Ravens and Cleveland Browns, though not for a lack of talent or worth ethic. Now his name was synonymous not with hitting but with injuries and unfulfilled dreams.

In 1998, Poindexter turned down a shot at the NFL and returned for his fifth and final year of eligibility at Virginia. Considered a "not higher than the second round" prospect by the NFL advisory committee that provides ratings for draft-eligible underclassmen, Poindexter opted to improve his stock with a fifth season.

The decision looked like a wise one early in the fall, when Poindexter continued to terrorize opposing running backs and wide receivers. Then, in a four-player scrum against North Carolina State in the seventh game of the season, he shredded three of the four ligaments in his left knee, jeopardizing his career.

Like many top college players, Poindexter had taken out a $1 million disability insurance policy that he could collect only if he did not play in a NFL regular season game. He kept his options open as long as possible, rebuilding the injured knee with the help of a trainer who had worked with All-Pro wide receiver Jerry Rice.

Drafted by the Baltimore Ravens in the seventh round in 1999—a far cry from his potential second round projection before the injury—Poindexter spent the 1999 season on the Ravens inactive squad and then voided the policy by playing in 2000. He played sparingly but earned a Super Bowl ring, even though he did not actually see action in Super Bowl XXXV against the New York Giants in Tampa, Florida.

"It was a risk, but I figured I was a young guy with a college degree to fall back on," Poindexter said. "I didn't want to look back years from now and wonder, 'What if I had pursued it?' Hopefully, I'll make things up financially."

Poindexter's comments were made at the Super Bowl in 2001 and his career ended the following fall when he was released by the Cleveland Browns with career earnings below a million dollars. Groh, who as an assistant under Bill Parcells was not allowed to speak to the media, imposed the same gag order on his assistants.

"Anthony is the saddest story I've had representing pro athletes," said Ben Dogra, an agent for SFX Sports who served as Poindexter's agent, and at the moment was recruiting Virginia linebacker Darryl Blackstock. "Anthony was never a great athlete. He was a great football player who made it on instincts. The injury cost him a half-step. If Barry Sanders or Deion Sanders loses a half-step, they're okay. Willis McGahee was a 4.3 guy (in the forty). Now he's 4.4 and that's still pretty good. But Anthony has never complained to me, never once saying 'I should have gone pro.'"

By hiring Poindexter as a graduate assistant for the 2003 season and promoting him to running backs coach for 2004, Groh created a highly visible cautionary tale for players weighing a decision to go pro early.

Though Groh hoped to keep his raw-but-promising linebackers from departing for the NFL as underclassmen, there were strong counterarguments in their midst in Poindexter and now defensive end Chris Canty, who turned down NFL money to return for a fifth season only to suffer a season-ending knee injury twelve days earlier against Syracuse.

Poindexter had become such a strong argument for going pro that players from other schools invoked his name when considering their options. Agents hoping to convince underclassmen to turn pro early mention Poindexter as Exhibit A. Michael Vick cited Poindexter when he left Virginia Tech early in 2001, becoming the draft's top overall pick when he was selected by the Atlanta Falcons.

"I had to look at it from a lot of different aspects," Vick said. "Maybe I would have had an injury that was career-ending. Maybe I would have had an injury that would have hampered me for two or three games and caused my stock to drop."

Of course, no coach would begrudge a consensus top pick like Vick from leaving early, regardless of reason. Groh was correct when he noted that, "If you go to the NFL (early), you might get hurt. If you play football at any level, you might get hurt. If you get scared of getting injured in college and go to a NFL team unprepared to deliver, you might get cut. Where does that leave you?"

Perhaps in a situation a lot like that of Anthony Poindexter.

Al Groh's office at the University of Virginia is a shrine to his thirteen years of NFL coaching experience, mostly as a linebackers coach under Bill Parcells. There are autographed photos from former players such as Clay Matthews, Mo Lewis, and Curtis Martin, a framed letter from Lawrence Taylor on the occasion of his Hall of Fame induction, thanking Groh for "making me into the best player I could be," and game plans from Groh's NFL days in binders color-coded green (New York Jets), blue (New York Giants), and red (New England Patriots).

The décor is less of an ego wall than it is a reminder to current and prospective players that Groh is in the business of acquiring and developing NFL-caliber talent. Like every college coach, he preaches that his primary focus is to educate young men and win national championships. In the competitive world of college football recruiting, where every high school star is convinced he's just four years—if not three— away from a career in the NFL, Groh makes full use of his program's vast NFL pedigree.

"We're used to coaching NFL players and we want to continue to coach NFL players," Groh says. "We just want to do it before they get to the NFL instead of after."

During the 2004 season, Groh was one of only eight head coaches in Division 1-A with NFL head coaching experience. Groh spent just one year as a head coach, leading the Jets to a 9-7 record in 2000 after taking over for Parcells. Like Parcells, his longtime mentor, he micromanaged everything and clashed with the media. Unlike Parcells, Groh did not have the track record of winning as a head coach or the larger-than-life personality to pull off such a style effectively. When Groh resigned to become head coach at his alma mater, few tears were shed.

"Yeah, we were 6-1 at one point, but a lot of that was despite the fact that Al was the coach," Kevin Mawae, the Jets Pro Bowl center, told the

New York Daily News upon Groh's departure. "He tried to micromanage, and a lot of guys tuned him out a long time ago. I don't think there's much heartache about Al leaving. Guys aren't hurt that he's gone. For the most part, guys weren't happy. It's hard to play for a guy when you're not happy."

Back at the college level, where he coached at Wake Forest from 1981 to 1986, Groh had not needed to worry about the happiness and feelings of handsomely compensated professional athletes. If players did not like Groh's system, well, they must not be cut out for playing at the highest level. Quotes posted on the door to Groh's office all but served as warnings.

From Ray Lewis, the Baltimore Ravens All-Pro linebacker: "Pain is only temporary, no matter how long it lasts. Don't use pain as an excuse. It's not important."

From Parcells: "I'm looking for big, fast guys who can play football, are aggressive, and have a passion for the game. I really don't like guys who don't like football and are not willing to do what it takes."

George Welsh, Groh's predecessor at Virginia, left the program in good shape when he retired after the 2000 season. Before Welsh took over in 1982, Virginia had produced just two winning seasons in twenty-nine years. Under Welsh, the Cavaliers became a perennial bowl game participant and put together a string of consecutive winning seasons from 1987 through 1999.

But Welsh, a graduate of the U.S. Naval Academy, who served as an assistant under Joe Paterno at Penn State before returning to Navy as head coach, never was comfortable having pro scouts around. NFL officials were allowed into practices, but Welsh made it clear he wasn't happy about it. The old salt was old school. The Cavaliers did not have their names on the backs of their uniforms and for much of Welsh's tenure wore white helmets without logos.

Welsh's staff usually consisted of career college coaches in their forties and fifties. Unlike Groh, Welsh did not have a vast network of NFL friends and acquaintances. He viewed sports agents with disdain.

If his program was not viewed as NFL preparatory, Welsh didn't care. He was pleased when players like Herman Moore, Aaron Brooks, and Tiki and Ronde Barber achieved stardom in the NFL, but he was more proud of their accomplishments at Virginia.

When Groh took over for the retiring Welsh in 2001, the first thing he did was put a professional stamp on the program. He slapped names on the uniforms and hired assistant coaches in their early 30s, most with NFL playing, coaching, or scouting experience. He fielded calls from agents and even brought them in for an "NFL Agents Meeting" to speak with players and their parents each summer. Groh hired a strength coach, Evan Marcus, who previously worked for the New Orleans Saints.

Ever the micromanager, Groh even took an active role in the production of the media guide, which no longer read "media guide" on the cover, but instead served as more of a glossy, high-end recruiting tool. The book had doubled in size and become a tribute to the NFL background of Groh and his staff.

The 296-page 2004 edition included hundreds of references to the NFL, including a page on the NFL Agents Meeting. Groh had invited a handful of agents that he respected to talk to his players. The group included Jimmy Sexton, the agent for Parcells and a number of NFL veterans; Brad Blank, who represented a long line of Cavaliers, including Moore and Slade; and Anthony Agnone, whose clients included Patrick Kerney, the former Virginia defensive end now with the Atlanta Falcons.

After the table of contents and two pages on the football stadium came the first of many references to Groh's NFL background:

When Virginia head coach Al Groh and his staff talk about what it takes to be the best in college and pro football, players listen. As a former NFL coach who has been to two Super Bowls, Al Groh is an expert at evaluating and developing exceptional talent.

Through his first three seasons, Groh had yet to take his alma mater beyond the level of the Welsh regime. In 2001, Groh's first year, the Cavaliers posted their first losing season since 1986 before winning nine games in 2002 and eight in 2003. Still, Groh had managed to raise the profile of the program. He convinced students to scrap the century-old tradition of wearing semiformal attire to games and wear orange T-shirts instead. A marching band replaced a ragtag pep group. Using his staff's NFL experience as a recruiting tool, he began landing blue-chip recruits such as Brooks and Ferguson.

Unlike many college coaches who restrict access to practice for fear of compromising game plans, Groh maintains an open-door policy all season long, except on Thursdays. The scouting reports his coaches file on Virginia's high school recruits are modeled after the NFL. During recruiting season, the coaches rank prep players on a board in a conference room just like NFL teams create a draft board.

The afternoon after Virginia defeated Clemson 30–10, to improve to 5-0, Groh pulled out a laminated scouting report. There were spaces for coaches to fill in remarks on objective information such as height, weight, and years as a starter. There were areas to note more subjective evaluations such as personality, character, work ethic, and competitiveness.

"All we've done is substitute the word recruit for draft," Groh said. "You have the same two categories as the NFL: tools and makeup. Tools are physical skills. The makeup category, that's the part that's going to help a player take advantage of the tools or the deficiency that doesn't let him take advantage. Each category is just as important in recruiting."

As if on cue, Groh's cell phone rang. He glanced at the caller ID and saw that it was Eugene Monroe, who ranked as the top prep offensive lineman in the country. Monroe had verbally committed to Virginia, but until he signed in February Groh and his staff needed to continue the strong sales pitch.

"Eugene, did you see the game last night?" Groh asked. "Did you see number sixty-six, D'Brickashaw Ferguson? That's your position, Eugene. We're like the Holiday Inn. We have a reservation in your name. . . . So how was practice? . . . Yeah, it was a big win. We played well, but we have a real challenge on our hands this weekend against Florida State."

Groh did not mean to suggest that Ferguson was leaving a year early, but that Monroe, too, eventually would play left tackle, the most valuable spot on the offensive line, because it protects the blind side of a right-handed quarterback.

Five minutes later, Groh said good-bye to Monroe. Groh's pro background did not come up during the conversation, though it often does during recruiting chats. It's a valuable card to play.

"If you were going to school, would you rather be taught by a teaching assistant or a full professor?" Groh asked. "Who would you rather be taught by?

"Look, evaluating talent is really the same at any level. I'm doing the same thing now that I was in the NFL. The only difference is that now I'm also the general manager and the player personnel director."

Like a NFL general manager, Groh spoke frequently to agents. Some college coaches all but unleash dogs on what the NFL Players Association calls "certified contract advisors." Not Groh. He uses his NFL experience to screen potential representatives for players, setting up the agents meeting himself and even arranging meetings between players and agents during the season. Some, like the ones he invited to the agents meeting, play by his rules and communicate through Groh. The rest contact players directly.

"Agents are going to talk to players, so you can pretend it doesn't happen or be part of the process," Groh says. "That doesn't mean you're controlling the process. I don't know if it can be controlled. It's going to go on. You can't tell the players not to have contact with agents, because the agents are going to contact them."

Some schools downplay the pro preparatory process. After all, student-athletes are enrolled to graduate and win college football games. Nobody is supposed to be thinking of going pro, right?

"I don't know if this is a progressive philosophy, but we're not having our heads stuck in the sand," Groh says. "We try to be a full-service organization. Whether it's academic or career counseling, within the NFL or out, agent selection and getting ready for the next level, we try and provide the best counseling based on our experience.

"When [NFL] draftable players are a big factor in your winning, you're going to get the attention of the next generation of players. That generation, besides wanting to win, wants to go to the NFL. They can look at us and say this is the place that knows how to train them."

Groh turned his attention to a television screen perched near his desk. There was game film to watch of Florida State, but his thoughts were never far from the pro game. Not that he was looking to get back to the NFL. It's just that when you're sixty years old and had spent thirteen of the previous seventeen years working for five different NFL teams, your network of friends in the league is enormous. He heard from many of them, perhaps a little more so this fall because of the NFL potential of many of his players.

Besides Parcells, Groh worked with Bill Belichick, the head coach of the New England Patriots, and New York Giants head coach Tom Coughlin. He coached alongside up-and-coming head coaching prospects such as Romeo Crennel of the Patriots and Mike Nolan of the Baltimore Ravens. Front offices around the league were full of former Groh colleagues, from scouts to strength coaches to guys like Giants general manager Ernie Accorsi, Baltimore GM Ozzie Newsome, and Scott Pioli, the general manager of the Patriots.

Groh also has sent several of his Virginia assistants to the NFL. The Jacksonville Jaguars staff included Bill Musgrave, Groh's offensive coordinator in 2001–2002; and Andy Heck, most recently Virginia's tight ends coach in 2003. Corwin Brown was in his first season with the Jets after three years as Virginia's special teams coach.

The University of Virginia's season was not even half over, the 2005 NFL Draft was nearly seven months away, but Groh knew the scouts and agents already had spent the last six months evaluating his players.

Chapter Five:

BIRDS OF PREY

Nearly two months before Eli Manning, Robert Gallery, and Larry Fitzgerald became the first three selections in the 2004 NFL Draft, preparations for the 2005 event got underway.

In March of 2004, NFL scouts and executives traveled around the country to college campuses for pro timing days, a sequel to the NFL scouting combine. At these events, referred to simply as "pro days," prospects for the 2004 draft were weighed, measured, and put through the familiar battery of tests designed to measure strength, speed, flexibility, agility, and quickness that they underwent at the combine.

With scouts already on campus, and with athletic department officials testing players anyway, many schools worked out their juniors immediately following the workout. Other schools waited a few weeks, but by the time the San Diego Chargers selected Manning on April 23, 2004, trading him immediately to the New York Giants, most every rising senior had been tested and initial reports filed.

Not that every team had to produce their own. Scouting is a grueling job. After spending most of the months between August and April on the road, scouts have their eye on vacations in May, June, and July, not the

2005 Draft. Thankfully, two national scouting services—BLESTO and National Football Scouting, Inc.—handle the heavy lifting.

BLESTO, based in Pittsburgh, formed in 1963 as a way for four teams—the Bears, Lions, Eagles, and Steelers—to share scouting expenses. National Football Scouting, or "National," is the other surviving combine of the 1970s. For the 2005 draft season, it had fifteen members, including BLESTO founder Philadelphia. BLESTO had a roster of twelve teams, including the Atlanta Falcons.

Five teams—Baltimore, Indianapolis, New England, Oakland, and Washington—were unaffiliated in 2004, preferring to do their own scouting. Though it might seem like these teams were being frugal—membership costs just one hundred thousand or so annually, along with, in many cases, the contribution of an entry-level scout—the teams are not at much of a disadvantage. Given the exhaustive nature of scouting, it's not difficult to assemble this early-stage information. Not only that, but unaffiliated teams end up acquiring the reports.

So, too, do agents, who use them for recruiting, as do a number of Internet draft gurus. For agents, the information is most useful because it includes player telephone numbers.

In mid-May of 2004, three weeks after the draft and following rookie minicamps, scouts from teams belonging to BLESTO and National convened in Florida. The BLESTO gang met in Orlando, the National contingent in Longboat Key, near Sarasota.

The scout or scouts who were in attendance at the junior days presents a report and a grade is assigned. BLESTO rates its players on a 1.00–5.00 scale, with the lower the score the better. National uses a 1.00–8.00 scale. The higher the number, the higher the rating.

Though the reports are anything but exhaustive, and don't begin to account for all of the character research teams will undergo over the next eleven months, they at least provide a starting point. They also, for the most part, provide a pretty good barometer of where many players will be drafted, barring a major injury or arrest, and not accounting for underclassmen that may enter the draft.

Here's a look at the top-rated rising seniors by position by BLESTO and National in June of 2004. BLESTO is on the left, National on the right. Draft-eligible underclassmen are not included in the ratings.

BLESTO AND NATIONAL RATINGS FOR THE 2005 DRAFT AS OF SPRING 2004

QUARTERBACKS

BLESTO	National
Dan Orlovsky—Connecticut—1.25	Charlie Frye—Akron—6.1
Charlie Frye—Akron—1.27	Dan Orlovsky—Connecticut—6.0
Andrew Walter—Arizona State—1.45	David Greene—Georgia—5.7
David Greene—Georgia—1.49	Andrew Walter—Arizona State—5.5
Ryan Fitzpatrick—Harvard—1.51	Jason White—Oklahoma—5.5
Matt Jones—Arkansas—1.55	Ryan Fitzpatrick—Harvard—5.4
Derek Anderson—Oregon State—1.57	Kyle Orton—Purdue—5.4
Timmy Chang—Hawaii—1.60	Derek Anderson—Oregon State—5.3
Jason White—Oklahoma—1.63	James Kilian—Tulsa—5.1
Darian Durant—North Carolina—1.68	Matt Jones—Arkansas—5.0

RUNNING BACKS

BLESTO	National
Carnell Williams—Auburn—1.16	Carnell Williams—Auburn—7.0
Cedric Benson—Texas—1.24	Ronnie Brown—Auburn—6.3
Ronnie Brown—Auburn—1.34	Cedric Williams—Texas—6.0
Walter Reyes—Syracuse—1.44	Kay-Jay Harris—West Virginia—5.8
Marvin Townes—East Carolina—1.44	Walter Reyes—Syracuse—5.6
Kay-Jay Harris—West Virginia—1.47	Anthony Davis—Wisconsin—5.5
Cedric Houston—Tennessee—1.53	Lydell Ross—Ohio State—5.5
William Brown—East Carolina—1.54	Marvin Townes—East Carolina—5.5
Anthony Davis—Wisconsin—1.57	Brandon Jacobs—Southern Illinois—5.4
Lionel Gates—Louisville—1.60	Jermelle Lewis—Iowa—5.4

FULLBACKS

BLESTO	National
Paul Jefferson—Penn State—1.45	Paul Jefferson—Penn State—5.3
Manuel White Jr.—UCLA—1.55	Manuel White Jr.—UCLA—5.0
Zach Tuiasosopo—Washington—1.57	Zach Tuiasosopo—Washington—4.9
Issa Banna—Northwestern State (LA)—1.8	Matt Phillips—Edinboro—4.7
Kevin Dudley—Michigan—1.8	Jeremy Thomas—Georgia—4.7

WIDE RECEIVERS

BLESTO	National
Craphonso Thorpe—Florida State—1.22	Braylon Edwards—Michigan—6.7
Terrence Murphy—Texas A&M—1.23	Mark Clayton—Oklahoma—6.4
Mark Clayton—Oklahoma—1.29	Terrence Murphy—Texas A&M—6.3
Braylon Edwards—Michigan—1.35	Craphonso Thorpe—Florida State—5.7
Josh Davis—Marshall—1.41	Josh Davis—Marshall—5.7
Fred Gibson—Georgia—1.41	Fred Gibson—Georgia—5.7
Craig Bragg—UCLA—1.43	Charles Frederick—Washington—5.7
Charles Frederick—Washington—1.47	J. R. Russell—Louisville—5.5
Brandon Jones—Oklahoma—1.47	Roddy White—Alabama-Birmingham—5.5
Courtney Roby—Indiana—1.47	Reggie Brown—Georgia—5.4

TIGHT ENDS

BLESTO	National
Alex Smith—Stanford—1.37	Alex Smith—Stanford—5.7
Vincent Jackson—Northern Colorado—1.49	Kevin Everett—Miami—5.5
Dave Kashetta—Boston College—1.53	Dave Kashetta—Boston College—5.4
Anthony Curtis—Portland State—1.63	Andrew Clark—Toledo—5.2
Kevin Everett—Miami—1.68	Anthony Curtis—Portland State—5.2
Billy Bajema—Oklahoma State—1.7	Gary Godsey—Notre Dame—5.2
Adam Bergen—Lehigh—1.72	Adam Bergen—Lehigh—5.1
Joel Dreessen—Colorado State—1.72	Alex Holmes—USC—5.0
Gary Godsey—Notre Dame—1.72	Steve Fleming—Arizona—4.9
Greg Estandia—UNLV—1.73	Eric Knott—Michigan State—4.7

OFFENSIVE TACKLES

BLESTO	National
Chris Colmer—North Carolina State—1.2	Alex Barron—Florida State—6.7
Alex Barron—Florida State—1.21	Ray Willis—Florida State—5.9
Khalif Barnes—Washington—1.28	Jeremy Parquet—Southern Mississippi—5.8
Adam Snyder—Oregon—1.32	Calvin Armstrong—Washington State—5.7
Adam Terry—Syracuse—1.36	Khalif Barnes—Washington—5.7
Ray Willis—Florida State—1.39	Michael Munoz—Tennessee—5.7
Jammal Brown—Oklahoma—1.42	Morgan Davis—Wisconsin—5.6
Michael Munoz—Tennessee—1.42	Wesley Britt—Alabama—5.5
Jeremy Parquet—Southern Mississippi—1.45	Jammal Brown—Oklahoma—5.4
Rob Petitti—Pittsburgh—1.45	Chris Colmer—North Carolina State—5.4

OFFENSIVE GUARDS

BLESTO	National
Chris Kemoeatu—Utah—1.34	Adam Snyder—Oregon—6.1
Marcus Johnson—Mississippi—1.36	Elton Brown—Virginia—6.0
David Baas—Michigan—1.46	Dylan Gandy—Texas Tech—5.7
Doug Buckles—Mississippi—1.47	Marcus Johnson—Mississippi—5.7
Elton Brown—Virginia—1.53	Claude Terrell—New Mexico—5.7
Dan Buenning—Wisconsin—1.54	Doug Buckles—Mississippi—5.5
Doug Nienhuis—Oregon State—1.57	Dan Buenning—Wisconsin—5.5
Dan Connolly—Southeast Missouri State—1.60	Chris Kemoeatu—Utah—5.5
Jonathan Clinkscale—Wisconsin—1.61	David Baas—Michigan—5.4
C. J. Brooks—Maryland—1.63	Cody Campbell—Texas Tech—5.4

CENTERS

BLESTO	National
Jason Brown—North Carolina—1.43	Vince Carter—Oklahoma—5.9
Ben Wilkerson—LSU—1.45	Ben Wilkerson—LSU—5.7
Raymond Preston—Illinois—1.59	Jason Brown—North Carolina—5.5
Matt Brock—Oregon State—1.68	Junius Coston—North Carolina A&T—5.4
Junius Coston—North Carolina A&T—1.73	Raymond Preston—Illinois—5.4

DEFENSIVE TACKLES

BLESTO	National
Shaun Cody—USC—1.25	Shaun Cody—USC—6.5
Mike Patterson—USC—1.32	Anttaj Hawthorne—Wisconsin—6.3
Lorenzo Alexander—California—1.40	Jonathan Babineaux—Iowa—6.0
Jonathan Babineaux—Iowa—1.44	Atiyyah Ellison—Missouri—5.5
Anttaj Hawthorne—Wisconsin—1.47	Ronald Fields—Mississippi State—5.4
Dusty Dvoracek—Oklahoma—1.50	Larry Burt—Miami (OH)—5.2
Atiyyah Ellison—Missouri—1.53	Jason Jefferson—Wisconsin—5.2
Ronald Fields—Mississippi State—1.60	Anthony Bryant—Alabama—5.1
Jason Jefferson—Wisconsin—1.62	Tim Bulman—Boston College—5.0
Tom Sverchek—California—1.63	Mike Patterson—USC—5.0

DEFENSIVE ENDS

BLESTO	National
David Pollack—Georgia—1.15	David Pollack—Georgia—7.0
Dan Cody—Oklahoma—1.26	Marcus Spears—LSU—6.0
Demarcus Ware—Tory State—1.33	Matt Roth—Iowa—5.7
Bill Swancutt—Oregon State—1.36	Demarcus Ware—Tory State—5.6
Matt Roth—Iowa—1.38	Kevin Huntley—Kansas State—5.5
Marcus Spears—LSU—1.38	Eric Moore—Florida State—5.5
Jimmy Verdon—Arizona State—1.41	Jimmy Verdon—Arizona State—5.5
Jonathan Jackson—Oklahoma—1.45	Vincent Burns—Kentucky—5.4
Chris Canty—Virginia—1.48	Dan Cody—Oklahoma—5.4
Eric Moore—Florida State—1.49	Jim Davis—Virginia Tech—5.4

MIDDLE LINEBACKERS

BLESTO	National
Roger Cooper—Montana State—1.45	Marcus Lawrence—South Carolina—5.8
Barrett Ruud—Nebraska—1.50	Robert McCune—Louisville—5.6
Robert McCune—Louisville—1.66	Adam Seward—UNLV—5.4
Kirk Morrison—San Diego State—1.68	Ronald Stanley—Michigan State—5.4
Nigel Eldridge—Alabama-Birmingham—1.69	Mike Goolsby—Notre Dame—5.3

OUTSIDE LINEBACKERS

BLESTO	National
Derrick Johnson—Texas—1.23	Barrett Ruud—Nebraska—6.5
Kevin Burnett—Tennessee—1.31	Kevin Burnett—Tennessee—6.0
Jared Newberry—Stanford—1.38	Derrick Johnson—Texas—6.0
Lance Mitchell—Oklahoma—1.40	Paul Walkenhorst—BYU—5.4
Jonathan Pollard—Oregon State—1.46	Jared Newberry—Stanford—5.3
Adam Seward—UNLV—1.47	Danny Triplett—Northern Iowa—5.3
Matt Grootegoed—USC—1.49	Roger Cooper—Montana State—5.2
Boomer Grigsby—Illinois State—1.51	Michael Boley—Southern Mississippi—5.0
Ryan Claridge—UNLV—1.52	Ryan Claridge—UNLV—5.0
Trent Cole—Cincinnati—1.59	Sarth Benoit—Southern Connecticut—5.0

CORNERBACKS

BLESTO	National
Antrel Rolle—Miami—1.17	Antrel Rolle—Miami—7.0
Corey Webster—LSU—1.21	Marlin Jackson—Michigan—6.3
Ronald Bartell—Howard—1.28	Ronald Bartell—Howard—6.1
Marlin Jackson—Michigan—1.32	Antonio Perkins—Oklahoma—6.0
Antonio Perkins—Oklahoma—1.46	Corey Webster—LSU—6.0
Abraham Elimimian—Hawaii—1.50	Karl Paymah—Washington State—5.6
Derrick Johnson—Washington—1.50	Cedrick Williams—Kansas State—5.6
Dustin Fox—Ohio State—1.52	Markus Curry—Michigan—5.5
Cedrick Williams—Kansas State—1.55	Vince Fuller—Virginia Tech—5.5
Karl Paymah—Washington State—1.58	Alphonso Hodge—Miami (OH)—5.5

SAFETIES

BLESTO	National
Jamaal Brimmer—UNLV—1.42	Jermaine Harris—South Carolina—5.5
James Butler—Georgia Tech—1.43	Jamaal Brimmer—UNLV—5.4
Aaron Francisco—BYU—1.43	Dustin Fox—Ohio State—5.4
Oshiomogho Atogwe—Stanford—1.49	Chris Harrell—Penn State—5.3
Jason Leach—USC—1.5	James Butler—Georgia Tech—5.2
Riccardo Stewart—Arizona State—1.5	Sean Considine—Iowa—5.2
Travis Daniels—LSU—1.56	Justin Fraley—Minnesota—5.2
Donte Nicholson—Oklahoma—1.57	Terry Holley—Rice—5.2
Sean Considine—Iowa—1.58	Jamacia Jackson—South Carolina—5.2
Marviel Underwood—San Diego State—1.59	Jason Leach—USC—5.0

Note: The author acquired copies of the BLESTO and National reports, but this grouping was assembled by Rob Rang for NFLDraftScout.com.

Here's a look at rankings of players at several schools with significant prospects for the 2005 draft:

AUBURN

Carnell Williams, RB, 7.0, 1.16
Ronnie Brown, RB, 6.3, 1.34
Carlos Rogers, CB, 5.0, 1.76
Jason Campbell, QB, 4.6, 1.85

FLORIDA STATE
Alex Barron, OT, 6.7, 1.20
Craphonso Thorpe, WR, 6.3, 1.22
Ray Willis, OT, 5.9, 1.39
Eric Moore, DE, 5.5, 1.49
Bryant McFadden, CB, 5.4, 1.64
Chauncey Davis, DE, 5.1, 1.75
B. J. Ward, FS, 5.0, 1.79
Chris Rix, QB, 4.9, 1.72
Jerome Carter, SS, 4.7, 1.85
Kylar Hall, FS, 4.4, 1.90
Travis Johnson, DT, 4.4, 1.85

GEORGIA
David Pollack, DE, 7.0, 1.15
Fred Gibson, WR, 5.7, 1.41
David Greene, QB, 5.7, 1.49
Reggie Brown, WR, 5.4, 1.51

VIRGINIA
Elton Brown, OG, 6.0, 1.53
Chris Canty, DE, 5.3, 1.48
Alvin Pearman, RB, 4.5, 1.80
Patrick Estes, TE, 4.4, 1.90
Jermaine Hardy, SS, 4.4, 1.88

The Atlanta Falcons college scouting staff is headed by Phil Emery, who joined the team on May 18, 2004 after a six-year stint with the Chicago Bears. He received a strong recommendation from Bears general manager Jerry Angelo, who had worked for more than a decade in Tampa with Falcons general manager Rich McKay and assistant GM Tim Ruskell.

Emery was one of several replacements in the scouting staff McKay and Ruskell had made since the 2004 draft. Compared to some new regimes, there was modest turnover on the seven-member scouting staff, with openings filled from within.

The group ranged in age from young Matt Berry, a former Falcons intern working his first year as an area scout, to sixty-seven-year-old Boyd Dowler, who played twelve seasons as a wide receiver in the NFL (1959–1971), mostly for the Green Bay Packers under Vince Lombardi.

In between, there was Billy Campfield, who spent most of his six-year NFL career with the Philadelphia Eagles; Bob Harrison, a veteran of thirty-three years of pro, college, and high school coaching; Taylor Morton, a former college assistant at Southern Miss and Auburn; Mark Olson, a former NFL advance scout, in his first year scouting the draft; and Bruce Plummer, a five-year NFL veteran who serves as the Falcons' BLESTO scout.

Dowler is the Dick Clark of NFL personnel, a man who could pass for his early fifties. At six-five, with thick gray hair, he's a testament to clean living, exercise, and good genes. He led the Packers in receptions seven times and still ranks among the franchise's all-time leaders with 448 catches for 6,918 yards.

Having played a key role on Lombardi's legendary teams, Dowler could be forgiven for being one of those crotchety ex-players forever bemoaning today's spoiled NFL stars. Instead, he has an uncanny knack of relating to the younger generations.

"He's just one of the guys," says Morton, who is three decades younger. "You forget how old he is until he starts telling some story about Bart Starr and Vince Lombardi."

Scouting is a thankless job. Starting in August, the area scouts visit college campuses, spending the bulk of the next eight months on the road, an average of about twenty nights a month.

Not all schools are created equal. Emery and Ruskell took the BLESTO reports and used them to narrow the field. A school chock-full of draft talent will receive three visits from an area scout, with Ruskell, Emery, and even McKay visiting key schools. For the 2005 draft, that group includes Auburn, Georgia, Oklahoma, Florida State, Miami, Southern Cal, LSU, and Virginia. A smaller school, such as Troy State, would get more attention than usual because of promising defensive end Demarcus Ware. The same was true of the University of Alabama-Birmingham, which featured wide receiver Roddy White.

Other schools, especially those not in Division 1-A, would receive one or two visits. Some perennial powers would get less attention, either because they were struggling or because the bulk of their talent was freshman and sophomores in 2004. That group included Arizona, Notre Dame, Penn State, and Pittsburgh.

When McKay and Ruskell arrived in Atlanta, they added another requirement to the scouts' workload. During the slower months of June and July scouts are to visit the top ten schools in their areas. It could be low-key. Take the wife and kids. Call it a mini-vacation. Most college towns are fun to visit in the summer. This way, the Falcons scouts get the first crack at coaches, before they've told the stories of players for the fiftieth time. Unlike during the season, when college coaches are distracted by game preparations and the intensity level is high, especially when a team is losing, coaches are more accessible.

"Schools actually liked seeing our guys," Ruskell said. "Someone from the outside world was actually visiting. There's not much to do during those periods, and it was a treat to have someone come in and visit. It got to the point where our guys were saying, 'Okay coach, I have enough here.' You couldn't shut them up."

In the fall, days typically begin at 7:00 A.M., with scouts rolling into a college football office armed with donuts or bagels for the coaching staffs. Scouts wear team-logo clothing, in part to help jog the memories of assistant coaches who don't always recognize the legions of visitors parading through the offices.

Much of the morning is spent watching film. Unlike video from actual broadcasts, the film is broken down by offense and defense. The first scout into the room gets control of the remote control. Getting the clicker means arriving no later than seven.

The goal is to watch film of the most recent game, plus that of the two toughest opponents. That's especially important with Division 1-AA schools, which might have only faced two Division 1-A foes.

Throughout the morning scouts check in with assistant coaches, strength coaches, academic advisors, NCAA compliance directors, graduate assistants, resident advisors in the dorm, tutors, secretaries, cops, and anyone else that can provide details on a player's work ethic, drive, personality, family background, academic performance, and disciplinary problems, if any. A scout's job is as much that of detective or investigative reporter as it is football expert.

"It's not enough to say, 'This is a good kid, he works hard and has no problems off the field,'" McKay says. "Not good enough. We want to know where he came from, what his parental situation was. We want to make sure the scouts have talked to the high school coach. We want to know about his education, so we talk to the academic advisor about every player. We want to hear from the position coach, the head coach, teammates, and ask their views of the player. Then obviously we want to know all the off-the-field issues. You're developing a whole picture and it takes a lot of time."

Sometimes a scout's investigation reveals that a player has been taking money from boosters or from agents, cardinal sins to the NCAA. The Falcons factor that in to their character evaluations.

"If this guy is that easily corruptible, it probably shows up elsewhere," Ruskell says. "Does he skip workouts? Does he come late to meetings? Has he gotten in trouble? It's a red flag that maybe this guy is a follower, that he's not his own man and doesn't have leadership skills. We're not going to just brush that off under the rug."

Scouts could watch film back at their team offices or at home, since many scouts live in the areas they cover. Falcon scouts do that in June and July to get an early look at players, and often as the season progresses. But it's tough to get a true read on a player's physique on television. Plus, there's a lag time between the end of a game and when the film is available for view outside of school. Colleges send the film to a dubbing center, where it's mass-produced for all NFL teams, but sometimes more than a month can go by before it's widely distributed.

If nothing else, by watching film on the same day they watch practice and interview school officials, they're able to write reports with all of the information fresh.

In the afternoon, scouts attend practice—a good indicator of how hard players work, though not as valuable as the two-a-day preseason practices in August, when players wear full pads all week long and are fighting to win jobs.

Access to practice, and to the football department in general, varies from school to school. Some old-school coaches, such as Penn State's Joe Paterno, restrict availability. Others, like Florida State's Bobby Bowden and Miami's Larry Coker, open the offices for part of the season. Some let scouts watch just the first part of practices, fearful that their game plans might be compromised. Others change their policies during the season, wreaking havoc on a scout's travel plans. Then there are coaches like Virginia's Al Groh, who provides unlimited access to scouts all season long, with the exception of Thursdays.

"I don't see how their doing their job hinders us from doing ours," Groh says. "The players are trying hard to prove themselves and we should give them an opportunity to showcase that."

In many respects, the job of a scout is similar to that of a sportswriter. Both groups spend their days interviewing sources and many nights writing. They endure marathon travel, preferring to stay at Marriott properties because of the company's attractive frequent traveler program. They spend many weekends in press boxes watching games, grabbing food on the go. Camaraderie develops among competitors in both fields.

Few are going to get rich in either profession. Though some veteran scouts can command $100,000 salaries, most earn less. The starting salary for young scouts is so low, there's even a name for it: "25 for 25"— referring to a twenty-five-year-old making $25,000.

Both groups rely on networks of reliable sources to provide off-the-record information. Scouts, many of which coached or played in the college ranks, turn to ex-colleagues first, gradually developing new sources. College coaches, working in a high-turnover profession, tend to be receptive to the scouts. Today's aggravation could be tomorrow's job lead, especially when an NFL general manager or scouting director rolls through the office.

Still, there's a fine line to walk. A college coach's recruiting of high school players depends in part on producing NFL players. An honest assessment of a college player to a NFL scout might hurt the kid's chances.

"They make their living on these decisions, so I'm not going to lie to them," says Florida State's Bowden. "I know I expect the high school coaches to be just as forthright with me. We all want to know the same things. What kind of kid is he? Is he dependable? Is he a slacker? Can you count on him? Is he an overachiever or an underachiever? If you sell a scout on a player and he's a complete flop, you lose all credibility."

"They're looking to invest millions of dollars in a guy and they want stability," says Georgia Tech head coach Chan Gailey, a former Dallas Cowboys head coach.

College coaches spend a lot of time talking about their "student athletes" and how they never want them looking beyond Saturday's game, let alone to a career in the NFL. Having logo-clad NFL employees roaming the halls of the football offices and standing on the sidelines during practice doesn't exactly reenforce the message.

Then again, scouts generally are expected to leave the offices before lunchtime, when players begin arriving. Scouts are forbidden from speaking to players beyond a friendly hello. Coaches figure that if players happen to notice scouts on the sidelines, they're more likely to work harder. At Florida State, Bowden has gone so far as to have a NFL scout speak to a talented underachiever.

"We'll have the scout tell the player what he's throwing away," Bowden says. "When we can't get him going, sometimes it helps for the kid to hear it from a guy wearing a shirt with an NFL logo."

The Falcons ask scouts to speak to a minimum of three solid sources, preferably five. If the first three say the same thing, that's enough to constitute a consensus. McKay and Ruskell urge scouts to step out of the familiar ring of the football staff and seek out those without a vested interest.

At Florida State, Ruskell turns to Brian Battle, the director of compliance. In that role, Battle helps players obtain disability insurance, assists juniors considering going pro by applying for a predraft rating from the NFL advisory committee, organizes an annual "Agent Day" meeting between Seminoles and agents, and even teaches a class called "A Career in Professional Sports," that's popular among players.

Battle, in many respects, gets to know more about the players than the coaching staff does. Since a player's success in the NFL depends in part on how fast he can process intricate schemes, the Falcons turn to people like Battle to find out how a player thinks. They prefer to do that than rely on the Wonderlic, the notorious, fifty-question aptitude test players take during the NFL scouting combine in February.

"You have to get outside the protective zone of the coaching circle," Ruskell says. "They protect the players, and you would too if you were a coach. After all, these are the guys that help me keep my job and make me look good and keep the winning tradition. A guy like Brian has a great perspective because he can speak to the intelligence level. Does the kid just sit there or does he participate in class? You want to know that because it eliminates the guess work. You don't have to rely on the Wonderlic."

After practice and dinner, scouts must translate a day's worth of information into reports. With scouts often hitting one school a day, the only way to keep up with the workload is to write at night in a hotel room, either in the same town or after driving to the next day's school.

"You have to get the reports done while it's all fresh in your mind," says Ruston Webster, the director of college scouting for the Tampa Bay Buccaneers, a holdover from the McKay-Ruskell regime. "You've worked all day, driven maybe three or four hours, and now you've got reports to write. It's tough."

It's not unusual for a scout to spend twenty nights a month on the road in the fall. There are long stretches in December, February, and April, where they work out of team headquarters, but that's the road, too, for most scouts, who live where they scout. The biggest grind is January and March, when the schedule of postseason all-star games and college "pro day" workouts is relentless.

"It takes a toll on you," says Ruskell, who paid his dues as an area scout in the CFL, USFL, and for the Buccaneers. "There's the stress of being away from the family and not being part of the office environment. You don't always feel like you're part of what's happening."

Falcons scout Taylor Morton, whose area in the fall of 2004 included Texas, Oklahoma, Kansas, Louisiana, and Arkansas, typically logs more than six thousand miles driving each fall. He hits the road four times for ten-day stretches, flying from his home near Atlanta to Dallas.

Boyd Dowler, who lives in Tampa, drives loops through his territory, which includes Florida, Mississippi, and Alabama, a fertile area for the 2005 draft, with schools such as Florida State, Ole Miss, and Auburn. Though Georgia belongs to Athens-based scout Bob Harrison, the state is thoroughly covered by the entire Falcons staff.

Dowler hits Georgia Tech and Georgia twice. When bad weather forces the Bulldogs to use the Falcons' indoor facility at Flowery Branch, any Falcons scout nearby is able to watch practice.

Tech attracts little attention, though that has less to do with the overall talent of Gailey's team as it does the lack of draft-eligible players. Five Yellow Jackets were drafted in the 2004 NFL Draft, the most in twelve years, and most of Gailey's talent is in the freshman and sophomore classes. If nothing else, Georgia Tech's downtown Atlanta campus is a popular destination for Falcons scouts—and the numerous agents that call the city home—because of home games against Miami, Virginia Tech, and Virginia.

Ironically, most scouts rarely see their own team play in person, since they're driving around the country visiting college campuses. At least they're able to listen to the games through Sirius satellite radio, which paid the NFL $220 million to broadcast all of its games for seven years, beginning in 2004.

The Falcons keep their scouts in the loop by assigning each one a position before the start of training camp. During the first two weeks of camp the scouts follow those players and coaches around to get a better feel for the scheme, existing personnel, and the team's needs at the position. Midway through camp they begin their tour of preseason college football practices.

During the fall, the seven scouts combine to write reports on more than twelve hundred players. They reconvene at Flowery Branch in December to make an initial cutdown of players, eliminating those that did not fit the Falcons offensive or defensive schemes and those that didn't pass the character filter.

Beginning in January, the scouts serve as cross-checkers. They go to bowl games, along with postseason all-star games such as the Senior Bowl, East–West Shrine Game, and Gridiron Classic—and concentrate on evaluating players at the position they focused on during training camp.

The area scout's grade and the cross-checker scout's rating form the basis of the first draft board, which is put in place prior to the NFL combine in February. The Falcons coaching staff serve as cross-checkers at the combine and during March pro days back at campus, but the idea is not to tweak the grade significantly. It's a lesson McKay learned from George Young, the late New York Giants executive.

"Be as loyal as you can to that first board," McKay says. "If you let it become too modified, then you've taken the art of scouting out of it and it becomes more of a groupthink process, and sometimes that's not a good thing."

The Falcons, in just one calendar year under McKay, have undergone a thorough remodeling. When Arthur Blank purchased the team early in 2002, head coach Dan Reeves ran the personnel department. Defensively, the team was a mess. Wade Phillips, the defensive coordinator, employed a 3-4 scheme (three down linemen, four linebackers), an effective setup for some teams, but not for the Falcons' smaller linemen. Defensive end Patrick Kerney, matching up against linemen forty pounds heavier, got pounded on a weekly basis. In 2003, the Falcons finished last in the league in passing defense and total defense and twenty-ninth against the run.

When Blank hired McKay, it was clear who ran the personnel department, especially since McKay would get to choose the head coach. The men agreed on the philosophy of the general manager, not the head coach, being in charge of the organization. Blank referred to the process as "looking for a GM or coach, not a king."

Just as McKay selected a former defensive coordinator, Tony Dungy, to rebuild the Buccaneers in 1996, McKay hired Jim Mora, who had spent five years in the role in San Francisco. Mora's father, also named Jim, was a longtime NFL head coach.

McKay's defense in Tampa had ranked among the league's best by using speedy defenders that some viewed as undersized. Mora and new defensive coordinator Ed Donatell scrapped the 3-4 scheme and installed a 4-3. Kerney benefited immediately, recording seven sacks in the Falcons' first four games in 2004.

Before the season, Mora and Donatell identified free agent Rod Coleman of the Raiders as the ideal fit at undertackle, the penetrating, pass-rushing position that was the key to an effective 4-3 scheme, a position Warren Sapp had filled in Tampa.

With a guy like Sapp or Coleman, it was possible to get by with almost anyone at nose tackle. In Tampa, Sapp's running mates included twelfth-round draft pick Brad Culpepper and Chartric Darby, an undrafted free agent.

"We could even play with Reggie," McKay would say, referring to Reggie Roberts, a burly man but more suited to his role as the Falcons public relations director.

Pat Dye Jr., Coleman's agent, knew things were changing in Atlanta when he took his reluctant client to meet with the Falcons. Coleman grew up a Giants fan in Philadelphia and wanted to sign with New York. There he met with a Giants position coach over dinner.

In Atlanta, Coleman broke bread with a fourteen-person Falcons contingent that included Blank, McKay, Mora, and Ruskell. Coleman signed a six-year, $27.8 million deal with the Falcons.

McKay preached speed to his scouting staff and spent his first Falcons draft pick on DeAngelo Hall, a cornerback from Virginia Tech who posted one of the fastest times in the forty-yard dash at the 2004 combine. Alex Gibbs, the new offensive line coach, wanted fast, athletic linemen modeled after those that played under him in Denver during their two Super Bowl–title seasons.

The most ambitious part of the makeover was the installation of a West Coast offense, which relies on finesse linemen in the Gibbs mold, but also a ball-control, precision passing game that didn't quite fit the talents of Michael Vick, the NFL's best running quarterback.

That was a work in progress. Tight end Alge Crumpler, a sure-handed tight end, fit the West Coast well. So did Warrick Dunn, a reliable receiver out of the backfield. Unfortunately, the Falcons did not have a big target at wide receiver. Vick, a fan of former 49ers quarterback and West Coast master Steve Young, was a willing pupil. Mora figured it would take a season or two to be fully implemented.

With the transition complete and the Falcons off to a 6-2 start in 2004 through October, Falcons scouts were well aware of what they were expected to locate for McKay. They were looking for smaller, aggressive, athletic linemen on both sides of the ball. They needed linebackers and defensive backs to bolster an improving defense. They needed a big wide receiver to help the West Coast offense. Above all, they needed fast, high-character players that were leaders, quick studies, overachievers, and solid citizens.

With all that in mind, it would be easy to narrow the field. By the time the Falcons scouting department convened in February, before the combine, they would have extensive reports. The area scout would have seen players three times: in August during two-a-day practices, after three games, and after the sixth or seventh game. Emery, the director of college scouting, would hit as many of the major schools as possible. Scouts would have cross-checked throughout January at the bowl and all-star games.

Ruskell and McKay would try to see as many games as possible, piggybacking trips to college games onto Falcons road trips. Before the Falcons played at San Francisco on September 12, Ruskell and McKay attended the California–New Mexico State game. When the team was home, they would watch games at Auburn, Georgia, or Georgia Tech.

Some scouting was as easy as walking downstairs from the Falcons second-floor executive offices to the locker room below. Though NFL players hesitate to reveal dirt on former college teammates, they also realize the potential impact the players could have.

Before the 2004 draft, the Falcons brass made it a point to ask Vick about Hall, a fellow ex-Virginia Tech Hokie. This year, the Falcons turned to young players such as rookie quarterback Matt Schaub, who as a University of Virginia senior during the 2003–2004 school year played with the members of the draft class of 2005.

"They want to make sure they're getting what they're paying for," Schaub said. "They'll ask about personality and character because that's such a big part of it. A guy can be a great player, but he might be lacking off the field and could hurt the team."

By the time scouts met before the combine, they would have a thorough understanding of a player's personality, family background, work ethic, drive, and integrity. The Falcons assign each player a double-letter grade that represents football character and personal character.

Football character refers to a player's ability to maximize his potential. A grade of A or B means the player works hard on the practice field, shows leadership qualities, learns quickly, plays through pain, commands respect from teammates, and instills fear in opponents. Personal character takes into account a player's history of criminal or disciplinary problems, if any. High-maintenance, diva players, no matter how talented, will score low in this area.

"We're looking for great character guys," Ruskell says. "If a guy is rated a D or below in that area, there's a possibility he's going to embarrass the franchise. At the very least, he's a guy who might just be too tough to get going."

Draft-eligible players that rate highly in football talent, character, and intangibles such as leadership are given a special "Falcon Filter" rating by Ruskell, a carryover from the "Buccaneer Filter" used in Tampa. When that player's card is posted on the "war room" ranking board, it's stamped with a team logo.

"You see five, maybe seven players a year where everything is so good we'll put the bird on the card," Ruskell says. "Those are exceptional guys, very rare. They lift the level of play of those around them. We make it hard to get. They might not be the greatest players, but they have exceptional intangibles."

Before the 2004 draft, Ruskell and his staff placed a Falcon Filter on Philip Rivers, the North Carolina State quarterback who was picked fourth overall, and Jonathan Vilma, the Miami linebacker picked twelfth by the New York Jets. In Tampa, Derrick Brooks and John Lynch earned Buccaneer Filters before their drafts.

"We're talking about the guy who everyone agrees is the leader of the team," Ruskell says. "Everyone rallies around him. He's the guy that organized off-season workouts. He's the guy that calls you when you're late. He's a natural leader and he lifts the level of play of everyone around him. You don't want to make him mad by showing a lack of effort, because he'll be right in your face. That's the guy you're looking for."

Chapter Six:

THE CHALLENGER

O n the afternoon of November 13, 2004, Frank Dorazio walked the sidelines before the University of Miami's game against the University of Virginia in Char-lottesville. As an area scout for the Tampa Bay Buccaneers based in Cleveland, it's Dorazio's job to cover the northeast.

It had been a grueling week for Dorazio, in his fourth season with the Buccaneers. He left home on Monday and drove to nearby Akron University. The following day, he visited Columbus and Ohio State, just as *ESPN the Magazine* published an article where former running back Maurice Clarett alleged that Buckeye football players were paid by boosters, provided with improper academic help, and given high-paying, no-show summer jobs. Ohio State officials denied the allegations.

After a tense day in Columbus, Dorazio traveled to West Virginia University on Wednesday and stopped at the University of Maryland on Thursday before arriving in Charlottesville on Friday.

Dorazio, forty-one, figures he drives between 20,000 and 30,000 miles over the course of a season, somewhere between 1,000 and 1,500 clicks a week. He was scheduled to spend 186 nights on the road in 2004. Like most scouts, he's put together a vast network of contacts from his previous gigs, and the one consolation for spending so much time on the road is getting to catch up with old friends.

A 1985 graduate of Ohio State, where he served as a manager for the football team, Dorazio worked briefly for the Cleveland Indians and Cleveland Browns before beginning a nine-year stint at Purdue University, working mostly on football recruiting. After that, he spent three years at Southern Cal as director of football operations before joining the Buccaneers before the 2001 season.

With such a journeyman resume, Dorazio runs into former colleagues almost everywhere. In Charlottesville, he visited with Luke Goldstein, his former roommate at USC, who now served as the Cavaliers' video coordinator.

Dorazio dutifully brings donuts or bagels wherever he goes, though he wonders if that tradition is waning. "So many coaches are on low-carb health kicks," he said. "I'm going to start bringing a fruit basket or something."

As the Cavaliers and Hurricanes underwent pregame drills, Dorazio searched for familiar coaches and kept an eye on players, making notes of body types. A chiseled guy is said to have a "beach body." Scouts obsess over hips and how loose or tight they are, since that will largely determine his agility and ability to generate power. Then there's a guy's butt or "bubble." Linemen need to have a big bubble.

"It's sometimes harder to get a read on guys at practice," Dorazio says. "Their jerseys are hanging out. Practice pants sometimes are baggier. This is more of a true read."

Al Groh and his Cavaliers still were in the hunt for the ACC championship. After an embarrassing, 36–3, loss at Florida State on October 16, Virginia rebounded to defeat Duke and Maryland to improve to 7-1. Elton Brown, the team's massive offensive guard, remained one of the top NFL prospects at his position. Scouts continued to keep an eye on Groh's talented underclassmen: linebackers Darryl Blackstock and Ahmad Brooks, tight end Heath Miller, and offensive tackle D'Brickashaw Ferguson. Senior Alvin Pearman, already a talented special teams player, had unseated Wali Lundy as the starting tailback and was drawing interest from NFL scouts.

Since Rich McKay and Tim Ruskell left the Buccaneers, things had changed in the scouting department under new general manager Bruce Allen. Ruskell's rating system had been streamlined. Unlike the Falcons, the Buccaneers do not have scouts serve as cross-checkers. With Ruskell's position still open, Ruston Webster, the director of college scouting, cross-checked the entire country.

Tampa Bay had a full arsenal of draft picks for the first time since

1999, having surrendered premium selections to acquire wide receiver Keyshawn Johnson in 2000 and head coach Jon Gruden in 2002. The Bucs acquired five more through trade, giving them a pair of picks in the third and fifth rounds, and four in the seventh, for 2005.

That made this year's draft especially important for the Buccaneers, who had gotten off to a 3-5 start after finishing the 2003 season 7-9. The glow of the 2002 Super Bowl victory had faded quickly. The following day, the Buccaneers would face the surprising Falcons, who were 6-1, in Atlanta.

Dorazio wouldn't be there. He planned to visit with Goldstein after the game and go into the football office on Sunday to watch film. Like most scouts, Dorazio had learned to root for the teams he had to visit the following week.

"Otherwise everyone is quiet and depressed—the coaches, secretaries, everybody," Dorazio says. "It's a bad atmosphere."

Chris Canty spent little time in the bad atmosphere of Virginia's postgame locker room. The Cavaliers, trailing just 17–14 heading into the fourth quarter, surrendered fourteen points and essentially were eliminated from ACC title contention by Miami.

Two Hurricanes juniors, both expected to turn pro early, did most of the damage. Frank Gore, enjoying a strong comeback season after enduring major surgeries on both knees, rushed twenty-eight times for 195 yards. Roscoe Parrish, a speedy five-ten wide receiver, scored twice in the fourth quarter, returning a punt sixty-two yards and hauling in a twenty-five-yard pass from quarterback Brock Berlin.

Canty, two months removed from knee surgery, watched the game on the sidelines, clad in the same orange-and-blue nylon running suits the Cavaliers wore to and from games. Technically, he still was a member of the team, though this was his first time back in Charlottesville since the injury. Sitting outside a reception for Cavalier football alumni afterward, he felt more like a returning graduate than an active player.

Canty was, after all, a graduate of the University of Virginia, having received his degree in May. After the injury, he dropped out of graduate school to undergo rehabilitation, first in Birmingham and then in Charlotte. Unlike other Cavaliers eligible for the 2005 NFL Draft, he was free to sign with an agent at any time, and had narrowed the field to four.

During the previous three weeks, the agents traveled to Charlotte and found their way to the Canty residence, a two-story brick home not far from downtown, in a tree-lined subdivision of houses built in the late 1980s. New homes in nearby communities began at four hundred and fifty thousand dollars.

Joseph Canty, Chris's father, works as a general contractor. His mother, the Reverend Shirley Canty, is pastor of the Calvary United Methodist Church.

Chris Canty had heard all of the stories of agents offering illegal inducements to players to sign, especially those players from modest backgrounds. Cars or cash in the form of "marketing guarantees," an advance against future endorsement earnings, income that only highly-drafted quarterbacks, running backs, and wide receivers ever see.

Canty said he did not receive those pitches, in part because he had his parents handle agents, and also because, unlike some NFL hopefuls, he does not come from modest financial means.

"Look around," Canty said during a visit to his home. "We've been blessed. My parents do very well making a living. By no means are we rich, but we're comfortable. Money, thank God, is not an issue for my parents anymore."

It wasn't always that way. The second of three sons, Chris was born on November 10, 1982, in the Bronx and raised in a part of the borough that Chris describes as "not right in the tough part of the Bronx, but right down the street from there."

Joe Canty worked for the city of New York Health Department, while Shirley served Methodist churches, first in Harlem and then in Queens. One afternoon in 1993, Shirley went to pick up the boys from school and returned to find their home had been robbed.

The family moved to Raleigh, North Carolina, soon after, settling in Charlotte three years later. With Charlotte booming, Joe's business blossomed in the late 1990s. Chris enrolled in the prestigious Charlotte Latin School, a private, 122-acre campus that passersby sometimes mistake for a small college.

Chris was more of a basketball player in high school, not even playing football until his junior year. Standing six-seven and at 215 pounds, he was too small to play power forward for big-time college programs. Still raw as a defensive end/tight end, he attracted little interest from Division 1-A programs, choosing Virginia over Boston College. Canty arrived in Charlottesville in the summer of 2000 with no aspirations of a career in the NFL, figuring he'd get a solid education and maybe contribute on the football field.

His first two years did nothing to change that view. George Welsh, in what would be his final year at Virginia, redshirted Canty as a freshman. Canty played as a backup in 2001, broke his leg during spring drills, missed the first two games of the 2002 season, and was not at full strength to start until the sixth game of the year.

By then, offensive linemen were struggling with the tall lineman with the huge wingspan and unlikely speed. He led ACC defensive linemen in tackles for the season, capturing second-team all-conference honors. By the end of the year he was getting mail from agents. Three seasons removed from high school, he was eligible for the 2003 NFL Draft.

Canty never considered it, returning as a redshirt junior in 2003, again leading the ACC linemen in tackles. By then, agents were swarming. Ethan Lock, the Arizona-based agent for former Cavaliers Tiki and Ronde Barber, was a frequent caller. So too was Brad Blank, who represented a long line of Virginia players, including Jeff Lageman, Herman Moore, and Chris Slade.

Canty let his parents deal with the agents. After the 2003 season, now weighing around 280, he applied for a predraft rating from the NFL's advisory committee and received an encouraging result: "not higher than the second round," the committee's second-highest rating. Canty considered signing with Blank and going pro, but again opted to stay in school. He already had disability insurance and re-upped for the 2004 season.

"I didn't think my skill level was as high as I wanted it to be," Canty said. "More importantly, I wasn't ready for that kind of lifestyle, being on my own and making financial decisions for myself. I was always a pretty responsible young man, but felt like I wasn't ready for that opportunity. Plus, Charlottesville is not a bad place to be. You can never get back that last year of college."

Lock and his Atlanta-based colleague Michael Brown told Canty about a training center in Arizona called Athletes' Performance, where the agency sent its clients to work out in the weeks before the NFL combine. During the summer of 2004, Canty and his parents traveled to Phoenix at their own expense and paid for Chris to train for a week.

By the time the 2004 season began, Lock was the front-runner to land Canty, now projected as a first-round pick for the 2005 draft. Lock was in the stands in Charlottesville when Canty blew out his knee against Syracuse on September 25, 2004, but like many who watched Canty helped off the field, he figured it was just a sprained ankle or knee.

Even when agents learned of the extent of the injury, few backed away, and the Cantys welcomed a parade of agents into their home in late October and November. There was IMG's Tom Condon. Brown and

Lock made a presentation. David Joseph, a Greensboro, North Carolina, agent who at the time represented Eagles wide receiver Terrell Owens, also came. Cary Fabrikant, a South Florida agent whose company represents twenty NFL veterans, rounded out the group.

The agents typically arrived after dinner and each spent the better part of three hours running through their qualifications, skills in negotiations, services, and how they would best prepare Chris for the NFL Draft. Some brought DVDs of their company, and Chris and his parents aired them on their big-screen TV, nestled in a corner across the room from Chris's diploma from the University of Virginia and several framed press clippings.

"There's always one key element that an agent says he can do better than anyone else in the world, whether that be financial advice, marketing, you name it," Canty says. "They all have an angle. The only thing you can do is pick the guy who best fits you, your personality. You've got to figure out what you need from them, whether it's a lot of attention or a little. It's who you feel comfortable with."

Canty said he managed to avoid the seamier side of recruiting. Many agencies send intermediaries, more commonly called "runners," to do the legwork. They set up shop in a college town, attach themselves to players, and, using whatever means necessary, deliver clients to agencies. Some runners are paid covertly, their relationships secret. Others are full-fledged agency employees, paying their dues until they became licensed agents themselves.

The NFL Players Association, which oversees the certification and regulation of agents, prohibits its "certified contract advisors" from offering financial inducements to lure players, but it's nearly impossible for the union to catch violators, since agents are permitted to loan or give money to players *after* signing them as clients. Proving when an inducement was made is difficult, especially with neither agents nor players serving as whistle-blowers.

At Virginia, head coach Al Groh tried to keep runners away from his players. He brought agents he believed acted aboveboard to his summer agent day to meet with players and parents. He installed security officers in the stairwells outside the parking garage at Scott Stadium. They checked that everyone entering the area outside the Virginia locker room—parents, alumni, friends—wore the appropriate wristband. Still, Groh knew, there was no deterrent any college coach could employ to keep runners and agents away from players, including talented underclassmen.

One floor above the garage, anyone could walk into the lobby, where Virginia football alumni had gathered following the Miami loss. Sitting alongside a check-in table, Canty felt ready to become one of the first members of the 2005 draft class to sign with an agent. All around him were former Cavaliers, most of whom never played a down in the NFL.

The decision looked like a lock. Ethan Lock.

While the Atlanta Falcons headed north on Saturday, November 20, 2004, to face the New York Giants the following day, assistant general manager Tim Ruskell opted to take a later flight so he could watch eighteenth-ranked Virginia face Georgia Tech in midtown Atlanta.

Ruskell arrived nearly two hours early at Bobby Dodd Stadium, located right on campus not far from Coca-Cola world headquarters. He met up in the press box with Falcons scout Bob Harrison, who is based in Athens and scouts the state of Virginia as part of a mid-Atlantic coverage area.

Ruskell and Harrison took the elevator down to the field, where they watched Virginia go through its pregame routine. They spent little time on Georgia Tech, partly because they see a lot of the hometown team, but also because Chan Gailey's roster did not have much draft-eligible talent for 2005. The Yellow Jackets draft prospects for 2006 and beyond looked promising, especially freshman wide receiver Calvin Johnson.

James Butler, Tech's senior safety, was rated highly by BLESTO and National before the season. ESPN's Mel Kiper Jr. ranked Butler as his top safety and number twenty-five prospect overall, but thus far, scouts had failed to see early-round talent in film and in person during his senior season.

Ruskell walked the sidelines, searching for familiar faces. Having scouted for nearly two decades, he knows at least a few people on every major coaching staff. Ruskell stopped to talk to John Garrett, Virginia's wide receivers coach, who spent three seasons in Tampa Bay's personnel department during Ruskell's early years with the Buccaneers.

Next Ruskell chatted with Tom Sherman, a longtime Virginia assistant coach who now worked in an administrative role for Al Groh's program. Before heading up to the press box, Ruskell spoke to Lynn Swann, the Hall of Fame wide receiver and ABC Television commentator.

Upstairs, Ruskell found his assigned seat in the scouts section of the press box. Few NFL team employees were on hand. Scouts generally prefer to watch games with draft-eligible talent on both sides of the field, though a game like this had its advantages, because scouts could focus on fewer players.

Unlike fans, who follow the ball as they watch the game, scouts concentrate on players. If a scout is watching, say, a group of defensive backs, he's unlikely to have much of a feel for how the offensive line is performing.

"You miss a lot of the game this way," Ruskell says.

Ruskell was making comments on a chart that had a dozen or so Virginia players listed. There was not a whole lot of space.

"You know those hard-boiled Easter eggs with all the tiny words written on them?" he says. "If this gig doesn't work out, I might look into that. I've gotten pretty good at writing small."

By now, nine games into the college football season, Ruskell had detailed reports from the Falcons' area scouts. The scouts had studied film and watched practices and games. They had visited each campus with significant draft talent multiple times, interviewing three to five people at each school for every player. On December 11, they would reconvene at Falcon headquarters in Flowery Branch to begin narrowing the field of scouted players.

Ruskell was not gung-ho about Elton Brown, Virginia's 330-pound, All-American guard who was projected as a first-round pick in the draft. The Falcons offensive coordinator, Alex Gibbs, preferred smaller, athletic linemen who could get off the line quickly and adjust on the fly with guys coming at them.

"Brown does not move well laterally," Ruskell says. "He's not a bender, which is to say he has tight hips. He doesn't drop his hips, and that keeps him from going side to side and changing direction well. It's more physical than a technique thing. He's going to be a quality player in the league, but probably not for us."

Ruskell, like a lot of NFL personnel, was bullish on Alvin Pearman, Virginia's five-nine running back. Pearman began the season as the backup to Wali Lundy, a junior, but seized the starting role after Lundy struggled in a loss to Florida State.

Scouts loved Pearman's versatility. He caught balls out of the backfield, played special teams, and even occasionally lined up as a wide receiver. Ruskell watched Pearman as he swung out to the right, hesitated, and then burst upfield.

"I'm becoming a big Alvin Pearman fan," Ruskell says. "He lets the play develop in front of him and lets his blockers do the work. He's slightly slower and smaller, so that helps. The problem is that he doesn't have that huge burst of speed once the play develops. You hear great things about his work ethic and character."

Ruskell also liked Marquis Weeks, a star running back in high school, who played sparingly at the position his first three seasons at Virginia behind Pearman and Lundy. Weeks now was lining up as a safety, but continued to thrive as a kickoff returner.

From watching film and talking to his Virginia sources, Ruskell learned that Weeks had the vision and cutback skills to thrive at the next level. Chiseled, with washboard abs, Weeks had a "beach body," along with speed.

In September, Weeks returned a kickoff one hundred yards for a touchdown against North Carolina. When asked about the play by reporters, he delivered one of the year's more memorable quotes.

"That was just instinct," he said, "kind of like running from the cops."

Weeks, at five-ten, was undersized, just like the five-nine Pearman. Just like Tiki Barber, the five-ten ex-Virginia back now playing with the Giants. Just like Warrick Dunn, Ruskell's own five-nine starter with the Falcons.

Barber and Dunn would square off the following day at Giants Stadium. Both were drafted in 1997, Dunn out of Florida State with the twelfth overall pick to Ruskell and the Buccaneers, Barber early in the second round to the Giants.

"Dunn showed a little more burst," Ruskell said. "He had the strength of a bigger man in a larger body. Tiki was a little undersized and looked slower. But it was pretty even. That might have been an example of with everything else being equal we went with the [local] Florida State guy."

Ruskell glanced up at a television to catch a replay. Since TV cameras follow the ball, broadcasts are of little help in scouting defenses, though replays help. For all of the talk about how the wider, HDTV technology would broaden the viewer's perspective, Ruskell hasn't found it to be much of an improvement, at least in scouting.

"There's no substitute for live games," he says.

ABC runs a note on Virginia center Zac Yarborough not allowing any sacks. "It means nothing," Ruskell says. "Nor do I believe it."

Yarborough was a prime example of how it's possible to be an outstanding college player and have little NFL potential. A three-year starter, he was under consideration for the Rimington Award, given to the nation's top center. At six-four, he had the size, though he needed some more bulk on his 276-pound frame. He had the bloodlines; his father Jim played ten years at offensive tackle for the Detroit Lions. Zach even served as Virginia's long-snapper on special teams, always a valuable skill in the NFL.

Like Elton Brown, Yarborough had stiff hips. Unlike Brown, he did not possess the raw skills to compensate for a lack of athleticism and mobility. If he got a shot at the NFL, it would come as an undrafted free agent.

Ruskell was thankful that all of the kickers and punters in the game were underclassmen. Teams rarely spend draft picks on kickers—the blanket term used for both positions—and scouts hate wasting energy writing reports on kickers. Unless a kicker has phenomenal leg strength or uncanny accuracy, most teams are content to sign free agent kickers.

Virginia led Georgia Tech 10–0 at halftime. Pearman provided a six-yard touchdown run. Connor Hughes, a junior already projected as one of the better kickers for the 2006 draft, chipped in with a thirty-three-yard field goal. As usual, junior linebackers Ahmad Brooks and Darryl Blackstock had dominated the opposition.

As a NFL executive, Ruskell faces fines for commenting specifically on juniors to the media, though he was keeping an eye on Virginia's talented cast of draft-eligible underclassmen, for future reference if nothing else.

"I'll say this," Ruskell said. "It's a very talented group."

Ruskell and Harrison departed in the third quarter with the rest of the modest scout contingent. Down on the field, Blackstock was enjoying himself, in the midst of a three-sack performance.

After each sack, Blackstock pointed to the sidelines and Chris Slade, the former New England Patriot who held Virginia's all-time sack record with forty. Slade, now retired at thirty-three and living in Atlanta, was one of Groh's all-time favorite players. Though Groh never asked Slade to lobby Blackstock to stay for a senior season, Slade made it a point to present the pros and cons.

"The NFL will always be there," Slade said on the sidelines as the final seconds ticked off on a 30–10 Virginia win. "But it's a personal thing. Nobody can make that decision for him."

After Groh met with the media and the players showered, they made their way to a bus parked alongside a plaza on the north side of the stadium. A small gathering of Virginia parents and fans offered congratulations.

There were no agents, even though Atlanta was a hotbed of "certified contract advisors," as they were referred to by the NFL Players Association. There was little interest in Georgia Tech's players, and plenty of more prestigious games going on throughout the country.

Atlanta-based Todd France, who a year earlier signed Tech linebacker Daryl Smith, was not at the game. But with the college season winding down, the young agent was getting into position to have a blockbuster 2005 draft.

By late November France was well on his way to taking his fifteen-month-old France Athlete Management Enterprises (FAME) company into the upper echelons of football agencies.

Like his competitors, France did not know for sure which players would sign with him. In four and a half years as an NFLPA certified contract advisor, he had learned not to consider a client his own until the signature was on the dotted line.

Nat Dorsey reminded him of that. In the fall of 2003, Dorsey was a promising junior offensive tackle at Georgia Tech who was considering going pro early. France thought he had him, at least until he signed with SFX agent Ben Dogra.

Dorsey should have stayed in school. He failed to impress NFL scouts prior to the draft, and lasted until midway through the fourth round, when the Minnesota Vikings took him. He received a signing bonus of $308,000. Combined with his 2004 salary of $230,000, he generated just $16,140 in commissions for Dogra and SFX Sports, which paid more than that for Dorsey's precombine training and lodging in Arizona.

The draft is funny that way. A player rated high by scouts and the media in the fall can see his stock plunge by April, even without an injury, arrest, or failed drug test. Sometimes, as in the case of Nat Dorsey, scouts get scared when a kid's motivation and drive do not seem to match the level of raw talent.

It still was a good draft for France. With the seventh pick in the second round, the Jacksonville Jaguars selected linebacker Daryl Smith, Dorsey's Georgia Tech teammate, and France negotiated a signing bonus of $1,872,000. Later in the round, the Denver Broncos drafted Darius Watts, a wide receiver from Marshall University. He received a signing bonus of $1,265,000. Along with their 2004 salaries, France would earn commissions of $107,910.

Still, France knew rival agents would use his lack of first-round representation against him, to say nothing of a pending lawsuit filed by his former employer, Career Sports Management, for resigning in 2003 and taking sixteen clients with him.

That does not stop France from aiming high. His four main targets were potential first-rounders: Auburn running back Ronnie Brown and cornerback Carlos Rogers; Roddy White, a wide receiver at Alabama-Birmingham; and Georgia safety Thomas Davis, a junior who seemed likely to leave school early. Though Auburn and Georgia had other promising players for the 2005 draft, France had made a presentation to just one other prospect, pitching Georgia's Fred Gibson a year earlier when the wide receiver was considering leaving school early.

France knows the key to getting considered by a client is to get in the door. The ultimate sales pitch is vital, and France has developed a reputation for having one of the most high-tech, DVD presentations of anyone in the industry, along with the requisite information on his success negotiating for clients.

He's at his best translating the glossary of NFL signing terms for players and family members. Phrases such as "option bonuses," "voidable years," and "escalators," quickly become simplified. France spent nearly a decade cutting big-time sports-marketing deals for Atlanta-based Career Sports Management, and his presentation includes the highlights of the deals he's done for clients.

Pat Dye Jr., the rival Atlanta agent, takes a preemptive strike against agents like France during his presentations. "Let's separate the sizzle from the steak," he tells parents and recruits, usually before detailing his seventeen-year track record.

France has learned quickly to tailor his presentations.

"You're selling your capabilities and establishing a comfort factor with the parents that you can take care of their son and do whatever it is you need to do. And that's not just the contract, that's everything. On field, off field, contract, someone they can trust—everything. Sometimes you're viewed as not having enough clients. Sometimes you have too many."

First, France needs help opening the gates, and that's where existing clients prove useful. Takeo Spikes, a linebacker from Auburn, is in the midst of a six-year deal worth $32 million. France's clients from Georgia include Bills left tackle Jonas Jennings and Kendrell Bell, a linebacker for the Pittsburgh Steelers. Both can become free agents at the end of the season.

If, say, Ronnie Brown is wondering what kind of marketing deals France could swing for him, he need only step into a wing of France's Atlanta office suites devoted largely to the many endorsement deals

Spikes, Bell, and Priest Holmes have landed, despite playing in small-market NFL cities.

Then there's the issue of finding the gatekeeper. Some kids delegate their parents to deal with agents and narrow the field. Others handle it themselves or enlist the help of a high school coach or friend.

"Sometimes the dad says everything is run through him, and meanwhile you find out he's not involved at all," France says.

In some cases, the college coach has his own agent and provides a point of entry to his representative. Jimmy Sexton has had good luck with client Nick Saban's players at LSU. More often that not, that connection proves irrelevant.

France spends most of the fall on the road. If he's not visiting recruits and families, he's flying off to tend to his current roster. He'll travel to an NFL city and visit clients on the home team on Friday and check in with any visiting clients at their hotel on Saturday. After the game on Sunday, he'll see the visiting team off on the bus before they fly out, have dinner with family members still in town, and then fly out on Monday morning.

"Nothing is easy," France says. "I won't be outworked and I just take care of my guys because it's a very nonloyal business. The famous agent line is 'Where's your agent?' implying that you're there and the agent is not. I've never said that to anyone, but I can see it happening. If you keep in touch and have a relationship, you can't worry about it."

Though France is a relative newcomer to the NFL agent business, the seeds of his involvement were planted nearly two decades ago. In 1986, Lonnie Cooper founded Career Sports Management, an Atlanta sports-marketing company that arranged appearances and endorsements for a small but growing client list of NBA coaches and players, including Atlanta Hawks head coach Mike Fratello, pint-sized guard Spud Webb, and power forward Cliff Levingston.

One afternoon, Levingston wandered into Marietta Toyota looking to purchase a 4Runner. Bob Pressley, the general sales manager, said he ran a credit check on Levingston and discovered all sorts of red flags. Levingston, like many generous pro athletes, had co-signed loans for others, some of whom never held up their end of the deals.

Cooper was summoned to straighten things out and Levingston was able to purchase the 4Runner. Cooper and Pressley also began discussions on what later would become a three-year deal for Fratello to serve as spokesman for Marietta Toyota.

In those days, long before seven-figure NBA coaching salaries became commonplace, Cooper realized that the marketing and endorsement side of the business could be every bit as lucrative as contract negotiations.

As Cooper's business grew, he kept things lean, but realized in 1990 that he needed help. He hired a young, aspiring sports marketer named Reed Bergman to shoulder some of the load.

France, born July 8, 1971, was enrolled at the University of Alabama, with a vague goal of working in sports. His family moved from Chicago to Atlanta in 1987, shortly before his junior year of high school, when his father was promoted from senior vice president to president of an Atlanta-based publishing business. Todd France graduated from Alabama in 1993 with a degree in communications, with a focus on advertising.

France paid his dues at the lowest rungs of sports. After graduation, he went to work for the Atlanta Knights, a minor league hockey team that performed downtown to sparse crowds at the Omni, and was best known for playing female goaltender Manon Rheaume for two games during the previous season.

Like most minor league sports employees, France did a little bit of everything. He sold sponsorships and advertising, hawked tickets, and pitched in whenever. He worked briefly for the Atlanta Fireants, a professional roller hockey team that played one season in Atlanta (1994) before moving to Oklahoma.

In April of 1994, Bergman hired the twenty-two-year-old France to work with him in the marketing department at Career Sports for seventeen thousand dollars a year. France threw himself into the job, working eighteen-hour days and immersing himself in the world of sports marketing. His specialty was consumer products deals, and he built relationships with companies such as The Keebler Company, Nestle, and SmithKline Beecham, makers of products such as Aquafresh and Tums.

France would approach the companies, ascertain their sports marketing goals, and put the deals together. Keebler's Cheez-It crackers became a sponsor of young NASCAR drivers Tony Stewart and Buckshot Jones. France negotiated the title sponsorship of the Cheez-It 250, a NASCAR race in Bristol, Tennessee. There were dozens of contests involving consumer products and sports-related prizes and CSM did everything from getting the point-of-sales materials designed to being on site to make sure the winners received everything. Typical was a trip France made to Disney World to greet three winners of a lunch with Jay Novacek, the former Dallas Cowboys tight end.

France helped negotiate a contract for ex-Georgia quarterback Eric Zeier to become a broadcaster at his alma mater. Zeier, who played six seasons in the NFL as a backup, was the closest thing Career Sports had to a legitimate football client when France approached Cooper in the fall of 1999 with the idea of starting a football agency division.

Cooper's practice still was dominated by NBA and college basketball coaches, along with a handful of baseball players, most notably Atlanta Braves pitcher John Smoltz.

After Bergman left in 1997 to form a marketing company with baseball agent Scott Boras, France was promoted to senior vice president of sales and marketing. Cooper continued to run the representation side of the business, though France was becoming increasingly interested in working as an agent.

He considered basketball and its eye-popping salaries, but NBA rosters were small and increasingly composed of players from all over the world, which made recruiting difficult and expensive. Plus, a handful of NBA agents held a virtual stranglehold on the league.

Baseball showed potential, and France was familiar with the field through Cooper, having made marketing-related presentations to potential CSM clients. With guaranteed contracts and commissions as high as 5 percent, baseball has made several agents multi-millionaires. There are few barriers to entry. As long as the aspiring agent has no felony convictions, and one client on a team's forty-man roster, he can be licensed by the Major League Baseball Players Association.

The NFL offers no guaranteed contracts, commissions of no more than 3 percent, and player careers that last an average of just three and a half years. To become a registered contract advisor, a would-be agent needs to possess a four-year degree from an accredited college or university, pass a background check, attend a two-day seminar, pass an exam, and fork over one thousand six hundred dollars. Then there's a dizzying array of licenses and fees agents face in order to operate legally in most states, though enforcement of such regulations often is spotty.

But the reason the number of football agents outweigh baseball representatives by nearly a four-to-one margin is because of the shorter gestation period between the time a player is drafted and when he reaches the big time.

Few baseball players ever have gone straight from draft day into the major leagues. Most spend four or five years toiling in the minors, during which time they make little money but expect their agents to provide them with equipment, shoes, and all manner of financial and moral support. Once they reach the majors, they're not eligible for a huge payday through salary arbitration until they've played three years. That's when more experienced agents swoop in and sign them, negating any work and investment the entry-level agents have made for years.

In football, players go right from draft day to a NFL minicamp, sometimes within a week, though contract negotiations last three months, until the start of preseason camp, and often beyond. Signing bonuses after the second round are modest, but there's an immediate commission, along with one off the rookie salary.

No wonder the ranks of football agents, or at least wannabe agents, had swelled. In the fall of 2004, there were more than thirteen hundred NFLPA-certified agents. More than two-thirds of them did not have a single client in the league.

The sudden paydays and soaring salaries have unleashed another agent subcategory on college campuses: financial advisors. Though most players will not earn enough money to make it worthwhile for investment managers, even at a management fee of 1 to 2 percent, to handle their portfolios, the financial gurus still recruit potential NFL clients with gusto. Like their agent counterparts, they see the route to riches beginning with one client.

"An agent's work is done pretty much when the career is over," says Bruce Smith, an Atlanta-based financial advisor. "A financial advisor relationship can go on for decades."

For football agents, the rising salaries come with a price. Greater competition among agents makes it possible for potential clients to ask for the world. NFL hopefuls now expect a full slate of predraft training services, and the poaching of clients is even more rampant than in baseball. Still, it's a heck of a lot easier for an agent to break into football than baseball.

Major League Baseball increasingly has become the domain of players from Latin America, requiring agents to foot the bill for expensive travel and assemble a bilingual staff. A football agent can set up shop in Georgia or Florida and recruit mostly out of his car. Agencies don't need Spanish-speaking employees, though most firms include both white and African-American agents.

"All Caucasian agents have that," says Darrell Wills, who worked for IMG until 2004, when the NFLPA revoked his certification when he tried to take six IMG clients with him and start a new firm. "They hire a guy to get them into the living room, but they never want him to get to the point of doing the contract."

Wills's claim is open to debate, though the issue of race permeates any discussion of draft recruiting. With the vast majority of NFL players African-American, it's perhaps not surprising that some of the more prominent agents—such as Carl and Kevin Poston, Roosevelt Barnes, and Eugene Parker—also are black. In Major League Baseball, where African-American players have become an even smaller minority over the last two decades, white agents dominate the field.

Not long after Wills left IMG, longtime football operations employee Chris Singletary, who is black, earned his agent certification and took a prominent role in recruiting for the 2005 draft, joining veteran agents Tom Condon and Ken Kremer, who are white.

At Momentum Sports, based in San Antonio, Jack Scharf and Jeff Griffin work in tandem. Scharf, who is white, and Griffin, who is black, received their agent certifications on the same day in 2002.

"The race card gets played by some agents, but most families, whether they're African American or white, see right through that," Scharf says. "I don't think it's nearly the factor some agents make it out to be, nor should it be."

Patrick Kerney, the defensive end for the Atlanta Falcons, recalls an amusing case of racial misidentification. Kerney was a relative unknown entering his senior season at the University of Virginia in 1998, projected as perhaps a fifth-round draft pick, but his stock rose with a solid senior campaign, and a flurry of communication from agents ensued.

"This one agency sent me a letter that read, 'Dear Patrick, we pride ourselves on providing the utmost service to you, the African-American athlete,'" Kerney says.

The same agent called one of Kerney's black teammates, defensive tackle Antonio Dingle, and suggested that the three of them meet in Charlottesville for a get-acquainted session. Dingle, having received a similar letter, knew the agent's angle.

"There's something about Kerney you might not understand," said Dingle, who went on to a brief NFL career.

"Oh, is he on the take?" the agent asked. "Has he signed with an agent already?"

"No," Dingle said. "Kerney is white."

Kerney, who signed with Maryland-based agent Anthony Agnone, shakes his head at the story. "I guess some people don't bother to look at the media guide."

France is a one-agent show, though he has an office staff of four to provide the level of concierge service that NFL players demand, including the negotiation of home and auto deals, travel arrangements, marketing and endorsements, everything down to wedding planning and wardrobe assistance.

Compared to that, the actual negotiation of contracts is easy and straightforward. Anyone armed with the pick-by-pick contract results from the previous year's NFL Draft can do a reliable job predicting what a team is willing to pay the following season, though that doesn't stop agents from trumpeting any tweaks they manage to negotiate to potential clients.

"I don't think it's brain surgery doing that structured thing that goes on in the NFL Draft," says Boras, who through loopholes and hard-line negotiating has fueled the escalation of baseball draft bonuses over the last two decades.

Boras has become such a powerbroker in baseball that teams sometimes pass up his clients in the draft rather than risk a protracted negotiation. In the NFL, where salary caps and slotting prevail, teams put far less weight on a player's representative.

"Any holdout that occurs after the first fifteen picks, you really have to ask yourself why," says Atlanta Falcons president Rich McKay. "These are pretty easy deals to do, especially after the second round."

France thought so, especially after nearly six years of negotiating sports marketing contracts. In February of 2000, at the age of twenty-eight, he became a certified contract advisor. His first client was Mareno Philyaw, a wide receiver from Troy State selected in the sixth round of the 2000 draft by Atlanta. Philyaw played only briefly in the NFL, but left a lasting legacy to France by introducing him to Falcons teammate Darrick Vaughn.

Vaughn, a cornerback drafted out of Southwest Texas in the seventh-round that year, was no more likely than Philyaw to enjoy a lengthy, high-paying NFL career. But in early 2001, Vaughn mentioned that a friend of his from Texas was getting out of college and was interested in pursuing a career in sports marketing.

France met with Vaughn's friend and, even though he could not offer him a job, tried to be encouraging. That might have been the end of it, if not for a phone call in early 2002. The kid had a buddy employed in the NFL, who was looking for new representation.

His name was Priest Holmes.

Holmes wasn't even drafted coming out of Texas in 1997. Back then, at five-nine and two years removed from a torn ACL, he was less of a prospect than Philyaw or Vaughn. After four seasons in Baltimore, he found the perfect home in Kansas City, which employed a zone-blocking scheme that showcased his patient running style. In 2001, Holmes led the NFL in rushing with 1,555 yards in his first season with the Kansas City Chiefs. With little notice, France met Holmes in Atlanta on a Saturday and after a brief presentation handed him a standard player representation agreement and a preaddressed FedEx envelope.

France knew only that CSM was one of four agencies Holmes was considering, and he wasn't especially confident of his chances. After all, it was rare to sign a client after just one meeting. But four days later, France received the signed contract back via FedEx.

No longer was France just another one of the dozens of faceless agents with a small stable of fringe NFL players. He now represented arguably the NFL's best rusher, a twenty-seven-year-old with high-earning years ahead of him. Holmes was signed through 2005, with his commissions going to a previous agent, but France was free to negotiate marketing deals.

The Holmes signing, via Vaughn and Philyaw, on July 26, 2002, reenforced France's belief in the power of the existing client network. Earlier that year, he signed Spikes, who had just finished his fifth season with the Cincinnati Bengals and was one of the more prominent free agent linebackers. Those two clients gave France credibility when he recruited college players for the draft. Until this point, his only significant draftee had been Kendrell Bell, drafted by Pittsburgh out of Georgia in the second round in 2001.

During the next two years, France built a client list of sixteen players, many from Auburn, Alabama, Georgia, and Georgia Tech. He kept a low profile, staying out of the media spotlight, and joked that he was not even the most prominent Todd France working in football. In 2002, a kicker from the University of Toledo with the same name entered the league as an undrafted free agent, signing with the Minnesota Vikings.

Still, by the summer of 2003, agent Todd France, former Atlanta Fireants salesman, had grown too big for Career Sports Management. On August 24, France declared his independence from Cooper, taking his football clients with him.

Cooper did not let France go quietly. On October 10, 2003, he filed a lawsuit in Fulton County, Georgia, Superior Court, against France. The suit claimed that Career Sports was entitled to all of the fees from the sixteen players for contracts consummated before September 9, 2003, and unspecified damages against France and his new company, France Athlete Management Enterprises (FAME).

Career Sports received sixteen faxed termination letters from NFL player clients, including Holmes, on September 4, 2003, the day after the Chiefs announced a four-year contract extension worth as much as $36 million.

Cooper, through Career Sports vice president of public relations Jamie

Sims, declined comment for this book. With the suit still unresolved as this book went to press, France had little to say, but hinted that his departure was due in part to wanting a bigger piece of the action at Career Sports.

"My preference was to stay where I was and keep doing things, but there comes a time where things need to be handled a certain way and you need certain securities with your job. If that's going to happen, great. If it's not, you consider alternatives. I don't know how much more I can say. I never envisioned myself doing this, but when it came down to it, when push came to shove, you've got to do what's best for you."

The affidavits and depositions filed as part of the suit provide conflicting accounts of France's role and the events leading up to his departure. The sides agreed that France proposed that CSM start a football representation arm of the agency in the fall of 1999. France and Cooper were agents of record for each player signed, though all commissions went to CSM. France, at the time of his resignation in 2003, earned a salary of approximately one hundred and seventy-five thousand dollars plus benefits, including a country club membership.

Beth Brandon, CSM's chief operating officer, said in an affidavit that when France proposed the football division, he asked that Cooper act as his "trainer and mentor until he was properly trained." Brandon said CSM agreed to the proposal with the understanding that France not neglect his sales duties in other divisions.

CSM paid all of the start-up costs of the NFL division, including salaries and benefits of other employees working with France, as well as all costs involved with France becoming a certified agent by the NFL Players Association, along with the various states that require licensing.

In July of 2003, according to Brandon, France asked for a new compensation package that included a doubling of his salary and half of the NFL player commissions. He also requested CSM pick up the lease payments, maintenance, and insurance on his Mercedes. The new salary alone, Brandon said, "would have come close to matching CSM's expected gross revenues in its NFL division for 2003 and would have exceeded the expected gross revenues for 2004."

Brandon also said in her affidavit that France neglected his other sales activities and focused almost exclusively on the NFL division. France's work on the NFL endeavor, Brandon said, "failed to produce any net profit for CSM for a substantial period," and his "neglect of his other duties and his initial failure to generate significant new NFL business" caused CSM revenues to drop and costs to escalate.

France, in his affidavit, said he continued to fulfill his sales and marketing responsibilities while creating the NFL division. He opened CSM sales offices in Los Angeles and Chicago. The bulk of the time he spent on the NFL division was on nights and weekends. France acknowledged that in lieu of receiving the fifty percent share of fees to which he was entitled under the NFLPA's standard representation agreement, he would be paid a salary by CSM.

But, France said in the affidavit, "At no time during my employment did I agree that this arrangement would continue upon the termination of my employment with CSM." France said he had not received a pay raise in more than five and a half years. France said that during a meeting on July 21, 2003, Cooper asked him to make a compensation proposal, but that France, not being privy to CSM's financials, was "not in position to fairly determine an appropriate salary increase."

A month later, France departed. Bergman, who says he reached his own settlement with Cooper after splitting in 1997, remains friends with France. "Lonnie took a chance that Todd could help him, and he clearly did," Bergman says. "Todd built an athlete representation practice for Lonnie and made him an awful lot of money."

Rival agents aren't so quick to paint France as a victim. "He was able to use Cooper's resources to build himself a nice little business, and once he got a foothold, he took off," says an agent with comparable experience in the field. "Most of us have to find a way to foot the start-up costs ourselves."

France's departure had overtones of *Jerry Maguire*, though unlike Maguire, who left with just one client, the entire football division joined France at FAME. France resigned on a Sunday night and one of his first calls was to Jennifer Krompass, who worked with France as CSM's new business coordinator. She resigned Monday morning and showed up at France's townhouse ready to work.

Realizing France had little more than a cell phone, pen, and paper, she took him to a Staples outlet to buy office supplies. As Krompass began loading a cart with supplies, France took stock of his pending start-up costs and put several items back on the shelves.

They operated out of France's home for six months as the agent incorporated, recruited for the 2004 draft, serviced his existing clients, located office space, and supervised the decoration. He settled on a black-and-silver motif for the FAME logo, ordered large images of his clients from various NFL photographers, and set up a marketing room that was part memorabilia gallery, part convenience store. The furniture was black leather and silver metal, the floors light hardwood.

When it was done, shortly before the 2004 draft, someone gave FAME a goldfish bowl for the entryway, a tribute to the one Jerry Maguire took from his previous employer on the way out the door. France and Krompass didn't fall in love like Maguire and his accountant, but oversaw a rapid start-up operation. France would be the only one involved in athlete recruiting.

"It's all me," France said. "Would I like to have help? It would ease the workload. Say I'm at a Georgia-Auburn game. I'll see agents from the same company planted on both sides in the stands. I'm on one side saying hello to whomever, then I have to sprint around to the other side and casually walk up to the other group. But I wouldn't have it any other way."

The CSM lawsuit seems to have no impact on France as he recruits clients for the 2005 draft. As usual, he must navigate the murky waters of state and university regulations regarding contact with players.

"Some schools don't want you talking to kids until after the end of the season," France says. "You can follow that rule, but you're not going to sign a kid ever. You'll be the only one following that rule. Why else would kids be signing right after their bowl games? You do the best you can to play by the rules.

"Different schools go different ways. Alabama used to have a rule that if you signed up as a registered agent, you can't talk to kids. I told the compliance guy that if your goal is to have agents sign up, it's not going to work. They'd rather not sign up, and talk to your players. Now you sign up and it doesn't say you can't talk to players. An agent list is just something they can provide to players, saying these agents have at least followed state and school rules. We're not recommending them, but they've registered."

Schools walk a fine line with agents. Be too strict and risk nobody following rules and protocol. Be too loose and risk agents plying players with illegal incentives.

Instead, most schools strike a happy medium. Instead of banishing agents from campus, which is impossible, school officials try to make them part of the process. That strikes some as letting the fox into the henhouse. But for schools like Florida State University, who have been embarrassed by agent scandals, it's a worthwhile tactic.

For most of the year, FSU and other schools try to keep agents away from campus. But for one day a year they throw open the doors and invite them to make their pitches.

They call it "agent day."

Chapter Seven:

AGENT DAY

P at Dye Jr. and Bill Johnson sat in desk chairs and smiled at Ray Willis, his wife Kimberly, and a roomful of Ray's relatives. It was November 21, 2004, and Dye and Johnson had thirty minutes to make their sales pitch to Willis, a Florida State offensive tackle considered a possible second or third-round pick.

The Willis camp sat in deep-cushioned garnet-red theater chairs with flip-up desktops, in Room 2302 of Florida State's massive football complex, a shrine to the big business of college football. During the season, the room was used for position meetings. Motivational signs were posted throughout. (YOU CAN'T LIVE SOFT AND FIGHT TOUGH.)

On this Sunday afternoon, the school had invited agents to sit down one-on-one with the school's draft-eligible players. It was the one day of the year that Florida State, like every other major football program, did not try to keep agents off campus and away from players.

"Agents drive us nuts," said Bobby Bowden, the school's longtime head coach. "They're probably the number-one problem in college coaching."

Bowden should know. A decade earlier, recruiters working for agents provided several of his top players with a free shopping spree at a sporting goods store. "The Foot Locker Incident" prompted a NCAA investigation that landed FSU on probation for one year. Steve Spurrier, head coach at rival Florida at the time, labeled FSU "Free Shoes University."

As part of Florida State's penance, it cracked down on agents and set up its agent day, where football representatives registered with the school and licensed by both the NFL Players Association and the state of Florida are allowed to submit names of players they wished to meet. The players then were asked to submit a list of agents they wanted to meet.

Brian Battle, the school's compliance director, matched up the lists and assigned agents rooms. Players rotated each half hour in a high-stakes job fair.

"We're not going to stick our heads in the sand and pretend that agents aren't constantly contacting our players," Battle said. "We know most kids, if they have any NFL potential at all, have narrowed down the agent selection process now, as they should have. Our goal with agent day is to give agents an open avenue to play by the rules, introduce themselves to our juniors, and give another pitch to seniors they might already be talking to. If they do that, then maybe they'll be less likely to do something stupid."

Dye and Johnson, based in Atlanta, had just three Seminoles on their dance card, but they were three of the school's top prospects for the 2005 draft: defensive tackle Travis Johnson, along with Alex Barron and Willis, both offensive tackles.

It had been a rough day for the agents. The meeting with Johnson was not promising. A California native, Johnson told Dye and Bill Johnson he thought highly of Gary Wichard, who was based in Pacific Palisades (and, according to *Jerry Maguire* director Cameron Crowe, a main inspiration for the movie).

Barron, considered a lock for the first round, appeared on the verge of falling asleep. "Two years of work down the drain," Johnson said afterward. "He's clearly going in another direction."

Dye, Johnson, and Willis were hardly strangers. Johnson had met Willis during the player's sophomore year, and they sat down formally for the first time at the agent day at the end of the 2003 season, when Willis thought of leaving school early for the NFL.

It helped that Dye represented Montrae Holland and Brett Williams, two former FSU offensive linemen drafted in the fourth round of the 2003 draft by New Orleans and Kansas City respectively. It also helped that Kimberly Willis was unlike any player girlfriend or spouse the agents had encountered.

Kimberly Willis, who is five and a half years older and nearly a foot shorter than her husband, was completing work at Florida State on a doctorate in sport management. Before the wedding, she taught a sports law class that often included Seminole football players, who were forever complaining to Ray about his fiancee's imposed workload.

To keep Ray focused on football Kimberly assumed the task of vetting agents. She logged calls, asked pointed questions, created spreadsheets, investigated agents through the NFL Players Association, and built thick files. She reminded some agents a little of Marcee Tidwell, the outspoken player wife in *Jerry Maguire* who wasn't afraid to challenge Tom Cruise's character to do more for her husband:

> We majored in marketing, Jerry, and when you put him in a Waterbed Warehouse commercial, excuse me, you are making him common. He is pure gold and you're giving him "Waterbed Warehouse" when he deserves the big four: shoe, car, clothing line, soft drink. The four jewels of the celebrity endorsement dollar.

Kimberly took her agent research a step further by interviewing several at length for various doctoral projects and developed a quick rapport with Johnson, a former marketing executive for the NBA's Orlando Magic, who had joined Dye's firm in 1998.

Johnson had become so friendly with Ray and Kimberly that he was invited to their wedding in June of 2004. When the Willis party entered the room for agent day, it seemed like a reunion between friends. Besides Ray and Kimberly, there was Ray's aunt Vanessa, the sister of his late mother; and her husband Chris. Two of his mother's cousins rounded out the group.

Ray Willis walked in on crutches, having sprained an ankle in a loss to archrival Florida the night before. Kimberly helped him squeeze into a desk. The rest of the Willis party took their seats.

Dye cringed. "Are you okay? I was listening to the game driving in, and almost drove off the road when I heard what happened. To me, it was kind of a microcosm of the whole season, very frustrating."

Everyone in the room nodded. Willis had endured a series of ankle and shoulder injuries at Florida State. The Seminoles, accustomed to ten-win seasons and New Year's Day bowl games, finished a disappointing 8-3, losing at home to Florida for the first time since 1986.

"Yeah," Ray sighed. The mood of the room grew somber.

"So," Dye said, smiling. "You ready to take it to the next level, start getting paid for it? I know they've been paying you well here at Florida State, but not *that* well."

Everyone laughed.

Dye took a deep breath and began his presentation.

It's difficult to overestimate the impact of college football. To much of the nation, schools such as Auburn, Notre Dame, Clemson, and Miami are thought of first as football teams rather than institutions of higher learning.

Florida State University does little to discourage such thinking. Doak Campbell Stadium, which seats 82,300 chanting, tomahawk-chopping fans, is attached to a series of offices and classrooms, and the combined structure is the largest brick building in the southeast. From the outside the complex looks like a giant castle, even a small college—contrary to popular belief, it does not hold the entire FSU campus—or perhaps, more appropriately, the world's largest house of worship.

The edifice is not far from the Florida governor's mansion, and some would argue that neither Jeb Bush nor his predecessors have wielded as much influence in Tallahassee as Bobby Bowden, Florida State's head football coach since 1976.

During the 2004 season, Florida State unveiled a nine-foot bronze statue of Bowden, the winningest coach in NCAA Division 1-A history. The statue stands at the entrance of the four-story Moore Athletic Center, a recent $32 million addition that houses the football offices, meeting rooms, and locker facilities, along with upscale amenities such as a grand atrium, hall of fame, trophy room, and theater, that have become must-haves in the college football arms race.

To top off the shrine to FSU football, school officials unveiled a thirty-by-twenty-foot stained-glass window prior to the Florida game, the day before the agent gathering. The image depicts Bowden gazing at the playing surface, recently renamed Bobby Bowden Field, and is one of the five largest stained-glass windows in America.

"I only know one other guy on stained glass," joked Kevin Steele, FSU's linebackers coach. "I see him every Sunday morning."

For Brian Battle, working in St. Bobby's Cathedral is a mixed blessing, one that crystallized for the Florida State compliance director prior to the 2004 season when he interviewed for a similar position at the University of Virginia.

On the surface, the job of a compliance director is to make sure the school is adhering to the volumes of NCAA regulations governing what athletes, coaches, administrators, and boosters can and cannot do.

That's a hectic, full-time position for anyone, and, not surprisingly, the gig usually is filled by a single, thirty-something like Battle, with a masters degree in sports administration.

The role of compliance director at many schools also has come to include everything that the vast football staffs would rather not handle. A player needs disability insurance to protect against a career-ending injury? Go see the compliance director. An underclassman wants a rating from the NFL advisory committee to determine his potential draft position and whether he should go pro? Go see the compliance director. Need someone to deal with agents? Get the compliance director on it.

Since arriving at FSU in 1996, Battle had fulfilled all of those roles, along with giving up his Tuesday nights in the fall to teach a class called "A Career in Professional Sports." Now held in the theater in the new Moore Complex, it's popular with athletes, who learn about such things as NCAA guidelines, sports agents, and the media.

For the princely adjunct professor stipend of two thousand dollars a semester, Battle helps ensure that the school avoids a repeat of the free shoes episode, for which the program received a year of probation. To illustrate his lessons, Battle focuses on actual college misbehavior. He'll show episodes of ESPN's *Outside the Lines* and distribute copies of landmark investigations in *Sports Illustrated,* including the report that detailed the free shoes incident.

"This is not a Jim Harrick Jr. course," Battle says, in reference to the former University of Georgia assistant basketball coach whose "Principles and Strategies of Basketball" class reportedly included such exam questions as *How many points is a three-point field goal worth*? "I've flunked some prominent athletes."

Battle spends an entire class on the rules of agent recruiting. That's probably more time than most students need, though with nearly the entire football team taking the class at some point, he knows it's not time wasted.

Battle explains how it's permissible for players and their parents to talk to agents, so long as nothing of value is accepted, not even a soda. He also explains the rules of engagement. Under Florida law, an agent may not make the initial contact with a player or parent. If a player or parent contacts him, all is fine. But if the agent calls first, he's breaking Florida law. The rule applies to every contact.

It's a rule, of course, that's flagrantly violated. Battle understands this, sees agents hovering around after games outside the players' exit, and realizes that he's powerless to enforce it. Almost every year, Seminoles players—along with those from the University of Miami and the University of Florida—sign with prominent agents not licensed in Florida. Still, Battle stresses to players that the agents who play by the rules probably are the most ethical.

Battle requires agents to register with him. All contact with players, whether via mail or by phone, is supposed to go through him, another regulation that's impossible to enforce. He and his boss, associate athletics director Bob Minnix, schedule agent day each fall, inviting dozens of agents to meet one-on-one with players. FSU was among the first to schedule such an event, and the nine-year-old program has been adopted by many schools around the country.

The irony of agent day is that it's held in late November. By then most players have been talking with agents for months and probably have narrowed the search to three or four representatives. Battle acknowledges this and believes agent day is more valuable for players who will be searching for agents the following fall. Unlike schools such as Miami, which hold a similar late-season event and restricts it to seniors, Battle lets juniors attend.

As for the draftees-to-be, "I tell guys if they haven't narrowed their search to three agents by November, then they must not be serious about going pro," Battle says. "If you want to be ready to train for the combine in January, you have to have these things in order."

A month before agent day, Battle sends invites to agents registered with FSU. He asks them for a list of players they'd like to interview and matches that up with agent lists he receives from the players.

"The whole process is kind of funny," says Ken Harris, a Tampa-based agent. "You know you'd better list everyone, in case there's some guy you thought you had no chance with who really wants to meet you. But usually you show up just to cover your butt. If you're feeling pretty good that you're going to land a certain guy, you know you'd better show up, since everyone else is going to be there."

Because Battle has been assigned or assumed so many ancillary roles, he gets to know Florida State football players well. By dealing with agents, submitting requests to the NFL advisory committee on behalf of underclassmen, and helping players apply for disability insurance— which is granted in part by a player's pro potential—he would have a good feel for where Seminole players stand in NFL eyes, even if he did not talk frequently to team officials.

People like Tim Ruskell, the Atlanta Falcons assistant general manager who got to know Battle during his time with the Tampa Bay Buccaneers, turn to Battle for character insight on players.

So, when Battle traveled to Charlottesville, Virginia, prior to the 2004 football season, he felt qualified to become the next director of compliance for the University of Virginia. Though head coach Al Groh was starting to produce more NFL talent, the school never would attract the beehive of agents that Florida State saw on an annual basis.

After interviewing with Groh, Battle realized the gig would be easier on other fronts. Groh, ever the micromanager, made it apparent that he and not the compliance director would organize such matters as agent day. Though Virginia players could petition the NFL advisory committee for an underclassman draft rating, Groh preferred to rely on his own vast network of contacts in the league. As for teaching "A Career in Professional Sports," Battle need not worry about *that* appearing in the course catalog at Thomas Jefferson's university.

Battle could not have felt more qualified; but he lost the job to an applicant from Vanderbilt, the prestigious academic school in Nashville, Tennessee, known for a sterling compliance record and for a football team that perennially finished at the bottom of the Southeastern Conference. Agents and NFL scouts spent relatively little time in Nashville.

"We're always going to struggle with that big football school image," Battle says. "I'm not saying it's undeserved, of course it is. But we've implemented a lot of things on the compliance front that a lot of schools might do well to emulate."

So Battle resumed his hectic schedule at Florida State. Though the Seminoles struggled during the 2004 season, at least by their lofty standards, they again fielded a roster of talent that made pro scouts and agents salivate.

Battle rose early on Sunday, November 21, 2004, the morning following Florida State's loss to Florida, to oversee agent day. Fifteen agents were to meet one-on-one with seventeen players. Battle produced a schedule based on which agents players wanted to meet with and vice versa, staggering thirty-minute meetings over a dozen rooms between noon and 5:00 P.M.

Alex Barron, the prized offensive tackle, surprised the agents by asking to speak with eight of them. Harris, the Tampa-based agent with twelve NFL clients, figured he scored a meeting by virtue of being invited by Battle to deliver an informational session to players' parents a month earlier.

Unlike most players, who brought an entourage of family members,

Barron met with agents alone. Like his meeting with Dye and Johnson, Barron said little during his chat with Harris and seemed on the verge of falling asleep. "A guy like Alex should have narrowed the field by this point," Harris said afterward. "My guess is he already has, but for whatever reason just wants to cover all of his bases."

Defensive tackle Travis Johnson was the next most coveted prospect, having enjoyed a breakout season in his first as a starter. Johnson's stock was soaring, despite character issues that included being arrested in April of 2003 and charged with felony sexual assault. A jury acquitted him after it was revealed that he had previous consensual relations with the woman.

Johnson's case illustrated how quickly a player's draft status can change. His pre-season scouting grades of 1.85 by BLESTO and 4.4 by National Football Scouting were those of a fringe prospect. Hundreds of players received higher grades. Now he was projected to go in the first round.

Johnson wasn't the biggest Florida State character risk for the 2005 draft, though he was the only one still enrolled. Adrian McPherson had started at quarterback for much of the 2002 season as a true sophomore before being arrested in late November of that year on charges of stealing a blank check and receiving nearly three thousand five hundred dollars after it was cashed. He was kicked off the team and three months later was charged with gambling on pro and college games. The six-three McPherson pleaded no contest to misdemeanor theft and gambling charges and spent the 2004 season playing for the Indiana Firebirds of the Arena Football League, where he was named the league's rookie of the year.

After Barron and Johnson, cornerback Bryant McFadden and wide receiver Craphonso Thorpe were the next most promising, at least at this stage, along with Ray Willis.

Though Pat Dye Jr. and Bill Johnson were the front-runners to represent her husband, Kimberly Willis was keeping their options open. Dye and Johnson were the first of four agencies on their schedule. Rich Moran, a former Green Bay Packers offensive lineman, would come next, followed by Roosevelt Barnes, who along with his partner Eugene Parker represented a long line of Seminoles, including Deion Sanders, Corey Simon, Peter Boulware, and Greg Jones. Phil Williams, a former Florida State wide receiver whose clients included ex-Seminole quarterback Brad Johnson, got the last meeting.

Battle and three colleagues played traffic cops, directing players to rooms and keeping warring agents away from one another. The most unpopular man on hand was Darrell Wills, who Battle allowed to meet with players, despite being decertified by the NFL Players Association seven months earlier.

Wills, who had reinvented himself as a player "manager," partnered with Matthew Couloute, who was a certified player agent, and brought him along with Thom Park, a former college football coach turned sports consultant and financial advisor. Wills scored three meetings, with McFadden, wide receiver Chauncey Stovall, and tight end Paul Irons.

Wills, wearing a gray suit and bow tie, kicked off his schedule by speaking to Stovall and his family. He revisited some familiar themes from a talk he gave to Battle's class in September.

"Most of the things you've heard about the agent business are bad," Wills told the Stovall contingent. "I'm not going to tell you it's any different. Most of these guys are crooks. You have twenty-one- and twenty-two-year-old kids. How do they know the difference? I'm about education. You always hear that saying, that what you don't know won't hurt you. That's completely false. What you don't know can and will hurt you. If you don't handle your business, the business will handle you.

"Fifty percent of players have no money after five years. What about the other half? They've lost a lot of it. I started a corporation to stop that. Seventy percent of NFL players are African American and 50 percent have no money after five years. So it stands to figure that a significant percentage of African-American players have no money after five years. It's a sad story. If you're going to take those violent hits for five years and have no money to show for it, you're an idiot."

Battle reluctantly granted Wills an audience with players. After all, he had twice invited the former FSU track captain to speak, to the class in September and to a gathering of players and parents in early October. From what Battle figured, the decertified Wills was playing within the rules as long as he had a certified agent with him.

Wills was just one of Battle's concerns. Early in the day, a young agent crashed the session, figuring he could just grab some players.

"This isn't a job fair," Battle told the man, escorting him out.

"How am I supposed to break into this business?" the agent asked.

"You're asking the wrong guy."

Battle shook his head as he stood in the atrium and watched the elevator and the would-be agent descend. Light reflected off the stained-glass Bowden window.

"Look, we're Florida State," Battle said. "You don't want players going with people who haven't been in the business that long. We have top-caliber guys and they should have top level representation. You don't want them going with people who haven't been in the business long. In our defense, we always try to bring some new people into the fold. Each year we invite a few up-and-comers. The fact is that there were no players that wanted to speak to the guy.

"I always tell players that the better your representation, the more likely you're going to get into a NFL camp if you're a fringe player. Of course, none of these guys think they're fringe players. They're all going to be NFL stars. But if you're in an NFL camp and get cut, at least that opens the door for NFL Europe, the Arena league, Canada. Dreams will be shattered in the next few months. Hopefully, the athletes have made the right choice to get someone to help them make it. You see some of these guys back around school a year or two later, not knowing what they're going to do. It's sad."

Back in Room 2302, Pat Dye Jr. addressed Kimberly and Ray Willis and his family. At this point, the player and his wife knew everything they needed to know about Dye and Bill Johnson, but they wanted to see what Aunt Vanessa thought.

"Let me give you an overview of who we are and what we're about. I'm Pat Dye, and I know you know a little about us. Bill and I grew up together in Greenville, North Carolina. I grew up in a football family. My father coached at Alabama under Bear Bryant and then was a head coach at East Carolina and finished at Auburn his last twelve years. So I've been around football literally all my life. I went to law school and decided I wanted to meld this legal training with my football heritage and be a sports attorney. My father wasn't too pleased with that, as you could imagine.

"That was seventeen years ago, and I've had the good fortune of negotiating hundreds of NFL contracts for several hundred-million dollars in total value. Bill and I have done a half billion dollars in the last five years alone. I've represented fifteen first-round draft picks in the last decade, twelve second-rounders. I've negotiated for players picked as high as the third pick in the draft, so nothing is going to come up that we can't handle, as far as a contract-negotiation standpoint. We have done landmark rookie and veteran contracts.

"As a coach's son, I have what I think are three distinct advantages. I know the game, can talk intelligently to Ray about it, articulate his strengths, address his weaknesses with teams intelligently, and with credibility, talk to the general managers, scouts, and coaches at any level. That gives us added credibility when we lead clients through the draft and negotiate contracts. I've been around major Division 1 programs all my life and I've seen the price someone like Ray has had to pay to get to this point. It gives me an even stronger sense of obligation to see him capitalize on this. Thirdly, and perhaps my most important advantage, is that because of being a coach's son and having this football heritage, imagine the network of contacts and relationships that I have. There are people that have known me since I was a little kid roaming the sidelines with my father.

"Al Davis came up to me at the Senior Bowl a couple years ago and said, 'Did you know I scouted your father at this game in 1960?' Those relationships help when we sit down at the bargaining table; we're seen as football people first and agents second, and that adds to our credibility. They don't care for agents; they think they're out there getting over on players, being a bad influence. But we have great relationships with people around the league. We're not looking to be golf buddies with them; they know we'll come strong to the table, be well prepared, and we'll show you that in our contract presentation. We're going to max out every opportunity for you.

"I started this firm eleven years ago. We have seven people, including myself, and we have fifty years of combined experience representing professional athletes. We have two attorneys on board. Bill is vice president and is independently qualified to represent Ray himself. You're getting two for one, and we work very closely together. We have a full-time marketing guy we hired away from IMG, which is the world's largest sports marketing company. All he does is bang that phone twenty-four/seven trying to get our guys free stuff. Free cell phones, free suits, free cars, Nike shoe contracts, paid personal appearances, trading card deals—all of those things. I'm not going to sit here and lie to you. The opportunities are going to be a little more limited for Ray because he's not scoring touchdowns. He's not throwing TD passes, and those kind of things, but there will be opportunities for him out there and we'll see to it that he'll maximize those, keeping in mind that he doesn't want to do too much, because we don't want to distract him from making his main income through football.

"We currently represent thirty-seven players on active NFL rosters. We've had eight different guys in the Pro Bowl in the last three years. That speaks to two things: the selectivity that we use when we recruit and also the caliber of our clients. With thirty-seven clients, that makes us the tenth or eleventh biggest firm in the country. We're not a small firm, but not too big. We're right where we want to be. We have enough leverage with our client base around the league that GMs treat us with respect. Yet we're not spread too thin with sixty or eighty clients.

"That's important, because we're in the personal service biz. We're accessible to our clients twenty-four/seven and the only way we can do that—because I have twenty-four hours in my day just like you do and Bill does—is we're very selective. A third of our base is first-round draft picks, and Ray is one of only two offensive tackles in the country that we're recruiting. The only other one is his teammate [Alex Barron], so we're not going to be out there hawking five or six different offensive tackles in this year's draft. When you get to that point, you're pushing too many guys. Two or maybe three, fine, but any more than that, you're stretching your credibility.

"Like I said, we're all about personal service. We have two young ladies in our office that handle the day-to-day services of our clients. Rental cars, limousines, dinner reservations. We're planning [Falcons linebacker] Keith Brooking's wedding right now. Our girls are out there looking for caterers, florists, photographers, churches, places to have the reception. We do it all from soup-to-nuts, and we'd do it for [Falcons guard] Steve Herndon, who you've never heard of and who never got drafted. We're a full-service operation, and if there's something we can't handle, we'll find someone who can. Bill and I have sat in with a dozen or more of our clients when they chose their engagement rings, making sure they didn't get taken advantage of by the diamond people. There are a lot of crooks in that business, too."

Kimberly Willis and the other women in the room nodded.

"We help with buying cars, buying homes—they see Ray coming and they'll try to cave his head in. Here comes the professional athlete with all this money in his pocket. They'll add all the bells and whistles, but then Bill comes in and works the deal and Ray walks out smiling. The car dealer isn't that happy about it, but that's what we're here for.

"We have a full range of predraft services. That involves going to scouts and getting a competitive, definitive assessment of his strengths, weaknesses, and providing it to Ray and his personal trainer, and doing everything we can to polish him up before he has a chance to go to an all-star game or go to the combine, or working out for scouts here for his pro day. We will map out a calendar of everything he's going to be doing, everything we'll be doing on his behalf leading up to the draft. That will also include us being there at different events: all-star games, pro day, and combine, not only for moral support, but to solicit feedback and continue lobbying and promoting him as the total package to scouts and GMs."

Most players leave school after New Year's to train for the NFL combine, the February event where they're stripped and tested in front of NFL personnel. The combine training period is geared to improve speed and strength quickly, and add or subtract weight if needed.

Agents must pick up the tab, which can be up to twenty-five thousand dollars, and over the last decade combine training has become a major perk NFL hopefuls expect.

"Part of the predraft process is identifying a good training solution for him," Dye says. "I'm sure we'll talk more about that later, but the thing I want to say about training is that we're not married to any one trainer. We'll send him wherever he wants to go. If he wants to go to Tom Shaw or Mackie Shilstone in New Orleans, Chip Smith or Velocity, they've trained our guys before. There's Cris Carter in Boca, [Mark] Verstegen in Phoenix. We get calls from all these people because they want to work with our clients. If Ray wants to visit these facilities, test drive the car if you will, we'll facilitate that. Once he plugs into that training solution, we pay for all the training fees, lodging, meals; he won't be coming out-of-pocket for anything associated with training. As much money as we invest in this process, we want to make sure he's with somebody that's outstanding and has a great track record. We don't want to waste our money."

Dye continued. "Our fees for all of these services is 3 percent of the contract. We don't charge for any expenses associated with training. We're going to go to these various events, fly around to see you play, take you to dinner—that's on us. That way, there are no hidden charges at the end of the year. You'll hear from guys who will say, 'Man, my agent threw me a slamming draft party.' Then at the end of the year he gets a bill for the chicken wings, beer, all that stuff. Not with us."

By now Dye was focused on Willis's relatives.

"We're all too conscious of the fact that he's not going to be doing this when he's my age. He'll be long out of the game. I'm forty-two. I can be doing this for the next twenty years or longer if I want to. Ray's got a limited window of opportunity to make it big, and we confess to being greedy on behalf of our clients. You know that movie *The Grinch Who Stole Christmas*, where the Grinch reaches down to get that last crumb away from Cindy Lou Hoo? We try to do that, recognizing that we're going to have to do business with that team again some day. There's the low end of reasonable and the high end of reasonable, and we like to be in the high end, plus a little bit. We're never going to burn bridges or take a scorched-earth approach to negotiations, but we are going to be a little aggressive, because at the end of the day he's judged by how many sacks he's given up. We're judged by how much money we get for a third-round pick, based on what the guys got above and below him, and we're very competitive like that. We're not out there buying and paying clients, and doing some of the things that our competition does to get clients. The only way you're going to get them is by your own clients bragging on you and showing good, solid results every time you negotiate a contract."

Dye leaned in toward Willis's relatives. "We're only going to have one or two offensive tackles in this year's draft. We might have one, we might get skunked, you never know. But he's very, very important to us."

Of all the rivalries in sports, few are as unlikely as the Atlanta Falcons and Tampa Bay Buccaneers. There's no track record of hard-fought games—neither team has a lengthy competitive history period—and there's no bad blood between players.

But when the Falcons arrived at Tampa's Raymond James Stadium on the morning of Sunday, December 5, 2004, they lit the fire of a growing rivalry fueled by two men who would not be wearing helmets that afternoon.

SOUTHERN FEUD, read the front of the *Tampa Tribune* sports section. MCKAY–GRUDEN SPLIT HAS TURNED DIVISION RIVALS INTO NFL'S HATFIELDS AND MCCOYS.

The headline topped a half-page cartoon featuring Falcons general manager Rich McKay and Bucs head coach Jon Gruden dressed as hillbillies and scowling at each other from the front porch of an old shack, divided down the middle.

Tribune sports columnist Martin Fennelly, channeling the prevailing pro-McKay, anti-Gruden sentiment of Buccaneer fans, wrote a tongue-in-cheek column projecting the futures of the two men. While Gruden struggled through a series of progressively lower-profile coaching jobs, McKay ascended to NFL commissioner, Florida governor, and U.S. president before becoming Pope Rich I.

Not even two years had passed since McKay, as Buccaneers GM, and Gruden stood on a podium in San Diego and celebrated a Super Bowl championship together after the Buccaneers routed the Oakland Raiders in Super Bowl XXXVII.

It didn't take long for the winning glow to fade. Gruden and McKay began feuding over personnel decisions, with Gruden favoring veteran free agents and McKay wanting to stay the course by building through the draft.

With the Bucs struggling late in the 2003 season, McKay resigned his longtime post on December 11. Four days later, he accepted a new job as president and general manager of the Falcons, whose next game was back in Tampa against the Buccaneers.

Television cameras zoomed in on McKay's suite frequently during the contest, usually catching him smiling. The Falcons won, 30–28, putting an end to the Buccaneers faint playoff chances.

That might have been the end of the rivalry, if not for the Falcons surprising 9-2 start and the Buccaneers 4-7 record in 2004. Gruden was diplomatic whenever McKay's departure was raised, as it frequently was leading up to the latest Falcons game, saying it would forever be a "sensitive issue." Still, Gruden bristled under the line of questioning, especially when an Atlanta reporter showed up at One Buc Place earlier in the year. To Gruden, it implied that McKay was responsible for the success of the Buccaneers and that the team might still be winning if he were still in Tampa. After all, the sports radio theorists argued, McKay quickly turned the hapless Falcons around.

Actually, the Falcons turnaround was more due to the return of quarterback Michael Vick, who missed much of 2003 with a broken leg. McKay, like Gruden, dodged the rivalry issue.

Others were happy to stoke the fire. When the Falcons defeated the Buccaneers in Atlanta three weeks earlier, head coach Jim Mora presented game balls to McKay, assistant general manager Tim Ruskell, and Reggie Roberts, the public relations director—all former Bucs employees.

Gruden made it a point not to let reporters bait him on the McKay issue, even when Gruden had a strong argument, like when someone asked him why the Bucs had the oldest roster in the NFC.

"I'm not criticizing anybody," Gruden told reporters early in the season. "But in the last ten or twelve drafts how many offensive players are [still] in the media guide? So you've got to fill the roster. If you look at the free agent list, the guys who make it to free agency are not twenty-six years old and they aren't cheap."

Bruce Allen, McKay's replacement as general manager, was careful not to say anything negative about his popular predecessor. But like Gruden he made it clear that the Bucs were hamstrung by an aging roster and the salary cap issues they inherited.

The Buccaneers traded two first-round picks in 2000 to acquire wide receiver Keyshawn Johnson from the New York Jets and dealt a pair of firsts and two second-round selections to Oakland as compensation for Gruden in 2002. Signing free agents such as quarterback Brad Johnson and defensive end Simeon Rice didn't help the cap situation.

Still, McKay didn't dispute Gruden's charge. In fact, it validated the argument he made when he became general manager of the Buccaneers a decade earlier. A team that's in constant flux, changing offensive and defensive coordinators frequently, will squander draft picks. A player that's drafted for one scheme likely will be a poor fit in another. The Buccaneers, from 1999–2001, had three different offensive coordinators and then brought in Gruden, an offensive-minded coach.

"When you have three coordinators in three years, then that's our fault," McKay said. "You let [Tampa Bay defensive coordinator] Monte Kiffin and his staff leave, bring in a new set of defensive coordinators, and I guarantee you that within three years you'll have nothing left. Nothing. Now do it every year for three years in a row. Good luck. Tell me what you have left.

"The thing I learned in Tampa that I say to owners all the time when they ask about how to have success in the league is that continuity matters. It's hard to adhere to sometimes, because you say, 'I could be better.' Yeah, you could be. But at what cost? You might get a little short-term gain, but you may have a long-term failure. We took a shot with Keyshawn with two ones. I don't regret the shot, because we felt like we had to force the issue. We were getting older and we had to hurry up and win, and then we continued to exchange schemes and accordingly had players falling out everywhere."

Russ Hochstein was part of the fallout. A fifth-round pick by Tampa Bay out of Nebraska in 2001, the guard spent his rookie season on the practice squad and then was cut early in Gruden's tenure. New England signed him, and the following season Hochstein started at left guard during the Patriots' win over Carolina in Super Bowl XXXVIII.

"He wasn't a pretty looking lineman," McKay says. "We threw him out immediately because we got a new staff in, and you know what? It was the right decision at the time. But that's what happens in that situation."

As for Tampa Bay's salary cap quandary, McKay viewed it as the cost of a Super Bowl championship. By acquiring veteran players such as Rice, Keyshawn Johnson, and Brad Johnson, the Bucs mortgaged part of the future.

"We never had a cap issue until we jumped into free agency, because we could feel our run coming to an end," McKay said. "You look back and say, 'Look at the cap problems.' It wasn't hard to see. Once we jumped into free agency it was going to happen, because those contracts are so much higher than the rookies. That's what you're going to get."

As for Kiffin, he remained as the Bucs defensive coordinator, though defensive pillars Warren Sapp and John Lynch had followed McKay out the door. Still, there was a strong nucleus, led by Rice, linebacker Derrick Brooks, and cornerback Ronde Barber.

The defense stifled the Falcons in Tampa, sacking Vick five times as the Bucs routed the visitors 27–0, keeping McKay and the Falcons from clinching a playoff berth.

Gruden had cut McKay's lead to 2-1.

The Renaissance Hotel in Orlando was the site of the 2004 Butkus Award, presented to the top linebacker in the nation. Like many Disney-area resorts, the Renaissance projects a faux tropical feel, with a ten-story atrium, palm trees, and a waterfall cascading into a goldfish pond. The Florida humidity gives it the feel of an upscale greenhouse.

Seven glass elevators, wrapped in red ribbon for the holidays, carry guests to and from their rooms. Early in the evening on Friday, December 10, 2004, an elevator descended to the lobby and out popped Al Groh, the University of Virginia's head football coach, clad in a black tuxedo and accompanied by Virginia linebacker Ahmad Brooks and his parents, Perry and Vergie Brooks.

Ahmad was a finalist for the Butkus Award, along with Derrick Johnson of Texas and Matt Grootegoed of Southern Cal. Groh and the Brooks family proceeded to a silent auction table laid out in front of the ballroom. There was plenty of Dick Butkus–signed memorabilia, certificates for various Orlando golf and lodging packages, items autographed by Arnold Palmer and Sandy Koufax, and a framed *Caddyshack* movie poster signed by Rodney Dangerfield, who had died two months earlier.

Groh surveyed the auction, focused as always on football. "I think the kid from Texas is going to win it," he said. "Then Ahmad will come back next year and win it."

Groh did not toss praise around lightly, but Brooks was an exception. The former NFL linebackers coach, who worked with Lawrence Taylor, already put Brooks in a special category. "I coached ten Pro Bowl linebackers," Groh said. "There's only one who had better skills."

Two weeks had passed since Virginia's regular season ended with a loss to Virginia Tech. Agents were circling around four of Groh's underclassmen: Brooks, linebacker Darryl Blackstock, tight end Heath Miller, and offensive tackle D'Brickashaw Ferguson.

Groh was asked how many of his underclassmen he thought would leave. "Why is it nobody asks a kid if he's staying? It's always, 'Are you going?' I think all of them will be back. Why wouldn't they? Look at the Mannings [quarterbacks Peyton and Eli]. They stayed four years. Why? Because they loved the college experience. The players will realize they're better off coming back."

That seemed like wishful thinking, especially with all four players getting a full-court press from agents. With so many departing seniors, including defensive end Chris Canty, guard Elton Brown, and running back Alvin Pearman, Groh could ill afford to lose underclassmen, especially after a disappointing 8-3 season. Ranked sixth in the nation in mid-October, with a 5-0 record, the Cavaliers were humiliated 36–3 at Florida State and lost two of their last three, falling to Miami and Virginia Tech.

Groh's job was secure, and his assistants were in the process of signing one of the nation's better recruiting classes. But if Groh hoped to keep the Cavaliers at the level where he wanted, contending for a national championship, he needed all of his underclassmen back.

Groh had reason to feel confident they'd all return, perhaps more reason than he had all year. Miller, who a day earlier had won the Mackey Award as the nation's best tight end, was suffering from a nagging abdominal injury. Though it had long been a foregone conclusion that the redshirt junior would leave, the condition could keep him from participating in the NFL combine and predraft workouts. Even for a talented, accomplished player, that could be enough to wait a year, though Groh knew it was a long shot.

Brooks, Groh knew, was coming back. Though he was eligible for the draft by virtue of spending a season in prep school, Brooks had played just two years of college ball. Money was not an issue, not with a father who had enjoyed a lengthy NFL career.

As for Ferguson, Groh was willing to bet the value of everything on the silent auction table he'd be back. Ferguson was the rare college athlete who had both NFL potential and aspirations of attending law school. An older brother had graduated from the University of Virginia. Ferguson was one of the more cerebral members of the Cavaliers, delivering quotes to the local media like, "I don't need anything deviating— or, excuse me—diverting my attention," as he told the *Roanoke Times and World News*.

The six-five Ferguson had finished his true freshman season two years earlier weighing just 260. But he put on thirty-five pounds and by the end of the 2004 season had become a favorite of NFL personnel people like the Redskins' Vinny Cerrato, who spoke frequently with ESPN draft guru Mel Kiper Jr. By November, Kiper was projecting Ferguson as a top-fifteen pick in the 2005 draft if he came out. *Pro Football Weekly* touted him as one of the best tackle prospects to come along in years.

Blackstock was the wild card. He was no scholar, unlike Ferguson. Unlike Miller, he still was a raw talent that could benefit from another year of college football.

There was another factor. Blackstock was the father of a son, Savion, born August 13, 2003. Blackstock shared custody with the mother, a fellow student, but they no longer were together. The linebacker estimated he had run up twenty thousand dollars in loans supporting the mother and child, but did so willingly. He wore his fatherhood proudly, with a tattoo of SAVION on his right wrist and STRONG DEDICATED DAD on his left forearm.

Groh had taken on Blackstock as a pet project from the moment the linebacker arrived in Charlottesville in 2002, following a year at prep school, where he earned a high school diploma. During the season, they would meet on Sundays at the football office to break down the previous day's game. They'd watch film, with Groh providing a candid assessment. Sometimes they'd line up head-to-head in Groh's office and walk through techniques.

Though Groh likened Brooks, who lost the Butkus Award to Johnson, to Lawrence Taylor, he assigned Taylor's number 56 to Blackstock, who had long since tired of the comparisons and asked to change numbers throughout the 2004 season.

Groh dismissed such talk, but finally relented before the Cavaliers appearance in the MPC Computers Bowl game against Fresno State on December 27 in Idaho, and had a number 1 jersey placed in Blackstock's locker.

The player remained noncommittal when asked by reporters if he would be going pro early. A week before Christmas, he said the bowl game would not be his last time wearing number 1, seemingly a telling indicator, since the NFL does not allow linebackers to don the number.

The statement was more in jest; Blackstock had not made a decision. But like the rest of the prospects for the 2005 NFL Draft, he knew that, if he did go pro, preparations for the draft would need to begin immediately.

Chapter Eight:

GOING PRO

Fred Gibson crouched down, pulled back his cue stick, and sunk the eight ball in a side pocket. It was early evening on December 30, 2004, and Gibson was shooting pool at Game Works, a video arcade and bar for adults in Tampa's popular Ybor City district.

Game Works was closed to the general public for a few hours while the football teams from the University of Georgia and University of Wisconsin had the run of the place as part of weeklong festivities for the Outback Bowl, which pitted the third-best teams from the Southeastern Conference and the Big Ten.

After devouring a dinner of pizza and barbecue—one of the few meals all week not catered by the Tampa-based Outback Steakhouse empire—most of the players fanned out to the state-of-the-art video games, all free for the evening.

Gibson and a few other teammates hung back at the pool tables near the buffet. Quarterback David Greene sat nearby playing a tabletop version of Ms. Pac Man, the type that was popular at Pizza Hut restaurants when the game came out in the early 1980s.

"I'm old school," said Greene, shattering the high score.

Gibson, known to teammates as "Freddy G.," racked up another game of eight ball. At six-four, he was a prototype NFL wide receiver, an attractive blend of size, speed, leaping ability, and good hands. On his good days, some scouts compared him to Minnesota Vikings star Randy Moss, minus the attitude and bad behavior. Unlike the perpetually scowling Moss, Gibson possessed a gregarious personality and a winning smile.

On his bad days, scouts compared him to, well, any number of athletic college stars who never cut it in the NFL. Gibson, some scouts believed, had a tendency to hear footsteps and lose concentration. Though he could leap and grab passes as well as any draft-eligible player—he also had played basketball at Georgia—he would drop easy balls caught against his body.

Gibson was an enigma in other areas. He could lock in on a game of eight ball or a pass through the air, but other times seemed unable to focus. Early in his college career a psychologist diagnosed him with attention deficit disorder, though Gibson never took medication for it. He struck everyone as a good kid, though he tended to be immature, or at least naïve. During a basketball game against Florida in 2002, he scored six points in a one-minute span, including four from the foul line. After the final free throw, he taunted Florida fans by clapping his arms in the school's "Gator chomp."

In May of 2003, he was suspended with eight teammates after they sold their 2002 SEC Championship rings. NCAA regulations prohibit athletes from reaping a financial benefit from their athletic fame. Gibson says he received four thousand dollars, but had to pay all of it back. The rings were recovered and he and his teammates were reinstated before the 2003 season.

Gibson was full of contradictions. Though he could come across as immature, he actually was one of the older members of the draft class of 2005, especially considering he never had a redshirt season. Born October 26, 1981, he grew up in a modest home next to the post office in Waycross, Georgia, the oldest of six children. Brenda Gibson gave birth to Fred when she was just thirteen and, according to Fred, never was around much. Dad was never in the picture either, and Fred was raised by his maternal grandmother, Delores Bethea, who had him repeat kindergarten.

"The first thing I want to do is buy her a big house with a lot of space for Christmas and Thanksgiving," Gibson says.

Still, it was not exactly a hardscrabble childhood. Early in high school, Gibson started competing in the privileged, quasiprofessional world of AAU basketball, playing on a Nike-sponsored team out of Atlanta that included Kwame Brown, the number-one pick in the 2001 NBA Draft. The team traveled the country and Gibson regularly went up against future pros, including Tyson Chandler, Eddy Curry, and Dajuan Wagner.

Gibson was the only member of his team not to accept a basketball scholarship, though he received offers from Auburn, Florida, and South Carolina. He verbally committed to Florida, but head coach Billy Donovan was reluctant to let him play football for the Gators. So Gibson headed to Georgia, where head coach Mark Richt had no problem with him playing both sports.

Gibson played just one full season of basketball at Georgia, averaging 4.9 points per game in a reserve role, before leaving the team early in his sophomore year to concentrate on football.

Throughout the 2004 season, Gibson was rated a strong prospect for the NFL Draft, as high as the first round by some analysts, though he was by no means a sure thing. At a lean but lanky 193 pounds, he was built more like a shooting guard than a wide receiver and still was a little raw on the football field. His biggest challenge in the months leading up to the NFL Draft would be to put on weight and shake the image of being a skinny basketball player.

Like most draft-eligible players, Gibson dealt with an endless barrage of phone calls and mailings from agents. Changing cell phone numbers helped. So did delegating much of the communication with agents to a close friend of the family.

The agents approached from all angles. Gibson says some agents—he won't say who—offered money and other incentives to get him to sign. A few sent attractive women his way.

"I don't care if agents were going to pay me a couple thousand dollars," Gibson said. "You can't buy me. If you were thinking of doing that, then I didn't trust you from the get-go. I didn't care if they had girls coming at me; they were wasting their time. I see pretty girls all the time."

At the end of 2003, Gibson's junior season, he briefly entertained the idea of going pro and met with Todd France, the young Atlanta-based agent. Pat Dye Jr. was in the running during Gibson's senior year, at least until Gibson found out that Dye and his partner, Bill Johnson, also were recruiting his fellow Georgia wide receiver Reggie Brown.

"That was a red flag right there," Gibson said. "I just stopped talking to them at that point. Do they think players don't talk to each other? How are they possibly going to sell the two of us?"

It's a common agent recruiting tactic to tell players that it's impossible for an agent to objectively represent two players for the draft at the same position, unless the difference in talent and pro potential is pronounced. The theory is that an agent, in marketing players to teams, will inevitably show favoritism. The problem with the argument is that teams are influenced little by a player's choice of representative, let alone the agent's efforts to talk up his client. Teams spend huge amounts of time and money scouting and will draft based on need and scheme. A team running a West Coast offense, for instance, will be more likely to go with a taller receiver than a shorter, faster one. Few players, even at the same position, are that similar.

France, as part of his presentation, shows a chart of prominent agents and how they represent multiple players at the same position.

"It's ridiculous to not go with someone because they have two players at the same position," France says. "I tell players not to do that, whether it be me or another guy. If you buy into that then, now you start thinking the agent affects your draft status. That's the biggest bullshit that's out there. We can affect them by the tools we give them to succeed—training before the combine, advice based on what we hear from contacts around the league—but I can't go convince Jerry Jones to pick one guy over another. He'd laugh at me."

Still, the *perception* of an agent having a conflict by representing two comparable players at the same position is enough to scare away most from even recruiting them.

"I can do it one of two ways," says SFX Sports agent Ben Dogra, who did not recruit Gibson. "I can recruit, say, the top five running backs and figure I'll get one and lose out on the other four, since the top five probably want bigger companies but don't want to go to the same agency. Or I can target the player I like best, spend more time with him, and not get caught up in the conflict game."

Two days before the Outback Bowl, Gibson had narrowed the agent field to two: Octagon and Joel Segal. Octagon, which represents athletes in many sports, has a football division based in Walnut Creek, California. Gibson had spent the most time with Demetro Stephens, a former Florida State linebacker based in Georgia, who worked for Octagon for two years recruiting athletes, becoming a certified agent just five months earlier. Stephens, as the junior agent of the firm, would defer to agent Doug Hendrickson to handle Gibson's contract negotiations.

Segal, based in Miami, is a one-man show best known for representing Atlanta Falcons quarterback Michael Vick. Gibson planned to make his decision shortly after the Outback Bowl, which kicked off the New

Year's Day marathon of bowls at 11:00 A.M. Two days later, he planned to be on a plane to Phoenix to begin training for the NFL combine.

Players cannot hire an agent—or commit to one orally—until after they've played their final college games. Some give less-than-subtle hints, though Gibson has played his cards close to the vest.

By revealing his choice of precombine training centers, the Phoenix-based Athletes' Performance, he tipped his hand, since Octagon is one of the seven agencies with a relationship with the training center. Segal, who previously sent clients there, no longer has such a deal.

"I think the two guys in the running probably have an idea," Gibson said between pool shots. "Bottom line is that an agent isn't going to get you drafted. *You* are going to get you drafted. An agent is there just to do your contract and make sure everything goes well. I don't believe all these agents calling me and telling me I'm going to go in this round. Agents are trying to sell you a dream and most kids get caught up into that."

Midway through the first half of the Outback Bowl, Greene rifled a pass to Gibson along the sidelines, hitting the wide receiver in the numbers. With Wisconsin defenders closing in, Gibson bobbled the ball. By the time he gained control, he had stumbled out of bounds.

In the press box of Tampa's Raymond James Stadium, two NFL scouts groaned.

"Fred, Fred, Fred," said one NFC scout.

The other scout, a twenty-year personnel veteran from an NFC team, shook his head as he picked at a complimentary "Bloomin' Onion."

"If he drops one ball early, he's done for the game,"

"I wouldn't even throw it to him," the first scout said. "He'll just break your heart."

The scouts scribbled their latest thoughts on Gibson. By now, they have spent five months watching film, practice, and live action of college players. Bowl games offer another glimpse of a player against top-quality competition.

For Fred Gibson, prototype wide receiver, world-class leaper, and all-around good guy, the scouting reports were not kind. *Pro Football Weekly*'s "Pro Prospects Preview," a widely read early-season scouting report, provided the consensus view:

Tall, lanky athletic playmaker with excellent size and natural athletic ability. . . . Has a thirty-eight-inch vertical jump. Lacks the polish of Randy Moss, but shows similar ability to stretch the field, sky for the ball, and make tough catches look easy. . . . Has been hampered by injuries and inconsistency throughout his career. Will show ability to adjust and make outstanding grabs but will also drop easy balls. . . . Not physical and does not like to be hit. Makes too many drops due to poor concentration and needs to take better care of the football. Will take some plays off. . . . Has first-round talent if he wants it badly enough, but has yet to show the toughness and consistency of a first-round receiver.

In the minds of many NFL scouts, Gibson was squandering his talent and needed to get his head in the game. He represented a typical dilemma for NFL executives, who spent much of their time trying to figure out if they were better off with a lesser athlete with mental toughness or a blue-chip talent who was inconsistent.

Greene represented the other side of the quandary. A calm competitor and leader who following Georgia's Outback victory would leave as the winningest quarterback in Division-1 history with forty-two victories, Greene lacked the bazooka arm and mobility of many NFL quarterbacks. *Pro Football Weekly:*

Makes good decisions. Good poise. Very good touch but lacks the arm strength to drill it on a rope, and struggles with deep accuracy. . . . Very intelligent and knows how to manage a game. Top intangibles. . . . At the very least, he can be a solid backup at the next level, but demonstrates the accuracy, leadership skills and mental toughness to develop into a starter.

If only NFL teams could put Greene's head and a few extra pounds on Gibson's body, they'd have Jerry Rice. If they could install Gibson's natural athleticism in Greene's physique, they would end up with Steve Young.

Later in the first half at the Outback Bowl, Greene overthrew wide receiver Reggie Brown, another NFL draft hopeful. Again the two veteran scouts groaned. Their teams didn't especially need quarterback help, but every player gets graded.

"David Greene? No thank you," one said, jotting down notes.

"He's no Jason Campbell," said the other, a reference to the athletic quarterback of the Auburn Tigers whose stock had soared over the course of the season.

Greene completed nineteen of thirty-eight passes on the day for 264 yards and two touchdowns. Gibson finished with four catches for 42 yards, including a touchdown grab. The Bulldogs won, 24–21, and by any measuring stick the two NFL hopefuls had a strong showing.

Up in the press box the scout section was empty. They had departed before the end of the third quarter to beat the traffic and drive to Miami to scout Southern Cal and Oklahoma, slated to play for the national championship three nights later.

The numbers Greene and Gibson compiled meant little, and their performances only confirmed the extensive scouting reports. It was New Year's Day, the start of a whirlwind tour for Greene, Gibson, and the rest of the Class of 2005.

That group included Georgia defensive end David Pollack, who recorded three sacks and was named the game's MVP, and Wisconsin defensive tackle Anttaj Hawthorne, the leading target of agent Jack "Show Me" Scharf.

Greene, Gibson, and Hawthorne soon would compete in the Senior Bowl, train for the NFL combine, work out at the late-February event, and again at a pro day held back at their respective schools in March. No longer were they off limits to NFL scouts, who would use every opportunity to interview them and pick apart their brains.

Greene and Pollack—who, by virtue of his blue-chip draft status, would skip the Senior Bowl rather than risk injury—took victory laps around Raymond James Stadium, shaking hands and posing for pictures with Georgia fans. Their college careers were over, but NFL scouts had only begun their analysis.

Pat Dye Jr. walked through a tunnel in the bowels of Raymond James Stadium. The Outback Bowl had ended a half hour earlier, and now Dye carried a satchel that contained two standard player representation agreements.

Autograph hounds lurked around the Georgia team buses. Nobody was more anxious to get a couple of Bulldog signatures than Dye was. He staked out a position in a corridor, not far from the team bus, and spotted Rick and Kay Greene, David's parents. The couple approached and invited Dye to a reception back at a condo they had rented for the week. Dye smiled. After three years of recruiting the quarterback, he finally would get a signature.

Dye excused himself and retreated into the corridor. Reggie Brown, the Georgia wide receiver, approached in a pack of teammates. Fred Gibson was among the group, but Dye knew he had no shot with Gibson, who the following day would choose Octagon's Doug Hendrickson over Joel Segal.

Brown told Dye they needed to get together back in Atlanta. Dye nodded back. He knew, from years of experience, that it did not mean anything until he got a signature. But he felt good about Brown, who had been recruited mostly by Dye's colleague Bill Johnson, who was in Jacksonville getting ready to sign Florida State lineman Ray Willis after the Gator Bowl.

Dye's euphoria did not last long. Thomas Davis, the gifted Georgia safety, who many believed would bulk up and become a Ray Lewis–style linebacker in the pros, was walking toward the bus with his mother . . . and agent Todd France. Davis, a junior, had two weeks to decide whether to renounce his final year of eligibility, a decision Dye and everyone else believed was a foregone conclusion.

Dye had spoken several times with Davis, not often, but enough to think he was in the running, at least before learning New Year's Eve that Davis was leaning toward France. Now it was official.

Dye shrugged, exhaled, and went to find Kay and Rick Greene. He would drive back to the condo with them, picking his car up later. It would be a raucous celebration, with three dozen friends and relatives toasting the end of David Greene's college career and the beginning of his professional one. Dye enjoyed the moment, but could not help but wonder how many other prominent autographs France would obtain.

France had gone to bed long before the ball dropped in Times Square in order to make a 6:00 A.M. flight from Atlanta to Tampa New Year's Day. As Davis boarded the bus, France told Davis's mother she could drive behind him back to the downtown Hyatt, where the University of Georgia was staying.

By dinnertime, France had signed his first client with legitimate first-round potential. He hung around long enough to celebrate with Davis, but soon excused himself.

There were more first-rounders waiting.

Two days after the Outback Bowl, January, 3, 2005, Jack Scharf was sitting in an apartment in Phoenix. He had gotten an early start on getting his clients situated at Athletes' Performance, the training center that would prepare them for the NFL combine in February.

The group was mostly athletes whose teams either played in early bowl games or none at all. There was Jovan Haye, a defensive end from Vanderbilt, who had left school as a junior; Washington cornerback Derrick Johnson; and Jonathan Pollard, a linebacker from Oregon State. J.R. Russell, a wide receiver from Louisville, would be arriving in Phoenix shortly. Scharf's most intriguing client was Richie Incognito, an offensive lineman kicked off the Nebraska football team after a series of disciplinary problems on and off the field. Two other clients, Arizona State cornerback Chris McKenzie and defensive end Jimmy Verdon, had opted to stay nearby on campus to train. Ronald Bartell, a cornerback from Howard University, rounded out the Momentum Sports draft class of 2005, though Jeff Griffin, Scharf's colleague, represented him.

It was a solid recruiting class for Scharf, though it lacked a surefire, blue-chip prospect. With Russell and Haye on board, Scharf had landed two of the four players from his early September recruiting trip to the East Coast. He lost out on Justin Geisinger, the Vanderbilt guard, but was still in the hunt for Anttaj Hawthorne, the defensive tackle from Wisconsin.

Scharf had jumped through hoops to recruit Hawthorne since meeting with the player's uncle, Ed Hawthorne, and family attorney Ed Walsh in Connecticut in September. Scharf was not to contact Anttaj unless instructed. Scharf, dubbed "Show Me" by the Hawthorne camp, followed along, only contacting the player on November 15 with a happy birthday e-mail, as Uncle Ed advised.

That was two days after Scharf had agreed to one of the more bizarre requests of his career. Ed Hawthorne asked him to go see his nephew play. There was to be no contact with the player, however, not even a hello after the game. So Scharf traveled from San Antonio to East Lansing, Michigan, and endured forty-degree weather to sit in the Spartan Stadium stands and watch Wisconsin lose 49–14.

Scharf might have blown the trip off, if not the recruiting of the player, were it not for his relationship with Ed Hawthorne. The two talked three times a week, not just the usual recruiting stuff, but about football, other sports, and each other's lives. As an agent, Scharf knew better than to read too much into a budding business relationship; he was a salesman, after all, but he felt this was different.

Two weeks later, when Anttaj was home for a week over Thanksgiving, the Eds summoned Scharf to New Haven, Connecticut. Finally, Scharf got to meet Anttaj and felt confident, especially since Uncle Ed prepped him for the meeting, which would include Anttaj's high school coach. So Scharf memorized Anttaj's high school accolades—first-team Reebok/ESPN All-American, number-nine prospect in the nation by *Tom Lemming's Prep Football Report*—and learned everything he could about Hamden High.

Scharf spent two hours with Anttaj Hawthorne, his girlfriend, the Eds, and the high school coach over pizza and beer. By the time Scharf departed for San Antonio, he felt good about his chances, but knew Tom Condon, the IMG agent and New Haven native, also was in the picture.

Shortly before the Outback Bowl, Ed Hawthorne told Scharf he would gather with Walsh and Anttaj at Walsh's law office to make a decision a few days after the game.

It had been quite an education for Hawthorne and Walsh. When they met Scharf in September, they knew little about agents and the predraft process. But as they interviewed eleven agents in person between July and October, always in Walsh's office late in the afternoon, it quickly grew repetitious.

"I'm a lawyer, I can negotiate a contract," Walsh said. "But I didn't know about incentives, escalator clauses, the salary cap. You learn that from the agents. Since they don't know if they're the first or the last to talk to you during the process, they go through everything. They show you their success stories. They all pull out their lists and say, 'Look what I got for this guy. He was drafted sixteenth in the first round. This guy was fifteenth and this guy seventeenth. I got my guy number-fifteen money. I jumped the guy in front of me and here's how I did that and why I'm the best.'"

The Eds marveled at the cutthroat competition. "As a lawyer, I can go at it with another guy and at the end of the day still have a degree of professional respect and friendliness," Walsh said. "With these guys, there's no union holding them together, no association, no bar or medical association. They're just a whole bunch of guys out there, half lawyers, half not, worried about who is stealing their clients. They all hate each other, and you can see why."

The Eds heard from twenty-five agents. There were others, but they were eliminated for continually calling Anttaj directly. To narrow the field, the Eds contacted the NFL Players Association, which, though not the equivalent of a bar association, serves as a governing body. Through that research, they eliminated agent David Dunn, who had eluded a two-year suspension from the NFLPA by filing for bankruptcy after a jury awarded his former boss, Leigh Steinberg, $44.6 million in damages.

(Though a federal appeals court overturned the decision on March 30, 2005, Dunn still would face discipline from the NFLPA.)

"How could somebody consider that guy, with all that was hanging over him?" Ed Hawthorne wondered.

The Eds also heard from Neil Cornrich, a Cleveland agent who represented Barry Alvarez, Anttaj Hawthorne's head coach at Wisconsin. The Eds eliminated Cornrich because he was under investigation by the NFLPA for working as an expert witness for General Motors and against the estate of deceased NFL player Derrick Thomas, who died in an automobile accident in 2000. (In January of 2005, the union would suspend Cornrich for one year for violating the NFLPA's agent regulations against conflicts of interest by accessing proprietary information on the union's Web site about the market value of NFL veterans and passing it on to General Motors. In August of 2005, an arbitrator upheld the decision and Cornrich began serving his suspension.)

The Eds narrowed the field to three: Scharf, Condon/IMG, and Joe Linta, a Connecticut-based agent. All three made their final presentations Thanksgiving week. Doug Hendrickson, the Octagon agent, managed to circumvent the rules about not dealing with Anttaj directly and staged a meeting with the lineman in Wisconsin.

IMG pulled out all the stops for its final presentation. Condon came, along with fellow agents Ken "Fuzzy" Kremer and Chris Singletary. Kremer, like Condon, was a former Kansas City Chief, having played nose tackle and defensive end from 1979 to 1984. Singletary, the only African American in the contingent, had played football at Michigan and for the last few years had helped with IMG's recruiting and precombine preparations, before becoming a licensed agent three months earlier.

The Powerpoint presentation was impressive, breaking down IMG's client list and the amount of money IMG had negotiated for its clients in recent years. Kremer, the former defensive lineman, took the lead, talking to Anttaj about the position. Singletary, who had played Big Ten football as recently as 1998, outlined the predraft preparation process. Condon pulled out a three-ring binder full of recent IMG football contracts, including the one for top pick Eli Manning the year before. Aware that Anttaj would fall a semester short of graduating at Wisconsin, Condon mentioned that they could require the team that drafts him to permit him to do his off-season conditioning work at Madison. They had inserted a similar clause in the contract of Chris Hovan, a Boston College defensive tackle selected in the first round by the Minnesota Vikings in 2000.

Six weeks later, sitting in Walsh's office, Anttaj made a decision. It would be IMG and Condon.

"Jack Scharf is a great guy," he said later. "He's really dedicated to his work, but Tom Condon has been around for a long time. He has a lot of connections in the NFL, played fifteen years [actually twelve] himself. I had to go with the experience."

Ed Hawthorne called Scharf's cell phone. Sitting in his apartment in Phoenix, Scharf knew it wasn't a good sign when he saw Hawthorne's number on caller ID. Had he been the chosen one, it would have been a conference call on speaker phone from Walsh's office.

"This is a tough call for me to make," Hawthorne said. "I couldn't make the decision for him. I didn't want him to come back to me later if it didn't work out and say, 'You told me to go with this guy.' It was his call. He's a man now, and it's time for him to stand on his own two feet."

Scharf didn't have to ask for an explanation. He didn't need to hear a listing of Condon's advantages again. Instead, they talked football and promised to share dinner and cigars at the Senior Bowl in Mobile, Alabama, at the end of the month.

"It's disappointing," Scharf said later while watching his clients train at Athletes' Performance. "I had the kid. I really thought I had him. But I can't compete with the client list of IMG. The bottom line was that Anttaj Hawthorne wanted to be a client of Peyton and Eli Manning's agent, of Marvin Harrison's agent, and you can't fight that. Plus, Tom Condon is from New Haven. So not only is it Jack Scharf up against the IMG giant, but also Tom Condon, local boy made good. At the end of the day he won, and second place means nothing. Can I accept that? Yeah, I guess I have to. I know I did everything I could and I know I made an impression. They saw the passion, the work ethic, and a guy who is going to be in this business the next twenty years."

That evening, Auburn defeated Virginia Tech, 16–13 in the Sugar Bowl in New Orleans. The Tigers capped a perfect 13-0 season and laid claim to the national championship.

For agents Todd France and Ben Dogra, there were bigger things at stake. They were hot on the trail of three of Auburn's top stars: running backs Ronnie Brown and Carnell Williams, and cornerback Carlos Rogers.

Brown and Williams somehow had done the impossible. They managed to put their egos aside and share the Auburn backfield without diminishing their stock in the eyes of NFL scouts. In fact, their willingness to set aside personal goals for the good of the team was one reason scouts referred to them as high character guys. Along with Cedric Benson of Texas, they were considered the best running back prospects for the draft.

France and Dogra were latecomers to the Brown/Williams sweepstakes. Though both backs considered going pro the previous year, neither agent recruited them. France began contacting Brown in the summer of 2004. Unlike Pat Dye Jr., who went after both players, France figured he needed to make a choice.

"I didn't know if they'd want to go with the same guy, or if they cared," France said. "But I figured they had been bunched together so long, I had to go with one or the other."

Dogra was even later to the party, not contacting Williams until October, and meeting just once with Williams and his family. That's unusual, but Dogra had gotten word that Williams, unlike many players, had not narrowed the field.

Dogra had no Auburn clients and attended no regular season games. He recruited no other Auburn players, not even Rogers, Williams's roommate. Dogra has a well deserved reputation among agents as a sniper, a tireless recruiter able to pick off top talent across the country at will.

He does not fit the agent profile, and not just because he is the only NFL player rep of Indian descent. With a squatty physique and thick black hair, Dogra is gregarious and polished without being slick. "Polite and cerebral," is how *Street & Smith's SportsBusiness Journal* described him in its annual ranking of forty sports powerbrokers under the age of forty. (Drew Rosenhaus was the only other football agent included.)

Dogra turned down an invitation to the magazine's "Forty Under 40" banquet at the Waldorf Astoria in New York before being told the date. He knew he would be working. Dogra, it seems, has not stopped working since his family moved to the United States from New Delhi when he was five. His father owned two restaurants outside Washington, D.C., and his mother cooked in them. At age ten he began working in the restaurants for no pay. He logged ten-hour days during summers in high school, and his parents expected him to take over the restaurants.

Instead, he graduated from George Mason University in Fairfax, Virginia, and enrolled in law school at St. Louis University because it was near Sports Management Group, a football agency run by Jim Steiner. After twice applying for an unpaid internship at SMG, he finally was accepted in his third and final year.

Dogra demonstrated his parents' work ethic, was hired full-time, and by 1997 was Steiner's equity partner. In 2000, they sold the company to SFX Sports, which was on a buying spree of boutique agencies that included David Falk's basketball practice and Arn Tellem's baseball/basketball business.

Steiner and Dogra continued to operate essentially independently, though with the marketing muscle and global power of SFX Sports, part of the Clear Channel Communications empire. Steiner let Dogra handle most of the recruiting and Dogra did not let up on his workload. He figures the closest thing to a vacation he's taken since law school was when his wife and two young daughters accompanied him to the Pro Bowl in Hawaii in 2002.

So when Dogra made his pitch to Carnell Williams and his family, he trumpeted not only his work habits, but also the marketing power of his company, no small concern to a player nicknamed "Cadillac." Dogra also mentioned his many successful running back clients, including Shaun Alexander, Warrick Dunn, and Deuce McAllister.

"Our company can bring a lot more to the table than a lot of other companies, and that gives us an advantage," Dogra says. "We can be a little more selective."

Dogra, like France, arrived in New Orleans fairly confident he was going to sign a client. Parents generally don't suggest agents attend otherwise.

The day after the Sugar Bowl, Dogra met with Williams and his family in New Orleans. The agent produced a standard player representation agreement, and Cadillac became the newest member of SFX Sports.

France, meanwhile, wasted no time. After the game ended around 10:00 P.M., central time, he hustled back to the New Orleans Hilton Riverside and waited for the players. Unlike the autograph hounds casing the hotel, France was in search of more valuable signatures. He signed Rogers first and then zipped down the hall to sign Brown.

As much as schools try to police agents during the season, all bets are off once the bowl game is completed. Many seniors do not even return to school with their teammates. Thomas Davis, the Georgia junior who signed with France following the Outback Bowl, drove back to Georgia with friends.

Brian Battle, the Florida State compliance director, makes it a point to sit sentry on the floor of the Seminoles' hotel during the week of the bowl game, just to make sure agents don't try to sign paperwork before the game.

When Florida State defeated Virginia Tech in the Sugar Bowl on January 4, 2000, clinching a national championship, the team hotel was a mob scene, with players, fans, and family members celebrating everywhere. Battle was returning to his room and found kicker Sebastian Janikowski standing in a stairwell with his soon-to-be agent, trying to sign some paperwork. Apparently there were too many people celebrating in Janikowski's room.

Battle rolled his eyes and pointed toward *his* room. At least they would have a level writing surface there.

Janikowski was a junior with a year of eligibility remaining. Before he signed the standard player representation agreement, Battle reminded him that there was no turning back once he signed. Janikowski nodded and signed. As an underclassman, he was required to notify Florida State within seventy-two hours of his intention to go pro. With Battle present for the signing, it was the quickest notification of all time.

Then, according to Battle, the agent pulled out a wad of hundred-dollar bills and laid out four thousand dollars for Janikowski on Battle's bed. Whether it was a loan or a signing bonus did not matter. Either way, it was legal through the NCAA, the NFL Players Association, Florida State University, and the state of Florida, now that Janikowski was a professional.

Battle shook his head and excused Janikowski and his agent. A player could accept cash, cars, and anything else from an agent, so long as it came *after* the signing, even thirty seconds later. Promising something beforehand was illegal, but the next time an athlete turns in an agent for making an illegal inducement, Battle knew, would be the first.

Back in New Orleans five years later, Todd France sat down for dinner at 11:30 P.M. with the families of Ronnie Brown and Carlos Rogers for a celebratory dinner in a private room of the hotel restaurant.

France picked up the check, which he now could do legally, and, he knew, he'd be expected to do so for as long as he represented the client. With Brown, Rogers, and Thomas Davis, he finally had not one but three legitimate, first-round draft prospects. France said he lost out on Roddy White, the wide receiver from Alabama-Birmingham, when he declined to accept a 2 percent commission if White landed in the first round.

Barring injuries to Brown, Davis, and Rogers, rival agents no longer would be able to rip France for not having represented a first-rounder.

"You work so freakin' hard, but it's so anticlimactic," France says. "You should take a step back and get excited, pat yourself on the back. But I guess not being satisfied, that makes you good. It's an asset and a liability, a liability because you should step back and smell the roses sometimes. I don't. It should surprise me or make me totally excited, it just didn't. Afterward, I went to bed. When it was done, it wasn't like I was a bachelor and there were two other guys and a girl and she made the decision and I had no clue. I kind of knew."

Rogers came to his decision shortly after Christmas, choosing France over Jeff Sperbeck, an agent for Octagon. Rogers said other agents brought up France's lack of experience representing first-round picks.

"Every agent has something bad to say about the others," Rogers says. "Todd France has no first-round picks. That didn't matter to me. Look at Priest Holmes and Takeo Spikes. They're Pro Bowl guys. A lot of guys are first-round picks, but they're not standout guys in the league. I didn't want to go with a big company. I wanted to go with the one I could get personal attention [from]. Todd was that guy."

Under NCAA rules, France and his competitors could not offer or promise players anything of value before they signed, with one notable exception. They could promise to send them to a training center to prepare for the NFL scouting combine in February. The agent could pick up the tab for the trainer and nutritionist, along with all lodging, meals, transportation, and related costs. Depending on the training center and lodging, it could run as much as twenty-five thousand dollars a player for three months.

It was a valuable inducement, though hardly an unusual one. These days, no agent recruits a player without a training plan in place. Players know they have to make a decision on an agent immediately in order to begin preparing for the late-February combine, where they'd be tested, poked, prodded, and interviewed by all thirty-two NFL teams.

Not surprisingly, the business of precombine training had mushroomed over the last decade. For Brown, Rogers, and Cadillac Williams, their college days were over, though they'd be reunited within a few days to prepare for the biggest test of their lives, the NFL combine.

Chapter Nine:

WORKOUT WARRIORS

E ach February, NFL scouts and executives gather in Indianapolis to take an in-depth look at the top three hundred or so prospects for the draft. The National Invitation Camp, known as "the combine," consists of four days of intense workouts, interviews, and drills.

How the players perform at the combine can mean the difference in several slots, or even rounds, in the April draft, which can mean a difference of hundreds of thousands, even millions of dollars in signing bonus money.

The NFL combine seems more like a track meet than a football-related event and, on one level, seems irrelevant to the game. But it provides a different perspective for NFL scouts and executives, who by the time the event is held in late February in Indianapolis have broken down long hours of tape, interviewed countless sources for background checks, and watched plenty of practice and live games.

The combine gives NFL officials a chance to get inside a player's head. Prospects travel to Indianapolis in four-day segments staggered over a week, depending on their position, and they are subjected to intense drills and interviews in which team officials try to assess their physical skills, mental acumen, and psychological makeup.

At the combine, the players undergo physicals, endure a Cybex test to measure their knee flexibility, take a fifty-question I.Q. test known as the Wonderlic, and go through a rapid-fire series of fifteen-minute interviews with teams.

They also complete seven drills, with players from certain positions excused from certain tests. Quarterbacks and wide receivers, for instance, do not have to bench-press, since their position is not one of raw power. Kickers and punters are excused from almost everything and spend their time at the combine demonstrating kicking ability.

Players have the option of doing all, none, or some of the drills. Some players, coming off injuries, do little more than interview with teams and take the Wonderlic, though there are plenty of able-bodied draft hopefuls who also sit out the combine. Some agents advise clients to skip all or portions of the event, and instead let their performances at individual school pro days in March serve as their showcase. Whether they perform at pro day and/or the combine, players go through the following:

- Forty-Yard Dash: Starting from a three-point stance, the player sprints forty yards and is clocked at increments of ten, twenty, and forty yards. Forty yards is the distance a player runs on punt coverage, Hall of Fame coach Paul Brown believed, or on long passes. The drill tests pure speed, along with power and explosion. The ten-yard split is especially important for linemen, who usually run no further on any one play.
- Bench Press: A player lies on a bench and presses 225 pounds off his chest as many times as possible. Though the drill tests nothing more specific than overall strength, scouts believe a poor performance on the bench shows a lack of dedication to the weight room and to conditioning.
- Vertical Jump: The combine uses a device called a "Vertec" to measure vertical leap. It's a pole with plastic flags that the athlete swipes with his hand at the top of the jump. The flags are spaced a half inch apart and rotate when hit. Before jumping, the player stands flat-footed and raises his arms straight up. The Vertec is lowered to the tips of his fingers. With the exception of wide receivers and defensive backs, for which there's a premium on leaping ability, the rest of the players are showing that they can generate explosion and power from their lower bodies.
- Broad Jump: In this standard drill from grade school gym class, the player leaps forward from a standing position on a line. Distance is measured from the line to where the back of his heels

land. The broad jump tests leg explosion and the player's ability to generate power by uncoiling his body. It's especially important for players working at or near the line of scrimmage: linemen, running backs, and linebackers.

- Three-Cone Drill: Three cones are placed on the field in the shape of an L, five yards apart from one another. Call them A, B, and C. The player begins in a three-point stance next to Cone A, runs to Cone B, bends down and touches the ground near the cone with his right hand. Then he runs back to Cone A, bends down and touches the ground with his right hand. He then runs back to Cone B and around the outside of it, weaves inside Cone C, then cuts around the outside of the two cones before sprinting back to Cone A. The drill tests change of direction and body control, especially valuable for running backs and the defenders chasing them.
- Short Shuttle (twenty yards): A player straddles a yard line on the field and places one hand down in a three-point stance. He can start by going to his right or left, though most players go to the right. He runs five yards to his right and touches the line with his right hand. He then runs ten yards to his left, touches the line, then runs back to the starting point. The short shuttle is a measure of change-of-direction ability and lateral control.
- Long Shuttle (sixty yards): A variation on the short shuttle, similar to basketball practice "suicide drills." Here the player runs five yards and back, then ten yards and back, then fifteen yards and back. He must bend down and touch the line at each interval for a total of six touches. This is less a test of lateral control as it is of overall conditioning and endurance.

As recently as the early 1990s, most players relied on their college strength coaches or a local weight-room guru to prepare them for the combine. The players worked out after class, continuing to progress toward their degrees, and pretty much enjoying the lives of pampered college athletes. That changed in the mid-1990s, when a few unsung players trained specifically for the seven events and dazzled scouts in Indianapolis.

The investment, paid for by agents, made sense. Not only could a player improve his draft position, thus earning more money, but by being drafted higher, he gave himself a better shot at a long-term NFL career. The more money a team invests, the more likely it is to be patient with a player. The lower a player is drafted, the more disposable he becomes.

By 2000 an entire combine preparation industry had sprung up. Agents, forever looking for an edge in recruiting, began sending athletes to these training centers. Much like high school students who spend months on expensive SAT prep courses, the players undergo grueling training regimens to give themselves an edge in the draft.

Most NFL draft hopefuls drop out of school after the fall semester to embark on a crash course on combine preparation. Some already have graduated, some never will. Others postpone their college educations for their NFL off-seasons. Some remain on campus working with their strength coaches, while others try to complete their coursework long distance.

Whatever route the player chooses, the most important class is Combine Preparation 101. The class is ungraded, the performance measured solely in numbers posted at Indianapolis and in dollars earned through the NFL Draft.

Mike Boyle figured it would be easy to beat the NFL combine. Working as a strength coach for Boston University in the mid-1980s, he became the football version of Stanley Kaplan, the popular service employed by high school kids looking to ace the SAT.

The way Boyle saw it, the combine was an open-book test, the questions provided well in advance. What if a player spent the weeks leading up to the mid-February event in Indianapolis training specifically to ace the test? Had nobody thought of this before?

"I was the first one to look at the test and realize you could cheat your ass off," Boyle said. "Then again, is it cheating if you're following the rules? I didn't think so, especially with the amount of gray area there is with these tests."

Boyle thought the vertical jump was the easiest drill to beat and it had little to do with training to jump higher. At the combine, a player's reach is measured from the ground to the tip of his fingers. The Vertec is lowered to that height to establish a benchmark. Plastic flags are attached higher up the pole, spaced a half inch apart, and rotate when hit. The player jumps straight up and hits as many plastic flags as he can.

During the initial reach, most players shrug their shoulders and reach as high as possible. Boyle taught his clients to do the opposite, depressing the shoulder blades, keeping the lat muscles of the upper back tight,

Top Left: Atlanta Falcons president Rich McKay. *(Courtesy of Jimmy Cribb, Atlanta Falcons)*

Top Right: Chris Canty, former University of Virginia defensive end. *(Courtesy of Eric Kelley, The Cavalier Daily)*

Bottom Left: University of Virginia head coach Al Groh.

Bottom Right: Brian Battle, Florida State compliance director during the 2004–2005 NFL draft season. *(Courtesy of Florida State University)*

Above: Jack Scharf, Momentum Sports football agent. *(Courtesy of Momentum Sports)*

Right: Tim Ruskell, Seahawks president and former Falcons asst. general manager (left) chats with Al Groh pregame.

Bottom: Chris Canty tore three of four ligaments in his left knee on September 25, 2004 against Syracuse. *(Courtesy of Danny Neckel,* The Cavalier Daily)*

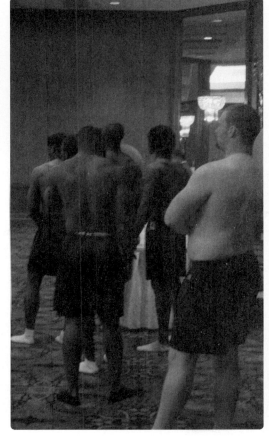

Top Right: Kimberly and Ray Willis, former Florida State offensive tackle.

Above: Fred Gibson, former University of Georgia wide receiver.

Right: Logan Mankins, former Fresno State offensive lineman, (right) and others line up for the weigh-in at the Senior Bowl.

Above: Roddy White, Cedric Houston, Cadillac Williams, and Fred Gibson stretch before Senior Bowl practice at Fairhope Municipal Stadium.

Right: Heath Miller, former University of Virginia tight end.

Below: University of Wisconsin defensive tackle Anttaj Hawthorne (middle) was guided through the agent selection process by family attorney Ed Walsh (left) and his uncle Ed Hawthorne.

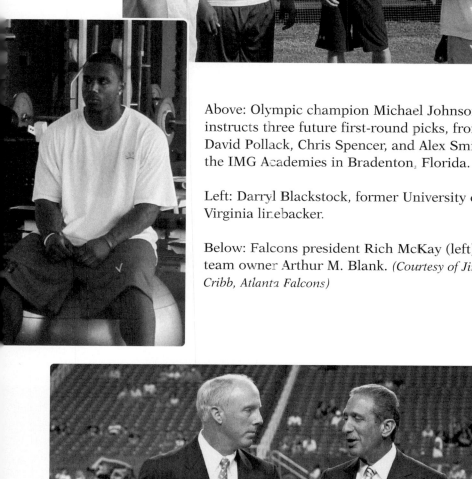

Above: Olympic champion Michael Johnson instructs three future first-round picks, from left, David Pollack, Chris Spencer, and Alex Smith at the IMG Academies in Bradenton, Florida.

Left: Darryl Blackstock, former University of Virginia linebacker.

Below: Falcons president Rich McKay (left) and team owner Arthur M. Blank. *(Courtesy of Jimmy Cribb, Atlanta Falcons)*

Above: Tim Ruskell (with helmet) is introduced as president of the Seattle Seahawks along with, from left, team owner Paul Allen, CEO Tod Leiweke, and board member Hoon Cho. *(Courtesy of the Seattle Seahawks)*

Right: David Greene speaks with the media at the NFL combine.

Below: Scouts take note of heights and weights during Florida State's pro day.

Top: Offensive tackle Ray Willis completes the forty-yard dash during FSU's pro day.

Above: Falcons assistant coach Brett Maxie (left) works out defensive backs during FSU's pro day.

Right: Seahawks president Tim Ruskell times players in the forty-yard dash at Auburn University's pro day.

Above: (From left to right) Agent Bill Johnson, Georgia wide receiver Reggie Brown, quarterback David Greene, agent Pat Dye Jr., and quarterback guru Zeke Bratkowski.

Right: Falcons owner Arthur M. Blank welcomes top draft pick Roddy White. *(Courtesy of Jimmy Cribb, Atlanta Falcons)*

Below: Todd France (top center), along with FAME staffers Jennifer Thatcher and Brushaud Callis. Bottom row: clients Carlos Rogers, Ronnie Brown, and Thomas Davis. *(Courtesy of France Athlete Management Enterprises)*

and extending the elbows. The beauty of it was that the player created the illusion of straining to reach as high as possible, even though he was establishing a base about four inches below where he would have been by elevating his shoulders. As a result, his vertical leap already was ahead of the competition.

There was nothing illegal about Boyle's advice. The only instruction players received at the combine, at least back then, was to extend their elbows. By keeping the lat muscles tight, it shortened the distance they could reach.

Like the Kaplan people, Boyle coached his clients on how to beat the tests. He looked at the twenty-yard shuttle drill and marveled at how players lost time with poor technique, not because they necessarily lacked lateral quickness and change-of-direction capabilities, which the shuttle is designed to test.

During the shuttle, performed on a football field, players must run five yards to one side and touch the line, then ten back to the other side and touch the line, and then five back to the other side. Boyle taught players to complete the drill in twelve steps, covering each of the five-yard segments in three steps and the ten-yard portion in six. Many players took extra steps so they could touch the line with the appropriate hand. That cost them precious time.

Even the bench press could be manipulated, Boyle felt. At the combine, players must bench 225 pounds as many times as possible. They're told not to bounce the weight off their chest. They also must "lock out" their arms at the end of each repetition.

In traditional strength training, coaches tell athletes to keep the bar in control. Often players are instructed to employ a slower routine (and lighter weights) to build strength and muscle. Boyle told his combine clients to toss that out the window and bench as fast as possible. Let the bar drop down quickly, as soon as the elbows begin to lock. That way, it was possible to create the illusion of the arms being fully extended.

Boyle had no reservations about his clients beating the bench press, especially since he saw the test as outdated and more a measure of endurance than strength, which was what it was supposed to test.

"A more telling measure would be if they had guys bench 275 or their body weight," Boyle said. "There are much better routes to find out how strong a guy is. If he's benching 225 for thirty or forty reps, that just means he has good endurance. But the NFL would rather do the same things they've been doing forever."

Even the forty-yard dash, the drill most associated with the NFL combine, could be tweaked in favor of the athlete, Boyle felt. At the combine, players were forced to place their feet six inches behind the starting line. At pro days, held later on the college campuses, the rule was loosely enforced and players could bring their front foot up to the line. In a three-point stance, the front foot and hand were on the line, the shoulders leaning ahead. (These days, the difference is one reason agents have clients skip the forty at the combine and run at school weeks later, though some combine coaches believe the foot placement makes little difference.)

"Some guys end up running forty-one yards," Boyle said. "The problem a lot of guys have is they try to learn from track coaches. But track coaches have no idea how to run the forty, because sprinters start with blocks. The shortest race they run is fifty-five meters, and it's run out of blocks. You want to have all of the weight forward, because you don't have a block to push off of."

Boyle found the easiest way to shave time off of a forty was during the first ten yards. A 4.5 time usually could be broken down to 1.5 seconds over the first ten yards, 1.2 for the next segment and .9 for each of the last two. Boyle trained his clients so they could run each ten-yard segment, especially the first, in just seven steps.

"You go back to the physics of running," Boyle said. "The average guy takes ten or eleven steps in the first ten yards, and that's a guy who is not putting a lot of force into the ground. Running is a function of how much force you put in the ground and how much horizontal vector that creates. When people do that correctly, they move further in fewer steps. So it's actually less movement in the same amount of time. But the illusion is that you don't see force production, how hard he's pushing against the ground, or how hard he's being propelled. You just see turnover. Some guys run like the Roadrunner; their wheels are spinning but they're not going anywhere, because they're not putting force into the ground. They look fast, but they don't run fast."

In 1986, Boyle began training Boston University athletes for the combine, a group that included wide receiver Bill Brooks and center Gary Walker. Brooks invited his young agent, Brad Blank, to stop by and check out his precombine program.

Blank packed a bag lunch and arrived at Boyle's "training center," a dark, windowless weight room of no more than three hundred square feet, nestled in the bowels of the BU athletic complex. Weights were locked in a cage. Nobody was around, so Blank ate his lunch, unimpressed with this early precombine facility.

An hour later Blank was a believer. He watched mesmerized as Boyle put Brooks and Walker through drills that, at the time, looked downright bizarre. Here was Brooks, trying to run with a harness around his waist and Boyle holding on to rubber tubing behind him to provide resistance. Boyle had the players jump up and down on platforms and boxes. When Blank asked for an explanation, Boyle pulled out a magazine called *Bigger, Faster, Stronger* and turned to an article on "plyometrics," a new regimen of jumps to make an athlete more explosive and powerful.

Boston University, which would disband its football program a decade later, was not exactly a finishing school for NFL prospects. With games against the likes of Holy Cross and New Hampshire, the team attracted few scouts. Boyle figured he could help BU's off-the-radar players make an impression at the combine and earn a spot in the twelve-round NFL Draft.

Brooks excelled at the combine, held that year at the Superdome in New Orleans, and caught the attention of the Indianapolis Colts, who selected him in the fourth round. (As a wide receiver, he caught sixty-five passes as a rookie and played eleven years in the league.) Walker, heeding Boyle's vertical-jump guidelines at the combine, leaped forty inches, an eye-popping result for a 270-pounder. The Colts took him in the fifth round.

"He got drafted solely off that jump," Blank said. "When that happened, Mike and I knew we were on to something."

Walker never played a down in the NFL, but teams kept biting on Boyle's workout wonders. In 1989, Mike Graybill arrived at the combine, having never played a down of college football. In other years, the Terriers basketball player might not have received an invite, but more than eight hundred players ended up at Indianapolis that year, the third year since the combine moved to the spacious Hoosier Dome and convention center.

Using Boyle's techniques and his own raw athleticism at the combine, Graybill sufficiently impressed the Cleveland Browns to take a flyer in the seventh round.

Graybill never advanced beyond the Browns practice squad. Stan Jones, a Hall of Fame lineman with the Chicago Bears, who as a prep star in the late 1940s was among the first football players to undergo a formal weight-training program, was the Browns strength and conditioning coach in 1989. He cornered Boyle at a convention and gave him grief for selling teams a bill of goods.

Boyle laughed. "It's not my job to watch film and figure out if they can play."

The 1989 draft also included the first of Blank's many clients from the University of Virginia to train with Boyle. Linebacker Jeff Lageman's stock rose after the 1988 season, with a strong performance at the East–West Shrine Game and the combine. Still, he was hardly a surefire first-round pick.

Until 1988, the NFL Draft was held on Tuesdays and Wednesdays at a series of hotels, most recently New York's Marriott Marquis. Now ESPN was in its second year of televising the weekend affair from a five thousand–seat theater at Madison Square Garden. The audience was dominated by rowdy Jets fans clad in full team regalia. When the Jets selected Lageman with the fourteenth overall pick, the crowd howled in protest.

Mel Kiper Jr., more combative in his early years working as ESPN's draft analyst, ripped the selection on air. "It's obvious to me the Jets don't know what the draft's all about," he said. (Lageman would go on to enjoy a solid decade-long career in New York and Jacksonville.)

Boyle remained under the radar, even after 1991, when he trained Eric Swann, who, coming out of high school two years earlier, was ruled academically ineligible to play at North Carolina State. He ended up playing for the Bay State Titans, a minor league football team in Lynn, Massachusetts. Dick Bell, the Titans coach who was serving as Swann's agent, brought the six-four, 300-pound lineman to Boyle.

The trainer put Swann through the usual routines and the lineman ran a 4.99 in private workouts for NFL scouts. Swann was so far off the radar screen that he wasn't invited to Indianapolis.

The Arizona Cardinals selected Swann with the sixth overall selection, four ahead of Herman Moore, the University of Virginia wide receiver and fellow Boyle trainee.

Even with Swann's unlikely background, his workout performance went largely unnoticed, and it might not have made a difference to Boyle's business if it had been noticed. Few reporters went to Indianapolis to cover the combine, and those that did were shut out of the Hoosier Dome, forced to loiter in the player hotel for scraps of information. The Internet was years away from widespread use. Few "draftniks" existed beyond Kiper and Joel Buchsbaum, the eclectic, well-connected Brooklyn hermit who wrote for *Pro Football Weekly*. Even ESPN had yet to expand its coverage into a full-blown, all-weekend affair.

So Boyle, working mostly with Blank's clients, continued to toil in obscurity. That changed in 1995. With interest and media coverage of the NFL Draft season mushrooming, an obscure Boston College lineman jump-started the combine training industry and caused NFL officials to rethink how they evaluated talent.

Mike Mamula was hardly a can't-miss prospect heading into the 1995 NFL Draft. As a redshirt junior for Boston College in 1994, he racked up thirteen sacks from the defensive end position and was named to the Big East's all-conference team.

Mamula, however, was a "tweener," a linebacker-sized player at defensive end. Though he possessed raw NFL potential, he lacked the fire, drive, and nonstop "motor" scouts like to see from players in charge of attacking the quarterback.

"The motivational level just wasn't there," Boyle recalled. "But once he was put in a situation where the combine mattered and he could make some money, he started concentrating and made this quantum leap."

Boyle had never encountered a player like Mamula, a talented but raw player with an upside. His precombine players typically had fallen into two categories. There were unheralded Boston University players such Brooks and Graybill, who parlayed strong combine performances into better-than-expected draft days. Then there were Blank clients with solid skills and athleticism such as Herman Moore and fellow Virginia Cavalier Chris Slade (second round, New England, 1993), who, as expected, went on to long careers in the NFL.

Boyle compared his work with the Moore-Slade group to polishing what were already fairly flawless diamonds. With Mamula, he had a hunk of rock to chisel.

Mamula had turned down his fifth year of eligibility, entering the draft as a redshirt junior. Unlike seniors, who are put through combine testing by NFL scouts in the spring before their final years of eligibility, Mamula had not produced any data. As far as combine testing, he was a clean slate.

Armed with Boyle's strategies, the twenty-one-year-old Mamula went to Indianapolis, and on February 10, 1995, dazzled more than three hundred NFL scouts and executives at the newly renamed RCA Dome, posting numbers never before seen at the combine by a man his size. Following Boyle's advice, he kept his lats and shoulder blades pulled down when he stepped up for the vertical jump, then leaped thirty-eight inches, a feat normally reserved for elite wide receivers and NBA players.

Six years after 270-pound center Gary Walker leaped forty inches, few players had caught on to Boyle's bait-and-switch reach technique. Only six of the other 230 players jumped higher than Mamula did.

Mamula bench-pressed 225 pounds twenty-six times, the same number as Tony Boselli, the six-seven, 323-pounder from Southern Cal, considered the best offensive tackle in the draft. Mamula broad-jumped ten feet, five inches—an inch further than Michael Westbrook, one of the best wide receivers in the draft. He completed the twenty-yard shuttle in 4.03 seconds, faster than every wide receiver, and even scored an impressive thirty-three on the Wonderlic, a stunning performance for someone who carried a C average at Boston College.

By the time Mamula stepped up to run the forty, he had become the focal point of the workout. Scouts sat poised, stopwatches in hand. Before a crowd that included Bill Parcells, then head coach of the New England Patriots, and longtime Miami Dolphins head coach Don Shula, Mamula took off.

He didn't appear especially fast, but covered the first ten yards in just seven steps and 1.55 seconds, better than some of the running backs. Many scouts couldn't believe their stopwatches. According to the official electronic timer, Mamula ran a 4.62, unheard of for a man his size.

When the combine ended, Mamula had soared up the draft boards. Never before had someone put up such eye-popping numbers, especially not a six-five, 252-pound lineman. By the time *Sports Illustrated* ran a two thousand, eight hundred-word Mamula feature by senior writer Peter King the week before the draft, Mamula's combine performance had become a legend.

"He's a rare athlete, the kind who comes along once every five or ten years," King quoted Ray Rhodes, then the first-year head coach of the Philadelphia Eagles. "I judge players by production, and he could be the most productive player in the draft this year."

A "real genetic freak," said Jerry Angelo, Tampa Bay's director of personnel.

Dwight Adams, the Buffalo Bills director of personnel, still was blown away by the combine showing. "If he'd done anything more, they'd have had to put a cape on his shoulders."

"As the combine showed," King wrote, "Mamula may be one of the most gifted pass rushers to enter pro football in the past decade."

Rhodes certainly thought so. On April 29, 1995, he made the first of several bad investments in Boyle's workout warriors, selecting Mamula with the seventh overall selection, five picks ahead of Warren Sapp, who fell to Tampa Bay at number twelve, after reports of drug use while at Miami, and well before future stars such as Michigan defensive back Ty Law (number twenty-three, New England) and Florida State linebacker Derrick Brooks (number twenty-eight, Tampa Bay). The Eagles even traded a pair of second-round picks to Tampa Bay in return for swapping draft slots and a third-round selection.

With their existing third-round pick, the Eagles drafted another Boyle combine star, Greg Jefferson, a defensive end out of the University of Central Florida.

Blank landed Mamula a four-year contract worth $7 million, a package worth at least $4 million more than Mamula would have received had he gone late in the first round.

That's where Blank believed he would have gone without Boyle's help. If nothing else, Blank knew Tom Coughlin was a Mamula fan and had the number eighteen pick. Coughlin, formerly Mamula's BC coach and now head coach and general manager of the Jacksonville Jaguars, drafted future five-time Pro Bowl offensive tackle Tony Boselli out of USC at number two and spent the number-eighteen pick on Tennessee running back James Stewart, who would go on to have a solid career with the Jaguars and Lions.

Others pegged Mamula before the combine as, at best, a third-round pick. When Mamula applied to the NFL's notoriously conservative advisory committee before making his decision to turn pro, he received a rating of "he will not be drafted higher than the fourth round."

Either way, Boyle, Blank's precombine training secret weapon, was exposed. Soon every player would want the equivalent of the Mamula program. Two years earlier, IMG had established the "International Performance Institute" for veteran clients in all sports, at its training complex in Bradenton, Florida. Mark Verstegen, the young IPI director, had urged IMG's head football agent, Tom Condon, to send his NFL Draft hopefuls to IPI. Condon, a former Boston College player who lost Mamula to Blank and Boyle, finally agreed for 1996.

By 1999, most top draft hopefuls were dropping out of school after their last football games and training full-time with Boyle, Verstegen, Chip Smith, Tom Shaw, and other "performance coaches" around the country. Smith and Shaw, operating out of Atlanta and New Orleans respectively, were best known as speed gurus, but soon put together versatile staffs to handle every part of combine training. Mackie Shilstone, a former 140-pound Tulane wide receiver known for his work with boxers and baseball players, launched a precombine program out of New Orleans.

Agent Pat Dye Jr., who spent nothing on precombine training in 1998, realized times had changed when Georgia offensive tackle Matt Stinchcomb asked him to foot the bill for Smith's services prior to the 1999 draft. Soon Dye and his competitors were spending fifteen thousand dollars or more per player for precombine training and expenses.

Boyle's precombine work and publicity fueled his growing Mike Boyle Strength & Conditioning business. He continued to work with the Boston University hockey program and served as the strength and conditioning coach for the NHL's Boston Bruins.

As for Mamula, he never lived up to the promise he showed in Indianapolis. A chronic underachiever on the field his first three seasons, he missed all of 1998 after tearing the ACL in his left knee during a preseason game. Remarkably, the Eagles responded by handing him a four-year, $11.5 million contract before the 1999 season. Even Blank and Mamula were stunned, figuring the player would need to try out for teams as a free agent.

Mamula saw only a fraction of that money. Andy Reid, who replaced the fired Rhodes before the 1999 season, was not nearly as enamored with the defensive end, and cut him after the 2000 season. Mamula soon retired. Sapp, named the NFL's defensive player of the year with Tampa Bay in 1999, often would cite Mamula whenever asked about the 1995 draft and the money Sapp lost falling to number twelve.

Under Reid, the Eagles would become a model for shrewd personnel decisions and building through the draft. Though Mamula still is cited throughout the league as a cautionary tale of irrational combine exuberance, Boyle does not consider it his finest work, or even Philadelphia's biggest blunder under Rhodes.

In 1997, the Eagles spent the twenty-fifth overall pick on Jon Harris, a six-eight defensive end from the University of Virginia. Rhodes compared Harris to former Cowboys star Ed "Too Tall" Jones and expected similar results.

Blank had signed Harris's teammates, linebackers James Farrior and Jamie Sharper, considering Harris a throw-in to his Virginia recruiting efforts. Like Mamula, Harris embraced Boyle's teachings and performed well at the combine, though not nearly as well as Mamula did.

Harris was projected as a fourth-round pick in most mock drafts, the fifth-best player out of his own school, behind Farrior, Sharper, and brothers Tiki and Ronde Barber. The New York Jets selected Farrior seventh overall, but Harris went ahead of everyone else, signing a five-year, $5 million deal.

Like Mamula, Harris never lived up to his combine performance. After two forgettable seasons in Philadelphia, he was dealt to Green Bay, where he was reunited with Rhodes. The Packers cut him a year later, and by 2002 Harris was out of the NFL.

In recent years, Boyle has scaled back his combine prep program, especially since Blank's pipeline of University of Virginia recruits has dried up. After Mamula, Boyle agreed to train Blank's clients exclusively, though after 1997 Blank allowed Boyle to accept other players.

"The one mistake I made was going exclusive with Brad," Boyle said. "Guys like Mark [Verstegen] and Tom [Shaw] saw what was out there and really capitalized on it."

In 2004, Boyle relocated to California to run the Carson branch of Athletes' Performance for Verstegen, but returned to Boston not long after the combine. Working with a full combine class for the first time in years, Boyle found the only thing that had changed was that now everyone knew how to beat the system. He wonders why the NFL refuses to tweak its roster of combine tests.

"NFL coaches have a Pygmalion complex," Boyle said. "They think they can take a great athlete and make him a great football player. In reality, it's easier to take a good football player and make him a great one. Jon Harris could run and jump and had a great body, but the bottom line was that he had limited football talent. It's funny. Every year you hear coaches say the combine doesn't matter and that it's more about talent and character. And teams like the Patriots actually believe that. But every year someone falls in love with a guy who blew up at the combine. As long as that keeps happening, combine preparation will be a booming business."

Nobody knew that more than Verstegen and his Athletes' Performance staff, who were training the equivalent of a college all-star team for the 2005 draft.

Chapter Ten:

FIGHTING FOR ALVIN PEARMAN

red Gibson parked his rented white Chrysler 300 in front of the Athletes' Performance training facility. It was Thursday, January 6, 2005, and Gibson was officially a professional. Shortly after the Outback Bowl he had signed with Doug Hendrickson, an agent with Octagon, and after a few days back in Georgia to gather his belongings, he boarded a plane to Phoenix.

Now, as he entered API—the pros used the full acronym for "Athletes' Performance Institute," even though the company had dropped the "Institute" from its name—he knew he was in a different world. The University of Georgia enjoyed one of college football's finest training facilities, and Gibson had viewed the DVD of Athletes' Performance that Hendrickson's colleague, Demetro Stephens, had provided. Still, the wide receiver was struck by the thirty-three thousand-square-foot facility, with its cavernous workout room, cafe, massage rooms, athlete lounge, and swimming pool.

Boxes of clothing and shoes were stacked up next to the front desk, having arrived via UPS or overnight delivery. The names were scrolled on the sides in black marker, and as Gibson surveyed the mail it looked like a college all-star-game roster. There were a lot of packages for Carnell "Cadillac" Williams, the Auburn running back.

Ronnie Brown, Williams's backfield mate, and teammate Carlos

Rogers, a cornerback, also were expected soon, having signed with agent Todd France after Auburn's Sugar Bowl win over Virginia Tech three nights earlier.

Two of the stars of the Oklahoma football team, wide receiver Mark Clayton and offensive tackle Jamaal Brown, were expected shortly, having just signed with Ben Dogra. (Southern Cal had routed the Sooners 55–19 in the Orange Bowl two nights before, to claim a share of the national title.) Dogra, who also had signed Williams, was in the hunt for Brodney Pool, a junior safety at Oklahoma expected to turn pro.

There was mail for Erasmus James, the defensive end from Wisconsin who, like Gibson, had played in the Outback Bowl. Marcus Johnson, an offensive lineman from Ole Miss, already was in the house, as was Andrew Walter, who was training in his backyard after quarterbacking Arizona State.

There were rumors flying about which other players might arrive at Athletes' Performance, all contingent on which agents they selected.

"You take the guys that are going to be training here, put us all on one team, and we'll win a Super Bowl in three years," Gibson said.

Gibson walked out to the pool and glanced at nearby Sun Devil Stadium, nestled between mountain buttes. Overhead was the steady cackling of traffic from Sky Harbor Airport. Near the pool there was a fifty-yard Astro Turf practice field and the Arizona State University softball stadium. The perimeter of the area was lined with pink oleanders and towering fan palms.

Octagon was paying ten thousand dollars to API to train Gibson for the combine in late February and for his pro day at Georgia in late March. The fee did not include housing for the three-month period—a pricey proposition in Phoenix during the winter—the Chrysler 300 rental, and meals not provided by the training center. Throw in nearly four months of spending money for the budding professional athlete and the bill easily could approach twenty-five thousand dollars.

Given that NFL agents worked on a commission of 3 percent—some worked for less—a player had to generate almost a million dollars in signing bonus and first-year salary to cover the costs of predraft training alone. Anyone drafted below the second round usually does not cover.

"With a lot of guys, you're working toward a long-term relationship," said agent Jack Scharf, who had six players training at Athletes' Performance for the 2005 draft. "If I do everything I can for my client and honor all promises, then they'll honor me for the second contract by allowing me to negotiate. By then I'll have no overhead."

Scharf used Nate Burleson as an example. Relatively unheralded coming out of the University of Nevada-Reno in 2003, Burleson trained at Athletes' Performance and was drafted by the Minnesota Vikings in the third round. He received a three-year contract with a signing bonus of $529,000, generating a 3 percent commission of $15,870 for Scharf. Burleson's salaries in 2003 ($225,000), 2004 ($305,000), and 2005 ($380,000) accounted for another $27,300 in commissions.

Deducting precombine expenses and the money Scharf spent recruiting, he figured he might make fifteen thousand dollars over the first three years of Burleson's contract. The wide receiver had emerged as a solid number two receiver, playing alongside Randy Moss, and was setting himself up for a huge payday after his third year in the league.

Yet that was no guarantee for Scharf, who like the rest of his thirteen hundred colleagues had to deal with the widespread practice of client stealing. After all, it was more cost-effective to grab a three-year veteran on the verge of free agency than pay the freight for the first three years. There also was the potential for career-ending injury; the average NFL career lasted just three and a half seasons.

Athletes' Performance was the most expensive of the combine training centers, and each year its draft class became more distinguished. In 2002, API trained one player that was drafted in the first round (offensive lineman Levi Jones, Cincinnati), three in 2003, and five in 2004, including top-ten picks Roy Williams of the Detroit Lions and DeAngelo Hall of the Atlanta Falcons.

Players quickly discovered how little precombine training resembled the work they did in the weight room back at school. There were some similarities; they were training to bench-press at the combine, after all. But they were just as likely to harness a sled weighted with plates across a field, balance on a giant rubber Physioball, or undergo a series of moving stretches that seemed more like yoga routines.

Unlike college strength coaches, trainers at Athletes' Performance were not just trying to bulk players up, though they could do that, too, for players that needed it. Instead, they concentrated on the player's hips, shoulders, and midsection, tapping into the power of the "core" region to generate ferocious power and explosion. An emphasis was placed on flexibility and lateral movement. Scouts were forever looking at hips to see how well a player, especially an offensive lineman or cornerback, could move.

Mark Verstegen, the founder and president of API, could not believe how his training center had become a negotiating tool in the cutthroat world of draft recruiting. It's not that he did not believe his product was the best. By limiting his combine training class to thirty players and offering a complete array of services—physical training, meals, nutritional supplementation, massage, physical therapy—all under one roof, he believed his ten thousand dollar-per-player cost was fair, especially given his staff's reputation for improving strength, speed, and overall performance at the combine.

What surprised him was how prominent a role the combine training industry played when athletes made their decision on agents. After all, the work of his twenty-person staff over the course of two or three months was a minor part of what could be a career-long relationship with an agent.

The thirty-five-year-old Verstegen, who wears his hair in a flattop and looks like a younger, more muscular version of the actor Ed Harris, briefly played football at Washington State until an arm injury ended his career. Not long after he opened Athletes' Performance in mid-2001, he sent out feelers to agents about combine training for 2002. Having run precombine programs as the director of IMG's International Performance Institute in Bradenton, Florida, for the 1996–1999 drafts, he had a strong resume.

In 1998, San Diego State's Kyle Turley was considered, at most, the fifth-best offensive tackle prior to the combine. Working with Verstegen, he gained fourteen pounds, lowered his time in the forty-yard dash, and dazzled scouts in Indianapolis. The New Orleans Saints picked him with the seventh overall pick. The following year, Notre Dame offensive tackle Luke Petitgout was projected as a mid-to-late-second-round pick. He packed on twenty pounds before the combine, impressed the scouts with his strength and speed, and was taken by the Giants with the nineteenth selection in the first round.

Between the success of the combine program and other clients such as baseball's Nomar Garciaparra, whom the trainer had met in 1993 while working at Georgia Tech, Verstegen began to feel the entrepreneurial bug. Not long after the 1999 draft, Verstegen, then thirty, and his wife, Amy, moved to Arizona armed with little more than a sponsorship agreement from Adidas and a dream of building an independent training center for elite athletes.

Verstegen, who as recently as 1994 was earning $22,400 a year at Georgia Tech, financed the facility to retain 100 percent ownership. The Adidas agreement helped. So did other sponsors and loans. While the building went up, Verstegen worked with a small group of athletes out of an old ASU building scheduled for demolition.

There was an old-school, Rocky Balboa charm to the temporary housing. Garciaparra, the no-nonsense shortstop in the midst of back-to-back American League batting titles, embraced the place, as did fellow Boston Red Sox teammate Lou Merloni.

Verstegen, with just his wife and two other coaches, attracted a modest combine class for 2000. The San Francisco 49ers selected Giovanni Carmazzi, a quarterback from Hofstra, in the third round. Tyrone Carter, a defensive back from the University of Minnesota, went to the hometown Vikings in the fourth.

The new building was not quite finished in time for the 2001 draft, though Verstegen trained Leonard Davis, a massive offensive tackle from the University of Texas, who was drafted by the Arizona Cardinals second overall after the Atlanta Falcons selected Michael Vick.

Amy Verstegen, serving as the original director of sales and marketing while wearing nine other hats, contacted agents in the fall of 2001 to "presell" slots for the inaugural Athletes' Performance draft class of 2002. In return for their commitment, the agents could use API's new facility as a recruiting tool.

It wasn't quite an exclusive arrangement for either party. API did not want ten clients from one agent, nor did agents want to foot the bill for high-end training for players with limited draft potential. API also wanted to leave a few slots open, in case an agent representing a top-ten pick came calling.

By the fall of 2004 API could be more selective. Most of the original agencies were still on board, though occasionally there was a replacement. Todd France and Octagon earned slots for the 2005 draft after Joel Segal and Eugene Parker opted to take their business elsewhere. Agents Pat Dye Jr., Drew Rosenhaus, and others called later asking for availability, but there was no more room.

"We can't continue to leave slots open," said Percy Knox, a former All-American track athlete at the University of Arizona who joined API in 2002 as director of athlete management. "We don't want agents to be using API as an incentive unless they're already in the fold. It's only fair to the guys that have been with us all this time."

Dye lost out on three Auburn clients—Williams, Brown, and Rogers—that opted to go with agents with slots available at API.

"I don't want to use that as an excuse, but I don't have any doubt that it made a difference," Dye said. "I know it did with Carnell. I was told his father said point-blank, 'You can't go with Pat. He can't get you into API.' I think it definitely made a difference with Ronnie [Brown] and Carlos

[Rogers], to the extent that they were locked in to going to Arizona, and knowing that I couldn't get them in there because the slots were filled."

Williams, who signed with Ben Dogra of SFX Sports, said that wasn't the case. "I wanted to come to API, and it influenced my decision a little bit, sure. I had heard different players talk about it and I wanted to be away from home, where nobody could bother me and I could focus on football and getting better. But that's not why I didn't choose Pat Dye. I just thought Ben could do a better job for me."

Dogra, who like France enjoyed a banner recruiting season for the 2005 draft, said the facility does not make that much difference in recruiting. In 2004, he represented first-round picks Lee Evans, a wide receiver from Wisconsin, and Vernon Carey, a guard from Miami. Neither trained at API, nor did clients such as 2005 draft prospect Jonathan Clinkscale, a guard from Wisconsin, or Bryant McKinnie, a first-round offensive tackle out of Miami in 2002.

Players from Miami and Wisconsin fall into their own categories, since those players almost always stay at school to train. Anttaj Hawthorne, the Badgers defensive tackle Jack Scharf lost to Tom Condon and IMG, was training in Madison and would not have come to API anyway. Erasmus James, Hawthorne's Wisconsin teammate who was at API, was the exception.

"This is just one piece of the puzzle," Dogra said. "I don't get players because of this facility. I would if I was the only one using it. I'm competing with a lot of these other agents that have slots here, so it neutralizes the training advantage."

"It might make a difference for some," said France, who also had clients training with Chip Smith's Competitive Edge and Velocity Sports, both in Atlanta. "But I'd like to think a kid isn't making decisions based on a six- or eight-week training program."

Dogra has a point. Sometimes even having slots at API was no guarantee for an agent. In January of 2004, cornerback DeAngelo Hall enrolled at the training center as a client of Ethan Lock. Hall fired Lock a few weeks later and signed with Joel Segal, who represented Vick, who, like Hall, played at Virginia Tech. At that point Lock asked API to kick Hall out.

Knox, as director of athlete management, let Hall stay, but made it clear to Segal that it could not happen again. Knox also crafted a new policy.

"I tell kids, 'You're here because your agent brought you here,'" Knox says. "If you go with someone outside the group, you can't train with

API. If it's within the group, it's okay only if the agents can work something out—or at least agree to disagree. If the original agent doesn't want the kid here, then the kid can't be here. Because, who am I here to protect—the athlete or the agent? That's a no-brainer. I get new kids every year. I'll work with the agents forever."

Hall was drafted eighth overall by the Atlanta Falcons. Defensive end Will Smith, a Segal client from Ohio State that trained at API, went to New Orleans at number eighteen. Segal's slots at API were grabbed by France for 2005.

Now, a week into combine training season, the Athletes' Performance staff had little time to spend wondering what impact they had on a player's selection of representation. It was all they could do to keep up with which players were coming. Though the thirty slots in the 2005 combine class had been sold for months, they still were being filled. Some players still had not selected agents—or, in the case of underclassmen, even decided if they were going pro.

At one point it looked like Braylon Edwards, the talented wide receiver from Michigan, was coming to API. But he signed with an agent (Lamont Smith), not affiliated with the training center. Dogra thought he had Miami cornerback Antrel Rolle, who, unlike most Hurricanes, would have come to API had he not chosen agent David Dunn. (Rolle, ironically, would fire Dunn and hire Dogra in mid-February, too late to start training at API.) At least two agents with slots at API had talked to D'Brickashaw Ferguson, the talented junior tackle from the University of Virginia who opted to remain in school.

Whoever ended up at API would be affiliated with one of seven agencies: SFX Sports (Dogra); Octagon (Hendrickson and partners Mike Sullivan, Ken Landphere, and Jeff Sperbeck); Momentum Sports (Scharf, Jeff Griffin); FAME (France); Professional Sports Marketing (Rich Moran); Lock, Metz & Malinovic (Lock); and Priority Sports (Ken Zukerman, Rick Smith, Mark Bartelstein).

By the morning of Friday, January 7, the API roster was still in flux. Lock, whose agency is based in Tempe, felt so confident in his chances of signing Miami's Frank Gore that API prepared a training binder emblazoned with the running back's name. The junior was expected to go pro and, for all the API staff knew, would be walking in at any time.

Back in South Florida, Gore placed a call to agent David Levine around three o'clock. "I want to get this done," Gore said. "Declare for the draft, sign with you. We can do it for the six o'clock news."

Levine's hard work had paid off. Though he represented only a handful of NFL veterans, he was no newcomer to the business, having been an agent since 1989. His clients had included former Hurricanes and NFL players Alonzo Highsmith, Winston Moss, and Darryl Williams. All three called Gore on Levine's behalf.

Levine contacted South Florida media outlets, setting up a press conference at the Coconut Grove home of Gore's mother, who had endured a history of kidney ailments and underwent dialysis three times a week. Gore himself had torn anterior cruciate ligaments (ACLs) in both knees during his college career, missing most of the 2002 and 2003 seasons. It was time to take advantage of his health and earning power.

By the time the media arrived at the Gore residence, a modest five hundred-square-foot bungalow the running back shared with his mother and two siblings, Lock had turned his attention to another running back from the Atlantic Coast Conference, one that was barely on the radar screen when the 2004 season started. But now Lock and Dunn were in a fierce battle to land Virginia running back Alvin Pearman.

Pearman wanted to train at Athletes' Performance.

Two days earlier, Ethan Lock had brought Pearman to API and Pearman came away impressed. It helped that he roomed for a night with Chris Canty, his former University of Virginia teammate who had signed with Lock and now was training at API.

David Dunn also wanted to represent Pearman, and unlike Lock did not have slots available to offer at the training center. Dunn also was in the hunt for Heath Miller, Pearman's former roommate at Virginia, who was considered the best tight end prospect in the nation. Miller, a redshirt junior, had yet to declare for the draft, and was having some second thoughts of turning pro after undergoing surgery for athletic pubalgia, a tear of the abdominal wall. Though not serious, it likely would keep him from working out at the combine in Indianapolis and during the school's pro day on March 23.

Miller had won the Mackey Award in December as the nation's top tight end, but wondered if he'd fall in the draft by not working out in the coming months. A training center with strong rehabilitation facilities was a must.

Late in the afternoon on Friday, January 7, one of Dunn's staff members called Athletes' Performance. He was told the facility could not make an exception and offer Dunn training slots in Arizona. But there was an alternative. API had a second facility on the campus of the Home

Depot Center, a 125-acre complex in Carson, California, near Los Angeles, that featured Olympic-caliber training facilities and playing fields for many sports, including soccer, track and field, and basketball.

The complex was owned by the Anschutz Entertainment Group, and API planned to build a training center there equivalent to its Arizona headquarters. Since 2003, API had operated out of a temporary facility that featured state-of-the-art equipment, a full team of performance specialists, and access to the entire Home Depot Center. But there was no way agents could convince potential clients that it was equivalent to the Arizona complex. Dunn had hired a trainer to work with his clients in California. Unable to get into the API facility in Arizona, he stuck with his existing program.

Pearman personified how a player's draft stock could soar in just a few months. As recently as mid-October, the thought of the five-nine Pearman attracting the type of agents that would pay twenty-five thousand to send him to Arizona and Athletes' Performance for combine preparation would have seemed preposterous. He began the year as the backup to Wali Lundy at running back, and though he was a solid college performer, contributing on special teams and in a reserve role, he projected as an undrafted free agent, lacking the speed, strength, and size needed at the next level.

That changed after Lundy and the rest of the Cavaliers were held to just twenty yards in an embarrassing loss at Florida State at midseason. Head coach Al Groh benched Lundy, and over the next four games Pearman rushed for 582 yards, continuing his stellar work at punt returner and even emerging as the Cavaliers' second-leading receiver.

Soon scouts were jumping on the Pearman bandwagon, comparing him to Brian Mitchell, the versatile back who played in the NFL for fifteen years, mostly for Washington, and ranked as the all-time career leader in total yardage. Groh began touting Pearman for ACC Player of the Year. Pearman didn't do anything exceptionally well, but he was the type of versatile performer NFL coaches loved to have in their running back rotation. A true scholar-athlete, Pearman majored in sports medicine and had graduated in just seven semesters.

By the end of November, *Sports Illustrated* was calling Pearman the most underrated player in the ACC. Scouts also began calling more frequently. Pearman, Miller, and their roommates did not have an apartment phone, relying on cell phones, and Pearman marveled at how Miller's rang incessantly. Now his was ringing nearly as often. Miller would spot an agent on his caller ID, ignore him, and moments later Pearman's phone would ring. Sometimes, after Pearman refused to pick up, the agent would call Miller again.

"We'd be watching TV and it was as if we had a land line, waiting for the other guy to get up and deal with it," Pearman said. "We just learned to ignore it."

Dunn had recruited both heavily, meeting with them together in Charlottesville late in the season. It helped that both remained close with Dunn's client Matt Schaub, the former Virginia quarterback drafted by the Atlanta Falcons in the third round in 2004.

Agents wondered how Dunn could recruit at all, given that he still was waiting for the result of his appeal of a jury award to Leigh Steinberg of $44.6 million in damages against him. (In fact, a federal appeals court overturned the decision on March 30, 2005, though Dunn still faced discipline from the NFLPA.)

With that hanging over Dunn, at least in January, not having slots at Athletes' Performance seemed like a minor issue. Pearman signed with Dunn and his agency, Athletes First.

"A lot of agents were using [the judgment] against him, and it was definitely an issue," Pearman said. "It was an issue that had to be discussed on a personal level, and it wound up that it wasn't going to affect my relationship with him, and vice versa, in the near future."

Miller, a soft-spoken young man from tiny Swords Creek, Virginia, disliked the agent selection process. He wasn't too fond of anything that drew attention and was happy to let his parents handle the process. They had narrowed the field to Dunn and IMG's Tom Condon and Ken "Fuzzy" Kremer.

Miller met with the IMG agents a few days after the Cavaliers' season ended with a 37–34 loss to Fresno State in the MPC Computers Bowl. Miller, like many of his teammates, figured they'd look back years later and wonder how a team with so much future NFL talent could finish the season 8-4. The tight end signed with IMG over Dunn, figuring Condon had the most high-profile contract experience, to say nothing of a training center that Verstegen himself had created before moving to Arizona.

"I felt like I couldn't go wrong with either choice," Miller said. "The entire process just wasn't very fun for me."

For Ethan Lock, losing Pearman and Gore stung, but he and his partners still had a solid draft class that included Erasmus James, Michigan lineman David Baas, Nebraska linebacker Barrett Ruud, and Charlie

Frye, a quarterback from Akron. Lock also had a Virginia Cavalier in Chris Canty, who, like Pearman, was emerging as one of the more unlikely stories of the 2005 NFL Draft.

Canty stood neck-deep in a small pool of fifty-five-degree water. It was late afternoon on Friday, January 7, and Canty, wearing swim trunks, was alternating between the "cold plunge" and an adjacent hot tub alongside the Athletes' Performance swimming pool. Most of his fellow members of the API precombine class had departed for the day, or at least were playing video games and Ping-Pong inside in the lounge. Canty had been at API just five days, but already he had established a pattern of being the first to arrive and the last to leave.

The idea behind the contrasts in pool temperature was to force the blood to move fast, from the organs to the skin and back again. That's a good thing, even for people who do not exercise. When done after a workout, the contrasts stimulate muscle recovery without much effort—though, as Canty had learned, sitting in a pool of ice water for up to two minutes takes some effort.

The cold plunge, in particular, decreases the natural inflammation in the muscles created by working out. Lifting weights creates tiny tears in the muscle fibers, which the body repairs in between workouts, leaving the athlete bigger and stronger. The contrasts jump-start the process.

Trainers at Athletes' Performance sometimes struggled with getting clients to put their full effort into the cold plunge. Some stood waist deep or jumped out before the interval was over. Nobody had to encourage Canty, who, despite one of the more grueling and painful precombine regimens, had embraced every element of the program.

Nearly four months had passed since Canty shredded three of the four ligaments in his left knee in the University of Virginia's game against Syracuse. While the rest of API's draft hopefuls dove right into training for the forty-yard dash, bench press, vertical jump, and the other tests they would face at the combine in Indianapolis in six weeks, Canty was on his own program.

Under the direction of Darcy Norman, an API physical therapist, Canty spent a lot of time doing plyometrics, a series of jumps and squats. Canty had undergone months of rehabilitation, first in Birmingham, Alabama, and then at home in Charlotte, North Carolina, but he still was in the early stages of preparing for the NFL combine. Much of the work at API took place in the swimming pool, where the water offered resistance but not a heavy impact on the knee.

"When you've had surgery, tissue atrophies," Norman said. "You spend your life developing tissue tolerance to activities, and after an injury you have to relearn a lifetime of tolerance, so that you're as good as you were. Guys have a tendency to come back too early and try and be a hero. If they don't have things taken care of, they're going to reinjure themselves, or another part of the body, trying to overcompensate.

"So much of rehab is psychological. You're going to react based on your experiences. If you've never had injuries, you're going to be sensitive to any pain or discomfort. Chris has had a laundry list of stuff, so he's able to push through the pain and move on. That's what makes him special. He's here every day doing whatever we tell him to do."

Canty already could train with the rest of the group on the bench press. The plan was for him to run in three weeks. It was too ambitious to think that he could run at the NFL combine, but the University of Virginia's pro day on March 23 was a possibility.

It also was imperative that Canty ace the Cybex test at the combine. In Indianapolis, every athlete is strapped into a chair and told to extend and pull back the leg. During the test, the machine is set at various speeds and it tests the player's ability to produce force in both directions. For players with healthy knees, the test is a routine procedure. But for those like Canty with knee issues, the Cybex is given considerable weight.

Canty already was well ahead of Willis McGahee, who tore three of the four ligaments in his left knee two years earlier in the Fiesta Bowl at Sun Devil Stadium, which Canty could see while seated in the cold plunge. McGahee, then a running back for the University of Miami, declared early for the NFL draft anyway, and still was selected in the first round by the Buffalo Bills. He was unable to play in his rookie season, 2003, but rushed for 1,128 yards in 2004.

"You've got to work very hard to make it back," Canty said. "The toughest part is not being able to do the things I was capable of doing. I've been blessed that so far the knee hasn't hiccupped even a little bit. It's not painful now."

When Canty considered applying for the NFL Draft in 2004, the league's advisory committee projected him as a "not higher than second-round" pick, which Canty interpreted as strong second-round potential.

"I'd like to get back to that, if not improve," Canty said. "And I think that's possible, once teams see how my body looks, the athleticism, and how hard I've worked to get back. All I can say is look at the tape. The tape doesn't lie. I'm a good player. I have confidence in my ability. If I'm not a first-round or second-round guy, as long as I get an opportunity to get into the league and prove myself, I know I'll be there for a long time."

Darryl Blackstock kept people guessing until the end about whether or not he'd go pro. On January 13, just days before the deadline to declare for the NFL Draft, the linebacker opted to leave the University of Virginia after his junior season.

Unlike Canty, Pearman, or Miller, Blackstock did not wear the student athlete title well, struggling at Virginia. His son, Savion, now was seventeen months old and he had to pay off the twenty thousand dollars in debt he accrued supporting the child and his mother by the end of the 2004 football season.

Not long after the Cavaliers season ended, Blackstock applied to the NFL's advisory committee for a rating on where he might go in the draft. Virginia head coach Al Groh didn't discourage underclassmen from doing this, but he didn't exactly encourage it either. He preferred to have players rely on him and his vast network of NFL sources. Given Groh's well-traveled NFL past, it was hard to argue with him.

Heath Miller did not bother with the NFL committee. Groh told him he was ready to be successful at the NFL level and that he would be one of the top tight ends taken, either in the first or second round. "That was good enough for me," Miller said.

Blackstock, however, wondered if Groh could provide an objective opinion on his status. After all, nobody believed that Miller, who was polished as a player and on track to graduate in May, should return for a fifth season. Blackstock, for all his skill as a pass rusher, still was a raw talent who could benefit from a fourth season in college.

Like many players, Blackstock interpreted his rating from the NFL advisory committee of "will not be drafted higher than the second round" to mean "strong second-round possibility." After all, the next-highest rating was "he will be drafted in round one." But the next-lowest rating was "he will not be drafted higher than the fourth round."

What Blackstock and others interpreted as strong second-round status really was a wide range, from early in the second round to late in the third round. During the 2004 draft, that was a difference in signing bonus of $400,000 and $2.3 million.

Blackstock called Groh and told him about his second-round rating.

"That's not what I'm hearing," said Groh, whose sources told him mid- to late-third round.

Until the letter, Blackstock still was on the bubble. He wanted to go pro, but didn't want to leave if it meant getting drafted low. He gave little credence to the predraft Internet hype about how he was the perfect outside linebacker for the NFL's increasingly popular 3–4 defenses, relentless in pursuit of quarterbacks, and equally capable of covering receivers out of the backfield. He thought little about the knee injuries to Canty and Anthony Poindexter, the Virginia running backs coach who, like Canty, gave up a chance to go pro after his junior year.

Given the NFL advisory committee's history of conservative ratings—nobody wants a player to be overly optimistic—Blackstock expected a third-round projection, which is what it was. But by misinterpreting the NFL's rating as strong second-round status, the decision was easy for a player with one foot already out the door.

"Any athlete that is good will tell you, 'You love football, man. That's what you want to do while you can do it,'" Blackstock said. "Can't nobody sit there and lie and tell you that school is first, football is next. That's a lie. That's just a big lie. Any athlete that really loves football—basketball, baseball, golf, hockey—you think about it all day long. You think about it all day. When you walk, you try and walk so you can plant at the corner. I'll be walking by people in the mall and they're thinking I'm crazy. It's something that comes with it. I love football. I'm not a school guy, anyone can tell you that. I have a problem doing things I don't like to do. It's not like a lot of stuff. It's not like I can only do this and hate everything else. Out of ten things, I won't like two. It's a matter of doing things you don't want to do."

Groh issued a statement that, while diplomatic, clearly lacked the hearty endorsement that he had given Miller days earlier.

"Darryl played a significant role in a lot of games that we have won," Groh said. "He is a talented player and we wish great success for him with this next challenge."

On Miller: "There is a significant difference between a player's being ready to be drafted and that of a player being ready to play well in the NFL," Groh said. "Heath clearly fits into both categories. We fully support his decision to start his NFL career."

Blackstock had spoken frequently with Chris Slade, the former Virginia defensive end whose school-record forty career sacks Blackstock had a chance of breaking by returning. Slade, who had played for the New England Patriots while Groh was linebackers coach under Parcells, stressed the benefits of an extra year of seasoning without lobbying for a return. "Ultimately, it's your decision," he said.

Slade made a strong pitch for his former agent, Brad Blank, who was actively recruiting Blackstock and trying to reestablish the Cavalier client pipeline he enjoyed for most of the 1990s. Blackstock considered Blank seriously before signing with SFX Sports agent Ben Dogra.

For Groh, who liked to think he had a big influence on his players' predraft decision making, Blackstock's agent selection meant not one of Virginia's five major draft hopefuls selected a representative from the group Groh invited to Charlottesville the previous summer.

That group included Blank and Anthony Agnone, who represented Atlanta Falcons defensive end and Virginia alumnus Patrick Kerney. There was Ralph Cindrich, whose forty clients included former Virginia linebacker James Farrior. There was Jimmy Sexton, agent for numerous NFL players and coaches, including Bill Parcells. There was Joe Linta, a Connecticut-based representative; and Alan Herman, who represented veteran wide receiver Ricky Proehl, who had played for Groh at Wake Forest.

In addition to Miller (IMG), Canty (Ethan Lock), Alvin Pearman (David Dunn), and Blackstock (SFX), guard Elton Brown chose Joel Segal. (Agnone signed defensive tackle Andrew Hoffman, considered a possible late-round selection.)

Groh said that in return for the access of agent day he asks agents "not to harass the players during the season, without asking them to put themselves at a competitive disadvantage."

"We play by Al's rules, not bothering players when Al doesn't want them bothered," Blank said. "I don't know. It seems if you play by the rules, you get shut out."

Not long after signing with Dogra, Blackstock flew to Phoenix, where he became one of the last members of the Athletes' Performance combine-training class of 2005 to arrive. He would have an opportunity to catch up quickly, since, as a junior, he was ineligible to play in postseason all-star games.

So, while Blackstock hung back at Athletes' Performance the last week of January with fellow juniors such as Brodney Pool and Richie Incognito, fifteen players left to showcase their talents for NFL scouts at the most prestigious of the postseason bowl games.

The Senior Bowl combined the medical exams and interviews of the combine with a week of practice and a game. It was a sort of Twilight Zone experience between college and pro football, and the first important signpost to the NFL Draft.

Chapter Eleven:

THE ALL-STAR
MEAT MARKET

Fred Gibson stepped off an escalator into the second-floor lobby of the Riverview Plaza Hotel in Mobile, Alabama, and suddenly felt like a rock star. Everywhere he turned someone wanted a piece of him. There were kids and adults looking for his signature on footballs, NFL scouts looking for a quick interview, and television crews hoping for a few sound bytes.

Having played four years of college football at the University of Georgia, Gibson was used to the attention. But this was something else entirely.

It was Sunday, January 23, 2005, the opening day of Senior Bowl week, the undercard to the NFL combine that would take place a month later in Indianapolis. One hundred and three of the top seniors were on hand for a week of interviews, practices, and glad-handing in the hope of improving their stock for the NFL Draft.

The Senior Bowl itself, played the following Saturday, would be anticlimactic, with most NFL executives long since departed, having watched a week's worth of practice. They would watch tape of the game later. The real action would take place on the practice fields and in the Riverview lobby.

Gibson negotiated his way through the crowd. Many teams had staked out tables, as if set up for a career fair, which in a sense it was.

The New Orleans Saints were alongside a local radio outlet, 93-BLX, "The Big Station." A potted palm separated the Saints from the Seattle Seahawks. The Washington Redskins and Chicago Bears carved out territory across the room.

Long white banners were posted on the walls, with the words FOOD WORLD in bold red type, the words separated by a globe, in reference to the local supermarket that served as the game's title sponsor.

Scouts, decked out in official team logo clothing, corralled passing players to fill out questionnaires. In the center of the room, Senior Bowl staff members handed out green credentials that were the same for everyone: agents, NFL officials, media, family members, hangers-on. Jerry Jones, the owner of the Dallas Cowboys, wore the same credential as David Levine, a South Florida agent who had no clients in the game but, like so many other agents, came to Mobile looking to tout his clients to NFL brass. (Levine's top client, University of Miami running back Frank Gore, had given up his final year of eligibility two weeks earlier. As a junior, Gore was ineligible for the Senior Bowl.)

All told, the Senior Bowl issued more than 1,200 credentials, including more than 700 to NFL officials (an average of more than 20 per franchise), 300 to agents, family members, and job seekers, and more than 200 to media members.

Though it was an impressive gathering of NFL talent and administration, there were few sportswriters on hand, as evidenced by the boxes of Krispy Kreme donuts in the middle of the lobby that had gone virtually untouched. NFL team beat writers had little interest in the event, since none of the players were yet affiliated with a pro franchise.

Not only that, but many writers were in Philadelphia for the NFC championship between the Eagles and Falcons, or in Pittsburgh for the AFC title game between the Steelers and New England Patriots.

Gibson walked by the Krispy Kremes. Players knew better than to grab an original glazed in full view of potential NFL employers, though Gibson might have been given some leeway. At six-four and 193 pounds, he needed at least seven more pounds on his lanky frame to compete in the NFL. As if to take the focus off of his frame, he wore a baggy gray Georgia sweatshirt, baggy white-and-blue shorts, and black Nike sneakers. A yellow badge worn around his neck—FRED GIBSON, UNIVERSITY OF GEORGIA—completed the ensemble.

Ever gregarious, Gibson worked the lobby like a politician. He hugged fellow players and his agents. He embraced other agents—most players got to know at least four or five well during the recruiting process—even reporters. Gibson spotted Georgia quarterback David Greene and greeted him with a sweeping handshake and embrace, as if he had not seen him in months, instead of hours. The lobby lights sparkled off Gibson's diamond stud earrings as he signed official thirty-five-dollar Senior Bowl footballs, among the many souvenir items available in the lobby.

"It's like Mardi Gras in here," said Gibson, unaware that the event had just kicked off in Mobile, site of the original Mardi Gras celebration. "I'm not sure how I'm going to get out."

Doug Hendrickson, one of Gibson's two Octagon representatives, watched him and smiled. "Fred is so outgoing. He loves people. When teams get to know him, they'll love the guy on a personal level. He just has to show teams he's consistent on the field. He's got great hands and doesn't have many flaws. If you look at receivers in the NFL, he can overcome any shortcomings through practice and repetition. And a year or two from now, he could weigh 220 pounds."

As Gibson signed for fans, professional autograph hounds jockeyed for position. Along one wall, Jim Dodson of Palm Beach Autographs worked out of a duffel bag. He spotted Kay-Jay Harris and cornered the running back from West Virginia University.

Harris, who had played three years of minor league baseball for the Texas Rangers, was no stranger to the autograph transaction. "I see these going for twenty-five bucks on eBay," he said.

"I'll give you seventy-five for twenty-five," Dodson said.

Harris shrugged and dropped to one knee beside a console table, a Luis Vuitton bag slung over a shoulder. Dodson handed him a black Sharpie pen and the first photo. Players, agents, NFL scouts, and reporters filed by, unfazed by the transaction. Scouts from the San Francisco 49ers and Carolina Panthers waited patiently for a Harris interview.

As Harris finished each signature, he handed the photo to Dodson, without looking up. Dodson shook each photo to dry the signature. It was an action shot of Harris running in his Mountaineers uniform. Harris completed his work in less than two minutes.

"Won't these photos be worthless once he's drafted?" Dodson was asked.

"That's the irony," Dodson said, opening his wallet and handing Harris the money. "You can't get to these guys when they're in school, but diehard West Virginia fans want the stuff of them in school. So you have to move fast to capitalize on the market."

At the moment, the market for Fred Gibson was white hot. The Miami Dolphins had taken over some key lobby real estate beyond the ballrooms, behind a piano. Two scouts escorted Gibson out of the main lobby fray, past the Alabama Ballroom.

Gibson poked his head in the door. Inside, more than a hundred scouts were watching the NFC championship on a movie theater–sized screen. The Eagles led the Falcons 20–10 at the start of the fourth quarter. As a Georgia native, Gibson felt a connection to the hometown team. His Georgia Bulldogs had practiced several times at the Falcons indoor facility during bad weather in Athens.

"It doesn't look too good." he said.

Inside the Alabama Ballroom, nine members of the Atlanta Falcons scouting department occupied a center table. They wore stylish black-and-red Falcons gear, their faces showing no emotion as their employer's unlikely storybook season ended one game shy of the Super Bowl.

Their boss, Falcons president and general manager Rich McKay, was scheduled to arrive the next day to oversee the scouting process. So was Tim Ruskell, the assistant general manager. Both would arrive disappointed, though no doubt consoled by having reached the NFC title game in their first full seasons since leaving the Tampa Bay Buccaneers.

Across the Alabama Ballroom, Buccaneers head coach Jon Gruden sat at a table with Monte Kiffin, his defensive coordinator. Gruden and Kiffin, like the players, were among the few people wearing yellow passes instead of green.

Gruden and his staff were on hand to coach the Senior Bowl's South team, a unit dominated by players from the Southeastern Conference and Atlantic Coast Conference. The Oakland Raiders, led by head coach Norv Turner, would coach the North squad.

For many years, Senior Bowl coaching duties were offered to the two teams with the best records that did not make the playoffs. It was a plum assignment, the opportunity to spend a week working with potential draft picks. Not surprisingly, teams that coached the Senior Bowl often selected players from the game, picks that often turned out well.

The Raiders and Buccaneers coached the game in 1999, and the Bucs produced a stellar draft that included defensive tackle Anthony McFarland in the first round, quarterback Shaun King in the second, kicker Martin Gramatica in the third, and safety Dexter Jackson, the future

Most Valuable Player of Super Bowl XXXVII, in the fourth. The Raiders picked up one of the draft's biggest steals, defensive lineman Rod Coleman, in the fifth round.

"Coaching the event gives you one more behind-the-scenes look," McKay said. "When you go into the colleges in the fall, you can see the kid practice, and talk to coaches. But even that, to a certain extent, can be staged, depending on the approach of the coach to protecting the players. Here, you can't hide and there's no question there's a benefit to coaching the game."

In recent years, the NFL has offered Senior Bowl coaching duties to the teams with the worst records. For the 2005 game, the invitation went first to the Miami Dolphins and San Francisco 49ers. Both teams declined, what with their staffs in flux with recent coaching changes. The NFL went down the line until Tampa Bay and Oakland accepted, thus pitting teams that had met in the Super Bowl two years earlier but finished 5-11 in 2004.

With 3:21 left in the fourth quarter, the Eagles scored again to push the lead to 27–10. The Falcons table did not flinch. Nor did Gruden, a former Eagles assistant who no doubt took some pleasure in seeing McKay fall short of a Super Bowl return.

With 1:47 remaining, the Eagles began celebrating. Head coach Andy Reid was doused with Gatorade. Two Falcons scouts stood up. Matt Berry, one of the younger members of the staff, shook his head as he walked out the room. "I didn't need to see that."

By the time the Atlanta Falcons season had officially ended, the scouting staff was back in the lobby preparing for 2005. Scouting director Phil Emery grabbed Ole Miss offensive lineman Marcus Johnson in the lobby and they sat down at a table abandoned by the Bears. Berry and Bob Harrison, the Falcons mid-Atlantic region scout, nabbed Virginia Tech cornerback Eric Green and escorted him to a semiprivate enclave of leather chairs off of the main lobby. Alex Page, who was not a scout but worked as a "college scouting assistant," pinned down Georgia quarterback David Greene for an interview.

"What other sports did you play in high school?" Page asked.

"Baseball."

"What position?"

Four hours later, the New England Patriots had defeated the Pittsburgh Steelers to advance to meet the Eagles in Super Bowl XXXIX. The lobby crowd had thinned and there were more empty tables. The Falcons had the largest presence in the room; all nine scouts continued to grab players for interviews. Perhaps it was because they missed time watching the NFC title game—or found added motivation because of the result.

"Not necessarily," said Taylor Morton, a younger Falcons scout who works the Southeast. "We'd love to be going to the Super Bowl, but our job is to get ready for the draft."

Morton stood in the middle of the lobby scanning for players, as if playing safety. He held a deck of business-sized cards with the Falcons logo and spaces to fill in an interview date and time. Like the rest of his colleagues, he was filling the dance cards of McKay and Ruskell.

"We'll do some interviewing here in the lobby, but later in the week we'll sit them down with Rich and Tim and go more in-depth," Morton said.

Fred Gibson reemerged in the main lobby and was nabbed by Boyd Dowler, who at sixty-seven was the elder statesman of the Falcons scouting staff and, technically, the tallest wide receiver at the Senior Bowl. At six-five, the former star of the 1960s Green Bay Packers had more than an inch on Gibson.

Dowler caught 448 passes for the Packers, was named to the NFL's All-Decade team, and served as an assistant coach for five NFL teams in the '70s and early '80s. Were this a hotel in Wisconsin, Dowler would have been the one signing autographs. Instead, he was stalking twenty-two-year-olds alongside scouts young enough to be his grandsons.

Not surprisingly, McKay and Ruskell put a lot of stock in Dowler's interview reports. All-star games like the Senior Bowl are the first chance for scouts to talk to players. Though they've been around the athletes for months, watching practices, standing on the sidelines before games, and watching games from press boxes, they never talk to players. By now they've spoken to coaches, tutors, compliance directors, and anyone else they think might hold a valuable opinion on the character and work ethic of a player. Now they get their first shot at hearing from the players firsthand.

"There are some con guys out there," Dowler said. "When the answers come out of their mouths before you're finished with the question, you know they've been prepped by their agent. They know what you're going to ask and they've got a canned answer, and you can tell. They try to tell us what they think we want to hear, not necessarily what they believe. They'll answer the question to make themselves look good to the scouts. Sometimes you notice, sometimes you don't. You won't know for sure what they're like until you've spent a few years around them. The goal is to have a pretty good idea between now and April."

Dowler wasn't entirely sold on Gibson. "He's a good kid and has the talent, but is he consistent enough to thrive in the NFL? I'm not sure."

After just three hours at the Senior Bowl, including an hour-long interrogation by the Miami Dolphins, Gibson was a veteran of the NFL scouting interview. Already the questions were becoming repetitious, in that sense not unlike the pattern of media queries he had endured for years.

"They want to know what you love most about football. Obviously, to win—that's a pretty simple answer. They ask about background. 'Have you been arrested? Do you have a valid driver's license—or has it been suspended?' They try to know everything about you because they're investing millions of dollars in you. They ask you, 'Who is the best cornerback you've ever faced? What are all the positions you played in college?' They ask, if I was a defensive back on the other team, what would worry me about Fred Gibson? What are his weak points?"

Dowler gave Gibson a Falcons card and a time to meet with McKay the following evening. "I feel like they've grabbed me ten times already, which is great," Gibson said. "I hope they're interested. They've asked me about my speed and ability to catch balls in a crowd. They asked for one weakness I could get better on. I said, 'I get all the hard catches, but some of the easy ones I miss. I try to run before I catch the ball, and I need to work on that.'"

David Greene emerged from another interview and signed a few autographs; the hounds never leave the lobby. He too had faced the Falcons scouts, though it was unlikely Atlanta would take the hometown quarterback. The team had superstar Michael Vick at quarterback, along with promising backup Matt Schaub.

"You never know," Greene said. "You have to assume everyone has sincere interest. What Georgia kid wouldn't want to play for the Falcons? The key is to be prepared for anything. Guys have different tactics. Some are informal, some are as formal as it gets, like an interrogation. You have to be prepared for both situations. It's almost like a good-cop/bad-cop routine. One guy loosens you up and the other one drills you. They want to see how you're going to react. It's really like an interrogation. 'Tell me about this. You ever been arrested? What do you hate most about football?'"

Greene had a clean track record, but Gibson had one major blemish.

In May of 2003 he was one of nine Georgia players accused of violating NCAA rules for selling their championship rings. The NCAA did not penalize the players, because of the lack of precedent and the unclear nature of the rules involved. Still, it's something NFL teams want to investigate, just to make sure Gibson is not a character liability.

"I'm up front about it," Gibson says. "You have to be. The teams know and they want to see if you're going to bring it up. They wait until the end of the interview and then ask, 'Anything else we should know?' So I explain everything. I gave it to one of my teammates. He said this dude wanted to buy it for four thousand dollars. I thought he was kidding, but I gave it to him and got four thousand dollars in cash. Someone's ring ended up on eBay and then it all came out. I had to pay the school back. You learn from your mistakes. Nobody is perfect. If that's the worst thing I've ever done, I don't think that should count too much against me."

At 10:30 on Monday morning, January 24, 2005, the Alabama Ballroom was packed. More than six hundred scouts had taken their seats, waiting for the meat market to begin.

A small dais was constructed in the front of the room, with an electronic scale. Tape was posted on the back wall, marked in increments from five-six to seven feet.

Outside the ballroom, the members of the South Team stripped down to identical black shorts and white socks. As the doors opened, a hush fell over the crowd and the players entered the room alphabetically, lining up stage right along the wall.

Senior Bowl officials had given out sheets with each player's name listed, along with their arm and hand measurements. There were spaces for scouts to fill in height, weight, and "body type," referring to whether the player was muscular or soft, lanky or fat.

The players were announced one by one. Each player entered from the right of the stage, stood on the scale, and then had his height measured. After his vitals were announced, he walked through the center of the room, giving scouts a closer look. All that was missing was a catwalk.

Over the years, players tried to stack the odds in their favor. There were stories of rocks hidden in pockets, multiple layers of socks. At least one player had wet his pants on the stage, having chugged too much water beforehand.

Fred Gibson, looking thinner than ever without a shirt, was announced at 6.035 (translation: six-three and five-eighths inches) and 194 pounds. David Greene, appearing even paler than usual amid the mostly African-American roster, was announced at 6.027, 223 pounds.

A few players flexed their biceps before leaving the stage, mimicking a boxing weigh-in. The scouts did not react; they had seen every attempt to lighten the mood through the years. When the players reached the back of the room, scouts approached to set up more interviews.

"It's like a meat market, which I guess is the point," Gibson said as he got dressed outside in the lobby. "I was proud of the way I looked. I didn't weigh what I wanted to, but nobody else did either. You're half naked up there, but that's how it is. Everyone's got to do it."

Greene nodded. "You've got the spotlight on the stage and you're in there with nothing but your shorts on. If you've got any flaws, you will be exposed."

The North squad came in next. Darren Sproles, a talented if undersized running back from Kansas State, showed no emotion as he endured the most embarrassing moment of the weigh-in. Since he fell just shy of five-six he had to wait as officials readjusted the height chart. If there was anyone in the room unaware of Sproles's lack of size, they had a few awkward seconds to consider it.

The verdict: five-five and six-eighths inches.

"It wasn't that bad," Sproles said afterward. "I've dealt with it all my life. When you're a running back, it really shouldn't matter. You have to run low to the ground anyway. I consider it more of an advantage to be so short. Look at Warrick Dunn in Atlanta and LaDainian Tomlinson with the Chargers. They're little guys."

Mike Nugent, a five-nine kicker from Ohio State, looked the most out of place amid the giants. He tried to appear confident as he took the stage. He tipped the scales at 179.

"Couldn't they have just given me the extra pound?" Nugent asked. "Like it's going to matter for a kicker. I might have just experienced the only time a guy would ever feel so inadequate about measuring five-nine and 179 pounds. I'm basically the size of the average American male. I guess they needed somebody like me up there to remind people of how huge everyone else is."

The road to the NFL goes through some unlikely places. On Monday afternoon many of the NFL's top executives and coaches drove fifteen miles east of Mobile to the town of Fairhope, and Fairhope Municipal Stadium, a field normally used for high school football games.

As school kids scampered through an adjacent playground and townspeople gathered around the fences, Jon Gruden's South squad got ready for practice. A five-lane asphalt track separated the fans from the field, which was ringed three deep by NFL executives, scouts, and media.

Among the luminaries were Dallas Cowboys owner Jerry Jones and head coach Bill Parcells, Indianapolis Colts head coach Tony Dungy, and Dick Vermeil, head coach of the Kansas City Chiefs. Agents walked circles around the field, talking on cell phone headsets.

The onlookers knew to keep a close eye on the action. Though the players were practicing in shorts, in theory going at three-quarters speed, they also were trying to impress NFL scouts. A year earlier, Falcons assistant general manager Tim Ruskell suffered a broken leg when he failed to get out of the way of players running out of bounds.

On this, the first day of Senior Bowl practice, the agent community was abuzz about young Todd France, the Atlanta agent who landed Auburn stars Ronnie Brown and Carlos Rogers, along with Georgia safety Thomas Davis—all projected as first-round picks.

Only Rogers was playing in the Senior Bowl. Davis, a junior who gave up his final year of eligibility, was ineligible. Brown, like a lot of projected top-ten picks, opted not to play in the game, figuring it could not help his draft status—and possibly hurt with a bad showing or injury. Interestingly, fellow Auburn running back Carnell "Cadillac" Williams, who competed with Brown for carries, had opted to play on the advice of his SFX Sports agent Ben Dogra, wary that the Buccaneers and Raiders, with early first-round picks, both were in need of running backs. Gruden, the coach of the South team, would get a chance to test drive a Cadillac.

The scouts carried roster sheets, though none were necessary. The players wore their college helmets, and, besides, the scouts had been watching them for six months already. The Senior Bowl was the last and most prestigious of the six postseason bowl games, and the talent pool was deep, though not as deep as it could have been.

Many of the top stars like Brown turned down invitations upon the advice of their agents, preferring to spend the week training for the NFL combine. Why risk injury or tainting a sterling college career with a bad week of practice for an exhibition game?

Blue-chip prospects could afford such a position, which explained the absences of Texas running back Cedric Benson and Michigan wide receiver Braylon Edwards. Miami cornerback Antrel Rolle did not accept his Senior Bowl invite. Nor did defensive ends David Pollack (Georgia) and Erasmus James (Wisconsin), or Alex Barron, the promising offensive tackle from Florida State.

The Senior Bowl was more attractive for players who had soared up the draft boards during the season and wanted to build upon that momentum. The South roster was full of such players, like Auburn quarterback Jason Campbell and Demarcus Ware, the defensive end from Troy State.

The week leading up to the game gave players a chance to address shortcomings in practice. Greene, the Georgia quarterback, needed to show athleticism. Matt Jones, who played quarterback at Arkansas, wanted to demonstrate that he could play wide receiver or tight end in the NFL. For Oklahoma's Mark Clayton, the idea was to show that a five-ten wide receiver was worth a first-round pick.

As the South practice ended, scouts, agents, and reporters swarmed the field. Fans and VIPs who had scored the familiar green passes also converged, pens and autograph material in hand. In a repeat of the previous night's lobby scene, scouts conducted flyby interviews and arranged times for more thorough investigations.

Todd Brunner, a scout for the San Francisco 49ers, managed to get an audience with Florida State cornerback Bryant McFadden between autograph seekers.

"Would you say you consider yourself a leader?" Brunner asked.

"Definitely," McFadden said, signing an autograph.

"Who was the vocal leader of the secondary? You? Jerome Carter?"

Jerome Carter played safety for the Seminoles. Unlike McFadden, who was projected as a first- or second-round pick, Carter was considered a lesser prospect. He played two weeks earlier in the Gridiron Classic, an Orlando game featuring players likely to get drafted in the later rounds, if at all.

"Mostly J. C., but both of us to some degree," McFadden said.

"How do you learn: classroom, film, on the field?"

"A combination of everything."

"What's your vertical [leap]?"

"Thirty-nine, forty [inches]." The players will be tested in the vertical jump at the NFL combine in Indianapolis.

"Think you can do that in Indianapolis?"

"Oh yeah."

All around the field, agents huddled with their clients. They were not there for any particular purpose, other than to offer congratulations on a fine practice, show support, and, perhaps most important, keep other agents from approaching their hard-earned, recently signed clients.

As Todd France chatted with Carlos Rogers, Pat Dye Jr. and his partner Bill Johnson spoke with two of their clients: Greene, the Georgia quarterback, and Ware, the defensive end from Troy State. Dye and Johnson already had touched base with Georgia wide receiver Reggie Brown and offensive tackle Ray Willis, whom they had successfully reconnected with during Florida State agent day in November.

Ware was Dye's prized signing, a product of the existing client network. Mike Pelton, who coached the defensive ends at Troy State, had played at Auburn for Pat Dye Sr. in the early 1990s. Dye Jr. represented Pelton during his brief NFL career.

Dye had heard the buzz about France and had taken note of the snickering about how the kid beat the veteran at Auburn and Georgia.

"He kicked our ass on three guys we wanted bad: Rogers, Davis, and Brown. I don't get it. He's never had a first-round player since he's been in the business, and to sign three top-twenty picks—wow, what a year! My hat's off to him. I told him congratulations. He works hard. I'll give him that. He's a hell of a lot smoother a talker than I am. This is my eighteenth draft and Senior Bowl, and I've had fifteen or twenty first-round picks and he's had none. If I'm one of those players, I don't know. I would have thought one of them signs with us. But I give the guy credit. He worked hard and I'm sure he'll do a good job for them. We'd been talking to those guys for two years. Between the two schools [Georgia and Auburn], we've got upwards of twenty-five clients from those two schools. Out of thirty-six guys we have on active rosters. That's two-thirds of our client base. But, hey, he's working hard. He's single. He doesn't have to worry about being on the road all the time, family. I was his age not that long ago."

Not that Dye had a bad recruiting season. Besides Greene, Brown, Ware, and Willis, he also signed Ben Wilkerson, a center from LSU. Still, in a year in which Auburn and Georgia were arguably the two most attractive colleges for agent recruiting, the agent that had dominated those schools for more than a decade couldn't help but feel defeated.

"We signed a good class. Ben Wilkerson is a top-rated center. Demarcus Ware, who many people have never heard of, is going to be a first-round pick. Reggie Brown is a climber in the draft, will go in the first two rounds, and David Greene is a freakin' icon in the state of Georgia. So it is a good class.

"But when you've got Thomas Davis, Ronnie Brown, Carnell Williams, and Carlos Rogers, all of whom we recruited very actively for two years, and don't get any of those guys, that is *very* disappointing and it's one of those things that just makes you shake your head on the rationale. I'm sure they have different reasons for not choosing us and I'm going to do everything I can in the next three months to learn why."

It was hardly time for Dye to panic. He had a solid draft class, to be sure, to say nothing of one of the deepest client rosters in the game. But as he told Greene his room number at the Riverview Hotel, he shook his head at the irony. No longer did he have a stranglehold on Auburn and Georgia, which presented a crisis of sorts for ProFiles Sports Management.

Dye was staying in room 911.

France's recruiting efforts also had yielded Kerry Rhodes, a safety from Louisville, Wake Forest cornerback Eric King, and Josh Davis, a wide receiver from Marshall. France did so well that he actually lost a client, Oklahoma State cornerback Darrent Williams, because Williams believed France could not give him the attention he needed while dealing with three consensus first-round picks. Williams fired France and hired Momentum Sports agents Jeff Griffin and Jack Scharf.

Williams was training at Athletes' Performance, setting up a potential replay of the previous year, when DeAngelo Hall fired Ethan Lock and hired Joel Segal after arriving in Arizona. Under the new rules, France could ask Williams to leave the facility, but he let him stay. Momentum, of course, would foot the bill.

France, having seen Carlos Rogers back to the team bus that would take the South squad back to the Riverview Hotel, made no apologies for his success.

"If I had just started in the business and had no clients and had never done any contracts and got a first-rounder, then even I would ask, 'How the heck did this guy do it? That's phenomenal. How did he do it?' I'm not going to sit here and pat myself on the back and say nobody without a first-rounder has ever gone out and gotten three first-rounders. It's hard work. They made their decision. I won; I almost won before, but being second doesn't count. The reality is I have a great list of clients, some big names, some medium, some smaller names. Some more well known. The reality is I've done good deals and have some big deals. I don't have to apologize for anything."

On Wednesday night during Senior Bowl week, Jack "Show Me" Scharf sat down at a table near the lobby bar at the Riverview Hotel with some unlikely companions: Ed Hawthorne, Ed Walsh, and Chris Singletary, an agent from IMG.

Nearly three weeks had passed since Ed Hawthorne called Scharf with the news that his nephew, Anttaj, would be signing with IMG agent Tom Condon. That decision cost Scharf a possible six-figure commission and his first surefire blue-chip client. Still, the men talked as if they were all old friends.

They sat near the foot of the escalator and watched as a parade of Mobile socialites and their husbands proceeded to the Alabama ballroom for the latest VIP reception. Actually, anyone with a green pass could attend, which included just about everyone. The buffet of fried foods was the same each evening, even if the sponsor and theme changed. Tonight's motif was "Seafood Jubilee," sponsored by a wireless phone company. A cloud of smoke hung over the lobby; Alabama had yet to ban indoor smoking.

"You're watching something that never happens," Scharf says. "An agent that lost out on a prominent client is sitting with the family. It never happens."

The group visited for more than an hour. Scharf picked up a bar tab in excess of one hundred dollars before the party broke up.

Of course, it's not uncommon for runner-up agents to keep in touch with would-be clients. Football players switch representatives frequently. Could Scharf have been jockeying for rebounding position?

"There might be a little bit of truth to that," he said later. "The bottom line is that it's rare in any profession when you have an opportunity to meet people you respect as much as I got to know Ed Hawthorne. It's very rare. I don't keep a relationship for the sake of it becoming fruitful in the business sense, bringing me some monetary reward. Though, if it happens, it happens."

Norv Turner's North team defeated Jon Gruden's South squad, 23–13, to win the Senior Bowl. Even in defeat, it was a good afternoon for David Greene, who completed eleven of sixteen passes for 102 yards and a touchdown. Fred Gibson caught two passes for 43 yards, but also fumbled a kickoff return.

Back in Tempe, Arizona, Chris Canty watched the Senior Bowl at his apartment after a brief workout at the Athletes' Performance training center. The place seemed empty, what with half of the NFL hopefuls in Mobile for the week.

That was fine with Canty, who for the last month had worked tirelessly to rehabilitate the knee he injured in September. So, while players like Gibson, fellow Virginia player Darryl Blackstock, and Auburn running backs Ronnie Brown and Carnell "Cadillac" Williams worked on their vertical leaps and forty-yard dash performances, Canty endured a grueling regimen of physical therapy.

The hard work was beginning to pay off. Training at Athletes' Performance began at 8:00 A.M. each morning. Canty always was the first player there, no later than 7:30. Though the combine was a month away, he felt confident that he would be ready to perform many of the drills in Indianapolis. Draft Web sites already were touting Canty's remarkable comeback.

Canty was, by his own admission, something of a loner. That had become more apparent during the season after his injury, when he no longer felt like a member of the Virginia Cavaliers. It was not that he was not friendly and approachable; his mother, Shirley, was a pastor in Charlotte, and Chris inherited her outgoing demeanor, but Chris preferred solitude, even living alone during his final year at school. After undergoing surgery in Birmingham in September, he returned home to Charlotte. Having graduated the previous May, there was little incentive to stay at the University of Virginia, not even the school's legendary reputation for partying.

It was Saturday night in Phoenix, the one night where Canty and the rest of the NFL hopefuls did not have to go to bed early to be ready for early-morning training. So he decided to accompany a few of his new friends to a pulsing, two-story nightclub called Axis/Radius, in Scottsdale. One of Canty's agents, Vance Malinovic, held a modest, indirect ownership stake in the club, having invested in a partnership that purchased several Scottsdale properties.

It's usually not a good idea for prominent athletes, especially larger ones, to enter a contained area where liquor is served. Canty arrived with Erasmus James, Jovan Haye, and Richie Incognito, all of whom stand at least six-two and weigh more than 270 pounds.

The club was packed when the group arrived around 11:30 P.M. and the players got separated. Canty and Incognito, a six-two, three hundred-pound lineman with a history of anger management issues, ended up in a VIP section upstairs. While navigating the area around

1:00 A.M., they brushed up against a patron sitting at the bar. The man jumped up and began yelling and waving a small flashlight in their faces.

Words were exchanged and accounts of what happened next vary, according to the Scottsdale police report. Canty said he and Incognito headed downstairs toward the exit after a profanity-laced exchange with the flashlight-wielding patron. Incognito said that the situation upstairs escalated into pushing and shoving, and bouncers escorted everyone downstairs.

Either way, Canty and Incognito were standing near the exit when Canty was struck in the face with a beer bottle. Canty says he never saw it coming; Incognito told a Scottsdale detective the assailant was the guy from upstairs. (Canty did not decide to press charges until days later. Incognito could not pick the alleged assailant out of a photo lineup and no arrest ever was made.)

In the darkness and cacophony of Axis/Radius, Canty fell to the floor. He reached up to his left eye and came back with a handful of blood. Someone helped him take off his shirt to apply pressure.

Though vision in his left eye was blurry, Canty assumed it was from blood trickling from his forehead or eyelid. It wasn't until an EMT took a look at the eye on the ambulance ride to the hospital that Canty grew concerned.

"Buddy, your eye has been cut," the EMT said.

From there, things seemed to proceed on fast-forward. Doctors were telling Canty he had a detached retina and they would need to operate momentarily. Two of Canty's agents, Malinovic and Ethan Lock, hustled to the hospital.

It was nearly 2:00 A.M. Mountain Time. Feeling disoriented and suffering from blurred vision, Canty managed two coherent thoughts. First, he did not want to call his father and mother, the Rev. Shirley Canty, and wake them up at 4:00 A.M. Eastern Standard Time.

Mom and dad eventually would understand, Canty knew, but as nurses prepared him for surgery, Canty wondered if he had not endured four months of agonizing knee rehabilitation, only to throw his NFL career away in a Scottsdale bar.

Chapter Twelve:

THE NEED FOR SPEED

C hip Smith is a devout Christian and a proud American. But when he's asked how he developed his training regimens to prepare for the NFL combine, he's quick to credit the former Soviet Union.

In 1987, Smith was part of a contingent of American trainers who visited the Soviet Sports Institute in Moscow to study the Russians' training methods. The facilities were every bit as drab and depressing as Smith expected, but their philosophies were cutting edge.

Unlike trainers in the United States, who at the time focused their efforts on making athletes big and strong, the Russians concentrated on sport-specific movement, athleticism, and especially speed.

"Their runners were among the fastest in the world," Smith says. "I figured if the Russians could make white guys this fast, they were really on to something."

At the heart of the Russian philosophy, Smith learned, was the notion of "overspeed" training. Children, from a young age, realize they can run downhill at extraordinary speeds. The brain triggers a neuromuscular response that keeps the body from falling.

The Russians discovered that it was possible to replicate that response, through training, by tricking the fast-twitch muscle fibers that fire first when movement begins.

"When you watched [sprinter] Carl Lewis, it looked like he'd accelerate in the middle of the race, leaving everyone behind," Smith says. "But what actually was happening was that he was maintaining that fast-twitch response and everyone else was decelerating."

In Moscow, Smith watched Russian athletes step into a harness attached to a motorized contraption that looked like the grill of a car. The machine would begin to reel in the athlete, who would need to continue that fast-twitch response to maintain his pace. As a result, he ran 10 to 15 percent faster than he normally could.

Back home, Smith simulated the device by using surgical tubing. Soon his athletes were working with harnesses and bungee cords. The muscles work harder while stretching the bungee, and when the cord contracts it produces overspeed, training the athlete to run faster.

"When you take the contraption off, the muscle fibers still think they have resistance," Smith says. "They fire just as fast."

By combining overspeed and resistance training, Smith found athletes could increase both the length and frequency of strides. Contrary to popular belief that speed was something an athlete was born with, Smith discovered it could be taught.

The training had obvious applications for football. After all, it didn't matter how strong a player was or how well he tackled if he couldn't catch the opposing player. The NFL, with its annual combine, became Smith's training ground.

Smith began preparing athletes for the NFL combine in the early 1990s, and when the market exploded at the end of the decade he was in position to capitalize. With a training center located just north of Atlanta in Duluth, he's conveniently located for players from Southern schools, to say nothing of the many agents operating out of Atlanta.

It's hard to overestimate the importance of speed. Ask any NFL rookie to explain the difference between the college and pro game and he'll inevitably talk about how everyone in the NFL is so much faster. It's why NFL scouts spend so much time on evaluating a player's raw speed and quickness.

Smith, fifty, touts his company as the largest preparer of NFL talent, estimating that he's trained more than six hundred players for the NFL combine. Agents who send clients other places use the larger numbers against him, arguing that it's impossible for any staff to provide hands-on guidance to a group of sixty or more kids each year.

The results would seem to indicate otherwise. In 2003, Smith trained the fourth, fifth, and sixth picks in the draft: Kentucky defensive tackle

Dewayne Robertson, Kansas State defensive back Terence Newman, and Johnathan Sullivan, a defensive tackle from the University of Georgia.

Then there was Brian Urlacher. After the 1999 season, agent Steve Kauffman sent the University of New Mexico player to Smith. Urlacher was hardly an unknown, but he was somewhat off the radar screen playing for the Lobos. Plus, he was undersized by NFL linebacker standards, weighing just 235.

Urlacher got a head start on his combine training, since the Lobos did not play in a bowl game after finishing the 1999 season 4-7. Two months of Competitive Edge training later, he weighed a chiseled 258. At the combine, he benched 225 pounds twenty-seven times and ran the forty in under 4.6. With fourteen of the future first-round picks sitting out the event, the fiery Urlacher stole the show. The Chicago Bears selected him with the ninth overall choice.

Smith tells potential clients that he can shave two-tenths of a second off their forty-yard-dash time, increase their bench press by four to five repetitions, improve their vertical leap four to six inches, and help them run faster shuttles.

"From the time I got back from Russia, I realized I could take a guy straight out of Division I football and have phenomenal results," Smith said. "In defense of college strength coaches, they don't have five or six hours a day to spend with players. But when you can get a kid off campus and put him in this focused environment, you can accomplish a lot in two months. Look, I'm not going to take credit for Brian Urlacher. He was a workout warrior who would have played in the NFL whether he met me or not. But I like to think of what I do as taking a diamond in the rough and polishing it and tilting it toward the sun so it sparkles."

Smith's 2005 draft class included Mike Williams, the former Southern Cal wide receiver who tried to enter the 2004 draft after his sophomore season. Williams announced his intention to go pro after a federal judge ruled in favor of Ohio State running back Maurice Clarett, who had challenged the NFL rule requiring that a player be three years removed from high school to enter the draft.

Williams trained with Smith before the 2004 draft, only to have Clarett's ruling overturned on appeal. The NFL managed to keep Williams and Clarett out of the draft and the NCAA refused to let Williams return to the college football ranks.

So Williams spent part of the fall semester training with Smith. Once the college football season was over, Smith's training center again filled up. There was Adam Terry, the offensive lineman from Syracuse, Clemson linebacker Leroy Hill, Kentucky defensive end Vincent Burns, Oklahoma quarterback Jason White, and Karl Paymah, a cornerback from Washington State.

Pat Dye Jr. and Todd France, the Atlanta agents who went head-to-head on Auburn and Georgia recruits, also had talent at Competitive Edge. France sent Auburn's Ronnie Brown and Carlos Rogers to Athletes' Performance in Arizona and Thomas Davis, the Georgia safety who turned pro early, to Velocity Sports, another Atlanta training center. Smith got Louisville safety Kerry Rhodes and Eric King, a cornerback from Wake Forest.

"Different players like different things, so I give them a choice," France says.

Dye believed in Smith and had sent players to him ever since Georgia offensive tackle Matt Stinchcomb asked for him to foot the bill for Smith's services prior to the 1999 draft. Dye sent many of his clients to Smith, including Georgia quarterback David Greene and Ray Willis, the offensive tackle from Florida State. Dye's top client, Troy State defensive end Demarcus Ware, was training at a Velocity center in Alabama.

At Competitive Edge, players train six hours a day, five days a week. Each day consists of two hours of weightlifting, two hours of speed and agility work, and two hours of position-specific training. The players are forever donning harnesses and bungees and weighted vests, whatever it takes to become stronger, faster, and more explosive for the combine.

Smith has versions of the Wonderlic, the fifty-question cognitive ability exam given at the combine, and has the players practice. To prepare players for interviews with NFL scouts, he brings in Ken Herock, a longtime personnel man for the Tampa Bay Buccaneers, Oakland Raiders, Atlanta Falcons, and Green Bay Packers. Herock puts the players through mock interviews and provides pointers.

Herock is not viewed by current NFL executives as the turncoat one might expect. Team officials realize agents hire interview coaches and figure they might as well use someone experienced in the process.

Herock worked in Tampa during John McKay's coaching tenure and later did a lengthy stint as general manager of the Falcons. No one is more familiar with Herock's work than Rich McKay, the Falcons current general manager, who still values the interview process, even if players are coached.

"It's very scripted, because you have the Kenny Herocks of the world out there giving seminars," McKay says. "But I still get a lot out of interviews. A lot of times 30 to 40 percent of what a kid says isn't true, and we know it's not true because we've done our research on the kid. How truthfully he answers is a pretty good indicator of his character."

There were no questions about Greene's character. A high school star growing up in the Atlanta suburbs, he won a record forty-two games in four years as the starting quarterback at Georgia. With a perpetual smile, self-deprecating sense of humor, and enormous in-state popularity, he could run for governor.

According to scouting reports, the All-American boy lacked quickness and foot speed, which trumped character in the minds of NFL officials. Dye asked Smith to work on those areas, even hiring a special quarterback coach to help. Zeke Bratkowski, a former Georgia player, NFL quarterback, and assistant coach, had developed a reputation as a predraft specialist for quarterbacks such as Michael Vick, Patrick Ramsey, and Philip Rivers.

Smith had his own quarterback guru, Roger Theder, a former San Diego Chargers assistant and University of California head coach. Between the three of them, they thought Greene's foot-speed issue was overblown. Still, Smith put Greene in harnesses and cords, even for some quarterback drills.

"We don't add so much resistance that he can't do a three-step drop," Smith said. "The idea is to work on muscle memory. You take off the resistance and the muscle fibers think it's still there. They fire just as fast."

Willis presented a different challenge. He still was recovering from the high left ankle sprain sustained during Florida State's final regular season game against Florida in November. Smith's staff went to work helping Willis rediscover his "proprioception," the system of sensors in the joints that helps the body maintain balance. After an ankle is immobilized or not used after an injury, the proprioceptive system needs to be reactivated.

Dye and his colleague, Bill Johnson, had told Smith about Willis, how he was married and possessed a maturity and work ethic unlike that of most football players. Not long after arriving in Atlanta, Willis asked Smith if he would work with him on Sundays and Smith agreed, showing up after church services.

"Ray's not blessed as a natural athlete," Smith says. "But he has a drive and a motivation that you see only in the great ones. His performance in the NFL won't be affected by a lack of effort, that's for sure."

Though Smith had one of the larger combine classes, with clients representing more than a dozen agents, he was working with just one consensus first-rounder in Williams, who, because of his failed early entry into the NFL draft, had undergone more precombine training than any player in history.

Down in Bradenton, Florida, a much smaller group of athletes prepared for the combine. There were just five of them, all clients of the International Management Group, and four had realistic first-round aspirations.

Michael Johnson opened the trunk of a rented Ford Taurus and pulled out a rope ladder. The man considered the fastest human in the world for much of the 1990s walked across a well-manicured grass soccer field, crouched, and laid out the ladder.

Temperatures already were approaching eighty degrees shortly before 10:00 A.M. on Thursday, February 3, 2005. Johnson was the first to arrive at the International Management Group's soccer fields, part of 190 acres of prime Bradenton, Florida, real estate. The IMG Academies are a sprawling complex of condominiums, private schools, and athletic facilities that attract kids with parents willing to pay up to one hundred thousand dollars a year for high-end, sport-specific training and accommodations.

In 1978, tennis coach Nick Bollettieri created a tennis academy on what was then a twenty-two-acre tomato farm. He welcomed students from around the world and trained young prodigies such as Andre Agassi, Jim Courier, and Monica Seles. In 1987 he sold the facility to IMG, the Cleveland-based sports colossus that represents hundreds of athletes, entertainers, and sports properties.

Over the next decade, IMG expanded upon Bollettieri's residential sports concept and transformed it into a major recruiting and development tool for young athletes in tennis, golf, soccer, baseball, and basketball.

IMG did not develop football players; high schools and colleges did an adequate job of that. Instead, it used the training center, specifically the coaches at the International Performance Institute (IPI), to help lure promising NFL hopefuls to IMG. Between IPI and the reputation of lead agent Tom Condon for representing top NFL players, IMG was able to land promising draft classes most every year.

Johnson checked his watch as two sport utility vehicles rolled up alongside the field. Out popped his pupils for the morning, IMG's 2005 NFL Draft class, clad in shorts, sneakers, and gray IMG Academies T-shirts that read "World's Toughest Playground."

It had been another good haul for Condon and his partner, Ken "Fuzzy" Kremer. The rookie-to-be class included Alex Smith, the quarterback from Utah projected as a possible number-one overall pick; David Pollack, the three-time All-American defensive end from Georgia; Heath Miller, the Mackey Award–winning tight end from the University of Virginia; Chris Spencer, a talented center from Ole Miss; and Rob Petitti, a 350-pound lineman from Pittsburgh. The other member of IMG's recruiting class, Wisconsin defensive tackle Anttaj Hawthorne, had opted to stay in Madison to prepare for the combine.

The players fanned out across the field. Brook Hamilton, a trainer at the International Performance Institute, guided the group through a series of stretches and movement drills.

Scouts referred to Pollack as a "high-motor" player, meaning his intensity level never wavered on the field—or off, according to his Georgia teammates. Pollack maintained a running commentary through the warm-up routine, with nobody off limits.

Petitti, sidelined with a foot injury, opened a can of Skoal and folded a pinch under his lip. "There's Rob Petitti and his precombine workout," Pollack said.

Pollack turned his attention to the Ford Taurus. How could a rental agency assign such an everyday vehicle to the world's fastest man? "Nice ride, MJ."

Johnson nodded. "I'm taking that car to Pimp-my-Ride."

At thirty-six, Johnson had assembled a full slate of postcareer endeavors, including television commentary, helping coach at alma mater Baylor, and launching a sports consultancy company. For the past few years, his former agency had brought him to Florida to train the football players how to best run the forty.

It was an odd pairing, a world-class sprinter with athletes that averaged more than 250 pounds, sort of like enlisting Warren Buffett to teach financial planning to college kids. IMG flexed all of its resources when it came to recruiting and preparing athletes for the NFL Draft.

Johnson, who won Olympic gold medals and world championships in the two hundred and four hundred meters, never ran forty yards for time. But he believed the mechanics and philosophies of running still applied. Johnson wasn't about to stay in Florida for the entire precombine season, but he flew in several times for three-day stints. Today was the first time the group would run the forty for time.

Besides his rope ladder, Johnson had laid out a forty-yard course. Johnson gathered the group in a huddle and recapped his main points from a previous session. The start was essential, especially because the players would not have the normal sprinter's luxury of blocks.

"You want to have maximum force coming out to propel you forward," Johnson said. "Once you start moving, the clock starts, so everything has to be moving as fast as possible. This is not a buildup. Your initial move sets up the rest of the run, so it's got to start off with aggression, force, and speed all together at the same time."

The players lined up to run, first a pair of twenty-yard dashes. Petitti sat out, along with Miller, who was nursing an abdominal injury sustained late in the season. Here, running on grass did not simulate the RCA Dome track they would use for the NFL combine in Indianapolis in three weeks, but that wasn't the point. Johnson was more concerned with their techniques.

Pollack, already in a lather from the heat, ran first. He assumed a three-point stance, with his right hand on the ground and left in the air. Unlike his football position, where he stared ahead at his opponent, he kept his head down. Pollack waited a few moments then lurched forward, barreling through the distance and walking back to Johnson for feedback.

The sprinter pumped his arms. "You've got to keep your hands by your hip, as if you're pulling a gun out of a holster each time."

Pollack nodded and walked away. Smith, the Utah quarterback, prepared to run.

"You have to use different types of analogies," Johnson said. "David tends to run with his chest out and his arms back, and they never come forward. You can't get very much power that way. You want it to come from further back every time. It's easier for him to remember if I say it's like drawing the gun out of a holster instead of saying, 'Make sure your arm always comes up in front of your body and passes by your hip.'

"To do what I need David to do, he has to keep his head down, and that's very difficult for a guy used to starting the opposite way. Linemen are used to having their hands at a certain position, and I need them to keep their hands down. It's only temporary. Whatever they do after I'm finished with them, it doesn't matter. But for that one day, those scouts want to see them run the forty as fast as they can."

Pollack watched Smith. "A lot of this technique is beyond what I've ever learned," he said. "I might have run forty yards on the football field ten times in my entire career. But it's a test to show how fast you are. You hear the word 'potential' used a lot right now. 'This guy has a lot of potential, a lot of upside.' Most of the evaluation should come from film, and most of it does; but this is something else they're going to look at. If I'm even with somebody else, this is going to push me over the top. So how can I not listen to the fastest human being to ever walk the planet?"

After Smith and Spencer ran, the trio waited a few minutes and ran twenty yards again. Johnson showed no emotion as he looked at his stopwatch.

"You can't measure progress by the watch, not after just fifteen days down here," Johnson said. "We've spent quite a bit of time on the start and the drive. Now we proceed into the full run, and the question is, how are guys going to make the transition? I'm looking at what he's doing right and what we have to work on. Which parts of this will he get and which ones will he not get, based on the time we have here? Which battles should I choose to fight?"

Pollack ran the forty first, pumping his arms and looking more like a gunslinger than previously. Johnson glanced at the stopwatch and then reset it.

"How'd I do?" Pollack asked.

"We're not worried about times."

"C'mon, how'd I do?"

"It's grass, man. Even if you ran a 4.3, I wouldn't tell you."

Two hours later, across the IMG campus, Steve Shenbaum prepared the IMG football class of 2005 for the interview portion of the combine. During their stay in Indianapolis, players would spend two evenings shuttling between hotel rooms to speak with NFL teams in fifteen-minute blocks. It was Shenbaum's job to make sure they put their best face forward.

Shenbaum was part of the growing number of consultants specializing in image-building and media coaching for professional athletes. The idea, borrowed from the corporate world, was to show pros how every interview contributed to their public image and to create strategies to get their messages across. A well-spoken, accessible athlete that avoided controversy but still projected personality and flair could generate millions in off-the-field endorsement money. He also could use the playing career as a springboard for lucrative retirement opportunities in business, broadcasting, coaching, or motivational speaking.

That was the big picture, anyway. For now, the players needed to impress NFL officials in Indianapolis in this high-stakes game of speed-dating. The key was to project confidence, respect, intelligence, passion, knowledge of football, and personality, without coming across as cocky, self-entitled, or coached.

Most agents hired media coaches to prepare players for the combine interview. Shenbaum was IMG's answer to the likes of former NFL executive Ken Herock, Chip Smith's guru. IMG, being an agency with its own training center, brought the interview process in-house. Shenbaum had relocated his Game On business from California to Bradenton and worked year-round with IMG's sports prodigies from a well-appointed office on campus. His top priority for the first six weeks of the year was combine preparation.

"Most of their college classmates are interviewing for real jobs," Shenbaum said. "This is a similar process, but there's much more money at stake."

Cynics, including those in the media and NFL officials, suggest people like Shenbaum don't build images so much as they sanitize them, creating vanilla personalities like IMG clients Tiger Woods and Derek Jeter that offer guarded comments and little insight into what makes them tick. In that sense, the industry is merely an advanced version of the famous bus scene in the baseball movie *Bull Durham*, where veteran catcher Crash Davis, played by Kevin Costner, lectured young pitcher "Nuke" LaLoosh (Tim Robbins) on how to handle the media.

"You're gonna have to learn your clichés," Davis said. "We gotta play it one day at a time . . . I'm just happy to be here and hope I can help the ballclub . . . I just want to give it my best shot and, the good Lord willing, things will work out."

The red-haired Shenbaum taught players how to act in Indianapolis, and he brought solid credentials to his work. He had a lengthy list of television and movie credits, with bit roles on *Married with Children* and *Will and Grace*, and a turn as "band camp director" in the second film of the *American Pie* trilogy. Still, Shenbaum bristles at the suggestion that there's anything disingenuous about interview coaching.

"Good actors are trying to be truthful, they're not trying to act. The basis of our program is for an athlete to be truthful. I don't want an athlete to try and be somebody he's not. If you don't go to church every Sunday, don't say you go to church every Sunday. If you're close to Mom, great. But if you don't talk to your parents then don't say you're close to your family. I'm not going to try and make Rob Petitti into a choir boy. That's not fair to him, and coaches and general managers are smart enough to know who is putting on an act."

Most bigtime football players think they're prepared for the combine interview, having undergone hundreds of sessions with the media in college. Unfortunately for Shenbaum and his competitors, they find that the constant media obligations have conditioned many players to spout the Crash Davis playbook on autopilot, rather than project the passion and personality NFL scouts and executives want to see, at least in Indianapolis. (Once they enter the NFL, the *Bull Durham* approach is heartily encouraged.)

Miller suffered from a version of the syndrome. A soft-spoken native of tiny Swords Creek, Virginia, with close-cropped hair, Miller came across as shy, expressionless, even disinterested. Teammates at the University of Virginia hung the nickname "Big Money" on him, mostly because of his reliable pass-catching skills, but also because he seemed like the last guy who would have such a flashy moniker.

So Shenbaum filmed an interview with Miller and had him watch it.

"Your issue is going to be that you don't come across as very dynamic," Shenbaum said. "But whose issue is that? Is it yours or the media's? I worked with Pete Sampras and he had this same problem. But do you think he's banging his head up against the wall with his $55 million in the bank and fourteen Grand Slam titles and a beautiful wife and child because he's called boring? Yeah, it hurt him for a while and it was frustrating, but whose issue is that? We ask athletes to be sportsmen and to be respectful and gentlemanly, and when they do exactly that, we call them boring. So don't worry about it."

Miller nodded. "I've always been the type of guy to deflect attention to the team. I don't really cherish the individual attention or the interviews." (It was no wonder Miller was one of Virginia coach Al Groh's all-time favorite players. Groh, like his longtime colleagues, Bill Parcells and Bill Belichick, prefers players that say little if anything that could be construed as colorful or insightful.)

"And that's a great attitude to have," Shenbaum said. "But look at yourself here. It's almost as if you're mourning a death. Let's work with what you've got. You've got a great smile; you're a good-looking guy. Talk about things that excite you. Use some facial reactions. The way you play speaks for yourself."

Shenbaum turned the video camera back toward Miller and began asking questions about his family. Miller relaxed, smiled, and spoke of family vacations to the beach. Shenbaum put the interview on screen.

"What's the difference?" Shenbaum asked.

"I'm smiling," Miller said.

"Of course you are. You're talking about something you enjoy. This is how it all starts. We're not going to make you into a silver-tongued Charlie, and that's okay. I don't need to tell you to smile more; you know that. Instead, think of things in your life that bring a smile to your face. Think of them as coins you can put in your pocket and take out when you need to smile."

Unlike other interview gurus working with combine players, Shenbaum did not have to spend time coaching his players on how to address questions about drug use, arrests, suspensions, and other red flags. Smith, Miller, Pollack, and Spencer were going to register high on any team's character evaluation; Petitti only had to address a hard-partying reputation.

Still, there was room for improvement, especially since Petitti was the only one of the group that had endured the nonstop interviews at the Senior Bowl. Smith, Miller, and Spencer, as juniors, were ineligible for the game. Pollack, who finished his college career with three sacks in the Outback Bowl and was considered among the top prospects in the draft, figured there was nothing to be gained by playing in Mobile.

Shenbaum worked with the players for four hours a week. There were one-on-one sessions and group workshops that included mock interviews, public speaking—even improvisation skits. There was plenty of discussion on typical combine questions—strengths and weaknesses, toughest opponent faced, biggest likes and dislikes about football—but Shenbaum drew upon his acting experiences to create a free-flowing classroom atmosphere. That way, players improved their communication skills instead of just memorizing what they thought scouts wanted to hear.

"We want them to be able to tell stories, not just provide canned answers," Shenbaum said.

Pollack represented a different challenge. He was always passionate and animated and shifted gears quickly in interviews, transforming from the smack-talking, alpha male of the locker room into a polite, "Yes sir," young man. Before his junior year, he declined a spot in Playboy's preseason All-American team photo, saying it conflicted with his religious beliefs. Prior to his senior season, he revealed to *ESPN the Magazine* that he planned to remain a virgin until marriage.

It was a shtick that struck some as a little too Mr. Goody Two-shoes. Pollack also had a tendency to credit God and his Christian faith frequently.

Pollack didn't worry if his public testimony rubbed some the wrong way. During Outback Bowl week in Tampa in January, he appeared at press conferences in a white T-shirt with a knocked off emblem of the NFL shield that read FML (For My Lord).

"I'm going to be outgoing about my faith," Pollack said. "That's the reason I'm here today. That's the reason I've been given this gift to play football. God has been so good to me in so many ways, and I love to share it. There's a difference between sharing it and telling people why you have that faith, and cramming it down someone's throat."

Shenbaum wasn't about to steer Pollack away from public testimony, though he did remind him of devout athletes who were skewered in the press for their transgressions. The former actor just hoped Pollack and the rest of the players found the happy medium in their combine interviews.

And the good Lord willing, things would work out.

On the morning of Saturday, February 19, 2005, one week before the NFL combine, Fred Gibson stepped on a scale. He weighed 196, just three pounds more than when he arrived at the Athletes' Performance training center more than six weeks earlier.

The trainers and nutritionists at Athletes' Performance prided themselves on helping athletes put on weight or take it off, depending on what they needed to perform in the NFL. Though the staff had less than two months between when an athlete arrived and when he needed to depart for the combine, the training and diet program produced dramatic results.

A year earlier, Shawn Andrews showed up weighing 401. By working out and eating properly, the right tackle from the University of Arkansas dropped 35 pounds in a little more than a month before the NFL combine. The Philadelphia Eagles selected him with the sixteenth overall pick.

Most players need to gain weight for the NFL, with its longer season and higher level of competition. Football players at Athletes' Performance consume six meals a day, including at least two protein-rich shakes. Among the facility's sponsors is EAS, the Colorado nutritional supplement manufacturer best known for producing the Myoplex shake powder popularized by the Body-for-Life fitness craze.

Carlos Rogers, the former Auburn cornerback, had gained 7 pounds since arriving at API, becoming such a believer in EAS that his agent Todd France signed a deal with the company to make Rogers an official spokesman. Running back Ronnie Brown, a fellow Auburn teammate and France client, received a similar deal.

Gibson was another story. He was lactose intolerant, which made it difficult to handle many of the shake mixes. He also tended to be a picky eater, even though the training center included an in-house chef and café that most of the players loved.

In college, players have access to special dining halls and world-class training facilities. Blessed with the hummingbird metabolisms of young adulthood, most eat whatever they please, never drawing a connection between what they consume and how it affects energy levels and performance.

"Very few athletic departments have hired sports nutritionists," says Amanda Carlson, the director of nutrition at Athletes' Performance. "College athletes spend all this time in the weight room, which is good, but some of those gains are never realized because of poor nutrition."

At Athletes' Performance, players learned the importance of regulating energy levels and creating an efficient, speedy metabolism by eating roughly every three hours. They're taught to consume a high-protein shake immediately after workouts to jump-start the muscle recovery and repair process. Carlson took some players on a field trip to the supermarket to examine food labels for future reference. At least in Phoenix, they could eat virtually every meal at the training center—as long as their agents picked up the meal option on top of the ten-thousand-dollar training fee.

Gibson, gregarious as always, didn't seem to grasp the magnitude of the training. He enjoyed the camaraderie of being around Brown, Rogers, and Carnell "Cadillac" Williams, and talking shop with Mark Clayton, the Oklahoma wide receiver who became something of a legend at the Senior Bowl when he did not drop a pass in practice all week.

API trainers tried in vain to convince Gibson that he needed to work harder; there were millions of dollars at stake. They wished he could be like Cadillac Williams, who despite consensus first-round status trained like a fringe prospect. "I might not even get drafted," Williams told the trainers, quite seriously.

Gibson shot pool in the player's lounge between workouts, once launching a cue ball through a window, which cost four hundred dollars to repair. The concept of this level of training was new to him. Having played both basketball and football throughout high school and early in his college career, Gibson never underwent a formal off-season football conditioning program.

"Scouts might look at him as not developed, but he does have upside, because there's so much room for improvement," said Darryl Eto, the

API coach who directed the speed and movement portion of the pre-combine training. "He's capable of a lot more physically. The thing that will be a challenge for Fred is seeing the value in strength training and work off the field. He'll go out and run routes and catch balls all day long. He goes beyond the call of duty there. But will that effort translate into working in the weight room or in the classroom in the NFL?"

By 1:00 P.M. on Saturday, the training center was virtually empty. Saturdays are considered "regeneration" days in the Athletes' Performance system, and players undergo just light workouts in the morning before being dismissed until Monday.

The lone football player still training was Chris Canty, just three weeks removed from suffering a detached left retina in the Axis/Radius nightclub in Scottsdale. Since the injury, he had worked out during off hours with physical therapist Darcy Norman, who had been overseeing his knee rehabilitation.

The left eye was bandaged, the area black and swollen. Canty looked like he had sustained a few blows from Mike Tyson. The ghastly appearance was the main reason Canty preferred to train alone, that and not wanting to keep recounting the episode.

He knew he would have to discuss it as many as thirty-two times, depending on how many teams wished to interview him at the combine in Indianapolis. Unlike the rest of the draft hopefuls at Athletes' Performance, Canty would not be flying to the combine.

To stabilize the retina, doctors inserted gas that would dissipate over the next eight weeks. Until then Canty could not fly. If he did, cabin pressure could cause the gas to expand and then things could get really ugly.

Canty did not plan to work out at the combine, but would be there to undergo interviews that now seemed more important than ever, especially with teams wondering if they had to worry about character issues on top of a rehabilitated knee and a detached retina.

Instead of flying, Canty planned to board a train from Tucson in just five days. An uncle would accompany him.

"I know I have to face up to this," Canty said, sitting in the lobby of Athletes' Performance after a brief workout. "I have to go in there and have the confidence to address these questions head-on. You always hear that for a football player the combine is the most important interview of your life. I don't know if I believed that before. I do now. And I've got a long train ride to think about it."

Chapter Thirteen:

INDIANAPOLIS

T here is no event in the NFL calendar that generates as much discussion, debate, and controversy as the weeklong National Invitation Camp, known more commonly as "the combine."

For seven days in late February, more than one thousand NFL coaches, scouts, executives, and even a few owners, descend upon downtown Indianapolis and fan out among the Westin, Hyatt, and Marriott hotels. A number of shrewd scouts, like their fellow Marriott point-collectors in the press room, book the hotel months in advance.

Indianapolis is a miserable place to be in late February, which is one of two reasons the city has served as an effective site for the event since 1987. Nobody cares that they're cooped up inside for a week; it's not like they'd be playing golf.

The other reason is that the RCA Dome, home of the NFL's Colts, provides a climate-controlled atmosphere for testing, and is attached to the Indianapolis Convention Center, an upscale shopping mall; and all three hotels connect by a labyrinth of indoor walkways. It's possible to go days without venturing outside, though many NFL officials find time to enjoy several popular restaurants.

The combine is an outgrowth of an earlier era when teams pooled information in the interests of saving money on travel and scouting departments. Just as combines such as BLESTO and National Football Scouting continue to provide subscriber teams with information that becomes the basis for their yearlong evaluations, the midwinter workout gives clubs another look at draft-eligible talent.

These days, teams spend enough manpower and resources on data collection to make the CIA envious. BLESTO and National serve a more modest role as an initial rating of draft-eligible talent. By the time teams gather in Indianapolis, they have spent thousands of man-hours on background checks, film evaluation, attending practices and games, and debating the merits of players.

The combine still serves a valuable purpose. Players undergo drug tests and thorough physicals. Drills such as the forty-yard dash, vertical and broad jumps, and shuttle runs, provide standardized "measurables" of speed, quickness, and strength, albeit not necessarily directly applicable to football. Given the preparation most players undergo in the seven weeks leading up to the combine, the tests arguably are as much a measure of the effectiveness of the trainers as of a player's athleticism.

"This is the president's physical fitness workout," said New York Jets head coach Herman Edwards, a former NFL cornerback. "When I was playing, I never worried about a guy that ran a 4.4 forty, if I watched the film and saw that he had 5.2 hands. Coach would say, 'What are you going to do if he runs by you?' I said, 'I won't worry about it too much, Coach, because he can't catch. I'll handle that guy all day.'"

Players do go through some football-related drills, though they're often overshadowed by the seven measured tests. In either case, teams know better than to fall in love with a workout warrior or dismiss someone who performs poorly.

The 2005 combine marked the tenth anniversary of Mike Mamula's legendary workout, and the former Philadelphia Eagle still served as a cautionary tale. On the other side were players like Ben Roethlisberger, who in 2004 looked less than impressive during quarterback drills in Indy. His passes lacked zip and he didn't appear to have the arm strength scouts coveted. Roethlisberger, from Miami of Ohio, lasted until the eleventh pick, behind Eli Manning and Philip Rivers, and proceeded to lead the Pittsburgh Steelers to a 15-1 record and the AFC title game.

If players needed another reminder of someone who overcame a poor combine, they only had to visit the set of the NFL Network, which was televising the 2005 event. Former Denver Broncos star running back Terrell Davis, a sixth-round pick out of Georgia in 1995, was serving as the cohost of the network's daily combine wrap-up show.

Then there was Tom Brady, a visible reminder that exhaustive scouting reports, and where a player is drafted, often mean little when it comes to predicting success. In 2000, the New England Patriots selected the Michigan quarterback in the sixth round, with the 199th overall pick.

The Patriots, winners of three Super Bowls in four years, were held up as the gold standard for building for the draft, though the Brady selection was mostly luck.

Rich McKay, the Falcons general manager, preached to his troops the importance of emulating the New England Patriots, along with perennial contenders the Philadelphia Eagles, by remaining committed to players. The Falcons arrived at the combine having narrowed their universe of draftable players to 225. Between the combine, the March pro day schedule, and three weeks of meetings in April, they would whittle the field to less than a hundred.

"The one thing the Patriots and Eagles do very well is stay committed to the players they draft," McKay said. "When they show up, players don't always look exactly the way they were projected to look. Maybe they're not quite as fast, or quite as quick, or pick up the scheme quite as fast, and I think, as an organization, those are two that have had a lot of success because they have stayed committed to it."

The combine is a blur for the players. With 332 invited to Indianapolis, they're staggered over the course of a seven-day period, with each group staying three nights. Offensive linemen and kickers, along with about half of the running backs, were the first to arrive on the evening of Wednesday, February 23. The players were given identical gray sweats, with either OL, RB, or PK on the left breast, along with a number. That number and the player's name also were on the back.

As usual, there were players who would not work out. Some, such as Virginia guard Elton Brown, Florida State tackle Ray Willis, and tackle Rob Petitti of Pittsburgh, were nursing lingering injuries. A few others, most notably Texas running back Cedric Benson and Michigan wide receiver Braylon Edwards, planned to just undergo physicals and submit to interviews.

Agent Drew Rosenhaus advised much of his contingent not to undergo full workouts, a group that included lineman Chris Myers from Miami, Oklahoma defensive end Dan Cody, and Vernand Morency, a running back from Oklahoma State. Roscoe Parrish, a wide receiver from Miami, planned to do everything.

Rosenhaus was among the agents who told their clients they'd be better off limiting their workouts to their pro timing days—better known as pro days back on their college campuses—where there would be less pressure and a more comfortable environment. Many players, especially those from Florida schools, were convinced—at least by their agents—that they were better off working out in the Sunshine State than indoors at the RCA Dome.

This kind of thinking drove team officials crazy. At the combine players had an audience of every decision-maker in the league. Every general manager and head coach showed up, along with dozens of scouts, assistant coaches, and executives from every front office. Many owners flew in to sit in on the interview portions or watch from the stands. Rarely did a college pro day attract more than one hundred scouts. They were an important part of the process, to be sure, but why not look at the pro day as a makeup exam for a poor combine performance? If they aced the combine, they could sit out some or all of the pro day.

"I don't see why anyone would come down here and not do all the drills," said Charlie Frye, the quarterback from Akron. "That's what we're here for, right?"

Agents made some compelling arguments to sit out. At the combine, players are put through a nonstop schedule of physicals, interviews, and tests. Sleep and eating habits get disrupted. It's hardly the formula for an ideal workout, especially if a player is suffering the effects of a lingering injury.

When each group of players arrived at the combine, one general manager addressed the group. Without mentioning agents by name, they implored the players not to listen to those telling them to sit out the combine.

Charley Casserly, general manager of the Houston Texans, drew the duty the first night. He didn't have to worry about punters and kickers skipping drills—they had a limited slate as it was—and he knew offensive linemen were less likely than running backs or wide receivers to be prima donnas. But he, along with his counterparts on other nights, made it a point to give the address every evening, regardless of position.

"This is like a job interview," Casserly said. "You have guys you grew up [with] and guys you went to college with and what are they doing? They're trying to find a job. So what are you trying to do? You're trying to find a job. You're auditioning for a job over the next couple of months. So let's start off there. Number one, be on time. Be honest with people.

When they ask you to do things, do them, okay? You're going to be pulled a million different ways during this combine and it's going to be tough on you, but think of it as a job interview.

"You're going to be told things like, 'Don't work out at the combine. It's not a good environment for you to work out in. It's not a good surface to run on.' I disagree and so do the general managers in the league on those points. Number one, you should work out. First of all, the surface? The surface is fast, men. It's an AstroTurf surface, indoors. Now, at the end of the day, when we're sitting in the draft room, we take your best performance in each individual category. We take your best time, your best jump, your tallest height if you will, your best weight. So the more times you do something, the more chances you have to do your best. If you don't work out here, some of us are never going to see you work out. But more importantly, head coaches aren't going to see you work out. Position coaches may not see you work out. So what you're doing, you're cutting your window down by not working out here. Number one, you're only giving yourself one workout and number two, you're limiting the number of people who are going to see you who are going to make the decisions on your career. That's what it comes down to, men. It's a dollars-and-cents thing. I can't be any more blunt than that about it.

"Don't pay attention to all these predictions about where you're going to be drafted. Men, we haven't finished our draft ratings. We have a rough draft board like everybody else in the NFL, but we don't have your physical. Some of you we don't have a time on. So, what we're saying is that none of this stuff you read in the paper is accurate. Because the people writing it don't make those draft decisions. So, conversely, don't get your hopes up or get deflated by draft predictions. Finishing up now, what are the points here that you want to come out of this with? Number one, it doesn't make any difference where you get drafted. Every one of you in this room has a chance to be Tom Brady. Don't worry about where you're drafted. This is a job interview process you're going through over the next couple of months. So be cooperative, be honest in the process. The next thing here we have is the combine. Work out and give yourself the best chance to get drafted, and make the money I talked about by giving yourself the best workouts. Why? Because we take the best workout. If you only work out once, maybe you're the guy who gets hurt in the warm-up, doesn't work out, and drops in the draft. It happened last year. It's going to happen this year, because somebody is going to make that mistake again. Don't you make that mistake."

When Casserly was through, the players were taken to Methodist Hospital for preliminary medical evaluations. Few players make it through college football careers without a significant injury, and it was the job of the doctors to address every concern, no matter how far removed from the injury the player was.

Chris Spencer, the lineman from Ole Miss who had been working out at IMG's training center in Florida, found doctors spending time on a wrist he had broken in the fourth grade.

"It happened so long ago, I didn't even remember," Spencer said. "I think I was playing football when it happened, but I'm not sure. I guess these background checks turn up everything."

The following morning, the players were awakened at 5:30 for urine tests. The league tests players for both recreational and performance-enhancing drugs. The league would send out letters to anyone that tested positive in April. (Two Wisconsin players, offensive guard Jonathan Clinkscale and defensive tackle Anttaj Hawthorne—the target of the Jack Scharf vs. IMG recruiting battle—tested positive for marijuana use.)

From there, it was off to the bowels of the RCA Dome for more extensive physical exams. Players with lingering medical issues could be sent back to Methodist Hospital for more X-rays or an MRI. After that, they were paraded in shorts and socks into an auditorium, a reenactment of the Senior Bowl weigh-in for those who were there. Unlike that event, where arm length and hand size numbers were provided beforehand, the measurement is taken at the combine.

The next two days go quickly. Players are brought to the press room in the Indiana Convention Center to answer questions from the media for fifteen minutes apiece. Maurice Clarett and Mike Williams drew the biggest audiences, with the media curious about how the two failed challengers to the NFL's underclassmen rule would fare at the combine.

The players spend their second and third evenings shuttling between hotel rooms on one floor of the Crown Plaza Hotel, interviewing with teams in fifteen-minute increments.

Then there's the bench press. NFL Network officials, televising the event extensively for the first time in 2005, quickly realized the bench press was riveting programming, especially with John Lott, the newly named strength and conditioning coach of the Cleveland Browns, running the show.

Before each group benched, Lott gathered them in a circle and implored them in his Texas twang to put on a show for the assembled scouts.

"Running backs, I'm going to hype you up today," he said. "You get off today on the bench press. After this, you don't have to lift a weight the rest of the spring, as far as the bench press. You concentrate on the skills and drills you have to do. Push yourself today. Talk to each other. Don't sit up there like some stinkin' mannequins. You've got one chance on this thing. Keep your elbows up and your head down and let's work. Every strength coach in the NFL is over there right now, every running backs coach, several coordinators, several head coaches and GMs—a lot of strong people over there right now. Fellas, it's first impression and it's a big impression. Get your stinkin' minds right and let's do this thing, all right?"

Finally, on the fourth day, the players take the field at the RCA Dome. Even with hundreds of NFL employees in the stands, the dome seems empty. It's quiet, except for when a player's name is announced or when he begins his forty-yard dash.

The forty is the first order of business. Each player runs twice. After that, he undergoes on-field, position-specific drills. Wide receivers catch balls, quarterbacks throw. Defenders run through simulated game situations. From there, it's back to the sidelines to complete the broad jump and vertical jump, followed by the three-cone and shuttle runs.

Then there's the Wonderlic, the twelve-minute, fifty-question test that measures cognitive ability and—depending on your vantage point—success or failure in the NFL.

More than 130 million people have taken a version of the Wonderlic Personnel Test (WPT). Developed in 1937 as a tool to measure the mental abilities of potential job candidates, it became part of the NFL scouting process in the mid-1970s. Tom Landry, the longtime head coach of the Dallas Cowboys, believed there was a correlation between cognitive ability and how a player processed data to performance on the field.

According to Wonderlic Consulting, the Libertyville, Illinois, publisher of the test, cognitive ability, or general intelligence, is the single greatest predictor of job success in any position. The Wonderlic provides employers with "quantifiable data about whether candidates can learn new skills, think effectively, and make important decisions under pressure."

NFL teams want players with such traits, though in the modern era of exhaustive scouting, where no stone is left unturned, few teams rely exclusively on the Wonderlic to gauge a player's ability to learn, let alone predict his future importance.

After all, the college football ranks are full of star players who, coming out of high school, struggled to post the requisite score on the Scholastic Aptitude Test (SAT) to be eligible to play. Many players who scored below the average NFL Wonderlic score of 19–20 went on to stellar NFL careers.

Dan Marino, for instance, posted a mere sixteen. Randall Cunningham scored just fifteen. Both showed exceptional abilities to quickly process information while performing the role of NFL quarterback, arguably the most stressful job in sports.

Brett Favre and Tim Couch both scored twenty-two. Favre, a second-round pick in the 1991 draft, is considered one of the smartest quarterbacks ever. The oft-injured Couch, the first selection in 1999, is viewed as one of the biggest busts of all time.

It's difficult to make sweeping generalizations about the Wonderlic, but one rule of thumb is that the closer a player is to the ball, the higher his score will be, or at least should be. Quarterbacks and offensive linemen will score higher than wide receivers. There does seem to be a correlation between academic intelligence and a high Wonderlic score. Pat McInally, a receiver/punter from Harvard, scored a perfect fifty in 1976. Players from prestigious academic schools often are among the high scorers.

Many of the questions are not especially difficult, but the challenge is to complete the exam in the allotted twelve minutes. In that sense, it mimics the NFL, where players must digest complex schemes, lengthy playbooks, and react quickly on the field.

Here are a few examples of Wonderlic questions, directly from the company's Web site:

1. When rope is selling for $.10 a foot, how many feet can you buy for sixty cents?

2. Assume the first two statements are true. Is the final one:
   1=True   2=False   3=Uncertain

   The boy plays baseball.
   All baseball players wear hats.
   The boy wears a hat.

3. Paper sells for 21 cents per pad. What will four pads cost?

4. How many of the five pairs of items listed below are exact duplicates?

Nieman, K. M.	Neiman, K. M.
Thomas, G. K.	Thomas, C. K.
Hoff, J. P.	Hoff, J. P.
Pino, L. R.	Pina, L. R.
Warner, T. S.	Wanner, T. S.

5. RESENT–RESERVE
   Do these words:

   1. have similar meanings?
   2. have contradictory meanings?
   3. mean neither the same nor opposite?

Answers:
   1. 6 feet
   2. True
   3. 84 cents
   4. 1
   5. 3

In addition to the Wonderlic, some NFL teams distribute their own questionnaires and psychological exams. The most notorious is the three hundred-plus question test given by the New York Giants, which includes the question, "If you were a cat or dog, which would you be?"

"I'm definitely more of a dog person," said David Greene, the Georgia quarterback.

Some questionnaires ask about a player's family history of heart disease or cancer. Others ask for the parents' height and weight; teams figure some players might still be growing.

"I thought it was kind of personal to ask how much your mom weighs," said Chris Myers, the offensive lineman from Miami. "I didn't want to disrespect my mom, so I left that question blank."

As for the Wonderlic, it's viewed by most teams the way they weigh the rest of the combine: a valuable exercise, but just part of a yearlong evaluation. In Atlanta, Rich McKay advises his scouting staff to include questions about how a player learns and processes information in every interview, and to seek out academic advisors and tutors as part of the background check.

"We don't consider the Wonderlic important at all," McKay said. "It's a marker to look at this issue in case it's there. But when you go back with guys with lower test scores and talk to coaches, you ask, 'How does he learn football? Is he a slow learner? What are the issues, if any?' We've never eliminated a guy because he was low or high. I don't know if it's even a tiebreaker. It's more of a red flag to make sure we've checked this guy out as much as we possibly can. More often than not, it's not a reference of how he learns."

"The Wonderlic is just another indicator," says Scott Pioli, general manager of the New England Patriots. "A guy isn't going to succeed or fail with us on the Wonderlic test. The range of socioeconomic backgrounds is so vast, and there are certain players from different parts of the country who, because of their backgrounds, may not test well. Maybe they have a learning disability or they just don't test well. The reason we have the interviews is because we want to spend time with players to find out if they get it or not. If you spend time with a person and ask the right questions, and you have a good feel for those kinds of things, you can figure out if a guy is smart enough for your system."

While most of the Atlanta Falcons contingent was settling in at the Indianapolis Marriott on Wednesday, February 23, 2005, Tim Ruskell was in Kirkland, Washington, being introduced as the new president of football operations of the Seattle Seahawks.

It had been a whirlwind few days for the Falcons' former assistant general manager. The Seahawks executive search committee called a week earlier. McKay, the Falcons general manager, gave the Seahawks not only permission to speak to Ruskell but also a hearty endorsement on his behalf.

Ruskell declined the overtures at first, telling the committee he did not want to talk until after the draft. If that meant he lost out on the job, fine. A year earlier, he left the Tampa Bay Buccaneers in mid-January to reunite with McKay in Atlanta. Changing teams so late in the draft preparation process was the toughest thing he ever did in his career.

Now the Seahawks were asking him to do it again, a month closer to the draft, and this time he wasn't going to be reunited with his closest friend in the game. He felt like he would be abandoning the Falcons at a crucial point in the draft preparation process. Not only that, Seattle's front office was in utter disarray.

More than a month had passed since the Seahawks had fired Bob Whitsitt, the team president. In that time, the general manager, vice president of football operations, and director of college scouting had departed. Head coach Mike Holmgren, who clashed with Whitsitt and once wore the dual title of head coach/general manager, remained, along with the scouts.

The Seahawks were persistent and called again. Ruskell was torn, and he turned to McKay for input. "I don't want you to be three months down the road feeling sorry that you didn't investigate it," McKay told him. "There's the money and security and the opportunity, but you've got to make that call."

Ruskell, forty-eight, soon realized it was time to leave. *Pro Football Weekly* recently had run a list of up-and-coming general manager candidates and tacked Ruskell's name at the end, noting that people throughout the league figured the accomplished talent evaluator would have such a position by now.

Steve Spurrier, during his brief tenure as Redskins head coach, had recommended the man he once knew as a Buccaneers ball boy to become GM. Ruskell had interviewed for several GM positions. Between the success of the McKay regime in Tampa and Atlanta, the phones were ringing more often.

Seattle was a good fit, with a team comparable to the Falcons roster McKay had taken over, not a rebuilding process but one in need of some minor repairs. Before the 2004 season, the Seahawks were a popular pick to reach the Super Bowl. But they finished a modest 9-7 and lost at home in the first round of the playoffs to the St. Louis Rams.

The move itself would not be a problem. As a kid, with a father in the military, Ruskell relocated every two years. He wanted his nine-year-old daughter and five-year-old son to be able to put down roots. The older they got, the tougher a move would be.

Negotiations proceeded quickly. Ruskell spoke several times on the telephone to Tod Leiweke, the team's CEO, and then met with Paul Allen, the billionaire cofounder of Microsoft who had taken a hands-off approach to running the Seahawks in his seven years as owner.

Speaking to reporters in Kirkland, Allen said, "It's safe to say that Tim has a strong and successful background in recognizing and securing talent, and communicating and motivating as a football executive."

Ruskell pledged to reunite the Seahawks front office.

"One of the keys is unifying," Ruskell said. "People working together where there are no walls, no agendas, and everybody's got a common focus on the goal, and that's winning. The answer is within. I know how it can go south when it's dysfunctional. What I'm hearing is we can do better."

For the first time in more than a decade, Ruskell would draft without McKay. They would not have their usual "popcorn night," where they would kick back and watch interview tapes of players from the combine. They would have to be guarded in their conversations, at least regarding the draft. On the flip side, Ruskell would have final say on draft picks.

In the past, when McKay and Ruskell would debate the merits of players before the draft, Ruskell sometimes would stop before wasting too much verbal energy. "I'm not going to say anything more," Ruskell would say. "I know one thing. You're never going to draft this guy."

Not that there were big disagreements. Having run their character-based draft evaluation for so long with an emphasis on background checks and interviews, they often came to the same conclusions on players. Now Ruskell would take that same system across the country.

He also would take an intimate knowledge of what the Falcons intended to do during the 2005 draft, although much of the final evaluation of players remained to be determined between the combine and during March, as players worked out one last time during campus pro days. Ruskell knew the Falcons' draft strategies to this point, knowledge that might be valuable, since the Seahawks drafted four picks before Atlanta. The information figured to be only so useful, since the teams had different needs and schemes.

If nothing else, Ruskell's anonymity was blown. Seattle sportswriters portrayed him as a hardworking mystery man operating in the shadows of the high-profile Rich McKay: son of John, team turnaround specialist, and future commissioner candidate. That soon would change for Ruskell, with much of the success or failure of an NFL club resting on his shoulders.

"This is a dream and a culmination of years of hard work," Ruskell told reporters in Kirkland. "Who would have thought twenty years ago that a struggling scout working in Saskatchewan would twenty years later be named to help run an NFL team?"

By Saturday, February 26, 2005, the lower level of the Indiana Convention Center was packed. In the hallways, NFL officials passed young girls attending a cheerleading convention, as well as those on hand for a gathering of the Indiana Association of Home Educators, as they shuttled between the RCA Dome, the press room, and their hotels. For some reason, a large number of Amish folks also were on hand, though the autograph hound contingent was modest. The main exhibit hall, adjacent to the RCA Dome and across from the press room, was set up in a country fair theme for the homeschooling crowd. Men wore stickers that read MY WIFE HOMESCHOOLS AND SHE'S MY HERO.

In the midst of the chaos, NFL Radio has set up a broadcasting center. The station, launched on the Sirius satellite radio network late in 2003, already has developed a huge following among NFL personnel, especially scouts driving hundreds of miles on fall weekends. Unlike Super Bowl week, where dozens of all-sports stations compete for guests wandering along "radio row," NFL Radio producers have no problem grabbing dignitaries for a few minutes of on-air chat.

In another room, there's a fitness industry trade show related to the combine. There are gym equipment suppliers, nutritional supplement manufacturers, and even Athletes' Performance, the precombine training center. Representatives of EAS, the Colorado-based maker of meal-replacement powders and protein drinks, hand out free samples. Already EAS displays advertising featuring former Auburn running back Ronnie Brown and cornerback Carlos Rogers, the top draft prospects represented by agent Todd France.

The media is confined to a large rectangular ballroom, which was assembled by opening the doors of four conference rooms. Unlike the Senior Bowl, where press coverage was modest and access virtually unlimited, a large contingent of reporters is kept at bay. Though the entrance to the RCA Dome is only a few hundred feet away, blue curtains block the view. Security people stand alongside signs that read CREDENTIALS ONLY.

The NFL's public relations staff brings a steady stream of players, head coaches, and general managers to the room for press conference–style interviews. The players wear numbered jerseys underneath their gray sweats, assigned by positions. Offensive linemen and running backs wear red, tight ends navy. Defensive linemen, quarterbacks, and wide receivers wear white.

The players stand on podiums at either end of the room. With so many players and more than two hundred credentialed media, the questions tend to be basic. Having undergone mock interviews at their training centers, the players know what to say, most answering in detached monotones. Everyone is willing to play whatever position or role an NFL team requests. Nobody has a preference of which team drafts them. Everyone is confident in their ability, but realizes they have a lot to learn.

Fred Gibson, the Georgia wide receiver, rolled in not long after weighing in (again) at 196 pounds. After seven weeks at Athletes' Performance, he had yet to put on more than three pounds. He strode to the podium and fielded questions.

Q: Who's the best cornerback you faced?
A: I'd have to say Carlos Rogers from Auburn. He has the speed. He's very strong in the upper body, just has the total package. He's the only defensive back that gave me a challenge.

Q: Did you have a lot of offers to play college basketball?
A: Yes, a lot of SEC schools: Florida, Georgia, Tennessee. I didn't start playing football until the eleventh grade. You find so many tall shooting guards in the NBA. You don't see too many six-four wide receivers in the NFL.

Q: Could you have been a NBA player?
A: I think so, if I would have dedicated myself and worked hard. I haven't played in two years. I kind of miss it, but football is my future now.

Q: Who do you compare yourself to?
A: I'd have to say Randy Moss. He goes deep, gets the deep ball, and I do the same things.

The oddest sight, aside from Bill Parcells weaving between reporters, the Amish, and prepubescent cheerleaders, is Gil Brandt, the former Dallas Cowboys personnel guru, cast as an NFL public relations staffer. Brandt spends much of the combine shuttling players between the dome and the press room, introducing the players to the media, and telling war stories to the many reporters who approach him. It's a role that would seem beneath the pioneer of NFL scouting and one of the architects of the Cowboys' early success, but Brandt embraces it, writing insightful columns for NFL.com and serving as all-around goodwill ambassador for the combine.

Though the combine is an NFL event, it's actually run by National Football Scouting, which at times creates some strange tensions. "National" is made up of NFL franchises, but the NFL has little control over the affair. Even the new NFL television network, a wholly owned subsidiary of the NFL, had to lobby for the right to televise portions of the workout. The 2005 combine marked the first time any portion of the event was televised live, and NFL officials credited the network for the large percentage of players that worked out.

For reporters who have traveled to Indianapolis to be confined to the press room, the lack of access is frustrating. They're reduced to watching the combine unfold on the NFL Network (in the press room—if not in their hotel rooms during the first two days of the combine, when the network broadcasts only a nightly wrap-up show) and that didn't always produce accurate reporting.

On Saturday, the combine finally moved to the RCA Dome field. The group that arrived Wednesday night, having completed their interviews with teams and the media, their medical tests, Wonderlics, and bench presses, would compete first.

Ronnie Brown and Maurice Clarett were among the first running backs to run the forty-yard dash. Clarett, who had unsuccessfully sued to enter the NFL Draft after his freshman year at Ohio State, was in the unusual position of attending his second combine, having not played in more than two years.

Clarett had become something of a pariah in college and pro football circles, not only for his defiant stance against the league and its draft eligibility rule but also for claiming in an interview with *ESPN the Magazine* that he had been given cash and grades he did not earn while enrolled at Ohio State, allegations the university denied. It didn't help that a year earlier, before a court ruled against him, he had come to the combine with a chip on his shoulder. By any measuring stick, NFL teams viewed Clarett as a major character risk.

Brown was among the first to run, clocking in at an eye-popping 4.32, at least according to the NFL Network. Clarett, running moments later, managed only a 4.82.

Or did he? The media soon learned that they were not watching *reality* television. An NFL Network official took the podium to announce that its times were unofficial. Later, the NFL released the official top five times among the group, and Brown's 4.48 ranked second, behind J. J. Arrington of California. In the interest of not embarrassing Clarett, or other low performers, the league did not reveal the other times. (Clarett ran a 4.78.)

Todd France, Brown's agent, could not have been more thrilled. The decision to hold Brown out of the Senior Bowl in favor of another week of precombine training looked like a wise one. With Cedric Benson opting to postpone his workout until his University of Texas pro day, Brown had managed to separate himself from the rest of the running back pack. Even Carnell "Cadillac" Williams, his former Auburn backfield mate, was now clearly behind him.

"Ronnie took the extra week to train, and look what happened," France said. "He's blown up the combine. There's no question that he's the top back in this year's draft. If anyone had any doubts, he eliminated them today."

Chris Canty almost missed the combine.

While the rest of his fellow NFL hopefuls at the Athletes' Performance training center took flights from Phoenix to Indianapolis, Canty and his uncle, Kenya Lee, drove to Tucson and boarded a train. A long delay caused them to miss their scheduled connector, so they got off in San Antonio, spent the night, and then got on another train to St. Louis, where they rented a car and drove to Indianapolis, arriving twenty-four hours behind schedule.

Canty showed up too late for physicals, but was able to interview with teams and take the Wonderlic test, which was all he had planned to do anyway given the condition of his knee—which, though much improved, was still not 100 percent. Canty scored a thirty-four on the Wonderlic, tops among defensive ends, and part of a strong showing by the University of Virginia. Heath Miller's thirty-nine was highest among tight ends and third overall. Alvin Pearman tied for the best running back score with twenty-six. (Virginia guard Elton Brown and linebacker Darryl Blackstock, however, managed only a thirteen and sixteen, respectively.)

Canty interviewed with nineteen teams in the Crown Plaza hotel over Saturday and Sunday nights. Like the rest of the players, he collected a bag of team logo goodies. The Seahawks, his first interview, gave leather briefcases. The Redskins and Rams handed out T-shirts, the Denver Broncos ski caps. The Falcons gave out a combination of ball caps and shirts.

"I hate the giveaways," Falcons president Rich McKay said. "It's ridiculous. It's not like we're recruiting them. We get to draft them."

Interviews were held each evening between six and eleven at the Crown Plaza, originally part of the nation's first "Union Station." Some rooms are converted from Pullman train cars, and the décor pays tribute to early 1900s figures such as Charlie Chaplin and Amelia Earhart. The

Pullman Restaurant, a small eatery and bar, is the only part of the facility not cordoned off for the week. Agents spend much of their time hanging out at the bar, waiting for updates from their clients.

NFL teams are assigned rooms on the first floor, with their logos placed in the window to the hallway. Players receive a spreadsheet of their meeting schedule, usually scheduled over two nights, and shuttle between rooms in fifteen-minute increments. A warning horn blows when there's one minute remaining and again when it's time to switch rooms.

Canty, trying not to appear self-conscious about the eye, addressed the issue head-on, providing copies of the police report and stressing that he did file charges. He also distributed copies of an eye report from a retina specialist in Arizona and a DVD from Athletes' Performance that showed him running and jumping.

Teams were willing to overlook Canty's poor judgment in heading to a nightclub in the midst of combine training; his otherwise impeccable character trumped one bad decision. But the eye, on top of the ailing knee and a history of injuries, gave some cause for concern.

You're never healthy. What's going on?

"I really don't have an answer for that," Canty told teams. "I'm a tough player. I play through injuries. I've had a lot of adversity and I've overcome it. If I do get hurt, it's only temporary, and I'll overcome the injury and I'm going to play. After every injury, I've come back stronger and a better player, and that's not just me talking. You can look at the tape. I'll always be a hard worker; it's been instilled in me and that's what I'll continue to do."

Canty could tell Al Groh and his Virginia staff had put in a good word for him. Teams that employed former Groh colleagues—Miami, Cleveland, New England—seemed to know everything about Canty. Four other teams—Houston, Jacksonville, Washington, and the Jets—employed assistant coaches who served on Groh's staff during Canty's time at Virginia. The Dallas Cowboys and Groh mentor Bill Parcells did not interview him in Indianapolis, but the team planned to fly Canty to Dallas before the draft.

The well-traveled Groh's sphere of influence had widened since the end of the 2004 NFL season. Already, he had former colleagues serving as head coaches in Dallas, New England (Bill Belichick), and New York (the Giants Tom Coughlin). The league's three new head coaches—Miami's Nick Saban, Cleveland's Romeo Crennel, and San Francisco's Mike Nolan—also had worked with Groh.

Bill Musgrave, Groh's offensive coordinator in 2001–2002, recently had left Jacksonville to join Joe Gibbs's staff in Washington. The Houston Texans had hired Groh's defensive line coach, Mike London, who became the fourth Groh assistant to join the NFL in three years.

"If you ever didn't buy into the way Coach Groh harps on the NFL experience of his coaching staff," said Miller, who bumped into Canty for the first time in more than three months at the combine, "you definitely realize it when you're at the combine."

Canty and the rest of the players shuffled between hotel rooms for two evenings. Upon arriving, they were given a schedule of interviews and times. Before 2003, NFL teams grabbed players as they could, much like at the Senior Bowl. To bring some order to the process, teams were asked to submit a list of no more than sixty players.

With 332 players, that does not sound like much, but teams already had interviewed many players at the Senior Bowl and other all-star games. The Falcons, for instance, had spoken extensively with wide receivers Roddy White and Fred Gibson at the Senior Bowl, and reserved combine slots for players like Canty and Georgia defensive end David Pollack, neither of whom they had interviewed. They also interviewed Miller and almost every junior of interest, since none had played in all-star games.

Besides quarterback, the last thing the Falcons needed was a tight end; Alge Crumpler had emerged as one of the league's best in 2004. But the Falcons did not want to dismiss Miller, whom they regarded as an intelligent, high-character player, the best tight end in the draft, and a perfect fit for their West Coast offense, having played it at Virginia. Matt Schaub, the Falcons backup quarterback who came out of Virginia the previous year, had shown Miller his playbook before his first minicamp. They figured more than 70 percent of the plays were run at Virginia.

The Falcons believed there was little downside to spending fifteen minutes chatting with Miller, a player who could play for them down the road. Miller, well-coached for the combine interview by IMG's Steve Shenbaum, was up for playing anywhere.

The interview process was more relaxed than Canty expected. The Falcons contingent, which included Rich McKay, head coach Jim Mora, scouting director Phil Emery, and a rotating cast of scouts and coaches, was eating pizza when he walked into the room. The Falcons ate pizza most evenings, and McKay believed it lightened the mood of the room. They even offered players a slice, which presented a quandary. No interview coach had addressed that situation.

Am I rude if I decline? I don't want to talk with my mouth full. Do they want to see how healthy I eat?

Canty turned down the pizza. Like most teams, the Falcons spent the first five minutes asking about the knee and the eye before querying him about schemes and fits. Canty, like every player, was willing to play wherever. If that meant bulking up twenty pounds and moving to defensive tackle, he was ready to do it. Having played the 3-4 defense (three down lineman, four linebackers) under Groh, Canty felt confident he could make an easy transition to the NFL, where an increasing number of teams played the scheme. He also, of course, told teams he would welcome the chance to play in the 4-3.

The Falcons had scrapped the 3-4 defense in favor of the 4-3 before the 2004 season, which had helped another former Virginia defensive end, Patrick Kerney. Instead of facing double teams each play, Kerney was freed up and recorded thirteen of the Falcons' league-high forty-eight sacks.

For the Falcons, Canty was not what teams call a great "scheme fit." Still, he was a tall, strong defensive end, and such players could fit any scheme to some degree. McKay liked what he saw on film, mostly from the 2003 season, since Canty was injured so early in 2004. If nothing else, he passed the Falcons' character filters—no small accomplishment.

"He's a nice kid," McKay said. "What happened off the field (in Scottsdale) is not an issue for us. Nobody says it was his fault. But the issue with the eye and the knee, those are serious things to consider. It's a shame. Without those, he doesn't last beyond the end of the first round."

If there were a Mike Mamula Award for the most unlikely, eye-popping performance at the 2005 combine, it would have gone to Matt Jones, the former University of Arkansas quarterback who posted a 4.40 mark in the forty-yard dash.

That's a great time for any player, let alone a six-six, 242-pound player without a position. Lacking the traditional bazooka arm, he didn't figure to play quarterback in the NFL. Some teams saw him as a wide receiver, others a tight end. A few projected him as a quarterback/receiver in the mold of Kordell Stewart, who had played the dual role for the Pittsburgh Steelers.

Jones, who had shot up the draft boards, wasn't the only player to earn money at the combine. Georgia defensive end David Pollack made his first appearance in front of NFL scouts since the Outback Bowl on New Year's Day a memorable one. Using Michael Johnson's gunslinger, arm-pumping technique, he completed the forty in 4.75 seconds, among the lowest times for defensive ends. He posted the best mark in the twenty-yard shuttle (3.94 seconds) at his position and scored a solid thirty on the Wonderlic. To nobody's surprise, he came across as confident and engaging in the interview rooms, expressing an interest in playing either linebacker or defensive end in the NFL.

"I had a great combine," Pollack said. "Nothing here surprised me at all."

Fred Gibson, Pollack's Georgia teammate, did little to distinguish himself in Indianapolis. He reached 38½ inches in the vertical leap, among the higher marks among wide receivers. But Reggie Brown led the field with a 41½ inch leap, further distancing himself from his former Georgia teammate. Gibson ran just a 4.55 in the forty, a slower time than twenty-one other receivers. That was significant, since scouts weighed the forty most prominently for wide receivers, because breakaway speed was a crucial trait at the position.

Gibson scored a nineteen on the Wonderlic, about average among receivers. After the forty, his most disappointing number was 196. Despite seven weeks on the weight-gain diet at Athletes' Performance, Gibson added just three pounds.

"I can't help it that I'm lactose intolerant," Gibson said. "I'm not able to put away protein shakes like everyone else."

David Greene put up solid, if unspectacular, numbers at the combine. The most puzzling one was his Wonderlic score (nineteen). With agent Pat Dye Jr. touting Greene's leadership and intelligence, trying to downplay his lack of athleticism, Greene's score was noticeable, especially considering that scouts tend to weigh the Wonderlic more heavily with quarterbacks. Top prospects Alex Smith, Aaron Rodgers, and Charlie Frye scored thirty-five or higher.

"I just didn't take it seriously enough," said Greene, who won an eighteen-thousand-dollar, post-graduate scholarship as the NCAA's National Scholar Athlete. "I'm not going to say I didn't try. I did, but I didn't prepare for it the way I should have."

"There's nobody around here that's going to question David Greene's intelligence," Dye said.

Darryl Blackstock's Wonderlic score (sixteen) was second-lowest among outside linebackers, which perhaps was not surprising for a player who struggled academically at Virginia. Still, scouts enjoyed their first postseason look at the pass-rushing specialist. Blackstock ran a pedestrian forty (4.70) but recorded a thirty-nine-inch vertical leap and twenty-five repetitions on the bench. Blackstock came across as engaging in interviews, though several of Al Groh's former NFL cronies challenged him about reneging on a promise to Groh to return for a senior year.

Blackstock never made such a pledge but spoke highly of Groh, while emphasizing his desire to play at the next level and provide for his young son.

Florida State's Ray Willis tipped the scales in Indianapolis at 327 pounds, third-heaviest among offensive tackles. Still hampered by the ankle injury suffered in November, Willis opted not to work out, though he bench-pressed 225 pounds a respectable twenty-seven times and scored a twenty-four on the Wonderlic.

Having arrived with the first group of players on the first day of the combine, Willis was able to leave on Saturday, February 26. That gave him just two and a half weeks to further rehabilitate his ankle and prove to NFL scouts that he was recovered.

Willis planned to return to Atlanta and train with Chip Smith. For guys like Pollack and Ronnie Brown who dominated the combine, the individual March workouts back on campus were meaningless. They'd sit out the bulk of those, standing by their combine performances, and perhaps undergoing position drills.

For Willis, the date of March 15, 2005, was the most important one on his calendar. On that day in Tallahassee he'd have to run forty yards and undergo the rest of the tests. He did not have the option of sitting out his pro day.

Chapter Fourteen:

PRO DAYS

rian Battle stood at the podium in the projection room in Florida State's Moore Athletic Center. The 180-seat theater was more than half full of NFL scouts and executives on the morning of March 15, 2005, for the Seminoles' pro day.

The side walls were decorated with images of FSU standouts such as Derrick Brooks, Warrick Dunn, Corey Simon, Deion Sanders, and Peter Warrick. Not that the NFL officials, comfortably seated in deep-cushioned garnet-red theater chairs, needed any reminder of the talent pipeline that had brought them to Tallahassee for a 9:00 A.M. meeting.

It was midway through the March pro day calendar, when schools staged mini-versions of the NFL combine to give scouts one last look at their prospects. By then, almost every player with any hope of being drafted had been weighed, measured, tested, and interviewed extensively at postseason all-star games and/or the combine, but team officials nonetheless scoured the country to get an additional glance at talent.

Many of the scouts on hand were regulars at Florida State, having visited several times during the season as part of their southeastern coverage area. Pro days also brought out general managers and head coaches trying to get another look for themselves. The morning's contingent included Pittsburgh Steelers head coach Bill Cowher, New Orleans Saints head coach Jim Haslett, and Floyd Reese, the general manager of the

Tennessee Titans, who was in the midst of a grueling tour of twenty-five pro days. With the sixth pick in the draft by virtue of a 5-11 record in 2004, and eleven selections overall, the 2005 draft was especially important to the Titans.

"Usually I'll go to eight or ten of these, but we have some extenuating circumstances," Reese said. "This year especially, you want to know what you're getting. You don't come to pro days to see anything real dramatic; it's more of a stabilizing act than anything. By now you expect to see something, and if you do, you leave satisfied that you had this guy pegged."

As with Agent Day in November, Battle planned to spend much of the day playing traffic cop. The school discouraged agents, friends, and family members from attending, but they showed up anyway. The weight room and projection room, where players would be weighed and measured, was the only part of the state facility they could effectively cordon off.

"I'm here to help you do your job," Battle told the group. "I have two police officers with me. If any agents or family members start hassling you, flag one of us down."

Jon Jost, the FSU strength and conditioning coach, took the podium next. Jost was the lone member of Bobby Bowden's coaching staff not on a Caribbean cruise. Jost outlined the day's protocol, which followed the NFL combine schedule and varied little from school to school. The players would enter the room for their height and weight and to have their hand size and arm lengths measured. They'd proceed outside for the forty-yard dash and then come back inside to the weight room for the vertical jump, broad jump, and bench press. From there, they'd go to another indoor room to run the three-cone and shuttle drills on artificial turf before heading back outside to the practice fields for position-related work.

Position work tended to be the most intriguing portion of the day. Many teams dispatched assistant coaches to pro days to work out players. Jost had no problem enlisting volunteers from the audience to work out the Seminoles highly regarded offensive and defensive linemen. A long silence followed when Jost asked for someone to work with the linebackers. FSU had nobody at that position that would hear his name called during draft weekend. Finally, someone accepted the duty.

Brett Maxie, the Atlanta Falcons defensive backs coach, raised his hand to work out the secondary. Maxie was part of a large Falcons contingent that included area scout Boyd Dowler, defensive line coach Bill Johnson, and offensive line coach Jeff Jagodzinski, recently shifted from tight ends coach when longtime NFL assistant Alex Gibbs moved to a consulting position with the team.

Following the combine, Falcons general manager Rich McKay and scouting director Phil Emery took their list of 225 players and assigned the coaching staff cross-checker scouting duties by position. The idea was for the coaching staff to provide input on whether the players were true scheme fits, along with an overall opinion.

Since the Falcons season ended in late January with the NFC championship game, Maxie had taken a crash course on top draft talent, like the rest of the coaching staff. He spent the weeks between the Senior Bowl and the combine watching film and reading scouting reports and now served as a cross-checker, writing reports on defensive backs of particular interest to Atlanta.

Secondary was a need for the Falcons, especially the safety position. But there were few blue-chip prospects at safety. The best of the bunch, Georgia's Thomas Davis, would be long gone by the time the Falcons drafted, and even he was projected by some teams as a linebacker.

The Falcons viewed defensive line, wide receiver, and linebacker as more pressing concerns, but McKay sent Maxie to a few pro days just in case. Two weeks earlier, Maxie came away from the University of Miami's pro day impressed with Antrel Rolle, even though the cornerback would not last until it was the Falcons' turn, picking twenty-seventh in the first round.

Later in the month, Maxie would head to the University of Iowa to take a look at Sean Considine, the Hawkeyes free safety. Maxie's primary assignment at FSU was to serve as a cross-checker for the Seminoles cornerback Bryant McFadden.

McFadden was a legitimate first-day selection, but Maxie would take a long look at the Seminoles' lesser secondary talents, having been in their position two decades earlier.

Maxie never expected to play in the NFL, let alone for thirteen years. During his senior year at tiny Texas Southern in the spring of 1985, he harbored no hopes of being selected in what was then a twelve-round draft. He planned to take his degree in biology and enroll in optometry school, but he made the New Orleans Saints roster as an undrafted free agent. He played nine seasons in the Big Easy before moving on to Atlanta, Carolina, and San Francisco.

Since retiring after the 1997 season, Maxie has retraced his playing career as a coach, working for the Panthers and 49ers before joining Jim Mora's staff in Atlanta.

"The one thing I've learned over the years is that a guy doesn't have to be the strongest, fastest, or tallest player, but he has to have some redeeming quality that catches your eye," said Maxie, who despite his earlier interest in optometry has shunned laser surgery and wears eyeglasses. "So you keep doing research and studying, talking to all your sources and gathering information. You can't overlook a guy just because he doesn't fit the physical mold."

Maxie planned to study Jerome Carter, the Seminoles strong safety. Despite a muscular physique honed by boxing in high school, Carter's strength did not translate on the football field and he tended to get overpowered by receivers. Still, he was regarded as one of the leaders on his team, always a plus in the Falcons' character evaluation.

"He has some redeeming qualities," Maxie said. "I like the way he approaches his craft, very businesslike. He's not the most athletic guy, but he has some size and some instincts. The things I'm going to look for today in the skill drills are how well he moves his body in space making plays on the ball. On film, I don't see the range."

Scouts from other teams figured that Bill Johnson, the Falcons defensive line coach, was on hand to get a look at Travis Johnson, the talented defensive tackle whose stock had soared during the 2004 season.

Though the Falcons needed help along the defensive line, they were unlikely to draft Travis Johnson, who between an acquittal on felony sexual assault charges in 2003 and a reputation for being a handful for coaches virtually disqualified himself from consideration under the Falcons character-based evaluation system. There was no denying his talent; most scouts believed he'd be long gone by the time Atlanta picked in the first round anyway.

Instead, Bill Johnson planned to pay close attention to Chauncey Davis, who unlike Travis Johnson had remained off the radar screen. Dowler, who scouted the state of Florida for the Falcons, believed Davis was a better prospect than Eric Moore, the more highly touted FSU defensive end, and perhaps a better long-term value than Johnson.

Dowler and Emery had met Davis in August while making an early visit to FSU. Though NFL officials rarely get a chance to talk to players during the season beyond a friendly hello, Dowler was able to have a brief conversation and was struck by the player's maturity and presence.

At that point, Davis was nothing more than a well-mannered college backup who had played just one season for the Seminoles, following two years at Jones Junior College in Mississippi. Once Davis got a chance to start in 2004, Dowler noticed a hardworking player who applied constant pressure on the quarterback, even if he did not rack up sacks. Dowler interviewed people throughout the school about Davis and tracked down his high school coach. Everyone, it seemed, had nothing but positive things to say.

"The more you watched, the more you liked the guy," Dowler said. "You're thinking, 'This guy could be a real solid pick on the second day. Not an instant star, but he'd be in the rotation.' He works his butt off, runs well, is a pretty good athlete. You see guys at the combine rated as some sort of future superstar and pretty soon you're thinking, 'I like this guy better.' He's probably playing just as good as the number-one draft choice tackle [Johnson]. But that guy is his own biggest fan. He's an attention-seeker, always putting on a show. He's not my idea of a real good teammate."

Davis was a prototypical McKay player: a late-blooming overachiever with plenty of upside. It also helped that McKay had a successful track record with FSU draft picks in Tampa, from first-rounders Derrick Brooks and Warrick Dunn to safety Dexter Jackson, a fourth-rounder in 1999 who would become Super Bowl MVP following the 2002 season.

The NFL officials in the room had been given nine-page packets of information produced by the strength and conditioning staff. There was a small grid for each player where scouts could write in height, weight, arm length, hand size, and performances in each of the drills.

Twenty-one draft-eligible Seminoles were scheduled to participate in the pro day, along with four special guests.

Linebacker Nate Hardage and quarterback Fabian Walker had transferred from FSU to Valdosta State (Georgia). Since the tiny school did not have a pro day, FSU welcomed them back. Former Seminole Stanford Samuels was signed as a free agent by the Indianapolis Colts before the 2004 season, but was cut in early September. Robert May, a linebacker, had played two seasons in the Arena Football League since leaving Florida State.

Samuels and May represented a sad fringe element of pro days—players desperately clinging to the NFL dream. Most schools require "additional players" to work out last in each session—or in their own group. Brian Battle, hoping to keep the event from deteriorating into an open tryout, limited pro day to those that had played for the Seminoles within the last two years.

Battle drew the line with Adrian McPherson, the quarterback who pleaded no contest to misdemeanor theft and gambling charges. McPherson and his agent, Leigh Steinberg, petitioned FSU to attend, and the decision was close enough that McPherson's name was listed in the scout packet.

McPherson's request did not seem that unreasonable compared to that of Maurice Clarett, who had the unmitigated gall to ask Ohio State if he could return for the Buckeyes pro day, even though he recently alleged that Buckeyes football players were paid by boosters, among other infractions, all of which the university denied. McPherson ended up staging his own workout for scouts at his Bradenton, Florida, high school.

"There were too many open wounds for us to have him back here," Battle said. "Apologies were supposedly given, but it just wasn't enough."

After Jost and Battle finished housekeeping duties, the players entered the projection room from the right in alphabetical order, dressed in shorts and either snug-fitting T-shirts—Under Armour being the brand of choice—or no shirt at all.

Offensive tackle Alex Barron, first alphabetically and in pro potential, led the line. As with the Senior Bowl and the combine, the audience remained silent. The players, most of which were now veterans of the drill, needed little prompting. Scouts announced height, weight, arm length, hand size, and the results of the "sit and reach," a test to measure hamstring flexibility.

Barron, wearing a sleeveless gray T-shirt, checked in at 6.073 (six-seven and three-eighths inches) and weighed 312 pounds. Travis Johnson walked in shirtless, heavily tattooed, and looking chubby. He measured 6.037 and 296 pounds. Ray Willis, wearing a snug red Under Armour shirt, stood 6.053 and 325 pounds.

The scouts dutifully wrote the numbers down out of habit. By now, they had seen most of the players poked and prodded. It's not like anyone was going to gain or lose significant weight from the combine three weeks earlier; certainly nobody was going to get taller. Still, the scouts wrote down data for everyone, even those with no hope of playing in the NFL.

"You never know who might be that one-in-a-thousand guy," said Reese, the Titans general manager. "Some of these guys don't go to an all-star game or combine. Some have been out a year. It's a long-shot, but you want to cover all bases. You're here anyway."

When the scouts were finished with Willis, the audience rose and headed outside. The forty-yard dash often is staged near the end of a pro day, but Jost moved the event up in the schedule with the threat of rain.

To get outside, the scouts walked through the Seminoles locker room, newly renovated at a cost of 2 million dollars. It sprawled out over eighteen thousand square feet and featured spacious locker stalls made of light-colored wood and a wide-open carpeted area with a Seminoles logo woven in the middle.

Scouts never ceased to be amazed at the college football arms race.

Few pro teams possessed such elegant facilities. "These guys are going to be in for a letdown when they get to our building," one scout quipped.

Outside, several hundred people had gathered at the track, a mix of family members, agents, students, and athletic department officials. Most of the scouts headed into the bleachers, sitting near the finish line of the forty-yard dash. A few sat or stood at the finish line, stopwatches poised.

At many pro days, the forty is anticlimactic. Those players that ran well at the combine sit out the pro day run since there's nothing to be gained. Players from the state of Florida historically have not run at the combine, believing it's advantageous to run in a warm familiar setting, away from the pressure of Indianapolis. The more promising the prospect, the more he and his agent can get away with such maneuvers.

Florida State's rubber track had a reputation for being fast, which helped explain the modest Seminole turnout for the forty at the combine. The school's top prospects—Barron, Johnson, McFadden, Willis, and wide receiver Craphonso Thorpe—sat out the forty, though Thorpe and Willis were nursing nagging injuries. Davis posted one of the better times among defensive ends (4.80) in Indianapolis and performed well in the other drills. Carter's time of 4.47 was among the best among strong safeties.

Unlike the combine, where players are clocked electronically, pro day times are open to interpretation. Each scout brings a stopwatch and after each run compares his time to those around him. At the end of the session, the scouts huddle to get a general consensus.

The process is more scientific than it sounds. Since most scouts have clocked thousands of players in the forty, their times are usually similar. It also helps that everyone follows the same routine.

The clock starts at the first sign of movement. Since players begin the sprint from a three-point stance, the hand moves first. Once the watch is triggered, the scout turns to the finish line, ignoring the player's progress. On rare occasions, schools will string a tape across the finish line, but usually it's up to the scout to decide when a player breaks the plane.

Dowler, at six-five, makes it a point to sit in the bleachers above the finish line. "Some guys sit on the ground, but I like to back off. I try to line up directly down the finish line. It helps if you can find a guy with a cap on and just line it up that way. When the player crosses the plane, you have to hit it fast. It takes good reflexes."

Having played or worked in the NFL for parts of six decades, Dowler knew better than to read too much into a player's time in the forty. Jerry Rice, after all, ran a pedestrian 4.6 at the combine in 1985.

"You have to be able to tell the difference between forty speed and play speed, and a lot of that has to do with other factors, physical mostly. You have guys that are stiff who can't change direction very well, who can't get in and out of a break very well. Either they're stiff or don't have balance, or they're not strong enough to carry the football uniform very well. So the timed forty is objective and play speed is subjective. You have to make a call. You might have a 4.6 guy who can do a lot of things well. He's a good athlete, has balance, body control, and he might play faster than a guy that runs a 4.5 or 4.55. While the time is good to look at, you need to be careful and watch him in person. Sometimes you can see a guy on tape and think he isn't fast. If he's smooth and is somewhat of a strider, smooth and not shaking his shoulders, not bobbing his head, thrashing arms and overexpending energy. You think that guy is hardly running. Then you get down on grass next to him and you think, 'He's a little faster than I thought.'"

For the purposes of the workout, Jost, the FSU strength coach, opted to treat every player equally. At Miami two weeks earlier, the Hurricanes top five prospects worked out separately, expediting the process for the scouts. They could leave at the end of the first session, and many did.

In Tallahassee, each of the twenty-five players would run a forty-yard dash before the first one ran a second time. Barron, running first, posted a 4.87 mark—at least according to the consensus from scouts who huddled up to compare notes later—an impressive mark for a man his size.

As the scouts checked their watches, Barron's momentum carried him into a cameraman who had gotten too close. The two tumbled to the ground. For a nervous moment, it appeared Barron had lost millions. Both were okay.

Travis Johnson, forever putting on a show, grunted through his 4.91 dash and screamed as he hit the finish line. "That's called running angry," Maxie said.

Thorpe ran a 4.38, which would have been one of the better times among wide receivers in Indianapolis. McFadden ran a 4.44, though Maxie clocked him closer to 4.3.

"You don't want to go by my watch, but he's fast," Maxie said, sighing. "He's kind of an enigma. When you watch him on film when the ball is in the air, you don't see that 4.3 speed, that second gear. That's the thing; track speed doesn't always translate on the field."

Willis, running last in the alphabetical order, posted a 5.18, a respectable time for a man his size. From the stands, Kimberly Willis cheered and smiled at agent Bill Johnson. Her husband finally was running well, adequately recovered from the ankle injury he sustained against Florida in November.

The Falcons scouts watched Willis, if for no other reason than because he had not worked out at the combine, but he already had been eliminated from consideration. With Alex Gibbs running the offensive line in 2004, the Falcons had adopted his philosophy of employing quick, athletic linemen who moved well laterally, who get off the line fast and run outside to block. That meant there was no need for the Falcons to spend high draft picks on powerful linemen like Barron.

Willis no longer was viewed as more than a third-round pick by most scouts, but he still didn't fit the Falcons mold. Though tightly built and a powerful blocker, he did not change direction quickly. His hips did not shift as fast as the Falcons would like. In scout-speak, he was not "a bender." Not that he had to worry; few linemen made the cut for Gibbs, the offensive line coach for the Denver Broncos during back-to-back Super Bowl title seasons in the late 1990s.

Once each Seminole completed two forty-yard dashes, the scouts huddled inside the track to compare times. Mickey Marvin, a bearded former Oakland Raiders lineman who now scouted for the team, loudly announced that reporters were not allowed to listen in on the session. A couple of sportswriters scurried away, shaking their heads at the unnecessary secrecy. The results would be leaked within hours and posted on various Web sites, which reported all predraft minutiae.

The crowd moved back inside to watch the players perform the three-cone and shuttle drills. From there it was off to the weight room—scouts and players only—for the bench press, vertical jump, and broad jump. Ninety minutes later everyone reconvened on the practice field for position drills. The weather, though overcast and windy, had remained dry.

Maxie took the defensive backs to one end of the field. The group included likely draftees McFadden and Carter, along with four other players, including Stanford Samuels, the free agent the Colts had released in September.

Maxie played the role of quarterback. There were no wide receivers; they were showcasing their skills with quarterback Chris Rix. Maxie simulated various quarterback motions—dropping back, scrambling, looking downfield—to see not only how the players reacted but how their bodies moved. Since cornerbacks must move both laterally and vertically in response to wide receivers, it's vital that they can shift their hips.

"I'm looking to see how good their feet are and how well they control their bodies in a short area," Maxie said. "I'm looking for explosion and transition. Then I look at their ball skills. I take them out on the edge and see how well they move their hips, in terms of zone and man-to-man, turning back across the body and just how they move their bodies in space."

The rest of the Falcons staff fanned out across the practice field. Dowler, like the other Falcons area scouts, was assigned a position to cross-check. Dowler, whose scouting area included Florida State, also was serving as cross-checker for wide receivers, having played the position for the Packers. Neither Thorpe nor Chauncey Stovall was big enough or talented enough for the Falcons, who needed a larger receiver, possibly with their first-round pick.

Jagodzinski, the offensive line coach, watched Barron and Willis, who worked together, alternating in the role of defensive lineman. Though neither Barron nor Willis fit the Gibbs philosophy, Jagodzinski still paid attention. If nothing else, he'd have a better feel for Barron if the Falcons pursued him as a free agent in the future.

Bill Johnson watched the defensive linemen. While much of the crowd focused on Travis Johnson and Eric Moore, he studied Davis. Like Dowler, he was impressed with the player's size and athleticism. Unlike Travis Johnson, who seemed intent on mauling the poor coaches conducting the drills, Davis took direction from the coaches.

Brian Baker, the defensive line coach for the Minnesota Vikings, was in charge of working Johnson through a thirty-second hand-deflection drill to test the player's reaction and balance. When the coach puts his hands on the player, the player must slap them away.

It's a routine drill, but Johnson takes it too seriously. He yells and grunts and even knocks Baker's cap off, which draws cheers from the fans and students watching.

It's not what teams want to see. "Whoever gets that guy will have his hands full," one scout says. "Is he going to take direction or just do his own thing?"

On the other side of the field, Maxie concluded his session with the defensive backs by having them go deep, as if defending a fly pattern. Afterward, he was ready to select McFadden with the Falcons second-round pick, though he knew the team had higher priorities.

"He moved a little better than I expected," Maxie said. "He showed a lot of short-area quickness, which is good. A lot of these guys aren't ready for the anaerobic stuff we throw at them, all of the starting and stopping and bursting. I wish I had thrown more deep balls than I did, but you'll kill them if you give them too many. It's kind of ironic. They've spent all this time training for the forty and the three-cone, and they're not as prepared as they could be for football."

The day after Florida State's pro day, Fred Gibson pondered his draft future over lunch. Rain pelted Gibson's white GMC Yukon parked outside the Taco Mac restaurant just off the University of Georgia campus in Athens. Gibson, along with fellow ex-Bulldog wide receiver Reggie Brown, was to have caught passes from David Greene, but the weather foiled those plans.

Gibson, as usual, was being a finicky eater. Though he skipped breakfast, he barely touched a burger and fries over a leisurely ninety-minute lunch. The staff at Athletes' Performance, the Arizona training center he left two days earlier, had given up putting weight on the skinny former basketball player.

It felt weird being back in Athens. Technically, Gibson and his fellow Bulldogs were still part of the Georgia football program, but, like most draft hopefuls around the country, had spent no time on campus the previous eleven weeks.

The time passed quickly. Gibson had flown to Phoenix shortly after the Outback Bowl and remained at Athletes' Performance, except for a week at the Senior Bowl in late January and four days at the NFL scouting combine in February. He left Arizona ten days before Georgia's pro day and planned to spend the bulk of the time preparing for the event with Greene, Brown, and Zeke Bratkowski, a former Georgia player, NFL quarterback, and assistant coach, who in recent years had served as a predraft quarterback instructor for players such as Michael Vick, Patrick Ramsey, and Philip Rivers.

Agent Pat Dye Jr. hired Bratkowski to work with Greene, who, though not in the same class as Vick, Ramsey, and Rivers (all former first-round picks), had the potential to hear his name called on the first day of the draft.

It was not all work for Gibson. After arriving back in Atlanta, he appeared at the Colonial Mall of America in Macon with Greene, Brown, and David Pollack for an autograph signing. More than fifteen hundred people showed up, many willing to pay thirty dollars for either Greene's or Pollack's signature. The two main draws earned almost twenty thousand dollars each for their efforts, duplicating a payoff from the previous day, when they signed at a mall in Douglasville with Georgia safety Thomas Davis and linebacker Odell Thurman.

Gibson and Brown, not nearly as in demand as Pollack and Greene, commanded just four dollars a signature in Macon, but that still came out to about thirteen hundred dollars per player. Gibson also attended the Southeastern Conference basketball tournament in Atlanta, though even there his mind was never far from the NFL. His date was Tiara Dungy, a student at Spelman College and the daughter of the Indianapolis Colts head coach. The two had met through a mutual friend.

"She said her dad was very strict," Gibson said. "I hope I didn't mess anything up with the Colts."

Now, five weeks before the NFL Draft, Gibson's stock was volatile. He had performed well during the Senior Bowl. Ever gregarious, he interviewed well both in Mobile and at the combine in Indianapolis, though his 4.55 time in the forty-yard dash was a concern. Overall, he could not shake the reputation as a work-in-progress, a skinny, inconsistent, ex-basketball player who could not put on weight.

Considered a potential second-round pick or even a late first-round choice before the 2004 season, the consensus now was that he would go late in the third round. It was not that Gibson had done anything wrong, but that comparable receivers such as Oklahoma's Mark Clayton and Mark Bradley, Vincent Jackson of Northern Colorado, South Carolina's Troy Williamson, Roddy White of Alabama-Birmingham, Indiana's Courtney Roby, and even Gibson's teammate Brown had done more to distinguish themselves. Those that lacked Gibson's height made up for it with strength, speed, size, and consistency. (Michigan's Braylon Edwards and Mike Williams, the former Southern Cal star, were considered more talented than the rest of the pack.)

"I don't know what more I can do to sell myself," Gibson said. "I went up against some of the top defensive backs at the Senior Bowl. I interviewed well, caught every pass at the combine. I ran a 4.55 at the combine, which was the only thing I was disappointed in. That's why I'm going to run here, so I can get that 4.4 I know I'm capable of."

Gibson was presented with some predraft magazines over lunch.

"I don't go searching this stuff out, because people are going to say what they want to say. Like [ESPN's] Mel Kiper. I had a scout say to me, 'Do you think we actually listen to Mel Kiper?' But go ahead. Tell me what they're saying."

"Tends to drop easy balls."

"I've dropped a few, sure. Sometimes I try to get up the field before catching the ball. I see a whole lot of wide receivers do that. Mark Clayton dropped a bunch of passes at the combine. He's a great player, but everyone drops passes. Randy Moss does, and he doesn't even block. C'mon man. Be real. That's why NFL coaches are going to be drafting me and guys writing magazines are not."

"Not very physical and does not like to be hit."

"What kind of crap is that? What receiver likes to be hit? I'm going to catch the football, and if they hit me, they hit me. I've been doing this for four years. Did you see any of this stuff they're talking about at the Senior Bowl? Stuff like dropping passes, coming off the ball slow, taking off plays? I played for Coach [Mark] Richt for one of the best teams in the country. If my coach saw me doing that kind of stuff, I don't think I'd be starting as long as I did. I might as well not show up."

Gibson picked at the French fries.

"Look, I don't think there's a player that's been interviewed more than I have, and I'm going to be talking to more teams in the next month. I've told everyone that I'm not going to bring any problems to their organization. If they draft me, they'll get a great person who loves playing wide receiver and will do anything to help their team win. I'll do anything— play special teams—it doesn't matter. Bottom line is that whoever drafts me is going to have one heck of a player."

The following day, Pat Dye Jr. was back at his desk in Atlanta. It was a busy time of year, between pro days and the beginning of free agency for veteran players. Dye had only a modest slate of pro days to attend. Bill Johnson had worked tirelessly recruiting for ProFiles Sports Management and, as Dye would be the first to admit, had as good a year.

Johnson had recruited Florida State's Ray Willis, Georgia wide receiver Reggie Brown, and Ben Wilkerson, a center from LSU. Dye landed David Greene and Demarcus Ware, the defensive end from Troy State who since the fall had soared from the level of midround pick to potentially a top-ten selection.

Dye and Johnson would attend Georgia's pro day together the following Tuesday. As for Monday, when Auburn's talented draft class would work out just a two-hour drive from the ProFiles office, Dye was free to take the day off.

It still bothered Dye that for the second consecutive year he had been shut out at Auburn, where he graduated and where his father coached for twelve years. This year really hurt. Running backs Ronnie Brown and Carnell "Cadillac" Williams, represented by Todd France and Ben Dogra respectively, were projected as top-ten picks. Cornerback Carlos Rogers, another France client, was climbing the charts, as was quarterback Jason Campbell, who had signed with Joel Segal, whose client list included Michael Vick, quarterback for the Atlanta Falcons.

Dye still was kicking himself for recruiting both Brown and Williams. Unlike most agents, he did not see a conflict of interest in representing two players at the same position for the draft. He knew he lost out on Campbell, since he also was recruiting Greene. Other agents represented multiple quarterbacks in one draft, but it was different with Campbell and Greene, having played in close proximity.

That was the thinking, anyway.

"It's no different than when a Realtor has two houses nearby," Dye said. "The buyer is going to buy what they want to buy. I'm not going to push one house over the other. I'm not going to play favorites; I'm trying to sell houses here. If I had Ronnie and Carnell, I'd have nothing but great things to say about both of them. They're entirely different running backs. One is bigger than the other; one is faster. One catches better, blocks better. This notion that you can't represent two guys at the same position is a fallacy created by agents."

Dye was hardly the first agent to struggle at a school he once dominated. For many years, Drew Rosenhaus was the heavy favorite to land the top players from his alma mater, the University of Miami. That had changed in recent years, with Rosenhaus representing just one of the five Hurricanes selected in the first round of the 2004 draft. Though Rosenhaus landed wide receiver Roscoe Parrish and offensive lineman Chris Myers for the 2005 draft, he lost out on the top two Hurricanes: cornerback Antrel Rolle and running back Frank Gore. Agent Jimmy Sexton, once the dominant agent at the University of Tennessee, had seen his fortunes shift there.

"What happens is that agents will call and say, 'I know you're going with Pat Dye' and they feel like they have to knock me out of the way to have a chance. That's not the case now, but for a long time it was," Dye said. "If you're a prospect and you hear from agents that Pat Dye is getting too big or he doesn't get his clients enough money and you hear that from enough sources, pretty soon that perception becomes reality. Who knows?

"Maybe I get too emotional when I'm in a presentation with an Auburn client. I've heard theories that players thought I talked too much about my father. They don't want to know about my father, they want to know what *I* can do for them. Fine, I've never gone around wearing that on my sleeve or anywhere else. I mention my father in the context of, I know I can't afford to screw up down there or do anything inappropriate. My father's name and legacy makes me more accountable for my actions."

With two young children, Dye knew he probably was not as aggressive on the recruiting trail as he was when he entered the business in his mid-twenties in the late '80s. Many of his competitors were his age or slightly younger, and still single. How could he strike a balance? It's a topic he discussed at the combine in Indianapolis over dinner with Dogra, the SFX Sports agent who landed Carnell Williams. Dogra is three years younger than Dye, but also has two young kids.

Dogra, who did not become a certified agent until 1995, wonders if Dye did not get spoiled in his early years of agent work, before everyone jumped into the business and players began demanding combine preparation and higher levels of concierge service.

"It's a time-consuming, high-service business," Dogra says. "When Pat got into the business, he was getting better clients for less work than he is today, and that's because the competition and the time intensity has driven it up. When you're married and have kids, as I do, something is going to have to give. Are you willing to pay the price? Pat has done it his way for so long, but everything changes. Ten years from now, when I'm forty-nine, I don't know that I'll want to spend all this time before the draft with eight players to make sure everything is right."

In any other year, Dye would have felt good about his recruiting efforts. The following day, he would drive three and a half hours to Troy, Alabama, to see Ware's pro day, which, in the absence of any touted teammates, would be essentially a private workout for NFL scouts. Ever since Ware, who stood six-three and a half, arrived at the Senior Bowl weighing 247 pounds, fifteen more than his listed weight, scouts saw him as the type of versatile end/linebacker who could fit any defensive scheme.

Now Ware weighed 251. Dye's other client, Greene, also seemed to be climbing the charts, to say nothing of landing endorsement deals, largely based on his Q rating in Georgia. Dye's marketing director, Michael Perrett, figured Greene would enjoy more than two hundred thousand dollars in extra income for 2005.

Greene had spent much of the previous two months working with Atlanta area trainer Chip Smith on his footwork and quickness. Like Ware, he seemed destined to overachieve on draft day.

"An agent that takes credit for a guy going higher in the draft is kidding himself," Dye said. "What we do is give our client great advice at every juncture—whether or not to play in the Senior Bowl or work out at the combine. We solicit feedback on their strengths and weaknesses from teams, and we excel on that because of the access of information from my father's career and from my career. We can tell Demarcus Ware that teams want to see him at 250 and not 239. With David Greene, team after team is telling me he needs to work on his speed, agility, and lateral quickness. So we feel like we're going to put them in the best possible position to get them drafted as highly as possible. But I'm not going to run the forty. I'm not going to bench-press or catch passes or convince a team that he's a better player than the one over here. They're going to make that determination on their own, but I hope that through everything we put into it with advice, physical and mental preparation, soliciting and passing along feedback, taking things off their mind in terms of scheduling—anything we can do to allow them to focus can translate into higher draft stock."

Based on his discussions with NFL officials, Dye believed Ware would go in the first half of the first round. Reggie Brown could sneak into the first as well. "He's certainly a two," Dye said. Ray Willis was moving into the second round, Dye felt, Greene the second or third. As for Wilkerson, who had been hampered by an injured knee, who knew? "He's all over, anywhere from third to sixth."

Dye shrugged. "That's a solid year. They're great kids. But having graduated from Auburn and my father having coached there, and the presence we've had there representing three or four times as many Auburn players as any other agent—with all that in mind, this year will always have an asterisk beside it."

Todd France pulled his black Mercedes CLK 430 convertible into a parking garage near the University of Georgia's Butts-Mehre Heritage Hall. It was March 22, 2005, which not only was pro day for the Bulldogs but also the twenty-second birthday of safety Thomas Davis, France's client.

To mark the occasion, France carried a giant chocolate chip cookie inside a box large enough to hold a pizza. Davis, as an elite athlete, would eat little if any of the cookie, but that wasn't the point. France, like his competitors, was all about personal attention.

France walked briskly through wind and light rain into Butts-Mehre, another multi-million-dollar shrine to the flourishing business of college football, complete with vast workout and meeting facilities, a Bulldogs museum, and decorated in an elegant style normally reserved for luxury hotels and high-end law firms.

The Bulldogs, coming off a 10-2 season, were winning the college football arms race, though the large contingent of scouts and prominent agents filing into the building served as a reminder of how hard-pressed they would be to reload for the 2005 season.

France, like the other agents, stood sentry by a bank of elevators near the meeting room that would serve as the briefing area for the scouts and Georgia officials. He nodded at rival Atlanta representatives Pat Dye Jr. and Bill Johnson, who did the same, and greeted NFL executives as they passed. France, unlike Dye, had spent the previous day at Auburn at the pro day of clients Ronnie Brown and Carlos Rogers.

Once the NFL officials were seated and doors to the meeting room were closed, France sidled up to Tom Condon, the IMG agent whose draft clients included David Pollack, the Georgia defensive end projected as a first-round pick.

Condon and France exchanged pleasantries. In France's young career, he rarely had gone head-to-head with IMG for a client; Condon landed Pollack ahead of Ethan Lock, whose Arizona firm of Lock, Metz & Malinovic represented Wisconsin defensive end Erasmus James and Virginia's Chris Canty, among others, for the 2005 draft.

France had only a five-person staff, unlike the hundreds employed by the worldwide conglomerate of IMG that represented athletes and sports properties throughout the industry, including a vast football client list headlined by Indianapolis Colts quarterback Peyton Manning, San Diego Chargers running back LaDainian Tomlinson, and Chad Pennington, the quarterback of the New York Jets.

But France had arguably as impressive a class for the 2005 draft. Condon and partner Ken "Fuzzy" Kremer represented Utah quarterback Alex Smith, projected as the number-one overall pick, along with Pollack and potential first-rounders Heath Miller, the Virginia tight end, and Chris Spencer, an offensive lineman from Ole Miss. France had three surefire top-twenty picks in Davis and his two Auburn clients.

Condon and France stepped back as the meeting broke up and scouts flooded into the lobby. Georgia officials, like their Florida State counterparts a week earlier, rearranged the schedule to account for the weather, moving the forty-yard dash first.

As the scouts and players headed outside, Tim Ruskell adjusted his Seattle Seahawks cap. It had been exactly a month since he left his job as assistant general manager of the Atlanta Falcons to become president of the Seahawks. The move included a huge increase in salary, though it didn't feel like such a promotion at the moment.

With the exception of Titans general manager Floyd Reese, who was continuing his iron-man schedule of pro day events, Ruskell was by far the highest-ranking official at Bulldogs pro day. Many team presidents, including his former boss Rich McKay, were in Hawaii for the NFL's annual meetings. Most general managers and head coaches also were there.

Though Ruskell was well up to speed on the 2005 draft with the Atlanta Falcons, he was looking at it from a new perspective, evaluating talent with different needs in mind. Not only that, he had inherited a skeleton Seahawks staff that since the beginning of the year had lost its vice president of football operations, general manager, and director of college scouting.

So, instead of going to Hawaii, Ruskell packed his stopwatch and new Seahawks logo sportswear and hit the road, with Auburn and Georgia two of his more prominent stops. Outside at the Bulldogs' track, he took a prominent position at the finish line of the forty-yard dash.

"I'm always going to approach this from a scout's perspective, because that's where I came from," Ruskell said. "If I didn't do that, then the Seahawks aren't getting the benefit of why they hired me."

The wind seemed to help the Georgia players. Fred Gibson ran between 4.42 and 4.48, depending on the stopwatch. Teammate Reggie Brown ran slightly faster. David Greene and Pollack opted not to run, standing with their times at the combine. Davis, the star attraction, ran between a 4.48 and a 4.55.

Doug Hendrickson, Gibson's agent, was convinced his client's stock was strong. "He's a late first, maybe the second round," he said. "He's shed the basketball image."

With the sky growing darker and the wind beginning to gust, the players proceeded to a practice field for position drills. Like most major football programs, Georgia had one field made of artificial turf. Instead of the knee-punishing Astroturf of the 1980s, it was a synthetic blend of sand and shredded rubber, topped by the equivalent of a giant green welcome mat.

Greene, wearing gray sweats from the combine, loosened up at midfield, flanked wide by Gibson and Brown. Zeke Bratkowski watched nearby, as did Mike Johnson, the quarterbacks coach for the Atlanta Falcons.

The last thing the Falcons needed was a quarterback. In December, the team signed Michael Vick to an eight-year contract extension worth $130 million through 2013. Matt Schaub, selected in the third round of the 2004 draft, had quickly grasped the West Coast offense, having played it at the University of Virginia, and the Falcons were confident he could fill in capably if Vick were injured.

Still, Greene intrigued the Falcons. He was a proven winner, having led the Bulldogs to forty-two wins, a record for Division 1-A quarterbacks. He was unflappable under pressure and a leader by any measuring stick. He also possessed the rare gift of being able to treat members of the media like old buddies without divulging secrets or saying anything remotely controversial.

Greene also had grown up in the Atlanta suburbs, which was no small matter for McKay, who believed having local products on the roster was grossly underrated. Even in the modern mercenary world of sports, with wealthy athletes often detached from their communities, McKay found fans were more likely to give a team and its players the benefit of the doubt if there was a local connection, no matter how tenuous.

In Tampa, McKay drafted heavily from the University of Florida and Florida State. Shaun King, a marginally talented quarterback selected in the second round out of Tulane in 1999, became a fan favorite despite his erratic play. King had grown up in St. Petersburg and, like Greene, lacked the traditional size and athleticism NFL teams demanded of quarterbacks.

That thinking was shifting, especially now that former sixth-round pick Tom Brady had led the New England Patriots to three Super Bowl titles in four years.

"Brady was on the lower end of physical ability," said Mike Johnson, who evaluated him in 2000 as quarterbacks coach in San Diego. "But he was high on the intangible side. Same thing with Greene. If you're a guy that lacks physical ability, you better have the smarts, intelligence, and decision-making ability. For a guy like Greene, it balances out."

As Greene fired passes to Gibson and Brown, Ruskell approached Pat Dye Jr. Unlike his former Falcons colleagues, Ruskell had a pressing need for a quarterback to play behind starter Matt Hasselbeck. He also liked Dye's client Demarcus Ware, though he knew the Seahawks would have no shot at Ware, picking twenty-third in the first round.

When Greene was finished, Ruskell asked him how he felt about playing for the Seahawks. The question is a typical conversation starter this time of year, whether in interviews at the combine or in more casual settings. Greene, who had never been to the West Coast, expressed enthusiasm for the Seahawks and related a story involving Hasselbeck.

It was a predictable response. With players coached for interviews, scouts rarely hear anything but excitement about playing for any team, no matter how cold the climate or how poorly the team has played in recent years. *Are you kidding? I'd absolutely love to play for the Lions!*

"You take it half-seriously," Ruskell says. "You run across players that clearly have a preference. Either they grew up as a fan of a team or want to stay close to home. But you can use it to gauge passion and how excited a guy might be to play for you. You can only fake it so much."

When Ruskell finished with Greene, a scout from the Green Bay Packers took the quarterback to the other end of the field for some more drills. Greene had learned not to read anything into which teams seemed to be giving him more attention.

"You've got so many different teams and different schemes, and they want to see how you fit, and I don't blame them," Greene said. "If you're going to invest all that money in someone, you want to check everything out. Guys get picked by teams that never spoke to them. They had no questions because they knew they were going to be great players. I don't even try and figure it out. It's like chasing your tail."

The star of the morning was birthday boy Davis, who was rapidly ascending in the draft. Davis performed both linebacker and defensive back drills. The vibe France got from teams was that half of them projected him as a safety in the NFL, the other half a linebacker.

The Falcons and Seahawks were among the teams that coveted Davis, but they knew he would be long gone by their twenty-third and twenty-seventh picks. He had the thickness of a linebacker and the speed of a defensive back, but though he had the physique of a bodybuilder, he lacked traditional weight room numbers.

After position drills, the crowd moved inside. Georgia, unlike most schools, allowed everyone into the weight room: agents, media, friends, family, students, and underclassmen. If Georgia officials were concerned about agents talking with underclassmen, they didn't show it. Representatives spoke freely with up-and-coming players alongside motivational signs such as THE DESIRE TO WIN IS WORTHLESS WITHOUT THE DESIRE TO PREPARE, DO YOU HAVE A BAD CASE OF THE WANTS?, and RULE NUMBER SEVEN: ASK GOD FOR HELP.

The weigh-in took place first. Fred Gibson again checked in at 196. Davis, who did not bench-press at the combine, managed only twelve repetitions, barely half that of players of comparable size (six feet, 230 pounds).

No matter. For players with the talent of Davis, weight room performance was irrelevant. Later, while Davis showered, France waited to take his client to lunch. He sat on a weight bench near the sign for rule number six—SEE YOURSELF MAKING A GREAT PLAY.

The rest of the agents, scouts, and players had departed. The draft was one month away, and for thirty-three-year-old Todd France it was all coming together.

Chapter Fifteen:

RED-DOT SPECIALS

The Atlanta Falcons draft room, like the rest of the Flowery Branch training complex, is first class. Those fortunate enough to be invited inside must go to the second floor, where they arrive at a marble landing with the inlay of the Falcons logo. To the left is a large, softly lit portrait of team owner Arthur Blank holding a football, flanked by action shots of linebacker Keith Brooking and running back T. J. Duckett. Across the landing is a portrait of general manager Rich McKay and head coach Jim Mora, surrounded by action images of running back Warrick Dunn and quarterback Michael Vick.

Straight ahead is the executive conference room. Down the hallway to the right is a room identified with a sign outside that reads simply DRAFT ROOM. The Falcons, like the rest of the league, as well as ESPN, have refrained from using the term "war room" since the United States invasion of Iraq in 2003.

Inside the draft room is an NFL fantasy leaguer's dream come true. The room is slightly rectangular and has perhaps one thousand two hundred square feet of floor space. Rows of tables face the front. The head table is reserved for Blank, McKay, Mora, and scouting director Phil Emery. Scouts and other personnel people occupy most of the other tables. Assistant coaches remain in their offices, available for insight if needed.

Two walls, the front and right, are covered from floor to ceiling with white magnetic board. The front wall contains two identical groupings of about five hundred magnetic strips. Each strip is roughly the size of a business card. It represents a player and includes his name, position, college, agent's name, height, weight, and Wonderlic score, along with his rating by the Falcons staff. That rating contains a number between 5.0 and 8.0 and a double-letter grade of AA to FF. The numerical portion is similar to that used by several teams and is a descendant of a system developed by Bucko Kilroy, one of the NFL's first full-time scouts in the 1950s.

The front board is arranged as a grid, with positions listed horizontally along the top and the numerical ratings vertically along the left side. Magnets are arranged accordingly. During the draft, scout Matt Berry will distribute the magnets onto two boards on the right wall, continuing a duty he once performed as an intern. One is a round-by-round board, the other a team-by-team. The final board ranks each team's top-three needs by position, which is a valuable reference when trying to determine if the teams drafting close by might take the Falcons desired player.

The rating system is identical to the one the Falcons use to update their existing roster, generally once every four games during the regular season. Unlike grades that are based on professional track records, the draft grades are computed using college performances and pro projections.

Most players fall into the 5.6-to-5.9 range and are rated as solid starters or "backbone" (5.9), backups or "contributor" (5.8), and fringe players or "depth" (5.6 to 5.7). Anyone rated 6.1 or higher is considered a star, a player who consistently makes plays that win games. Though the numbers ranged from 5 to 7, scouts referred to them as if the decimal places did not exist. A guy is a "sixty-two" or a "fifty-seven."

Within the 5.7-to-5.9 range, players also can receive a plus or minus, depending on the projected period of transition. A 5.8-plus, for instance, might be a player that's on the border of being a starting player, either already as a veteran or, in the case of a drafted player, down the road. The plus/minus system also is a reflection of how well a player fits the Falcons' offensive and defensive schemes. No plus or minus is given at 6.1 or higher, since players projected that high inherently fit schemes and should need little transition time.

It's a tough grading system. Falcons such as linebacker Keith Brooking and defensive end Patrick Kerney, whom during the 2004 season many fans would have called stars, warranted only 5.9 ratings at the beginning of the year, but were bumped up to 6.2s after Pro Bowl campaigns. Quarterback Michael Vick, considered by some the best player in the league, or at least the "playmaker" most capable of transforming a game, is a mere 7.0, though the Falcons brass believes he can ascend to the 8.0 level. Alge Crumpler, the team's All-Pro tight end, is a 6.7.

McKay and his staffs, first in Tampa Bay and then in Atlanta, have typically assigned a rating of 6.1 or higher to just fifteen to twenty players heading into the draft. Not surprisingly, the players receiving such ratings for 2005 projected as high picks, including Georgia safety Thomas Davis (6.4), Auburn running back Carnell Williams (6.3), Troy State defensive end Demarcus Ware (6.2), Miami cornerback Antrel Rolle (6.2), and Roddy White, a wide receiver from the University of Alabama-Birmingham (6.2).

The two-letter ratings, from A to F, represent "football character" and "personal character," respectively. A player receiving a grade below a C in either category has little chance of getting drafted by the Falcons.

"With football character, we're not looking for Mr. Goody Two-shoes or guys that always do the right thing," McKay said. "That's the second grade, personal character. The first grade is about a million different things. It's about toughness, desire, work ethic. How many off-season workouts did he attend? How did he handle and play through injury? Does he command respect from teammates and instill fear in opponents? What did his coach say about his ability to learn football? Not math or science, but football. All of that goes into football character."

Personal character is a measure of citizenship. If a player has a criminal record, a history of disciplinary problems, or poor performance in the classroom, the Falcons believe he's more likely to be a distraction in the locker room and will not make the most of his talent.

"The object is to make sure you know very well who it is you're bringing in, and you accept both from the coaches' standpoint and the organization's standpoint, whatever the weaknesses are," McKay said. "Are we okay with that, and, if we are, what's our plan to manage it? Once you know the whole person you're dealing with, you're okay. It's surprises that crush you. It's not that we've set the bar so high we've eliminated everybody. It's just we want to know everything there is to know. There are certain guys, because of what we know, we're not going to take them."

Though McKay does not identify such players, it's clear where certain players rank in the Falcons character-based system. Adam "Pac Man" Jones, a highly rated cornerback and Atlanta native who played at West Virginia, was involved in a 2002 bar fight that led to a malicious assault charge, a felony that was later reduced to a misdemeanor. (Jones received a suspended sentence, along with probation and community service.) Richie Incognito, the former Nebraska lineman, had a history of suspensions from his college team. In February of 2004, he was charged with three counts of assault following a fight at a party and was found guilty of one misdemeanor assault charge. Then there was Odell Thurman, the Georgia linebacker with a history of troubles, including a suspension from the team as a freshman for a series of incidents, including a bar fight. Later he was arrested for underage possession of alcohol and having an open container of alcohol in a vehicle. These charges were dropped, and he was given a fine for a traffic violation.

Jones, Incognito, and Thurman were among the dozens of talented players eliminated from consideration by the Falcons' character filter.

The Falcons' character ratings are even more stringent than the numerical rankings. Davis, rated a 6.4, earned a CB rating. Rolle, the 6.2, ranked BC. Chris Spencer, a 5.9-plus center from Mississippi that the Falcons thought of highly enough to bring to Flowery Branch for an interview, was rated CC. Ware, the Troy State defensive end whose stock had soared between an impressive performance at the Senior Bowl and by gaining twenty pounds, rated AA. Nobody, it seemed, could find anything negative to say about Ware, a studious athlete, weight room warrior, and all-around good guy.

Then there was Williams, the Auburn running back nicknamed "Cadillac," who received an "AA" rating from the Falcons. Gregarious, humble, a team leader, and a tireless worker, Williams was a younger, more talented version of Warrick Dunn, a model citizen who could both run and catch out of the backfield.

Of course, the Falcons already had Dunn on their roster. Between Dunn, Duckett, and Vick, a constant threat to take off, running back was a low priority for the Falcons. Still, Cadillac's magnet in the Falcons draft room was one of just eighty stamped with a red dot.

At the moment, the eighty red-dot magnets were scattered along the front draft boards, across positions, and from 5.7 and up vertically. Barring something unforeseen, like a highly rated player that took a precipitous drop, the Falcons' eight picks would come from among the eighty.

They were not the eighty most-talented players or the eighty rated highest by the Falcons. After all, the Falcons, like everyone else, had to make late-round selections. But the eighty players were those that best fit the team's needs and schemes, while earning high grades as prospects and in both football character and personal character.

Which players would land in the Falcons lap depended on a host of factors. It was not as simple as ranking the group one to eighty and crossing players off as other teams drafted. McKay had tried that in

Tampa, and it only created problems if he decided to pick a player when there were five or six remaining on the list ahead of him. The list opened up the room for debate and gave scouts fodder to argue for players from their scouting regions, even during the draft.

Instead of drafting vertically, McKay chose horizontally, based on the 8.0 scale. During the draft, as magnets were transferred, it was easy to see which players remained at the highest levels across all positions. If, for instance, the team needed both a defensive tackle and a linebacker, the highest-rated player at either position usually would get the nod. The Falcons generally would wait until the next selection to address the other need, unless, of course, a more highly rated player at another position of need remained on the board. Scouts quickly learned McKay's mantra, "We do not want to drop down a level to draft a player."

That helped explain how the Carnell Williams magnet ended up with a red dot. Most mock drafts projected Williams going to Tampa Bay with the fifth pick. Though nobody put much stock in mocks—examine enough of them, and it's possible to find most players going to any of a half dozen teams, more in the later rounds—the Williams projection looked solid. Tampa Bay head coach Jon Gruden, who coached the running back during the Senior Bowl, made no secret of his feelings. Williams was the player to jump-start the Bucs' moribund running game.

At the same time, the offensive-minded Gruden could never have enough wide receivers and quarterbacks. Mike Williams, the Tampa native and former Southern Cal receiver, had made an impression. The Bucs needed an upgrade at quarterback, and there was talk of a trade up to land Alex Smith, the Utah junior.

It had become fashionable in NFL circles to suggest that running backs were disposable commodities. The Denver Broncos seemed to create a new backfield star each season. Still, if Cadillac made it past the Buccaneers, it was highly unlikely that he would fall to the Falcons at number twenty-seven.

Since Williams was such an ideal scheme fit, and a perfect AA character, the Falcons placed a dot on him. Former teammate Ronnie Brown, another AA character who even received the team's highest rating, the Falcon Filter, also had a dot, though there was even less chance he'd be available at number twenty-seven. The red dots also included tight ends Heath Miller of Virginia and Alex Smith of Stanford, both solid fits for the team's West Coast offense. Both figured to be available when the Falcons picked, though it made no sense for the Falcons to select either, with Crumpler entrenched at the position.

The Falcons even hung a dot on David Greene, the Georgia quarterback. The last thing the team needed was a quarterback. Greene, a high-character local product, would be tempting at the end of the draft if he was available. McKay figured he'd go in the third or fourth round, but that's what he thought in 2000, when Georgia Tech quarterback Joe Hamilton slid to the seventh round and McKay drafted him for the Buccaneers.

Players like Williams, Brown, Miller, Smith, and Greene were more the exceptions. Of the eighty red dots, about seventy were truly in the mix to become the next Atlanta Falcons.

Williams compared favorably to other smaller NFL backs, such as Tiki Barber of the Giants and Washington's Clinton Portis. But they were both second-round picks, in part because of size concerns, and teams rarely spent a first-round choice on the position, unless they lacked a featured back.

Cadillac was a long shot for Atlanta. The only way he would wear a Falcons uniform was if twenty-six teams passed. McKay would not be trading up to grab a running back, sacrificing future draft position and picks.

He would, however, consider trading up to land two of the biggest red dots on the Falcons board: Ware or Davis. Having played, respectively, at Troy State University (in nearby Troy, Alabama) and the University of Georgia, the players had plenty of exposure to Falcons scouts. The Falcons viewed Ware as a defensive end, unlike much of the league that saw him as a linebacker. As for Davis, the Falcons did not care if he played safety or linebacker, though the latter position was less of an immediate need with the signing of free agent Ed Hartwell from the Baltimore Ravens a month earlier. Davis, the Falcons believed, was a future star at either position.

McKay had his limits, however. If he could trade up from number twenty-seven to, say, number twenty to grab Davis or Ware, he would do it. Any higher and teams would command a number one or number two in the 2006 draft, a price McKay refused to pay. He wasn't about to do what Buffalo did in the 2004 draft, sending its number-one pick in 2005 to Dallas, along with second- and fifth-round picks in 2004, for the chance to draft quarterback J. P. Losman in the first round in 2004.

Buffalo's former first-round pick now was, ironically, the twentieth selection. With the Cowboys drafting eleventh and twentieth, and head coach Bill Parcells remodeling his defense into a 3–4 scheme, there was a good chance the versatile Ware would go to Dallas. McKay could live with that; he had learned never to stake too much on the selection of any one player.

"It becomes very pricey," McKay said. "What everyone tries to do in a trade up is they're hoping you've fallen in love and they're hoping you're willing to put next year's one or two on it. Not for me."

It had come to this, just eighty players, seventy really. From a pool of thousands that Falcons scouts began evaluating in May, they had narrowed the field to 225 by the combine. Through cross-checking and meetings, they had culled the list to eighty players.

Once pro days ended, roughly four weeks before the draft, the scouting staff reconvened at Flowery Branch. They spent the first three weeks going through the 225 players, rereading every one of the now voluminous files. They repeated the process the final week before the draft with head coach Jim Mora, defensive coordinator Ed Donatell, and offensive coordinator Greg Knapp.

During the process, McKay paired up scouts and assistant coaches to do a ranking of players at each position. Tim Ruskell came up with the idea before he left for Seattle. The idea was to take another close look at the players while also building camaraderie between the coaching and scouting staffs.

The process of elimination was now complete. At times, McKay cautioned his staff from taking it further. With players so thoroughly scouted by now, everyone had a few warts.

"Let's not kill everybody on the board," he said. "There are some guys who can be Falcons."

How much of the eighty-player list was a reflection of character evaluation? In the early 1990s, McKay believed teams weighed character just 10 percent in their overall ratings. These days, he figured it was up to 40 percent—more than 50 with the Falcons.

However, the Falcons' double-letter character grade did not serve as a tie-breaker during the draft. If it came down to two comparable players with the same numerical grade, McKay would call in the appropriate position coach to see if one player was a better scheme fit.

"The letters are confusing because we emphasize character so much," McKay said. "We're not going to draft anybody *because* of character, but we may *not* take somebody because of character. We're not going to draft because of these letter grades. But it plays a key role in the process of elimination."

McKay preached to his staff to watch what they said in the weeks leading up to the draft, not just to other teams, but to the media. He wasn't as paranoid as Parcells and New England head coach Bill Belichick, who did not allow their assistant coaches to speak to the press. But McKay didn't want anyone to be able to glean information about who the Falcons planned to pick.

On the Monday before the draft, McKay sat with Falcons beat writers Matt Winkeljohn of the *Atlanta Journal-Constitution* and George Henry of the Associated Press. Few sports executives are better at the give-and-take of informal interviews with writers than McKay, who, like his late father, is insightful, self-deprecating, and quick with one-liners. He appreciates journalists who try to better understand the personnel decision-making process and the salary cap implications of each move. The financial structure of a football roster is more complex than those of the other three major sports, which was why, upon taking the Atlanta job, he held a seminar for Falcons media on the salary cap.

Sitting with Winkeljohn and Henry in the office belonging to public relations director Reggie Roberts, McKay held court for forty-five minutes without addressing any draft prospect by name.

"I'm not going to talk about specific players," McKay said. "I don't think it's appropriate for me to grade them and scout them right here. Because then if I draft a guy and I had said something bad about him, you'll kill me. If I said something good and we didn't, you'll kill me. I'm not big on grading specific players."

Winkeljohn was familiar with McKay's tactics. "What about Shaun Cody?"

"Cody?" McKay asked. "What school did he go to?"

McKay figured he had done a successful job keeping a lid on the Falcons' plans, because most of the mock drafts were not coming close to predicting what the team planned to do.

The team had brought in four players for interviews in the weeks before the draft—Oklahoma defensive end Dan Cody, Alabama-Birmingham wide receiver Roddy White, Clemson cornerback Justin Miller, and Ole Miss center Chris Spencer—and even they were not drawing much attention in mock drafts.

Brodney Pool, the safety from Oklahoma, was a popular pick. Many predicted a defensive lineman, such as Iowa's Matt Roth or Shaun Cody from Southern Cal. *USA Today*'s mock draft had the Falcons taking Davis at number twenty-seven, an ambitious pick McKay gladly would have accepted. Paul Zimmerman, the longtime football writer for *Sports Illustrated*, projected White, the UAB wide receiver.

The hometown *Atlanta Journal-Constitution* threw out six names:

Pool, Roth, Cody, Tennessee linebacker Kevin Burnett, tight end/wide receiver Matt Jones of Arkansas, and Bryant McFadden, the cornerback that Falcons defensive backs coach Brett Maxie worked out during Florida State's pro day five weeks earlier.

Without a glaring need at any position, McKay could play his cards close to the vest. With the exceptions of quarterback and tight end, the Falcons were open to upgrading at any position. Between the roster McKay inherited in December of 2003, the 2004 draft, and several free agent acquisitions, he was in position to use the 2005 draft essentially to choose a developmental squad. The draftees would play, as backups and on special teams, but nobody needed to start immediately. They could be eased into the system slowly.

It was easy to sell patience in Atlanta, especially after a surprising 11-5 season in 2004. Atlanta never will be described as a rabid sports town. Fans were mostly ambivalent, even when it came to the Braves, a dominant team for more than a decade. In New York, Philadelphia, or Chicago, fans would be calling for major free agent acquisitions to put the team over the hump after a season like the Falcons had in 2004.

There were smatterings of discontent. Terrence Moore, sports columnist for the *Atlanta Journal-Constitution*, wondered in the days leading up to the draft if McKay wasn't overestimating his talent pool.

"He apparently has nerves of steel," Moore wrote. "That's because he doesn't see what I see, and that is an overachieving team that went to the NFC championship game last season by overcoming a lot of things. I'm talking about things such as a secondary that rarely was gouged by a deep pass, but that relinquished so many yards through the air that you figured the Falcons would get a certifiably awesome defensive back from somewhere. They didn't.

"Elsewhere, you have the Falcons' receiving woes. In a tribute to the NFL's Stone Age that featured Bronko Nagurski, three yards and a cloud of dust, and the forward pass only as a last resort, starting wideouts Peerless Price [forty-five catches] and Dez White [thirty-five catches] were virtually invisible. You know you're offensively impaired when your tight end [Alge Crumpler] is your go-to receiver, and nothing has changed."

McKay knew the wide receiver position needed to be addressed. He much preferred drafting at the end of the first round. That meant the team had done well the season before and probably had no pressing needs. The worst place to be was at the end of the first round with a glaring hole, as McKay had been in 2001, with the Buccaneers in dire need of a left tackle.

Not only did McKay have to surrender his second-round pick for the right to move up from number twenty-one to Buffalo's number fourteen in the first round, the Bucs were forced to start that player, University of Florida junior Kenyatta Walker, immediately. Walker quickly alienated teammates and coaches with his underachieving play, poor work ethic, and by voicing his complaints to the media.

"If we didn't get a left tackle, we didn't have anybody to line up there," McKay said. "That is very, very nerve-racking. Because now you're going to watch every card come off, from number five through fifteen, before you can get into range to move up, and that is not fun. You always want to pick last. The next place you want to pick is second to last. And you move up from there."

Picking later in the round requires a different mind-set. From the Buccaneers' first draft in 1976 through 1997, McKay's third as general manager, the team often selected among the first ten picks, including number one five times. As the team improved in the late 1990s and began drafting later, McKay, Tim Ruskell, and Jerry Angelo realized they had to change their thinking. A player they previously considered an early second-round pick needed to be viewed as a late first-rounder, especially with the additions of four new franchises between 1995 and 2002.

So, as the Falcons examined their eighty red-dot players for the 2005 draft, they needed to get an idea of where they might go by round, keeping in mind their late draft position.

The Falcons had pegged Courtney Roby, a wide receiver from Indiana, as a third-round pick. But the more they spoke to teams around the league, the more it became apparent that somebody would take him early in the third round. If the Falcons wanted Roby, they'd have to grab him with their pick at the end of the second—if they did not take a wide receiver in the first.

McKay believed there was danger in picking late in the round, especially the first round, because you're more likely to take a player who chronically underachieves, even though he has tremendous talent. The further he falls, the more of a bargain he appears.

"It's very tempting, because his card will be sticking up on that board and it'll have a fast time, and he'll jump real high. He's going to look great when he comes in here. The only thing is, he's got to go out and play, and he didn't quite do that in college, otherwise he'd have been picked higher."

Though eighty players was a small universe of players in a draft of 255, the red dots were spread out evenly across most positions, with quarterback and tight end being the exceptions. At linebacker, the Falcons had six red dots, all of which projected to go in the second or third rounds.

That group included Jordan Beck of Cal Poly, Southern Cal's Lofa Tatupu, Nebraska's Barrett Ruud, Matt McCoy and Kirk Morrison of San Diego State, and Michael Boley of Southern Miss. Technically, the group also included Davis and Ware, though the Falcons viewed Davis as a safety and Ware as a defensive end. Both would be long gone by number twenty-seven.

Which of the remaining six would fall to the Falcons? In a sense, it didn't matter. Each player fit the Falcons 4-3 defensive scheme, was sufficiently talented to warrant drafting in the second or third round, and passed the team's stringent character evaluations.

Though the Falcons needed help at linebacker, at least from a depth standpoint, there was no guarantee they'd select one in the second round. It depended on which players remained at the higher levels, regardless of position.

Two days before the draft, McKay took a piece of notebook paper and scribbled down the players he thought the Falcons would likely select. It was not a true best-case scenario—no Thomas Davis or Demarcus Ware—but a best case, given the players likely to be available at the end of each round when the Falcons selected.

It was a routine McKay followed every year. For all of the draft's variables and surprises, he usually manages to guess most of his team's selections.

First round: Roddy White, wide receiver, Alabama-Birmingham
Second round: Jordan Beck, outside linebacker, Cal-Poly
Third round: Chauncey Davis, defensive end, Florida State
Fourth round: Marviel Underwood, safety, San Diego State
Fifth round: DeAndra Cobb, running back, Michigan State
Fifth-sixth round: Kevin Dudley, fullback, Michigan

For each pick, McKay kept a "hot list" of five or six names. The idea was to identify players that were good values at each spot and have several contingency plans depending on how other teams drafted. Not even the scouts saw the hot list, just McKay, Blank, Mora, and Emery, the scouting director.

The Falcons first-round hot list consisted of Ware, Davis, White, Georgia defensive end David Pollack, and Marcus Spears, the LSU defensive end. Pollack wasn't the greatest scheme fit; many teams viewed him as a linebacker. Plus, Falcons scouts had learned from other Bulldogs that Pollack wasn't the most popular guy in the locker room, though even then it was hard to poke holes at a guy who rated an AB in character. Pollack's drive and intensity reminded McKay a little of Warren Sapp. There was no way Pollack would accept anything less than success.

Spears, like Pollack, was not a great scheme fit. Plus, there were some lingering concerns about a knee injury suffered during precombine training.

If all five players were gone by the time the Falcons picked, McKay planned to entertain offers to trade down. The top names on the trade-down list were Mike Patterson, the defensive tackle from USC, Fresno State guard Logan Mankins, and Chris Spencer, the center from Ole Miss.

So much of the draft was a chess game of trying to discern which teams would pick players at what spot. Nobody wants to pick a player earlier than they have to, no matter how highly they think of him. Emery and the scouts spent a lot of time gathering intelligence on who teams wanted.

"You never want to overpay," McKay said. "Sometimes coaches will say, 'If we want them, why don't we just take them? It doesn't matter what round.' That's like going to the grocery store really hungry; you'll come out with way too many groceries. Don't do that. Take them where they're supposed to be taken. If somebody else takes them, move on. Take the next guy."

McKay did not go too deep with his projections. He placed Dudley in the fifth- or sixth-round range, in part because the Falcons had two fifth-round picks, having acquired one from Denver in September in exchange for defensive tackle Ellis Johnson.

Most mock drafts had the Falcons taking a defensive player with their first choice, and even McKay publicly acknowledged the team's draft would be heavy on defenders. He still kept his eyes on wide receiver, his Achilles' heel for nearly a decade. No matter how he acquired one—draft, trade, free agency, or inheritance—the player ended up creating headaches.

In Tampa, McKay spent his second number-one pick in 1997, behind Dunn, on Florida's Reidel Anthony. In 1998, without a first-round pick, he chose Gator wide receiver Jacquez Green in the second. Neither became a consistent deep threat.

Free agency proved equally dangerous. In one of McKay's first acts as general manger in Tampa, he signed Alvin Harper away from the Cowboys. Without Michael Irvin by his side, Harper struggled and lasted just two seasons.

Bert Emanuel had posted three consecutive years of nine hundred-plus yards receiving in Atlanta when McKay signed him prior to the 1998 season. Emanuel didn't reach nine hundred yards combined in his two years in Tampa. His Buccaneer career ended appropriately, with disappointment. With the team driving against the Rams late in the fourth quarter of the 1999 NFC championship, Emanuel's catch was ruled incomplete when instant replay showed that the tip of the ball touched the field.

With the Bucs so close to the Super Bowl, McKay surrendered a pair of first-round picks in the 2000 draft to the Jets in exchange for the talented but high-maintenance Keyshawn Johnson, who continued his self-indulgent act in Tampa. Johnson spent the week leading up to one of his first games bashing new Jets head coach Al Groh and former teammate Wayne Chrebet. Johnson called himself a star, Chrebet a flashlight.

Groh issued Jets-logo flashlights to his team and, in one of the highlights of his brief tenure as head coach, the Jets held Johnson to just one catch, a shovel pass for one yard. Chrebet, meanwhile, caught the winning touchdown to cap an unlikely Jets comeback. (Groh keeps one of those flashlights on display in his office at the University of Virginia.)

Johnson, who as a rookie in 1996 authored the book *Just Give Me the Damn Ball,* was forever complaining in Tampa about Tony Dungy's conservative play-calling. Even when Jon Gruden brought his offensive wizardry to the Buccaneers in 2002, Johnson's mood rarely improved, even with a Super Bowl victory. The following season, McKay spent his last weeks as general manager refereeing the Johnson–Gruden feud.

The Bucs did not have a pick until the third round in 2002, having sent their first two selections to the Raiders for Gruden. McKay drafted Michigan wide receiver Marquise Walker in the third round, trading him a year later to the Cardinals for Thomas Jones. Walker made no impact for either team.

At least McKay could point to Joe Jurevicius, who played a key role for Tampa Bay's Super Bowl squad after signing as a free agent before the 2002 season. But even that had an unhappy ending. In the second week of the 2003 season, Jurevicius collided with teammate Mike Alstott, tore a ligament in his knee, and along with Alstott missed most of the season.

In Atlanta, McKay inherited Peerless Price, who parlayed a ninety-four-catch, 1,252-yard 2002 season in Buffalo into a seven-year, $42 million contract. Price caught thirty fewer balls in 2003 and only forty-five in 2004. This, after the Falcons surrendered their first-round pick in the 2003 draft to get him.

In his first draft in Atlanta, McKay targeted the wide receiver position. With the number-eight pick, the Falcons were ready to take Texas wide receiver Roy Williams or Virginia Tech cornerback DeAngelo Hall. When the Lions drafted Williams, the Falcons selected Hall, who had a promising rookie season. But not as promising as Williams, who caught fifty-four passes for 817 yards and eight touchdowns.

Meanwhile, Tampa Bay finally discovered a deep threat. Michael Clayton, the LSU wide receiver the Buccaneers took with the fifteenth pick, outperformed every rookie not named Ben Roethlisberger, catching eighty balls for 1,193 yards and seven touchdowns.

The Falcons traded up to draft a wide receiver with their second first-round pick, grabbing Ohio State's Michael Jenkins—rated AA in character and a Falcon Filter—at number twenty-nine. For the right to do so, the Falcons gave up their second, third, and fourth selections, also receiving the Colts' third-round choice.

Jenkins caught just seven passes as a rookie, but played a prominent role on special teams. McKay thought it was premature for anyone to pass judgment on Jenkins, who, unlike Tampa Bay's Clayton or Williams in Detroit, was not called upon to start in 2004.

With Vick as quarterback, it was difficult to judge the Falcons' receiving corps. Did receivers underachieve because Vick, the best running quarterback in the league, did not look to them enough? Or did he lack the precision touch to get them the ball more? Or was he forced to run more because he did not have enough downfield threats?

Whatever the reason, it was clear by the end of the 2004 season that Price and Dez White, the number-two receiver, were not the long-term solutions.

The 2005 draft did not offer as many promising receivers as 2004, when seven were chosen in the first round. Michigan's Braylon Edwards clearly was the class of the 2005 bunch, though he would be long gone before the Falcons picked.

So would Mike Williams, the former Southern Cal receiver who had missed a season following his unsuccessful attempt to enter the draft early. The Falcons had plenty of inside scoop on Williams, who grew up in Tampa not far from where McKay used to live and where scout Boyd Dowler still resided. During McKay's tenure in Tampa, Williams visited

Buccaneers headquarters as a guest of Keyshawn Johnson, who was pushing him toward USC.

Even if Williams fell to the Falcons, he wasn't a good fit. He reminded Dowler of Kellen Winslow, the Hall of Fame tight end whose son, Kellen II, was drafted in the first round in 2004. Dowler looked at how Williams's frame had thickened over the last two years. He still had a lean, powerful physique, but it was morphing into that of an H-back or tight end. That was of little use to the Falcons, with All-Pro Crumpler in the house.

Dowler, the former Packers receiver for Vince Lombardi, scouted the southeast for the Falcons in the fall and served as a cross-checker on wide receivers in the spring. By March, the Falcons had five wide receivers pegged as first-rounders: Edwards, Williams, South Carolina's Troy Williamson, Oklahoma's Mark Clayton, and Roddy White of Alabama-Birmingham.

Williamson's stock had soared. A six-one speedster, he left South Carolina with a year of eligibility remaining. The Falcons knew he would be long gone by the time they picked. They loved the sure-handed, five-ten Clayton, but felt they needed someone bigger.

That left Sharod "Roddy" White, whom Dowler had seen a lot of during the 2004 season, visiting the UAB campus three times and watching the Blazers game at Florida State. With UAB playing in Conference USA, the nonconference game against the Seminoles was by far the toughest competition White faced all year.

Dowler did not place too much weight on level of competition, remembering how some scouts knocked Randy Moss in college because his school, Marshall University, did not play the most imposing schedule.

"You could see where Moss dominated the competition," Dowler said. "Roddy White was clearly getting beyond the secondary, and it's not like he was playing 1-AA football."

Dowler visited UAB three times, once more than he visited Alabama, which had no blue-chip prospects for the 2005 draft. Following McKay's guidelines of interviewing five sources, Dowler spoke to everyone at UAB—coaches, strength coach, trainers, and academic advisors. He delved into White's high school days—White was a two-time all-state wrestling champion—and even rounded up a couple of youth coaches.

White was hardly perfect. He wasn't much of a blocker and his work ethic wasn't the greatest. He rated just a CC on the Falcons scale for football and personal character. But that was outweighed, the Falcons believed, by a huge upside and fiery determination.

"Everybody I talked to, going back to playing baseball as a nine- or ten-year-old, talked about how competitive he is," Dowler said. "He doesn't like to lose and he definitely doesn't like to look bad."

Dowler and the rest of the scouts had followed McKay's orders to be thorough in their background checks. Taylor Morton reached a point with Spears, the defensive end from LSU, where he almost felt like a member of the family.

Morton began his investigation in June of 2004, making an early visit to Baton Rouge. He returned in September and November. LSU was one of a handful of teams that had two pro days, and Morton attended both. Along the way, he spoke to anyone he could find that could provide insight into the defensive end.

"I met his dad three times and he knows me by name," Morton says. "I can tell you his sister's name, what his fiancée does, where he went to high school, and who his high school coach is. You get so much data, you hit a wall where you say, 'I know this guy.' But that's the level Rich wants you to be familiar with these players."

By mid-April White had emerged as the Falcons' most likely first-round draft pick. Other receivers passed the team's character filters and fit the West Coast offense, most notably Indiana's Courtney Roby, but the Falcons did not believe he warranted more than a third-round pick. Roby would serve as a fallback position in case the Falcons missed out on White in the first—or someone more desirable at another position fell to them at number twenty-seven.

The Falcons were not pinning everything on White. As with the other rounds, McKay had options for the first-round pick.

"One philosophy I've stayed with is to treat the draft just like a trial," McKay said. "Go into it with the idea that everything is put to bed. There are no surprises. Just realize that there will be a surprise or two involving trades."

McKay had whiffed on wide receivers with either a first-round pick or his first overall selection in three of the previous eight drafts, four if Jenkins was counted. Even McKay's wife, Terrin, got on him about his track record picking receivers. Other positions offered safer options, but McKay felt confident he'd finally catch a break at receiver with White.

Chapter Sixteen:

DRAFT DAY

E SPN's coverage of the seventieth NFL Selection Meeting, better known as "the draft," began at noon on Saturday, April 23, 2005. The broadcast unfolded with a flurry of graphics, ominous tones, Chris Berman voiceovers, and hyperbole. The theme was "Wall Street," and ESPN had brought many of the projected first-rounders to the floor of the New York Stock Exchange earlier in the week to pose, scowl, and boast in front of the camera.

"If value is what you're after, you better pick me," said Alex Smith, the Utah quarterback.

"I've put in the work already," Cal quarterback Aaron Rodgers said. "You just have to call my name."

Soft-spoken tight end Heath Miller of tiny Swords Creek, Virginia, and the University of Virginia, seemed the most uncomfortable following ESPN's scripted Wall Street smack talk.

"I feel there are no risks in drafting me," he said.

Back at the Falcons training complex in Flowery Branch, things were quiet. Rich McKay, clad in dress slacks, white shirt, and red tie, watched the broadcast unfold from the draft room along with the scouting staff, clad in team logo polo shirts. Team owner Arthur Blank, nattily tailored as always in a dark suit and red tie, stood in the back of the room with friends and invited guests. Lunch was available in the back of the room.

Downstairs, the media room was quiet. With teams allotted fifteen minutes per pick, the first round proceeded at a painstaking pace. The Falcons did not figure to pick for at least five hours. Still, technicians were working in small chambers off the press room, hooking up live video feeds for ESPN and The NFL Network, prepared in the unlikely event of a trade.

Like most sporting events, the draft did not start as scheduled. ESPN's Chris Berman, Chris Mortenson, and Mel Kiper Jr. spent the first thirteen minutes setting the stage, which for the first time since 1995 was not at Madison Square Garden's Paramount Theater. With Cablevision, the owner of the facility, and the New York Jets arguing over a proposed West Side stadium for the Jets, the NFL moved the event to the Jacob K. Javits Convention Center.

The Falcons table was occupied by video director Mike Crews, logistics manager Spencer Treadwell, and sixteen-year-old Hunter McKay, continuing his father's Tampa tradition of relaying picks via telephone.

At 12:13 P.M., NFL commissioner Paul Tagliabue strode to the podium and announced that the San Francisco 49ers were on the clock. The 49ers, under new head coach Mike Nolan, spent nearly their entire fifteen minutes deliberating, which allowed ESPN's Suzy Kolber enough time to interview IMG agent Tom Condon, who represents Alex Smith. Condon told Kolber he had not heard from the Niners in a day and a half.

Finally, at 12:26, San Francisco selected Smith, who smiled as he walked to the podium to greet Tagliabue, don a 49ers cap, and mug for the cameras.

That put the Miami Dolphins on the clock and Ronnie Brown on camera, chatting with agent Todd France. It had been a busy couple of days for France, who, as the agent for three top draft prospects, had become a story himself. In the weeks leading up to the draft, France's office fielded more than a dozen requests from media outlets looking to tag along with him and Brown in New York.

France knew there was a fine line between providing access that's beneficial to the client and generating unnecessary publicity that makes the agent look self-promotional. Guys like Drew Rosenhaus and Leigh Steinberg were forever pushing the envelope on that front. France knew other agents would be gunning for him after a blockbuster 2005 draft, and the last thing he wanted to do was provide them with more ammunition. The story, France believed, was Brown, Rogers, and Davis, not their agent.

In the end, France listened to his four-person staff. Maybe the exposure could help them add to the considerable endorsements they already had landed for the trio. France let the hometown *Atlanta Journal-Constitution* accompany him and Brown, not because France was based in Atlanta but because Brown is a Georgia native. As for the sports-business writers looking to explore the agent angle, he opted for ESPN.com and reporter Darren Rovell.

Brown and France checked into the Westin Times Square on Wednesday night. They spent Thursday shopping along Fifth Avenue, enjoying a one-thousand-dollar, please-sign-with-us buying spree at Niketown, listening to a Reebok sales pitch, and stopping in at Saks Fifth Avenue.

On the morning of the draft, France told Brown not to look disappointed if the Dolphins did not select him at number two. After all, cameras would be rolling. He and Brown arrived at the Javits Center at 11:00 A.M. and sat in a backstage green room, along with the agents and family members of the other five invited players.

After Smith was selected, France clasped his hands, as if in prayer. The second pick in the 2004 draft, Robert Gallery, received a package that included $18.5 million, guaranteed.

France, wearing a blue suit, stayed calm. He reminded Brown that the Dolphins could opt for Braylon Edwards, the wide receiver from Michigan. Instead, with just a minute remaining on the clock, the Dolphins selected Brown.

Brown stood, hugged his mother, and then France, who wiped away a few tears. The agent spent the next three picks following Brown around to his various media obligations. Dolphins beat writers asked France if he thought the rumored return of running back Ricky Williams from a one-year hiatus would affect his client's negotiating leverage. France deflected the queries, keeping one eye on the draft.

The Cleveland Browns selected Edwards with the third pick. Cedric Benson, the Texas running back, went to the Chicago Bears at number four. The Tampa Bay Buccaneers, to nobody's surprise, selected Cadillac Williams fifth.

France's decision to recruit Brown, who backed up Williams at the beginning of the 2004 season, paid off. Back in Flowery Branch, scout Matt Berry moved the Williams magnets to the right wall. For all the talk of McKay and Buccaneers head coach Jon Gruden differing on draft philosophy, the Bucs took a player at the top of the Falcons' chart.

In New York, with Brown now a Dolphin, France turned his attention to client Carlos Rogers, the Auburn cornerback. France believed Rogers could go in the top ten, but after five offensive picks, he needed some other corners to come off the board. Floyd Reese, the Tennessee Titans general manager who attended two dozen pro days, obliged by drafting Adam "Pac Man" Jones from West Virginia.

The Minnesota Vikings, using a pick acquired from the Oakland Raiders for Randy Moss, selected a potential replacement: Troy Williamson of the University of South Carolina, a favorite of Falcons scout Boyd Dowler. The Arizona Cardinals then took another cornerback, Miami's Antrel Rolle.

With reporters still interviewing Brown backstage, France left his client to watch Tagliabue announce the ninth pick. At 2:13 P.M., Tagliabue announced the Redskins took Rogers. France, standing next to Rovell, the ESPN.com reporter, pumped his fist and screamed, "Yes! Yes! Yes!"

France called Rogers, "I'm so, so, so, so happy for you . . . How fired up are you baby? . . . Just like we talked about!"

The next pick produced the day's first surprise, albeit a mild one. Mike Williams, the Southern Cal wide receiver who sat out the 2004 season after his ill-fated attempt to go pro after his sophomore year, went to the Detroit Lions, who for the third consecutive year took a receiver with a top-ten pick.

The night before, Williams ate dinner with Tampa Bay general manager Bruce Allen and now was hosting a draft party in his native Tampa at a restaurant around the corner from Raymond James Stadium.

"I really feel like it came down to me and Cadillac Williams, and they had a better feel for Cadillac Williams," Mike Williams told reporters.

With Mike Williams off the board, France and SFX agent Ben Dogra, who represented Cadillac Williams and Rolle, were the only agents with a pair of top-ten picks. It was nothing new for Dogra, whose client list included Lions wide receiver Roy Williams, the seventh pick in 2004. For France, it was more significant. No longer would rival agents be able to say he never had represented a first-round pick.

At that point he had two, with a third—Thomas Davis—waiting in the wings.

Back at Flowery Branch, McKay took a break from the draft room. He walked down the hall, over the marble Falcons inlay, past the Arthur Blank portrait, and into his office, where he kept an eye on a flat-screen television on his desk tuned to ESPN.

So far, the draft had unfolded as expected. The Falcons were fans of many of the first ten picks, especially Brown, Cadillac Williams, and Rolle, though they knew they had no real shot at any of them, especially after Williams went to Tampa Bay. Six weeks earlier, they believed they had a legitimate shot at Rolle.

"You've got to be prepared for anything," McKay said. "Who's to say someone doesn't call us and say we love one of your players and we're going to give you a one, and that one is the twelfth pick in the draft? Because of that, you can't treat players any differently. But when it comes to the end and you get within a week of the draft, things change. We're not spending any time in the last two weeks on Antrel Rolle. But before, when we looked at it, we did. Because you just don't know. The last thing you want to be is unprepared."

McKay remembered 1998, when Randy Moss began to fall toward the Buccaneers, who held the number-twenty-three pick before trading it to Oakland for a pair of second-round choices. Many teams had character concerns about Moss. Unlike 1995, when the Bucs investigated Warren Sapp, they had not done as thorough a job with Moss, believing he'd never fall so far.

"Had he come to us, we would have had an issue," McKay said. "The issue was that we hadn't done as much work as we would have liked. You should always be prepared, because you never know."

At the moment, the Falcons had not lost any of the players on their short list for number twenty-seven. Roddy White, McKay's projection, was still there. So, too, were Thomas Davis, David Pollack, Marcus Spears, and Demarcus Ware, though McKay knew what was coming next.

Tagliabue stepped to the podium and announced that Dallas had selected Ware. McKay shook his head. Ware didn't come close to falling to twenty, striking distance for a trade. "They got Ware, huh?" McKay said. "Good pick."

The selection of Ware salvaged the draft for Pat Dye, Jr., who watched as three Auburn clients, including two represented by France, went in the top ten. Ware's selection capped a meteoric rise for a player who, coming out of high school, was a 165-pound wide receiver with few scholarship offers. Now he was a dominant 251-pound player who could play linebacker or defensive end.

In Seattle, Tim Ruskell crossed Ware off his board. Ruskell viewed Ware as a defensive end and he needed one desperately. It was another example of how difficult it was to land a premium player at that position.

"The good ends go early," Ruskell said. "Just look at Ware. He had just one great year of production, at Troy State of all places, and we're not even sure what he'll be in the NFL. And yet we all wanted him."

The San Diego Chargers selected Shawne Merriman, a defensive end from the University of Maryland, at number twelve. Merriman was not a scheme fit for the Falcons; Maryland and the Chargers played in a 3–4 alignment. He also did not pass the Falcons' character filters.

At 2:53 P.M., the New Orleans Saints traded up with Houston at number thirteen and selected Jammal Brown, an offensive tackle from Oklahoma and the third Dogra client of the day. The Falcons, following the Alex Gibbs philosophy of not spending high picks on offensive linemen, had no interest in larger lineman like Brown or Florida State's Alex Barron.

France knew if he wanted to accompany Ronnie Brown to Miami, he could only stay at the Javits Center for one or two more picks. A car was waiting to take them to LaGuardia Airport. At 3:05 P.M., France stared at a television mounted on the wall in the green room. The Carolina Panthers took Davis at number fourteen.

France reached his client in Shellman, Georgia—one of France's staff members was attending the draft party—and congratulated "T. D." on his selection. "How happy are you?" he asked Davis. "Are we on it, or what?"

After a brief conversation with Davis, France leaned back against the wall. His eyes moistened. Given the information the agent had before the draft, Brown, Rogers, and Davis each had gone as high as he believed possible.

"We got [number] two," France tells Rovell, the ESPN.com reporter. "We got nine. We got fourteen. I'm fired up. But I'm absolutely drained."

The Davis pick ended any thought of the Falcons' best-case scenario taking place. It also caused the first nervous moments in the Falcons' draft room. Twelve selections remained before number twenty-seven. The key, the scouts knew, was for two quarterbacks to come off the board. Aaron Rodgers, the Cal quarterback, was the last of the six players remaining in the green room at the Javits Center. The NFL had invited Rodgers to New York for draft day, along with Smith, Ronnie Brown, Edwards, Benson, and Rolle. There were reports that the Redskins, who four days earlier traded their number-one pick in 2006, and two other choices, to Denver for the number-twenty-five selection, were interested in Jason Campbell, the Auburn quarterback.

Then there was the Ruskell wild card. The Seattle Seahawks president, having traded down with the Raiders from number twenty-three to number twenty-six, and also receiving Oakland's fourth-round selection, was just two months removed from Falcons' employment and one selection in front of his former team.

The picks began to fall in Atlanta's favor. The Chiefs selected Texas linebacker Derrick Johnson at number fifteen—too pricey for the Falcons' linebacker needs, and not a good scheme fit. Houston grabbed Florida State defensive tackle Travis Johnson, who did not pass the Falcons' character filter.

The draft already was more than three and a half hours old, with just sixteen picks on the board. Nobody was more impatient than McKay, who, as cochairman of the NFL's competition committee, had lobbied hard to cut down on the time spent on each selection

"I've tried three different times to move the first round to twelve minutes and the second round to eight, or doing something. But we haven't gotten there yet. I would even consider trying to say that the first sixteen picks be fifteen minutes and then the next fifteen be ten. I just don't think pick twenty-four requires fifteen minutes. It's very annoying. I have no idea how [ESPN] fills in that much stuff.

"If you want agony, just try doing it the year when your first- and second-round picks are traded away. Our first pick that year [2002] was at 9:00, maybe 9:30. We'd sit in [Ruskell's] office and we'd say, 'You know what? Let's go sit in my office.' We'd go over and hang out there. Then we'd go back in the draft room. We just couldn't do anything, nothing. And you can't leave. Somebody could call and say, 'We're going to trade you Bronco Nagurski.' So you've got to stay and there's nothing going on. You call other people. Hey, how's it going? You having fun? We're not doing anything. It is very, very, very tough."

After Johnson, there was a run on defensive ends and an offensive tackle. Pollack, the Georgia end who grew up in the Atlanta suburbs, went to the Bengals. At number eighteen, the Vikings selected Wisconsin defensive end Erasmus James, a player the Falcons did not view as a good scheme fit. The Rams then took Barron, the Florida State offensive tackle.

Dallas, still looking to revamp its defense, selected Spears, the defensive end from LSU, leaving McKay with just one player on his hot list: Roddy White, the wide receiver from Alabama-Birmingham, with seven picks to go.

At number twenty-one, the Jaguars provided the day's first surprise, taking Matt Jones of Arkansas. Jones, who played quarterback for the Razorbacks, but thrilled NFL scouts at the Senior Bowl and combine at wide receiver, soared up draft boards in March. The Falcons were intrigued with Jones, but like many teams saw him as a tight end. No need there.

The Baltimore Ravens drafted sure-handed wide receiver Mark Clayton from Oklahoma at number twenty-two, giving Dogra, the SFX agent, his fourth first-rounder of the day. The Falcons loved Clayton's character and performance, but felt they needed someone taller than five-ten in their West Coast offense. At number twenty-three, the Raiders selected

Nebraska cornerback Fabian Washington, who didn't pass the Falcons' character filters.

When it came to defensive backs, there were few among the Falcons eighty red dots. Besides Davis and Rolle, there were cornerbacks Bryant McFadden (Florida State), Dominique Foxworth (Maryland), and Justin Miller (Clemson). The Falcons thought enough of Miller to have brought him to Flowery Branch for a predraft interview. Miller had pleaded guilty to a drunken driving charge in July of 2002, and the Falcons were willing to give him the benefit of the doubt. However, Miller didn't help his character rating with a disorderly conduct arrest a week before the draft.

The Falcons were even choosier when it came to safeties. Besides Davis and Marviel Underwood, McKay's projected fourth-round pick, the only other red-dotter was Sean Considine of Iowa.

After spending nearly five hours in the green room, Rodgers finally got to come to the podium, the newest member of the Green Bay Packers. Washington, as expected, made it two quarterbacks in a row, drafting Auburn's Campbell.

Then the only thing standing in the way of the Falcons was Ruskell. It was tough to read Ruskell, who knew much of the Falcons' draft plan, having been employed at Flowery Branch until February 21. But though he sat in on the defensive team meetings, he left before the offensive side of the ball was discussed. McKay could not recall ever talking to his friend about Roddy White.

Like McKay, Ruskell had hoped to trade up, preferably to take a defensive end like Ware, to upgrade a defense that ranked twenty-sixth in the league in 2004.

When that didn't happen, Ruskell did not have any ends on the board that warranted the number-twenty-six pick. The Seahawks, like the Falcons, were not about to drop down a level to draft a player. Instead, the first draft pick of the Tim Ruskell Era in Seattle was Chris Spencer, the center from Ole Miss.

Ruskell, dressed in a suit and tie at the team's headquarters in Kirkland, Washington, anticipated the fallout. "It wasn't a flashy pick," Ruskell told reporters, "so I figured I'd be flashy."

McKay and the Falcons had no interest in using the number-twenty-seven pick on Spencer, whom they rated a 5.9-plus, CC player; Ruskell rated him higher in Seattle. The Falcons liked Spencer enough to have brought him in to Flowery Branch for an interview, and he was on the team's short list, in the event they could not get anyone rated sufficiently high at number twenty-seven and traded down.

Instead, they proved *Sports Illustrated*'s Paul Zimmerman correct and grabbed Roddy White, a 6.2 CC player and an excellent value at number twenty-seven. White was the last player on McKay's hot list. Had White been gone and had he been unable to trade down, he would have taken Southern Cal defensive tackle Mike Patterson, or Logan Mankins, a guard from Fresno State. Those players were the last two picks of the first round, going to Philadelphia and New England, respectively.

McKay was surprised how little his phone had rung throughout the first round; there was little trade action from teams looking to trade up or down. Before he could savor the White selection, he took a call he feared would come soon. His brother, J. K., was on the line from Tampa with the news that their mother, Nancy "Corky" McKay, had died after a four-year bout with cancer.

As the widow of John McKay, the former Southern Cal and Buccaneers head coach, Corky McKay understood the importance of draft day. Three days before the draft, Rich McKay traveled to Tampa and stayed for twenty-four hours before she ordered him back to Atlanta to be with his team. "We talked a long time," McKay said later. "I would have liked to have been there, obviously."

With the first round finally over after six hours, teams were given just five minutes per pick. The Eagles, selecting third in the round, took Georgia wide receiver Reggie Brown, giving Pat Dye Jr. his second client in the first thirty-five. Brown, once considered the second-best Bulldogs receiver, had gone before Fred Gibson.

The Buccaneers, picking next, selected Barrett Ruud, the linebacker from Nebraska, and another one of the Falcons' eighty red dots. The Bucs, McKay wryly noted, were thinking along the same lines as the Falcons, at least with their first two selections.

Now McKay was hunting for a linebacker. He looked at his hot list. His projected second-round pick, Cal-Poly linebacker Jordan Beck, still was on the board. So, too, were defensive ends Dan Cody of Oklahoma and Southern Cal's Shaun Cody. Miller, the Clemson cornerback, was still there, along with Iowa defensive tackle Jonathan Babineaux.

Other teams obliged, with a run on cornerbacks and wide receivers, though McKay's hot list suffered a blow when Shaun Cody went to Detroit. Ruskell, also needing linebacker help, traded up nine picks with Carolina to select Southern Cal's Lofa Tatupu, projected by many as a third- or fourth-round pick.

McKay and Ruskell had watched USC's blowout of Oklahoma in the Orange Bowl in Miami, and McKay came away infatuated with Tatupu.

It seemed like he touched ten passes. When Tatupu, a junior, decided to go pro, they watched tape on him together.

After Ruskell's conservative first-round selection of a center, the drafting of Tatupu in the second was stunning.

"For Tim to take Tatupu is not fair. I found him," McKay quipped. "Tim will catch criticism for where he took him, thinking maybe he could have gotten him later, but he's going to be a good player."

With the Seahawks out of the way, the board began to fall in favor of the Falcons. The Dolphins took Matt Roth, the Iowa defensive end, and the Jets stunned their Javits Center faithful by making Ohio State's Mike Nugent the highest-drafted kicker since Florida State's Sebastian Janikowski in 2000.

ESPN producers cued the tape of Kiper's comments in 1989. "It's obvious to me the Jets don't know what the draft's all about," the younger Kiper says. The older Mel is kinder to the Jets and Nugent.

The Bengals, drafting next, took junior Georgia linebacker Odell Thurman, whose history of disciplinary problems took him out of consideration by the Falcons.

McKay looked at the board. There were ten picks remaining, and most of his second-round hot list remained on the front wall. That changed when Baltimore, selecting six picks before the Falcons, drafted Dan Cody. McKay looked at the team-needs board toward the back of the room and saw a nice problem developing. Babineaux and Beck both stood to be available for Atlanta.

Sure enough, the next five picks consisted of a running back and two wide receivers—no interest there—along with a cornerback (Darrent Williams of Oklahoma State went to the Broncos) that did not pass the Falcons' character filter. (Williams's resume included a positive test for marijuana as a freshman and not endearing himself to the coaches with his bad attitude.)

Momentum Sports agents Jeff Griffin and Jack Scharf had two picks with Williams and Howard cornerback Ronald Bartell, selected by the Rams three picks before Dan Cody. Scharf technically still was looking for his first drafted client; Griffin was the lead agent-of-record for Bartell and Williams.

The Jets, picking before the Falcons with their second choice of the round, took Clemson's Miller.

That left McKay with Beck and Babineaux. Both were rated 5.9 on the Falcons' board. Beck fit the McKay profile, a dynamic leader and classic overachiever who made the most of his talent. He earned a perfect AA character rating, along with the rare Falcon Filter designation. Babineaux had a solid CB character rating. Picking Beck looked like the logical move.

McKay preached to his staff that character was not to be used as a tie-breaker on draft day, but as a way to whittle down the universe of players beforehand. Perhaps Beck, his projected second-round pick, could last until the third round. If not, he had other red-dot linebackers for later in the draft, albeit ones for later round hot lists.

The Falcons did not expect Babineaux, unlike Beck, to last until the end of the second round. In that sense, Babineaux was the better value. Besides, the Falcons always were looking for athletic defensive tackles that fit their one-gap system. Babineaux, at 286 pounds, meshed perfectly. McKay, having missed out on USC's Mike Patterson when the Eagles took him at the end of the first round, snapped up Babineaux.

The rest of the second round took out some popular players in the Falcons' draft room. Wide receiver Vincent Jackson, the Northern Colorado favorite of scout Boyd Dowler, went to San Diego, though with the selection of White in the first round it didn't matter. The Steelers grabbed McFadden, the cornerback that Brett Maxie, the defensive backs coach, worked out at Florida State's pro day. The consensus in the room, however, was that McFadden warranted no more than a third-round pick. The Eagles, again thinking like the Falcons, chose San Diego State linebacker Matt McCoy, who was on McKay's third-round hot list.

With the draft now nine hours old, the 49ers led off the third round by selecting Miami running back Frank Gore. Three picks later, the Tennessee Titans went with Courtney Roby, the Indiana wide receiver the Falcons correctly predicted they'd have to take with their late second-round pick (had they not chosen White and still wanted a receiver.)

Tampa Bay, picking seventh in the round, chose "the other" Alex Smith, the tight end from Stanford. That inspired Buccaneers head coach Jon Gruden to quip that the rumors of the Bucs interest in Alex Smith had been correct after all. Back in Flowery Branch, scout Matt Berry moved the Smith magnet over to the right wall board, where it became the third straight red-dot player for the Bucs. Though Smith had a red-dot, he was never hot-listed since the Falcons did not want to spend such a high pick on a position where they did not need help.

The same was true for David Greene. With Matt Schaub entrenched behind Michael Vick, there was almost no scenario—barring Greene falling to the seventh round—that would have caused the Falcons to pick the former Georgia quarterback.

That wasn't out of the question for Greene, whose lack of quickness and arm strength scared off many teams. Unlike many players, Greene did not have a draft party, preferring to watch the event at home with immediate family, and politely turned down requests from Atlanta media to view the draft with him.

He need not have worried. Ruskell, who needed a backup quarterback in Seattle, selected Greene with his third-round pick, the eighty-fifth overall. Greene, speaking to Seahawks writers via a conference call, addressed his lack of arm strength yet again.

"There are a lot of guys in the NFL that have had great careers and didn't have the strongest arms, because they were able to throw on time and they were accurate. I'd rather have accuracy over arm strength any day of the week."

For Pat Dye Jr., Greene joined clients Demarcus Ware and Reggie Brown as draft overachievers, at least by their projections on New Year's Day. In Flowery Branch, Greene's magnet gave the Seahawks, like the Buccaneers, three of the Falcons' red-dot players, along with Spencer and Tatupu.

Five picks later, the Falcons still had a choice of red-dot linebackers. The Raiders took red-dotter and third-round hot list member Kirk Morrison at number seventy-eight, but Beck remained on the hot list. So did Chauncey Davis, the Florida State defensive end and McKay's projected third-round selection.

This time, McKay chose Beck, a two-year team captain at Cal Poly, with a nonstop motor on the field and tireless work habits in the weight room. Projected as a fourth- or fifth-rounder in some mock drafts, Beck found himself looking at a signing bonus of around four hundred and thirty thousand dollars, double what he might have received as a fourth-round pick and more than triple what a fifth-rounder would get.

Then there was Maurice Clarett, who went to Denver with the one hundred and first selection, the last of the third round. The pick jolted the ESPN crew, showing fatigue from eleven hours of coverage. Many teams figured Clarett would go in the sixth or seventh round, if he was selected at all. Instead, he was drafted by a team with a deep stable of running backs.

"His slate is clean and we're giving him an opportunity," Broncos head coach Mike Shanahan said.

As ESPN signed off on the first day of draft coverage, other players wondered where their opportunities had gone.

Chapter Seventeen:

DAY TWO

Suzy Kolber took over for Chris Berman as lead host of ESPN's draft coverage on Sunday. ESPN's panel of Chris Mortenson, Mike Golic, and Mel Kiper Jr. continued to analyze the shocking selection of Maurice Clarett the night before. Denver head coach Mike Shanahan appeared via teleconference to defend the pick.

Kiper presented his list of the top twelve remaining draft prospects. Anttaj Hawthorne, the Wisconsin defensive tackle who had tested positive for marijuana use at the combine, was number three. Ray Willis, the Florida State offensive tackle, was number six and Chris Canty was number eight. Fred Gibson, the Georgia wide receiver, was not on Kiper's list.

Willis was back in Tallahassee watching the draft alone with his wife Kimberly. They weren't especially surprised when he didn't hear his name called the first day. Agents Bill Johnson and Pat Dye Jr. had tempered their expectations. With Ray's ankle injury and history of ailments, it was hard to make a prediction.

At the Seattle Seahawks draft headquarters in Kirkland, Washington, Tim Ruskell was glad to see Willis still available. Ruskell, still only two months on the job as Seahawks president, had one of the more confusing draft rooms. One board was set up using the Atlanta Falcons' mold, another with the Seahawks' existing system.

Freed from the constraints of the Alex Gibbs offensive line philosophy, Ruskell used the fourth pick in the fourth round on Willis, a player deemed too tight and not athletic enough to play for the Falcons.

"I like him a lot as a person," said Ruskell, who used the pick he acquired from Oakland for trading down in the first round to draft Willis. "He's got toughness, character—and he's relentless when it comes to effort. For me, that's what being an offensive lineman is all about. Guys like Ray aren't always pretty, but they're tough and they usually pan out better than others. He's a quiet guy, but he's smart and there's a passion that comes out on the field."

Six picks later, the Arizona Cardinals selected Virginia guard Elton Brown, considered a first-round lock for much of the fall. But Brown left the Senior Bowl and combine early with a knee injury and then pulled a hamstring while working out during his pro day in Charlottesville. No player fell further since the end of the season without failing a drug test.

It had been a disappointing draft all around for the Virginia Cavaliers. Heath Miller became the school's first player to go in the first round since 2000, but he fell to Pittsburgh and the thirtieth pick because some teams had concerns about the tight end's abdominal injury. Linebacker Darryl Blackstock, who left school early in part because he misinterpreted his "not higher than the second round" rating from the NFL advisory committee, did not go until the end of the third round to the Arizona Cardinals.

Alvin Pearman, the fast-rising running back who was the target of the fierce recruiting battle between agents Ethan Lock and David Dunn in January, also was still seeking employment, though that was not unexpected.

Kiper suggested Brown needed to be more aggressive, while praising the Virginia program. "That's a talent-laden team at Virginia," Kiper said. "Al Groh has done a great job of recruiting."

Green Bay, with the fourteenth pick in the fourth round, selected Marviel Underwood, the San Diego State safety that Falcons general manager Rich McKay had projected as his fourth-round pick prior to the draft. A pair of Florida State players went next (wide receiver Craphonso Thorpe to the Chiefs, and safety Jerome Carter to the Rams), giving the Seminoles six picks on the day.

The Jacksonville Jaguars, with former Virginia assistant coach Andy Heck working in a similar role, selected Pearman, the versatile Cavalier running back, with the twenty-sixth pick in the fourth round. The Falcons, drafting next, chose Florida State defensive end Chauncey Davis, McKay's projected third-round pick.

The Falcons considered Davis at the end of the third round but did not want to pass up linebacker Jordan Beck. The Davis pick continued McKay's long tradition of drafting Seminoles, and he likened Davis to Greg Spires, a late-blooming former FSU end who was drafted in the third round by New England in 1998 and played a key role on Tampa Bay's Super Bowl team in 2002.

"We feel like Davis is on the upswing," McKay said. "He's a great kid, definitely has some pass rushing skills. He's just going to get bigger and stronger. He's not close to where he's going to be strength wise. He's a high-motor guy. You watch tape and he goes a hundred miles per hour on every play."

Back in Waycross, Georgia, Fred Gibson remained at his grandmother's house in his old bedroom, watching the draft with a cousin. The community center would not be hosting a day-two draft party; nobody had planned for it.

The Arizona Cardinals called early in the day, telling Gibson they might be selecting him, but they chose Elton Brown instead. Now he watched more wide receivers come off the board. With the thirteenth pick in the round, the Houston Texans chose Jerome Mathis, who played Division 1-AA ball at Hampton (Virginia) University, but ran a combine-best 4.28 in the forty. Kansas City chose FSU's Thorpe with the thirteenth selection and New Orleans selected California's Chase Lyman at seventeen, making him the sixteenth wide receiver drafted.

Two picks after the Falcons selected Davis, San Diego drafted Darren Sproles, the tiny running back from Kansas State. That put the Pittsburgh Steelers on the clock and it was then that Gibson's cell phone rang. He would be joining a team that finished 15-1 the previous season with rookie quarterback Ben Roethlisberger at the helm. The Steelers needed a tall receiver, having lost the six-five Plaxico Burress to free agency and the New York Giants.

"I can't wait to get to Pittsburgh and start catching the football," Gibson said. "I want to go out and prove everybody wrong."

The Steelers chose Gibson in the midst of Suzy Kolber's teleconference interview with David Pollack. Kiper didn't miss a beat.

The Steelers "lose one tall receiver in Plaxico Burress and get another one in Fred Gibson, who goes about six-four. What he needs to do is fill out that frame and become a little more consistent."

In Charlotte, Chris Canty waited patiently as the Philadelphia Eagles were on the clock. Or were they? His cell phone rang and he learned that he was the newest member of the Dallas Cowboys, who had traded up to get him.

Bill Parcells continued the overhaul of his defensive line, having already selected Demarcus Ware and Marcus Spears in the first round. ESPN showed a shot of a triumphant Dallas draft room, noting that Parcells had not officially committed to switching to the 3-4 defense that Canty had played under Parcells's protégé Groh at Virgina. Still, with Ware, Spears, and Canty on the roster, the 3-4 looked inevitable.

Canty was glad to be off the board and headed to a team where he was a perfect scheme fit. Still, he remained in shock. He thought he would be chosen in the second round, certainly no later than the third.

"I'm happy to be drafted," Canty said, "but this wasn't the excitement that I hoped for."

Still, the Canty household was downright jubilant compared to the scene at Ed Hawthorne's home in Connecticut, where his nephew, Anttaj, was watching his once-lofty draft status plummet.

When the Tennessee Titans drafted Tulane wide receiver Roydell Williams with the last pick in the fourth round, Anttaj Hawthorne's name moved to the top of Mel Kiper Jr.'s list of best available players.

That's where it remained throughout the fifth round. When the Philadelphia Eagles selected Brigham Young guard Scott Young, with the third-to-last pick in the round, Hawthorne was the only player left from Kiper's ten highest-rated players from the start of the day.

Hawthorne was among four players, including Wisconsin teammate Jonathan Clinkscale, to test positive for marijuana at the NFL combine in Indianapolis. Before the season, Kiper rated Hawthorne the best defensive tackle prospect for the draft and the eleventh-best overall.

From a character standpoint, Hawthorne rated high. Down-to-earth, levelheaded, and immensely popular with his teammates, "this kid could run for president," proclaimed one Internet scouting service. Still, scouts were concerned about Hawthorne's dropoff in production from the 2003 season. He could be a disruptive force, but at times seemed to take plays off. The positive drug test raised a red flag.

"One of the biggest knocks on Hawthorne is that he plays lazy, takes snaps off, and does not give great effort on every down, despite his natural physical talent," wrote *Pro Football Weekly*'s Nolan Nawrocki on April 12 when the test results became public. "The test results could give scouts a reason to explain his effort."

It didn't help that most teams identified Hawthorne strictly as a two-gap defender, which limited his stock. In a one-gap scheme, the lineman attacks a hole and either goes after the running back—if he comes that way—or proceeds to the quarterback. A one-gap lineman tends to weigh at most 290 pounds, and is quick and athletic.

In a two-gap scheme, the lineman must read the play, anticipate which gap a running back will choose, and fill the hole. A two-gap lineman tends to be heavier, like Hawthorne, who's 325 pounds.

No team plays either scheme exclusively, though almost everyone tends to lean on one or the other. A team playing a 3-4 defense, with three down linemen and four linebackers, tends to use a two-gap system more often. A 4-3 team like the Atlanta Falcons, with four down linemen, tended to use the one-gap more.

Hawthorne was highly regarded as a two-gap defender, at least before the drug test.

"When he went to the combine, you had the impression that he was going to go somewhere in the second round, because for a lot of schemes like ours, he doesn't fit," Rich McKay said. "Now, the two-gap scheme he fits and fits it well. So he's got twenty teams to choose from probably and there are twelve of us who he probably doesn't fit real well. And obviously the test positive did not help him."

According to Ed Hawthorne, IMG agent Chris Singletary remained in close contact with Anttaj throughout the spring, checking in by phone once or twice a week. Though Anttaj opted to train for the combine mostly at Wisconsin, instead of joining fellow IMG clients such as Alex Smith, David Pollack, and Heath Miller full-time in Bradenton, Florida, Singletary stayed in touch.

Ed Hawthorne says his nephew used marijuana following the Out-back Bowl at a party in Tampa and knew about the positive drug test for three weeks before it came out.

"He didn't tell anybody," Hawthorne said. "Not me, his attorney, or his agent, until it came out in the paper three weeks later. He was so worried about what I was going to say that he went into a shell. He knew that he'd let me down, and he let everyone else down because of all the work we put into this thing, and he goes and does something stupid like that—even though he's been lectured one hundred times that 'you're high-profile now. Whatever you do is going to end up in the newspapers. It's going to be in there.' He just figured he had enough time to clean up before the combine. I guess he didn't."

Ed Hawthorne said IMG did not call during draft weekend. (Condon, head of IMG's football division, said he called Anttaj the day after the draft.)

Jack Scharf, who had remained in touch with the Hawthornes, did call. "I'm so sorry," he told Ed. "I can't believe what's happening. I don't know what to say."

Finally the wait ended. The Oakland Raiders, no strangers to drafting and acquiring players with baggage, selected Hawthorne with the first pick of the sixth round. Head coach Norv Turner and his staff, who coached Anttaj during the Senior Bowl, remained fans of the defensive tackle.

Ed Hawthorne did the math. Players selected early in the sixth round in 2004 received signing bonuses of around eighty-five thousand dollars. It was a far cry from the seven-figure bonus Anttaj figured to receive for much of the fall, when everyone from Kiper to IMG to Scharf viewed him as a first-rounder.

"If you learn from your mistake, you'll be a better person," Hawthorne told his nephew. "If you don't, then you're an idiot."

Late in the afternoon, Roddy White arrived at Falcons headquarters with his mother and younger brother for a news conference. As far as sports media events, nothing is more mundane than the player introduction. There's the inevitable praise lavished by team officials, the jersey presentation photo-op, and a brief question-and-answer period.

For Arthur M. Blank, former image-conscious chairman of The Home Depot and now the image-conscious owner of the Atlanta Falcons, no media event is ever mundane. Much planning and preparation went into the White introduction.

Reggie Roberts, the team's public relations director, sent a file of bio information to Kim Shreckengost, the executive vice president of operations for the AMB (Arthur M. Blank) Group, LLC. Shreckengost previously worked as Blank's vice president of investor relations at Home Depot and knew the importance of projecting a rosy, upbeat outlook to the media at all times, no matter how trivial the information presented.

By the time Blank approached the podium in the Falcons' media room, dressed impeccably as always in a black blazer, gray slacks, white shirt, and red team-logo tie, he had a detailed speech that he delivered as if it were off the cuff. The theme of the speech was family, and how White now was a treasured member of the Falcons tight-knit community.

Oddly enough, the wide receiver was not the first Roddy White in the organization. The Falcons employed a Roddy White as director of event marketing and client services.

Falcons beat writers Matt Winkeljohn of the *Atlanta Journal-Constitution* and George Henry of the Associated Press sat at their cubicles, views obstructed by a phalanx of television cameramen and reporters appearing at Flowery Branch for the first time in six days. Earlier in the day the beat writers were asked to leave the press room briefly while Blank sat for an updated portrait.

White's "background is really very interesting," Blank said. "Today, the young man to my right is 207 pounds. When he entered his first days of high school at James High School in South Carolina, he was 112 pounds. He joined the wrestling team, which is a tradition—a part of the DNA in their family (they have five members who were all state wrestling champs in South Carolina)—and he became a two-time state wrestling champion himself, the first time at 152 pounds and the second time at 182 pounds. So Roddy has grown up a good bit physically, and obviously matured a great deal in high school as well, and on through college.

"In high school he was an all-time state selection as a football player, broke all the school's receiving records, and was listed among the top receivers on a national basis. He's seven courses away from getting his [college] degree in sociology. His mother has made it very clear to me that Roddy will complete his college degree; and Roddy, we're here to make sure that we can help you in any way to do that, and we're as excited about you being that close to your college degree as you are today.

"So I want to welcome Roddy to our Falcon family. He's an exceptional young man on the field, off the field. We're thrilled that he's here, we're thrilled about the contributions he's going to make to us. I promise you, Roddy, that you'll get tremendous support from the coaching staff here. I promise you'll get tremendous support from this organization in every aspect.

"When you're part of our family, you're part of our family, and we're going to care for you on the days that your mom is not here, which I know she'll be here to watch you every Sunday or Monday night, or whenever we're playing. I promise you, the rest of the staff here will be supporting you and really treating you as family as well. So thank you for being here. We're excited about you being a Falcon. Come on up here and say hi to your new family."

White thanked God, Blank, Rich McKay, the coaching staff, and his family, before taking a few questions from the media. Head coach Jim Mora said the addition of Roddy would help open up the Falcons' languishing passing game.

"Right now you'd say we're a team that runs the football and throws to the tight end," Mora said. "We'd like to be a team that can beat you any number of ways, and that's why you want to keep adding quality players like Roddy to your program, and give a great player like Mike [Vick] more weapons, more places to deliver the ball, and more threats up the field."

With two selections in the fifth round, the Falcons had some flexibility. The draft had unfolded nicely, McKay believed. Glancing at his predraft predictions, he had landed his first-round pick (Roddy White) as expected, and grabbed Jordan Beck and Chauncey Davis, each a round later than projected, which meant he was getting good value for his draft position. Picking up Jonathan Babineaux in the second round was an added bonus.

Having selected wide receiver, defensive tackle, linebacker, and defensive end, McKay had addressed the Falcons' primary needs. A safety would have been nice, but after the like-minded Eagles took Sean Considine with the first pick in the fourth round and the Packers nabbed Marviel Underwood, nobody else jumped out at the Falcons.

McKay looked across the Falcons' draft board. Michael Boley, a linebacker from Southern Miss, was looming high with a 6.0 rating. The 6.0 was a wild card, sort of the sergeant-major of the Falcons' rating system. A 6.0 was not necessarily better than a 5.9 player, but had a much higher upside.

The Falcons called the 6.0 the "elevator grade," since the player had a high ceiling and a low floor. There were only a few 6.0 grades per draft, and they fell into three categories. The first was the "special specialist," the rare special teams player that commanded a premium draft pick. For the 2005 draft, there was only one such player, Ohio State kicker Mike Nugent.

The second category was a player that scouts were having a hard time putting a grade on, because he played at a lower level of competition, had recently switched positions, or would be expected to learn a new position in the NFL. Troy State's Demarcus Ware fit the bill in the fall, before he gained twenty pounds and solidified himself as a NFL-caliber defensive end with a strong predraft season. Already in possession of an AA character rating from the Falcons, he had been bumped up to a 6.2 long before the draft.

The final category consisted of players with bigtime potential who thus far had not made the most of their talents. McKay's character-based draft system frowned on underachievers. By thoroughly researching a player's football and personal character, the Falcons hoped to eliminate any potential problems down the road.

Boley received a CC in character, the same grade as White and Davis. He was a raw talent with a lanky frame and a reputation for not working hard in the weight room. On the field, he got by more with athleticism than proper technique. At least he had a long resume of community service endeavors, always a plus with the Blank-owned Falcons.

McKay still wanted an offensive tackle. Going into the draft, he didn't plan to take one, but figured if he did it would be in the fourth or fifth round. Using the stringent Alex Gibbs parameters, the Falcons had few red-dot linemen, and only three remained on the board. Tackles Anthony Alabi (Texas Christian) and Frank Omiyale (Tennessee Tech) were on the fifth-round hot list, along with Robert Hunt, a center from North Dakota State. DeAndra Cobb, the Michigan State running back and McKay's projected fifth-round pick, remained available.

With two fifth-round choices, just three picks apart, McKay could afford to play chess.

Boley and the 6.0 rating, in some respects, contradicted the core of McKay's draft philosophy, but then there was the cardinal rule of never dropping down a level to draft a player. Boley was, by far, the highest-rated player left on the Falcons' board. McKay could afford to spend a fifth-round pick on a 6.0 and let him develop on special teams and in a backup role for at least a year.

Whenever McKay considered a 6.0 player, the name Santana Dotson came to mind. In 1992, McKay was participating in his first draft with the Buccaneers as vice president of football operations. Head coach Sam Wyche had final say on personnel decisions, and that year the Bucs had two selections in the fifth round. As the rounds went on, the Bucs drafted 5.8 players, even though Dotson, a 6.0 defensive tackle from Baylor, remained on the board.

Finally, with their second pick in the fifth round, the Bucs drafted

Dotson, who recorded ten sacks as a rookie and went on to a productive, decade-long career with the Bucs and Packers. Michael Boley, like Dotson, was a player viewed as a potential underachiever.

"One of the things that hurts Michael is people want more out of him," McKay said. "He's such a good athlete and moves so well, you look at every play and say, 'Boy, he could have done this or he could have done that.' But every tape you watch, you see nothing but production."

McKay pulled the trigger on Boley. The Jets, picking next, chose Andre Maddox, a safety from North Carolina State. The Dolphins then chose an offensive tackle, Alabi, leaving the Falcons with Omiyale of Tennessee Tech, a Division-II school.

The run on offensive linemen continued with the next pick, as San Diego drafted Wesley Britt, a tackle from Alabama. The Colts then took Hunt.

McKay marveled at the intelligence-gathering operation of scouting director Phil Emery and his staff. Through their own evaluations and by talking to other teams before the draft, they identified three linemen that fit the Falcons' scheme and were fifth-round-caliber players. The rest of the league agreed, drafting the players in a span of four picks late in the fifth round. It was the draft equivalent of missing the Powerball Lottery by one number.

The art of the draft, McKay believed, was not just identifying talent but spending time with other teams to determine leaguewide value. The danger was that scouts would come to second-guess their own grades, which wasn't such a bad thing if it caused them to make one last check of the files. More often than not, the process provided the type of intelligence that gave McKay the confidence to wait an extra round on a Beck or Davis.

"You want to buy wholesale," McKay says. "You'll pay retail, but you never want to pay the marked-up price. Problems occur if you get your rounds all wrong and you start overpaying. Just because you like a guy doesn't mean you should take him in the second when you can get him in the fourth."

The Falcons believed they got good value in Omiyale, who showed an uncanny ability to explode off the line of scrimmage for a man his size (six-four and 310 pounds), a good fit for the Gibbs system, even if he was huge. The Falcons had depth on the offensive line, and McKay planned to give Omiyale the equivalent of a redshirt season in 2005, letting him learn the Falcons' system in practice.

Omiyale was something of an unknown, in that he seldom had played against top-level competition. But he showed tremendous upside, along with a mean streak, and posted a solid CB on the Falcons' character rating. Omiyale also possessed thirty-six-inch arms, believed to be among the longest in the NFL. "I don't know where you get that shirt," McKay said.

In the sixth round, the Falcons picked up McKay's projected fifth-rounder, Michigan State running back DeAndra Cobb. With Warrick Dunn and T. J. Duckett entrenched in the backfield, the Falcons had no interest in spending a higher selection on a running back.

Cobb, at five-nine, 196 pounds, was in many respects a younger version of Dunn. He was a skilled kickoff returner and figured to get a chance at that role, and as a third-down back as a rookie. Married, with a daughter, he also earned the second-highest character rating (BB) of any Falcons draft pick. With a rating of 5.8-plus, McKay believed he got a deceptively fast runner and a tremendous value in the sixth round with Cobb.

"He ran a 4.5 at the combine, but I defy you to look at any tape you want and tell me he runs a 4.5," McKay said. "He certainly looks like he runs a lot faster than that, because his play speed is really impressive."

Anttaj Hawthorne was not the only person disappointed in the sixth round. Florida State's Eric Moore, once rated among the better defensive ends, lasted until the twelfth pick and the New York Giants.

Two players that agent Jack Scharf and Momentum Sports spent ten thousand dollars apiece just to train at Athletes' Performance, not including housing and other expenses, lasted until the sixth. Jovan Haye, the defensive end who left Vanderbilt with a year of eligibility remaining, went to Carolina with the fifteenth pick. Cornerback Derrick Johnson of Washington—the other Derrick Johnson in the draft—went to San Francisco with the thirty-first selection. Neither player figured to generate enough in commissions in 2005 to cover their combine training. Nor would Louisville wide receiver J. R. Russell, drafted in the seventh round by Tampa Bay, or Oregon linebacker Jonathan Pollard, who went undrafted.

Hawthorne was not the lowest-drafted IMG client. Rob Petitti, the mammoth offensive tackle from Pittsburgh who was sidelined throughout the spring by turf toe, lasted until the Dallas Cowboys took him with the thirty-fifth pick, one of eight compensatory selections tacked onto the end of the round.

Though it had been a disappointing weekend for University of Virginia players at the front end of the draft, Al Groh's network of NFL contacts paid off for lesser prospects. Defensive tackle Andrew Hoffman, who was not even invited to the combine, went to the Cleveland Browns and new head coach Romeo Crennel, a fellow Parcells assistant with Groh with the Giants, Patriots, and Jets. Crennel planned to install a 3-4 defense similar to the one Hoffman played at Virginia.

Tight end Patrick Estes, another noninvite to the combine, who had played in the shadow of Heath Miller, went in the seventh round to San Francisco. There he would play for new head coach Mike Nolan, who in 2000 had served as defensive coordinator for the New York Jets during Groh's one season as head coach.

The Falcons concluded their draft by selecting Darrell Shropshire, a six-two, 301-pound defensive tackle from South Carolina. Shropshire received a 5.8-minus grade from the Falcons, which meant he wasn't the greatest scheme fit. Like White, Davis, and Boley, he received a CC character grade. Shropshire didn't figure to play much, not with promising second-yearman Chad Lavalais, a fifth-round selection in 2004, moving into an expanded role. Then there was Babineaux, the second-round pick.

"We just felt like we needed one bigger-bodied nose tackle to make sure we're stout enough inside," McKay said. "We believe we are inside with Lavalais and Babineaux, but neither is as big-bodied as this guy. He can eat up space inside."

Shortly after 7:00 P.M., once the draft was over, McKay met with the small Falcons press corps one more time in his office. Down the hall, the scouting staff worked the phones. It was time to pick free agents off the scrap heap of undrafted players, a process that would take no more than an hour.

Nobody wanted to stay on the phone long, especially with disappointed agents who would have to explain to their clients why they went undrafted.

Some agents prepared for the moment before the draft ended. Agents Bill Johnson and Pat Dye Jr. maintained close phone contact with Ben Wilkerson, the LSU center whose injured knee kept him from undergoing full workouts all spring.

By the time the seventh round got underway, the agents told him he'd be better off not drafted. At least then they could be selective and try and find the team that most needed a center. Wilkerson signed with Cincinnati shortly after the draft.

After the media departed, McKay examined his draft picks.

Roddy White, WR, Alabama-Birmingham—6.2, CC
Jonathan Babineaux, DT, Iowa—5.9, CB

Jordan Beck, LB, Cal-Poly—5.9, AA
Chauncey Davis, DE, Florida State—5.8-plus, CC
Michael Boley, LB, Southern Miss—6.0, CC
Frank Omiyale, OT, Tennessee Tech—5.7-plus, CB
DeAndra Cobb, RB, Michigan State—5.8-plus, BB
Darrell Shropshire, DT, South Carolina—5.8-minus, CC

For a team that placed such a premium on character, there were a lot of C grades on the board. McKay was okay with that—a C was an average grade, after all—so long as the area scout had investigated the player thoroughly. Getting a C in personal character was worse than in football character.

"If you give a guy a C in personal character, you go back and look at him from A to Z to make sure we know all the issues," McKay said. "If there's no alert, then you turn to the area scout and say, 'You're ready on this guy?' And if [the scout] is ready to go, then you're ready to go, If he's interviewed his three, preferably five or more sources, you're fine."

McKay's draft showed how little value the Falcons place on the Wonderlic. Only three players scored higher than the league average of 19: Boley (30), Beck (27), and Omiyale (20). McKay was fine with that, too, since among the variables that went into the football character grade was how well a player learned football.

Looking around the Falcons' draft room, most teams had at least one selection with a D or F grade in football character or personal character. It wasn't difficult to find the teams that shared the Falcons' philosophy. The magnets representing Tim Ruskell's first three picks in Seattle—Chris Spencer, Lofa Tatupu, and David Greene—had red dots. Ruskell's fourth pick, Florida State offensive tackle Ray Willis, did not have a dot, because he didn't fit the Alex Gibbs scheme, though Willis did receive a lofty BB character grade from the Falcons.

The first three magnets on the Tampa Bay board also had red dots, representing Carnell Williams, Barrett Ruud, and Alex Smith. For all the talk of how much McKay and Buccaneers head coach Jon Gruden differed philosophically, McKay could find little wrong with his former employer's draft, at least at the front end.

The Chicago Bears, led by general manager Jerry Angelo, McKay's longtime friend and colleague, did not have a red dot on their board, led by Texas running back Cedric Benson.

McKay shook his head in mock disappointment. "Jerry has abandoned us."

As McKay glanced at his own board, he liked what he saw. The Falcons had addressed their depth issue at defensive line and linebacker. They had a legitimate home run threat at wide receiver in White and an exciting addition to their already potent running game in Cobb. They drafted strong character players, receiving good value in each round.

Best of all, none of the players, with the possible exception of White, would be counted on to make significant contributions in 2005. They could play backup roles and on special teams, learning the system and advancing gradually into more prominent duties in 2006 and beyond. When that time came, McKay would be able to jettison aging, higher-priced veterans, thus managing the salary cap and keeping his team young and yet experienced.

Already he could look at his 2004 draft class, which collectively accounted for just ten total starts in 2004—and see the players stepping into more prominent roles in 2005. DeAngelo Hall, the first-round pick, would start at cornerback. Fourth-rounder Demorrio Williams, a linebacker, and fifth-round defensive tackle Chad Lavalais, projected as starters. So, too, did Michael Jenkins, the wide receiver selected late in the first round after Hall.

Even third-rounder Matt Schaub, who didn't figure to play much behind Michael Vick, had mastered the West Coast offense to the point where coaches were comfortable with him in the event of an injury to Vick.

That's why it didn't matter to McKay what 2005 draft "grades" the Falcons received from football writers and Internet pundits the following morning.

"How can you grade a draft? I hope the people in the top ten got better players than we got. They better. They had every advantage and in every round—and they should. Last year, when we had a number-eight pick, we should have had a very good draft grade, unless we screwed it up.

"Look, if you give me a C every time, I'm thrilled. If you give me an A, it means we didn't have a very good team and you're able to look at our draft and say that these two guys are going to have an immediate impact. That's great, but it also means we're not very good right now."

After reaching the NFC title game three months earlier, the Falcons appeared very good, but McKay knew how quickly that could change. The NFL maintained parity by giving the better teams low draft picks and tougher schedules. The Falcons had never produced back-to-back winning seasons, not even after appearing in the Super Bowl following the 1998 season.

Mastering the draft is the only way a team can stay on top. That's why there would be little time to rest for the Falcons scouting staff. By 8:00 P.M. they were heading out the door, through the press room. They had rounded up a dozen free agents, including Kevin Dudley, the Michigan fullback McKay had projected as a fifth- or sixth-round pick for the Falcons.

In just a few weeks the scouts would meet in Florida with the rest of the teams that subscribed to the National Football Scouting service; McKay planned to drop out of BLESTO and rejoin the combine he belonged to in Tampa.

In Florida, the scouts would discuss rising seniors and give them grades. Those ratings would become the starting point for the 2006 NFL Draft.

No matter how deep the scouts dug, some players would fail to live up to expectations. McKay's office includes a large framed action photo of Ricky Bell, the former USC running back the Buccaneers drafted ahead of Tony Dorsett in 1977 with the first overall pick. John McKay coached Bell at Southern Cal, and the running back was one of Rich McKay's all-time favorites. He hung a photo of Bell in his dorm room at Princeton and has displayed one at every office since.

Bell no doubt would have scored an AA character rating, had the younger McKay's system existed in 1977. McKay believes it's unfair to second-guess the selection. Nobody knew Bell would suffer from a rare heart condition that would take his life at age twenty-nine. Besides, Dorsett never had to run behind the lousy offensive line the Buccaneers fielded during Bell's rookie year.

The photo serves as a tribute to Bell and the Buccaneers, the room's only indication that the man that occupies the office is connected to the Tampa Bay franchise. It also serves as an unintended reminder that even the most gifted, high-character player does not always pan out, for whatever reason.

"The draft is not an exact science," McKay says. "But in my naïve thinking, there are two things we need to focus on: character and scheme fit. To give the player the best chance to succeed, he needs to fit what you do and what you're going to ask him to do. If you can get that person and get the character side of who you want to be a Falcon, then from a work ethic and durability standpoint, you give yourself the best chance of success. It's not a perfect system, but it gives you that best chance."

Chapter Eighteen:

AFTERMATH

The 2005 NFL Draft produced the highest draft ratings ever for ESPN. The show was the most viewed cable program during the month of April among men eighteen to thirty-four, eighteen to forty-nine, and twenty-five to fifty-four. Overall, a whopping 34.4 million people tuned in to at least part of the eighteen-plus hours of coverage.

The network's selection of a Wall Street theme for its 2005 coverage was an appropriate one. In the year between the 2004 draft and the time the San Francisco 49ers selected Alex Smith with the first pick in the 2005 draft, the stock of many players went up and down dramatically.

Anttaj Hawthorne, once regarded as the best defensive tackle prospect for 2005, fell to the sixth round, largely for testing positive for marijuana at the NFL combine in February. Chris Canty, rated a "not higher than the second round" talent by the NFL's advisory committee in the spring of 2004, and as a potential first-rounder by some prognosticators before the 2004 season, plunged to the end of the fourth round after suffering torn knee ligaments in September and a detached retina in January.

Ray Willis, though never as highly rated as Canty or Hawthorne, dropped at least a round, to the fourth, because of a nagging ankle injury that figured to be completely healed by the time he played in a regular season game for the Seattle Seahawks. Ben Wilkerson, once the draft's highest-rated center, never overcame a torn left knee patella tendon suffered late in LSU's season. Undrafted, he was signed by the Bengals as a free agent and cut when he failed a physical.

Fred Gibson did nothing from a strictly football standpoint to hurt his draft stock, though he ran a slow forty-yard dash at the combine and failed to put weight on his skinny frame. Like a stagnant company that fails to provide Wall Street analysts with consistently better earnings reports, he fell behind more than a dozen wide receivers that suddenly looked more promising.

At least Gibson was drafted. C. J. Brooks, an offensive guard from the University of Maryland, was rated highly by BLESTO during the preseason, and once was ranked by ESPN's Mel Kiper Jr. as the top guard prospect for the draft. Brooks did not impress scouts in 2004, however, and went undrafted.

James Butler, the Georgia Tech safety, was rated among the nation's top draft prospects by BLESTO, National Football Scouting, Kiper, and numerous draft gurus for much of the fall of 2004. Butler did not get hurt, fail a drug test, or participate in a nightclub scuffle, but he failed to deliver on the promise that he showed in his junior season.

For every David Pollack or Carnell "Cadillac" Williams that maintained a blue-chip rating throughout the twelve-month draft cycle, there was a Gibson or Butler that failed to provide NFL investors with enough promise to warrant a "buy" rating. For every Hawthorne or Canty that lost millions on draft day, there was a Matt Jones or Travis Johnson that parlayed a strong senior year or postseason run into a spot in the first round.

Given such volatility, it's no wonder NFL personnel people are mindful of the first rule of investing, the disclaimer that's included at the end of investment ads:

Past performance is not indicative of future return, and investors can and do lose money.

"It's not what you say about them in the fall, it's what you say about them on draft day," says Tim Ruskell, the president of the Seattle Seahawks. "James Butler had a high draft rating by the combines and the media, but at no time in Atlanta or Seattle were we that excited about him. We put him on the board based on the numbers from our combine, but that wasn't our opinion. But what happens is that initial opinion stays out there, and TV announcers keep talking it up when, in fact, what was really happening was that once people started looking at him, they weren't that high on him. I think that happens more times than any dramatic interview or bad combine workout."

At least NFL teams have until draft day to make an investment decision. Agents must commit much earlier. In September of 2004, Jack Scharf of Momentum Sports spent six thousand dollars and a grueling week of travel recruiting four players: Vanderbilt defensive end Jovan Haye and left tackle Justin Geisinger, Louisville wide receiver J. R. Russell, and Hawthorne, the defensive tackle from Wisconsin.

Russell was drafted in the seventh round, the rest of the group in the sixth. Scharf landed two of the four, Haye and Russell, and spent approximately forty thousand dollars on their expenses and training at Athletes' Performance prior to the NFL combine. Scharf's total commission for their signing bonuses and 2005 salaries will be less than twenty thousand dollars. Scharf and Jeff Griffin, his Momentum Sports colleague, can write off the losses against their two second-round clients, Ronald Bartell (Rams) and Darrent Williams (Broncos).

Haye and Russell, drafted by Carolina and Tampa Bay, respectively, still could recoup Momentum's investment, though few sixth- and seventh-round picks enjoy significant NFL careers.

Many players go into the draft with an overly optimistic view of where they're going to be drafted. After all, confidence and a belief in their skills have gotten them to that point, and most agents base part of their sales pitch on an ability to best position their clients to NFL officials. It's difficult for an agent to give his client anything other than the rosiest scenario, not with competitors lurking in the background promising more.

The irony, of course, is that no NFL team takes into account a player's agent, let alone his predraft marketing campaign. Players tend to ignore obvious red flags leading up to the draft—better all-star game and combine performances by players at the same position, their failure to address concerns about weight, strength, etc.—and they believe their college reputations will carry draft day.

No wonder that there's rampant postdraft agent-shuffling among disappointed players who thought they were going higher.

"There's so much hype in getting a college player now, that it's almost impossible to live up to expectations," says veteran NFL agent Brad Blank, who did not represent anyone for the 2005 draft. "It's gotten to the point where most guys don't stay with their first agent for the duration of their careers. I prefer to just wait and get guys the second time around."

Gibson stopped short of firing his agent, Octagon's Doug Hendrickson, but made it clear to him he wasn't pleased.

"He told me I could go either late first round or early second," Gibson said. "He really didn't give me a good explanation of why things happen the way they happen. I was kind of upset about that. You know how agents are. They tell you one thing, they tell you the world, I tell you that."

Hendrickson said he told Gibson that several teams were considering him for picks toward the end of the first round or early in the second, but that he could go as late as the third.

"I never envisioned him lasting to the end of round four, but I always tell clients that the draft is a crazy process," Hendrickson said. "I never tell clients they're going in the first round, unless I know for sure. Fred's situation was all over the board, and by no means did I tell him anything other than there was a *possibility* he could go in round one. All you can do is give your client a range, because there are only ten or fifteen guys you can ever be certain are going in the first round. For everyone else, it's a crapshoot."

The phrase "crapshoot" isn't thrown around during recruiting season, when agents go to great lengths to show how they can best position players for the draft and improve their stocks in the minds of NFL officials. But there's a difference, Hendrickson says, in preparing a player for the draft and promising to magically improve his status.

"Teams spend millions on scouting," Hendrickson said. "All we can do is prepare the players for the Senior Bowl, combine, Wonderlic, interviews—everything. They take it from there. No agent can get a guy drafted higher. That's just unheard of."

Even at the top there are no guarantees. Hendrickson and his Octagon partners represented Aaron Rodgers, the Cal quarterback who was invited to New York for the draft because of leaguewide assumptions that he'd go among the first ten selections. He lasted until Green Bay chose him at number twenty-four.

Hendrickson is right; the draft *is* a crapshoot. For every supposedly sure thing like Ryan Leaf who bombs, there's a sixth-round success like Tom Brady. The Pro Football Hall of Fame is full of players drafted in the third round or later, such as Johnny Unitas, Joe Montana, Steve Largent, Mike Webster, and Dan Fouts.

On Sunday, August 7, 2005, as the members of the draft class of 2005 underwent their first NFL preseason training camps, the Hall of Fame inducted Dan Marino and Steve Young.

Marino was the sixth quarterback chosen in the first round of the 1983 draft, behind standouts John Elway and Jim Kelly, but also after such forgettable names as Todd Blackledge, Tony Eason, and Ken O'Brien. The entire NFL, or at least the teams with first-round picks, also overlooked Texas A&I's Darrell Green, the future Hall of Fame cornerback chosen after Marino by the Washington Redskins with the last pick of the first round.

As for Young, he spent time in the USFL, played briefly for the Tampa Bay Buccaneers, and served four seasons as Montana's backup before achieving stardom after his thirtieth birthday.

A list of Hall of Famers that overcame being drafted low provides little encouragement for today's low-drafted players, who know there's no guarantee of a second contract in a league where the average career lasts less than four seasons. Not only that, the size of the first contract is proportional to the amount of leeway they will be given in ensuing seasons. The greater the investment, the less likely the team will be to cut ties.

Gibson figured there was no point to a protracted contract negotiation and was among the first picks to sign. The Steelers paid him a $296,000 signing bonus, along with salaries of $230,000 in 2005, $310,000 in 2006, and $385,000 in 2007. Unlike many draft picks that are forced to sign five-year deals, Gibson inked a three-year pact that makes him eligible for free agency earlier.

"It's not where you get drafted, it's where you end up," Hendrickson told Gibson. "If you are the player you know you can be, you can make up that money in three years instead of five."

Frank Gore, the Miami running back, didn't wait for the draft to fire his agent, unloading David Levine in favor of David Dunn. Levine, who won a spirited recruiting battle over Ethan Lock to land Gore, and hired a trainer to help the running back lose thirty-two pounds prior to the draft, received his termination letter by fax. Gore, who had overcome major surgeries on both knees, went to the 49ers with the first pick of the third round, and signed a three-year contract with a signing bonus of $599,500.

"Nothing's ever a surprise in this business," Levine said. "No matter how hard you're working, and the result, players are always wondering if there's another guy who could have done better. And there's always someone there to convince them there is. Plus, there's no penalty for switching agents."

There is some recourse for the agent who wants to recoup his pre-draft expenses. He can appeal to the NFL Players Association and an arbitrator, though typically the player asks his new agent to pick up the cost as a condition of switching. Levine also receives his commission on the marketing deals he negotiated for Gore, mainly from trading card companies.

"As bizarre as it sounds," Levine said, shortly before training camp, "I'm still Frank's marketing agent."

Canty, drafted near the end of the fourth round by Dallas, fired Lock via FedEx and hired IMG's Tom Condon.

Canty said he was disappointed at how Lock and his colleagues handled his medical issues, and wondered if they could have better communicated his progress to NFL teams.

"I was not satisfied," said Canty. "It was best that we move on."

Lock said that he felt "very comfortable and confident" about how he disseminated information on Canty's medical condition, drafting a six-page, single-spaced document that he sent to all thirty-two NFL teams that detailed his client's progress. Lock said several NFL teams commended him for being so thorough.

Lock said his firm spent between twenty and twenty-five thousand dollars on Canty in the months leading up to the draft, including providing him with a two-bedroom apartment in Phoenix during precombine training so his parents would have a place to stay. Lock said he spent three separate weeks leading up to the draft dealing exclusively with Canty at the expense of his other clients, which included Erasmus James, who was drafted in the first round.

"I've been in this business twenty years and did more for that kid than for anyone else in my entire career," Lock said. "I can't tell you how disappointed I am."

Condon negotiated a five-year deal for Canty, with a signing bonus of three hundred and ten thousand dollars. Canty was hoping for a three-year deal, which would have given him the right to become a free agent earlier, and that's essentially what Condon delivered, negotiating the last two seasons as "voidable years." That allows Canty to become a free agent after the 2007 season, if he reaches certain incentives based on minimal playing time.

IMG and Condon should be glad that Canty, before switching agents, didn't seek out Ed Hawthorne's opinion on IMG's predraft communication skills. A month after the draft, his nephew, Anttaj, fired Condon. Ed Hawthorne said he and his nephew were disappointed with IMG's advice to not talk to the media following the news that Anttaj tested positive for marijuana at the combine.

Ed Hawthorne pointed to Luis Castillo, the Northwestern defensive tackle that tested positive for steroids at the NFL combine. Castillo sent a letter to all thirty-two NFL teams saying that he was frustrated that an elbow injury wasn't healing properly, and used steroids to perform better at the combine. Castillo put up strong numbers at the combine and was selected by San Diego late in the first round.

Anttaj "got some bad advice, and we believe that's why he dropped in the press," Ed Hawthorne said. "He didn't say anything to anybody, and that's not what the NFL wanted to see. So he got taken off a lot of people's draft boards because he didn't respond to it. If we did respond, he might have dropped a round or two, but not to the sixth."

Ed Hawthorne said IMG agents never called Anttaj on draft day or afterward. "They never called to say 'Keep your head up. Don't worry.' The writing was on the wall. They were basically saying, 'You don't meet our criteria anymore.'"

Condon, head of IMG's football division, said he called Anttaj Hawthorne within a day of the draft and had every intention of continuing to represent him. Condon said the player wondered if, as a sixth-round pick, he would get the attention he needed from an agency that had four first-round picks. Condon assured him he would.

" 'Taj is going to be a starter in this league by his second year," Condon said. "Why wouldn't we want to keep representing him?"

About six weeks after the draft, Anttaj Hawthorne hired Jack Scharf, the runner-up in the recruiting process. Scharf, after all, had plenty of experience guiding players with baggage. Scharf represented Richie Incognito, who was suspended several times and finally kicked off the team at Nebraska for disciplinary problems. The Rams selected Incognito in the third round.

Scharf's Momentum Sports colleague, Jeff Griffin, represented Darrent Williams, the Oregon State cornerback who was drafted in the second round by the Denver Broncos and carried a similar reputation as a problem child.

Before the draft, Griffin and Scharf worked to paint positive pictures of their clients, sending teams packets of information that included recommendations from coaches and professors. Scharf said a similar approach should have been taken with Hawthorne, who signed a five-year deal with a signing bonus of $157,500, a fraction of what he figured to earn before the failed drug test. The deal is loaded with incentives based on playing time and Pro Bowl appearances, though he's bound to the Raiders for five seasons.

"You have to do some damage control," Scharf said. "If Anttaj Hawthorne had come clean and addressed the issues with teams, he might have been able to overcome a lot of it, like Luis Castillo did. Would he have been a first-round pick? No, not based on what teams perceived as a lack of speed and strength his senior year. But he was too much of a talent to last beyond the first day."

Condon said IMG sent a letter to all thirty-two teams saying that Anttaj would give back his signing bonus if he failed another drug test. "We thought we did the appropriate thing," Condon said. "I couldn't give you a reason for why he chose to go in another direction."

For Scharf, the 2005 draft was a bit of a disappointment. It's not that he didn't think the world of his players, even those that were drafted late or not at all. His efforts yielded eight clients, but only one (Incognito) went on the first day.

Scharf was inching closer to his first huge payday, now that the Minnesota Vikings had traded wide receiver Randy Moss to the Raiders. That made Scharf's client Nate Burleson the number-one receiver in Minnesota heading into the 2005 season, the third and final year of his rookie deal.

Still, for all of his tireless recruiting efforts, Scharf had failed to land a blue-chip talent for the 2005 draft, though Griffin signed a pair of second-rounders in Williams and Bartell.

With the late signing of Hawthorne, Scharf landed three of the four targets of his September 2004 recruiting trip, but none of them went higher than the sixth round.

"I batted .750 on that trip, and a lot of agents would take that percentage," Scharf says. "But the thing is, you're dealing with so many unknowns, especially in September. All you can do is do your research and hit the road hard."

Scharf already was racking up frequent flyer miles for the 2006 NFL Draft before NFL training camps broke for the season, albeit with a different approach than for 2005. He planned to recruit only ten or twelve players, with more of an emphasis on consensus blue-chippers.

His targets included his alma mater (UCLA) and Marcedes Lewis, ranked as the second-best tight end, according to BLESTO. There was Arizona State wide receiver Derek Hagan, LSU offensive tackle Andrew

Whitworth, North Carolina State defensive end Manny Lawson, and Boston College's Will Blackmon, a cornerback who planned to play wide receiver as a senior.

As usual, Scharf would recruit promising juniors. His 2006 draft-eligible targets included N.C. State's Mario Williams, Jason Hill, a wide receiver at Washington State, and Joe Newton, an Oregon State tight end.

Scharf already scoured most of the country, but for 2006 planned to expand his efforts into Florida, perhaps the most hotly contested agent-recruiting ground in the nation. He aimed high, targeting Florida State's Ernie Sims. Though only a junior, Sims had developed a reputation as a ferocious hitter and a likely early entry into the 2006 draft.

It was only the second week of August, and Scharf still was negotiating a deal for Incognito with the Rams, but the forty-five hundred dollar Armani suit was out. There were red-eye flights to catch, presentations to make, Jaguar XJ8s to rent, parents and gatekeepers to woo.

"The only players I'm attempting to establish contact with are first- or second-round picks," Scharf said. "I'm not going to go after guys that are projected second-to-fourth-round and hope that they improve with a great combine. It's too much. Instead of signing eight guys, I'd much rather sign three studs."

Many of Scharf's rivals would be flocking to Charlottesville, Virginia, where Al Groh again had a promising crop of draft-eligible talent. Linebacker Ahmad Brooks, a redshirt junior, and senior offensive tackle D'Brickashaw Ferguson were projected first-round picks, at least before the 2005 season. Scouts and agents also had their eyes on running back Wali Lundy and kicker Connor Hughes.

A school-record seven Cavaliers were drafted in 2005, second only to Oklahoma and Florida State. In four seasons back at his alma mater, Groh had yet to take the Virginia program beyond the perennial eight- or nine-win showing of his predecessor, George Welsh.

Still, the emergence of more NFL draft talent confirmed the beliefs of school officials that Groh was raising the level of the program, even if it had yet to translate into additional victories. With coaching salaries soaring across the country, Virginia rewarded the sixty-one-year-old Groh, on August 19, with a six-year contract extension worth $10.2 million. The annual salary ($1.7 million) more than doubled Groh's previous income of $765,000. No wonder Welsh, seventy-one, who was enshrined in the College Football Hall of Fame a week earlier, was expressing interest in getting back into coaching after five years of retirement.

Groh's contract was negotiated by Neil Cornrich, who on August 10 began serving a one-year suspension by the NFL Players Association. Arbitrator Roger Kaplan upheld the NFLPA's decision to discipline Cornrich for violating the union's conflict of interest policy by working as an expert witness for General Motors in a lawsuit brought against the automaker by the estate of Derrick Thomas, the late Kansas City Chiefs linebacker.

The NFLPA suspension had no bearing on Cornrich's coaching representation. Groh hired Cornrich upon the recommendation of Bill Belichick not long after Groh's previous agent, Craig Kelly, died of pancreatic cancer in 2003.

Cornrich "is smart, hard-working, and has integrity," Groh said. "So if that's what a player is looking for, he might want to consider him."

With Cornrich suspended, the draft class of 2006 would have to look elsewhere for representation. So apparently would any of Cornrich's clients in need of free agent negotiation. Nate Clements, the Pro Bowl cornerback for the Buffalo Bills who could become a free agent after the 2005 season, left Cornrich and hired Todd France, who was a little late getting out of the gate for 2006 draft recruiting. His negotiations with the Miami Dolphins for Ronnie Brown, the number-two pick in the draft, took up much of the summer before they agreed on August 15 to a five-year contract worth $34 million, including about $20 million guaranteed. It was the richest deal for a nonquarterback in draft history.

During recruiting season for the 2005 draft, rival agents noted that France never had represented a first-round pick. As negotiations for Brown dragged on, there were rumblings that France was waiting for number-three pick Braylon Edwards to sign with Cleveland, because France wanted a benchmark for negotiations. Edwards did indeed sign five days before Brown.

France laughed off the criticism. All he had to do was look at the money given to the number-two pick in 2004 (Robert Gallery, $18.5 million guaranteed), account for the annual increase across the board, and strike a deal. In that sense, baseball agent Scott Boras is right about the NFL Draft. It's not brain surgery.

"Negotiations are negotiations," France said. "If anything, I thought [first round] negotiations were easier because the market is set. It wasn't that confusing. It's a recruiting thing. 'He hasn't done a first-round pick.'

That notion is so overrated it's unbelievable. For me, it's harder to establish a market for a free agent tackle and not know who else the team is talking to and how far you can push it. Are they talking to other free agent tackles, too? What are they willing to pay? It's wide open. Here you're boxed in and have some parameters. I like free agency better, because your negotiation skills are called upon more. You have far less leverage in the draft. What are you going to do? Tell the team you're going back in the draft?"

Throughout the FAME office there were monuments to a blockbuster year. In the conference room were blown-up images of Brown, Rogers, and Davis, each holding their new jerseys at introductory press conferences. A large blowup of a two-page Reebok advertisement featuring Brown that appeared in national sports magazines waited to be hung, alongside a life-sized cardboard standup of Priest Holmes.

In the marketing room hung the EAS ads featuring Brown and Rogers, alongside posters of Takeo Spikes representing Taco Bell and Kendrell Bell for Subway. There was a rack of DVDs, each featuring one of France's clients, that were given to potential marketing clients.

It was Friday, August 19, 2005, a week shy of France's second anniversary of resigning from Career Sports Management. Lonnie Cooper's lawsuit against France continued to churn through Fulton County Superior Court. In early August, the judge handling the case denied motions by both parties for summary judgment. That left the case either to be settled or to go to trial.

In the meantime, the commissions paid by former CSM-turned-FAME clients for deals struck during France's employment remained in escrow. Not that France worried much about that, given his recent earnings.

In the last six months, France had negotiated $140 million in contracts, between the three draft choices and new deals for veterans Bell, Jonas Jennings, and Jason Craft, a defensive back with New Orleans. Almost $65 million of that was guaranteed, giving France a commission of almost $2 million. Two days earlier, he visited the Bills training camp to begin negotiations on a contract extension for his newest client, Clements.

Again, the existing client network paid off for France, who has a history of representing Buffalo players. France already was hinting that Clements, who could become a free agent following the 2005 season, wanted to be the highest-paid cornerback in the league.

Then there was the 2006 draft. Once again, Auburn and Georgia were loaded. Marcus McNeil, an Auburn tackle, was considered one of the top-ten prospects, at least before the season. Georgia featured guard Max Jean-Gilles, safety Greg Blue, and cornerbacks DeMario Minter and Tim Jennings.

Unlike Jack Scharf, France was keeping his targets close to the vest, though with the additions of Brown, Rogers, and Davis, his existing client network at Auburn and Georgia had grown stronger. France was starting with a list of twenty-five to thirty targets and would whittle it down as the season progressed, inevitably adding a few others. Rival agents already had him pegged as the frontrunner for Leonard Pope, a junior tight end at Georgia. France already was behind on 2006, though at least rivals no longer could say he never had negotiated a first-round contract.

"I know how hard I work," France said. "I sacrifice my personal life to do this job, and my philosophy is that I will never be outworked. I don't care who it is. I'm up so early and in bed very late. Starting your own company and putting your head down for two years and sacrificing your personal life and to have it all pan out. . . ."

He let the thought linger. Standing in the lobby of his office next to the *Jerry Maguire* goldfish bowl, France flipped through a photo album. There was a kaleidoscope of images from the last year, mostly of France with clients at various events.

It had all gone so quickly. With the Brown signing four days earlier, he finally could close the book on 2005. France placed the album next to the goldfish and headed out the door in pursuit of talent for the 2006 NFL Draft.

Much had changed for France and other figures from the 2004–2005 NFL draft season. Ruskell had gone from a behind-the-scenes role with the Atlanta Falcons to president of the Seattle Seahawks. Shortly before the 2005 college football season began, Brian Battle resigned from his job as compliance director for Florida State to take a similar position at Georgetown University.

It seemed like a lateral move—Georgetown does not field a Division-1 football team and is more than a decade removed from its "Hoya Paranoia" dominance in basketball—but Battle received the title of "associate athletic director." Unlike in Tallahassee, where he reported to Bob Minnix, Battle will run the Georgetown compliance department.

As the 2005 NFL season began, the Dallas Cowboys appeared to have found a bargain in Chris Canty, who had overcome his knee and eye injuries to take a prominent role in the team's new 3-4 defense, along with first-round picks Demarcus Ware and Marcus Spears.

Anttaj Hawthorne wasn't so fortunate. The Raiders cut their sixth-round pick a week before the season opener, citing depth at the position. Considered by some to be the best defensive tackle among college players a year earlier, he cleared waivers and was re-signed to the Raiders practice team, an eight-man taxi squad that serves as the last chance for NFL hopefuls.

Practice squad players can be moved onto the active roster and are free to sign with other teams. They can only remain on the squad one season, do not travel with the team to away games, and don't dress for home games. They earn roughly $4,700 a week, a fraction of the $230,000 rookie minimum for players on fifty-three-man rosters.

Fred Gibson also found himself relegated to a practice squad at the beginning of his rookie season. Gibson struggled to learn the Steelers' playbook and ran poor routes. At times he seemed to run away from the football. One of the highest-drafted players cut, he signed on with the Miami Dolphins as a practice squad player.

Still, Gibson remained upbeat. As was the case throughout the pre-draft season and the draft itself, Gibson continued to believe he ranked with the rest of the receivers in his class, though he now seemed to recognize the work ahead of him.

"It's going to come, just like in college," Gibson said. "I had to learn the offense my freshman year, and it's the same thing here. It's a different level; everyone's good here. It all starts in practice. Practice pays off. The thing you've got to do is separate yourself from everybody else."

ACKNOWLEDGMENTS

've always read acknowledgments and wondered why an author needed to hit up so many people just to get a book done. After writing this book, I know. Trying to weave together the perspectives of NFL teams, college football programs, agents, and athletes was at times like trying to solve a Rubik's Cube.

I did not obtain a publisher for this book, by design, until shortly before the 2005 NFL Draft. I'm grateful to Marc Resnick and the staff at St. Martin's Press for offering me a chance to tell this story. I'm even more thankful for the army of football publicity people and executive assistants who opened the gates to a guy without either a book contract or extensive experience covering the NFL and college football.

That group includes Reggie Roberts, Frank Kleha, Ted Crews, Ryan Moore, Sammie Burleson, and Tina Reinert of the Atlanta Falcons; Rich Murray, Michael Colley, Nancy Bourne, and Darlene Craig at the University of Virginia; Rick Korch at the University of Miami; Jeff Kamis, Tony Morreale, and Julia O'Neal of the Tampa Bay Buccaneers; Harvey Greene of the Miami Dolphins; Rich Gonzales of the Seattle Seahawks; Claude Felton at the University of Georgia; Jeff Purinton, Stacy Wilkshire, and Rachel Curran at Florida State University; Allison George at Georgia Tech; Kirk Sampson at Auburn; Mike Schulze at the Outback Bowl, Joe Galbraith at Florida Citrus Sports, Vic Knight at the Senior

Bowl, Judith Ordehi at the East/West Shrine Game; Ben Crandell at the IMG Academies; the NFL's Steve Alic; Carl Francis of the NFL Players Association; Seth Palansky of the NFL Network; ESPN's Rob Tobias; Dan Bell of Fox Sports; and *Sports Illustrated*'s Rick McCabe.

I'm especially grateful for the more than 150 people who agreed to be interviewed for this book, especially those that let me into their lives frequently during a year. Only one person declined my requests, which I found puzzling, since agent Drew Rosenhaus never turns down a media opportunity. Rosenhaus hinted he might be working on his own draft-related book. We can only hope he finds the time to write a sequel to his memorable 1997 memoir, *A Shark Never Sleeps*.

In the interest of giving credit and full disclosure, I must mention that this book is partially an outgrowth of my work with Mark Verstegen, the founder and owner of the Athletes' Performance training center in Tempe, Arizona. I have coauthored three fitness books with Verstegen, including two that come out in 2006. As recently as February of 2004, I helped players training at Athletes' Performance for the combine to prepare for their interviews with NFL officials. During that time, I met agent Jack Scharf and his Momentum Sports colleague Jeff Griffin and became intrigued by the yearlong process that goes into the evaluation of talent by NFL teams, the recruiting of players by agents, and the often-dramatic shifts in a player's stock between the end of the college football season and the NFL Draft four months later.

Though Verstegen and I continue to write fitness books, and in fact worked on one concurrently while I worked on this project, I agreed that I would not take advantage of my familiarity with his staff and access to his facility. Though I interviewed Scharf and players Chris Canty and Fred Gibson twice each for brief periods at Athletes' Performance in early 2005, I interviewed all three extensively throughout the country between September of 2004 and August of 2005.

Combine preparation is a small but essential part of *The Draft* story, which is why in the interest of balance I twice visited IMG's International Performance Institute in Bradenton, Florida, where Verstegen previously worked. I also interviewed Chip Smith by phone about his precombine work with David Greene and Ray Willis, and spoke extensively with combine prep pioneer Mike Boyle.

Percy Knox, the tireless director of athlete relations at Athletes' Performance, made sure I did not overstep my bounds in Tempe, while at the same time providing insight into combine preparation. I'm grateful for his assistance.

I'm a graduate of the University of Virginia, but my decision to follow the Cavaliers was based solely on the pro philosophies Al Groh has instilled in every aspect of his program, his vast NFL network, and the fact that Virginia uncharacteristically ranked among the top schools for draft talent during the 2004 season. Admittedly, there are few better places to visit on fall afternoons.

Only a few books have tackled the history of the draft, but they were invaluable resources. They are *Sleepers, Busts & Franchise-Makers* by Cliff Christl and Don Langenkamp; *The Meat Market* by Richard Whittingham; *America's Game* by Michael MacCambridge; and the exhaustive *Sporting News Pro Football Draft Encyclopedia*. I'm especially grateful to Christl, who sent me a photocopied version of his hard-to-find book, which a smart publisher would be wise to put back in print.

Several team-related books also were helpful, most notably *When Pride Still Mattered* by David Maraniss, Peter Golenbock's *Cowboys Have Always Been My Heroes, Tales from the Bucs Sideline* by Chris Harry and Joey Johnston, and *Patriot Reign* by Michael Holley.

Many friends generously offered or provided lodging during the writing of this book, keeping me from blowing my advance accruing Marriott points. Special thanks to Becky and Joe Lettelleir, Ed Giuliotti, Margee and Tim Mossman, Melissa Mikolajczak, Beth Knowles and Brooks Rathet, Etch Shaheen, and Julie and Brett Benadum.

I'm grateful to old pals Tim Mossman and Bruce Greenbaum for keeping me awake on long drives through Georgia and Florida, providing feedback and insight via cell phone. As for my former collaborator Mike Veeck, a man who does not even watch the Super Bowl, thanks for the proper dose of perspective.

I also owe a debt of gratitude to many media colleagues, including Frank Cooney, who writes for *USA Today Sports Weekly* and runs the fabulous draft Web site NFLDraftScout.com; Neil Stratton, whose InsideTheLeague.com site has a much-deserved following of NFL insiders; Nolan Nawrocki of *Pro Football Weekly;* Russ Lande, who provided me with a copy of his exhaustive *GM Jr.* draft guide; Bill King of *SportsBusiness Journal,* a closeted draft geek whose story of ESPN's draft coverage in 2000 partially inspired this book; Scott Reynolds and Jim Flinn at *The Pewter Report;* I. J. Rosenberg of Score Atlanta; Mark Maske of the *Washington Post;* Roger Mooney of the *Bradenton Herald;* John Romano of the *St. Petersburg Times;* Martin Fennelly and Joe Henderson of the *Tampa Tribune;* and fellow freelance mercenaries Mark Didtler and Bob Andelman, a onetime book collaborator with Arthur Blank.

Since I could only be at one place on draft day, and chose to watch the draft unfold from Atlanta Falcons headquarters, I reconstructed much of the New York action through interviews and ESPN's always-thorough coverage. I'm also grateful for Darren Rovell and Ken Sugiura for providing blow-by-blow accounts of agent Todd France's day on ESPN.com and in the *Atlanta Journal-Constitution,* respectively.

A hearty thank you goes to Falcons scribes Matt Winkeljohn of the *Atlanta Journal-Constitution* and George Henry of the Associated Press, who, during draft week, made me feel like an honorary member of the small but hardworking Falcons media corps.

This book might not exist were it not for Scott Smith and Jonathan Woog at Street & Smith's sports annuals. They provided the assignments and credentials to get me where I needed to be. For many years, NFL teams prepared for the draft with little more than Street & Smith's publications. I am honored to have worn the magazine's credentials at the Outback Bowl, Gridiron Classic, Senior Bowl, and NFL combine, and to have contributed to Street & Smith's wonderful new draft-preview publication. Thanks also to Street & Smith's publisher Mike Kallay and staff writer Matt McKenzie.

Having spent so much time around football agents and players trying to select representation, I am reminded that I have *the* best agent in any field. David Black is everything a writer could hope for, treating this undrafted free agent like a first-round pick. Special thanks to David's All-Pro staff, especially Gary Morris, Dave Larabell, and Jason Sacher.

Then there was my wife, Suzy, who handled my frequent absences while pregnant and with a toddler in tow, never wavering in support of this project. To borrow a phrase from the scouting world, I've over-achieved in marriage.

APPENDIX

THE 2005 NFL DRAFT
Round by Round

KEY

Number in parentheses is the overall selection.

Underclassman =*.

Agent as of August 15, 2005 in parentheses.

Key figures in *The Draft* listed in bold type.

FIRST ROUND

San Francisco (1), *Alex Smith, QB, Utah (Tom Condon)

Miami (2), Ronnie Brown, RB, Auburn (Todd France)

Cleveland (3), Braylon Edwards, WR, Michigan (Lamont Smith)

Chicago (4), Cedric Benson, RB, Texas (Eugene Parker, Scott Parker)

Tampa Bay (5), Carnell Williams, RB, Auburn (Ben Dogra)

Tennessee (6), *Adam Jones, CB, West Virginia (Michael Huyghue)

Minnesota (7/from Oakland), *Troy Williamson, WR, South Carolina
    (David Canter)

Arizona (8), Antrel Rolle, CB, Miami (Ben Dogra)

Washington (9), Carlos Rogers, CB, Auburn (Todd France)

Detroit (10), *Mike Williams, WR, USC (Tony Fleming, Mitch Frankel)

**Dallas (11), Demarcus Ware, DE, Troy State (Pat Dye, Bill
    Johnson)**

San Diego (12/from New York Giants), *Shawne Merriman, DE, Maryland (Kevin Poston)

New Orleans (13/from Houston), Jammal Brown, OT, Oklahoma (Ben Dogra)

Carolina (14), *Thomas Davis, S, Georgia (Todd France)

Kansas City (15), Derrick Johnson, LB, Texas (Vann McElroy, Jeff Nalley, Graylan Crain)

Houston (16/from New Orleans), Travis Johnson, DT, Florida State (Gary Wichard)

Cincinnati (17), David Pollack, DE, Georgia (Ken Kremer)

Minnesota (18), Erasmus James, DE, Wisconsin (Ethan Lock)

St. Louis (19), Alex Barron, OT, Florida State (Roosevelt Barnes)

Dallas (20/from Buffalo), Marcus Spears, DE, LSU (Jimmy Sexton)

Jacksonville (21), Matt Jones, TE, Arkansas (Dave Butz, Alan Herman)

Baltimore (22), Mark Clayton, WR, Oklahoma (Ben Dogra, James Steiner)

Oakland (23/from Seattle), *Fabian Washington, CB, Nebraska (Brian Mackler, Jim Ivler, Jason Chayut)

Green Bay (24), *Aaron Rodgers, QB, California (Mike Sullivan)

Washington (25/from Denver), Jason Campbell, QB, Auburn (Joel Segal)

Seattle (26/from New York Jets through Oakland), *Chris Spencer, C, Mississippi (Ken Kremer)

Atlanta (27), Roddy White, WR, UAB (Neil Schwartz)

San Diego (28), Luis Castillo, DT, Northwestern (Mike McCartney, Rick Smith, Mark Bartelstein)

Indianapolis (29), Marlin Jackson, CB, Michigan (Doug Hendrickson, Mike Sullivan)

Pittsburgh (30), *Heath Miller, TE, Virginia (Tom Condon, Ken Kremer)

Philadelphia (31), Mike Patterson, DT, USC (Gary Uberstine)

New England (32), Logan Mankins, OG, Fresno State (Frank Bauer)

SECOND ROUND

San Francisco (33), David Baas, OG, Michigan (Ethan Lock)

Cleveland (34), *Brodney Pool, S, Oklahoma (Ben Dogra)

Philadelphia (35/from Miami), Reggie Brown, WR, Georgia (Bill Johnson/Pat Dye)

Tampa Bay (36), Barrett Ruud, LB, Nebraska (Ethan Lock, Vance Malinovic)

Detroit (37/from Tennessee), Shaun Cody, DT, USC (Harold Lewis)

Oakland (38), Stanford Routt, CB, Houston (Vann McElroy, Jeff Nalley, Graylan Crain)

Chicago (39), Mark Bradley, WR, Oklahoma (Danny Bradley)

New Orleans (40/from Washington), *Josh Bullocks, S, Nebraska (Josh Luchs, Steve Feldman)

Tennessee (41/from Detroit), Michael Roos, OT, Eastern Washington (Cameron Foster)

Dallas (42), Kevin Burnett, LB, Tennessee (Ricky Lefft)

New York Giants (43), Corey Webster, CB, LSU (Jimmy Sexton)

Arizona (44), J. J. Arrington, RB, California (Fletcher Smith, Kennard McGuire)

Seattle (45/from Carolina), *Lofa Tatupu, LB, Southern Cal (Fletcher Smith, Kennard McGuire)

Miami (46/from Kansas City), Matt Roth, DE, Iowa (Brad Leshnock, Joe Flanagan)

New York Jets (47/from Houston through Oakland), Mike Nugent, K, Ohio State (Ken Harris)

Cincinnati (48), *Odell Thurman, LB, Georgia (John Michels)

Minnesota (49), Marcus Johnson, OG, Mississippi (Rich Moran)

St. Louis (50), Ronald Bartell, CB, Howard (Jeff Griffin, Jack Scharf)

Green Bay (51/from New Orleans), Nick Collins, CB, Bethune-Cookman (Dave Butz, Alan Herman)

Jacksonville (52), Khalif Barnes, OT, Washington (Ken Zuckerman, Rick Smith, Mark Bartelstein)

Baltimore (53), Dan Cody, DE, Oklahoma (Drew Rosenhaus, Jason Rosenhaus)

Carolina (54/from Seattle), *Eric Shelton, RB, Louisville (Peter Schaffer)

Buffalo (55), *Roscoe Parrish, WR, Miami (Drew Rosenhaus, Jason Rosenhaus)

Denver (56), Darrent Williams, CB, Oklahoma State (Jeff Griffin, Jack Scharf)

New York Jets (57), *Justin Miller, CB, Clemson (Eugene Parker)

Green Bay (58), Terrence Murphy, WR, Texas A&M (Doug Hendrickson)

Atlanta (59), Jonathan Babineaux, DT, Iowa (Jack Bechta)

Indianapolis (60), Kelvin Hayden, CB, Illinois (Fletcher Smith, Kennard McGuire)

San Diego (61), Vincent Jackson, WR, Northern Illinois (Neil Schwartz, Jonathan Feinsod)

Pittsburgh (62), Bryant McFadden, CB, Florida State (Roosevelt
Barnes)

Philadelphia (63), *Matt McCoy, LB, San Diego State (David
Caravantes, Bus Cook)

Baltimore (64/from New England), Adam Terry, OT, Syracuse (Ken
Landphere)

THIRD ROUND

San Francisco (65), *Frank Gore, RB, Miami (David Dunn)

St. Louis (66/from Miami), Oshiomogho Atogwe, S, Stanford (Doug
Hendrickson, Ken Landphere)

Cleveland (67), Charlie Frye, QB, Akron (Eric Metz, Vance Malinovic)

Tennessee (68), Courtney Roby, WR, Indiana (Peter Schaffer)

Oakland (69), Andrew Walter, QB, Arizona State (Jeff Sperbeck)

Miami (70/from Chicago), *Channing Chowder, LB, Florida (Joel Segal)

Tampa Bay (71), Alex Smith, TE, Stanford (Ken Landphere, Doug
Hendrickson)

Detroit (72), Stanley Wilson, CB, Stanford (Ken Zuckerman, Rick
Smith, Mark Bartelstein)

Houston (73/from Dallas), *Vernand Morency, RB, Oklahoma State
(Drew Rosenhaus, Jason Rosenhaus)

New York Giants (74) *Justin Tuck, DE, Notre Dame (Ken Landphere,
Doug Hendrickson)

Arizona (75), Eric Green, CB, Virginia Tech (Craig Domann)

Denver (76/from Washington), Karl Paymah, CB, Washington State
(Rocky Arceneaux)

Philadelphia (77/from Kansas City), *Ryan Moats, RB, Louisiana Tech
(Mike McCartney, Rick Smith, Mark Bartelstein)

Oakland (78/from Houston), Kirk Morrison, LB, San Diego State (Leigh
Steinberg, Bruce Tollner, Ryan Tollner)

Carolina (79), Evan Mathis, OG, Alabama (Kirk Wood, Archie Lamb)

Minnesota (80), Dustin Fox, CB, Ohio State (Neil Cornrich)

**St. Louis (81), *Richie Incognito, C, Nebraska (Jack Scharf, Jeff
Griffin)**

New Orleans (82), Alfred Fincher, LB, Connecticut (Kristen Kuliga)

Cincinnati (83), *Chris Henry, WR, West Virginia (John Frederickson)

New England (84/from Baltimore), Ellis Hobbs, CB, Iowa State (Kevin
Omell)

Seattle (85), David Greene, QB, Georgia (Pat Dye, Bill Johnson)

Buffalo (86), Kevin Everett, TE, Miami (Brian Overstreet)

Jacksonville (87), Scott Starks, CB, Wisconsin (Jason Fletcher)

New York Jets (88), Sione Pouha, DT, Utha (Ken Vierra)

Carolina (89/from Green Bay), Atiyyah Ellison, DT, Missouri (Jim Steiner)

Atlanta (90), Jordan Beck, LB, Cal Poly (Leigh Steinberg, Bruce Tollner, Ryan Tollner)

Tampa Bay (91/from San Diego), Chris Colmer, OT, North Carolina State (Jonathan Feinsod, Neil Schwartz)

Indianapolis (92), Vincent Burns, DE, Kentucky (Hadley Engelhard)

Pittsburgh (93), Trai Essex, OG, Northwestern (Roosevelt Barnes)

San Francisco (94/from Philadelphia), Adam Snyder, OG, Oregon (David Dunn)

Arizona (95/from New England), *Darryl Blackstock, LB, Virginia (Ben Dogra)

Tennessee (96/compensatory selection), Brandon Jones, WR, Oklahoma (Craig Domann)

Denver (97/comp selection), Dominique Foxworth, CB, Maryland (Jim Ivler, Brian Mackler)

Seattle (98/comp selection), Leroy Hill, LB, Clemson (Bill Strickland)

Kansas City (99/comp selection), Dustin Colquitt, P, Tennessee (Jimmy Sexton)

New England (100/comp selection), Nick Kaczur, OT, Toledo (Vance Malinovic)

Denver (101/comp selection), *Maurice Clarett, RB, Ohio State (Steve Feldman)

FOURTH ROUND

Philadelphia (102), Sean Considine, FS, Iowa (Rick Smith, Mike McCartney, Mark Bartelstein)

Cleveland (103), Antonio Perkins, CB, Oklahoma (Danny Bradley)

Miami (104), Travis Daniels, CB, Louisiana State (Albert Elias)

Seattle (105/from Oakland), Ray Willis, OT, Florida State (Bill Johnson, Pat Dye)

Chicago (106), Kyle Orton, QB, Purdue (David Dunn)

Tampa Bay (107), Dan Buenning, OG, Wisconsin (Mike McCartney, Rick Smith, Mark Bartelstein)

Tennessee (108), Vincent Fuller, FS, Virginia Tech (Mitch Frankel)

Dallas (109), *Marion Barber, RB, Minnesota (Craig Domann)

New York Giants (110), Brandon Jacobs, RB, Southern Illinois (Justin Schulman, David Dunn)

Arizona (111), Elton Brown, OG, Virginia (Joel Segal)

Minnesota (112/from Washington), *Ciatrick Fason, RB, Florida (Joel Segal)

Tennessee (113/from Detroit), David Stewart, OT, Mississippi State (Bus Cook)

Houston (114), Jerome Mathis, WR, Hampton (Kevin Poston)

Green Bay (115/from Carolina), Marviel Underwood, FS, San Diego State (Jack Bechta)

Kansas City (116), Craphonso Thorpe, WR, Florida State (Matt Couloute)

St. Louis (117), Jerome Carter, SS, Florida State (Dave Butz, Alan Herman)

New Orleans (118), Chase Lyman, WR, California (Marvin Demoff)

Cincinnati (119), Eric Ghiaciuc, C, Central Michigan (Craig Domann)

Washington (120/from Minnesota), Manuel White Jr., FB, UCLA (Leigh Steinberg, Bruce Tollner, Ryan Tollner)

Carolina (121/from Seattle), Stefan Lefors, QB, Louisville (Jerrold Colton)

Buffalo (122), Raymond Preston, C, Illinois (Craig Domann)

New York Jets (123/from Jacksonville), Kerry Rhodes, FS, Louisville (Todd France)

Baltimore (124) Jason Brown, C, North Carolina (Harold Lewis, Kevin Omell)

Green Bay (125), Brady Poppinga, OLG, Brigham Young (Michael Hoffman, Gary Uberstine)

Philadelphia (126/from Denver, through Cleveland, Seattle, Carolina, and Green Bay), Todd Herremans, OT, Saginaw Valley State (Joe Linta)

Jacksonville (127/from New York Jets), Alvin Pearman, RB, Virginia (David Dunn)

Atlanta (128), Chauncey Davis, DE, Florida State (Kevin Conner, Robert Brown)

Indianapolis (129), Dylan Gandy, G, Texas Tech (Scott Smith)

San Diego (130), Darren Sproles, RB, Kansas State, (Gary Wichard)

Pittsburgh (131), Fred Gibson, WR, Georgia (Doug Hendrickson, Demetro Stephens)

Dallas (132/from Philadelphia), Chris Canty, DE, Virginia (Tom Condon, Chris Singletary)

New England (133), *James Sanders, SS, Fresno State (Steve Feldman, Josh Luchs)

St. Louis (134/compensatory selection), Claude Terrell, G, New Mexico (Steve Feldman, Josh Luchs)

Indianapolis (135/comp selection), Matt Giordano, FS, California (Steve Baker)

Tennessee (136/comp selection), Roydell Williams, WR, Tulane (Jeff Guerriero)

FIFTH ROUND

San Francisco (137), Ronald Fields, DT, Mississippi State (Josh Luchs, Steve Feldman)

Kansas City (138/from Miami), Boomer Grigsby, ILB, Illinois State (Vance Malinovic)

Cleveland (139), David McMillan, DE, Kansas (Craig Domann)

Chicago (140), Airese Currie, WR, Clemson (Carl Poston)

Tampa Bay (141), Donte Nicholson, SS, Oklahoma (Ben Dogra)

Tennessee (142), *Damien Nash, RB, Missouri (David Canter)

Green Bay (143/from Oakland), Junius Coston, C, North Carolina A&T (Bardia Ghahremani)

St. Louis (144/from N.Y. Giants through San Diego and Tampa Bay), Jerome Collins, TE, Notre Dame (Mike McCartney, Rick Smith, Mark Bartelstein)

Detroit (145/from Arizona through New England), Dan Orlovsky, QB, Connecticut (David Dunn)

Philadelphia (146/from Washington), Trent Cole, OLB, Cincinnati (Richard Rosa, Anthony Agnone, Edward Johnson)

Kansas City (147/from Detroit), Alphonso Hodge, CB, Miami (Ohio) (Ken Harris)

Indianapolis (148/from Dallas through Philadelphia), Jonathan Welsh, DE, Wisconsin (John Temple)

Carolina (149), Adam Seward, ILB, Nevada-Las Vegas (Michael Hoffman, Gary Uberstine)

Tennessee (150/from Kansas City), Daniel Loper, OT, Texas Tech (Leonard Roth)

Houston (151), Drew Hodgdon, C, Arizona State (Leo Goeas, Craig Domann)

New Orleans (152), *Adrian McPherson, QB, Florida State (Leigh Steinberg, Bruce Tollner, Ryan Tollner)

Cincinnati (153), Adam Kieft, OT, Central Michigan (Dave Butz, Alan Herman)

Washington (154/from Minnesota), Robert McCune, ILB, Louisville
(Ken Harris)

Tampa Bay (155/from St. Louis), *Larry Brackins, WR, Pearl River C.C.
(Bus Cook, Don Weatherall)

Buffalo (156), Eric King, CB, Wake Forest (Todd France)

Jacksonville (157), Gerald Sensabaugh, SS, North Carolina (Kevin
Conner, Robert Brown)

Baltimore (158), Justin Green, FB, Montana (Andrew Baker)

Seattle (159), Jeb Huckeba, OLB, Arkansas (Drew Pittman)

**Atlanta (160/from Denver), Michael Boley, OLB, Southern
Mississippi (Ethan Lock, Zeke Sandhu)**

New York Jets (161), Andre Maddox, SS, North Carolina State (Jason
Waugh, Derrick Harrison)

Miami (162/from Green Bay through Kansas City), Anthony Alabi, OT,
Texas Christian (Vann McElroy, Jeff Nalley)

Atlanta (163), Frank Omiyale, OT, Tennessee Tech (Mark Slough)

San Diego (164), Wesley Britt, OT, Alabama (David Dunn)

Indianapolis (165), Robert Hunt, C, North Dakota State (Kevin Omell,
Harold Lewis)

Pittsburgh (166), *Rian Wallace, ILB, Temple (Edward Johnson,
Anthony Agnone, Richard Rosa)

Green Bay (167/from Philadelphia), *Michael Hawkins, FS, Oklahoma
(Alex Balic)

Arizona (168/from New England), Lance Mitchell, ILB, Oklahoma
(Mason Ashe)

Carolina (169/compensatory selection), Geoff Hangartner, C, Texas
A&M (Leonard Roth)

New England (170/comp selection), Ryan Claridge, OLB, Nevada-Las
Vegas (David Dunn)

Carolina (171/comp selection), Ben Emanuel, FS, UCLA (James Ivler,
Bill Heck)

Philadelphia (172/comp selection), Scott Young, OG, Brigham Young
(Patrick Pinkston, Jeff Courtney)

Indianapolis (173/comp selection), Tyjuan Hagler, OLB, Cincinnati
(Craig Domann)

San Francisco (174/comp selection), Rasheed Marshall, WR, West
Virginia (Ralph Cindrich)

SIXTH ROUND

Oakland (175/from Philadelphia through Green Bay and New England), Anttaj Hawthorne, DT, Wisconsin (Jack Scharf, Jeff Griffin)

Cleveland (176), Nick Speegle, OLB, New Mexico (Jack Bechta)

San Diego (177/from Miami), Wes Sims, OG, Oklahoma (Robb Nelson)

Tampa Bay (178), Anthony Bryant, DT, Alabama (Archie Lamb, Kirk Wood)

Tennessee (179), Bo Scaife, TE, Texas (Kevin Robinson)

Green Bay (180/from Oakland), Mike Montgomery, DT, Texas A&M (Brian Overstreet)

Chicago (181), Chris Harris, SS, Louisiana-Monroe (Albert Elias)

New York Jets (182/from Arizona through Oakland), Cedric Houston, RB, Tennessee (John Michels)

Washington (183), Jared Newberry, OLB, Stanford (Doug Hendrickson, Ken Landphere, Richard Newberry)

Detroit (184), Bill Swancutt, DE, Oregon State (Vance Malinovic)

Jacksonville (185/from Dallas through Oakland and New York Jets), Chad Owens, WR, Hawaii (Leo Goeas, Craig Domann)

New York Giants (186), Eric Moore, DE, Florida State (Adisa Bakari)

Kansas City (187), Will Svitek, OT, Stanford (Steve Baker)

Houston (188), Ceandris Brown, SS, Louisiana-Lafayette (Chad Wiestling, Rich DeLuca)

Carolina (189), *Jovan Haye, DE, Vanderbilt (Jack Scharf, Jeff Griffin)

Cincinnati (190), Tab Perry, WR, UCLA (Jeff Sperbeck)

Minnesota (191), *C. J. Mosley, DT, Missouri (Harold Lewis, Kevin Omell)

St. Louis (192), *Dante Ridgeway, WR, Ball State (Roosevelt Barnes)

New Orleans (193), Jason Jefferson, DT, Wisconsin (Ron Slavin, Brad Leshnock)

Jacksonville (194), Pat Thomas, OLB, North Carolina State (Jason Waugh, Derrick Harrison)

Green Bay (195/from Baltimore through New England), Craig Bragg, WR, UCLA (Michael Hoffman, Gary Uberstine)

Seattle (196), Tony Jackson, TE, Iowa (Cary Fabrikant, Brian Levy)

Buffalo (197), Justin Geisinger, OG, Vanderbilt (Rick Smith, Mark Bartelstein, Mike McCartney)

New York Jets (198), Joel Dreessen, TE, Colorado State (Jeff Sperbeck)

Kansas City (199/from Green Bay), Khari Long, DE, Baylor (Vann McElroy, Jeff Nalley, Graylan Crain)

Denver (200), Chris Myers, OG, Miami (Drew Rosenhaus, Jason Rosenhaus)

Atlanta (201), DeAndra Cobb, RB, Michigan State (Andrew Baker)

Indianapolis (202), Dave Rayner, K, Michigan State (Paul Sheehy)

Cleveland (203/from Tampa Bay), Andrew Hoffman, DT, Virginia (Anthony Agnone, Noel Lamontagne, Edward Johnson)

Pittsburgh (204), Chris Kemoeatu, OG, Utah (Ken Vierra)

San Francisco (205/from Philadelphia), Derrick Johnson, CB, Washington (Jack Scharf, Jeff Griffin)

Detroit (206/from New England), Jonathan Goddard, DE, Marshall (Adam Heller)

Carolina (207/compensatory selection), Joe Berger, OT, Michigan Tech (Tom Tafelski)

Dallas (208/comp selection), Justin Beriault, FS, Ball State (Alan Herman, Dave Butz)

Dallas (209/comp selection), Rob Petitti, OT, Pittsburgh (Ken Kremer)

St. Louis (210/comp selection), Reggie Hodges, P, Ball State (Roosevelt Barnes)

Philadelphia (211/comp selection), Calvin Armstrong, OT, Washington State (Ethan Lock)

Oakland (212/comp selection), Ryan Riddle, DE, California (Josh Luchs, Steve Feldman)

Baltimore (213/comp selection), Derek Anderson, QB, Oregon State (David Dunn)

Oakland (214/comp selection), Pete McMahon, OT (Jack Bechta)

SEVENTH ROUND

San Francisco (215), Daven Holly, CB, Cincinnati (Andy Simms, David Lee)

Miami (216), Kevin Vickerson, DT, Michigan State (Anthony Hilliard)

Cleveland (217), Jon Dunn, OT, Virginia Tech (Ken Harris)

Tennessee (218), Reynaldo Hill, CB, Florida (Ian Greengross)

Minnesota (219/from Oakland), Adrian Ward, CB, Texas-El Paso (Jim Grogan)

Chicago (220), Rodriques Wilson, SS, South Carolina (David Canter)

Tampa Bay (221), Rick Razzano, FB, Mississippi (Jack Reale)

Washington (222), Nehemiah Broughton, FB, The Citadel (Harold Lewis, Kevin Omell)

San Francisco (223/from Detroit), Marcus Maxwell, WR, Oregon (David
   Caravantes, Bus Cook)

Dallas (224), Jay Ratliff, DE, Auburn (Mark Slough)

Tampa Bay (225/from New York Giants), Paris Warren, WR, Utah
   (Derrick Fox)

Arizona (226), LeRon McCoy, WR, Indiana (Pa.) (John Rickert)

Houston (227), Kenneth Pettway, OLB, Grambling State (Will Jordan)

Pittsburgh (228/from Carolina), Shaun Nua, DE, Brigham Young (Don
   Yee, Steve Dubin)

Kansas City (229), James Kilian, QB, Tulsa (Bob Lattinville, Joe Hipskind)

New England (230/from Minnesota through New York Jets and
   Oakland), Matt Cassel, QB, Southern California (David Dunn)

Tampa Bay (231), Hamza Abdullah, SS, Washington State (Mark
   Bloom)

**New Orleans (232), Jimmy Verdon, DT, Arizona State (Jack Scharf,
   Jeff Griffin)**

Cincinnati (233), Jonathan Fanene, DE, Utah (Angelo Wright)

Baltimore (234), Mike Smith, ILB, Texas Tech (Gary Glick)

Seattle (235), Cornelius Wortham, OLB, Alabama (Mark Slough)

Buffalo (236), Lionel Gates, RB, Louisville (Ken Sarnoff)

Jacksonville (237), Chris Roberson, CB, Eastern Michigan (Anthony
   Agnone, Richard Rosa, Edward Johnson)

Kansas City (238/from Green Bay), Jeremy Parquet, OT, Southern
   Mississippi (Reggie Rouzan)

Denver (239), Paul Ernster, P, Northern Arizona (Brett Tessler)

New York Jets (240), Harry Williams, WR, Tuskegee (Harold Lewis,
   Kevin Omell)

**Atlanta (241), Darrell Shropshire, DT, South Carolina (David
   Canter)**

San Diego (242), Scott Mruczkowski, C, Bowling Green (Jack Bechta)

Indianapolis (243), Anthony Davis, RB, Wisconsin (Brian Mackler, Jim
   Ivler)

Pittsburgh (244), Noah Herron, RB, Northwestern (Mike McCartney,
   Mark Bartelstein, Rick Smith)

Green Bay (245/from Philadelphia), Kurt Campbell, SS, Albany (New
   York) (Andrew Baker)

Green Bay (246/from New England), Will Whitticker, G, Michigan State
   (Reggie Smith, Jim Ryan)

Philadelphia (247/compensatory selection), Keyonta Marshall, DT,
   Grand Valley State (Angelo Wright)

San Francisco (248/comp selection), Patrick Estes, TE, Virginia (Ron Del Duca)

San Francisco (249/comp selection), Billy Bajema, TE, Oklahoma State (Drew Pittman)

St. Louis (250/comp selection), Ryan Fitzpatrick, QB, Harvard (Jimmy Sexton, Kyle Rote)

St. Louis (251/comp selection), Madison Hedgecock, FB, North Carolina (Tim Irwin)

Philadelphia (252/comp selection), David Bergeron, ILB, Stanford (Josh Luchs, Steve Feldman)

Tampa Bay (253/comp selection), J. R. Russell, WR, Louisville (Jack Scharf, Jeff Griffin)

Seattle (254/comp selection), Doug Nienhuis, OT, Oregon State (Bill Heck)

New England (255/comp selection), Andy Stokes, TE, William Penn (Joe Linta, Tom Klein)

INDEX

FALLING TOGETHER

ALSO BY MARISA DE LOS SANTOS

Belong to Me
Love Walked In

Falling Together

MARISA DE LOS SANTOS

WILLIAM MORROW
An Imprint of HarperCollins*Publishers*

FALLING TOGETHER. Copyright © 2011 by Marisa de los Santos. All rights reserved. Printed in the United States of America. No part of this book may be used or reproduced in any manner whatsoever without written permission except in the case of brief quotations embodied in critical articles and reviews. For information address HarperCollins Publishers, 10 East 53rd Street, New York, NY 10022.

HarperCollins books may be purchased for educational, business, or sales promotional use. For information please write: Special Markets Department, HarperCollins Publishers, 10 East 53rd Street, New York, NY 10022.

FIRST EDITION

Library of Congress Cataloging-in-Publication Data has been applied for.

ISBN 978-0-06-167087-9 (hardcover)
ISBN 978-0-06-210635-3 (international edition)

11 12 13 14 15   OV/RRD   10 9 8 7 6 5 4 3 2 1

For my first family,
Arturo, Mary, and Kristina de los Santos,
with all of my heart

FALLING TOGETHER

CHAPTER ONE

*P*EN WOULD NOT USE THE WORD *SUMMONED* WHEN SHE TOLD
Jamie about the e-mail later that night. Additionally, she would
not say that the e-mail dropped like a bowling ball into the pit of her
stomach, and at the same time fell over her like a shining wave, sending
arcs of sea spray up to flash in the sun, even though that is precisely
how it felt.

Across from Jamie at dinner, forkful of rabbit halfway to her mouth,
Pen would cock an eyebrow, cop a dry tone, and say, "Leave it to me
to get the e-mail of my life while wedged between Self-Help and True
Crime, listening to Eleanor Rex, M.D., recount her career as a paid
dominatrix."

The truth is that Pen was not giving Dr. Rex her full attention, even
though she should have been. She liked Eleanor. She liked her Louise
Brooks bob, her large, smoky laugh, and her impeccable manners. In
the nine hours she had spent driving Eleanor around to radio interviews, stock signings, and an appearance at an upscale but vampire-
den-looking private club called Marquis, Pen had come to view the
dominatrix gig—no sex but a lot of mean talk and costumes—as an
utterly valid and even sort of nifty way to put oneself through medical
school. Even if she hadn't, she should have been listening. As a general
rule, she listened to all of her authors. It was part of the job.

But this evening, Pen was unusually tired. She stood with her head tilted back against the bookstore wall, her ears only half hearing a description of how to single-handedly lace oneself into a leather corset ("There's an implement involved," she told Jamie later. "There always is," he said.), her eyes only half seeing the otherwise lovely store's horrible ceiling, paste-gray and pocked as the moon, while the weary rest of her began to fold itself up and give into its own weight like a bat at dawn.

Yesterday, Pen's daughter, Augusta, had come home from school with a late spring cold, and Pen had recognized, her heart sinking, that they were in for a rocky ride. Augusta's sleep, disordered in the best of circumstances, could be tipped over the edge and into chaos by any little thing. To make matters worse, it was her first illness since Pen had purged their apartment of children's cold medicine following newly issued, scarily worded warnings that it might be harmful to kids under the age of six. When Jamie got home at 2:00 A.M., he had found Augusta cocooned in a quilt on the sofa, wide awake, coughing noisily but decorously into the crook of her arm the way she had been taught to do in school, and a pale, wild-haired Pen staring into the medicine cabinet like a woman staring into the abyss.

"I hate the FDA," Pen had spat viciously. "And don't tell me I don't."

"I would never tell you that," said Jamie, backing up. "Noooo way."

In the bookstore, Eleanor's voice grew fainter and fainter, and Pen was so completely on the verge of sliding down the wall and curling up on the hardwood floor that she was planning it—how she would tuck her knees under her skirt, rest her head on a very large paperback book, possibly some sort of manual—when she felt her phone vibrate against her rib cage. Jamie, a sucker for gadgets, had given her the phone just a few days earlier—a "smartphone" he'd called it—and he had since realized what Pen had known the second he'd handed it to her: that it was far, far smarter than she required or deserved.

A hummingbird, Pen marveled through her sleep fog, *in my purse.*

A second later, she thought, *Augusta*, and then, *Oh no*, and her heart began to do a hummingbird thrum of its own. Generally, Pen's girl was as healthy as a horse, and her cold had been of the messy but aimless variety. But anything could happen. A couple of months ago,

Pen had sent Augusta to her father's house for the weekend and, apparently seconds after Augusta had stepped over his threshold, her flimsy sore throat had flared like a brush fire into a serious case of strep.

"Pustules all over her tonsils," his wife, Tanya, had hissed. "*Pustules. Everywhere!* And you never *noticed*? I've got news for you, lady: strep can turn into rheumatic fever. Just. Like. That."

Anything could happen with children. No one had to tell Pen this. Anything could happen with anything. Pen didn't even bother to check the message before she was punching in her home phone number and snaking her way through the small crowd of people who had gathered at the back of the store to hear Eleanor. In every bookstore audience, there were those who stood on the fringes instead of taking a seat, even when seats were plentiful, folks Pen called "lurkers." Usually, this label was both unkind and unjust, simple snideness on her part, but in the case of Eleanor's lurkers, perhaps not so much.

One ring and Jamie picked up.

"Jamie," Pen whispered frantically into the phone. "What? Fever? Pustules? What? Just tell me."

"You," Jamie told her calmly, "are insane."

Pen breathed, and her eyes filled with tears of relief. She swiped at them with her finger.

"Well, you *called*," she said, clearing her throat. "Naturally, I was worried."

"I called?" There was a brief pause and then Jamie said, "You didn't check the voice mail, did you? You didn't even check the *number* of the person calling, even though it was right there on the screen. Just hauled off and called me in a panic like a crazy person."

All true, but Pen was not going to say that to Jamie, so instead she said, "Not that many people have this number, Jamie. It's new, remember? You and Amelie and Patrick and Mom and Augusta's school. The school is closed; Mom's in Tibet or wherever the hell; Patrick never calls in the evenings; and I just talked to Amelie twenty minutes ago. That leaves you."

There was a small silence as Jamie considered this, then he said, a sly note sliding into his voice, "Let me ask you this."

"No," Pen said. "Whatever it is, no."

"Did your phone even ring?"

"It didn't ring," Pen corrected. "I'm in a bookstore. It whirred."

"Repeatedly? Or once? One long whir?"

"Who knows? Could've been one whir. Maybe. So *what*?" She gave her phone an accusatory look.

Jamie groaned. "E-mail." He enunciated the word as though it were composed of three distinct syllables. "Didn't we go over this? Check your e-mail, Penelope. We're fine. Augusta's fine. No fever and she ate like a champ. We had a long, and I'm talking about crazy-long, dance contest, and then she conked."

Pen swiped at her eyes again. "Oh. Well, thanks. Sorry."

Quietly, Jamie said, "The world doesn't spin out of control the second you turn your back, Pen."

Oh, yes it does. That's exactly what it does. You know that as well as I do. Pen thought this, but she didn't say it.

Jamie sighed. "Listen, if she busts out in pustules, I promise you'll be the first to know."

After she hung up, Pen almost didn't check her e-mail. She glared at her phone and stuffed it into her handbag. Contrary to what Jamie probably thought, she knew how to check it, but anyone who needed urgently to reach her would call, and the mere thought of pecking out an answer on the phone's microscopic keyboard made her fingers inflate to the size of baseball bats. Besides, she needed to get back to Eleanor.

Pen was walking toward the rows of chairs when she heard someone ask, "So I know you're, like, retired? But do you ever, you know, make an exception if the guy's, like, really special? Like really cool or whatever?" The person's voice had an unfinished, squawking quality: a boy, about twelve years old, thirteen at the outside. He was talking to Eleanor. Pen winced, stopped in her tracks, and there, in the heart of the Animals and Pet Care section, she checked her e-mail. The new one was from Glad2behere, an unfamiliar moniker but one that struck Pen as cheerful. *Good for you,* she thought.

Dear Pen,
I know it's been forever, but I need you.
Please come to the reunion. I'll find you
there. I'm sorry for everything.
                              Love,
                              Cat

Pen did not draw a blank or have a moment of confusion or have to read the message twice. She didn't think, *Cat who?* There was only one Cat. What she did was sit down on the floor between the shelves of books, shut her eyes, and press the cell phone to her sternum, against her galloping heart. Out of the blue sky and after more than six years of waiting—because no matter how hard she had tried not to wait, that is exactly what she'd been doing—Pen had been summoned. As soon as the merry-go-round inside her head slowed its whirling and jangling enough for her to think anything, she thought, *Oh, Cat,* followed by, *Finally.*

CHAPTER TWO

$\mathcal{C}$AT WOULD BEGIN IT: "WE MET CUTE."

"No," Pen would correct. "We met terrifying."

"And hostile," Will would add.

"I wouldn't say 'hostile,'" Pen would say.

"You were yelling," Will would remind her. "And swearing."

"And pushing," Cat would add. "Although not that hard."

"How would you know?" Pen would demand. "And I wasn't the only one swearing."

"I *know*," Cat would insist. "You were hostile. *I* was cute."

"You were terrifying," Will would correct.

"Through no fault of your own," Pen would concede.

"But cute," Cat would assert, "nevertheless."

And no one would disagree.

This was the way they told their story.

IT WAS THE FOURTH DAY OF THE FIRST WEEK OF THEIR FIRST YEAR OF college, immediately following a lecture on *Beowulf*.

Weeks afterward, when their friendship had become an ageless and immovable fact, Will would remark that he had noticed Pen during the lecture, specifically the way her hair had looked all of a piece, a glossy brown object hanging next to her face as she tilted her head to write.

"God," Cat would say, grimacing, "don't tell me you were checking her out. Don't tell me that Pen piqued your sexual interest. Because the thought of that is just nauseating."

"Thank you," Pen would say.

"Nope," Will would assure them. "It was just that hair. It was so brushed that it didn't even look like hair. Who has hair *that* brushed?"

"No one," Cat would reply. "No one has hair that brushed. And no one cries over *Beowulf.* No one but Pen."

Pen had not cried exactly, not out and out cried, not during the lecture anyway. She had cried the night before when she had gotten to the part about Beowulf's death. It wasn't so much the death itself, since Beowulf had never, during the hours she'd spent reading the poem, felt particularly real to her. Instead, it was the moment immediately following his death, a still and private moment near the end of an epic's worth of action and fighting, appearing suddenly and taking Pen off guard. The smoke cleared, and there was Wiglaf, the youngest of Beowulf's warriors, exhausted and blood-spattered and out of options, sprinkling water on the face of his dead king to wake him up.

During the lecture, Pen had waited for the professor to cover this moment, its bottomless sadness, but he had not even mentioned it. Still, while he spoke in cool tones about Beowulf's death marking the beginning of the end of an entire civilization, Pen had envisioned the boy's cupped hands full of water and had not burst into sobs, thank God, but had felt her eyes flood with tears. Her embarrassment at displaying emotion in front of what appeared to be hundreds of strangers was compounded by the fact that she was wearing mascara for the second time in her life. Her high school boyfriend, Mitchy Wooten, had liked her lashes "plain," but he had abruptly broken up with her fewer than twenty-four hours before they'd left for their respective colleges. Mascara was part of the new, college Pen, but as her dampened eyelashes began to gum, Pen vowed to throw the stuff away forever, a vow she would keep.

However, before its absolute exit from her life, the mascara had a role to play because when the professor ended the lecture a half hour early so that the class could break into small groups and meet with their respective teaching assistants, Pen did not go directly to her assigned classroom. Instead she wandered through the belly of the old, neoclassical, externally gracious, internally dank building in search of a bathroom in which to repair her smeary eyes. It took some time, but she found one, and as soon as she opened the door, she found Cat.

The bathroom was tiny, just two stalls, one sink, a paper towel dispenser, a trash can, and a large radiator. Lying on the scarred black and white tiles, face-up, her head jammed against the radiator, was a small girl in big trouble. Pen did not immediately identify the exact kind of trouble because the second she opened the door, the scene slammed into her senses, scattering them: a spill of black hair, limbs in terrible motion, a rigid face, a gasping, prolonged moan, a banging, banging, banging.

Pen yelped and fell back against the paper towel dispenser. For a few seconds, her hands flapped stupidly. Then she squatted down and took hold of the girl's thin ankles. She had expected them to stop moving, but they bucked inside her hands like two animals.

"Oh, God," Pen squeaked. "It's okay, it's okay, it's okay." But it wasn't.

Pen leaped up, wheeled around, and shoved open the bathroom door.

"Help," she said, not as loudly as she'd meant to. She saw a sweatshirt, grabbed it, and pulled it into the bathroom. Inside the sweatshirt was a boy.

"Shit," the boy said breathlessly and with what Pen would later discover was a relatively rare display of profanity. "She's seizing."

"Of course she is!" Pen shrieked, even though, before the boy said it, she had not hit upon a name for what the girl on the floor was doing. "We have to call 9-1-1!"

"Wait," said the boy.

"Wait?" squealed Pen.

"She's got one of those bracelets."

"A bracelet? Are you insane?"

The boy *was* insane she decided. Insane and useless. She yanked open the zipper of her backpack, fished wildly inside it, and snatched out a pen.

The boy pulled off his sweatshirt.

"Oh, great. Are you *getting warm*?" yelled Pen. "Are you a tad *uncomfortable*?" She pushed past the boy and leaned over the girl.

"What are you doing with that pen?" demanded the boy.

"You're supposed to put something in her mouth, so she doesn't swallow her tongue."

To Pen's amazement, he grabbed the pen out of her hand.

"That's a myth, the tongue thing," he snapped. "You'll hurt her."

Pen launched into a rant about the boy not being a doctor, damn it, and about how everyone knew the tongue thing was true and about how he needed to return her pen right now, this second, but the rant petered out before it really got started because what the boy did next was drop to his knees and tuck the sweatshirt under the girl's head, placing part of the shirt on the floor, part of it between her head and the radiator. It was among the most restrained and gentle gestures Pen had ever seen.

"Look," the boy said softly. "She's stopping."

Pen and the boy stayed still, waiting, and in a few seconds the noise emptied out of the room and was replaced by an opalescent quiet.

Eventually, the girl's eyes batted open. She looked from the boy to Pen, bewildered. She turned her head to the side, looked at the base of the sink, and groaned.

"Oh, bloody hell," she said hoarsely. "Give me a minute, okay?"

"Sure," said the boy, and Pen added, ridiculously, like a person on TV, "Take all the time you need."

Minutes passed. The girl might have fallen asleep, she lay so still. Her blouse was gauzy and peacock blue, scattered with yellow flowers. Pen caught sight of her own reflection in the mirror and gave a start at how haggard she looked, before she realized it was mostly because of the smudged mascara. Surreptitiously, she touched her forefingers to her tongue and rubbed under each eye. It helped a little.

When the girl opened her eyes again, she said, "So tell me who you are."

Relief and the sudden sound of the girl's clear voice sent Pen's adrenaline flowing again.

"Pen," she said. "Penelope, actually. Calloway. My grandmother's name. Penelope, I mean. Not Calloway. She was my mother's mother, so you know, different last name." The words hopped out one by one, *flip flip flip*, like goldfish out of a bowl. Pen sighed.

The girl smiled, and Pen noted that the smile managed to look exhausted and sparkling at the same time. "Got it," the girl said.

The boy wiped his hand on his gray T-shirt and held it out.

"Will Wadsworth," he said.

The girl's eyes widened.

"Get the hell out of here!" she cried.

Will froze for a second, then put his outstretched hand on the back of his head and rubbed. When Pen looked at him, she saw that under his tan, his cheeks were turning red. "Oh, right," he said. "Yeah, yeah. Sure. No problem."

He started to stand, made a slight move in the direction of the sweatshirt, still underneath the girl's head, then seemed to change his mind.

"So, uh, I'm glad you're okay and all," he said and turned sideways to squeeze past Pen and head for the door.

Pen giggled, a slightly hysterical sound, and Will Wadsworth turned toward her, startled.

"What?" he said.

"I don't think she meant for you to really get the hell out," Pen told him, still giggling. "I think it was an expression of incredulity. Disbelief."

"I know what 'incredulity' means." Will looked at the girl on the floor. "Yeah?" he asked.

The girl smiled again. "It was the name!" she sang out. "Will Wordsworth! Like the poet!"

"Uh, it's Wadsworth, actually," said Will, his face relaxing. "Like the other poet."

The girl laughed, a chiming sound, and said, "Well, you sure know how to make a first impression."

Will crouched down next to Cat, his elbows on his knees.

"When *I* first met *you*," he pointed out, "you were having a grand mal seizure."

The girl laughed again and sat up, her back against the radiator. She hooked her tangled hair behind her ears with her fingers, a snappy movement.

"Tonic-clonic," she told them, inscrutably but with great charm, her black eyes twinkling. "And I'm Cat."

WHEN CAT, PEN, AND WILL EMERGED, IN THAT ORDER, FROM THE over-conditioned air of the English-department building and stood blinking in the sudden sunlight, Pen stood and looked out at the saturated greens of the grass and trees, the white columns blazing against the red brick of the buildings, the cobalt sky stretched tight as a tarp overhead. Ever since she had arrived at the university, she had walked around, heavy (like a soaking wet pathetic tea bag, she'd e-mailed her mother) and dull, missing her parents every waking second and also in her sleep. She had watched the other new arrivals, resenting the pact of eager chipperness they all seemed to have signed. Now, standing between Cat and Will, a veil lifted; she felt engulfed by the electric beauty of everything around her. She gasped. It was a loud gasp.

"I *know*," moaned Cat. "The *heat*! Ugh."

"It's like walking through Jell-O. Hot Jell-O," observed Will, shedding the sweatshirt he had put back on only minutes before.

Pen peeled off her red cardigan sweater and said, "It really is awful, isn't it?" But she didn't feel awful. She tipped her face to the sun and smiled.

Will carried Cat's backpack. He offered to carry Cat herself.

"Not to be a jerk or anything," he said to Cat slowly, "but do you think you can make it walking? Because I can carry you, no problem."

Cat looked at Pen and rolled her eyes. "God, that was jerky, wasn't it? What an offer."

Pen peered at Will. "Do you know what 'jerk' *means*?"

Will laughed. "Okay, okay. Just answer the question. Carry or no carry?"

"No," said Cat thoughtfully. "I used to be one of those small people who liked to be carried. Up on people's shoulders usually. I'd also sit in laps. But I'm done with all that."

"Gave it up for college?" asked Pen.

"Exactly."

"I gave up not wearing mascara, but then just a little while ago, I gave up wearing it."

"Good choice. With your kind of eyelashes," said Cat, squinting at Pen, "mascara just muddies the waters."

"Good choice to you, too," said Pen, and the three of them, Will and Pen with Cat in between, set off together, amid the people, under the bright sky, and straight into the whites, greens, reds, and blues of the day.

THAT EVENING, THEY ATE A CHEESE PIZZA ON THE LAWN IN FRONT OF Pen's dormitory. Plain cheese was Pen's favorite kind of pizza; she found it pure and unencumbered. But in the argument that preceded the placing of the pizza order, Pen had not advocated for cheese. As Jamie had pointed out to her for years, it was a boring preference, reflecting underdeveloped, kindergarten-like taste. So she kept quiet about cheese and let Will and Cat battle it out to a stalemate.

"Forget it," Will finally said. "I'd rather have no toppings at all than eat anchovies."

"She did have a little bit of a rough day," Pen reminded him. "Maybe you could tough it out this once?"

"No chance."

"Hatred of little fish is a reflection of a little mind," said Cat primly. "But fine. No toppings. Cheese me, man. Let's do it."

They ate, slathered in citronella and sitting atop Pen's bed-spread on the cropped, prickly lawn. Late summer life—young and gold-edged—crackled around them: footballs and Frisbees cutting parabolas into the sky, club music undulating out of someone's window into the humid air, and it seemed to Pen that she, Will, and Cat were part of the action and also separate from it, so that when Will leaned back on his elbows and laughed, the sound rang through the quiet the three of them had made at the same time that it was just another noise.

"Tell us what's funny," Pen ordered.

"'Are you *getting warm*?'" said Will. He shook his head in amazement.

Pen put her pizza slice down and covered her face with her hands.

"Oh, no," she said from behind the hands. "I was a nightmare, wasn't I? Totally inept and screeching."

"Oh, yeah."

"What are you talking about?" demanded Cat. "No fair you two knowing something I don't know."

"That's what she said," explained Will. "In the bathroom. When I took off my sweatshirt."

"Oh, God," said Cat to Pen. "You said that?"

"I was a little freaked out, Cat."

"You were *enraged*," corrected Will.

"That's what happens when I get freaked out," said Pen, truthfully. "I get enraged."

"And hurl insults," added Will.

"I'm sorry," said Pen. She looked at his face in the fading light and realized that ever since she had met these two people, she'd been too busy at first and then too comfortable later to really notice what they looked like. Will's hair was wavy, but the rest of him was all straight lines: straight eyebrows, a straight mouth, his cheekbones two arrows pointing to the straight line of his nose. Even his eyes were somehow straight. It was a good face, but severe. When he smiled, though, with his straight, straight teeth, everything softened and lit up.

He smiled and said, "No problem. It got pretty scary there for a while."

"Wait! I don't think I thanked you guys, did I?" cried Cat. "Oh, God, I didn't!"

Pen looked at her, too, and found that she was bird-boned and broad-faced, not pretty in an ordinary way, but a joy to look at. Her delicate brown hands danced when she talked. She knee-walked over to throw her arms first around Pen's neck, then Will's, planting kisses on their foreheads.

"That doesn't usually happen," she said, "the tonic-clonic thing. Grand mal. I haven't had one in aeons. But I got thrown off last night."

"How?" asked Pen.

Cat wrinkled her nose. "Ooh, well, a little party happened in my dorm, I guess."

"You drank?" asked Will, then quickly added, "Not that you shouldn't. I meant does drinking do it?"

"I don't know if it was the drinking exactly. I think it was more of a triangulation."

"Like in trigonometry?" asked Pen.

"Of course not," said Cat. "I hate math. As in three things." She counted them on her fingers. "I drank three beers, even though I hate beer. I stayed up too late. And I forgot to take my medicine."

"So maybe you shouldn't do that anymore," ventured Will. "You think?"

"I definitely shouldn't," said Cat, nodding. "But I probably will."

Then she reached out, grabbed one of their hands in each of hers, and squeezed. "Thank the Lord in heaven you didn't call an authority figure. Or 9-1-1! Gosh, that would've been bad."

Even in the heat, Pen felt her face grow hot, as her own voice yelling about calling 9-1-1 echoed in her head. In a flash, she pictured the ambulance screaming up to the building, Cat being slid into it like a batch of cookies, the hordes of gaping undergrads, Cat known forever after as the girl who mysteriously malfunctioned in the English building. Pen shot a don't-rat-me-out-please look in Will's direction, but he was already talking.

"It was pretty stupid of us not to, given the fact that we didn't know what was wrong with you. A kid at my high school had epilepsy, so I sort of thought the seizure would be over fast. But we didn't know for sure."

Pen smiled her thanks at him. She wasn't ready to tell Cat the whole story, yet, but she knew that she would tell her before long. Maybe tomorrow. Maybe the day after that. There was plenty of time. She watched the sunset settle itself into dark pink and apricot layers behind the faraway trees.

"Your bed's going to smell like citronella for weeks," remarked Will.

"I don't mind," said Pen.

CHAPTER THREE

*Y*OU'LL GO," TAUNTED JAMIE, LEANING BACK IN HIS CHAIR. "You know you'll go. You know-know-know you'll go-go-go." He played the kitchen table like a conga drum, ending with a flourish.

Ignoring him, Pen focused on the food on her plate. It smelled winey and still held the shape of the take-out container: a tiny, brown, glistening mesa. Pen wheeled her knife and fork like birds looking for a place to land, poked wearily, took small, snapping bites. She set the knife and fork down with a bang.

"Why rabbit?" she asked irritably. "Why French? Again? I mean, I appreciate your bringing me leftovers, but enough with the rabbit and the snails and the congealed butter and the soggy crepes. Crepes don't travel well; I thought we'd established that."

Jamie shrugged. "It's Nancy. She thinks if it's not French, it's not sophisticated, and if it's not sophisticated, it's a bad date."

Pen narrowed her eyes. "If it's not *French,* it's not *sophisticated*?"

"Yeah, yeah, I know."

"Why work so hard to please Nancy, anyway? Isn't she just one of the Jims?"

"She was." Jamie snagged a bite of Pen's rabbit and grinned, chewing. "I just tonight asked her to call me 'Jimmy.'"

Pen shook her head. "You are hopeless. Hopeless and bad."

Roughly two years ago, shortly after Pen and Augusta had moved into

Jamie's apartment in what was meant to be a temporary arrangement, Jamie had devised a system that he called a work of genius and on which he congratulated himself with a glee and a frequency that Pen believed spoke volumes—and nothing good—about his moral development.

Upon first meeting a woman, he would introduce himself as James. At some point in their relationship, and this point could come within minutes or after several dates, whenever Jamie decided it was time for a phone number exchange, he would ask the woman to call him something else: Jim, Jimmy, Jay, or Jamie. For example, he might tell her, "I always introduce myself as James, but, actually, my friends call me Jim. I think maybe we should be friends," or something along those cornball lines. Occasionally, if the relationship continued for long enough and the necessity arose, Jamie would initiate what he called, obnoxiously, "an ancillary nomenclatural shift."

While the women took the changes to be a sign of growing intimacy, they were actually unknowing participants in a scheme that involved a reluctant Pen and the use of a code. In the drawer of the telephone table that had once belonged to their grandmother, tucked beneath the folder of take-out menus, Jamie had placed a laminated sheet ("Laminated?" Pen had said upon seeing it. "Are you kidding me?") delineating the code:

```
        If she asks for . . .


  Jimmy:   act like an aggrieved girlfriend; demand
           to know the identity of the caller; request
           that the caller refrain from future calls;
           in the best of all possible worlds, you will
           cry, yell, and/or hang up on the caller;
  Jim:     don't identify yourself as girlfriend,
           but be terse and businesslike when
           taking message; take message even if Jim
           is home; if asked your identity, say "I
           live here" in an ambiguous tone;
  Jay:     be friendly; if Jay is home, turn the
```

```
             phone over to him; if asked to identify
             yourself, say "Penelope";
   Jamie:    identify yourself in a friendly manner
             as Jamie's sister, Pen; turn the phone
             over to Jamie if he is home; feel free
             to submit funny anecdotes from childhood
             or beyond that speak well of Jamie's char-
             acter.
```

Most of the callers asked for "Jim." There had been just three Jimmys (Pen had neither cried nor hung up on any of them) and two Jays, although Pen knew that the number of callers did not accurately reflect the number of women Jamie had met or dated because the majority of those women did not progress past the James stage. In two years, Pen had never once fielded a call from a woman asking for Jamie.

Pen was ashamed of her participation in the system, and every few weeks, she railed at Jamie for his treatment of women in general and for the system in particular, saying things like "You will burn in hell for this," or "You suck," or "You are hopeless and bad." Just once, after a particularly fragile Jim had broken down on the phone, sobbing apologies to Pen, she had said solemnly, "Jamie, what would Dad say? He treated Mom like gold. He treated everyone like gold," but when she saw Jamie's eyes change, she knew she had gone too far.

The truth is that when Jamie first proposed the system—he had a brainstorm one day as he watched her answer the phone: "Hold on," he said, squeezing his eyes shut, pointing at her with one hand, pressing his other palm to the side of his head, "I can use this. I *know* I can use this"—Pen hadn't felt repulsed, but touched, even grateful. That her older brother would invite his emotional wreck of a sister and her sleep-disordered toddler to live with him at all was kindness enough, but that he would figure out a way to view Pen's presence as an asset, something to high-five her over, rather than as the liability it clearly was, moved her nearly to tears, even now, whenever she thought about it. It was such a quintessentially Jamie thing to do.

When Pen was twelve and the despairing victim of mean-girl awfulness, sixteen-year-old Jamie had scooped her up and let her live for a whole fall in the reflected glory of his perpetual coolness, even letting her walk around the track at football games with him and his beautiful friends. Pen could still see Mary Anne Riddle's evil face in the dazzling stadium lights, the dual stripes of her blush, her jaw actually dropping in an expression of envy and shock. Jamie had not discussed beforehand with Pen his decision to do this, had not set down ground rules or made her feel like she owed him. She was pretty sure he hadn't even thought about it much. Under Jamie's lawyer suits and caddishness, Pen knew he was still that carelessly generous boy, so that even when she called him "hopeless and bad," she never really believed it.

"So we were talking about how you're going to the reunion," said Jamie. "How there's no-no-no way you're not going."

Pen pushed her plate in Jamie's direction. "Take it," she said. "I'm through."

"I thought you'd be eating dominatrix food with the dominatrix anyway," said Jamie, digging in.

"She was tired and decided to order room service."

Through a mouthful of rabbit, Jamie said, "I *thought* you'd be eating with her, but just in case you weren't, I got you your own order of profiteroles. Check out the white box on the counter."

Pen hooted with joy and began to sing a rough approximation of "La Marseillaise." She paused and said, "Chocolate sauce?"

"In its own separate container for do-it-yourself, type-A-freak drizzling."

While she was in the middle of chewing the first ungodly good profiterole, Jamie said, "It's your ten-year college reunion, which is a big deal, right? Why weren't you planning to go even before you got the e-mail?"

Pen swallowed, her throat suddenly tight, and, briefly, pressed her fingers to her eyes.

"You know why," she said.

"The kid and no husband thing? Forget about it. Patrick sucks. Augusta's awesome. You made out like a bandit with that deal."

"You think I don't know that?" demanded Pen, her eyes flashing. "And who gives a nit about what anyone thinks?"

Jamie smiled at "gives a nit," one of their mother's stock phrases, along with "shut the cluck up."

"Good. So why not go?"

"Don't pretend you don't know."

Jamie looked down at the table for a few seconds, fingering his napkin. Pen watched his brow furrow and relax. The sound of a siren swirled in the distance, first faint, then louder. Jamie's eyes met Pen's.

"It's not like it's on the same day as the thing for Dad."

As soon as Jamie said the word *Dad,* Pen saw her father's face, yellow under that streetlamp, felt the stillness of his hand inside hers. She remembered the way he lay on his side, as though he were asleep. She put her hand over her mouth.

"Come on, Pen," said Jamie, sighing.

" 'Come on, Pen'?" Of its own volition, her voice rose. Jamie glanced over her shoulder at the hallway that led to Augusta's room. Pen took a breath and said more quietly, " 'The *thing* for Dad'? The *thing* means he died two years ago. Remember that?"

Jamie ran a hand across his forehead. "Yeah, I remember."

"Do you?"

Jamie shook his head, picked up the plate with the remains of Pen's rabbit on it, and pushed back from the table. Pen watched him as he scraped, then rinsed the plate, first one side then the other, and slid it into the dishwasher. Jamie had always performed small tasks this way, ever since he was a kid, as though he were being graded for thoroughness.

"I'm sorry," said Pen. She looked down at the profiteroles, the chocolate sauce in its plastic cup, and she ached for Jamie and herself and her mother in Tibet, and her father, who deserved better than to die on the dirty ground.

Jamie leaned on the counter with both hands, his shoulders hunched.

"You think I don't miss him?" he said finally, without turning around. "You think you're the only one?"

"No."

Jamie turned around and looked evenly at Pen. "Forget moving on or getting over it or whatever because who does that? But I gotta tell you, it would be really good if we didn't have another anniversary like last year's. Good for Augusta, especially."

At this mention of Augusta, Pen turned her face away sharply, as though she'd been slapped.

Jamie's voice softened. "Good for you, too. Right? For all of us."

Pen didn't look at him, but said, "I know."

"The bike ride is supposed to be a way to celebrate Dad, right? Everyone together?"

"I *know*. All right? I know. I don't have any plans to fall apart again, so you can stop worrying." Pen's voice was bitter, but she wasn't mad at Jamie.

Their father, Ben Calloway, had been a passionate cyclist, getting up before daylight for decades to ride with a group of people who, over the years, had become like family to Pen and Jamie, a tribe of aunts and uncles with sunglass tans and articulated calves. The rides would begin and end at the Calloway house in Wilmington, Delaware, and for Pen's whole childhood, before she got old enough to ride with them, Saturday mornings meant watching for her dad and his friends through the screen door and then coming outside in her pajamas to greet them. She loved it, the clack of their shoes on the front walk, the way they'd drop onto their backs on the lawn and squirt her with their water bottles, her mother coming out to laugh and offer them breakfast.

To mark the anniversary of Ben's death, two of the riders, David and Tracy Hersh, had organized a long bike ride through the countryside. More than thirty people, including Pen and Jamie, had met that May morning in front of the house. Pen would never forget how perfect it felt just before they took off: the dewy grass, the laundered scent of her mother's lilacs, everyone poised, one foot on the ground, ready to begin.

Pen's mother, Margaret, was still home then, hadn't yet been chased off by grief or loneliness to faraway places, and the last thing Pen saw before she set out was her mother standing on the porch with Augusta half-asleep in the crook of one arm, her free hand pressed to her mouth, then waving in the air.

But a few miles into the ride, as they came around a curve and the trees opened up to a vista of fields and stone barns and streaked-silk sky, Pen was overcome by a bleakness that made it hard to breathe, a comprehension that this road, this sky, the bikes rounding the curve together, swooping like a flock of birds, even the faint twinge between her own shoulder blades and the air filling her lungs, all of it belonged to her father, was rightfully his, except that he was dead, and so it be-longed to no one and meant nothing.

Pen had not finished the ride. She had slipped to the back of the pack and stopped her bike by the side of the road, willing the others not to notice, to keep going, but they turned back, all of them.

"I don't feel good," she explained, forcing a smile. "A stomach thing. You guys keep going. I'll be fine."

Even though she had tried to avoid looking in Jamie's direction, he had pulled alongside her and stopped, leveling a gray-eyed stare at her that was fierce and pleading at the same time.

"Stay. You have to," he'd said in an urgent voice that only she could hear.

But she had turned around, gone back to the house, stumbled past Augusta who sat at the kitchen table, a cup of milk in her hand, her eyes round and surprised, past her mother who stood at the counter, coiling dough into cinnamon rolls, and up the stairs into her old bed-room. She tossed her body onto the bed like bags of sand, and she stayed there for the better part of three days.

When her mother tried to coax her to get up, she cried and said that she was too tired. When Jamie raged at her for being selfish and for scaring Augusta, she turned her face to the wall. When Pen woke to find the hard knot of her child jammed against her back, she turned over, put her arms around the little girl, and said, "I'm sorry, baby. Mama's sick," in a hoarse, remote voice that even she knew was the opposite of comforting. For weeks afterward, after they were home in Philadelphia and back to their regular routine, Pen would catch Au-gusta watching her with a mixture of hope and worry, an expression no one should ever see on a four-year-old's face.

"I wouldn't do that to Augusta again," said Pen, more to herself than to Jamie.

"You sure?"

Pen rested her chin on her palm and looked at the vase of flowers in the middle of the table, tulips, barely open, like little folded hands in white gloves.

"I didn't get it," she said. "For that whole first year, I knew that he was gone from us and how unfair and sickening and sad that was. But I didn't get that what was worse, the very worst thing, was that he was gone from himself and all the things he loved. The day of the bike ride, it fell on me like an avalanche."

She looked up at Jamie and shrugged. "So now I know. And it can't fall on me again."

Jamie got a bag of coffee beans out of the freezer and poured them into his expensive coffeemaker with its built-in grinder and timer. Pen listened to the oily click of the beans, waiting.

"Your reunion doesn't start until, what, a week, week and a half, after this year's ride?" said Jamie finally. "So if you're not planning to be incapacitated, why don't you go?"

Pen stood up, slapping crumbs off her skirt in annoyance. "Why are you so sure I'd want to see Cat, anyway? It's not like I've been holding my breath until she and Will came back."

"Uh, actually, if you think about it, that's exactly what it's like."

"Nice," said Pen. "Very nice. They walked out on me. Why would I want to see either of them?"

"Because they're Cat and Will." Jamie flopped onto the sofa and snagged a remote control out of the bafflingly large collection on the coffee table. Before he began pushing buttons, he added, "And you're you."

WHEN PEN WAS STILL NOT ASLEEP AT 3:00 A.M., SHE GOT OUT OF BED and walked, as silently as she could, into Augusta's room, a thing she almost never did. For Augusta, the state of sleep was a frail construction, something you could send toppling with a misplaced footfall or clearing of your throat. But every now and then, Pen risked it. Now, she closed the door behind her and stood, allowing her eyes to adjust to the powdered-sugar sifting of moonlight and streetlight on the windowsill and the thin blue glow of the nightlight that Pen allowed as a concession to Augusta's fear of the dark, even though she'd read that nightlights could cause nearsightedness later in life. Glasses later, she decided, beats terror now, hands down.

Augusta lay in one of her customarily untranquil positions, as though she'd been struck by sleep mid-snow-angel, her duvet and sheets heaped in drifts on the floor around her bed. Pen resisted touching her, but leaned in close to listen to her breath and smell her smell: honey soap, apple shampoo, and a fundamental Augusta scent that reminded Pen of dandelion stems.

Without taking her eyes off her daughter, Pen lowered herself by increments into the chair next to Augusta's bed and thought what she had thought so many times before: *How can Cat and Will not know you?* For weeks after Augusta was born, Pen had expected them to come, even though, when the three of them parted ways, first Cat leaving, then Will, they had all agreed to make it final, to never get in touch, not years later, not ever.

"We're all or nothing," Cat had said, tears streaming down her face. "We can't be fake or partial or now-and-then. That would be wretched." Pen hadn't been so sure, but she had agreed to it anyway.

Even so, and even though she had no clear idea of how they would've found out about Augusta's birth even if they had wanted to, she had waited for them to come. She had waited again after her father died. At the funeral, she had sat between her mother and Patrick, Augusta on her lap, feeling broken and absent, her body numb inside her black dress, and had suddenly felt them there, behind her, the certainty of their presence running like electricity along her shoulders and up her neck. She had stood and spun around, searching through the crowds of people who had loved her father, for Will and Cat who had loved him as much as anyone. Nothing.

After that, over and over, for two years, Pen had imagined what she would say to them if she ever saw them again, all the ways she would be angry or indifferent, clever or cool. But from the beginning, from the very first day each of them walked out and for every second since, what she would have said if she were speaking truthfully was this: "Since you left there's been a you-shaped space beside me, all the time. It never goes away."

"All right, then," whispered Pen into the darkness of Augusta's room. "What the cluck. She wants me to be there, so I'll go."

Chapter Four

W ILL COULD STILL CONJURE THEM UP. LIKE NOW, FOR IN-
stance, as he worked at his desk, he could look through the
window and watch them emerge from between the guesthouse and the
japonica bushes and walk across his backyard, past the weird village of
staked birdhouses his mother had set up, past the crab apple snowing
white onto the grass. Pen all spare, pliant lines, with her hair pulled
back, her hard cyclist's legs. Tiny, animated Cat with her usual bird-
of-paradise plumage: lapis-blue scarf, flame-red dress, green shoes.

Sometimes, he had nothing to do with it; they showed up out of
nowhere, with the fast sting of a static electric shock. Just yesterday,
after he'd gotten the e-mail, he had seen Pen's long, oval-nailed fingers
wrapped around a stranger's coffee cup in the Bean There, Done That
Café. These visitations didn't happen often, a few times a year maybe,
but they always left Will a little out of breath, the sudden yank backward through time: Pen's surprising, childlike laugh bubbling up over
restaurant noise or her almost comically perfect posture ("Tut, tut!
Chin up, shoulders back, stiff upper lip," Cat would tease in a very
bad British accent. "For God and Empire, you know.") inhabiting the
back, neck, and shoulders of a woman across the room at a party.

Once, a couple of years ago, as he stood in line for a movie, he had
heard Cat's voice, winsome, tinny, and unmistakably off-key, singing
a song he didn't know but that was exactly the kind of sappy love song

Cat would adore. He had left his place in line to find the singer, who turned out to be teenaged and blue-haired with a nose piercing that looked fresh and painful, a detail that had annoyed Will unaccountably, almost to the point of anger. How stupid of him, he had thought, how moronic, after so many years, to look for Cat and find this silly, attention-hungry kid instead.

Now, though, he let himself fall into the act of imagining them, of hearing Cat's silver bangles add themselves to the morning music—birds and, already, a distant lawnmower—of watching them balance each other the way they always had, Pen shortening her fluid, stalking stride, Cat stepping fast and light, like a sandpiper, so that she seemed, from this distance, to just skim the ground.

Will shifted his gaze to the bulletin board on the wall next to his desk. He had read Cat's e-mail once, then printed it out and pinned it to the bulletin board. Pinning e-mails to the bulletin board wasn't something he usually did, and he didn't analyze his reasons for doing it now. "You're trying to make it more actual," his mother had said when she'd seen it. "You're filling a space," which was just the kind of thing his mother said these days, although in this case, as in others, he had to admit that she might have a point.

```
Dear Will,
I know it's been forever, but I need you.
Please come to the reunion. I'll find you
there. I'm sorry for everything.
                                    Love,
                                    Cat
```

It didn't sound like Cat. Will had thought this as soon as he'd read it. A flat, sparse e-mail from a girl (Will still thought "girl" when he thought of Cat) who was never either of those things. The Cat Will had known was effusive and playful, hardwired for flirting. "Buckets of love," Cat would have written. "Aeons, oceans, and mountains of love forever and ever." "I need you," though, that sounded like Cat.

The e-mail was pinned next to a poem that Kara had given him, left for him to find there on the bulletin board, when they had first started dating. "I Knew a Woman" by Theodore Roethke. Funny, Will had thought at the time, for his girlfriend to give him a love poem in the voice of a man worshipping a woman. "This is what I want," the gift suggested. "Love me like this."

Will liked the poem for its rhymes and because it didn't praise the usual body parts—eyes, lips, et cetera—but the woman's body in action, her specific way of moving or of holding still. After Kara had gone, moved out without ever having entirely moved in, Will had left the poem where it was. In his mind, it had never had all that much to do with Kara, who was pretty and smart, but not exactly graceful, a fact she freely acknowledged. Still, when the man in the poem asserts, parenthetically, more to himself than to anyone else, "(I measure time by how a body sways.)," Will had always known exactly what he meant.

" 'I'm sorry for everything,' " Cat had written in the e-mail. *Why should you be sorry?* Will thought, and looked out the window again to see, not Cat or Pen, but his mother, in the flesh and saluting the sun. Even though she had been this woman for almost five years, Will still felt amazed at the sight of her, sturdy, lean, and clear-eyed. She traced arcs in the air with her arms; her gray hair flashed. Abruptly, she broke her posture to wildly shoo a fly away, hands flapping, elbows stabbing the air. When she gave the retreating fly the finger, Will grinned.

He remembered the conversation they'd had on the first anniversary of her sobriety. They were celebrating at the summerhouse where his mother had lived year-round since the divorce. His sister, Tully, was upstairs napping with her new baby; his brother, Philip, and Tully's husband, Max, had driven into town for lobsters, corn, tomatoes, and blueberry pies. Will had been working at his computer on the porch. He liked it out there, even though it was smotheringly hot and breezeless that day, the wind chimes hanging, listless, in the sticky air. His mother had come up behind him and pressed a cold glass of iced tea against the back of his neck. When he reached around for the glass, she'd given his hand a little slap.

"Talk to me," she had ordered, "or no drink for you."

Will had laughed, closed his laptop, jumped up, and pulled out a chair for her, into which she settled like a cat, tucking her feet underneath her, leaning forward, and eyeing him determinedly.

"Oh, man, what are you up to now?" Will said warily.

"I asked Philip and now I'm asking you."

"Uh-oh."

"It's just this: I've done a lot of changing this past year, and I'm wondering how you feel about it all."

Her eyes were hazel, like Will's, coppery brown near the pupils, shading to amber and ending with rims of dark green, and they were looking at him with a combination of patience and insistence. *We will have this conversation,* the look said, *if it takes a hundred years.*

"Good," answered Will. "I feel good."

The eyes waited, unblinking.

"Proud of you," he went on. "Relieved. Uh, happy at how happy you are. I'm glad you're painting."

"Thank you," said his mother. "All very nice. What else?"

"Else?"

"Yup."

He slapped his neck. "Mosquitoes."

"William."

"What was Philip's answer?"

"William."

Will thought for a few seconds, looking out at the wide lawn, the blue-purple hydrangeas and thick, leaning stands of black-eyed Susans, the blown-glass hummingbird feeders hanging from the trees, and, yards away, the vegetable garden looking like a tiny campground, with its stakes and bean teepees. He loved this place. It had been the setting for some intense family ugliness over the years, and this very porch was the spot where his friendship with Pen had ended, smashed to smithereens, but the place itself had stayed pure, calm and unstained. Will felt oddly glad for it, glad that its days of bearing witness to meanness or betrayal or to the icy, cutting conversations that had been his father's specialty were over.

"Okay, how about this? Sometimes, I worry that you'll change so much I won't know you anymore," he had said finally. "Some of those friends of yours, they're nice, but they're a little . . ."

"Humorless?" his mother offered. "Annoyingly earnest? Overly huggy?"

"Yeah, that," said Will, laughing.

"Say more. What else worries you?"

"Apart from your maniacal insistence on openness and communication, you mean?"

"Yes." She folded her hands and smiled innocently, waiting. "Apart from that."

"All right, all right." He thought for a few seconds, listening to the bees hum like tiny engines. "I'm getting used to the yoga and the vegetarianism. I can see the point of them. But the really hard-core New Age stuff makes me—" He searched for the right words (*itch uncontrollably, vomit, run like hell*), then gave up. "I want you to be happy, and you should do whatever it takes. I'll adjust."

"But from a purely selfish perspective . . . ," prompted his mother.

"You should get a job with the KGB. Seriously."

"I believe the KGB was dissolved some time ago. As you were saying."

Will picked a leaf of mint off the surface of his iced tea and chewed it.

"From a purely selfish perspective, I'd say that I just want to keep feeling like we speak the same language. And I want you to stay funny."

His mother slapped the table and laughed. Then she leaned toward him and said, "How about this? Yoga, vegetarianism, and maybe just a bit of Buddhism. Tibetan. The joyful kind. But no crystals, personal gurus, or star charts."

Will raised his eyebrows. "Goddesses?"

"Nope."

"Vortices?"

"Don't know what they are."

"Wicca?"

"Never."

"What's your position on modern medicine?"

"All for it. Deal?"

"Deal."

Now, out in his backyard, his mother finished her sun salutation, started walking toward the house, and then leaned forward, squinting, her hands on her knees. Will wondered what she was looking at. It was so much brighter outside than it was in his office; no way could she see him. Then she smiled and blew a kiss in his direction. Will was highly skeptical about things like sixth sense and intuition, but when it came to her kids, his mother could be downright uncanny. This hadn't always been true, but it was true now. Even though he didn't believe she could possibly see him do it, he waved.

She didn't come straight to the office but went instead to the kitchen. Will heard her turn on the water, then clatter around, unscrewing the lids off the small, round metal canisters that held her loose tea leaves and herbs.

Will knew that she would come into his office in a few minutes, would lean against the doorjamb in her paint-streaked shirt, and tell him that she'd finished the last illustration for his new book. She had been close to finished last night, and he was pretty sure she had gotten up before sunrise that morning to paint. It amazed him, how little sleep she needed now, especially since one of the primary ways he remembered her from his childhood was as a long, sloped lump under sheets. He could see himself—he could transport himself into himself—at six, ten, fifteen, standing next to the guest-room bed or next to the couch in what she called her studio, even though she almost never used it for making art, staring at her and churning with worry and anger, his hands dangling, as full daylight sliced in around the drawn curtains.

Soon she would come in with her tea, say she had finished the painting for the book, and tomorrow or the next day, he would drive her to the airport and she would go back to the summerhouse. This visit had been her longest, almost four months. During the last book, she had come for three and had been staying in the guesthouse when Kara finally left him for good.

Having his mother, or anyone else, around to witness firsthand his getting dumped should have been a nightmare of humiliation and awkwardness, but it wasn't. He remembered how she had waited a few days, staying nearly invisible and quiet as a cat, before weighing in on the breakup. Then all she'd done was tilt her head to one side and say, "I liked her."

"She liked you, too," said Will. It was true. Some women might have minded—might have *detested*—having their boyfriend's mother living in the backyard, but Kara had repeatedly told him how much she loved it, even going so far as to ask her to eat dinner with them nearly every night, an invitation that, most of the time, his mother graciously refused. In fact, Kara seemed to have a crush on his mother, blushing in her presence, agreeing with her about the smallest things, asking her what kind of perfume she used ("Eau de paint" his mother had said, laughing). Once, Will had come home to find Kara wearing the cardigan his mother had left in their kitchen the night before. Will hadn't completely understood this enthusiasm, but sincerely hoped— and almost believed—that it had nothing to do with what Kara had once referred to, with a complete and disturbing lack of irony, as his mother's "pedigree."

"I liked her," his mother continued, "but, if I may be blunt, I didn't think she would stay."

"Why not?" Will had asked. Forty-eight hours earlier, he might have asked this defensively, but now he felt more exhausted than anything else. Besides, he was curious.

"The way she cleared out a separate shelf in the pantry for her own food, instead of mixing hers up with yours. I thought it was a bad sign."

"Oh."

"Also, she always seemed to be a little mad at you."

Actually, Kara had seemed more than a little mad, a fact that Will had asked her about exactly five times during the nine months they were together. The first time, she had laughed it off. The second time, she had cried and apologized and blamed her anger on her own moodiness. The third time, Kara had yelled, thrown a magazine in his direction (it didn't hit him), and slept in the guesthouse (his mother wasn't staying in it at the time), but at four that morning, he'd woken up to her hands pulling up his T-shirt, her mouth on his chest. "Forgive me," she'd murmured, and he had.

But then, just days later, when her anger came slashing toward him out of nowhere again, and he'd asked her about it, she had pressed her lips into a line, walked out of the room, walked back in, and said matter-of-factly, "You're just a closed-off person. That's your right, of course. But I'm passionate; I wear my heart on my sleeve. Sometimes, I get frustrated that you aren't the same way."

This had surprised Will because he had never considered himself closed-off. He wasn't a secret keeper, for the most part; he disclosed. He expressed his feelings when it seemed important to express them. When he tried to explain these things to Kara, she had cut him off, tenderly, saying, "Please. I didn't mean to put you in the position of having to defend yourself. You are who you are. I love you, and I value you, and I'm sorry," which pretty much put an end to that conversation.

Then, one night, on their way out to a dinner party, he had kissed her and said, "I love you in that dress," and she had pushed him backward with both hands, slapped the kitchen table, and snapped, "Well, that's just great, Will. That's just peachy," shoved her handbag over her shoulder, and slammed her way out the front door. Will had stood in the kitchen, listening to the screen door creak on its hinges in the aftershock of her slamming, suddenly feeling his own anger nearby, crouching, like something misshapen and ugly in his peripheral vision.

He had looked down at the kitchen chair in front of him, a fragile thing, and gripped it to steady himself, even as the urge to lift it up over his head and hurl it against the wall rushed up from his hands, into his arms and shoulders.

He'd done the breathing, the visualizing, employed all the strategies he hadn't had to use in years to calm himself down. Then he'd gone out to the car, where Kara sat in the passenger seat, opened the door, and said quietly, "Why are you so mad at me all the time? The real reason."

Kara had stared straight ahead for a long time before looking up at him with sad, sad eyes and saying, "I lied."

"What?"

"That time I said you were closed off, not passionate enough."

Will knew all at once what she was going to say, the general gist of it, and he braced himself.

"You do wear your heart on your sleeve," she told him in a hollow voice. "It's right there. You just don't love me as much as I love you."

"Kara," Will began, then stopped.

"You love me," she clarified. "But only a little bit. Not enough."

WILL'S MOTHER STOOD IN THE DOORWAY TO HIS OFFICE.

"How's the tea?" he asked.

" 'It tastes like licorice,' " his mother said, smiling. " 'That's the way with everything.' " It was a Hemingway quotation, one Will had been hearing for as long as he could remember. Even though it made no sense for his mother to love Hemingway (Woolf maybe, Austen definitely, Hemingway no), she always had. She knew that particular story, every word, by heart, and could quote whole chapters from *The Sun Also Rises*. When Will had finally read those stories on his own— he'd been in tenth grade—it had made his stomach hurt to think about his mother feeling so at home with all those unhappy, disappointed, disconnected characters.

"I finished the last painting," she said. Jokingly, she threw her arms out to the side and said, "It's brilliant!"

"Same as always. Thanks, Mom."

She leaned over and kissed the top of his head.

"Have I told you lately how I adore you?"

"Yep."

"Adore," she said. "Not just like a lot."

"Adore. Got it."

"Good."

"You still need to do the book cover," Will reminded her, "for the novel."

"I'll come back," she said.

She turned to face the bulletin board, and Will knew she was reading the e-mail again.

"It still says what it said the first five times, Mom."

"You know, it's really too bad Cat ever left in the first place," she said.

"She wanted to get married," said Will. "It seemed like a fair enough reason to go."

His mother turned around and said suddenly, "You know, I thought that after she left, you and Pen might fall in love."

Will leaned back in his chair, startled.

"Oh, yeah? I never knew you thought that."

"I guess it wasn't in the cards, though?"

Will straightened some papers on his desk. He could feel her watching him.

"Nope. We were friends." He gave a half-baked smile. "Until we weren't."

His mother's cheeks reddened, and she made a gesture with one hand, as though she were brushing away the past.

"Anyway, I think you should go." She tapped a finger against the e-mail on the bulletin board. "Cat needs you. That's not a small thing, is it? Even after so long?"

"No," admitted Will.

"You never could say no to Cat. You and Pen. Could you?" She was smiling.

"I don't know. No," said Will, with a shrug, "I guess we never could."

CHAPTER FIVE

*A*S PEN PARKED HER CAR AT THE CURB IN FRONT OF AUGUSTA'S father Patrick's house, or in front of the uniformly rainforest-green ocean of lawn on which Patrick's house floated like a distant ship, Pen thought what she had thought the very first time she had seen the house and every time since: Patrick was living the wrong life.

Although it's true that this thought initially came to her during a time in her own life when thinking such a thing was suspiciously convenient, she persisted in thinking it long after she'd stopped wanting Patrick to live a different life in a different house with a radically different wife, a thing Pen had wanted ardently for a while there, or at least had thought she wanted. It was clear to her now: she had been confused and only *thought* that she wanted to be married to Patrick—although she had to admit that, at the time, thinking and actually wanting felt like one and the same.

But Pen couldn't imagine anyone who knew Patrick reconciling him—perpetually messy, boyish, slouchy Patrick—with all this new-ness and gleam: the dazzlingly white driveway lined with still-scrawny trees, the landscaping carefully choreographed for staggered, three-season blooming (crocuses, then forsythia, then tulips, then azaleas, then a bewildering sequence of flowers and flowering bushes, then, finally, dahlias and mums, and somewhere in there, for years, twined

delicately around the mailbox, clematis—starry, purple, and hopeful—until Tanya had declared it "folksy" and had it yanked).

The first time Patrick had shown her the house, Pen thought he
was joking. She had given his shoulder a playful shove and said, "Yeah,
right. Now take me to the real house."

"What do you mean?" he'd asked, with what Pen had assumed was
faux surprise. "That's it. That's our house."

This remark would only sting later, after they'd driven back into
the city and she was lying next to him on his simultaneously rock-hard
and rickety Ikea futon in his small, unbeautiful, rented South Philly
row house, watching him sleep. He had only been living in the house
for a few weeks before Pen met him, but already it looked more lived-
in than the apartment a few blocks away where she'd lived for years:
houseplants on the kitchen windowsill, *New Yorker* cartoons stuck
to the refrigerator door, a grove of candle stumps above the imitation
fireplace, the mantel studded with coins of wax.

"That *was* our house," he should have said, or "That's *her* house,"
or even better, "That's the house I barely remember living in for two
years, if you can call what I was doing before I met you living."

Pen had watched his eyes move under the heartbreakingly thin skin
of his eyelids and tried to remember what she knew about REM sleep.
He was dreaming, right? Watching things invisible to her. It seemed
possible that in such a state, his brain might be especially susceptible
to suggestion. "You live here," she had whispered fervidly. "Got that?
Here."

But because at the time, sitting next to Patrick in the car, Pen
thought the whole thing was a joke, she had laughed and said, "Trust
me, that is not your house."

"It is," he'd insisted. "I lived in it for two years."

"Please," she'd said, rolling her eyes. "You did not live there."

"Why do you say that?"

"Because people don't really live in houses like that. It's not possible."

"Houses like what?"

"You know like what. Like oversized and soulless and planted in the middle of what used to be someone's cornfield."

They both looked at the house. Because Patrick had slunk down in the passenger seat to hide from the neighbors (although why he bothered was a mystery to Pen, since the neighboring houses were set so far away that, unless the people living in them had high-powered binoculars, they couldn't have seen a 747 landing in Patrick's yard, or what Patrick was pretending was his yard, which was almost large enough to accommodate such a landing, should one ever occur), he had to scoot himself up so that his eyes were just above the base of the window.

It had been July, just after twelve noon, and the high white sun pounding down wasn't doing the house any favors. Pen remembered imagining how, in mellow afternoon light, the stucco might have looked buttery instead of bad-teeth yellow and the tall windows might have seemed welcoming rather than flashing and blind. Despite her old-house snobbery, Pen might have found it sort of pretty or at least impressive. As it was, the house appeared creepily phony, like an enormous photograph thumbtacked to a vast blue wall. Even the flowers looked plastic.

"I think it's fake," Pen had said in a stage whisper. "I think if you went up to it and pushed it with one finger, it would fall down flat."

"I guess I can see how it wouldn't be everyone's cup of tea." Something in his voice caught Pen's attention because it sounded like sadness. But before she could ask him about it, the yard was suddenly alive, blossoming with tiny, silvery, geranium-flower-shaped fountains and crisscrossed with rainbows.

"Whoa," breathed Pen.

"Hey!" said Patrick, sitting up in his seat. "That's not supposed to happen." He didn't sound sad anymore; he sounded concerned.

"I guess it's the sprinkler system. For the grass?" said Pen, figuring it out. She felt a bit deflated. For a few seconds there, the lawn's abrupt transformation had seemed like a minor miracle.

"Yeah, but it's set for morning and evening. If you water in the heat of the day, the sun soaks it all up. Tanya must have set it wrong before they left for the beach."

Pen stared at the back of Patrick's neck.

Crap, she thought, *crappity crap crap shit.*

"Um," she said in a small voice. "So, gosh. You really did live here, in this place I just completely demolished?"

"Until I was thrown out on my ass, yes." He turned and smiled at her. "Demolished? You doused that sucker with gasoline and set it on fire."

"I'm sorry. I really and truly didn't think it was yours."

Patrick took off his ancient Phillies cap, put it in his lap, and looked at it.

Pen said, "Guess I was pretty harsh."

Patrick looked back at the house, "You really think it's soulless?"

Absolutely and entirely soulless, thought Pen, *barren and treeless and pretentious and soulless.* "I shouldn't have said 'soulless.' "

"Because that's the house Lila's growing up in, you know?"

At the time, Pen hadn't yet met Lila, who was three years old, and whenever Patrick mentioned her, Pen experienced an odd and intense mix of reverence, curiosity, jealousy, and irritation. It was just the way she had felt back in elementary school, when her devoutly Catholic friend Shelby talked about the Blessed Virgin. ("We have the Virgin Mary, too," Pen could remember protesting. "You don't pray to her, do you?" Shelby had shot back. "And if you don't pray to her, you don't have her. You have God and Jesus, that's *it.*")

Pen looked at Patrick's longish curly hair, the stubble on his face. His T-shirt was transparent in spots and so decayed that the figure on the front looked more like a Cat in the Hat zombie than the Cat himself, and his Phillies cap was a dull pink, the ratty white buckram poking through all along the brim.

"I don't know. I guess I just can't imagine you in that particular house," ventured Pen finally.

"Why not?"

"Patrick, you shave once a week, tops. And look at you. Every single edge on you is frayed."

Patrick looked down at himself, fingering the hem of his khaki shorts.

"I'm clean, though. I make a point of being clean." He smiled at her, but his eyes weren't happy.

"You are. You do."

"I let Tanya pick the house. She cared, and I really didn't. Besides, it was mostly her money."

Pen wasn't sure that this was true. Despite his threadbare appearance, Patrick was a partner in a marketing and design firm that even Jamie (who had loathed the Patrick situation from the beginning) had grudgingly acknowledged "did well." But Patrick liked to think of himself as a "regular Joe," a trait Pen had found endearingly down to earth, initially, and annoyingly affected later. ("I should have known he wasn't trustworthy," Pen told her friend Amelie, after Patrick had broken off their engagement and gone back to Tanya. "The first time I saw him in a mechanic's shirt with another man's name on it, I should have known.")

The house seemed to suit Patrick no better now, almost six years after he'd left her and gone back to it the first time, two since he'd gone back to it for good, than it ever had, but now Pen had her own reasons to regret calling it soulless, since, for one weekend out of every month, Augusta was growing up here, too.

Before she got out of the car, Pen smoothed her already smooth hair and put on lip gloss, stabbing at her mouth with the sponge-tipped wand and cursing herself between clenched teeth for caring, even a little, about Patrick's and Tanya's opinions of her. She started to check for food in her teeth, then stopped. *Enough,* she thought, *enough, enough, for God's sake,* and she set off briskly down the long driveway, *pat pat pat,* her dark red ballet flats flashing against the white. It was strange, Pen thought, how coming to this house never got any less awkward, especially strange when you considered that she hadn't hated Tanya for a long time, not for years, and was ashamed that she ever had.

The trouble was that Tanya still hated Pen. She hid it, most of the time, or, rather, camouflaged it as cold dislike or stony indifference or mocking disdain (the woman had Joan Crawford eyebrows and knew how to use them), but then, as sudden as a slap, it would hit Pen: a blazing, palpable, ever-fresh hatred that whipped around and raged inside Tanya's eyes like twin electrical storms. *If you ever get diagnosed with terminal cancer, if you get hit by a freight train or just drop dead for no reason at all,* the look told Pen, *I would rejoice in my soul.*

Certainly, this was disturbing, but Pen had to admit that she found it kind of admirable. She could imagine sustaining certain emotions at that pitch for that long—love absolutely, grief probably, guilt maybe—but hatred was exhausting and gave so little back. Once, after her father died, Pen had tried to keep hatred alive, but it kept losing its firm shape, kept smudging and blurring until it became an immense, black, impossibly heavy sadness that lived inside her body and made it hard to move, so she had given it up. Sometimes she missed it, though.

When Tanya opened the door, the eyebrows were telegraphing a patronizing impatience, but nothing more.

"Finally, she arrives," said Tanya.

Pen didn't apologize or glance at her watch. Her habitual lateness was a fiction Tanya had maintained for years, despite the fact that Pen was chronically, even annoyingly punctual. ("It has to end," Amelie had ranted once. "This arriving *on the dot.* Good Lord. It's an *affront!*") But Pen couldn't help it. It was family law. Her parents had caught her young and brainwashed her. Even Jamie was never late.

"We said five," Pen reminded her. Then she made the snap decision to smile and did it, slowly, beginning with her eyes, ending with the corners of her mouth, throwing a tiny nose crinkle in for good measure. What the hell; she had a favor to ask Tanya and Patrick and could use a boost, even a cheap one. She held the smile for a few seconds, letting it ripen on her face like a peach. She waited. Whenever Pen was friendly to Tanya (and sometimes she was even friendly by accident, rather than by design), she got the same response: Tanya was thrown off her game entirely, sometimes freezing up, sometimes spluttering incoherently, sometimes stomping out of the room. Whatever her response, for a few moments anyway, Pen had the upper hand.

Her face still beaming post-smile warmth, Pen watched Tanya

take a step back and clear her throat. "*We* have a *dinner* reservation with Lou and Bev *Byatt* at a *tapas* place. We ordered the special rice dish, *not* risotto"—she paused, searching for the word, then shaking her head, impatiently—"in *advance* because it takes an extremely long time"—her voice rose as she finished—"*to prepare!*"

Tanya didn't say, "So there," but with her raised eyebrows and fist on her hip, she might as well have. Pen had to stop herself from smiling again.

"You mean paella?" asked Pen. "Lucky you. You'll love it."

"Oh, I've had it," Tanya told her. "Many, many times!" Then she twisted her neck to bellow over her shoulder, "Lila! Time for Augusta to go!" And she turned on her heel and was gone.

Pen leaned against the foyer wall, feeling more guilty than satisfied. The truth was that Tanya was not a ridiculous person, not most of the time, anyway. She was smart, generous, and community-minded, a former ob-gyn who now worked for a women's health advocacy group. Pen had met a few of her former patients over the years, and they all worshipped her. She was pretty, too. Five years older than Patrick, which meant that she was ten years older than Pen, but no one would ever have guessed it. She had an aquiline nose and the kind of coloring that Pen's mother called "autumn redhead," auburn hair, tawny skin, and eyes the color of whiskey.

Pretty, hardworking, and good, Pen thought, *and you had to push the one button that turns her into a blithering idiot.*

She hates you, Pen reminded herself in her own defense.

Understandably, she argued back.

Understandably, maybe, but not justifiably. Look at the facts.

It was an old argument. In its first incarnation, Pen had been arguing with her mother instead of herself.

"She's a mother. And you're threatening her family. Of course, she hates you," her mother had said.

"Look at the facts," Pen had retorted. "He didn't leave her for me. She called him a self-centered bastard and threw him out. I met him afterward, when he was living by himself because she *threw him out!*"

"Even so."

"She changed the locks!"

"Oh, Pen."

The kindness in her mother's voice had been too much for Pen, who was alone, jobless, and, although she didn't know it yet, pregnant. She had begun to cry, then to sob, clenched and bent over like an old woman. Her mother had pulled her into her lap and stroked her hair.

"I wanted to keep him," Pen sobbed. "And I gave him back. I loved teaching, and she got me fired, even though I gave him back."

Her back against the wall in Tanya's cold foyer, Pen closed her eyes, remembering.

"Hey there, uh, Pen." It was Patrick, slipping into the foyer in his slinking, barefoot manner, saying her name the way he always did, as though he didn't quite have the right to say it.

"Hello."

Reluctantly, Pen opened her eyes, saw Patrick in the vintage Replacements T-shirt she had bought him when they'd first started dating, thought, *Oh, God,* and shut them again. The Replacements had been Jamie's favorite band all through college (even though they had been broken up for years even then) and, therefore, Pen's favorite, too, although Pen really only liked their major-label albums. She opened her eyes and took another look. Paul Westerberg, the first of her scrawny, shaggy-haired crushes, gazing moodily out at her from the chest of her last. *Wonderful.*

"You want to come in? Sit down or something?" asked Patrick.

Pen didn't. She preferred the peripheries—the yard, the foyer, the driveway—and rarely ventured into the rest of the house ("the family quarters," she joked to Jamie, "the inner sanctum," "the bowels"). In the five years since Augusta was born, she had never gone upstairs once. Today, she needed to talk to Patrick, though, so she nodded and followed him into what she knew was called "the great room," cavernous, a tsunami of sun cresting through the gigantic windows, drowning the room and everything in it. Pen recoiled like a vampire, arms in front of her face.

"I know," said Patrick. He made his voice flat and instructional, "Don sunglasses before entering."

Pen smiled. *Don.*

"It's actually a pretty room," she said, blinking and looking around. "Sweeping. Gracious. All those words. I've always thought so." She meant it. She couldn't imagine living in such a room, but she liked the *idea* of wall-lessness: everything happening in one place, everyone together. And despite its vastness and stark light, Tanya's decorating, or her decorator's decorating, had given it warmth. Cream, sand, and sage, punctuated with garnet and Delft blue, large vases of real flowers, walls the color of coffee ice cream.

"Nah," said Patrick, with a sidelong grin, "I've seen the nest. I know your hermit thrush ways."

Pen stiffened.

Suddenly, it was winter, her parents' house, back when it was still her house, too, the first time Cat and Will came home with her for a weekend. Will and Cat seeing her old room for the first time: the bunk beds, the white swivel egg chair with the red cushions. Will pointed to the bunk beds and asked, "You and Jamie shared a room?"

"God, no," said Pen, making a face and ducking backward into the chair. She looked up at them, her legs swinging. "I just like bunk beds. Upper bunk. I used to pretend I was sleeping in one of those train compartments from a Hitchcock movie." She thought for a second. "Actually, I still do pretend that."

Will eyed the bed. He rapped his knuckles lightly on the fiberglass shell of the chair and nodded.

"You're a nester," he'd said. "You like to fold yourself into little spaces. Armchairs. Library carrels. I've noticed this."

"Restaurant booths!" added Cat, catching on. "I like an open table myself, but you!" She leaned over and poked Pen's forehead with her finger. "You always want the booth! I bet you get in the bathtub and close the shower curtain."

"Tea parties *under* the table," said her mother's voice from behind them. Pen couldn't see her, but could hear her mother smile, and swiveled around to look.

"I think they're on to me," said Pen to her mother.

Her mother pointed to the wardrobe against the far wall of the room. "That's got a deep, low shelf, for shoes, maybe, or blankets. But when Pen was little, she used to climb out of her bed and sleep on it. The first time it happened, Ben and I were scared to death, looked for her everywhere."

"Like I said," said Will, "a nester. A hermit thrush."

After graduation, a week after the three of them had moved to Philadelphia together, Pen had come home to the apartment she shared with Cat to find that they had made her a nest. A window seat rigged with a wooden curtain rod, a green curtain, and a matching cushion, so that she could curl up inside, draw the curtain shut, and look out at her little piece of city. Pen had still lived in the apartment when she'd met Patrick, even though, by then, Cat was long gone.

So unfair, Patrick's fingerprints on her funny stories, her pet phrases, on people he never knew.

This is what you get, she berated herself, *for handing everything over.*

She had felt the same way when Cat and Will left. "I gave you two my life," she had raged at Will the last time she saw him. "My childhood, my parents, the things that scare me, the books I love, the *sentences* I love from the books I love. You went on bike rides with *my dad.* And you're *leaving*? Are you *kidding* me?"

Keep the T-shirt, she wanted to tell Patrick, *but everything else, everything pre-you, forget it; erase it from your clucking hard drive.*

"Have a seat," Patrick offered.

Pen looked at the sofas, the deep armchairs, and the love seats and could not imagine doing that kind of sinking down and leaning back in Tanya and Patrick's house.

"How about over here?" She was already walking toward the kitchen, which lay at the distant end of the great room, rising up out of the earth tones like a city, all steel, edges, and glass, its appliances mammoth, its countertops shining like lakes. She sat on one of the high stools that flanked one of the counters, feeling out of place and rigid, her back straight, her hands in her lap, becoming prim the way she often did when she felt out of place. She shook her head when Patrick offered her something to drink.

"So," she began, but Patrick grabbed her "so" and ran with it, in the last direction Pen wanted to go.

"So, *yeah*," he said, widening his blue eyes, "tell me about the weekend at your mom's. The bike ride and all. It go okay?"

Just like that: *Tell me about.* Pen stared at him. Tell *you*? *Tell* you? *He cares,* she tried to remind herself. *He has no tact and is presumptuous, but he does care.* And he had taken Augusta for an unscheduled weekend so that Pen and Jamie could go alone to the anniversary ride. *You're about to ask him for another unscheduled weekend,* Pen thought. *Suck it up.*

"I guess it went okay," she said. "It was crazy-sad, but we got through it. And it felt like the right thing to do."

"Was it different from last year?"

It had been. Jamie had been too loyal to tell Patrick about Pen's little breakdown last year, and Pen had been too ashamed, but Patrick had picked up on the fact that it had been an ordeal for everyone. This year had been different, maybe not easier, but hard in a different way. Last year, Pen hadn't been able to finish the ride; this year, she hadn't wanted it to end. With the road unspooling under her bike wheels and the trees leaning in on either side, Pen remembered doing the same ride with her father, a memory of such detail and vividness that, for several sweet miles, she almost believed he was there with her, riding just outside of her peripheral vision, his voice tugged out of earshot by the wind. But when the ride ended, he was as gone as ever, and Pen was left raw, windburned by loss.

Then, afterward, eating catered food in her parents' house with their friends, Pen kept expecting her mother to appear, to come down the stairs in a linen dress and lipstick. Pen had known she wouldn't be there (she had called the night before from Greece), but Pen kept watching for her anyway. "It's awful," she'd told Jamie. "Like phantom limb syndrome."

But to Patrick, who had lost his right to know about such things, she said simply, "Yes."

Patrick nodded his trademark nod, a movement not just of his head, but of his shoulders and chest as well. Full-upper-body empathy. *Please know that I, and my entire torso, are right there with you.*

"Cathartic, right?" he prompted. "Healing? I bet you have that wrung-out but good-wrung-out feeling, right?"

Pen stared at him. He had not always been like this; she swore he hadn't. Back when they were together, he'd had a far more distracted approach to conversation, losing track of threads, doodling while they talked, playing his own knee like a techno-pop keyboardist. Back then, he had a trick of nodding with apparent interest even as he zoned out, then zoned back in, saying, maddeningly, "So, *yeah*. Wow. *Any*way."

Somehow, since their final split two years ago, he had become a talk-show host, a conversational lobster eater, cracking open shells, twisting off legs, trying to get at every soft and hidden thing. His bright blue eyes were lit with over-interest, and Pen had to stop looking at them, focusing instead on the pepper grinder in front of her. It was a foot and a half high and appeared heavy as lead.

"Man felled by pepper grinder in own kitchen," she said.

"What?" Patrick's full-body nod stopped midbend, and his neck turned scarlet. "Oh, okay. Boundaries, right?" They'd had boundaries conversations before.

"Right."

"Sorry." He gave a little laugh, but his face shifted into the kind of puzzled hurt that you usually only see on the faces of small children. Once Pen had crumbled before that expression. Even now, her first impulse was to take back what she'd said, but she resisted. Instead, she smiled a lopsided smile at him, and said, "Man apologizes in nick of time."

Then, sailing toward her from across the room: "Mama!"

High-pitched, even squeaky, it was the most soul-catching sound Pen knew. She was turning in its direction before she had even slid off the stool, and, when she saw the girl bounding rabbit-fashion through the great room, she felt what she always felt, her body opening toward her daughter in a great whoosh of breathless blooming.

"Sweetpea," she whispered, smiling, and then Augusta flew against her with a whack, and Pen knelt down to gather all of the child into her, pressing her cheek into the cloud of dark hair, her palms against the narrow back. At five, Augusta was already losing her baby softness, was becoming pared down, almost sinewy, her back a delicate landscape of spine and shoulder blades that Pen could feel through her shirt.

"I am so happy to see you," said Pen.

"My heart leaps up, Mama." It was what they always said.

"My heart leaps up, too."

She drew back and looked at Augusta's face, which was smeared with colors, brilliant, glittery, and iridescent as a hummingbird's neck. For the first time, Pen noticed the child's outfit: black go-go boots so big they were merely drifting around her calves, a scratchy pink tutu, a silvery tank top slipping off one scrawny shoulder.

"Hey there, Pop Star."

Augusta shimmied her shoulders and sang a few lines from a song about going out with her girlfriends and leaving the boys behind.

"Sounds good to me," said Patrick.

Pen could imagine her before-kids self being utterly disapproving of this, the little girl in makeup and grown-up clothes thing, the pre-pre-pre-tween fascination with fabulousness. But seeing it in action, she found it didn't bother her. Little girls were magpies and butterflies, gaga for everything shiny, in sheer, giggly, joyful love with transformation. Pen looked at Augusta, so at home in her body, so convinced of her own gorgeousness. *Keep it up, honey,* she thought. *Hang on to it with both hands.*

"Hi, Pen." Lila stood behind Augusta, smiling and tugging at her T-shirt in a way that made Pen's heart ache. At nine, Lila barely qualified as chubby, but, despite her parents' efforts to celebrate her good points, which were many (smarts, big blue eyes, and an uncommon sweetness), self-consciousness was setting in.

"Hey, lovely," said Pen, standing. Lila's eyes widened with happiness. Pen did not spend enough time with Lila for the two of them to really be close, but Pen knew Lila regarded her with the kind of shy, eager interest that verged on adulation. She remembered feeling that way herself, about her fifth-grade teacher, her friend Sydney's teenaged sister who began loading her neck with rosaries (to her family's deep and everlasting horror) and her arms with rubber bracelets before most people in Wilmington even knew who Madonna was. Pen could not imagine Tanya's enjoying Lila's crush on Pen, but to her credit, she had never tried to squelch it.

"You guys have fun this weekend?" Pen asked.

"We totally did," said Lila, reaching out and giving her sister's hair a gentle tug. "Can Augusta come back soon?"

"You know what? I was just about to talk to your dad about another visit. You think you could help Augusta change and get her stuff together, while we discuss it? That would be a huge help."

"Definitely!"

Pen and Patrick watched the girls zigzag through the furniture and out of the room, hair flying.

"Lila's a doll," said Pen. "Aren't they supposed to get mean by the time they're nine?"

"Yeah, she seems to be sidestepping that stuff so far. Hope it lasts." He folded his arms across his chest. "So what's up? You need another weekend?"

"My college reunion, ten year. It's in two weeks."

Patrick smiled at her. "Ten year, huh? I forget what a baby you are."

"Oh, come on. You're five years older than I am, which is nothing." Five years wasn't nothing really, not necessarily, but Pen had never felt the age difference between them. Most of the time, she felt as though she were the one who was older.

"Hey, you think you'll run into Cat? It's been ages, right?"

Pen hesitated, then told him about the e-mail. He'd known what Cat had meant to her. It might give him some extra incentive to persuade Tanya to take Augusta for another weekend. Tanya liked Augusta, never failed to make her feel welcome, but she was fiercely protective of "family time" on weekends. On weekdays, too. She and Patrick both made a point of being home by 5:30 and ruthlessly screened incoming phone calls in the evenings. A couple of years ago, Tanya had asked Pen not to call, unless Augusta had a "life-threatening emergency." Wincing at the phrase "life-threatening" appearing in the same sentence with her daughter's name, Pen had quickly agreed.

"I think it'll be fine," said Patrick. "I'll talk to Tanya. But I hope that Will guy won't show up."

"Oh, Patrick."

"Seriously. I've heard enough about his temper to think you're not safe around a guy like that."

It was ridiculous, this protective posturing, this misplaced, left-over, and far too easy chivalry. When Pen had met Patrick, Cat and Will were newly gone, and Pen was still reeling, her sadness still fresh and shot through with anger. She'd told Patrick too much, probably, and he had fixated on Will in a way that she'd briefly found touching, but that made no sense. Not safe with Will. *Will?* With whom had she ever been safer?

"He never directed any of that stuff at me. He wouldn't in a million years. You know I've told you that."

"I'm not so sure. Sorry, but I just don't think he's trustworthy."

What about you? You walked out on me and our newborn baby. You gave up custody of her because your wife made you. How trustworthy are you? Pen felt like saying these things, but mostly only because they were true, only to defend Will. She wasn't really bitter anymore, not bitter-bitter, a fact that still surprised her.

"He probably won't be there, anyway," said Pen, although she knew that if Cat had written to him, too, he probably would be. Not probably. She didn't know who Will had become in the past six years, but if he was now a person who could turn down a cry for help from an old friend, Pen would eat her hat.

"It's been a long time. Do you still think about them? I mean, more than once in a while? Do you miss them?" said Patrick.

Lobster eater, thought Pen, shaking her head, *lobster eater, lobster eater, lobster eater.*

"Not really," she said.

CHAPTER SIX

$\mathcal{T}$HE LITTLE BOY IN *COUNTING BACK TO LIAM* TURNS INTO A
monster when he's angry. The monster is huge and gloriously
ugly, toothy as a shark, carpeted with spiky slime-green hair, sporting bat wings, stegosaurus plates down his back, and a head that is an
amalgamation of buffalo, werewolf, and Gila monster. When a man
walking in front of Liam and his mother down a city street unwraps his
sandwich and throws the wrapper on the ground, the monster erupts
into thundering life, charging down the sidewalk—clunking into innocent bystanders along the way—and confronting the man with a
roar that shakes the buildings around them, shattering the window of
a bakery storefront, toppling the cakes. Then the monster stomps on
the man's foot. The man is hopping and stunned. The people on the
sidewalk are appalled and rubbing their elbows and heads and other
places the monster has bumped. The mother's head is drooping, her
hand over her eyes, and in this gesture and in the wilt of her shoulders,
there is a profound discouragement, a near hopelessness that tells the
reader that this is not the first time something like this has happened.

When the boy turns away from the man, he is Liam again, small in
his T-shirt and jeans, shaky, drained of triumph, frightened by his own
loss of control. In bed that night, he tells his mother, "I thought the
man was bad, but maybe I'm the one who's bad." And his mother tells
him, "You? No, you are my funny sonny, my curious, story-loving,

cookie-sharing boy. That monster, *he's* the one who's bad." And the boy says, "The monster makes me lonely. I mean he makes me feel alone." "The monster makes me lonely, too," his mother says.

Liam and his mother visit a wise woman. In the wordless illustrations that follow, Liam talks, sometimes laughing, sometimes sad, sometimes pressing his face into his mother's arm, and the woman listens. Then she says, "I'm not a fairy godmother, you know. I don't have a magic wand, and what a silly thing, to think that magic lives inside a wand!" "It doesn't?" asks the boy. "Magic lives in here," the woman says, placing one hand on Liam's head. "And here," she tells him, pointing to his heart. "And you are full of it and courage, too." "Courage?" asks Liam. "I don't think so. Me?" "Of course," says the woman. "Now, listen: I think I know a way to get that monster *gone*."

Pen read this book for the first time four months after her father died. She was sitting in Pollywogs, her favorite children's bookstore in Philadelphia, a place to which she had escorted so many writers that she'd become friends with the owner, a Mrs. Piggle Wiggle look-alike named Selena Bass. Selena had invited her to come just after closing to help create some displays of new books.

It was one of Pen's first ventures out of the apartment for anything other than work since her father had died, and she had walked the whole way there, a long walk. At first, she had almost turned back, shaky and tired, street noise loud in her ears, but after a few blocks, it had felt good to be out, walking among strangers, anonymous. She crossed streets, stopped at corners, shrugged her handbag more securely onto her shoulder, an oddly reassuring movement. On the busy sidewalk, she could have been anyone, someone who was grieving or not, had a father or didn't. If Selena hadn't been watching through the door of her shop, Pen might have walked right past it. She might have walked all night.

Inside, the shop was cozy and purple-walled. A former elementary-school teacher, Selena had whipped off freehand, typeface-quality signs with colored Sharpies, each sign featuring a quotation from a famous children's book (one notable example from *Winnie-the-Pooh*: "If the person you are talking to doesn't appear to be listening, be patient. It may simply be that he has a small piece of fluff in his ear"), while Pen had unpacked picture books, feeling moved and reverential, running a hand over each glossy cover before placing the books on the display shelf of the little backroom reading space called the Cuddle-upreadalotorium.

She was remembering a conversation with her father.

"Here's what happened: you got fired, then you got discouraged. Who wouldn't?" he had told her a few days before he died. "Then you started driving the writers around, you and that cute Amelie, and you liked it pretty well, and then you had Augusta, and you went with the flow. Makes sense. But my bet? You'll be back in front of a classroom one of these days."

"How do you know?" she'd asked him.

"I know because I know," he'd answered.

Holding the new books in her hands, she missed teaching kids how to read. She missed having someone know her the way her father had.

Pen didn't see Will's name on the front of the book at first. She had been too arrested by the cover: jewel and earth tones soaked in light, looking more like a Vermeer than like any children's book cover Pen had ever seen, the monster standing with one vast, clawed hand over its eyes, the other hand in the air, three fingers raised, counting.

"Ooh, that's a good one. Brand-new and bound for greatness. It'll win every kids' book award under the sun," said Selena, glancing over. "Why don't you sit down with it for a minute?"

Pen had sat. From the beginning, the language was wonderful, clean, vivid, leaping upward into poetry at just the right moments, especially in the second half of the book. Liam and his mother wait in line at the post office, their arms full of packages. Outside the window, low afternoon light rests on the snow-covered street; pearly caps of snow top fire hydrants and parked cars and the wool hat of a woman who bustles into the post office with her own tower of packages. Snow caps the tower of packages. "Excuse me," the woman says huffily. "I'm late for a very important appointment! I'm sure you won't mind!" And she steps in line in front of Liam's mother.

Slowly, Pen had turned the page and winced to find what she'd been afraid she would find. The little boy Liam is gone, replaced by the monster, who begins to take a step toward the woman, his awful, thick green leg hooked in the air, his arms raised menacingly. And then, quite suddenly, he freezes, and he puts his foot back down, the effort that it takes to do this written on his face. Then he closes his wild eyes—red lizard eyes with the dash-shaped pupils of a goat—and in a few moments, the walls of the post office fall away, the people and their packages and the snowy city turn translucent and disappear, and there is the monster, standing in somebody's backyard. It is early summer and the yard is flush with blooming; a sprinkler glitters in the background, a giant oak tree cradles a wooden tree house in its branches, purple pansies with their tiny, winking faces bloom in a pot beside the backdoor of the house, and framed by an open window—it seems to be a kitchen window—is the face of a woman, Liam's mother's face.

Liam's mother smiles at the monster, who puts one hand over his eyes. He begins to count, and something amazing begins to happen. "Five . . ."—the monster shrinks to boy-size. "Four . . ."—his bristly fur silvers, turns to dandelion fluff, and blows across the sky. "Three . . ."—each stegosaurus plate along his back detaches, folds itself into an origami bird and flies away. "Two . . ."—the bat wings of the monster who is almost not a monster anymore close themselves like black umbrellas. "One . . ."—and then they *are* umbrellas and Liam holds one in each hand.

On the next page, Liam is back inside the post office in his winter coat, packages at his feet, and he takes the two umbrellas and slips them into the umbrella stand beside the post office door. Then he walks up to the woman who cut in line and taps her lightly on the arm. She turns disdainful eyes on him and asks him what he wants. Liam says, "Excuse me, but my mother and I have been waiting a long time. Our packages are heavy, just like yours. I think you should go to the end of the line. I think it's only fair." And, for a moment, the woman's face twists in anger. She seems about to speak, then stops, closes her eyes, and takes a few deep breaths.

"You're right," she tells the little boy. "I'm having a hard day, but that is not your fault. Not your mother's, either. And, yes, it's only fair." And she steps to the back of the line. Then Liam's mother smiles as loving a smile as Pen had ever seen on any person, living or painted, and carefully bends her knees to set her bundles on the floor. She opens her arms to Liam, who fits himself inside them. "Liam 1," she whispers to him, "Monster 0."

Pen had not consciously known that Will had written *Counting Back to Liam* until she shut the book and saw his name on the cover, but what she would swear to be true forever after was that before she knew that she knew, she knew. About three-quarters of the way through the book, she had gotten the strange and specific sensation of a small light turning on inside her chest, lifting itself out of darkness like a miniature dawn, and starting to brighten and grow, so that by the time she'd found his name on the cover, she wasn't stunned the way she might have expected she'd be. Her heart didn't take off like a racehorse. Instead, she sat in the child-sized blue plastic chair and felt like one of the paintings in the book, imbued with a warm, lemon-colored radiance. It took her a few seconds to realize that what she felt was happy.

Good for you, Will, she had thought, hard. She meant for writing the book, which was wonderful, for writing it in spite of his father, who would never have given his blessing to such a thing, but more than that, she meant good for him for getting better, for learning how to get the best of his temper, which had been so nightmarish and had made him feel so bad. Because that's what the book meant, Pen understood. She lifted the book and leaned her forehead on it, briefly, eyes closed, in honor of the promise it gave that her friend was okay.

"It's gorgeous, isn't it?" said Selena.

"Yes. It's gorgeous and moving and funny. I love it," said Pen. "I know him."

"Will Wadsworth?" asked Selena. "Is he a friend of yours?"

"He was," said Pen, but the words sounded wrong, so she added, "We went to college together." Still wrong, too limited and small. It had seemed very important to find the right words to describe Will's position in her life, but the story was too long to tell. "I adore Will, actually. Just haven't seen him in a while."

"Oh," said Selena. She had smiled, head tipped to one side, and blinked her twinkly eyes. *You need a hat,* thought Pen, thinking of Mrs. Piggle Wiggle, *a boater hat and an apron.* Because she was picturing this, it took her a moment to process what Selena said next, "Then you must know his mother?"

Will's mother. Mrs. Wadsworth. Pen had flashed back to her, then, seeing her as she'd been the few times Pen had met her: flushed, faintly smiling, extremely quiet except for, now and then, a surprisingly witty remark, the fact of her drunkenness revealed only in her occasional shaky and incongruous bursts of laughter and in her clumsy hands. Pen had eaten three meals with the woman in her life, and at all three, she had knocked over a glass. But mostly, she was so lacking in presence, so overshadowed by Will's father that it had been hard to tell that she was drunk at all.

"If I didn't know your mom was an alcoholic," Cat had said once, "I wouldn't know she was an alcoholic. I don't think I've ever seen her drunk."

"You've never seen her not drunk," Will had said dryly. "Trust me on that."

The last time Pen had seen Will's mother, she had been different. It was at the summerhouse, not long after Cat had left, the only time Pen had ever been there with Will's mother and without Cat, a weekend that had started out calm and lovely and that had ended in disaster. She had been newly separated from Will's father (Mr. Wadsworth, Pen always called him, even though he had asked her more than once to call him Randall), and there was something wild in her. Pen remembered her as loud and frenetic, in constant motion, laughing, whirling across the living room, sitting on the lap of a man just a few years older than Will, a painter she had met in an art class. Damon Callas.

Pen's face had felt hot as she answered Selena, "I didn't know her. Not well. She and Will weren't really close." Again, her words felt wrong. Will and his mother hadn't been close the way Pen and her parents had been. There was no confiding, no easy camaraderie, and none of the starry-eyed hero-worship that marked Cat's regard for her father, but what was written all over Will's face whenever he spent time with or talked about his mother, while it might have been broken and sad, was clearly love.

"No?"

"You sound surprised," said Pen. "Do you know her?"

"Oh, no," said Selena. "But the illustrations and the words, they're so wonderfully matched, so one with each other. It's surprising to hear that they're not close."

Pen felt confused, trying to make sense of Selena's pronouns. Then she looked down at the cover of the book again and saw what she had missed the first time. There, below Will's name: "Illustrations by Charlotte Tully Wadsworth." Pen read the name again, tracing it with her finger. What a wondrous thing.

Pen had gone back and paged through the book, then, through each glowing, intricate, color-drenched illustration, and had stopped at the picture of the monster, mid-transformation, the dandelion fluff touched by the sun into a kind of filigree, each feathery filament of each tiny blowing seed parachute precisely shining, the whole picture full of an almost palpable lightness. Pen looked, next, at the mother's watching face in the kitchen window. The illustration had blurred, as Pen's eyes filled. She smiled. If Charlotte Tully Wadsworth had walked into the bookstore right then, Pen would have hugged her, something she had never done in real life.

"You're right," she'd said to Selena, nodding, her fingertips resting on the beautiful thing that Will and his mother had made together. "Something must have changed a lot for her to be able to do this."

Selena capped her Sharpie with a flourish. "Good. Better than good. The world could use more of that, couldn't it? Kids and parents getting closer, instead of breaking apart and losing each other." Then Selena pressed the back of her hand to her mouth for a few seconds and shook her head. "Oh, God. I'm sorry, dear heart," she said. "I wasn't talking about you and your dad, who were as close as any people could be. I didn't mean—"

Pen reached out and squeezed Selena's hand. "I know what you meant. And it *is* better than good. That's just exactly what it is."

◆ ◆ ◆

AFTER PEN HAD SPENT TEN MINUTES INTERCEPTING DIRTY LOOKS from her fellow diners, including one from a child in an Elmo T-shirt who feigned gagging himself with his finger, and watching Kiki Melloy, nonstop talker and bestselling mystery author, try to simultaneously talk nonstop and cut her enormous rib eye without losing her grip on the unlit cigarette chopsticked between two fingers of her left hand, she said, "Kiki, maybe you should just put that thing down."

Kiki's gaze became patient and long-suffering. "Penny, honey, no one ever said personal protests were easy. Ask Dr. King about that."

Kiki's mysteries featured amateur detective Hildy Breen, an occasionally clairvoyant exotic small animal vet (fire-bellied toads, sugar gliders, bearded dragons, and the like), living in an adorable, if corpse-riddled, southern town. People categorized her books as "cozy mysteries" but there was nothing cozy about Kiki, not Kiki's exterior anyway. Her interior was quite a different matter. She had been one of Pen's first clients and had teased out of Pen the whole story of Patrick and Tanya and of how, after a long talk with Tanya, and after talks with other parents who had talked with Tanya, the headmaster at Pen's school had suggested that she take leave from teaching to deal with her "disheveled personal life." Kiki's rapid-fire, profanity-laced excoriation of Tanya, Patrick, the headmaster, and all of "Purifuckingtanical, hypofuckingcritical, soy-slurping, 100 percent testicle-free upper-middle-class America" had caused Pen to laugh out loud for the first time in months.

Pen ignored the Dr. King remark, along with Kiki's calling her "Penny." Calmly, she said, "All I'm saying is that more of your outrageously expensive steak is flying off the table than is going into your mouth, for which your circulatory system is probably thanking you. From the bottom of its heart."

"My father said that if a steak didn't weigh more than the family Bible, it wasn't worth his time, and the man's going gangbusters at eighty-six."

"Good for him, but you've still got twenty bucks' worth of red meat sitting in your lap."

Kiki closed her eyes and issued an extravagant groan. "Have you *read* the Bill of Rights?"

"Life, Liberty, and the Pursuit of Lung Cancer? That part?"

Kiki turned to the pregnant woman at the next table, who had been shooting her murderous looks since she'd sat down. "How about you? Have *you* read the Bill of Rights?"

"You're a lunatic," said the pregnant woman.

"Only if being crazy about freedom counts," whooped Kiki. "That baby of yours will have a better future because of lunatics like me, lady."

Pen sighed. "I do not, do not, do *not* want to talk about this, but the data regarding the harmful effects of secondhand smoke are looking pretty solid."

A thoughtful expression stole over Kiki's face; her chewing slowed. " 'Data *are*,' " she echoed. "Sounds wrong. Is it?"

"I don't think so. Possibly, you can use 'is,' too. Probably."

"Interesting," said Kiki, nodding, then she jabbed the air with her fork to signal the end of their grammar facts sidebar. "Anyhoo. Data potata. Folks who don't want to expose their candy-ass asses to hazards should stay the hell home. The world is dangerous. Deal with it, people."

"I said I didn't want to talk about it. Remember?"

The pregnant woman and her friend began ostentatiously slapping their napkins from their laps to their table and signaling their waiter.

"Oh, fine. Fine, fine, fine," growled Kiki, and jammed the cigarette into the pocket of her immaculate pink Oxford shirt. Kiki swore like a dockworker, but she dressed like a Junior League president. Amelie called her a "Lilly Pulitzer fever dream."

Kiki sawed off a chunk of meat and wedged it into her mouth, squinting at Pen as though sizing her up.

"What?" asked Pen.

Through meat, Kiki said, "Tell me about this Cat character, the one who dropped you like a hot potato and is whining for your help. Whine, whine, whine."

Pen had told Kiki about the reunion by way of explaining why Amelie, not Pen, would be escorting Kiki to her speaking engagement at a big hospital benefit the following day ("the Lyme disease lunch," as Pen and Kiki liked to call it).

"You're gearing up to give me the 'You're Too Nice for Your Own Good' speech, aren't you?" Pen asked.

"No, I am not. Honest Injun."

"I don't think people say that anymore."

"Good Lord, whatever. Cross my heart, then," said Kiki, crossing her heart with her steak knife and alarming vigor. "Look, I strongly suspect that you are being too nice for you own good, but I *get* friendship, undying loyalty, all that crap. It's one of the few varieties of crap that I do get."

Because she knew this to be true, Pen thought for a moment, and then said, "Cat is the single most charming person I have ever met. She is beguiling. Bewitching. She pulls you in."

Kiki frowned. "One person's charming is another person's full-of-shit, if you know what I mean."

"I do know what you mean, and Cat likes attention, for sure. She likes to be fussed over and cuddled and adored and taken care of. She's a kitten. But she's a *real* kitten. She's genuinely sweet, but in good way."

Kiki chuckled. "Sounds like something I'd say. Okay, so what about Will? What was he like?"

Pen laughed, remembering. "Once, Cat asked Will if he was the WASPiest man on the planet."

This had been in the spring of their freshman year. Without missing a beat, Will had said, "I used to be, until my brother, Philip, showed up."

"Isn't your brother, Philip, a high school sophomore?" Pen had demanded. "Are you saying that you were the WASPiest man on the planet until you were just three years old?"

Will had nodded and said, "It was a good run, though. A really good run."

Kiki laughed when Pen told her this, then said, "I've known WASPy men. Stone face, good manners, cold hands. Getting all distant and

Episcopalian on you the second the going gets tough. Bad genes, too. Those Mayflower types are as inbred as the stinkin' Amish."

Before Kiki finished her list, Pen was shaking her head. "No. Good manners, yes. He was maybe a little old school, but not in a phony way. And maybe a little quiet. Not with us, mostly in big groups. But funny, dry-funny, and creative—he's an amazing writer now—and the main thing about Will is that he always had—what do I mean?" Pen rooted around for the right words for what Will had always had.

"An extremely large penis?" suggested Kiki.

"Quiet." Pen held up her hand. The right phrase came to her and she blushed at the thought of what Kiki would say about it.

"Spit it out," said Kiki.

"You'll make fun of it."

"Very possible."

"A generous heart."

Kiki absorbed this and then said, "You're saying he was nice, but in a good way?"

"And I don't know about inbreeding, but he did not get his niceness from his father, that's for sure."

"Mean?"

"Hideous."

"Hitting-mean?"

"No. But I'm pretty sure the guy was a sociopath. Or a narcissist. Not sure what the difference is, but he thought he owned other people. Or more like he didn't have any idea that other people *were* other people, especially his family. He thought they should all behave according to his will, and when they didn't, he got mean. I think Will hated him."

"Bummer. So tell me this." Kiki leaned in, her necklace of fat, unmistakably real pearls falling forward to rest on her steak. "Were you doing it?"

"Kiki."

"The three of you. You were doing it, right? Not all the time, not *nightly,* but it happened."

Pen rolled her eyes. "You aren't the only person who's wondered that."

"I'll bet."

"We weren't doing it. We were *friends*."

Kiki deflated a little and she said wistfully, "Yeah, I didn't really think you were doing it. I mean, I *hoped*. But I was almost 100 percent sure that you weren't."

"Hold on. Almost 100 percent? And why would that be?"

"Oh, come on. Why else? It's you. You're wholesome. A good girl. No getting around it. More's the pity."

"Thanks."

It was something Cat used to say, one of a few things she'd said to Pen that truly stung. "Our resident girl next door," she would sing. "Our pink-cheeked, long-lashed, straight-A, stand-up gal!" "The original brown-eyed girl!" "America's Sweetheart!" "Little Miss Perfect!" "The kind you bring home to mother!" Once as a joke, she had copied out the Girl Scout Law in semi-calligraphy on a piece of poster board and taped it to Pen's wall.

"Euphemisms for boring," Pen had observed, once, unhappy but tentative, not wanting to hurt Cat's feelings.

Cat had thrown her arms around Pen, pecked kisses onto her cheeks, and shrieked, "Never!" But she hadn't explained or taken it back. Pen hadn't stayed mad, though. She was never very good at staying mad at Cat, and she had to admit that Cat wasn't the only one calling Pen a good girl, squeaky clean; it was the sort of thing people had said, in varying tones of voice, for Pen's entire life.

"I don't feel like that inside," Pen had told Will, once.

"Of course, you don't. Why would you?" he'd said.

Now, she told Kiki, "I had an affair with a married man. Twice. Same man both times, but still. I was fired from my job for my rule-breaking ways. I have a *child* out of *wedlock*. I am an unwed mother, for crying out loud."

"Well done, too, all of that. Even so, doesn't change who you are. I guarantee that you'll go to that reunion, and Cat and everyone else'll tell you you haven't changed a bit." Kiki dabbed primly with her napkin at one corner of her mouth and shrugged. "Sorry, sister."

Pen lifted a forkful of salade Nicoise to her mouth, then put it back down on her plate. What if she and Cat and Will had changed too much? How was it that in all the years the three of them had been apart, Pen had never once, not for a moment, considered this possibility? Abruptly, she put her elbow on the tabletop and dropped her forehead into her open hand.

"Kiki."

"What?" asked Kiki, alarmed. "Oh, God. Bad tuna?"

"What if we don't know each other anymore?"

"Oh, sugar. You'll catch up. Gab, gab, gab. It's a reunion! Don't you worry."

Stricken, Pen lifted her head and looked wide-eyed at Kiki.

"No, what I mean is, what if we aren't knowable to each other anymore?"

"People don't change that much. Usually."

"What if we have? I don't know what I'll do." She had no idea.

Kiki reached across the table, pressed her tobacco-scented hand briefly against Pen's cheek, and looked at Pen in way that reminded her, with a pang, of her mother.

"Here's what you'll do," said Kiki sternly. "You'll have a quick, no fuss, no muss, three-way roll in the hay and come on back home. Understand?"

This was in no way like something her mother would have said and was at the same time exactly like something her mother would have said. Pen felt a smile start in the middle of her chest and spread to her face.

"I do," she said, and she gave Kiki a double thumbs-up to show that she did.

Chapter Seven

Driving down to the reunion, Pen remembered this: Halloween, junior year. Cold; the smell of wood smoke, rotting leaves, and beer; a fat and jaundiced moon.

The fraternity party was bad, but not as bad as most. The music was moody and decent and playing at a less-than-bone-jarring level; someone had actually made an effort, however feeble, with the decorations (jack-o'-lanterns, dry ice in a plastic cauldron, wobbly rubber bats hanging from the ceiling, fake cobwebs making their woolly way across walls and windows and the cracked bathroom mirror); and there was even—and this was the crowning glory—promotional beer from a new local microbrewery.

"Just wait," Will warned. "What begins as Beck, Luna, and amber ale will be grain punch, vomit on the dance floor, and 'Louie, Louie' by the end of the night. It's the way of all things."

They were there because of Cat, who adored fraternity parties as she adored any activity involving dim lights, music, noise, and boys. "Don't you feel it?" she would ask Pen, with a shiver. "The singing in your veins? The electric zing of possibility in the air?" And, often, Pen did feel it, not so much at the party or the club or the bonfire or the concert, but beforehand, getting ready with Cat, trying on clothes, splashing the rejected scarves, tops, and dresses onto Cat's bed, shimmying around the living room with a glass of wine. They'd walk out their apartment door, with their lipstick fresh and their hair and eyes lit by the streetlights, and anything, *anything* would seem possible to Pen.

Thirty minutes into the party, Cat left with a mummy. He had a blanket tucked under one arm and the other arm around Cat, who blew Pen a kiss and smiled a devilish smile. Cat had a rule to never, ever go upstairs with a boy at a fraternity house. This made sense to Pen (technically, she had this rule, too, although the opportunity to enforce it had yet to arise), but going outside in a flapper dress to lie on the cold ground with a guy wrapped in toilet paper struck her as a fairly bad idea, as well.

An hour or so later, after two brief, desultory, and shouted conversations, the first with a vampire Pen recognized as the guy from her British lit class who'd made a compelling argument linking the metaphysical poets with early Motown songwriters, but who turned out to be both a personal-space invader and a person who spit when he talked, and the second with a Jolly Green Giant who was losing leaves at an alarming rate and really just wanted to score some Ecstasy—("Do I look like a drug dealer?" Pen had asked, slightly flattered. "No," the Giant had said. "You look like the kind of person who'd be too polite to refuse drugs from others and would put them in her pocket to dispose of at a future time.")—Pen was ready to leave.

Her wig itched. Her false eyelashes itched. She had succumbed to Cat's demand that she be Holly Golightly, mainly because she owned a black dress and had no imagination for things like Halloween costumes. "Halloween costumes should be *scary*," she'd protested to Cat. "I hate it when women use Halloween as an excuse to glam up. All those Catwomen and go-go dancers, and flappers in tiny dresses with fringe."

"Ooh, *flapper*!" Cat had squealed. "I'm being that!"

Pen spied Will at the other end of the room flipping through CDs with his friend Gray, a guy he knew from boarding school. Gray was the guitarist for Elephants Gerald, a band that specialized in punk covers of Gershwin and Cole Porter songs and that was perpetually purportedly on the verge of being signed by a major label. Pen liked the band's name and found that there was something appealing about watching a kid with facial tattoos scream out the lyrics to "It's De-lovely," but she worried about the band members' complete lack of musical training. "When we first got together, we put our names in a hat to decide who would play what. It was totally random," Gray had once told her. He had seemed to consider this fact an asset, but Pen had her doubts.

Pen caught Will's eye and made an inquiring doorward motion with her head. She watched Will nod, give Gray a good-bye clap on the shoulder, and begin to make his way toward her. She smiled. Will's costume consisted entirely of a black eye patch and a fake yellow bird pinned to the shoulder of his shirt.

"I don't get it," Cat had said, when they'd picked him up.

"I'm a pirate," said Will.

"You're wearing a rugby shirt," said Cat.

Pen had touched the bird on his shoulder. "I think this is a canary."

When Will got to Pen, he flipped the eye patch up and rubbed his eye. "This patch is making me unexpectedly nauseated. Is that weird?"

Pen considered, then said, "It would've been weirder if you had ex-pected nausea and worn the costume anyway. Because, really, it's not that great a costume."

"I expected limited vision. Disorientation, *maybe*. Nausea, no. I don't know how the pirates did it."

"Maybe they got used to it. Maybe being on ships all the time made them immune to nausea. Maybe not having the two-eye option made a difference. I'm just guessing here."

"What else can we do but guess?" Will's gaze shifted to something behind Pen. "Uh-oh," he said.

"What?" She turned around to see the mummy swaying in the open doorway, his toilet paper raveled and torn, his expression simi-larly frazzled, even stunned. But in the few seconds she looked at him, she witnessed the party soaking into his consciousness: a dopey grin wormed across his face, and he began to bob his head and pop his chest in and out to the music, first absentmindedly, then with increas-ing vigor.

"Yo, Jason!" shouted one of his compatriots from across the room.

"Squid Man!" bellowed Jason the mummy. "I have been overtaken by a great and powerful thirst!"

Pen glanced at Squid Man, who was sitting atop a beleaguered upright piano in one corner of the room. He was dressed as a skeleton, not a squid. Pen was struck by the fleeting thought that, as far as she knew, squids did not even have skeletons.

"Shut the damn door!" roared Squid Man.

And Jason turned around and flung the door shut, without Cat's having walked through it.

"Oh, no," groaned Pen. "Where is she?"

She and Will didn't need to consult each other; they made a beeline together through the grinding, gyrating, drink-spilling crowd. At some point the music had become earsplitting and horrible; Pen could feel the bass thumping inside her sternum. They caught Jason mid-bellow, "I repeat: I find I have been overtaken by a great and powerful—" Will thumped him on the shoulder and said, "Where's Cat?"

Jason blinked. "Who?"

"Cat," said Pen. "The girl you left with?"

Jason screwed up his face in a look of concentration that struck Pen as remarkably authentic, as though he had actually forgotten Cat. Suddenly, Pen began to feel scared. *Let him just be drunk,* she thought. *Let him not be some psychopath out of a Flannery O'Connor story.*

"Oh," said Jason finally, snapping his eyelids open, "the Hispanic chick."

"Filipino," corrected Pen automatically. Her heart was beating fast. "Half Filipino. Her dad's side. Filipina, actually, is what you'd say. But she's, you know, from Houston."

Will shot her a look that said, *For the love of God, stop.*

"Where is she?" Will asked Jason, but Jason didn't answer him.

Instead, he said to Pen, "Houston? Ha. She's from Crazyville is where she's from."

"What?" said Pen.

"That is one spooky chick," said Jason. He scratched his ear and shook his head for emphasis, then said, "Seriously."

Pen saw Will's hand around Jason's upper arm. "What are you talking about?" asked Will. His voice was icy.

Jason tried to shrug Will's hand off and said, "We're just down in the Crater, hanging out or what have you, and she goes totally freaky on me. Sits up, says, 'Hold on a sec,' and then lies back down and gets all stiff, like a freaky-ass"—he searched for the word that would describe the freaky-ass thing Cat had become—"board."

"Oh, man," said Pen, turning to Will. "She had a seizure."

"No," said Jason, "she wasn't throwing herself around or anything. She just got stiff and kind of shook, tremored or whatever, and, like, disappeared, so to speak. Scared the shit out of me, if you want to know the truth. Ow! Dude!" He slapped at Will's hand, which had evidently tightened its grip. "Get off me."

"You left her?" Will's voice was quiet and deliberate, but scary. Pen looked up at his face, which was scary, too, taut, the muscles working beneath his skin.

"You would've done the same thing, man," avowed Jason. "Believe me. Anyway, I'm sure she's fine."

"Oh, you're sure she's fine," said Will. "That's good."

"Ow! What the hell?"

Pen yanked on Will's wrist, trying to pull his hand away from Jason's arm. "That's not helping," she said, trying to catch his eye and failing.

She turned back to Jason. "Just tell us where she is."

"The Crater. Like I said."

The Crater was a large, shallow, scooped-out field in the middle of fraternity row, part beach, part playing field, a place where droves of students hung out on sunny days. In snow, it was a fairly lame but very popular sledding and peppermint-schnapps-swilling destination; in wet weather, to Pen's eternal disgust, it morphed into a mud-wrestling pit. "The very last—and I mean *very* last—people on the planet you would want to see shirtless, covered in mud, and slapping their bellies together are shirtless, covered in mud, and slapping their bellies together," she'd told Cat, shuddering, after once having walked past it after two days of spring rain. "Goody!" Cat had cried, grabbing her jacket.

Pen tugged at Will's shirtsleeve and said, "The Crater. Let's go."

"Show us," said Will, his eyes never leaving Jason's face, "exactly where she is."

"Naw, man. You'll find her."

In a single, violent motion, Will turned the doorknob and sent the door flying open with one kick. He caught it before it rebounded shut again, took Jason by the shoulder, and shoved him out of it.

"Whoa!" Jason lost his balance and fell sideways, grabbing at the first thing he found, which, unfortunately, turned out to be the arm of a rocking chair. He went down hard on the porch and the chair somersaulted onto him with a whack. For a moment, everything seemed to go still. Pen heard some people standing in the yard start to laugh, and then Will was yanking the chair off Jason and telling him to get the hell up.

"What is your problem?" Pen hissed at Will. "Enough with the Bruce Willis crap. Let's just go!"

When Will didn't even look at her, she turned her back on him, yanked off her black pumps, and, with one in each hand, took off across the lawn in the direction of the Crater, gaining speed until, before she realized it, she was running full tilt, flying by startled face after startled face, the cold burning her eyes and filling her chest. She knew she must look insane, but it didn't matter. Her legs pistoned; her breath clattered; her heart banged.

"Audrey!" someone yelled after her. "Late for breakfast?"

Let her be there, she thought. *Let her be there. Let her be safe.* A sob rose in her throat, and she thought, *This is what it feels like to be a mother*, which only struck her as a peculiar thing to think later, when everything was over.

Her wig slid backward, and she pulled it off, faintly aware of the scrape of hairpins. In the same way that she could leave off being herself and become the act of bicycling, she became the running. Even when she thought she heard someone running behind her, she didn't turn around, didn't do anything but fling her body forward through the night, until she found herself on the rim of the Crater. She stopped short and wiped her eyes with the backs of her hands.

It was hard to see anything inside the Crater. The moon was high and its light didn't clarify, but stretched tightly over everything, like the skin on hot milk, making what lay under it appear liquid and uncertain. Pen realized that she was light-headed. She dropped her shoes, and leaned over, her hands on her knees. When she straightened back up, Will was beside her, Jason a few stumbling steps behind.

Jason, who was having a manifestly bad night, knocked his fist against the seismic heaving of his chest. His breathing had an alarming seal-bark quality to it, and when she glanced his way, even in the dark, Pen could tell that he was looking bad, slack-faced, pale, and sweating. If he had been a sixty-year-old man or even a forty-year-old man, Pen would have dialed 9-1-1 without a second thought.

"Where?" demanded Will.

Jason flapped his hand weakly in the direction of the Crater's center. Pen squinted into the dark and couldn't tell for sure, but thought she saw a small spot where the darkness condensed.

"Okay, we'll take it from here," she said to Jason, although her words were really meant for Will, whose face was marble-hard and cut with shadows, more full of barely contained rage than ever, but when Will started off down the hill, he took hold of Jason's shirtfront and towed him along behind.

As Jason went by, the expression on his face startled Pen. She thought he would look pissed off, even dangerous, but what she saw was much worse: a bleak and weary resignation. *He looks kidnapped,* she thought, and, for a moment, Pen wondered if that's what he was. Then she ran down the hill, leaving Jason and the Will who wasn't Will behind.

Cat was curled up and wrapped in a gray blanket, her black hair fanned on the grass and catching light.

"Oh, thank God," whispered Pen. Cat was not confused and wandering in the dark alone. She wasn't being hurt by drunken strangers. No one had taken her, although Pen thought that anyone could have, could have so easily lifted her up like a rag doll and carried her away. In the big field, she looked tiny and abandoned, like a toy forgotten on a beach.

Pen dropped to her knees next to Cat and lifted a flap of blanket away from her face. Cat's eyes were open and she looked confused, as though she'd been sleeping, which she probably had. Pen saw that she was crying without making a sound, tears falling sideways down her face and into the grass.

"Please don't cry, Catsy. You knew we'd come to get you, didn't you?"

Cat smiled. "I like it when you call me 'Catsy.'"

She sat up and put her arms around Pen's neck. "It happens sometimes," she said, "after a seizure. Tears for no reason."

Pen thought to herself that being left alone mid-make-out-session, mid-seizure in an empty field in the dead of Halloween night would be reason enough for anyone to cry, but she didn't say this out loud. Over Cat's shoulder, she saw Will coming toward them, Jason behind him, slumped and shadowy, and she put up her hand and said, "Don't."

Will stopped.

She pulled back and scanned Cat's face. "You're okay?"

"Tip-top."

"Promise?"

"Yes."

"See, man. Told you she was okay." It was Jason.

Pen held her breath, thinking, *You are dumber than krill.*

"What happened next was like the moment in the movie when the grenade flies through the window and lands on the floor and everything stops. I swear to God, even the crickets stopped chirping. And then the grenade exploded, except that it was Will instead of a grenade, and the whole night blasted open, and everything got surreal and slow motion, and it was the wildest thing I ever, ever saw."

Cat would say this over coffee the next afternoon to a group of students from her and Pen's Twentieth-Century Women Writers class. It was how she would tell the story to other people in other places for years, and, even though Pen would be repulsed every time by the excitement gleaming in Cat's eyes, she wouldn't say a word because what had happened that night belonged as much to Cat as it did to Pen.

But what Pen knew was that it wasn't like a grenade or a movie. It wasn't surreal or exciting. It wasn't like anything but what it was: one wholly human body slamming into another one, packed dirt and spit flying and animal grunts and sobbing and the sickening sound of a fist hitting skin and bone.

It was the first time Pen had ever seen Will lose his temper, although "lose his temper" never seemed like quite the right way of describing it. What got lost was everything else, all the things that made Will himself: empathy and patience and decency, his sense of humor, his sense of justice, everything fine and good deserting him in one ugly rush.

Before that night, she had only seen the fallout. After a visit from his parents (his father handing him a box of condoms, saying, in front of his mother, who was drunk, "Learn from my mistakes, Will. One slip-up and I'm stuck with this pathetic cow for life."): broken hand, cracked windshield. After a phone call from his father ("Drop the creative writing bullshit. I'm not paying for any faggot courses."): scabbed knuckles from punching a tree. Smashed dishes. Broken chair. A ragged hole in the plaster where he'd yanked out a light fixture with his hands.

He had told Pen and Cat about how he had been suspended twice in eighth grade and had been kicked out of one boarding school after six months for fighting. But Pen had never been able to reconcile that information with the Will she knew, and assumed he had been that person in the same way that Jamie had spent his seventh-grade year as a skate punk (bad haircut, an anarchy "A" inked onto the bottom of his sneakers).

For at least a whole minute, all Pen could do was watch. Jason was a big guy, broad-chested, with the meaty muscles of someone who spent a lot of time in the weight room. Will was over six feet tall and just this side of slight, no more than 175 pounds, but he was strong and had the advantage of being both sober and unhinged by rage.

As she watched, though, Pen saw that he was not wildly out of control. After they had rolled over a few times, they ended up not ten feet away from Pen, with Will on top, his left hand against Jason's chest, the right angle of his right elbow jutting out again and again. *Not wildly out of control,* Pen thought, *controlled out of control,* which was somehow much worse.

Pen watched that methodical punching, heard Jason yell, almost scream, "Stop!" and was herself walloped so hard by a sense of wrongness that she felt dizzy. It didn't matter how much Pen loved Will, how much they both loved Cat, didn't matter that Jason had put Cat in danger and had forgotten about her like she was nothing. The why of what was happening was weightless compared to the what: a person on top, hitting, a person on the bottom, not fighting back, defeated.

Pen stood up and threw her full weight against the side of Will's rib cage, knocking him off Jason. For a second or two, she lay sprawled on top of Will, before she scrambled up and pinned him to the ground by sitting on his chest. There was no way he was getting back to Jason. She expected him to struggle, to try to get up, but he lay still, except for the sharp, fast rise and fall of his ribs.

She could feel the bones and muscles of Will's chest, could feel his heart beating under her hands, but she didn't look at him. Instead, she watched Jason painfully clamber to his feet, openly sobbing, spitting what Pen knew must be blood and hoped did not include teeth. "Thank God," she said hoarsely, so relieved that he could stand, that he wasn't unconscious or worse.

Jason walked unsteadily backward, wiping his face with one hand and pointing at Will with the other, yelling, "You're a fucking maniac. I didn't do shit to her. I put the goddamned blanket over her, you fucking maniac. I will kill you. I will bring my buddies back and kill your ass. I didn't hurt her. I put the blanket over her. I will sue your ass from here to fucking eternity, I swear to God."

He turned around and ran up the hill, out of the Crater, and away.

"Are you okay, Will?" asked Cat in a tremulous voice. She was still sitting where Pen had left her, the blanket bunched around her shoulders and coming up over the back of her head like a hood.

Will didn't answer. Suddenly, Pen didn't want to be touching him. She slid off his chest onto the sparse grass and realized how cold she was. In the name of costume authenticity and foolhardy vanity, and because they'd assumed they'd only be walking to and from the party, not sitting around for what seemed like hours inside the Crater while Will pounded a fellow human being into the ground, she and Cat had eschewed outerwear. Pen's bones felt brittle. She tucked in her knees and pulled the skirt of her dress as far over her bare legs as it would go.

"Will?" asked Cat, again. "Are you okay? Did he hurt you?"

"Did he hurt him?" Pen said bitterly. "Is *Will hurt*?"

"Stop it," said Cat.

"I don't think Will's hurt, Cat, but I'll tell you what; he is definitely not okay."

"*Stop* it!"

"I'm sorry," said Will. Even though she could hear the misery in his voice, Pen didn't look at him.

"Don't be sorry!" cried Cat. "The guy was an asshole. You were right to do it!"

Pen pressed her palms to her eyes and shook her head.

"I didn't mean to," said Will.

Pen looked down at his face, which was white against the grass. Pen saw that his lip was bleeding and that his face was familiar again. Will's face was his face, his voice was his voice, and it would have been so easy for Pen to warm to him, to tell him not to worry, that she understood. But she couldn't, and she didn't really think he would want her to anyway, not that what he wanted mattered to Pen just then.

"What does that mean: you didn't mean to?" she said, struggling to keep her voice low and even. "You did it. I tried to get you to leave him alone, back there at the party, and you wouldn't stop. How could you not *mean* to?"

"Pen, let it go," pleaded Cat, getting up and coming to kneel down beside Will. Tenderly, she placed a hand against the lean slope of his cheek, but he flinched, and she took it away.

"You're right," he said, looking straight at Pen. She didn't want to be right.

"Oh, Will," she said, and silence sprawled out between the three of them after she said it. Except for shivering, nobody moved. Pen could hear laughter and shouting spilling toward them over the edge of the Crater from what felt like a very long distance away.

"I don't know what to do." Will's voice was hollow. "I don't know how to fix it."

Because Pen didn't know, either, she unfolded herself and stretched out next to him on the grass. Cat did the same, flaring and settling the gray blanket out and across the three of them. They lay like that, not touching or speaking, in the center of Crater, with the moon like a white balloon and the ground like a cupped hand, holding them, and after a little while, they got up and walked home.

PEN TURNED UP THE MUSIC. IN A CHARACTERISTIC COMBINATION OF thoughtfulness and mockery (and because he was just a guy who liked to make playlists), for the trip, Jamie had made her a playlist of the music she had listened to in college. "The sound track of your youth. Total-body nostalgia immersion," he'd intoned, dangling the iPod in front of her nose. "You know you want it."

Because her car didn't have an iPod hookup, she had taken his Land Cruiser, mammoth, black, and gas-gulping, a ridiculous vehicle for any non-outback dweller, but particularly for a man who walked to work and almost never had cause to take his SUV out of the shockingly expensive garage in which it languished. (In moments, Pen imagined it there, waiting, like a lonely, shiny hippopotamus.) It was Pen's habit to make relentless fun of Jamie for owning it. "Who do you think you are, Puff Daddy?" she'd asked the first time he'd shown up with it, which had made Jamie shut his eyes and say, "Nobody calls him that. Nobody. For well over a decade, not one person has even considered calling him that." Even so, Pen loved driving it. She felt like a badass driving it (and she was not someone who got a lot of opportunities to feel like a badass), and the playlist was marvelous, just what the doctor ordered.

Just as Pen came to the place in the highway where the mountains appeared like magic—up and over a hill, around a curve, and there they were in lines and layers, ghostly and blue-gray, more like clouds or billows of smoke along the horizon than like mountains—she remembered how Jason had never followed through on his threats. He hadn't shown up on Will's doorstep with a gang of fraternity brothers out for blood or with a lawyer out for damages. He hadn't confronted Will at all, even though they had expected him to, Cat and Pen, fearfully, Will with a fatalism that, in Pen's opinion, bordered, disturbingly, on hopefulness.

Instead, a week or so later, Jason did something entirely other: he walked up to Cat as she sat drinking coffee with Pen in a campus café and, with a great, serious sheepishness and a ducking motion that was almost a bow, handed her a letter. They hadn't known who he was at first, having only seen him at night and dressed as a mummy. He could have been anyone: a big kid in a dark blue sweatshirt and brown cords, clean shaven, his blond hair newly cut, patches of pale skin beneath the sharp line of his short sideburns.

It was only when Pen noticed the partially healed cuts on his upper lip and the faded green half-moon bruises under his eyes and saw a wary expression replace Cat's initial smile that she understood who he was. Pen and Cat looked at each other, then down at the white envelope in Cat's hand.

"What's this?" asked Cat.

"Just something I needed to say to you," Jason said, shoulders high, hands shoved into the pockets of his pants.

Pen bristled and was preparing to say, "*You* needed? Do you think anyone here gives a shit about what you need?" when Jason surprised her by adding, in the small, taut voice of someone possibly about to cry, "I mean, something I hope you'll read, even though I wouldn't blame you if you didn't feel like it."

Cat's eyes widened, and, absently, as though it had a mind of its own, her hand lifted and started to reach out in the direction of Jason. *Oh no, you don't,* thought Pen. *Do not do it.* As though it had heard her thoughts, the hand drew back and landed in Cat's lap. Cat shrugged.

"All right," she said. "If I feel like it later, I'll read it."

Jason's mouth gave a twist, and he seemed about to say something else, but then he just tugged a hand out of his pocket, lifted it in a good-bye wave, and walked out of the café. Through the window, Pen saw him take off running the instant he was out the door, the white bottoms of his sneakers flashing.

Cat set the envelope on the table gingerly, as though it were fragile or dangerous.

"My name's not on it," she said a little forlornly. "Maybe he forgot it."

"Maybe he doesn't know how to spell it."

Cat smiled.

"What do you want to do, sweetheart?" asked Pen.

"Split a cinnamon bun."

"Okay. What else?"

"Tell Jason to shove his stupid letter up his stupid ass."

"Good."

"Then throw it away without reading it."

"Yeah, right. That sounds like you." Pen smiled.

Cat laughed. "How about this: call Will, get him to meet us at our place, and read it together?"

"Well." Pen paused. "Why don't we call and tell him we're coming to his place?" she said, raising her eyebrows. "Just in case."

She waited. The subject of Will's temper had come up a few times since Halloween, and they had always handled it with circumspection and gravity. In fact, there wasn't one thing funny about it, and, although she didn't tell Cat or Will this, Pen found the whole of Halloween night physically, chest-tighteningly, stomach-knottingly painful to discuss. ("Do you think he could have killed that guy, if you hadn't been there to stop him?" Cat had asked once. "Of course not," Pen had said, almost as sure as she sounded, but not quite.) But since the inherent seriousness of a subject had never stopped them from joking about it in the past, Pen thought it might be time to try.

Without missing a beat, Cat nodded. "Just in case he decides to throw a refrigerator through the wall."

"I like our refrigerator," said Pen. "It's shiny."

"And it has an in-door ice dispenser," Cat reminded her. "Which is extremely handy."

THEY SPLIT THE CINNAMON ROLL THREE WAYS. CAT WAS TOO NER-vous to read the letter aloud, and no one brought up the idea of Will's reading it (he seemed averse to even looking in the direction of the white envelope), so the duty fell to Pen. The letter was unexpectedly long and, more unexpectedly, lucid. Although everyone hated to admit it (and didn't admit it out loud for some time), it was quite a good letter, particularly the end:

> Like a lot of people, even though I knew
> I could be a jerk at times, I always
> thought of myself as a good guy, but
> after what I did to you, I can't think
> that anymore. A good guy does not leave
> a girl by herself outside on the ground
> at night (even if she does have a blan-
> ket over her), period, let alone having
> a seizure. I've done a lot of thinking
> since Halloween and I realize that I am
> turning into someone I don't want to be.
> I think a big part of the problem is
> drinking, so as of one week ago, I quit
> for good. I know you probably don't care
> about that in terms of my health or well-
> being because you probably wish I would
> drop dead (justifiably), but I wanted you
> to know that I will never do to anyone
> else what I did to you. I am sorrier than
> I can explain.
>
> Sincerely,
> Jason Rogers

P.S. I have a younger sister and if any shit-for-brains did to her what I did to you I would summarily kick his ass.

LIKE THE MUSIC POURING OUT OF JAMIE'S RIDICULOUSLY SOPHIS-ticated sound system, the past seemed to come at Pen from all sides, sharp and clear and real, and, momentarily, she felt the urge to turn the SUV around and head home. *Nerves,* is what her mother would have said, *just a minor nerve-quake.* Pen decided to buy herself some time. She steered off the main road and drove through an ancient town of woods, upright, stoic houses, and what might possibly qual-ify as the most charming post office on the planet.

She was surprised at how well she remembered the letter. Partly this was due to, after that first, breathless, trisected cinnamon-bun read-ing, many subsequent readings (mostly in Cat and Pen's apartment, mostly by Cat, who would, for months, interrupt Pen's eating, or tele-vision watching, or studying—once even her sleep—with an "Okay, listen to this," followed by an excerpt from the letter), and partly due to the fact that bits of the letter became, irresistibly, stock phrases for all three of them, and eventually for their friends and family members, for a ridiculously long time. (Just last month, Pen had scolded Jamie by saying, "You shouldn't stuff your sweat-drenched running clothes into the hamper, period, let alone having a seizure.")

But more than any of that, Pen knew that the reason Jason's letter had stayed with her so resolutely was that reading it out loud that day had triggered in Pen what could only be called an epiphany, although she had never called it that to anyone but herself, suspecting, as she did, that what had hit her, at age twenty, like a ton of bricks, was an under-standing that most people acquired much earlier in their development. It was simply this: for the first time, she understood that it was possible to form an opinion about a person, an opinion based on solid evidence and a vast quantity of justified self-righteous anger, to even have this opinion reinforced by trusted colleagues, and to be, at least partially, wrong.

Actually, this was something Pen had already known to be true about other people. Other people could and often did form wrong, negative, vehemently held opinions about their fellow human beings. But as Pen read Jason's letter, she was shocked to discover that she, Cat, and Will—*she, Cat, and Will*—were fallible in exactly the same way everyone else was. If a boy they had branded, once and for all, as a complete and irredeemable cad could reveal himself to be an incomplete and potentially redeemable one, what else might be possible?

With more than ten years gone and oceans of water under the bridge, Pen couldn't help but regard the long-gone college-boy Jason in yet a different way: as somebody's son. For someone out there, Jason had been the sun and moon, the basket into which someone had placed innumerable eggs, a walking, talking universe of promise and heartbreak. *You screwed up in a way that you should not have screwed up, but good for you writing that letter,* the mother in Pen said. *Well done.*

With the Replacements jangling, growling, and banging around her, Pen thought again about Halloween night, the moment after Will had told her that she was right, that he had done, on purpose, the ugliest thing that Pen had ever seen up close. She remembered the hard ground and the burning moon and the stillness and the cold seeping into them all. For Pen it had been a moment of truth, a fulcrum moment. She had stood on the fine point of all that had just happened and she had teetered. *I could walk away,* she had considered. *Get up, brush the dirt off my dress, and go.* The thought was appealing. It caught her by the wrist and pulled, but at the last second, she had stopped teetering. She had yanked herself loose from the idea of leaving and had stayed. *I'm in. For better or for worse.* She had sat on the ground thinking those words, making a vow. *For better or for worse.*

Pen realized now that she had never regretted it, not even after Cat left, after Will left. It mattered, being a person who stayed, who counted herself in, for good. Paul Westerberg rasped out a song Pen had always loved, "Hold My Life." With a sigh, but without bitterness, Pen thought, *When did I ever do anything else?*

CHAPTER EIGHT

WILL WAS WISHING LIKE HELL THAT HE HADN'T COME. NOT that he hadn't come to the reunion weekend itself because it made no sense to regret doing something that, if left undone, would have caused him to wallow in regret for the balance of his natural life. He wished he hadn't come here, to Alumni Hall, his REUNION CELEBRATION REGISTRATION LOCATION! as the massive banner over its massive white doors declared it to be, but which he realized, too late, was not only a mouthful, but also a misnomer, since his actual registration had taken place at home, online, so that his schedule and map, even his name tag (which he had no plans to wear; he and Cat would know each other if they met in their nineties in a snowstorm, and Cat was the only reason he was there), were all already neatly printed out and tucked inside a folder back in his hotel room.

Will didn't love crowds, but he didn't mind them that much, either. Still, the prospect of seeing Cat after so long had set him so on edge that, for a long minute or two, standing just inside the doors, next to the inevitable bust of Thomas Jefferson, he felt like bolting, his pulse revving up, his palms right on the verge of sweating.

Chaos, he thought, looking out at the crowd. *A seethe, a hatch.* He remembered a spider's egg sac he had kept in a jar when he was a kid, how right in front of his eyes, the white ball, tidy as a planet, had erupted into a boiling mass of bodies. This was like that, he thought, but with squealing and goody bags.

Even after the initial urge to leave had subsided, he recognized that this was no place to be, the last place he would want to reunite with anyone, let alone Cat.

Still, as he turned to go and someone's hand tugged at his shirt from behind, he felt hopefulness flash through him and spun around, ready for Cat's face, almost already seeing it, her black eyes, the distinct shape of her smile. Instead, because he was looking downward, Cat-ward, he found himself looking directly at a tall woman's breasts. They weren't bare breasts, and Will wasn't exactly looking down the woman's shirt (although if he had, it would not, technically, have been his fault), but because they were definitely breasts and definitely there, inside a thin, blue, sleeveless sweater, and because they definitely did not belong to Cat, they were an unexpected and arresting sight all the same. For a few seconds, Will stared, immobilized.

"Will Wadsworth." The voice wasn't squealy like the rest of the voices piercing the air, but languid, stretching the vowels of his name out like caramel.

Will snapped his gaze upward, to the woman's face. She was pretty, honey-skinned, blue-eyed, blades of blond bob cutting toward the corners of her glossed mouth. Pretty and vaguely familiar. Will ransacked his memory and came up with, "Kirsty?"

Her smile swung open slowly, like a bank vault. White teeth gleamed.

"You remember me."

In the nick of time, a few details floated to the surface. Sophomore year. Two months of dating. Maybe less. Winter. It had been winter. Will flashed back on a moment of holiday awkwardness: Cat and Pen studying at Will's apartment; Kirsty showing up with a gift wrapped in silky, heavy gold paper. Will had noticed that it was embossed with pears and was the kind of paper his mother and her friends used for one another, hostess gift paper, not college kid paper. Because Kirsty had insisted, he had unwrapped it right away, in front of all three girls:

a scarf the color of pumpkin soup, obviously handmade. "To match your eyes," Kirsty had explained, throwing her arms around his neck.

Mid-hug, over Kirsty's cashmere-covered shoulder, he had watched Pen and Cat wrinkle their noses, their faces bunching with stifled snickering. Will shot them a "grow up" look, but they had known he wasn't really mad. Will could stand in his living room locked in Kirsty's arms all day, but everyone knew, with the possible exception of Kirsty who at the very least suspected, where he really stood. When Pen looked at him and mouthed, *Orange eyes?* Will knew before she said it exactly what she was going to say.

Will smiled. "Sure, I remember you."

"You weren't leaving without your goody bag, were you?" scolded Kirsty. She lifted the blue drawstring bag next to her face and set it swinging like a pendulum, and Will remembered that about her, the way she could turn the smallest act into a flirtation. "Because I think that would be a really bad idea."

"Oh, yeah? Why?"

She leaned in, lifting her eyebrows, half-whispering, "Lanyard," then leaned closer, "Car magnet."

Will laughed. Had she been funny back in college? Will didn't think so, although it was possible that he just hadn't noticed. When he remembered college, only Cat and Pen were sharp, four-color, foregrounded. (He remembered the exact smell of Pen's shampoo, the sweater Cat's father sent her for her twentieth birthday.) And it wasn't just the way he remembered things; it was the way things had been. Cat and Pen were the people with him on the train; everyone else was the blur outside the windows.

But here, in this moment, stood Kirsty, being funny and looking extremely good. *Stay in this moment, dipshit,* Will commanded himself.

"Do you have a plan for your lanyard?" asked Will.

"A lanyard plan?"

"What do people do with lanyards? What do people who aren't high school football coaches hang on a lanyard?"

Kirsty wrinkled her forehead, thinking. "An ID card?"

"So is that your plan? Hang your driver's license around your neck so you don't lose it? Because I'm having trouble picturing it."

Kirsty laughed. "You want to know what I think?"

"Yes."

"I think we should go out for a drink and discuss it."

Will hesitated, thinking of Cat.

"Unless you're with someone," said Kirsty quickly. "Like a wife or someone."

"I'm wifeless."

"You mean, you're wifeless here?"

"Wifeless everywhere. You?"

"Equally wifeless." Kirsty smiled. She waggled her ringless left hand in front of his face.

"But I'm supposed to meet someone later," said Will, then added, "A friend." Even though this was perfectly true because Cat was certainly a friend, Will felt a twinge of guilt at saying it that he could not explain.

"At the reception?" Kirsty looked at her watch. "Because we have three hours before the reception. Three hours and eleven minutes."

Kirsty raised her arm to show him the time. Her watch was bracelet-thin and as expensive looking as the rest of Kirsty, gold against the darker gold of her skin. He looked at her fine-boned wrist, but, without wanting to, what he saw was Pen's wrist, her long hand. He had to keep himself from circling the wrist with his fingers, turning it over to see the paler underside, and it startled him, this sudden emergence of Pen. *Get a grip,* he told himself. Here was a flesh-and-blood woman, asking him to have a drink.

"Sure," he said, meeting Kirsty's arch blue gaze. "Let's do it."

"Kirsty!"

Kirsty turned around to see another blond, tan woman across the room. The woman smiled a gargantuan smile and waved with her skinny brown arm shot straight up in the air, in the manner of a first-grader frantic to be called on.

Kirsty waved back and, sideways, through the closed teeth of her bright smile, said to Will, "Oh, God, it's Sissy."

"Sissy is very, very happy to see you."

"I fooled around with her boyfriend, senior year. She never knew. I can't not say hi to her."

Will didn't question the logic of this. Feeling equal parts disappointment and relief, he said, "Hey, we'll do the drink another time. No problem."

Kirsty swiveled on her heel. "Oh, no you don't." She poked his chest with a pink-nailed finger. It wasn't a light poke. "You wait right here."

As Will watched Kirsty walk across the room like a woman who knows a man is watching her walk across the room, thoughts tumbled toward him, one after the next. He thought about Cat, small, bright, and in trouble, waiting for him somewhere out there in their old college world, thought about how little he needed the complication of a Kirsty this weekend, then followed up that thought by thinking that thinking of her as "a Kirsty" was a reprehensibly asshole thing to think, and the fact that he'd thought it reflexively (without thinking) did not make it less reprehensible. Then he cursed himself for overthinking, reminding himself that, whatever had brought him to the reunion (not only Cat, but the possibility of Pen, a possibility that leaned, slender as a birch tree, in a far corner of his mind, casting a shadow he tried to ignore), he was still a wifeless guy at a reunion and was therefore practically obligated to have drinks with a blond blast from the past. Across the room, Kirsty and Sissy shrieked and fell into each other's arms.

Will averted his gaze from the two women and found himself looking straight into the marble eyes of Thomas Jefferson. The eyes seemed disapproving, accusatory, and cold, and not just because they were carved out of stone.

This is not a big deal, Will told Jefferson silently. But Will had the uneasy sense that going for drinks with Kirsty was some kind of betrayal, although he wasn't sure what he might be betraying, or who.

You owned slaves, he told the statue. *Remember that?*

Then Kirsty was back, slipping her hand into the crook of his arm, saying, "Ready?" And even though he wasn't, even though he thought he should just go back to his hotel room until the reception or maybe jump on the bike he'd stuck on top of his car at the last minute— actually pulling out of his driveway, then pulling back in and stomping impatiently into the garage to get the bike—and ride for a couple of hours, maybe do the hilly ride past the old church that he used to do with Pen, Will didn't know how to say any of this to Kirsty, so he just said, "Why not?"

THEY CALLED IT A "RUMP SLAP." ACTUALLY, THEY CALLED IT NOTHing for a long time, didn't even acknowledge that such a thing existed between them, even though they all knew that it did. Then one day, Cat said something about a soccer player Pen had a date with that night, and Pen jumped up out of the hideous armchair Cat had bought at a fire sale ("lung-pink" Pen had declared when she'd seen it), pointed at Cat, and shouted, "Rump slap!"

Later, Pen would say that it hadn't been the soccer player but the Tri Delt who had asked Will to her spring formal that had provoked the comment that provoked the birth of "rump slap," but Will knew it was the soccer player. He remembered the soccer player's name and exactly what Cat had said about him, which was, "Trent Bly's legs are so exquisitely dreamy that I don't even notice the front teeth thing anymore."

"What front teeth thing?" Pen had asked.

"I'm sure it's not his fault," demurred Cat.

"What's not his fault?"

"It probably has to do with the way they're shaped or the way they're set or something."

"Elucidate."

"I'm sure he brushes. Of course, he does."

"Cat."

"I shouldn't have brought it up."

"Cat!"

And Cat had sighed and done the thing she did to indicate resignation that was half-shrug, half-Charleston shimmy, pointed to her front teeth, and said, "Food."

"Food? In his teeth?" said Pen.

"Always."

"I never noticed that."

"He sat next to me in psych last semester." Again, she pointed to the place where her two front teeth met. "Spinach. Bread. Lunch meat. Just the teensiest bit. But every day. Without fail."

Will laughed, and that's when Pen jumped up and said it: "Rump slap!"

She was referring, it turned out, to the Old West practice of hanging a man by setting him on a horse under a tree, dangling a noose (possibly a lasso knotted noose-fashion, possibly an ordinary rope, if there was a difference; Pen didn't know; none of them knew for sure) from a tree branch, looping it around the man's neck, and then slapping the horse's rump to make the horse run out from under the man, causing his neck to snap like kindling.

"Although I'm not sure why I think this happened in the Old West. Maybe it only happened in westerns," mused Pen.

"Do you watch westerns?" asked Will. "Because I've never watched you watch a western."

"You've never mentioned watching them," added Cat. "In all the time I've known you, not one mention."

"So maybe it only happens in novels about the Old West. I don't know which ones. I don't even know if I've ever read that kind of novel, but I must have," said Pen.

"Doubtful," said Cat. "You really aren't the type."

Pen groaned with impatience. The source of the rump-slap scenario wasn't the point. Historical accuracy wasn't the point. The *point* was the no-going-back comment, the irretrievable, irreversible, eternally damning remark, the one that broke the relationship's neck, sometimes even before the relationship *had* a neck.

"Trent Bly could cure cancer, negotiate peace in the Middle East, and reunite the Beatles, and he'd still be the guy with food between his teeth," Pen said.

"Per*pet*ually," Cat added. "Food between his teeth per*pet*ually."

"See?"

"I do see," said Cat thoughtfully. "I wonder if I rump slapped Trent on purpose. I guess I might have. I'd rather have you stay home and play with me than go on dates with Mr. Food Teeth."

"Like that thing Pen said about the Tri Delt who asked me to her formal," said Will. "Eliza."

Pen winced, blushing.

"Ha!" shouted Cat, clapping her hands. "Eliza of the constantly erect nipples!"

"Rump slap," said Will.

"I just worried that maybe she had, you know, circulation issues. Or trouble maintaining a normal body temperature, like a condition or something," explained Pen. "And I thought she could benefit from a different kind of bra."

"Pen was only thinking of Eliza's needs, Will," said Cat.

"Too bad she never told Eliza about her concerns directly," said Will. "Since, last time I checked, and I do check, she was still walking around with her high beams on."

"I should have told her," said Pen, a smile teasing around the corners of her mouth. "I was actually going to, but then I thought that having constantly erect nipples wasn't something a person could do and not notice. I mean, you'd notice at some point, right? Even if no one ever pointed them out to you, you'd at least see them in photographs and know."

"Oh, she knew," said Cat, nodding. "She definitely knew."

"You really didn't want to go to that formal, anyway," Pen reminded Will. "Remember?"

"I guess I remember that."

Pen turned down the corners of her mouth and sighed. "I shouldn't have said it."

None of them should have said, ever, what they said about each other's dates, boyfriends, girlfriends, or potential dates, boyfriends, and girlfriends, but that never stopped them.

Now, sitting at the hotel bar with Kirsty, Will remembered her rump-slap moment. It wasn't the scarf; the scarf was not insurmountable. You could still date a girl who believed you had orange eyes. It was the kind of thing that you could spin as a charming idiosyncrasy, that best men joked about in wedding toasts, not that Will ever considered marrying Kirsty or even, really, going away with her for the weekend, something he remembered her pushing for more than once.

What snapped the neck of the Will/Kirsty alliance was the voice-lowering habit, *habit* being the noun Will, Pen, and Cat had finally agreed upon, even though Cat swore that it was so euphemistic as to be nearly worthless. Will disagreed, although he did admit that, while the Will/Kirsty neck had been unusually flimsy, the voice-lowering habit would have spelled doom for even the strongest, most promising neck on the planet.

Apparently, the habit had staying power, too, because less than an hour into Will and Kirsty's conversation over drinks, there it was.

Until that moment, things had been going well. The funniness Kirsty had exhibited back at Alumni Hall turned out to be part of a bigger-picture change, which was that somewhere along the line (she had moved from the wealthy suburb of Atlanta in which she'd grown up to Atlanta itself, had been married briefly to a guy who owned "of all things!" a vegetarian restaurant, and had ditched law school after a year to become a buyer for a shoe boutique), Kirsty had acquired an edge. She swore; she had only recently quit smoking; she liked art house films "in moderation." In addition, her debutante flirtatiousness of old had grown feline and sinuous: she laughed with her head thrown back; she trailed her hand up and down her own bare leg as she spoke; she narrowed her eyes like Lauren Bacall.

At the bar, she insisted on buying Will's beer.

"I'm just so glad you decided to start drinking," she said, giving his hand a congratulatory pat. "In college, you were Mr. Club Soda with Lime, which was, to be honest, a little boring."

"You're getting me mixed up with someone else. I was Mr. Ginger Ale," corrected Will. "Way more exciting."

Most people who had known him well enough to know about his mom had figured that she was the reason for his teetotaling ways. But somehow Will had never worried about becoming an alcoholic, had intuitively understood that he was not one, and luckily for him, seemed, in fact, to have dodged that particular genetic bullet. What he had worried about—and only Pen and Cat had recognized this—was messing with what little control he had over his temper. If he could beat the living shit out of an oak tree (or a frat boy) sober, what havoc might he wreak drunk? By now, he had figured out enough about managing his anger so that he wasn't Mr. Ginger Ale anymore, but he still didn't trust himself to have more than a couple of drinks.

In the light of the hotel bar, Kirsty was soft-edged and golden. Will was bad at noticing this kind of thing, but he could swear that her hair was blonder than it used to be. *Less goldenrod, more canary,* he thought, and smiled to himself. Pen and Cat spent years making gloating, gleeful fun of him for almost only ever dating blondes.

"It's inspiring," Pen had told him dryly, "the way you're dating your way through the whole yellow section of the Crayola box."

"Better than the whole purple section," he'd answered.

"I don't know about that," snapped Pen. "I can definitely picture a future between you and a woman with purple mountains' majesty hair."

Only once, after a few drinks, had Cat said, "You're dating blond girls because they are markedly un-us. If you dated girls who were more obviously Cat-and-Pen-like, the possibility would exist that you could at some point be interested in dating one or both of us, which, of course, would mean . . ."—she'd paused dramatically—"Total. Friendship. Apocalypse."

Even though that had been everyone's cue to laughingly agree or disagree, for several beats too long, nobody had. Nobody had met each other's eyes or said a word, and Will was torn between urgently wanting and urgently not wanting to know what the other two were thinking.

Will didn't know if it was the beer or the mellow light or the new

and edgier Kirsty, but he found himself relaxing, the tangle of anticipation that had been knotting inside him for weeks loosening enough
so that when Kirsty asked, "So who are you meeting later?" Will said,
"Cat."

When Kirsty found out that Will hadn't seen or spoken to Cat and
Pen for years, her eyes (cerulean? cornflower?) widened, and she said,
"I'm stunned," and then, "Actually, I'm not that stunned."

"Why?"

"It's hard to imagine you guys maintaining that level of . . ."—she
paused—"intimacy forever," she said. "But it's also hard to imagine
you being normal adult friends."

Will didn't say anything.

"Oh, come on," said Kirsty. "Dinner parties? Exchanging the occasional e-mail? Cookouts with your significant others? Significant
others, period?"

She was right, of course, but he didn't feel like telling her that.

"Why did you break up? What was the inciting incident?" There
was a challenge in her voice.

Will thought about not telling her or about making something up,
but what would be the point? He shrugged and said, "Cat wanted to
get married."

"Ha! Go on."

"We were a pretty self-contained entity, I guess. And I guess we
could be a little hard on people who weren't part of that entity."

"On outsiders, you mean."

"I guess."

"No kidding!" Kirsty laughed. "I don't think clubs that exclusive
are even legal! I think they're in violation of the Bill of Rights!"

"You could sue," suggested Will, smiling.

"I haven't ruled it out."

"Cat wanted to give her relationship a real shot, she said. So she
broke off our friendship and moved away with her fiancé."

"What about you and Pen?"

"Without Cat around, we couldn't figure out how to stay friends."

"Oh, I'll bet you couldn't," said Kirsty, laying on the sarcasm.

Will didn't know what she meant and didn't want to know, so he ignored this and, thoughtfully, popped a couple of peanuts. "I don't think we meant to be exclusive. The three of us just knew each other in a way that made it hard to know other people very well."

Kirsty narrowed her eyes. "Biblically? Did you know each other in the biblical sense?"

Will laughed. "I just talked to my friend Gray the other day. He asked the same thing in those exact words."

"Gray who was in that band?"

"Yes."

"The one who dated the"—and then Kirsty did it, did what she had done not only once but twice in a single conversation with him, Cat, and Pen over ten years ago: lowered her voice to a whisper and said— "*black* girl?"

Rump. Slap. Snap.

I'LL FIND YOU THERE IS WHAT CAT HAD WRITTEN IN HER E-MAIL, BUT after assessing the reunion demographic as it was represented inside the giant white party tent stretched over a good quarter of the university's central green lawn, Will figured that discerning one tall, lean, brown-haired thirty-two-year-old man wearing a navy jacket and khaki pants in that crowd would be a lot like finding the real Will in a house of mirrors.

So Will spent the first thirty minutes of the cocktail party looking for Cat. Actually, he spent the first thirty minutes trying to look for Cat while also trying to remain invisible to any person there who might know him, especially Kirsty. It was hard. For one thing, although Cat, small, dark, dressed like a flock of butterflies (assuming she still looked the way she used to look, which Will did assume), would stand out in that crowd, the fact remained that she didn't literally stand out in any crowd because Cat standing was not a lot taller than most people sitting. Avoiding Kirsty was equally tough since every third woman there could have been her.

After spending a half-hour skirting the edges of the party, dodging blondes, and attempting unobtrusive, chest-level crowd scanning, Will felt too stupid to continue—and too hungry. He threw caution to the wind and cut a straight and reckless path through the crowd to the food table.

Plate loaded, a ham biscuit halfway to his mouth, he turned around and saw her, no more than twenty feet away in a dark blue dress: bare arms, straight back, smooth hair, clavicles like open wings, and Will didn't need to see her face to know her: Pen.

He had tried not to think about what it would be like to actually see her, but on the few occasions that he had slipped up and imagined it, he had gotten it all wrong. He wasn't numb or frozen or panicked; he didn't feel like he had been punched in the stomach or was having a minor heart attack. Right then, Will wasn't searching for a word for his reaction, or doing anything except looking at Pen, but later, he would recognize what he felt as wonder, the kind of baffled awe you would feel if a statue in your house came alive or if the music playing on your iPod in the next room turned out to be an orchestra.

He wasn't ready for her to see him see her, yet, and knew he would have to look away, at least briefly, but for one attenuated moment, he took her in. She was looking to the side, searching through the crowd the way he'd been doing a couple of minutes before, and he saw an earring dangling, the long tendons in her neck, her jaw's clean swoop, and when she moved, shifting the white Chinet plate from one hand to the other, looping her hair behind her ear, Will saw that she still moved the way she always had, with a fluid, all-of-a-piece grace that was unexpected in a person so lacking in softness, so sinewy and sharp-jointed.

As Will stood watching Pen, just before he turned away, his initial astonishment shifted into something quieter. *Soon, she will see me; we'll sit someplace and talk*, he thought. He felt like a kid who falls asleep on a long car trip, wakes up, and looks out the window to find that he's in a new place, or home, and that it's morning.

Chapter Nine

IN THE MOMENTS BEFORE SHE TURNED AND SAW WILL (AND IT
was more a shifting of the gaze than an actual turn, a movement
the slightness of which would strike her as remarkable, even breathtaking, later), Pen had begun to get angry. Actually, before she had
begun to get angry, she had begun to get sad because this party, like all
parties, reminded her of her father.

Pen realized that not everyone would understand this because her
father had not, in any obvious way, been a life-of-the-party kind of
man. He didn't dance outside of his own living room, would hold the
same scotch on the rocks until it went the color of weak lemonade,
and was much more likely to be the (often underdressed) guy talking
to one other person in a corner of the room for hours than the one in
the center, telling stories, making everyone laugh. "A glower, not a
sparkler" is how Pen's mother described him. But once Pen had asked
Jamie if parties reminded him of their dad, and he had said instantly,
"Yeah. Because Dad *believed* in parties," and Pen had hugged Jamie
right then and there because that was it exactly. For their father, any
place full of people talking to one another over food and drink qualified as hallowed ground.

Pen had stood under the peaked, snow-white sky of the tent, in
the middle of the brightness and noise, with the wide-open, breath-

ing spring night just outside, thinking about her dad and had felt the old sadness plodding toward her on its big, square feet. *Oh no,* she thought, *nope, not here, are you kidding,* and, as fast as she could, she had whirled away from it and chosen anger instead.

Once she had decided to fume, it was easy to start because it was so like Cat, so *exactly* like her to decide to meet Pen again, after so many years, at an enormous party, in front of an audience of strangers and, worse, non-strangers. And it was so like Pen to go along with the idea, to do things Cat's way, instead of suggesting an alternate plan. Even as she thought these thoughts, getting angrier and angrier, Pen realized that they had little basis in fact. Although Cat had always loved parties, she had a firm sense of appropriateness and privacy, especially other people's privacy, and though Pen had been occasionally happy to indulge Cat's flights of fancy, she had never gone along unquestioningly when it came to something really important. In fact, it was the very abruptness and oddness of Cat's request that had caused Pen's uncharacteristic compliance, caused her to send an e-mail saying nothing but I'll be there. Still, however makeshift, the anger felt good, coursing through her like a stiff drink and sending the sadness, shoulders hunched, clomp, clomp, clomping away.

I could be home, Pen growled silently. *I could be in my apartment, right this second, with Augusta.* It had hurt to leave Augusta. It always hurt. Even the usual monthly weekend good-byes set a hard sadness thrumming inside Pen's chest every single time, and this month, there had been more than one good-bye.

Augusta had been okay this time, though, which wasn't necessarily to be expected. She didn't balk often at being left at Patrick's, but when she did, it was invariably high and excruciating drama. Last time it happened had been awful: Augusta wrapping herself around Pen, python-fashion, wailing like a blizzard, Patrick's face crossed with sorrow, Tanya feigning applause in Pen's direction, saying, "Nice. Very nice."

Pen had been especially worried about this go-round because whenever Pen left, Augusta insisted upon knowing precisely where she was going, and, perhaps because she had so little in the way of a past, Augusta had had difficulty comprehending the concept of a reunion. In the end, this had probably worked in everyone's favor, since, inside her imagination, Augusta had tidily substituted the unwieldy reunion idea with one of her own and decided that Pen was going to meet friends at the Union Street bakery in Wilmington where Augusta had loved to go with Pen's mother.

Pen had driven Augusta over to Patrick's in the early morning, with long, pink-stained clouds still floating low in the milky sky and with her child, bread-warm and messy-haired, sleeping in the backseat, and had prayed that the powers that be not mistake her recent uptick in leave-takings for a lack of love. *This is it,* she had vowed. *It, it, it. For a long time, all summer; except for Patrick's weekends, this is the last time I'll spend a night away from her.* On Patrick's doorstep, as carefully as Pen had tried to make the transfer—one palm cupping the weight of Augusta's head, the other arm supporting the curled rest of her—Augusta had awakened and reached for her. Pen had held her breath, but, instead of launching into a tantrum, Augusta had smiled, blinked extravagantly like a cat, and said, "You will bring me some jam-spot cookies like I like, right, Mama?" And Pen had asked Patrick, "How can I, how could *anyone* walk away from that?"

But she had. Because Cat had said that she needed her, Pen had left Augusta, and now here she stood, mute and rigid as a stump, her head full of noise, remembering the curve of her child's perfect skull in her hand, and waiting for someone who was either taking her damn time (Pen hadn't worn a watch in years and her satin wristlet bag was too small for her phone, so she didn't know how long she had been waiting but knew it was unforgivably long) or who was never arriving at all. *God, I must be insane,* she thought, *or stupid.* And then she turned her face—what was it? fifteen degrees? ten? less?—and saw Will.

He wasn't looking at her, was at such an oblique angle to her that his face was little more than a sliver, but she knew him at once. "It was like reading," she would try to explain later, and she wasn't talking about phonics. She didn't break him into syllables—shoulders, hair, shirt collar, hand, nose, cheekbone—and put him back together again; she didn't sound him out. He was a language she knew, and it was whole-word recognition: Will.

He looked at her and smiled, not a wry or wary smile, but an easy, sudden gift of a smile, like someone handing her a pear, a smile that only a crazy person would fail to return. But that's just what Pen did. Not only did she fail to return it, but she stared at Will, frozen, for a long time, a fiery blush shooting up her neck and face, finally lifted one finger in a forlorn and inane gesture meaning *I'll be right back,* then spun around and went careening—erratic, batlike—through the crowd of people and out the back of the tent.

Once outside, she kept walking, blindly, cursing herself, cursing the ridiculously high heels that sent her wobbling, knock-kneed, across the grass like a baby giraffe, then teetering down a brick sidewalk, clicks echoing like gunshots in the night.

"Idiot!" She bit the word out through clenched teeth. "Idiot, idiot."

After a few more steps, she stood still, squeezed her eyes shut, and a thought came to her that was perfectly calm and in the voice of her mother, *You are overwrought and you need to sit down.* She opened her eyes and got her bearings: a long, beautiful serpentine wall made of bricks, a white gate. One of the university gardens. "Let it be unlocked," Pen whispered, and it was.

Inside, plum trees stood in a row, flowers lifted their pale throats to the moon and stars, a magnolia held its tight-closed buds like white candles in its green hands. The place was so orderly, so full of grace that Pen hated to disturb it with her idiocy and her burning face and her raucous pulse, but then she saw a white bench, so she sat down.

She hadn't walked far, but she felt like she had. The party was still there, right around the corner. She could hear it but not see it, and she took a few seconds to imagine it as a big, white, hoop-skirted ghost floating away over the grass or one of those Mississippi riverboats, its paddlewheel turning languorously in the brown water, carrying the music and laughter, the corseted women and wild-eyed gamblers farther and farther downstream. *You are weird, girlfriend,* thought Pen, shaking her head. *As weird as they come. A closet weirdo.* But the ghost and the riverboat called her back to herself enough so that she could sort out just what in the hell had happened back there at the party, to enumerate all the reasons (and she was sure there were legions of them) why she was an idiot.

It had happened fast. What had happened fast? Will had done a small, normal thing: he had looked at her and smiled. But as soon as he did it, the instant Pen really and truly saw him, she was overtaken, sucker punched, not once but twice: first by a terrible, rawboned loneliness, then by desire. For Will. Desire for *Will.* Although *desire* was too breathy a word for what she felt, and too narrow. Because it wasn't just sexual desire (although it was that, too), but a voluminous, all-purpose longing. If Will hadn't, by the grace of God, been too far away to hear her, she might have said it out loud: "I want you in every way a person can want someone."

"Holy shit," Pen whispered, panicked, into the stillness of the garden. "What have I done?" And then she remembered that, apart from running out of the party like a lunatic, she hadn't really done anything. "Calm down, sweetheart," she told herself, doing her best to channel her mom. "Chill the cluck out. Think."

After briefly undertaking what she imagined to be yoga breathing, she did think, taking on the loneliness first, touching it cautiously, examining it, and she discovered that the loneliness was nothing new, but had been there all along. It was just that, before the moment at the party, she hadn't been aware of its magnitude. She hadn't been conscious of all the pieces of it—loneliness upon loneliness—all at the same time: her lost friendships, her misbegotten hopes for Patrick, her father's dying (and, for a bad split second, sitting in the garden, she was that woman again, her father's girl, kneeling next to him, asking him to wake up), her lonely windswept desert of a heart at her father's funeral, the lost, folded-in-on-itself solitariness she felt when she rode her bike, the way she missed her mother, the way she missed Augusta every time she left her.

Stop it, she told herself, disgusted. *Cut the crybaby crap. You have*

Jamie. And Amelie. You have Kiki and plenty of other people. And for God's sake, you have Augusta.

It was true that there was no way to be with Augusta and to feel alone. Just the sight of her girl holding a cup with her two hands, just the sound of her voice in the hallway outside their apartment not only connected Pen to Augusta, but turned Pen's boundaries deliquescent, let some of the world flow in. But the rest of the time? *The rest of the time,* Pen understood, startled, *I am outside of life. I am sad. I spend so much time missing people.* She turned the idea over, parsed it out, tried it on—"Penelope Calloway is a sad and lonely person"—and found that it fit. How in the world had she let this happen?

For a few bleak seconds, she reeled, before snapping back to herself, or to herself-as-her-mother, or, more specifically, to herself-as-her-mother-on-an-especially-impatient-day. *Don't be silly. You will fix it,* she told herself sharply. *Of course, you will. It's not too late.* Pen would do whatever people did to fix themselves, and even though she had no clear idea of what this was or where to start, just thinking the word *fix*—the short, no-nonsense briskness of it—made her feel competent. She sat up straighter on the bench. She clapped her hands together like Mary Poppins: spit-spot, that's done.

As for her wanting Will, just because something felt like a revelation didn't mean it was one. Wanting a man she hadn't set eyes on in six years? *You don't even know him,* she told herself meanly, but she didn't really believe it. In any case, whether she knew him or not, whether the desire was a fleeting or a permanent condition, wanting wasn't nothing, but it wasn't all that much, either. It wasn't love. *You have always loved Will,* a voice in her head reminded her. *That's different,* she shot back with fierce practicality. *And you know it.* Then the garden gate creaked and there he was.

Neither one of them said hi. After a single, superfast, peripheral glance, Pen didn't look at him, not even when he sat down on the bench next to her. She sat gazing vacantly at the flowerbed, unmoored, possibly not breathing, thoughts fluttering like moths through her brain— *Are those daylilies? Are daylilies supposed to bloom at night? Who are you, the daylily police?*—and listening to what might have been a mockingbird braid its long, rippling strands of shine in the magnolia tree (*Were mockingbirds supposed to sing at night?*), but mostly listening to the annoying bass line of her heart in her ears. Will was so still that, for all Pen knew, he might have been doing the same (daylilies, bird, even her own heart because it was that loud).

When the mockingbird finished singing, Will said, "So, are you gonna eat that?"

For the first time, Pen noticed that she still had the small Chinet plate. It sat in her lap. A piece of ham the size of a silver dollar sat on the plate, all that had survived her mad rush from the tent to the garden. *Intrepid ham scrap,* was her desultory thought. *Scrappy scrap.* She envisioned herself, trailing hors d'oeuvres; then as her mind cleared enough for Will's question to register, she smiled.

"It's all yours."

"Awesome."

She laughed and gathered herself and looked at him. To her relief, she wasn't gobsmacked by desire. She didn't burst into tears. There was Will, sitting on the bench, chewing ham, and the sight of him made her happy.

When he finished, he grinned a semi-shy, close-mouthed grin and said, "Hey, Pen."

At the sound of her name, Pen flashed back to the Pen of a few minutes (five? twenty? more?) ago, hightailing it out of the tent in her cocktail sandals, and groaned.

"What?" Will asked.

"I guess I was hoping you wouldn't recognize me."

"You? Oh." And then he smiled his true, guileless, transfiguring smile, the one he had given her back in the tent and so many times (how many?) before that, back when his smile was just an ordinary part of her life, like her books or her coffeemaker or the view from her window. "I would know you anywhere. Sorry about that."

Pen shrugged. "It's okay."

"But, hey, did you see that woman back at the party? Blue dress? Ran out of there like a jackrabbit."

"Whew." Pen rolled her eyes. "Total nutjob."

"Maybe, but fast. Her speed, and not just her speed, her *acceleration* was *very* impressive."

"You think?"

"Oh yeah. In heels? And with a death grip on that little white plate? Not a lot of people could've pulled that off."

Pen considered kissing him, then, not kissing him-kissing him, which would have been madness, but leaning over and kissing the plane of his cheek because, with an impossibly light touch, he had gotten them through it, set them both safely down on the other side. Not kissing him-kissing him, but kissing him because he was kind and funny, because he was a man who deserved to be kissed. *Ha! Forget it,* Pen told herself, derisively. *I don't trust you as far as I can throw you.*

Instead of kissing Will, she placed her hands in her lap, fiddled with the tassel on her satin bag, and said, "Have you seen her?"

"Not yet. Have you?"

"No." Then Pen had a thought. "You mean you haven't seen her here or you haven't seen her since she left?" She'd almost said "left us" but stopped because it sounded both too plaintive and too final. "Left us" made it sound like someone had died. "I mean, since she moved away."

"Both."

Pen let slip a sigh, a drawn-out sigh, an *oceanic* sigh, of relief.

"Hey," said Will, surprised. He looked at her until she looked back. "You didn't really think we were out there somewhere being friends without you, did you?"

"Oh, no. Of course not." But she found that her voice was shaky. "Okay, maybe. Once or twice, in my darkest hours."

Will didn't say anything. Then he said, "I'm sorry."

"It's not your fault."

"No. I'm sorry you had darkest hours."

Pen swallowed. This wasn't the time or place to talk about her darkest hours. There might be a time and a place later; she even hoped there would be, but not here in this serene and otherworldly garden, not now.

She said, "I just got an e-mail from out of the blue. It didn't say much."

"Mine said, 'I know it's been forever, but I need you.' "

Pen's eyes widened. " 'Please come to the reunion. I'll find you there.' "

" 'I'm sorry for everything.' "

"What did she have to be sorry about?" asked Pen, and immediately wished that she hadn't, since who among them should be sorry and for what were untouchable topics, the very last ones she wanted to discuss.

Maybe Will felt the same way because he jumped in quickly with, "Weird how she sent us identical e-mails."

"It is weird. And that e-mail just didn't sound like her."

"I thought the same thing."

"It was flat."

"And colorless."

"And not at all long-winded." Pen and Will exchanged a quick smile because Cat's long-windedness was legendary, but then Pen frowned. "Honestly, the way she said what she said worried me more than what she said."

"I know. I don't like to think about what might have happened to Cat to make her write a flat, colorless, short-winded e-mail."

Pen shivered and said, "You know what? We should . . . ," but before she finished, they were both standing up.

"Yeah," agreed Will. "We should go back to the party, see if she's there."

But as they left, first Pen, then Will, and as Will closed the gate behind them, Pen felt her heart sink a little.

"I like that garden," she said, picking her painful, tottering way across the bricks. "I could live in that garden. Pitch a tent under that big magnolia tree and live there. Just so you know."

Will nodded. "I can see how you would. Although if you're planning to live in a tent, you should probably consider some different shoes."

Pen said, "Ha ha, very funny," and slapped Will's chest with the Chinet plate, and poof, there they were, the Pen and Will of ten years ago, twelve years ago. Then, without breaking stride or making a big deal about it, Will offered her his arm, and because when someone offers you his arm, you take it, that's what Pen did.

If Will leaping, after six years, into a full-bodied, radiant being out of the chaos of a party was one thing, Will leaning back on his elbows in the grass under an ordinary noon sky turned out, to Pen's profound relief, to be quite another. Longing didn't jump up and seize her by the throat; she was not a voice crying in the wilderness; the "come live with me and be my love" nonsense from the night before did not evince itself for a second, having been washed out, apparently, by a flood of normalness and daylight. Even when she checked in with her body (*like a person poking a rattlesnake with a stick*, she thought), it seemed to be behaving itself.

It wasn't that he didn't look as good in the light of day. Pen knew that his austere angularity wasn't everyone's cup of tea. (Once, in the throes of taking Intro to Architecture, Cat had declared Will's looks as "either totally Bauhaus or totally Frank Lloyd Wright!" "Better figure that out soon," Will had advised. "I *will* be on the midterm.") Strictly speaking, he wasn't even Pen's cup of tea, since her taste in men had always leaned toward the lush-featured and swarthy. But, in a detached way, on the rare occasions when she'd thought about it, she had always found him oddly beautiful. Now, plopped down next to him on the grass, she had to admit that, while pretty much anyone could look good in a moon-soaked garden, Will was holding his own in the sunshine, and still, no fuss, no lust. All she felt was happy.

Cat never had shown up the night before. But, after sidling uneasily up to the party, an interesting thing had happened to Pen and Will: they had had fun. They'd eaten; they'd mingled. Will had run into a hallmate of his from freshman year, a guy they had all called Huey and whose dual claims to fame had been wearing cowboy hats and the ability to quote *Raising Arizona*—not bits and pieces, but the entire script—by heart. Now, Huey went by his given name, Paul, was a nurse-anesthetist with Doctors Without Borders, and was headed, in three weeks, for a two-year stint in Sierra Leone.

"You make me feel like a deadbeat, Paul," Will had said.

"Don't worry about it, man," Paul had replied. "I make everyone feel like a deadbeat." Then he squinted his eyes and drawled, " 'Son, you got a panty on your head.' "

"Thanks," said Will. "That helps."

Pen spoke with three separate women named Jennifer, one of whom now owned a designer resale shop in Richmond called Déjà Ooh!, a woman named Lane Lipton whom everyone had known would become a high-powered Washington attorney and was one, and a very drunk redhead whom Pen remembered not at all, but who tearfully apologized for having told "at least ten people" that a friend of a friend of hers had walked in on Pen, Cat, and Will having a threesome.

"Forget about it," said Pen.

"I can't!" the woman wailed. "Were you? Having them?"

Afterward, in the sleepy, easy quiet of Will's walking Pen to her car, Will said, "I hate to even say this, but what if she doesn't—" and Pen cut him off, saying, "I know. I hadn't even considered that. I mean, until right now."

"She'll come," said Will.

They walked a few more steps and Pen said, "My stupid feet are on fire," and she stopped and slipped off her shoes, and, fleetingly, considered throwing them at something, the streetlamp by the side of the road, a passing car.

"Where the hell was she?" she almost yelled, making her voice angry even though what she really was was disappointed and worried. "We come all the way here and she doesn't *show*?"

For a few seconds, she and Will stood rooted to the sidewalk, not looking at each other. Pen stared at their two shadows stretching down the sidewalk as though they'd been flung from a bucket, then at the streetlamp that was casting them, shining yellow through a haze of bugs.

"That," she said, "is a lot of bugs for this early in the summer." Her eyes were filling with tears, which annoyed her.

"It is a lot of bugs," agreed Will in a tired voice. "She'll come."

"What will we do if she doesn't?" The childishness of this question deepened her annoyance, but she waited for Will's answer anyway.

"We'll think of something," said Will. "And anyway, she'll come."

They started walking again. Pen's shoes dangled from her fingers. A car quaking with bass trundled by, and Pen saw a child-skinny arm dangling out the passenger-side window, the orange pin-dot glint of a cigarette.

Finally, Pen said, "She might not."

"Yeah," said Will. "She might not."

But when Pen got back to her hotel room, she found the gumdrop of a message light on the oldfangled phone blinking, and even though, when she hit the button and braced herself for the sound of Cat's voice, it never came, relief washed over her because it was a message from Cat all the same. The man working the front desk read it to her: "Sorry I couldn't make it tonight, but I will see you at the barbecue tomorrow."

"Is that a note that someone dropped off?" As she asked, Pen was already slipping her shoes back on so she could run down and get it, was already seeing Cat's curvaceous handwriting, capital "S" like a swan, but the man said, "No. Jonah the guy with the shift before mine took it. I'd know his chicken scratch anywhere. Must've been a phone call."

Pen opened her satin evening bag and took out the napkin with Will's cell number on it. When she saw that he'd written "Will W." above it, she smiled. As if she wouldn't know. As if she'd been collecting phone numbers from men named Will all night. And then she smoothed the napkin with her fingers and felt a twinge, below her sternum and on the back of her neck, of what she had felt when she had first seen him in the tent.

"Don't be a sap," she snapped. "It's a *name* on a *napkin*."

Then she called Will, said, "Listen to this," and read him the message.

"I got the same thing," he said, and for a moment, they basked in their shared relief, not saying anything. Then Will said, "Hey, you didn't bring your bike with you, by any chance?"

◆ ◆ ◆

PEN HAD FORGOTTEN HOW QUICKLY IT HAPPENED, HOW YOU ROUND a corner, pass a Shell station and the Kingdom Hall, go up a hill, and enter another world: sloping wooden porches, dogs chained to stakes in yards, dense trees, steep, thigh-burning hills, and the occasional valley farmstead opening up like an exhale. Once, years ago, Pen had hit a broken patch on the road and fallen and, with her bike on top of her, had been amazed to see children—white blond hair, knobby heron legs—materialize from between the trees to call, shyly, "Hey, lady! Hey, lady! You okay, lady?"

Pen and Will took a lunch break in the yard of the ancient gray church, leaning their bikes against an oak tree, tossing down their helmets and sprawling gratefully on the hard, balding lawn. Will had stopped at a deli on the way to pick up Pen at her hotel, and after he'd caught his breath, he unzipped his backpack and started to hand Pen a sandwich wrapped in white paper, but when she tried to take it from him, he got a look of concern on his face and didn't let the sandwich go.

"What's wrong?"

"I should've asked."

"Asked what?"

"About your current relationship with brine-cured meat."

"You got me a sauerkraut-less Reuben?"

"I did." Will's expression turned unexpectedly shy. "But, you know, it's been six years. I shouldn't assume."

"My love for brine-cured meat has endured the test of time," said Pen, yanking the sandwich out of his hand. "My heart belongs to brine-cured meat now and for all eternity."

The Reuben was slightly leaky but otherwise perfect.

As Will began unwrapping his sandwich, Pen said, "You're a whole other story. No love. No loyalty. Total sandwich promiscuity. You could have anything in there."

Will grinned and bit into ham and Swiss with hot mustard on pumpernickel. "We're talking about sandwiches," he observed, after an interval of chewing. "We haven't seen each other in six years."

"You're right." She watched two dark birds wheel against the powder blue sky. Vultures, she figured, although they didn't look ominous or even hungry, just lazy. An idea hit her and she slapped her palm on the ground. "I thought of a way to do this."

"Do what?"

Pen raised an arm and made impatient, circular, flapping motions with her hand. "*This!* This-this. What other this would I mean?"

"Okay. So what's the way?"

"Four sentences," she said smugly.

Will waited, then popped the stopper of his water bottle with his teeth and drank.

"Brilliant, right?" said Pen.

"Four sentences. That's all you're going to say."

"Oh, come *on*."

"I got nothing." He held out his empty hands.

"You used to be better at connecting the dots."

"It's been a while since I've been around your dots, remember?"

Pen sighed. "Six years in four sentences. No questions, no comments. Four sentences from each of us and we consider ourselves caught up."

"Fine," Will said slowly. "You first."

"Oh, no," said Pen. "I thought of it. I did the legwork."

Will laughed and kept eating. "No questions or comments," he said. "And that would apply to the person who did the legwork, too."

"Right."

Pen was suddenly nervous. As she redid her ponytail, she felt a rising urge to babble her way into and through the silence of Will's thinking, and instead of fighting the urge, she decided to give in.

"My hair's hot." She petted her head. "You know how you have those things that you measure the start of a season by? Not you-you, but people-you. One, I guess. *You* might or you might not. But anyway, like if you wear gloves *and* a scarf, that means it's winter? Like that?

Well, even if, technically, it's not summer, not, you know, summer sol-stice summer, I always feel, personally, that it's summer when I sit in the sun and my hair gets hot."

"I write books for kids, for a living," said Will. "I live in Asheville, North Carolina, sometimes with my now-sober yogi/painter mom, sometimes by myself. When I get mad, I no longer go apeshit. My dad, whom I haven't spoken to in about four years, has a girlfriend who had a baby last year, so I have a little brother I've never met, whose name, apparently, is Randall Junior, a.k.a. R.J."

Pen absorbed this for a moment, her heart in her throat. *It's been so long*, she thought. *It's been no time at all.* In a soft voice, she said, "Am I allowed to say that I love your books?"

Will ducked his head, smiling. "No."

Pen lay back on the grass with her eyes shut, feeling the sun on her face, pressing like warm thumbs against her eyelids, thinking how she could fall asleep there, with the sun and with Will and that old church watching over her, and it would have been so easy to do, even for Pen, who had trouble falling asleep in her own bed, but, instead, after a minute or so, she started talking, without sitting up or opening her eyes or even imagining what Will was thinking as she spoke.

"I have a daughter named Augusta who turns five in July. I am not now, nor have I ever been married. Augusta and I share an apartment in Philadelphia with Jamie. My dad died two years ago." It wasn't hard after all. She released the sentences carefully, evenly, like someone placing leaves, one by one, onto the surface of a stream, letting the water carry them slowly into the trees and out of sight.

Will didn't make a sound. Pen couldn't hear anything except the tide of her own breathing and the sequined clamor of birdsong, but as she sat up, she kept her eyes closed, thinking, *Please don't let him be crying. If he's crying, I might cry, I might roll over on the ground, bury my face in my arms and fall to pieces, and he will feel like he needs to say something or hug me, but he won't know if I want him to, and it will be a disaster.* So great was Pen's need for Will not to be crying that it ceased, for a few seconds, to matter that he almost certainly wouldn't be. Will had never been a crier, not even when he was a kid.

This was something Pen knew, and, sure enough, when she opened her eyes, he wasn't crying. He was almost not moving. The only giveaway that he was sad (a thing Pen had forgotten about Will until this very second) was a pair of parentheses etched into the corners of his mouth.

"Am I allowed to say I loved your dad?" Will said finally.

Pen caught his eye and smiled. "No."

A red pickup truck with a German shepherd in the bed drove by.

"It's been a long time since I've seen a dog riding in the back of a truck," said Pen. "Is that even legal anymore? You'd think not, with all the seat belt laws and car seat laws and so forth. I remember how when we were little, we'd take, I don't know, ten kids to the pool in my mom's Volvo station wagon. We'd lie in the back, head to foot, like sardines. Not that I'm not all for the new laws. They're great. I just wonder if they apply to, you know, dogs."

Pen stopped for breath, and Will said, "No feet."

Pen looked at him quizzically.

"Sardines."

"Oh. Right. Anyway—"

"So hold on," Will broke in. "You *live* with *Jamie*?"

"Hey! No questions! Remember!" But Pen was laughing, and even though she knew that Will didn't really expect her to explain why she lived with Jamie, that it was just his way of breaking the tension and navigating them away from the towering subject of Pen's father's death, she answered it anyway, surprising herself by beginning at the beginning, with Will and Cat leaving and with Patrick's knack ("perverse knack" she said, even though she had found his arrival lifesaving, or close to lifesaving, at least once) for showing up at Pen's most vulnerable moments.

"You didn't meet cute," said Will, resurrecting their old joke right on cue. "Tell me you didn't."

"I wish I could. *I* was sour and mopey, but pretty much everything Patrick does is cute. We met cute and irresponsible and slightly deceptive, which is Patrick in a nutshell." Guiltily, she jumped in with a revision. "Well, except for the deceptive part. Well, I mean, he *is* deceptive sometimes, but he doesn't really plan to be."

"Spontaneous deception is much better," said Will.

"I had just finished up my last requirements for my master's in education," began Pen.

"I remember you were studying to be a reading specialist. Congratulations."

"Well, and I was feeling sorry for myself because I didn't have anyone to celebrate with." She shot him a look.

"Yeah. Sorry about that."

"I guess I could've found someone. Jamie or one of the people in my program or someone, but I really just wanted to wallow. I did a fair amount of wallowing after you and Cat left."

"I'm familiar with wallowing," said Will.

"And I'm drinking coffee as morosely as I can and reading a book, a really sad book about a child murder because if you're feeling glum you might as well go all the way, and this person sits at my table and says, 'Is it okay if I sit here?' Except he was already sitting, so I said, meanly, 'I guess, but there's a seat right over there,' and he said, 'Oh, I know, I was just sitting in it.'"

"You're right. Cute." Will pretended to gag.

"See? And then he said, and this was the deception part, 'I was waiting for a friend who never showed, and I hate to drink coffee alone.' And I said, 'On the other hand, I like drinking coffee alone,' and he said, 'Not to be insolent or anything, but you don't look like you're liking it. In fact, you look miserable.' And it made me laugh that he said 'insolent' so we ended up talking."

"I get how that was nauseatingly cute and spontaneously deceptive, since I gather he didn't really get stood up, but how was it irresponsible?"

"His wife had thrown him out of the house just five weeks earlier. They had a three-year-old daughter. And while he was busy hitting on a random girl in a coffeehouse, he missed a meeting with his attorney regarding their breakup."

"Wow," said Will. "That's hard-core."

"I know. But I was worse because even after I found all that out, I didn't send him away."

"I wouldn't say worse," said Will. "He was the one with a wife and kid."

"I know, but he's just *like* that. Careless. I'm not, but I threw myself into it, even though I knew better. I allowed myself to become criminally smitten."

Will smiled at "criminally smitten."

"I even let it affect my career. One day, Patrick said there was a reading specialist job at his old private school in the suburbs, the one he went to from the age of four until he graduated, and because it was his school, I applied for it. I'd been all set to work in a city school, and I got all goo-goo-eyed and dropped that idea in a flash. I think I'd known him for two weeks."

"Still: wife, kid."

"We were together five months that time, before I made him go back."

"You felt guilty?"

"Yes, but also, he was pining for them, both of them. Anyone could tell that."

"What do you mean 'that time'?" asked Will.

Pen kept going, leaving out nothing, or almost nothing. How Patrick and Tanya had shown up at her school, Patrick's alma mater, one day without warning, Patrick having forgotten to mention to Pen—having possibly forgotten altogether, knowing Patrick—that he and Tanya had always planned to send Lila there. How the admissions director stopped into the reading center as part of the tour and how Pen had kept her cool, pretending not to know them, but how Patrick had turned into a red-faced, stammering idiot so that Tanya knew something was up, and how the next day, the headmaster suggested that Pen take a semester's leave of absence. Pen could still recall the way the icy doom settled in her stomach as she walked down the hallway to his office.

"Did you go back?" asked Will. "After that semester?"

"No. I found out I was pregnant soon thereafter. But I'd decided not to go back even before I knew. I was—disheartened."

"I'm sorry you were disheartened. The whole thing sucks."

Patrick had come back after Augusta was born. He hadn't come to the hospital for her birth, which had earned him Pen's parents' and Jamie's disdain until the end of time, but which was actually a relief to Pen. Patrick slouching among the nurses and Pen's family members, with his uneasiness and his big hands in his pockets and his guilt-stricken eyes, asking her for whatever it was he needed from her—and there would've been something—while Pen tried to give birth would have been a distraction, one thing too many. Plus, there was a tiny, barbed part of her that had been glad he was missing it, glad that their baby's sliding whole and gorgeous into the world would never belong to him.

It was ten days later, less than an hour after Pen's mother had gone home ("What were you doing, spying on us?" Pen had asked. "Yes," Patrick had replied.) that Patrick had shown up on Pen's doorstep, unshaven and gaunt, his nails bitten to the quick, and Pen, her edges worn down by ten days of sleep deprivation, breastfeeding, and titanic love, had let him in and, when he begged to stay, had let him stay. Pen didn't tell Will how Patrick had set his daughter gently back into her bassinet, then had fallen onto his knees in the bedroom, sobbing, how she could still close her eyes and remember the sight of him in the half-light with his face in his hands, and the raw and honest sound of his weeping.

"I didn't really love him. I didn't even feel the charmed infatuation I had felt when I met him, but we spent our days in Augusta's glow. She made things seem possible. So when he asked me to marry him, even though he wasn't divorced yet, even though I didn't have that much faith that it would work out, I said I would."

She broke off a piece of her Reuben and tossed it to a couple of brown birds that were hopping near by. With affronted squeaks and a melodramatic agitation of feathers, they bounced backward and flew away.

"I shouldn't have done it," said Pen, sighing. "It made him really happy, though, and Patrick when he's happy is just this big, positive force of nature, so I let down my guard and let myself start to believe in our happy little family, and as soon as I did that, the next day maybe, Tanya threatened to take Lila."

"What do you mean 'take' her?" asked Will.

"She said she'd say anything; she'd lie and get other people to lie. She'd do whatever it took to get full custody. The day Patrick found this out, I came home to find him on the couch, looking like he'd been run over by a tractor, and even before he told me, I knew he was gone."

"Man, Tanya sounds like a piece of work."

"The thing is, though," said Pen, "he would've left anyway. I like to think I would have come to my senses and broken it off eventually, but even if I hadn't, I don't think he would've gone through with it."

"Why not?"

"He loves Tanya. It's a fact. He loves Lila, too, of course. Lila alone might have been enough reason for him to leave us, but he is stone-cold, crazy in love with Tanya."

"What about you? And Augusta?"

"Oh, he loves us, too. He told me one time, at a really low point, that he was cursed to be in love with two women. But he loved Tanya first. And best, which in a way is only fair because she loves him back in a way that I never did."

Then, in a thin, strained voice, Pen said, "He did come back one more time, though." She started talking fast to get it over with. "He showed up at my dad's funeral, which wasn't a bad thing because I was a wreck that day, and Augusta was three years old and needed a parent who didn't collapse into tears every five minutes."

Pen swallowed. *You got this far,* she said to herself. *Don't fall apart now.*

"He came back to Philadelphia with us, and somehow he just stayed." She caught herself. "On my couch, I mean. He told me he was thinking he'd made a mistake, that he wanted to try again. I don't know why, except that maybe I was such a mess that he thought I needed him, and he loves to be needed. I didn't say yes or no. I hardly heard him. I was so tired and sick at heart. He took care of us for a week, maybe a little more, cooking and doing everything for Augusta, and then Jamie showed up, and got furious (you wouldn't even have recognized him), and threw Patrick out, and took me and Augusta home with him, and sent some guys later to pack up our stuff. And we ended up staying. Somehow, it worked. It works. For now, anyway."

Will didn't say anything for so long that Pen began to get anxious. There she went again, handing everything over, entrusting, like a five-year-old, and to what end? *Good grief. Did you really think,* she asked herself, *did you honestly think that you and Will could just pick up where you left off?*

"Maybe we should go," she said stiffly, and started to clean up, brushing crumbs off her bike shorts, balling up the white sandwich paper in her fist.

"Wait," said Will. "Can I say something?"

Pen's hands stopped moving at the sound of his voice, which was grave and formal. *Oh, God,* thought Pen. His jaw, his shoulders, even the skin around his eyes looked taut; he had the aspect of a man steeling himself. *Just say it, say that this is all too much,* thought Pen. *Get it over with.* Then he shook his head and laughed, a short, self-mocking sound, more like a bark than a laugh, but it did the trick, dissipated the tension and Pen's worry, sent them evaporating into the bright blue air.

"I'm not used to being nervous when I talk to you," said Will. "I'm not used to talking to you."

"Well, and I threw a lot at you: the rise and fall of my doomed love affair, the birth of my illegitimate child, my near breakdown after my father's death. My life as a Russian novel. Way to give a guy some breathing room, Pen." Pen gave Will a quick glance, then began the careful and important project of unballing the sandwich wrapper in her hand and smoothing it flat against the grass.

"You don't have enough names for a Russian novel. You need to have at least six names," said Will.

"And three nicknames."

"I wasn't talking about that, the breathing room thing. I was going to say: no pressure, but—"

Pen looked up at him.

"You can say no to this," Will started over, riffling his hair with the palm of his hand, "and if you were thinking we'd just hang out here and then go back to business as usual, post-reunion, that's fine. Or not fine, but I'd respect it. I mean, of course, I would. But I was just going to say that I think I should meet Augusta, before she turns into one of those what-do-you-call-'ems, girls with ironed hair and Ugg boots, who text instead of talk."

"Tweens," Pen said. She smiled. "She already has Uggs because Patrick has no freaking idea of how to say no to her. But okay."

" 'Okay'? That's it?"

"If I said more it would be something like, 'Your meeting Augusta is not only okay, but would right a grievous and cosmic wrong,' which might sound overblown."

Will shrugged. "I'm okay with okay."

"Good," said Pen.

THE BARBECUE WAS TURNING TO SAND IN PEN'S MOUTH.

"What if she's sick? What if she has cancer? What if there's some complication with her epilepsy? What if she's crazy? Not Cat-crazy, but seriously mentally ill? We've been here an hour, Will. What if she doesn't come?"

Pen's voice was shrill, about to tip over an edge into frantic and desperate, but she couldn't help it. The tent tonight was smaller, and, at some point earlier in the evening, humid air had rolled in from someplace, the Amazon rain forest maybe, and the party, just an hour old, had already hit the glazed-face, mosquito-y, warm drink, sticky-red-checkered-outdoor-tablecloth phase that every summer party gets to if there are enough people and if it goes on long enough. And still, no Cat, no Cat.

Flushed and tugging at the neck of his white T-shirt, Will said irritably, "What do you want me to say, Pen?"

Pen saw him, then, striding purposefully, eyebrows hawkishly lowered, toward them through the crowd. He was a little thinner than when she'd last seen him, softer bellied, but still big, blond, and boy-faced.

"Oh, for the love of God."

Will didn't turn around to look, but put down his knife and fork and stared at Pen. "Cat?"

"Cat's husband," said Pen drearily.

"Pen. Will. It's been a while." Same voice.

Will stood up to shake his hand. "Hey, Jason. You want to join us?"

"Oh, I do. Most definitely." Jason pulled out a chair and sat down. Pen didn't like the look on his face: smug, challenging, a little mean. She didn't like his pink, short-sleeved button-down or his sunburned ears or his hammy forearms, either. How, oh how, could Cat have married this person?

"Where's Cat?" demanded Pen.

At the question, Jason's demeanor cracked, just briefly, a flinch, a flash of alarm in his eyes, before the bravado was back.

"You tell me," he said. "That's"—he made two guns with his fingers and pointed them at Pen and Will (*God, you're an idiot,* thought Pen)—"why I brought you here."

Chapter Ten

OU." Pen exhaled the word more than spoke it.

"Yup," said Jason, with an upward, confirming chin-jut jerk
of his head. "Me." He leaned back in his chair and crossed his freckled
arms.

Pen wished with all her heart that she could say, "I knew it!" or "I
thought so," or at least, "I didn't really believe that e-mail came from
Cat," or even, "As much as I wanted to believe Cat had written that
e-mail, as much as I expected, every second, to turn around and find
her standing next to me, I harbored, nevertheless, a small, slender, va-
porous sliver of suspicion that it wasn't really from her at all." But none
of those would have been the truth. The truth was that she had fallen
for Jason's trick hook, line, and sinker. The truth was weeks of happiness and worry and anticipation and nervousness and waiting and
hope like a blazing light.

Pen wanted to hit him. Not just hit him. Pen who had never hit
anyone in her life (since childhood anyway, and then it was only Jamie)
wanted to slam Jason over backward in his chair, leap on him like a
wolverine, and beat the crap out of him with her fists. She was picturing it, filling in the details (the clonk of his head against the ground,
his nose fountaining blood), when, suddenly, she became aware of Will
across the table, perfectly unmoving, his silence hissing like a live wire,
his hands flat on the table at either side of his plate, and hitting didn't

seem like such a good idea anymore. *Don't,* she thought in Will's direction. *He's not worth it. You've come so far. Please don't.*

But when she forced herself to look at Jason, the urge to hit and for him to be hit came back. Belligerent and neckless, hair like toothbrush bristles. The way he lolled his head to one side and had his hands shoved under his forearms so that his biceps strained against the sleeves of his shirt made her want to scream. *You are not LL Cool J, you posturing moron!* she imagined herself yelling. *You pink, doughy, unripe strawberry of a man! Yup? Yup?*

"You shit," she said instead. "You complete and total asshole." She didn't scream it. Her voice was low, but she could feel herself gathering steam. "You must be pretty proud of yourself, right? Sending us down here, worried out of our minds about Cat? What was it, some kind of joke to you?"

"Pen," said Will.

"Some kind of sick game to get back at us for—what? *Not liking you* six years ago, you stupid overgrown baby?"

Jason's face went from hostile to stunned to enraged. He turned alarmingly red, clamped his lips together, and began to breathe hard out of his nose. *Bull!* thought Pen.

"Pen," said Will.

"I left my *daughter.* I left my job. I drove all the way the hell down here for some cat-and-mouse bullshit *game?*" When she said "game," Pen slapped her hand down on the table, making the plates jump and her nearly empty plastic water bottle flop over and roll across the table. It stopped in front of Jason, who didn't even look at it.

It wasn't until Will put his hand over her hand to stop its trembling that Pen realized it was trembling, not only her hand, but her entire body. *I am shaking with rage,* she marveled.

"Hey," said Will gently.

She looked up at him and he gave her a little encouraging nod, so she took a deep breath and began to count backward from ten, like the child in Will's book. By five, Will's hand was gone—she wished it weren't, even with all that was happening, she had the momentary presence of mind to wish it weren't—and he was staring at Jason with piercing eyes. Pen remembered, then, how Will could narrow his already long narrow eyes an almost imperceptible bit and turn their gaze to steel. "Like Clint Eastwood looking down a gun barrel," Cat used to say. "The eye equivalent of gritted teeth."

"Cat left you," said Will. Even before what he said sank in, Pen admired the flatness, the absolute, matter-of-fact calm of his voice.

Then what he had said sank in, and Pen thought, *Of course, she left him!* followed by, *Wait. What?*

"No," Jason shot back viciously.

"She left you, and you thought she came to us."

Pen stared at Will, bewildered. Then she heard it again, the part that had gotten lost in her outrage at Jason for tricking them into coming, in her sorrow at Jason's being Jason instead of Cat: her own voice asking, "Where's Cat?" and Jason's answer, "You tell me."

"You don't know where she is," said Pen in a wondering voice.

"You don't know shit," said Jason.

"She left you," said Will again.

"Not *me*," said Jason, pointing at his own chest with both forefingers. "She might have left, but she didn't leave *me*. She thought I was"—he paused, searching for the word—"awesome."

Will shifted his gaze from Jason to the tablecloth, the trail of water.

"We were happy," said Jason. "You might not believe it, but fuck you. We were a happily married couple." And at "happily married couple," even Pen, who still hated him, had to look away because he sounded so querulous, querulous and defensive and about six years old.

Maybe he sounded this way to himself, too, because, with one windshield-wiper swipe of his arm, the water bottle flew off the table, and he was standing up.

"Forget it," he said. "I don't have to defend myself to you shitheads."

But he just stood there, not leaving, breathing hard, rubbing his forehead with one hand, and staring out over the party, looking, with his sunburned ears, exactly like a guy in a lifeboat, scanning the ocean for land or boats or dorsal fins. As Pen watched him, she found herself remembering the e-mail, the words she had thought for so long were Cat's, but were really Jason's:

I know it's been forever, but I need you.

"Wait," she said to Jason.

"*You* wait," he said. He jerked his arm back as though she'd touched him, even though she hadn't.

Pen sighed. "Just—sit. Okay? Please." The "please" was an afterthought, a giving in, a tiny offering to his childlike blustering and his sad red ears. But she didn't think he would sit, not immediately, anyway. He was the kind of guy who would sit later, on his own terms.

"I need a beer," said Jason. Pen watched him stomp his way toward the beer table in his shorts and loafers, his arms slightly bowed at the elbows, his hands in loose fists. She recalled his vow in his old apology letter to never drink again and wondered what other promises to Cat he might have broken.

"I can see what Cat sees in him," Pen said, nodding. "Absolutely."

"'*You* wait,'" said Will. "Nice comeback."

Pen slumped, cradling the sides of her face in her hands and looking wide-eyed at Will. "Holy, holy, holy shit."

"I know."

"I can't believe it was him all the time."

"Yeah. Not only did I think it was her, I thought she'd be here. Even when she didn't come last night, I would have bet money she'd show up before it was all over."

"You think we should've suspected?" asked Pen.

"I don't know. I think we really wanted it to be her."

"And not only is she not here, she's missing."

"She left," Will said quickly. "That doesn't mean she's missing."

"I hope not. He's worried, though. You can see it in his face. And think about that e-mail. He's scared."

After a somber moment, Will grinned. "He should be scared. I thought you were about to jump up and break your chair over his head."

"Remember that night when you lost your marbles and pounded him into the Crater? I miss that night."

"Me, too. But maybe we should try to be nice, so he'll tell us what happened to Cat." Will shook his head. "What happened *with* Cat, is what I mean."

"He's a hard man to be nice to."

"Just until he tells us about Cat. Then you can clobber him."

"Here he comes."

This time, Jason didn't just sit, he yanked the chair around backward and straddled it, a startling gesture that would have been more impressive had it not placed him too far away from the table to put his beer down. After one attempt, he propped it on his knee instead. *Stumpy arms,* thought Pen. *T-rex.*

"Sorry I lost my temper," she said, attempting a smile of mollifying self-deprecation. "It was a shock, you showing up instead of Cat." At least this was true.

"Yeah, I'll bet," snorted Jason. "You guys always hated me."

Pen almost said, "And this is all about you." Instead, she didn't confirm or deny what he'd said. Neither did Will.

"Please tell us what happened," said Pen.

"Her dad died, like, six weeks ago, give or take," said Jason, darting his eyes from Pen's face to Will's, as though watching for their reaction.

Instantly, Pen's eyes filled with tears, both because her eyes always filled with tears at the mention of dead fathers and because the dead father in question belonged to Cat.

"She was crazy about her dad," said Will.

"How did it happen?" asked Pen, trying not to picture her own father, curled on his side, his cheek slack against the cement.

"Heart attack," said Jason. He squinted at them. "You're telling me you didn't know? Her dad died and she didn't tell you."

"How would I know?" said Will. "I haven't talked to Cat in six years."

"Neither have I," said Pen.

"Yeah, right," said Jason snidely. "I forgot."

"What's that supposed to mean?" asked Pen.

"It means I don't believe that, no matter what Cat said. I'm not an imbecile. Not one phone call? Not one e-mail?" said Jason. "It means I think you're all a bunch of liars."

"Cat, too?" snapped Pen, forgetting to be nice. "Cat who thinks you're awesome and would never leave you? You're calling her a liar, too?"

Jason tensed and opened his mouth, but nothing came out. His right knee started to jitter, causing his beer to slosh out of the glass and down his leg. "Fuck."

Will handed him a napkin, and he slapped at his leg with it.

"Her dad died," prompted Will. "Go ahead."

Jason tossed the napkin onto the table and said, "She lost it. It was weird."

"Weird to lose it when your dad dies?" said Pen. Will shot her a look.

Jason glared at her. "Believe it or not, I was *sensitive* to the fact that she was grieving. I was *there* for her. And, at first, you know, she was dealing with it the way you'd expect."

Pen tried to imagine how Cat would deal with something as big and final and grim as death, Cat of the twinkling eyes and sly sweetness and witty quips. Cat, who so much of the time, had seemed to float.

"I don't know what I'd expect," said Will. "I haven't seen her in a long time, and when I remember her, she's usually laughing."

A cloud passed over Jason's face. "Well, you know, she's an adult now. No one stays like that."

"So tell us," said Pen, "how she reacted."

"When she first heard, she was sad. Understandably, right? She said stuff about how she didn't know him that well, even though he was the only family she had. Which was true, by the way. She thought he was the greatest thing since sliced bread, and I guess he was charming and all, but he wasn't exactly a guy who showed up, if you know what I mean."

Pen thought that she did. She and Will had only met Dr. Ocampo twice (which in itself said a lot), once at their graduation and once in

Philadelphia when he came to lecture at a medical conference at Penn, and both times, Pen had liked him. It was impossible not to. He had been one of those compact people who fill up a room, a person who shimmered with charisma. It was there when he shook your hand, there in conversation, when he talked and even more when he listened, giving you his steady, absorbed attention, his eyes alive with intelligence. She still remembered the conversation they'd had about neuroscience and teaching kids to read. "You have learned, through experience and fine-tuned observation," he had told her, so animated he seemed to crackle, "what science is only just beginning to give us!" Pen had felt understood, cherished, and at the same time, gleeful, like a baby tossed into the air, and all the while, there had been Cat, rapt, flamelike and flickering in her father's presence, her face full of dazzle.

But he was the kind of father who was good in the flesh, but bad at a distance, who almost never returned Cat's phone calls, who sent extravagant birthday gifts two weeks late, who forgot the classes Cat was taking, the names of her friends ("Persephone!" Cat told Pen once, hooting with laughter. "He thinks you're the Queen of the Underworld!"), and, at least twice, the day and time of her arrival home for Christmas break (she called him from baggage claim, he sent a town car). "It's not his fault. He never learned *how*!" Cat had once explained. "Blame my mother, who kept track of everything, everything, everything for him!" Later, alone with Pen, Will had said, "Cat's mom died when she was two. The guy's had seventeen years to learn how," but neither of them said it to Cat.

"She said she thought they'd have a lot more time to get to know each other, but then he died. Plus, she said she was an orphan, which is big, having no family. There's her mom's sister out in Oregon or someplace, but Cat hardly knows her. So she was sad," Jason went on. "For like forty-eight hours, she even let me take care of her, which you guys know isn't easy for a person like Cat."

Pen's and Will's eyes met, and Pen knew that he was thinking what she was thinking and that he was thinking it in the same way, without a trace of resentment, *What was ever easier for Cat than letting someone take care of her?*

"But then we flew to Houston for the funeral, and she was her old self and then some. Totally took charge of the arrangements, organized this big after-party at her dad's house, ordered the food, flowers, talked to all the people, shaking hands like frigging Jackie O. No crying. She was amazing." Even in the midst of her shock at hearing about this unfamiliar, take-charge Cat, Pen had to smile at "after-party."

"That does sound amazing," said Will.

"It does, right? And then I flew home and she stayed for another week or so, getting his estate in order and whatnot. Meeting with his lawyer, sorting through his stuff, getting the house ready to sell—"

Jason broke off, stared into his nearly full cup of beer, bolted it the way you'd bolt an espresso shot, and then stared into the empty cup. Pen waited for him to crumple the cup in his fist, but he didn't.

"I couldn't stay," he said, looking at them defiantly. "Cat was a student, so she could leave for a week, get incompletes or whatever, but I had a *job*."

"Makes sense," said Will.

"I'm an accountant," said Jason. "This was April, for God's sake."

"What was Cat studying?" asked Pen. She was surprised to hear that Cat had gone back to school because, as smart as she was, Cat had loved everything about college *except* school.

"Physical therapy. She thought about nursing, but it would've taken forever. As it was, she had to take a bunch of undergrad science courses before she could even think about PT."

If Jason had said that Cat had gone back to school to be an elephant trainer or a pole dancer, Pen could not have been more flabbergasted. (In point of fact, pole dancing was a stretch only because it did not, as far as Pen knew, involve costumes covered with spangles and feathers; she wasn't even sure if it involved costumes at all.) In Philadelphia, Cat had worked as a salesperson in an upscale men's clothing store, a job she had adored. "It's like a game!" she'd said. "A dance! A play!" And Cat wrinkling her nose at the fit of a pair of pants, recommending charcoal over navy as though the fate of humanity depended on it, saying, "You would be completely out of your mind not to buy that tie," *that* was Cat. But Cat healing the injured? Cat laying her tiny, perfect hands on imperfect bodies? Cat taking *science* courses? Pen's mind boggled. As a physical therapist, she would wear what? Sweats? *Scrubs?*

"Anyway, she came back different," said Jason in a very tired voice.

"Different in what way?" asked Pen.

"Every way. She basically stopped eating. Not even candy. Not even *pastries*."

Pen smiled, remembering Cat, sighing with bliss over éclairs, napoleons, palmiers, chocolate croissants, and, especially, scones, the ones from her favorite Rittenhouse Square bakery, hockey-puck-heavy, studded with currants, and blanketed in Devonshire cream.

"And she didn't sleep," said Jason. Cat, who could sleep anywhere, on a kitchen chair, on a subway, at a Phillies game, as instantly and peacefully as a cat in a shaft of sun.

"She got really careless about her medication."

"For the Cat we knew," said Will, "that wouldn't have been much of a change."

"Yeah," said Jason. "It's not like she was ever great about it, but she got worse. In fact, she got really bad. I even yelled at her about it once, that's how bad it got, and she just gave me this thousand-mile stare. It was spooky."

Pen felt a pulse of something uncomfortably like affection for Jason, so obviously still riddled with guilt for having yelled.

"But if she wasn't crying, she was like that, a million miles away, even when she was right there. Distracted. And then she'd leave for hours, say she'd been driving or at a friend's. Then a few days before she left, she got better. Still really distant, but she got calm, started taking care of herself. And then whammo: she left me a note saying she had to get away for a while, to please not try to find her."

"But you did." Pen sounded judgmental, although she didn't mean to. She wasn't even sure if she felt judgmental. She knew from experience that just because someone wanted to be alone with grief didn't mean they should be. But maybe Cat didn't want to be alone; maybe— and this was abundantly easy for Pen to believe—she just didn't want to be with Jason.

Jason's face hardened. "Have you seen her? That's all I want to know."

Pen shook her head.

"No, man. Sorry," said Will.

"And she didn't tell you where she was going."

Pen and Will shook their heads.

"I guess I have no choice but to believe you."

"Guess so," said Pen.

"Then it looks like my work here is done," said Jason.

"Will you let us know," said Will, "when you find her?" Pen could tell by Will's face what it cost him to ask this favor of Jason.

"Oh, I'll find her," said Jason, lapsing into a cocky nonchalance that, again, filled Pen with the urge to slug him. "No worries there. I got it covered."

He started to drum on the back of chair and look around the party. He actually yawned.

Why doesn't he leave? thought Pen. *What's he waiting for?*

In the midst of her exasperation, a thought began to take shape.

"Hold on," she said. "Give me a second."

Will and Jason looked at her. She closed her eyes.

"You know what?" she said to Will, opening her eyes.

"What?" he asked.

"It doesn't make sense." She reached across the table and took hold of Will's wrist. "It doesn't."

"Okay," said Will, waiting.

"Think about it," Pen said, getting excited. "If he really suspected we were with Cat or had seen her or knew where she was, how could he have thought his trick would work? 'I know it's been forever, but I need you.' See?"

Will looked puzzled; then his face cleared.

"We wouldn't have believed the e-mails were from her," he said, "because we would've been in touch with her."

"That's right! We wouldn't have come down to see her if we were *with* her or knew where she was!" Pen dropped back in her chair, breathless.

"Everything happened so fast I didn't even think of that," said Will.

Pen's heart started to race. What if Jason was insane? What if he had hurt Cat and was just pretending she'd left him? Then she remembered that the only reason she thought Cat was missing was that Jason had said so. Maybe she wasn't. Maybe she was. Maybe Jason was a psychopath. Psychopaths existed. Maybe Jason was one of them. Pen felt sick to her stomach. But when she turned to face Jason, he didn't look like a psychopath. She reminded herself that this didn't mean he wasn't one. But, red-faced and squirming in his seat, Jason looked embarrassed, near tears even, like a third-grader who has been caught in a lie.

"What the hell?" said Will in a flat voice.

Jason opened and closed his mouth a couple of times without saying anything.

"Did you do something to her?" blurted out Pen.

Jason's eyes went wide. "No! Of course not. God!"

"What, then?" said Will.

"I figured that—" Jason ran a hand down the center of his sweating face. "I figured that if she was with you, she'd make you come, okay? To see who was pretending to be her. Except more than likely, she'd know it was me. Even though I didn't use my own e-mail address, she'd figure sending that e-mail to try and find her would be something I'd do, and she'd send you to the reunion. Or maybe she'd even come with you."

"Why would she do that?" asked Pen, whose head was beginning to hurt with trying to follow Jason's train of thought.

"To laugh at me. Why else? You three could have a big old chuckle together at my expense. But at least I'd get to see her, maybe talk her into coming home."

Pen and Will sat staring at Jason for a long, stunned moment. Then Will said, "You sent e-mails to us pretending to be Cat so that Cat would know it was you pretending to be her and would come down here, even though she'd left and asked you not to look for her? Jason, that's"—Will scratched his head—"pretty complicated."

With wonder, Pen noted that there wasn't a single mocking note in

Will's voice; more than anything, he sounded kind. *Wow,* thought Pen. *Kindness? Now?*

But Jason didn't seem to hear it that way because he jumped up and hissed, "You know what? Go to hell."

At this, Pen flared. "That must be some marriage you've got, Jason."

"Fuck you, you condescending fucks," said Jason, spit flying out of his mouth with each "f." He threw his plastic cup on the table and left.

For at least half a minute, Pen and Will just stared at each other, or in each other's general direction, since they were both lost in their separate, if overlapping, thoughts, with the party whirling to a blur around them. A woman came up and asked if she could take Jason's chair, and Pen didn't even look at her, just nodded.

"I think he likes us," said Will finally.

Pen sighed. "I'm sorry."

"Why are you sorry?"

"That last thing I said about his marriage. It was a low blow."

"It wasn't anything he didn't know," said Will.

"I know, but he's a sad and desperate case, setting this whole thing up the way he did. He's lost."

"We believe him, then?"

"I don't know," said Pen. "I'm confused. I'm dumbfounded."

"Maybe we should get out of here," said Will, "take a walk. Unless you wanted to stay, hang out, have a beer, maybe go for a whirl on the dance floor." He smiled.

"That sounds fun," said Pen, standing up, and together they walked out of the tent.

"Do you mind if we don't talk for a little while? My brain is so full it hurts," said Pen.

"Brain indigestion," said Will.

Even outside of the tent, the air was so humid that Pen felt as though she were wearing the night like a coat of paint. They ended up at the university chapel, a small, stone Gothic Revival structure that Pen had always loved, perched moodily as it was, all its eyebrows arched, amid the gleaming neoclassicism. As if by agreement, she and Will stopped walking when they got there, Pen dropping onto a wooden bench, Will standing around awhile like a person waiting for a bus, then sitting on the brick walkway in front of her, elbows hooked over his knees, arms dangling.

"We're mosquito bait," he said. "You know that, right?"

"Little vampires." Pen sighed heavily. "I'm too discombobulated to care."

"You want to talk about what we're thinking?"

"Maybe," said Pen. *No.*

"What are you thinking?"

"You first."

Will leaned back on his elbows and looked at the sky. Pen waited for Will to start the conversation about Cat and Jason but wished he wouldn't. She wanted to keep it at a distance for a few more minutes.

Will said, "I'm thinking it's way too muggy for June. That moon looks like it's suffocating."

Pen looked at the hazy moon. "It looks like an Alka-Seltzer dissolving."

"You're right. So what else are you thinking?"

She closed her eyes and rested her head against the back of the bench. "I'm thinking how I've always liked this chapel."

"And your little friend who lives in it," said Will. Pen could hear him smiling.

"Edith," said Pen.

For the most part, the chapel's stained-glass windows were lovely but generic, sporting geometric patterns or expressionless religious figures with blue robes, iconic noses, and bony, rectangular feet. But the first week Pen had arrived at college, before she met Will and Cat, when she was homesick and drowning in lonesomeness, she had wandered into the chapel and found herself drawn to one high, almond-shaped window (she'd find out later that it was called a *mandorla*, a beautiful word) that seemed different to her: a girl's face, intimate-eyed and human and looking straight at Pen. Pen figured that she was supposed to be an angel, but to Pen, she looked like a regular person, a girl like herself, shy, brown-haired, smart, out of breath, slightly lost. Something about the girl, about being alone with her in the dim, high-ceilinged hush of the chapel made Pen feel less lost, befriended even.

Though she knew that having an imaginary friend at the age of eighteen meant she'd hit a point so humiliatingly low that she must never, ever tell anyone about it, one night, she told Cat and Will. They made fun of her, of course, but they liked it, and, straightaway, the two of them, especially Cat, wove the girl into the fabric of their friendship. "Edith says hi," Cat would say, or "I couldn't finish my sandwich, so I gave half to Edith." On the bench under the fizzy moon, Pen held Cat's voice in her head, cradled it in the palm of her memory.

"I miss her," Pen said sadly, a sob in her throat. "I was so sure I would see her."

"It'll be okay," said Will quickly, and Pen remembered how worried he'd always gotten when anybody cried.

"I know it will," said Pen, rubbing her eyes and sitting up. "You know I was always a crier."

"You always were," he agreed. "I was sure we'd see her, too."

"You want to know the truth?" Pen said. "The truth is that, all these years, I have missed both of you more than I can describe. I have pined for you. I wanted you back the whole time."

Pen felt lighter after she'd said it. She had not planned to say it. In fact, she had planned *not* to because what in the world would be the point? To make herself as vulnerable as a newborn chick? To make Will uncomfortable? To put him on the spot? And still: this lightness. Something about the night, about having listened to all that Jason had said and to be sitting in this precise spot under this precise sky thinking about Cat with Will made saying what she harbored in her heart feel natural. She didn't expect him to say it back or to even acknowledge it. She just wanted him to know.

"You know what," said Will after a long moment. "I was in town for my friend Gray's wedding a couple of years ago, not at the chapel, at an inn down the road, and I stopped in to see Edith."

"You didn't."

"Yep. I did, and there happened to be a tour going on, so I asked the tour guide about her."

"You asked about Edith?"

"Turns out she's special."

"Of course, she is!"

"Hers is the only Tiffany window in there. The others were made by someone else. And it also turns out that she's a real person."

"Of course, she's a real person."

"I mean, she was. The window's a portrait of a real girl. Who lived."

Pen considered this information. "Was her name Edith?"

"No."

"Then don't tell me about her. I don't want to know."

"Well, yeah, I was pretty sure you wouldn't."

Pen thought about Will stopping in to see Edith, asking about her, two years ago, four years after Pen and Will had last seen each other. She thought about how there was more than one way to say, "I missed you, too."

"Thank you," she told Will, "for checking on her."

"No problem."

"Do you believe Jason's story?" Pen asked. Time to dive in.

"I think I did, until you pointed out that his reasons for getting us to come down here made no sense. That made me doubt everything he'd told us."

"And the thing he said afterward. When you described it back to Jason—how he pretended to be Cat so that Cat would know it was him pretending to be her, et cetera—it sounded so convoluted. Convoluted to the point of crazy."

"Can you think of another reason, though? His real motive for setting us up?" asked Will.

"No. I tried. It made my head hurt."

"I had one idea," said Will slowly. "It's pretty far-fetched, though, and grim."

"You think he hurt her?"

"It's probably just too much *Law and Order,* but I had the thought that if he did something to her, looking for her afterward would be a way to make it look like he hadn't done it."

Pen shivered and wrapped her arms around herself. "Do you think he would hurt her?"

"Do you?"

Pen thought about this and said, "No. I don't, and not just because I can't stand to think it. Remember that letter he wrote after he left her in the Crater? As much as I loathe being around him, I think he's decent at the core. What do you think?"

"I think he loves her," said Will. The word *love* coming out of Will's mouth caused a brief fireworks display to go off in Pen's chest. She ignored it. "When he was talking about her, that's the impression I got. It's what I always thought about him: he's a huge pain in the ass, but he loves Cat."

"Still," said Pen, "maybe we should check out his story. Maybe Cat's safe at home, and he made all this up for a mean joke. Because he hates us."

"After all this time?" said Will.

"Maybe," said Pen. "Maybe the thought of us wanting Cat not to marry him rankled and rankled his soul for six years. Probably not, though."

"I hope she's safe at home," said Will. Then, in a hesitant voice, he asked, "Do you know where home is? Do you know where Cat lives?"

Pen's rib cage tightened at the question and her cheeks got hot. She looked down at her hands. "We weren't supposed to look for each other. We weren't even supposed to google. Those were Cat's rules."

"I remember."

"I guess you could say"—Pen paused and took a breath—"I broke them."

"Oh."

"For the first year, I googled you both. Often. Obsessively often, I would go so far as to say. I didn't know you'd moved to Asheville, but I know you ran a 10K there in March of 2004. For example."

"How'd I do?"

Pen smiled. "Not bad, but not great. 42.47."

"I was out of shape," protested Will. "My friend Jack—I moved down there to work with him after I bailed out of Wharton—he *made* me do that race. I'm way faster now."

"Sure, Will. Sure you are," said Pen.

"What about Cat? You find out anything about her?"

"Not really. We knew she and Jason were moving to Tampa when they left Philly. I saw their wedding announcement, I guess, but after that, nothing, and, as I said, after a year, maybe a little more, I stopped. I started following the rules."

"Any particular reason?"

"Augusta was born. I got busy, and also"—Pen gave a nervous laugh—"I was on the verge of becoming a stalker. I wanted my daughter to have a mother with a little more dignity than that."

Pen could remember the day, typing Catalina Rogers (Cat had sacrificed her musical name for Jason's, a semi-tragic misstep, in Pen's view) into the narrow box, then looking down at Augusta asleep in her Moses basket next to Pen's desk. Augusta had stirred, her arms flying outward, her hands startling open into two stars, and for some reason, that had been the sign Pen had been waiting for without knowing she'd been waiting. "Enough!" She had said it out loud and had not only deleted the name, but had turned the computer off altogether, then had rested her forehead on the desk in front of her.

"But then you went and became a famous writer," said Pen, grinning, "and all bets were off."

"You started stalking me?" Will asked hopefully.

"No, but I buy all your books, and I looked at your website a few times."

"Yeah?"

"It's nice, all those interactive games and great graphics, but there's no picture of you. That was kind of disappointing."

"Don't want to scare off the kids."

"Ha ha," said Pen. "So, anyway, I don't know if they're still in

Tampa or not." Then, tentatively, she asked, "What about you? You ever break the rules?"

When he answered, Will's voice was odd, tight and fast, as though he wanted to put the question behind him, get rid of it. "No. It seemed easier that way."

"Oh."

She waited for him to say more, but he didn't, and Pen felt rebuffed, even though she couldn't think why he would resent her question, when he had just asked her the same thing. In the brittle lull that followed, Pen watched a couple walk past about thirty yards away, coming from the direction of the reunion, the man talking fast and eagerly, telling some kind of story, his hands in motion, the woman walking with her head tilted back, languidly fanning herself with a newspaper. *Give it up,* Pen thought about telling the man. *No way she's interested.* And because she was distracting herself from the little wall—not wall, she thought hopefully, hedge, low hedge—that had sprung up between herself and Will by imagining the inner lives of these strangers, she didn't realize that the man walking a short distance behind them, his shoulders slightly bunched, his hands in the pockets of shorts, was Jason, until he was cutting across the grass toward them, a stone's throw away.

"Jason," she whispered to Will. "Behind you."

When he got to them, he didn't sit down, but just stood, a few feet away, and there was something about him, not his face, which Pen couldn't really see, but his posture—duck-footed, slump-shouldered, backward leaning, his hands in his pockets, his elbows jutting—that was so old-mannish and forsaken that Pen wanted, almost, to hug him, to put her arm around him and lead him back to the bench.

"I'm glad you're back," said Pen kindly. "We were just talking about you."

"Yeah, I bet," said Jason. "My ears were burning."

Because his attempt at belligerence was so halfhearted and because she remembered that his ears really were burned, hot pink and peeling, Pen's heart softened a little bit more, and she said, "You want to sit down?"

"That's okay," said Jason. "I just want to say something."

"Go ahead," said Pen.

"The thing I told you back there, about why I e-mailed you. It wasn't the real reason."

"We wondered about that," said Pen.

"You know, I thought there was an off-chance all that would happen, that she'd know it was me and come down here with you. An off-off-chance. But really what I wanted—" He pulled a hand out of his pocket and slapped at his arm. "Damn mosquitoes are out for blood tonight," and then he looked at Will and Pen and smiled. "Literally. Since they're mosquitoes, right?"

"The little suckers," said Will.

Jason chuckled. "So anyway. It was the reunion that made me think of it, of getting in touch with you guys. After Cat left, I happened to find the stuff about the reunion that came in the mail, and thought, *Okay, so maybe this is the way to go.*"

"The way to go?" asked Pen.

"Backward, I guess," said Jason. "Into the past. Because the present wasn't really panning out."

"What do you mean?" asked Will.

"I'm really worried about her," said Jason. "Running off that way, all distraught."

"That is worrisome," said Pen. "I agree."

Jason squatted down next to the bench. "So the deal is I was hoping you could help find her."

Pen and Will looked at each other.

"I guess I'm wondering," began Will carefully, "why ask us? We haven't seen her in a long time."

"Trust me," said Jason sardonically. "If I hadn't exhausted all my other possibilities, I wouldn't have. I talked to a cop buddy of mine, but there's no sign of foul play, and he said that a wife's allowed to leave her husband, *not* that that's what this is. Anyway, they might've checked into it, but she got in touch with this friend of hers, who told me she's okay."

"She did?" Pen said, startled. "Well, then why don't you just ask her friend where she is?"

Jason snorted. "It'll shock you to hear that Cat's friends aren't all that fond of me. Samantha won't tell me a thing, apart from that Cat's supposedly safe."

"Jason," said Pen, "maybe she just needs a little time. Maybe you should just wait for her to come home."

Jason squeezed his eyes shut and shook his head. "The best I can explain it to you," he said, "is that I have a sense of foreboding."

"You do?" asked Pen, impressed at his use of the word *foreboding*.

"Look," said Jason, standing up again, "you guys knew her better than anyone. I think she's in trouble. I want your help." He took a deep breath and held out his hands in a gesture that could only be called beseeching. "I'm *asking* for your help. Please."

Ten, maybe twelve seconds went by, a few heartbeats—Pen and Will looking from Jason to each other, getting their bearings—before Jason was taking off across the grass so fast he was almost running.

"You know what?" he yelled over his shoulder. "Forget it. My bad."

"Jason!" called Pen, jumping to her feet. "We'll help!"

Jason slowed to a walk, then stopped, his back still to them, his arms hanging at his sides.

Pen turned to Will, saying, "We'll help, right?" but he was already moving past her. She watched Will run his long, loping run to where Jason stood, watched him put a hand on Jason's shoulder, talking to him, turning him around, bringing him back.

CHAPTER ELEVEN

K IKI CALLED," SAID AMELIE, "WANTING TO KNOW WHETHER the three of you, um, connected."

She lifted one sculpted eyebrow and smiled.

"Ha," said Pen. "Kiki's never used a euphemism in her life. What'd she really say?"

Amelie sorted through the phone messages, which were written on random scraps of paper, napkins mostly, a few receipts, the front page of the *Philadelphia Inquirer.* It was one of Amelie's quirks: to be meticulously organized in some ways and almost pathologically messy in others. Once, Pen had found a used paper coffee cup on her desk with "Call your (yummy!) brother" scrawled across it in lipstick, along with the precise time and date he had called.

"Here it is." Amelie plucked a take-out menu from the pile. " 'Need details on the group sex, pronto, Henny Penny. Hope you didn't turn chickenshit on me.' "

"Charming," said Pen. "Subtle."

Amelie tapped her pencil lightly against her pursed lips and looked at Pen.

"What?" said Pen. "No!"

Amelie put the pencil down and sighed. "No?"

"No. I told you the whole story. Cat wasn't even there."

"So you're saying that if she had been there—?"

"No!"

"Fine," said Amelie lightly. "Fine, fine, fine. The subject of you, Cat, and Will is officially closed."

Sure it is, thought Pen. She waited, watching Amelie pretend to sort through the phone messages, then to examine her fingernails, which were perfect. She looked up at Pen, opened her mouth, closed it, then searched for a pencil and tucked it behind her ear.

"Oh, for crying out loud," growled Pen. "Just say it."

Amelie leaned back in her chair and folded her hands on the desktop. "I think you should tell me what happened between you and Will, way back when, why you stopped being friends. I think it's time."

"You do, do you?"

"Not for me," said Amelie, her eyes widening with empathy. "For you."

"Gosh," said Pen, "you're so thoughtful."

The weird thing is that Pen found that she wanted to tell. She had never, in six years, told anyone, not Jamie or her parents, not the therapist she had seen a handful of times in a tired, haphazard, halfhearted (not even half: quarter-hearted, sixteenth-hearted?) manner at her mother's insistence after her father's death, not Amelie all the other times she had asked. But suddenly, she felt like telling.

She didn't know why. Maybe it was because, after the reunion, the story of the end of Pen's friendship with Will was no longer the story of the end of Pen's friendship with Will. Maybe it was because she needed to set the story free from her own head, where it had circled for so long like a fish in a bowl, getting bigger and bigger and more and more neurotic, and send it swimming out into the narrative of her life with everything else. Maybe she needed closure or release or absolution so that she could move forward. Mostly, what she felt was, "Oh, go ahead and tell, for cluck's sake."

Pen knew that, in the grand scheme of things, it wasn't such a terrible story, not especially shocking or sordid. Even so, it was the story of the worst thing Pen had ever done. If she could go backward in her life and change one thing (excluding—oh, God—everything she had done, everything everyone had done on the day her dad died), it would be pushing Will away, even though, she reminded herself, the real problem hadn't involved pushing away, but pulling toward (her hand against the back of the man's neck, her fingers in his hair), when she should have done anything but.

A COLD MARCH, CAT TWO WEEKS GONE, TWO WEEKS OF PEN feeling as empty as Cat's closet, as relinquished and obsolete as Cat's twin bed, which drifted, with its flower-splotched Marimekko comforter, like a parade float in the middle of her empty room. Pen avoided her (their) apartment, went to classes in sweatpants, sat through gloomy meals of take-out food and self-blame with Will. With sadness, she noted that the two of them, unused to being the two of them, were awkward around each other for the first time ever. "Patience. You will adapt," Pen's mother assured her, and Pen believed her. He was still Will, after all; she was still Pen. But it hurt her, how moments of quiet between them felt, for the first time, like silences.

Things got better in the car. Even though Cat's absence rode along with them the way her presence always had, unbelted, leaning forward between them from the backseat, even though the bottle of wine in the paper bag in the trunk was Cat's favorite Pouilly-Fuisse (she'd left it in their refrigerator, further proof, Pen told Will glumly, of her eagerness to get the hell away from them as fast as her little legs could carry her), Pen and Will regained something like their old ease.

Maybe it was the act of putting the city in which they'd been a trio (the word they had long ago agreed upon, less loaded, God knew, than *triangle* or *threesome* [although *threesome* got Cat's exuberant vote], less commanding, but more accurate than *triumvirate,* Pen's personal favorite) behind them. Maybe it was the near impossibility of face-to-face conversation, of reading each other's eyes. In any case, Will's old red Saab, which, even in their college days, had hovered somewhere between being a classic and a piece of crap, was on its best behavior, and as they flew along the road, the still-bare trees and billboards and pearl gray sky streaming by on either side, Pen was glad that Will had suggested going to his family's summerhouse on Boston's North Shore for a few days. "It'll be colder than here and grayer than here," he'd said. "It might suck. But at least it won't be here."

They talked. Their conversation veered and backpedaled and bounced and stalled out and, from time to time, rocked to a rest, featherlike, before taking off, herky-jerky, in some unforeseen direction, which is to say that it was, for them, an ordinary conversation, apart from the fact that it was between two people, instead of three. Pen realized that others had often found the way she, Will, and Cat talked to each other annoying. "It's like goddamn conversation bumper cars," one of Cat's boyfriends had said. "I get motion sick just listening." But for Pen, talking this way with Will, the faint, familiar, pleasant-bad cracked-leather-dusty-attic-with-a-hint-of-street-vendor-peanuts smell of the car around them, the chilly air wailing through the permanently one-inch opened right rear window, was relaxing. More than relaxing. A homecoming. For the hours of the car ride, Pen was a creature in her natural habitat.

And though they didn't exactly skirt the subject of Cat, they didn't do what they'd been doing nearly every day back in Philadelphia: wallow in it, throwing around anger and sadness and what-ifs until the very furniture seemed saturated with regret. They talked about Cat, yes, but also about Roald Dahl, their favorite smells (Pen: the cold cream her mother used and bread baking; Will: coffee and the ocean), dyslexia, whether watching television makes kids overweight, Lance Armstrong, the Salem Witch trials, and why some people love horror films while others don't.

When a solemn, smoke-colored dusk began to fall, Will brought up the subject of his parents' marriage, a drawn-out, ugly thing that had recently begun coming to what would surely be a drawn-out, ugly end.

In mid-January, while Will's father, Randall, was on a three-day business trip to San Francisco, in a burst of initiative and activity that shocked everyone who knew her, Will's mother, Charlotte, had changed the locks on the family home, hired a lawyer, and enrolled in a painting course at the local arts college. She was two weeks sober, which didn't sound like much, Will said, until you considered that it was two weeks longer than she had ever stayed sober before.

"Two weeks!" Pen had blurted out, then, "Do they recommend that, making so many life changes so fast? She didn't waste any time cleaning house, did she?"

"Not unless you count the thirty years she spent married to the guy," snapped Will.

Since then Pen had trodden lightly. Will had visited his mother in Connecticut twice, and both times had come back bearing a hopefulness in his face that was so simultaneously glowing and cautious that it broke Pen's heart a little to see it. But right after he got back from the second visit, Cat had left, and, as they rode in the car together now, as Will said, "So Tully says the lawyers have made it so my dad can't get anywhere near my mom's money. Which is going to kill him," Pen realized, with shame, how long it had been since she had asked about his mother, the extent to which she'd let Cat's leaving usurp every other thing.

"You sound pretty busted up about that," said Pen.

"We all are," said Will. "Philip actually opened a bottle of champagne. I just wish I'd been there to see my dad's face when he got the news."

"No, you don't. Remember: *he* was there when he got the news."

"You're right. I wish someone had taken a picture of his face and sent it to me."

Even as Pen saw Will's smile flash in the growing darkness, she noticed his right thumb thrumming against the steering wheel, always a sign that something was wrong.

"How's your mom?" she asked.

"It's getting cold in here," said Will. "You want to stop and get your jacket out of the trunk?"

"I'm wearing it," Pen said, holding out her arm to show him. "You got it out for me at the last rest stop, remember? You said, 'Pen, time for this.'"

"Your teeth were chattering, and your lips were turning blue. Science tells us that these are signs it's time for a coat."

Pen was beginning to get nervous. From long experience, she knew that the intensity of Will's worry would be directly proportional to the length of time he spent on aimless chatter, rather than on answering her question. *Go ahead, Will,* she thought, *give me an answer.*

"Damn window," said Will, giving the window a baleful glance over his shoulder. "I should get it fixed."

"It's been broken for seven years."

"I've been taking the laissez-faire approach," said Will. "I'm the Ayn Rand of broken windows."

"You hate Ayn Rand." *Please don't let it be that she's drinking again,* thought Pen.

"Okay, then I'm the Alexander Hamilton of broken windows. Nobody hates Alexander Hamilton."

"Except that one guy."

"Except for him, but he was just one guy."

"He was," said Pen, truly scared now. "He definitely was."

Then Will said, "Tully's worried."

Pen shivered inside her coat. "Oh. Does Tully think she's—" Pen found that she couldn't say the word.

"She doesn't know. She hasn't found direct evidence. Those were Tully's exact words, 'direct evidence.'"

Will's sister was in law school, a superfluous, if necessary, step, Will and his brother, Philip, liked to joke, since Tully had been born a lawyer. "When has Tully *not* been in law school," Will had said when he got the news she'd been admitted. "It's like Mephistopheles and hell. Wherever Tully is is law school."

"But if she's drinking," Will went on, "she's different from how she used to be. Tully's word was 'agitated.' Never sitting still, talking in long bursts, not sleeping, starting things and not finishing."

"Like paintings?

"Paintings, meals, gardening. She dug holes in the side yard to plant bushes or something, which had to be hard because it's still so cold, and then she left them there, empty, for days. The mailman stepped in one."

"Oh, no."

"Nothing broken and my mom's lawyer says she's in the clear because he shouldn't have been walking across the yard in the first place. Not that the mailman threatened to sue. Actually, he was apparently really nice about it."

"But she checked with a lawyer anyway? That maybe sounds a little paranoid."

"Tully checked with the lawyer," said Will. "Tully was born a little paranoid."

"So maybe Tully's seeing a problem with your mom when there's really not one?"

She heard Will draw in a long breath, then let it out. "It's not just Tully. I talked to my mom a couple of days ago. She said something odd."

"What?"

"She said she doesn't know how to live."

Pen thought about this and said, "Without your dad? Because that would make some sense. Yes, he was jerk, but they were married for a long time."

"That's what I asked her. I said, 'You mean without Dad?'"

"And what did she say?"

"She said, 'I mean period.' Her voice when she said it—" Will broke off, shaking his head.

Without thinking, Pen unhooked her seat belt and reached out to hold on to Will, her forehead on his shoulder, her arm across his chest. It's what she would have done for anyone she loved, for Jamie or Cat or her mother, and for a few seconds, everything was normal. She smelled the cold wool of his coat, felt its roughness against her face and her hand, and then something happened: Will took one hand off the steering wheel and rested it against the back of her head.

Pen knew that it was nothing Will would not have done for Tully or Cat or anyone, something he probably *had* done for Pen herself, without her blinking an eye. She knew that it was an acknowledgment, a thank-you, Will being nice, but the fact of her knowing these things did not stop the touch from feeling different from any way Will had touched her before. It startled her. She tensed. Within seconds, she was detaching herself from Will, pressing her back against her seat, her hand lifting involuntarily to the spot on the back of her head where his hand had been, even as she scolded herself for being so foolish, ridiculous for imagining weirdness into Will's hand on her hair, especially at a time like this. *He's thinking about his mother,* she thought. *He's worried. He's not hitting on you, you ridiculous person.*

"Thanks," said Will, and for a moment Pen thought he meant for understanding that he hadn't been hitting on her. Then she realized he meant for the hug.

"*De nada,*" she said.

With her peripheral vision, she saw him looking at her. "Hey," he said.

"What?" said Pen too quickly, pulling her hand off the back of her head and slapping it into her lap.

"Buckle up."

Because Pen worried that the quiet that followed might be awkward, even though Will seemed fine, because she was concerned that, distracted by the hug/hand/hair event (non-event), she had dropped the subject of Will's mother prematurely, Pen decided to say something, and because she wanted to say something appropriate and natural, she fell headfirst into cliché.

"She'll be fine eventually." She hated the stilted sound of her own voice. "It will take time. Change is hard."

"Don't worry about it," Will said, his sarcasm making everything the way it should be. "I didn't know what to say, either."

They had never arrived at the house in the dark before; they had never come in March. Usually, it was early evening and spring or summer, the sky like a slice of nectarine to the west, low light striping the porch boards, the air smelling like black dirt and flowers. Pen had always loved the moment of arrival, the way the place opened its arms to her. She expected it to be different at night, with nothing in bloom, nothing singing in the trees, and, on the surface, it was different, drained of color and still. But the outline of the roof against the sky, the sigh of the wooden screen door were so familiar, Pen could have cried, and the house's essence, as it settled over her, was the same as ever: clean and old and incandescently peaceful.

Pen dropped her bag in the hallway and leaned against the wall.

"I love this place," she said.

Will was fiddling with the thermostat, and Pen heard the radiators start to hum.

"I called and asked Lacey and Roy to turn the heat on for us," he said, "but I think their idea of warm enough might be different from yours." Lacey and Roy were the caretaker couple who lived in town.

He turned around and looked at Pen. "You always say that as soon as we get here," he said, "that you love it."

"Because I always love it." Pen turned around and planted a kiss on the wall, loving its chalky, bleached-seashell whiteness, the bumps in its thick plaster.

"Cat was less sold," said Will, smiling.

"She loved it *some*. Definitely, she loved being here with us. You know Cat can't love any place entirely that doesn't have central air," said Pen. "Comes from growing up in Houston."

Will walked through the house, turning on lights as he went, the heavy switches thunking. Pen stayed in the hallway with her eyes closed, breathing the place in. The house seemed to breathe, too. *Leave it to this house,* Pen thought, *to not feel shut down or forsaken in the winter, to just be sleeping.*

"Are you hungry?" called Will.

"No," Pen called back. "I'm too tired to be hungry."

"Are you hungry if there's a pie?"

"Are you kidding?"

At the enormous, scarred dining room table, they ate shamefully large slabs of Lacey's apple crumb and drank the milk she had left in the refrigerator. Basking in gladness, Pen took in the room around her as she ate, the tall windows, the defunct brick fireplace, the great bronze, low-hanging octopus of a chandelier. The house wasn't a showplace by most standards, but it was perfect nonetheless. The kind of house in which you'd look up to see sprigs of dried lavender in a glass milk bottle exactly, smack-dab, where sprigs of dried lavender in a glass milk bottle should be. The kind of house whose cramped, hot kitchen was rendered moot by the faded hydrangea-print wallpaper in the guest room and the sleeping porch's view of the backyard.

"This and my parents' house are the only places I drink milk," said Pen.

"Same here," said Will.

THE NEXT DAY WAS SERENE, SUNLIT, AND CONSUMMATELY BEAUTI-ful. Pen woke up to white curtains full of light, and she and Will spent the daytime hours in an easy weaving between being together and being apart. They went for a morning run, parting ways after mile four, then drove to the market in town and bought green beans, new potatoes, and lamb for Pen to butterfly and rub with olive oil, garlic, and rosemary from the backyard and for Will to throw on the grill for dinner.

In the afternoon, Pen sat on the porch in a trapezoid of sun and read an ancient copy of *The Golden Bowl*, turning the frail, sepia-colored pages with care and, stopping, now and then, to unknot a sentence, reveling in the opulent commas and old-book smell. Afterward, while Will worked at his computer, she walked on the rocky beach with a bucket to search for sea glass, an addictive, squatting, neck-kinking enterprise that consisted of Pen vowing to stop, then finding, at the last second, something rare—an aquamarine kidney bean frosted over with nicks, a needle of saffron-yellow—and keeping on until her eyes swam with black spots and shooting stars.

It was only after dinner, when Will and Pen sat down to watch *The Graduate*, one of the DVDs from the crazily random selection (*Mad Max, To Kill a Mockingbird, The Unbearable Lightness of Being* . . .) that had accumulated at the summerhouse over the years, that a little awkwardness set in, at least for Pen. While Will crouched in front of the television cabinet, coaxing into action what could have been the DVD player prototype, Pen got herself a glass of water. When she came back into the living room, Will was sitting on the sofa, and Pen stood, water in hand, socked feet rooted to the rug, immobilized by uncertainty about how to sit in front of a television with Will without Cat.

Don't be stupid, she berated herself, *you've done it before*. Even though she knew that this was true, had to be true many times over, standing there, she couldn't remember a single instance. What she remembered was Cat, with her instinct for cuddliness, plopping her head into Will's lap and throwing her legs across Pen, Cat curling against one shoulder or another, Pen and Will sitting on the sofa with Cat on the floor, her arms hooked over their knees. When it came to sitting in front of a television or a fireplace or on a picnic blanket at an outdoor concert, they hadn't been a triangle; they'd been an "H." Now, every place Pen considered sitting seemed either too close to or too far away from Will. Too close to Will? Before this moment, such a thing had not existed. Pen didn't understand why it should now. From the edge of the living room, she watched Benjamin Braddock ride the moving walkway, the white tile wall gliding by behind him, Ben's shell-shocked profile going nowhere.

"What's up?" asked Will. "You're having second thoughts about the movie?"

"No," sputtered Pen. "What do you mean? Why would you think I was having second thoughts about the movie?"

Will gave her a mild, squinty "Are you crazy?" look, and said, "Because you're not watching it?"

"I'm listening to the sounds of silence," said Pen. "Hold your horses." To show herself who was boss, she strode across the room and sat next to Will on the sofa. There was about two feet of space between them, maybe two and a half, not that Pen was keeping track. *Calm yourself, missy*, she thought.

When Benjamin took Elaine, with her shining hair and lily-white jacket, to the strip club and she looked up in mute misery, the tears in her big, angelic brown eyes rendering them bigger, more angelic, more brown, Will said, "Remember how Cat used to say you were Elaine?"

"Cat and her backhanded compliments," growled Pen. "The passive-aggressive midget."

"I'm glad she's gone," said Will, throwing a pillow into the air and batting it toward the television like a volleyball.

"Oh yeah," said Pen. "Way glad. Cat never did see my inner bad girl."

"Hello, darkness, your old friend."

"Damn right."

"You don't really have an inner bad girl, do you?"

"Nope," said Pen. "But I'm working on it."

"Uh-oh," said Amelie, when Pen got to this part of the story.

"I know," said Pen. "Famous last words."

The next day, after a leisurely breakfast and another trip to the market, Pen and Will filled travel mugs with coffee, a paper bag with a lunch of leftover pie, packed up a blanket and the newspaper, and drove to the sandy beach on the other side of the peninsula. With the lambent bay before them, flat and silver as a platter, they sat back-to-back and ate and read, silently trading sections of the paper. Then they walked along the shore and talked about plovers, whether Will should quit business school, and Cat. In the almost-heat of the afternoon, Will rolled up his sweatpants and waded into the water, and Pen took off the Irish wool sweater she'd found in the guest-room closet and tied it around her waist. After a while, they walked back to the car, where Will stripped down to shorts, put his running shoes on, and took off down the road. Pen drove home, wrapped in tranquility and the smell of warm mothballs.

From the road, even before the blond stones of the driveway were crunching under the Saab's tires, Pen saw the car, a long gray Mercedes with Connecticut plates. Before she had time to consider who it might be, a note of unease began sounding in her head, faint, barely audible, but throwing the harmony of the past thirty-some hours out of whack. She wondered who it was, although anyone would've been less than welcome in Pen's opinion, now, when she and Will were leaving the next morning.

"You couldn't have waited just one more day?" Pen asked the Mercedes, as she pulled up next to it.

If someone apart from herself and Will had to be there, she hoped it was Philip, whom she loved for being a goofier version of Will, or Tully, whom she loved for being part twenty-three-year-old girl, part cranky old man ("Andy Rooney in Juicy Couture" is how Cat summed her up). But the man sleeping in the rocking chair on the porch with his feet, in gigantic, beat-up, paint-splattered black Chuck Taylors, propped on a milk crate wasn't Philip or Tully. He was older, maybe late twenties, with a long narrow face, Frida Kahlo eyebrows, and a head of oil-black Shirley Temple curls. One hand was tucked inside his toffee-colored Carhartt jacket; the other one dangled off the arm of the chair and was large and elegant and stained with something purple.

"Excuse me," said Pen.

Possibly it had something to do with his oversized hands or his extravagant hair, but Pen expected the man to wake up dramatically, maybe kick over the milk crate or shout with surprise. But he didn't move at all.

"Excuse me," she said again more loudly, and, this time, the man lifted a hand very slowly and rubbed the back of it back and forth across his still-shut eyes. It was only after he'd dropped the hand heavily into his lap and had, with great languor, tilted his head from side to side, as though working the kinks out of his neck, that he opened his eyes. They were an unexpected cloudy bluish gray, like the eyes of a newborn baby. The man smiled at Pen, a fast-twitch smile that made the cheek muscles in his thin face pop out like two golf balls.

"You caught me napping," he said. Actually, what he said was, "Yih cawt me nappin'," all the edges of his words smoothed away by a southern accent so lush it was almost comical.

"I see that," said Pen. She couldn't help smiling back at him. He was at best an interloper, at worst a serial killer, but he was cute.

He stood up. Due to his immense height, this was a multistage unfolding activity that reminded Pen of setting up a music stand. The man rubbed his hands down the front of his jacket and offered the right one to Pen. "Damon Callas."

Pen shook his hand. "Pen Calloway."

"What sort of a name is 'Pen,' if you don't mind my asking?"

"A nickname. For Penelope."

"Good Lord, girl, you're Greek!"

"No. Sorry."

"Where'd you get a name like that, then?"

"It's from *The Rise of Silas Lapham,* a book no one in the world but my mother loves. Penelope is Silas's daughter, the plain, brainy one."

"I'm sure only the latter adjective applies to you." Somehow— maybe it was the accent—he could say this without sounding like a complete phony. "Does she get her man?"

"She does, actually."

"I believe it." He winked. Pen was not a fan of winking, and she averted her gaze, but Damon was the kind of person whose eyes never leave your face during conversation. When she looked elsewhere, he leaned so that he could keep looking at her.

"Hmm," sniffed Pen.

"Sounds like she got a better deal than the other Penelope. Mrs. Odysseus."

"Yeah," said Pen, "you really never want to be the one who gets left behind."

"I was thinking more about the loyalty, the fidelity." He sagged his bony shoulders and made a bored face, "The chastity."

"The never-ending sewing project." Pen smiled.

"That, too." He smiled back at her, not a quick smile like before, but a molasses-slow, whole-face event. He crossed his arms across his chest and kept smiling.

"So," said Pen.

"Right," he said, still smiling. "So are you one of Charlotte's neighbors?"

Partly because of the way Damon pronounced "Charlotte," partly because Will never referred to his mother by her first name, and partly because Pen never suspected that this sublime scarecrow of a man could have anything to do with Will's mother, it took Pen several seconds to figure out what Damon was asking.

"Oh," she said finally. "No. I'm a friend of her son Will. We're just up for a few days."

"Will." Damon nodded. "The one in Philadelphia, right?"

"Yep, him."

Damon continued to nod. Pen thought Damon might be the most unhurried person in the world. Standing before her, nodding in the sun, he had the aspect of someone who could stand there nodding in the sun all day long.

"Are you a friend of Will's mother?" she said.

"I am," he said. "We're visiting for a few days, too. She's upstairs having a little lie-down. Long car trip and all. Plus, we were up late last night."

Something about the way he said "we" caused Pen to begin formulating a complicated word problem inside her head: if Will was twenty-six and the oldest child, which he was, and if Charlotte had gone to college, which she had, and if she'd gotten married after graduation, which Pen was pretty sure she had, even if it had been *right* after graduation, which it might have been, and even if she had been slightly pregnant at the time, which Randall Wadsworth liked to insinuate when he was feeling mean, how old would that make Will's mother? Mental math was not Pen's strong suit, but, eventually, her brain managed to eke out a number: forty-nine.

Will's mother was, at the very youngest, forty-nine years old, and, unless Damon were a vampire—which was possible, since he sort of looked like a vampire—he might have been thirty at the very oldest, which would mean he was dating (and this word seemed entirely wrong, although Pen realized it should not), *if* he was dating her, a woman at least nineteen years his senior. And that woman was Charlotte Wadsworth, Will's mother. When Pen, using emotional calculus, factored in the two measly months Will's mother had been separated from Will's father, along with the two measly months plus two measly weeks Will's mother had been sober, assuming she still was sober, plus

Will's sky-high hopes and bone-deep worry for his mother, the only answers she came up with were these: a vision of her friend Will running, fleet and unsuspecting, toward a mountain of fresh worry and her own heart beating out the words, *Oh, Will. Oh, Will. Oh, Will.*

Pen's finding Damon Callas sleeping on the porch of the summerhouse marked the point at which things got weird, but things did not progress from weird to surreal until after Pen got drunk.

Pen got drunk. Not falling-down drunk, but not just tipsy, either, which meant that she got drunker than she ever usually got. She didn't plan to get drunk at all, but after she, Will, and Damon got back from their walk to the sea glass beach—a weirdly unweird excursion—while Will and Damon sat in Adirondack chairs in the yard, making conversation in a weirdly normal way, Pen went into the house to get herself an apple and found the bottle of Pouilly-Fuisse on the counter, open and half-empty. It should not have been on the counter, open. It should have been in the refrigerator, unopened, the way Pen knew it had been when the three of them had left the house, with Will's mother still asleep upstairs.

Pen panicked. She could not let Will see the bottle. She could not let Will's mother drink any more of it. With shaking hands, she got a large wineglass, a goblet really, out of the china cabinet in the dining room, poured herself a glass of the wine and gulped it down. Then she poured another big glass, draining the bottle, and hid the bottle in the cabinet under the sink behind dishwashing soap and two boxes of scouring pads. For a moment, she leaned on her hands against the counter, her stomach burning, her head bowed, and whispered an already drunken prayer inspired by the box of scouring pads, "S.O.S., S.O.S., please S.O.S." Then she picked up the glass of wine, drank it, washed the glass, put it away, and walked outside.

◆ ◆ ◆

"WHY DIDN'T YOU JUST POUR IT OUT IN THE SINK?" ASKED AMELIE.

"I should have, but, honestly, for some reason, I didn't think of that."

"That reason possibly being your subconscious desire to have a drink?" said Amelie.

"Or two," said Pen ruefully.

WHAT PEN SAW HAPPEN IN WILL WHEN HE GOT BACK FROM HIS RUN had struck her as both marvelous and chilling: after she'd raced out to meet him on the driveway, giving him a rushed explanation, as much as she had one, for Damon Callas's presence on the porch, and after she'd watched confusion followed by anxiety followed by revulsion followed by anger pass over his face and she'd heard him spit out the words, "Oh, for fuck's sake," he had pulled out what Pen would later describe as "the big WASP guns." He had slid his emotions into some noiselessly opening and shutting WASP filing cabinet, turned his face into a blandly friendly WASP mask, and put on good manners like a suit of clothes.

Instead of pounding Damon's towering, scrawny body into the summerhouse yard, Will had made conversation, which is how Pen found out that Damon taught at the art school where Charlotte was taking a class ("Not my class, of course," he'd told them with a quickness and a reassuring tone that effectively turned "Not my class, of course" into "Will, I am banging your mother."), that he was a painter and collagist, that his hands were purple from dyeing cloth for use in one of his pieces, that he was "six-foot-six in stocking feet" but had not played basketball in high school or anyplace else.

When Damon asked if they'd mind showing him around a bit, Will had taken him to the sea glass beach, the two men walking ahead, talking in mellow tones about the history of the North Shore, and Pen following behind, fighting off the urge to fall to her knees on the stony beach and wail, "Will, let's go home!"

It wasn't until Pen had disappeared the wine and was walking unsteadily out of the house that she saw Will's remote demeanor crack, just for a second. He looked hard at Pen's face and said, "Everything okay?" The question made Pen want to weep.

She scraped together a feeble smile and said, "Should we start making dinner?"

"That reminds me," said Damon, giving his forehead a light smack. "There's a cooler of wine in the car I need to unload. Give me a hand, Will?"

Pen reeled at this, but everything else—Will, the house, the birds in the trees—seemed to stand still. She could see Will's face, which was not full of rage, but of sadness.

"Oh, Will," she said.

He turned toward Damon and said, "I don't think that's a good idea."

"Why not?" asked Damon.

"I guess you don't know that my mom's a recovering alcoholic. She hasn't had a drink in over two months."

Damon drew his heavy brows together, confusion all over his face, then he closed his eyes and sighed. "I'm sorry," he said. "I don't know how to tell you this."

Before he was even finished saying it, Pen had walked over to Will and taken his hand. "Don't," she told Damon.

The screen door sighed its sigh, and Will's mother stepped onto the porch. She was tall and straight and wore a long, loose sweater dress and boots. Pen noticed that she'd cut her hair; it hung at either side of her high-cheekboned face, blunt and expensive-looking.

"Why don't you say I'm a work in progress, Damon?" she said brightly. "Like all of us."

"Mom," said Will. His cheeks were red; he looked the way he looked when he had a fever, but his voice was ice-cold. Pen wanted to put her arms around him and take him away; she wanted to make his mother and Damon and the last couple of hours disappear off the face of the earth. Oh, please, she prayed, let it end, make them leave.

"Hello, darling," said his mother. "I didn't know you were coming. Lovely to see you."

"Lovely to see me?" said Will.

"You and Pen, both," said his mother, smiling. "Hello, Pen."

"Hello, Mrs. Wadsworth."

"Charlotte, please."

"Charlotte," said Will with a raw laugh. "That's great, Mom. Very hip. Like your new boyfriend and your cooler of wine."

"Please don't be rude," said Charlotte.

Will turned to Pen and said, in a low voice, "I need to get out of here before I lose my mind."

"I'll go get our stuff," said Pen.

"No, I mean right this second," said Will. "I need to drive. Or something. I'll come back."

"I'll go with you," said Pen.

"No," said Will, shaking his head and letting go of her hand.

"Why not?"

Will gave her an exhausted look with something scarier hovering behind it, "Because I really can't talk to you right now about why in the hell you're drunk and when you got that way."

Pen took a step back, her eyes stinging. "Will!"

"You have the keys, right?" He held out his hand, and Pen gave them to him.

"Promise you'll be careful. Promise you'll come back," she said, but Will was already turning away from her and running toward the car.

IN ALL OF THE BIG HOUSE, PEN COULD FIND NO PLACE TO BE. SHE'D started out in the guest room, but its door, like most of the doors in the house, was too warped by salt air and age to shut properly, and the music, along with the laughter and voices, poured hotly into the room just as the moonlight poured coolly through the white curtain to pool on the floor and make shadows on the wall. Pen gulped water and tried to read, but the words swam in front of her eyes, and all she could do was lie on the bed, trying not to hear the noise from downstairs, straining to hear the sound of Will's car. Emotions washed over her:

mostly anger—at Charlotte, drinking wine, dancing while her son's heart broke somewhere out in the dark; at Damon for letting her drink, for dancing, for being attractive, for being here at all; at Will for leaving her alone with them—but also sorrow and worry and something else, a cut-loose reckless feeling that might have been desire if it had any suitable object to fix on.

At midnight, Pen could not stand it a minute longer. She pulled on her shoes and the fisherman's sweater, yanked the quilt off the bed, and crept downstairs, wincing at every creak the steps made, wanting to be invisible. From the landing she could see Will's mother in the living room, dancing with surprising grace across the floor to sit in Damon's lap. *How could you?* she thought. *How* could *you?* She had to stop herself from shouting the words. Later, she would remember this righteous indignation with shame.

They didn't see her. Pen let herself out, the sound of the screen door reminding her of how arriving at the house just a couple of days ago had felt like a blessing. She had planned to sit in the porch rocker, but it was too close to what was happening in the house and, when she looked at the chair, she remembered seeing Damon there, asleep, so she went out into the backyard to get one of the Adirondack chairs and clumsily carried and dragged the big, awkward bulk of it to the grass a few yards out from the porch, a spot that gave her a clear view of the driveway. Then she cocooned herself in the quilt, tucked her hands deeply into the cuffs of the sweater, and sat down to wait for Will.

She woke, or half-woke, to the feeling of hands on her shoulders.

"Will," she whispered, with sleepy gratitude. "You're home." She opened her eyes.

Damon knelt on the grass in front of her, his face close. Pen blinked and leaned away from him, confused.

"Hey there," he said, smiling. "You must be cold out here."

"Where's Will?" Her voice was a croak.

"Not back yet," said Damon. He took his hands off her shoulders and put them on the wide, flat arms of the chair and said it again, "You must be cold."

Then he kissed her, and, after a numb few seconds, his warm mouth began waking her up, and the restless free-floating wanting that had been moving through her for what she now realized had been days, weeks even, contracted and concentrated to the point at which their two mouths met. She didn't think about Charlotte or Will or even Damon, because the man kissing her wasn't Damon. Or he was Damon and at the same time wasn't. It didn't matter. When he began to pull away, she put her hand on the back of his neck and pulled him back to her. She kissed him because he was there. She kissed him because he was kissing her.

"TRANSFERENCE," SAID AMELIE.

"What?" said Pen.

"You transferred your desire for Will onto Damon. Clearly."

"Except that I didn't have desire for Will."

"Oh, please."

"Trust me, he was my best friend. I definitely would have noticed if I had desire for him."

"Or maybe," said Amelie smugly, "that's why they call it the subconscious. Because it's subconscious."

SHE MIGHT HAVE PUSHED HIM AWAY. SHE MIGHT HAVE SLID FROM THE chair to the grass, opened the quilt, and pulled him inside with her. Pen would never find out because what broke, ragged, through the night was Will's voice, saying, "How could you do this?" And just as quickly as they'd come together, Pen and Damon broke apart, Damon dropping back to sit on the grass.

"Will, man," said Damon, but Will didn't even glance in his direction. Will stood in the darkness just beyond the circle of porch light so that Pen couldn't see his features, but she knew he was looking at her. In alarm, she jumped to her feet, shucking the quilt off her shoulders and starting toward him.

Will held up his hand. "Stop."

Pen stood still. "I'm sorry," she said.

Will took a step toward her and the light fell on his face. His expression, not closed and angry, as she had expected, but wide open as a child's, stunned and hurt, made her hate herself.

"Him?" said Will.

"I don't know why I did it," Pen said pleadingly. "I'm so sorry."

"You—" Will broke off and just looked at Pen. "That's not something you would do."

"I didn't mean to."

"What does that mean?"

Pen didn't know what to say.

"It means you're down here making out with my mother's whatever-the-hell he is. Boy toy. It means I don't know who you are."

"Yes, you do." Pen was crying. "You know you do."

"Will, brother. It was just a kiss," said Damon, with an attempt at a laugh, and Pen shut her eyes (had he really said "brother"?), waiting for an explosion.

But when Will answered, his voice was simply cold. "My mom is what? Passed out someplace? Seemed like a good time to give old Pen here a go?"

He shook his head in disgust, then ran up the porch steps. Before Pen realized what he was doing, before she could stop him, Damon was trotting up after him. He put one giant, bony hand on Will's shoulder. *Oh, God,* thought Pen, her chest tightening, *whatever you're about to do, don't, don't don't.*

"Listen," said Damon, with a smile that was probably meant to be kind and ingratiating, but under the circumstances, just looked smarmy, "I want you to know that there's no betrayal going on here. Nothing like that. Your mom and I are a no-strings operation, strictly casual."

A frozen second. Then the bottom dropped out of the world, and all of them crashed downward into a roaring nightmare, worse than a nightmare because it was so real, so flesh and blood. Pen's voice screaming "stop" might have been a fly buzzing. Nothing stopped. It went on and on. Until: Will's mother on the porch in a yellow bathrobe, yelling, "William, William"; Will turning his head to look at her; Damon catching him off guard and, like a battering ram, knocking him across the porch and into the corner of a railing.

Will lay still, his head bleeding onto the gray-white boards of the porch.

Pen ran to him—stepping over Damon, who sat slumped against the wall of the house, holding his rib cage and gasping—with a single throbbing thought: *If he is dead, I will die.*

Will's mother got there first. She dropped onto the porch next to him, put her face close to Will's, and pressed her fingers to the side of his neck. "My baby. My darling boy," she cried out. "I am so sorry."

Pen's heart seemed to stop, but she saw Will put his hand on his mother's hand and hold it for a few seconds. When he let go, he sat up, pressed his hand to the side of his head, groaned, then twisted sideways and vomited over the edge of the porch into the bushes.

"Forgive me," said his mother in the most regretful voice Pen had ever heard. "It's all my fault."

"Not all," said Pen. Will took his hand away from his head and stared uncomprehendingly at his wet red palm, and Pen saw that it wasn't the time to sit around talking about blame.

"You're going to the hospital," she said.

Will turned his battered face up to her, and, to her amazement, laughed a short, bitter laugh.

"What?" asked Pen.

"Who will drive me?" said Will. "You're all drunk."

"I'm not," said Pen. "I drank that wine hours and hours ago. I'm as sober as I can be."

She watched the archness fall away from his face and the hurt flash back into his eyes. She knew what he was thinking as surely as if he'd spoken the words aloud: *You kissed my mother's piece-of-shit boyfriend, and you weren't even drunk.* Pen quashed the useless impulse to apologize again and said, "Can you walk to the car?"

Pen heard a long groan from behind her and turned to Damon. "What about you? You need to go, too?"

"I don't think so," he said, working his way slowly up the wall, until he was standing, hunched and still breathing hard. He shot a glance at Will. "You're crazy," he said, with a strange lack of anger. "You're going to get yourself killed one day."

"Maybe," said Will.

"Go inside the house," said Charlotte to Damon. "Go on."

When he was gone, she started to help Will to his feet, but he picked up her hands in both of his and moved them off him, impassively, as though they weren't his mother's hands or hands at all. He reached for the porch railing and pulled himself up, wincing every time he shifted position. Blood was running down his neck and the front of his shirt.

"Wait," said Pen. She ran into the house, catching a fleeting glimpse of Damon on the living room sofa, ran upstairs to the linen closet, and grabbed an armful of thick white towels.

Back on the porch, she handed Will a folded-up towel for his head and took hold of his arm.

"I don't need help," said Will balefully.

"Yes, you do," said Pen.

THEY DIDN'T TALK ON THE WAY TO THE HOSPITAL. PEN DIDN'T TALK because she couldn't think of anything to say that wasn't scolding or apologizing, and she assumed Will didn't talk because he was too busy hating her and bleeding. He had refused to lie down in the backseat and sat with the towel between his head and the front passenger-side window, leaning as far away from Pen as it was possible to lean. The ride lasted twenty minutes, twenty minutes of silence, Pen catching glimpses of Will's unmoving face in the occasional beams of light from outside, and by the end of the ride, Pen found she had reached an odd, wrung-out state that was almost like peace. The tumult of blame, anger, confusion, worry, regret was all gone, everything was gone, except for love, of course, from which there was no relief.

The emergency room was quiet, and the nurse took Will back right away to be triaged. Under other circumstances, Pen would've gone, too, but without asking, she knew Will didn't want her with him.

She sat in the waiting room for what felt like hours, paging through months-old magazines and watching close-captioned CNN, until a nurse came in to say that Will's head was stitched but that he had a concussion and needed to remain there for observation.

"Does he want me?" said Pen.

The nurse gave her a concerned smile, looking, for a second, like Pen's mother. "Not right now," she said gently. "Are you his girl-friend?"

Pen started to cry, mostly from sheer exhaustion. "His friend," she said. "His best friend. But he's mad at me right now."

"I'm sorry," said the nurse. "He said you should go on home, and he'll call when he needs you."

"Can I stay?" said Pen, wiping her eyes. "For a little while more?"

"Sure you can," said the nurse. "He's not the boss of the waiting room, now is he?"

Pen fell asleep, her cheek leaning against her hand. When the nurse shook her awake next, Pen saw on the television that it was 7:05. Morning.

"Hey," said the nurse, "I told Will you were still here. You want to come on back?"

Pen nodded.

The sight of Will sitting in the hospital bed in a blue-sprigged gown, the white sheets over his legs, flooded Pen with relief, even though he looked surpassingly bad, unshaven and weary and the color of oat-meal, apart from a purple, swollen cheekbone and a black eye. Pen saw that a patch of his hair had been shaved on the right side and had a short caterpillar of stitches running across it. But he was breathing. He was safe. She had known he would live, of course, but the ugliness of the night before had shaken her up, twisted her imagination into irrational shapes. Looking at him, she realized she had been afraid, ter-rified even, that she would never see him again. But here he was.

"Hey," said Pen softly, smiling.

"Hey," said Will.

"Nice haircut."

"Yeah. You like it?"

Pen felt fear steal over her because nothing was the way it should have been. The words she and Will said to each other were more or less normal, but everything else was wrong: the distance in his voice and in his eyes, the way he didn't smile back at her. She thought it might have been the first time ever, since they'd met, that he hadn't smiled back at her. He wasn't angry anymore, at least she didn't think so, but he wasn't Will, either. Will would have rushed to meet her halfway. He would have understood that this bright room, everything clean, a world away from the squalor and the bloodstained porch, was meant to be the place in which they would fall back together. They'd had a very bad night, but now it was morning.

She tried again. "You hit your head pretty hard, friend. You didn't, by any chance, suffer memory loss. Maybe lose the last fifteen hours or so?"

Still, no smile. He said, "You didn't have to stay."

"You don't think so?" Pen asked. "Really?"

Will didn't answer. He looked down at his hands, turning them over and back on the sheet in front of him, as though noticing the white bandages on them for the first time.

Pen walked to the side of the bed. She wanted to touch Will but was afraid he would stiffen or move her hands away the way he had his mother's the night before, so instead, she held on to the metal arm of the hospital bed.

"Won't you forgive me?" she asked. "You have to know how sorry I am."

Will turned his tired, faraway eyes on her and said, "Don't ask me that. It's not about forgiving you."

"*What's* not about forgiving me?" asked Pen, gripping the bed rail. "Can there just not be an 'it'? Please? Can we make it go away?"

"I don't want to talk about this right now."

"When, then?" Pen ordered herself not to cry. She wasn't sure why, but she understood that her crying would doom the conversation. She needed to stay calm and optimistic and as normal as possible if there was any chance of ending the moment on a happy note. And Pen thought that if the moment didn't end on a happy note, she would not be able to stand it.

With gratitude, she saw Will's gaze soften a little, and he said, "Soon. All right?"

"All right."

The next second, though, he was all business. "I called Philip. He's on his way."

"So when he gets here, we'll go home," said Pen.

"I can't," said Will. "Phil and I need to stay with my mom, figure out what to do. You drive my car home, okay? I'll take a train later."

At the thought of driving home alone, the panic from the night before came back, the fear that, if she left him, she would never see Will again. On impulse, she placed her hand on top of his bandaged one and carefully curled her fingers around it. "Let me stay. I don't want to leave without you."

He gave her a long, complicated look, his clear hazel eyes taking in her face bit by bit, a look that she would spend hours and months afterward trying to decipher. She would never figure out what he was thinking, but, eventually, what she understood was that, while other good-byes would follow, this look Will gave her was the real end. He leaned over and kissed her forehead.

"It'll be okay. Go home." He smiled at her, then, which should have made her feel better, but it didn't. She didn't want to go home, she didn't think anything would be okay, but she let go of his hand and left.

AMELIE SAID, "CAN I STOP HERE TO POINT OUT THE ELEPHANT IN the room?"

"I know what you're thinking," said Pen. "And why you're thinking it. I've even considered it myself, but nope, it's not there. It's not a real elephant."

"When it comes to your personal life, honey, you wouldn't know a real elephant if it bit you on the ass."

"You didn't know us."

"*You* didn't know you," Amelie said. She sighed. "What happened next? After he got home."

"You know what happened. He left. Eight years of friendship up in smoke."

"Did you try to stop him?"

Pen told Amelie how she had yelled at Will the way she had never yelled at anyone. She had gone on and on and ended with:

"That's it? That's *it*? I watch you totally lose your mind and beat the shit out of another human being, *twice*, which I have to tell you is pretty fucking terrifying, and I don't leave you. I don't not forgive you. I know I shouldn't have kissed that man, that I betrayed you and your mother and probably my mother and God knows who else, and I am sorrier than I have ever been about anything but come *on*! I lose my head for five minutes, after being a goody two-shoes *my entire life*, and you're *leaving*?"

"What did he say?" asked Amelie.

Will hadn't yelled back. He hadn't even been angry. He'd been generous and loving and in pain about how much he was hurting Pen, from the second he arrived back home until the second he got into his car and left Philadelphia for good, but he was immovable as a mountain.

"He said, 'I forgive you. I feel stupid even saying that. Of course, I forgive you. It's not about that.'"

Pen could close her eyes and see him saying this to her and still feel what she'd felt then: the lights going out with a bang, total hope blackout. She knew right then that he wouldn't stay, no matter what she said, but still she asked, "What is it about, then?"

"Pen," he'd said, sighing, "my family is a disaster. I'm a disaster. I hate my dad. I hate business school. Damon"—he paused, and Pen flinched at the sound of Damon's name—"was right when he said I was going to get myself killed one day. I need to get away and start over, figure out my life."

But he didn't meet her eyes, and when she said, "Do you hear how little sense you're making? How none of those are reasons for leaving *me*? Don't lie about this," he didn't contradict her. He leaned back in his chair with his hands on top of his head, staring at the ceiling. *He's trying to think of how to say it,* thought Pen, bitterly, *how to let me down easy.*

After a long time, Will reached across Pen's tiny kitchen table, lightly raked his fingers down her cheek once—a ghost of a touch, there and gone—and slowly and carefully, with such kindness and sadness in his voice that Pen felt that maybe all wasn't lost after all, he said, "The thing is, this won't work, just the two of us."

"We can make it work," said Pen.

"I can't." In frustration, Will pushed his chair back from the table, so that he was suddenly far away, out of reach.

"So—what?" Pen lashed out at him, put words in his mouth that she knew weren't true. "You're saying that Cat's the only reason you and I were friends? If it's just me, it's not worth it?"

"No. No way. Of course not. But Cat kept us—in balance."

Pen was not above begging. If she hadn't been sitting at the table, she might have gotten down on her knees. Instead, she reached out as far as she could and put her hands on the table in front of Will, palms up, as though asking him to take them. He didn't, but she just left them there.

"We're still here, together. Cat's leaving was bad enough. It was a nightmare, but I could stand it if you were still here. You're my best friend," said Pen. "I love you."

She realized they were words that she and Will never said. Cat had said them all the time, and they had said them back to her, but never to each other.

Will didn't say them now. He said, "I don't know how to be with you without her."

"I don't know what you mean," wailed Pen.

"I know," said Will. "And I'm so sorry."

When Pen told Amelie this, Amelie knocked on Pen's head and said, "Hello. Is anyone in there?"

"Stop it," said Pen seriously. "We were friends. It was as big a deal as being in love." She tried to think of a way to make Amelie understand. "It was a revelation, being friends like that. God, it was *holy* to me. But it wasn't being in love."

"Fine," said Amelie. "And what about now?"

"We're talking. We're plotting," said Pen. "Coming up with a plan to try to find Cat. Will's going to talk to a neighborhood friend of hers."

"You already told me that, and you know what I'm asking," said Amelie impatiently. She waved her hands around. "What about *now*? Six years later. You're both adults. Bygones are bygones. No Cat around to distract you at the reunion."

"We wanted Cat around," Pen reminded her. "A lot."

"Still, she wasn't there."

Pen shrugged.

"So how did it feel to be with him again? Different? Come on, it had to feel different."

Pen raised her eyebrows at Amelie. "You want me to say I'm in love with him. After seeing him for two days."

"No, I don't." Amelie grinned.

"You want me to say that I was struck by the thunderbolt realization that he is the love of my life."

"Nope."

"Yes, you do. That's how you are. But here's a thought: it takes two to tango."

"Ha! So you *are* in love with him!"

"Not what I'm saying, and you know it."

"Oh, he wants to tango all right."

"I don't think so," said Pen. "I didn't see a single sign, not that I was looking."

"History tells us you're not so good at seeing signs. But let's put tangoing aside. Were you attracted to him? Simple question."

"I might have been, but not continuously. In flashes."

"Why say 'might'? You were."

"Seeing him again was overwhelming. A shock. I can't be sure of what I felt."

Amelie gave her a skeptical look.

"And even now," said Pen, "I can't quite believe in him."

"You don't trust him?" Amelie ruffled her cropped blond hair in dismay. "Why not?"

Pen shook her head. "I trust him. Or I trust him in all ways except that I'm not completely sure he won't disappear again. But what I meant was I can't quite believe that those two days happened. You know what I did?"

"What?"

"On my way back from the reunion, I pulled off the road to call him because I needed to make sure he was real."

Amelie smiled at her and said, "Was he? What did he say?"

"He said, 'I was about to call you. I just passed a dead possum the size of a Volkswagen. I knew you'd want to know.'"

AFTER HER CONVERSATION WITH AMELIE, PEN WALKED HOME DIS-tracted and brimming with feeling, half of her still in the past, the other half walking homeward through the here and now. Outside her apartment door, Pen stopped to listen to Augusta, who was inside singing a song from her spring concert, when suddenly, above the bubbling clarity of this, she heard one word, like a bird landing on a branch, "Beautiful!" *Oh, my God,* she thought. Pen was fumbling with the key in the lock, when Jamie threw open the door with a smile like Christmas morning.

"Mom?" said Pen, stepping inside.

Pen's mother sat in the leather armchair in a blue T-shirt with Augusta on her lap. The breath seemed to fly out of Pen's body. *Everyone, everyone is coming back to me,* she thought.

"My girl," said her mother, holding open her free arm. "I missed you every day."

"Your heart leaps up, Mama!" said Augusta, clapping her hands. "Right?"

All Pen could do was nod.

"Come here, right this second," said her mother, and Pen went.

CHAPTER TWELVE

$\mathcal{S}$AMANTHA DENHAM-DREW MADE WILL WANT TO SMOKE. NOT in the same way that *Casablanca* made him want to smoke every time he saw it; chiefly because he was sitting on his back steps not seeing Samantha, just talking to her on the phone, but her luxurious, intriguingly placed inhaling pauses and her drawn-out velvet exhales sounded so satisfying that Will could feel them in his own chest. Will had smoked for eight weeks at summer camp when he was fifteen, exclusively on sloped roofs and exclusively at night, which caused him to associate the smell of cigarettes forever after with sliding and the sound of frogs, but, apart from that, he had never been a smoker and had no interest in becoming one. Still, Samantha Denham-Drew was a woman who knew her way around a drag.

Jason had e-mailed Samantha Denham-Drew's number to Will and Pen (not from the Glad2behere address, which was apparently a dummy account Jason had set up to fool Will and Pen into thinking he was Cat, a username choice that Pen called "such a clear case of wishful thinking it makes you want to throw up or cry," but from CoolTaxDude, which Will found equally wishful, if considerably less poignant), and they had flipped a coin to decide which one of them had to call her. Actually, Pen had flipped a coin while the two of them were talking on the phone and had given a short victory cheer that went something like, "I won I won I won," after which she had put Amelie ("friend, business partner, coin-flip witness, hot blonde") on the phone.

"I really am hot," said Amelie. "And she really did win."

"You'd lie for her," said Will. "Admit it."

"All day long." Amelie's voice shifted from snappy to buttery. "But you should be the one to call anyway. You have a great voice. Very commanding. Very persuasive. Any woman on the other end of the line from you would be putty in your hands."

"Oh, yeah," said Will. "Putty. As you and Pen are demonstrating."

"Abundantly," corrected Amelie. "Abundantly demonstrating."

So he had called.

Sam answered the phone by exhaling smoke and saying, "This is Sam."

"Hi, Sam," said Will. "This is Will Wadsworth. You don't actually know me, but—"

Sam cut him off. "If you're calling on Joe's behalf, forget it. Joe's a sonofabitch."

"I'm not calling on Joe's behalf."

"Fool me once, shame on you. Fool me twice, shame on me." Inhale. Will watched a little brown bird with a tail like a tongue depressor take a brief but entire bath in the birdbath Will's mother had put up in his backyard. Exhale. "Tell that to your friend Joe."

"I don't know Joe."

"I don't know you, and you don't know Joe. Is that your story?" Inhale.

"I guess it is."

Exhale.

"Fine. I'll play along. So if you know neither me nor your sonofabitch friend Joe, how did you get my number?"

"From a guy named Jason Rogers."

"Aha. Jason." Inhale. "There's another sonofabitch." Exhale. Will smiled. It would take more than a colossal lungful of smoke to keep Samantha Denham-Drew from calling Jason a sonofabitch.

"I agree," said Will. "Not that I know the guy all that well."

"If you're agreeing that he's a sonofabitch, I'd say you know all there is to know," said Sam. "So why are you calling me?"

"I'm an old friend of Jason's wife, Cat."

Inhale, quickly followed by a hairball cough. "Hold on. What did you say your name was?"

"Will Wadsworth."

"You are so egregiously full of crap."

Will laughed. "Sometimes. But not right now."

"Will Wadsworth." Sam's voice dropped to a hoarse whisper. "Mother Mary."

"So you've, uh, heard of me?"

"You? Of course! You're a living legend."

"You're not thinking of the poet, are you?"

"What poet? I've never heard of a poet named Will Wadsworth."

"Well, yeah, there's not one, but—"

"You're Will Wadsworth, the friend! College Will! Philly Will! The Pen-and-Will Will!"

Will smiled. "That's the one."

"And you got my number from *Jason*? I thought you and Pen hated Jason."

Will flashed back to Jason standing outside the chapel, his hands open, hollow-eyed under the moon. "Well, I wouldn't say 'hate.'"

" 'Despise.' 'Despise' was Cat's word. Although she also said you beat the shit out of him the first time you met him, which sounds a little hotter under the collar than—what's the noun form of 'despise'? Despisery?"

"I don't think so, but nothing else really springs to mind," Will said.

"Huh! I thought you were English majors, you, Pen, and Cat."

Will laughed. "Anyway, it was a long time ago, when I did that."

"You've cooled off, you're saying?"

"Yes, and I shouldn't have done it in the first place."

"Oh, I don't know about that. So how did Jason come to give you my number?"

Will gave her a condensed version of the story, after which she was silent, except for the sounds of smoking.

Finally she said, "Question: Why? Are you and Pen looking for her for you and Pen or for Jason?"

Will puzzled over this. "I don't know. We were worried about Cat because Jason said he was worried about Cat, and he was pretty convincing. But Pen and I haven't really discussed why, even though we talk about finding her all the time."

He thought for a while more, aware of the lengthening phone silence and wishing he had a cigarette to fill it. "So I don't know, but knowing me and Pen, it's for us, not Jason. Or it's for Cat. Cat's dad died. She was distraught. She took off. I guess we didn't discuss why we were looking for her because it just seemed like the only thing to do. If that makes sense."

Will heard sniffles.

"Are you—crying?" he asked nervously. He stood up as though to make a getaway.

More sniffles, one gulp, and then, tearfully: "That just has to be one of the sweetest things I've ever heard. So sweet and *so you*!"

"You don't actually know me," Will reminded Sam.

"I know," she said. A bout of unusually staccato smoking followed. Puff puff puff. When it was over, Sam was calm and snarky again. "Sorry. I'm prone to emotional outbursts, having only recently broken up with my lying, cheating boyfriend." Will sat back down.

"Joe," supplied Will. "The sonofabitch."

"See? You do know him." Sam laughed. "Cat would love it that the two of you are looking for her. She'd be over the moon."

"You think?"

"But she'd be jealous as hell that you guys are back together without her."

"Do you," said Will slowly, "know where she is?"

"I knew where she was going. I know that she got there. Which isn't the same as knowing where she is at this precise moment. And then there's the matter of how she is, which I also don't know. Although not so good would be my guess."

"Where she was going is a start, though. Will you tell me? I would really appreciate it."

More smoking. Unless Sam's cigarettes were a foot long, she'd lit another one without Will's noticing, although Will doubted that a woman who smoked like Sam was capable of soundless cigarette-lighting. He would have imagined a big snapping Zippo or the loud, luscious cinematic *scrape-whoosh* of a match.

"On one condition," said Sam.

"Okay. What?"

"I tell you in person. How could I pass up a chance to meet the famous Will in the flesh?"

"Seriously? I live in Asheville, North Carolina, and you're outside of Cincinnati. That's got to be at least six hours, one way."

"You'd do it, though. You'd make the trip. For Cat," cajoled Sam. "You know you would. You know you would."

Will groaned. "Fine."

"Ha! I knew you'd do it. Cat would love that, too," she said. "But look, I don't have a lot going on right now, to tell you the truth. A long drive could be therapeutic. How about we do a little Mapquest magic, pick a spot, and meet halfway?"

"How about you tell me where Cat is now, and you and I will plan a get-together for another time?"

"Ha! Nope."

"All right, all right. I'll meet you halfway."

"You think there's any chance Pen could come, too?"

For one clear instant, Will pictured Pen in the passenger seat next to him, reaching with one long golden-brown arm to close the air-conditioning vent. "I doubt it. She has a five-year-old daughter."

"What?" shrieked Sam. "Is Pen married? Are *you* married? Oh my God, you're not married to *each other*?"

"Maybe," said Will. "Maybe not."

"You're not telling me? Are you kidding?"

"I'll tell you when I see you," said Will coolly.

"Ah. Payback."

"Not payback. Insurance," said Will. "Three hours each way is a long way to drive just to see me in the flesh. As enticing as I am."

"Modesty! Sarcasm!" Will heard a sound that might have been Sam slapping the table in front of her. "That is just so *you* of you! Can I tell you how excited I am at how you you are?"

"Well, thanks. I'm sure you're very you, too."

"Oh, I am," said Sam. "I totally, totally am."

THE NEXT DAY, AS HE HEADED OFF TO JELLICO, TENNESSEE, TO MEET Sam, Will found himself remembering the conversation he had had with his mother on the day he got home from the reunion. After he'd walked through his front door, but before he had closed it behind him, the phone had started ringing.

"Welcome back, sweetheart," she'd said.

"What do you have?" Will had said. "Spies staking out my house?"

"Intuition," said his mother.

"You're deeply, deeply creepy," said Will. "I just want to go on record with that."

"Done," said his mother. She got down to business: "Now, tell me, did you see her?"

"Yes," Will had said. "I mean, no."

He had told her the whole story. It was the fourth time that day he had told it, since Philip, Gray, and his Asheville friend and former boss Jack, all of whom apparently lacked either his mother's patience or intuition or both, had called him while he was on the road coming home. Unlike the other three, his mother didn't punctuate his telling with "No fucking way," or "Holy shit," or similar expressions of surprise. Unlike the other three, she didn't ask him if Pen was still hot. In fact, his mother had stayed almost perfectly quiet, and when Will had finished, the first thing she said was, "Isn't it interesting how, in the years you've been apart, all three of you have lost a father?"

Will was caught off guard by this and didn't say anything.

"Sad, of course," his mother went on, "but there's also something beautiful there, something synchronous. Maybe you're coming back into each other's lives to help each other heal."

Will had thought about pointing out that his own father wasn't actually dead, unless you counted his heart and soul, or that you had to first have a father in order to lose one, or that his father's exit from his life had left nothing that required healing. But Will suspected that even though his mother respected Will's right to think these things about his dad, it bothered her to hear them. His mother, who had been more despised, more broken by Randall Wadsworth than anyone, had forgiven him.

Once, four years ago, Will had asked her how she had accomplished this. She had reached out to cup the side of his head in her hand, her eyes full of tears, and said, "Oh, my darling, compared to forgiving myself, it was easy."

"How, though?" Will had persisted.

"I did for your dad what I did for me," she'd said. "I didn't decide that his behavior wasn't that bad or erase the memory of it from my mind, but I threw away the idea that he was a monster. I acknowledged his humanness. There's a light inside every human being; I chose to honor his inner light."

"When?" asked Will. "How long did it take?"

His mother had given him a crooked smile and said, "When? Every morning when I get up and every night before I go to bed. Same as I do for myself."

"Like brushing your teeth."

"Yep."

"I'm a long way from that," said Will. "Probably, I won't get there."

"Maybe you won't, and that's okay," said his mother. "But I don't think you're giving yourself enough credit. After all, you forgave me."

She believed that he had forgiven her because she had asked him, once, and he had said yes, which he had been glad about because the answer had made her so happy (nothing he had ever done or said in his entire life had ever made anyone even close to that happy), but, in truth, he didn't know if *forgiveness* was the right word for what had changed between himself and his mother after she'd stopped drinking. He hadn't deliberately forgiven her. He had never thought the word *forgive*. Instead, gradually, without really meaning to, he had turned himself over to her, had begun to love her without wariness or sorrow.

"Oh, come on," Will had said. "Dad is—. You don't need to hear what I think Dad is, but I'll tell you what: he's not you."

"Okay," said his mother, "but for your sake, if not for his, I hope you'll forgive him one of these days."

"I might." Will had shifted uncomfortably, then. "Whether I do or don't, though, I figured something out."

"What's that?"

"I need him gone," Will had told her, looking her straight in the eye. "For good. No seeing him. No more phone calls or e-mails. Nothing."

He had braced himself.

"Good," said his mother firmly. "Cut him out."

"Really? I thought you'd be upset."

"Of course not," said his mother. "Whatever you need to do to take care of yourself, do it. And good riddance."

"Hold on," Will had said. "I thought you forgave him."

"I did. I do. I let go of my anger and blame, but I know him." She had given Will a look of such fierce tenderness that he knew he would never forget it. "And you are my child, and, unless that man undergoes a radical change, which could happen because miracles do happen, but which I'm sorry to say seems unlikely, he shouldn't be anywhere near you."

Now, four years later, Will was no closer to forgiveness, unless not caring much anymore counted as forgiveness, and Will's father, if not dead, was as gone as ever, not as gone as Pen's father, as Cat's, but only technically. Will could still see Pen lying on the ground outside the old gray church, could still hear her voice saying, "My dad died two years ago," and he knew that his father was gone in a way that Pen's and Cat's would never be.

But when his mother said that, about how they had all lost fathers, Will hadn't launched into a conversation about degrees of fatherlessness or grief. Tired from his drive, his head full of Pen and Cat, he had looked out his window and said, "I think my lawn has grown a foot since I left. Is that possible?"

Will's mother said, "Ben Calloway was an uncommonly good man."

"Yeah," said Will. "I wish he hadn't died."

"You wish it for Pen's sake and for her family's sake the most," his mother went on, not noticing, or more likely ignoring, his terseness. "But also for your own. He was more a father to you than your father ever was. I know how you loved him."

Sometimes, he thought, *you are too much.* Time to pull back. Time to set limits. "I haven't seen him in a long time," he said.

"Honestly, William, *time*?" his mother had snapped. "*Distance*? Those things have nothing whatsoever to do with love. Who knows that better than you?"

It happened the way it always happened: Will set limits and his mother rolled over them like a tank mowing down a picket fence.

Will hadn't bothered bringing up his overgrown lawn again. He smiled a resigned smile, shook his head, and said, "Nobody."

In the middle of the drive to Jellico, Pen called.

"Where are you?"

"Driving."

"Where?"

Will looked around him. Highway. Hills.

"In my car."

"Your *speedy* car," said Pen, who had seen Will's car at the reunion and given him the kind of look you'd give a traitor. "How could you?" she'd said. "This car is shiny and speedy and blue! The only thing it has in common with your old red Saab is that it's German." When Will told her that Saabs weren't actually German, she had refused to believe it, saying, "Why would I have thought all this time that Saabs were German if they're not?" to which Will could find no answer.

"I hope you're not speeding," said Pen.

"If by 'speeding,' you mean exceeding the speed limit. Grandma, then I am."

"I don't blame you," said Pen giddily. "I can't wait until you pick the brain of Samantha Denham-Drew. I bet the anticipation is killing you."

"I wouldn't say 'killing,'" said Will.

A couple of days before, Pen had e-mailed Will a list of fifteen questions for Sam with the instruction that he should add them to his own, checking, of course, for redundancy and preferably arranging them in a subtly rising arc of intimacy and importance. Will had reminded Pen that nobody showed up to a conversation with a list of questions; went on to say that, as far as he could tell, Sam was the kind of person who would talk for hours, in detail, about any subject, especially Cat, *unless* a man were to hand her a list of questions and instruct her to answer them; and had added, "Besides, all we really need to know is where Cat went, right?" To which Pen had hollered, "Are you insane? It's been six years! You have to find out everything! How can that happen if you're *not prepared*?"

Now, as he had known she would, Pen asked, "Did you bring the list of questions?"

"I e-mailed them to her in advance," said Will. "She's putting together a PowerPoint presentation on the last six years of Cat's life that she'll project onto the wall of the barbecue joint."

"Shut up," said Pen, laughing her laugh. "So you'll never guess what happened."

"What?"

"Guess."

"You said I never would."

"Guess."

"Uh, Augusta lost a tooth."

"That's mean, Will," reproached Pen. "If you saw her perfect, little, square white baby teeth, you would know how mean it was."

"Sorry," said Will. "So what really happened?"

"My mother came home."

Something in Pen's tone was familiar to Will, and it occurred to him that maybe the tone was a universal, the way you sounded when your mother came back: like a little kid and so glad that you shine, even over the phone. Maybe he had heard Tully sound that way. Or Philip. Maybe he'd heard himself.

"Wow," said Will, "that's great news! You must be really happy."

"I'm beside myself with happiness," said Pen. "And gratitude. And relief. I just came home from work and saw her sitting there with Augusta, and it took my breath away. It was like someone fixed my television."

For a second, Will considered saying what he figured most people would say to this, something like, "Man, you must really like television," but the fact was that he knew immediately and exactly what Pen meant. "Colors got brighter," said Will. "Edges got sharper."

"Everything gleamed," Pen said. "Like sometimes happens after it rains."

"How is she?"

It took Pen a little while to answer, and when she did, something uncertain had edged into her buoyancy. "You know," she said. "She's fine."

"Good. But if she's fine," said Will, "then why do you sound like that?"

"Like what?"

"You tell me."

Pen sighed. "Worried? A little?"

"About what?"

"Listen, are you driving with one hand while we're talking? Because that's dangerous."

"I have a Bluetooth phone."

"You have to know that I have no idea what that is."

"I just talk. No hands required. So why don't you tell me what you're worried about."

"Okay. I know this sounds crazy," said Pen, "but she's almost too fine. If you had seen her when she left——. I mean, my father had been gone for over a year and a half, but she seemed sadder than she was right after he died. More than just sadder. She was heartsick, despondent." Pen quickly added, "And, Will, you know I would've given anything to make things better for her."

Will remembered the last visit he'd made with Pen to her parents' house, how he and Pen's father had just come back from a bike ride and could hear, from the driveway, even before they'd gotten off their bikes, Pen and her mother singing in the kitchen: Michael Jackson's "Ben" at full volume, their voices stretching for the high notes near the end, then collapsing into laughter.

"Sure, you would have," he said. "You don't even have to say it."

"But there's something about her now that's more than what I expected," said Pen. "I expected peace, acceptance. But she seems so *actively* happy. She has this—this luster to her."

"She was in India and Tibet, right? Maybe she had some kind of spiritual awakening. Or maybe she's just glad to be home." Will could see how a spiritual awakening and coming home to Pen could amount to the same thing.

"Jamie, Augusta, and I are driving her home tomorrow morning. She mentioned that she has something she wants to tell us."

"Could be the meaning of life," said Will.

Pen laughed. "I'll keep you posted."

LEAVE IT TO CAT, THE MOST DRAMATIC PERSON WILL HAD EVER known, to have a friend who walked into a tiny barbecue joint in a tiny Tennessee town at twelve thirty on a June afternoon looking like a head-on collision between Marilyn Monroe and Johnny Rotten: white halter dress, white sandals, red lipstick, orange sea urchin hair. As every person in the restaurant—mothers and toddlers, men nursing beers at the bar, people on their lunch break—turned to look at her, Sam whipped off her enormous black sunglasses and flicked her green gaze over the room. Will started to raise his hand (he was that sure of who she was), but her eyes didn't rest on him for more than a split second before she strode across the room to the bar, grabbed a giant of a man with a ZZ Top beard and a John Deere cap by his copious shoulders, cried, "Will Wadsworth, you are exactly what Cat described!" and kissed him, Euro-style, on both cheeks.

For a second, the man stared at Sam. Then, as the other men at the bar erupted into hoots and laughter, he removed, with great delicacy, Sam's hands from his shoulders, stood up, took off his hat, and said, "Ma'am, I believe you have me confused with somebody else."

Sam's eyes widened, and she gave the man a smile that had the grace to be abashed and that confirmed Will's suspicion, from their phone conversation, that Sam Denham-Drew was a little out there but was overall a good egg. Gesturing toward Will with one red-nailed hand, she said, in a further demonstration of good-eggedness, "Sir, I was playing a little joke on my friend here, pretending I didn't recognize him, and I am mortally sorry if it embarrassed you. I can be thoughtless."

The man, and every other person in the restaurant, looked over at Will, and, feeling suddenly scrawny and overgroomed, Will stood and gave the man a forlorn thumbs-up.

"Me as him, huh?" said the man, chuckling. "That *is* funny."

"See?" said Sam to Will, as though the whole display were part of some conversation they'd been having. "Funny!"

"Hilarious," said Will.

When Will put out his right hand to shake Sam's, she batted it away and grabbed his left.

"Ha! No ring!"

She narrowed her eyes at him. Up close, Sam's face was pretty in a surprisingly ordinary way, bare, apart from the lipstick, snub-nosed, pale and freckled, like eggnog sprinkled with nutmeg.

"Unless," she said, "you're one of the ones who refuses to wear one?"

"I'm one of the ones who refuses to wear one because he's not married."

"God, I hate those guys," seethed Sam. "Expect your wife to sport an 'I'm taken' diamond that can be seen from space but won't wear jackitty shit yourself."

Before he could catch himself, Will laughed.

"What?" said Sam.

"You're just so—mad."

"I know," said Sam, sighing. "Hi, nice to meet you. I'm full of rage."

"Will you hit me if I ask you if you want to sit down?"

Sam appeared to consider this, then wrinkled her nose and said, "Nah, I'll sit."

Will walked around the table and pulled out a chair for her. She stabbed a finger in his direction. "Don't even start with the gentlemanly crap," she said. "I'm in a vulnerable place."

"Sit the hell down," said Will.

"That's better."

A teenaged female server in a T-shirt with a pink pig face on it and the words HOPE YOU'RE BIG ON PIG walked over. Her hair was dyed a sooty, shineless black. Will would've bet money that she hated having to wear that T-shirt. Will waited for Sam to order a drink and was relieved when she asked for a Diet Coke with lemon.

"The lemon's not an affectation," she told Will. "I really like it better that way."

"I believe you," said Will, and ordered a ginger ale. As the server walked away, Will saw that the other end of the pig was on the back of her shirt. "I think I was expecting you to get bourbon," he told Sam. "Possibly a double."

"Because of the rage thing," said Sam, nodding. She mimicked throwing a drink in his face. "A 'Take that, asshole!' kind of drink."

"And because of the smoking," admitted Will, with a grin.

"Oh, I only smoke on the phone," said Sam. "It's one of my rules."

"I see."

"And when I drink, which I do from time to time, I hate to say it, but I lean toward the pink and frilly," she said and quickly added, "But I know you don't drink at all."

"I do, actually," said Will. "Not a lot, but sometimes." He smiled. "Not in the middle of the day when I have to turn around and drive two hundred miles, but if you'd ordered that double bourbon, I would've had no choice."

"Can't stand to be outdone by a girl?" asked Sam. "Or can't let a lady drink alone?"

"Both," said Will.

"Whoo!" said Sam, snapping her fingers. "Cat would *hate* it that I know you drink and she doesn't. Know, I mean. Not drink. Which she does. Not like a fish or anything, but if you were married to Jason, you'd throw back a glass of wine now and then, too."

"I'm sure I would."

"You said you'd tell me about Pen's kid. So tell."

"Her name is Augusta. She's about to turn five."

"Is she yours?" asked Sam, clasping her hands pleadingly under her chin.

"Nope," said Will. "I've never even met her."

"Oh, yeah." Sam snorted and rolled her eyes. "Like that means anything. Like fathers who have never met their kids aren't a dime a stinkin' dozen. Stinkin' deadbeats."

"Rage, again," observed Will.

"Sorry," said Sam.

"Maybe you should just run over Joe with your car," said Will. "Get it out of your system."

"I just might," said Sam. She folded her hands primly on the table. "Pray, continue. About Pen and her kid. She's married, I take it."

"No."

"Oh, no, she's a widow." Sam pressed her fingers to her lips, a reckless move, Will thought, considering her lipstick.

"Not a widow," he said.

Sam's eyes widened in amazement. "Well, I'll be damned. Divorced? Little Miss Perfect is divorced?"

"That's not a name Pen really embraces," said Will, "believe it or not. And no."

The server came back and handed them menus. "We have a couple of specials today."

Impatiently, Sam waved her away with the menu, as though she were a fly. The server gave Will a look with her black-rimmed eyes that said *What the fuck?* as clearly as if she'd said it out loud.

"Sorry," he said. "Would you mind coming back in a few minutes?"

She lifted one painfully thin shoulder, mumbled, "So be it," spun around on her heel, and left.

"Whoa-ho-ho-ho, Nelly! I am stunned. I am *thunderstruck*," said Sam, her jaw dropping open. After several seconds, she closed her mouth and said, breathlessly, "Our Penelope has joined the ranks of the unwed mothers. Holy frijole."

"He wanted to marry her," said Will and immediately felt stupid for defending Pen, who didn't need defending, although he couldn't resist adding, "She wasn't interested," which wasn't the complete truth but which felt pretty good to say, nevertheless.

"Cat would fall. Over. And die," said Sam and did a dance in her chair.

"Speaking of Cat," prompted Will.

"All in good time, my friend," said Sam with a laugh. "We haven't even ordered yet."

They both ordered the pork barbecue, a.k.a. "enough pig to pop your buttons," which caused Sam to merrily point out that she didn't have any buttons, standing up and turning around to reveal their absence along with a generous expanse of freckled back, which caused the server to appear to contemplate stabbing herself in the jugular with her pencil.

"Take your time," said Will to the server, in an attempt to cheer her up. "We're not in a hurry." It was the only thing he could think of to say.

The server didn't even look at Will, but lifted two listless fingers in a "V" that certainly did not stand for victory. "Your meals come with your choice of two vegetables," she said.

Will ordered fried okra and slaw. Sam ordered French fries and macaroni and cheese. "Mac and cheese," she said, clapping her hands. "My favorite vegetable."

"Got it," said the server in a voice of bottomless despair.

When she had slumped away, Will said, "Okay, we ordered."

Sam began to talk about Cat.

◆　　◆　　◆

As soon as he had pulled out of the barbecue joint parking lot, Will called Pen, who answered with lightning speed and by saying, "How is our girl?"

Will smiled. "How" not "where"—even in the middle of their burning quest to find Cat, "how" came first. *That is just so you of you*, Will thought in Pen's direction. He wished he had a better answer for her.

"Still funny, according to Sam," said Will, deciding to start with the positives. "Still 'the cutest little fairy princess person in the whole world.'"

"I assume that's a direct quote?"

"The entire thing was something like, 'How could you and Pen have let the cutest little fairy princess person in the whole world marry that box of rocks?'"

"We tried! We did everything we could, and it only made things worse," protested Pen. "Did you tell her that?"

"I think the question was mostly rhetorical. When I pointed out that Cat hardly ever made up her mind, but when she did, she was about as easy to stop as an elephant stampede, Sam knew what I was talking about."

"So: funny, stubborn, fairy princess," said Pen nervously. "All good, but there's more to it, right? I can tell by your voice."

"Well, yeah," said Will, "I guess there is."

"Tell me that Jason wasn't hurting her."

"No. Nothing like that," said Will.

"Thank God," said Pen vehemently. "I mean, I didn't really think he was, but thank God all the same."

It felt suddenly wrong to be talking to Pen but looking out the windshield at the highway with its ruffle of flimsy trees and occasional cataracts of kudzu on either side, its green signs and billboards (DON'T LET DARWIN MAKE A MONKEY OUT OF YOU said one). For a moment, Will considered heading north, driving without stopping until he got to Philadelphia so that he could sit in the same room with Pen as he told her what Sam had told him about Cat's life since they'd last seen her. Not that it was an unusually tragic story. It wasn't unusually anything, really, and this had struck Will, as he knew it would strike Pen, as the saddest thing about it: their bright star of a friend spending the last six years living a life of ordinary disappointment.

"Tell me," said Pen, sighing, "plain and straight."

"She didn't like living where she lived," said Will.

"Oh, no. Was it awful?"

"Not by most standards. Strip malls, subdivisions, chain restaurants, typical midwestern suburban stuff."

"Hell, by Cat standards, in other words."

" 'Soul-killing' was what Sam said she called it."

"Except, you know what?" said Pen quickly. "It didn't have to be. You know how it is: places are places, but more than anything, they're the people you're there with. So I'm guessing that means she and Jason weren't happy together."

She said this thing about places as though it were self-evident, when it was something Will had never even thought about before. He wasn't sure she was right, not universally right. Certainly, he knew New Yorkers who didn't really believe life happened anywhere else or people in Asheville who couldn't imagine living without hills and co-op groceries and a shiny downtown like something out of a movie. In truth, he suspected that his own mother was one of those people for whom place in and of itself mattered. But, as he considered all of this, Will realized that he agreed with Pen: there were people he could live with anywhere and have that place be home.

"Will?"

"Sorry. Driving."

"Oh, good. Safety first, sonny boy. I need you in one piece."

Will smiled at this. "Getting back to your question about Cat and Jason. I think Jason was pretty happy. Cat wasn't. Sam said she fell out of love a couple of years after they moved to Ohio."

"Nobody falls out of love," scoffed Pen. "They just realize they were never in love in the first place."

"Nobody?"

"Nope. Nobody, nobody. Especially if they're Cat and they're married to Jason."

Will laughed.

"I hate thinking of Cat unhappily married," said Pen. "Cat *hated* being unhappy. Why didn't she just leave him?"

"Well, she did," Will reminded her.

"I mean earlier. What kept her there? They didn't have kids, right?"

"That brings us to the next thing Sam told me."

Sam had cried at this part of the conversation. When Will had gone to the bar and gotten her a fresh napkin to dry her eyes with, she'd only cried harder and ordered him to "Stop being gallant, goddammit."

"It's like what you said," Sam had told him, once she'd settled down. "When she really made up her mind, Cat was unstoppable. Getting pregnant became a project with a capital 'P.' Nothing mattered more. Maybe nothing else mattered, period."

"They had trouble?"

"It just kept not happening. Or happening and then un-happening. Over and over. It wore her to a frazzle, physically, mentally, spiritually. I hated watching it."

"Was it because of the epilepsy?"

"They didn't think so, but they didn't really know. That was the worst of it, not knowing why. She and Jason tried everything, spent thousands of dollars, tens of thousands, on in vitro. And then there were the charts and the Internet support groups and the herbs—chaste tree and cohosh and whatever the hell else—and the acupuncture and the homeopathy. I think she would've tried witchcraft, if there'd been a witch around to show her how, which there wasn't where we live." Sam had taken a long sip of Diet Coke and eyed Will. "You probably have witches where you live."

"Entirely possible," Will had said.

Sam had begun to tear up again, then, waving her white napkin in front of her eyes as if she was either fanning them dry or surrendering.

"I remember the day—and this was just less than a year ago—when she came over to my house to tell me that the doctor had advised them to give up and start looking into adoption. 'Some things just aren't meant to be,' he had told her, like he knew. Like he was God or Fate or whatever. Cat was completely racked with sobs, this little tiny thing in a flowered dress bent over double. Broke my heart. I just gathered her up in my arms like a puppy."

"I'm glad she had you there," said Will.

When he told Pen about this, she said, "I wish we'd been there, Will. My poor, poor, beloved girl. Thank God for Sam." Then she said, "I'm trying to think of how to say something without sounding cold-hearted."

"Like maybe it was nature's way of saying that a guy like Jason has no business trying to transmit his genes in the first place?"

"Ouch!" said Pen. "Not that cold-hearted. Geez, Will. I was thinking more along the lines of: Why would Cat work so hard to have a baby with Jason, when she didn't even like him that much?"

"Oh, that. Yeah, I said the same thing to Sam. And she had apparently, at some point, *not* when Cat was bent double with sobbing—she was clear about that—asked Cat a similar question. Although what she said was something like, 'Do you want a baby so much because you think it will save your marriage?' "

"Bully for Sam. And what did Cat say?"

"Sam said Cat gave her a look like the thought had never occurred to her, and she said, 'This isn't about me and Jason. It's about being a mother. I've been stockpiling love for my baby for years. You can't even imagine how much.' "

"Oh," said Pen. "That's a little disturbing, right?"

"Kind of makes you wonder where Jason fit in."

"I think I need to put that away and think about it later," said Pen. After a silent few seconds, she said, "And then, on top of everything, her dad dies. It must have shattered her."

"It sounds that way," said Will.

Pen growled in frustration, "How could this have happened? When I think about the Cat we knew—. I mean, who ever gave off more light than Cat? Her future should have been shining; it should have been *resplendent*. Or at the very least, fun. I will never, never, in a trillion years understand why she married Jason."

"I'd like to know," Sam had asked Will at one point in their conversation, "what's your take on why Cat married Jason?"

"Who knows?" Will had said. "He was definitely crazy about her. I thought it was a little creepy even, the way he worshipped her, all the presents and the surprise trips and showing up wherever she happened to be. Borderline stalking is what Pen and I thought, but Cat loved it. So maybe that was it. Except that he wasn't the first guy to fall for Cat that way, and he probably wouldn't have been the last."

"She is inherently adorable in every sense of the word," Sam had declared.

"Exactly. But he didn't just adore her. He deferred to her in everything. He asked her advice about any decision he had to make: what to order for dinner, how to vote. It's true that she was smarter than he was, and he was smart enough to know that. Still, it was kind of nauseating to watch. What amazed us was how Cat ate it up."

"Now, don't get mad at me for saying this," said Sam, "but maybe it felt good because maybe no one had ever treated her that way before."

"We listened to Cat," said Will. "We always wanted to hear what she had to say."

"Of course, you did! I do, too. Her take on things is always funny and kind of weirdly brilliant. But I'm talking about asking her advice, looking to her for wisdom and suchlike. That's different, right?"

Will had sat and considered this for a long time. "I don't know. Maybe," he said. "But the thing is that, back then, Cat was, I don't want to say 'careless'—"

"Impulsive?" suggested Sam. "Flighty?"

"Not a lot of looking before she leaped. She got herself into some tough situations that way. So, if we didn't trust her judgment that much, it was probably because she didn't use it very often." Will felt bad saying this, but it was true.

"You want to know what I think?" Sam had raised one very pale eyebrow very, very high.

"Sure."

"Cat married Jason because she wanted a chance to be the grown-up."

Will had set his fork down and stared at Sam, letting this sink in. When it had, his first impulse had been to get defensive, but when he thought past this urge, he had to admit that Sam might be right. When he told Pen about this part of the conversation, she was quiet for a long time, just as he had been, and he could feel her thinking.

When she finally spoke, her voice was subdued, almost ashamed. "Remember how Jason said Cat took care of all the funeral arrangements after her dad died the same way she took care of everything?"

"I do remember that," said Will.

"We babied her, didn't we?"

"We took care of her," said Will. "Everybody did. She was just that kind of person."

"You know what Jamie said once?" said Pen with an embarrassed laugh.

"What?"

"He said that it was like we were the parents and Cat was our child." Pen laughed again. "At the time, I wanted to kill him, but . . ."

Will didn't know how to answer this.

Pen said, "Listen, maybe we took care of her, but if we did—and I'm really trying not to be defensive when I say this—it's because she wanted us to. It was how things were, and it worked."

"But you could see," Will said carefully, "how it could have stopped being what she wanted. And how she couldn't see any other way out of it but to leave."

"Leave?" Pen said. "But we *loved* her."

Pen's voice filled the air inside Will's car, and the pain and sincere bafflement in it sent Will to where he had, for so long, tried to avoid going: back to Pen's tiny kitchen table, to her telling him, with that same painful confusion, that he could not leave—*how* could he leave?—when she loved him. The second he got there, saw her again, with her outstretched hands and her stunned disbelief, he realized that this was who Pen had always been, a person who believed that people who loved each other were different from everyone else, from the world in general, exempt from the usual pressures of time and change, of growing older or of growing up. When it came to love, Will's friend Pen was that rare and dangerous thing: a true believer.

"I want us to find her," said Pen resolutely.

"I figured," said Will.

"Where did she go? Across town? Across the country? Not that any place is too far away to look."

Shit, thought Will, regretting so hard it felt almost like anger that he didn't have an easier answer to give her.

"Across the world," he said. There was nothing to do but say it. "Cebu City, where her dad was born. The Philippines."

CHAPTER THIRTEEN

PEN HAD SPENT TWO YEARS WAITING TO BE HAUNTED, AND IT hadn't happened. True, her father was always there, inside Pen's mind, sometimes standing squarely in its center, everything else side-stepping or flowing around him, other times as a reassuring but nearly anonymous presence, like the lit windows of the apartment building across from Jamie's that Pen would look at, parting the curtains of the window next to her bed for a quick glimpse, when she couldn't sleep. Anything—a windbreaker, a bicycle helmet, a man with his hair parted a certain way, the joke the weatherman on Channel 10 made about fog—could send him flaring like a torch into a three-dimensional, walking, talking memory. But if these moments were vivid and if they bruised and embraced Pen at the same time, they were memories all the same, she knew, incorporeal, evanescent. Actually seeing her father or hearing his voice or feeling his hand on her shoulder, even sensing his physical nearness had never happened, no matter how patient she had tried to be, no matter how much she had longed for him to come back to her, even for a second.

The day she and Jamie brought their mother home, entered, for the first time in months, the house they had grown up in, was no differ-ent, though the house even looked sort of haunted, with every shade and curtain drawn and pale sheets over the furniture making a moon-scape of the living room. Pen knew that the Wexlers next door had been coming over now and then to check on things and to adjust the thermostat so that the pipes wouldn't freeze in the winter, and that they had been sending their teenaged son, Alec, to weed Pen's mother's flowerbeds and mow the lawn, but the house had the hollow, echo-filled atmosphere of a long untouched place. Standing in the dim entryway, Pen imagined cobwebs into the corners, even though she knew there wouldn't be any because she knew that, just as Margaret Calloway would never have asked her friend Astrid Wexler to do a little tidying up from time to time, Astrid Wexler would never have not, from time to time, tidied up her friend Margaret Calloway's house.

As she and her mother went room to room, dusting and vacuuming, raising blinds, lifting or cranking open windows so that light cut pathways across the floors and new air drifted in (with Pen dogged, the whole time, by the idea that doing so should have felt a lot more metaphorical than it did), Pen kept a part of her psyche (small, upright, and hyperalert as a meerkat) attuned to the possibility of her father's presence. She had to admit that it made her feel foolish. She had never believed in ghosts, not even as a kid. It was only in bursts that Pen believed in an afterlife at all.

The thing was, though, that if the dead could come back to visit the people they loved, her father was exactly the kind of person who would do it. Alive, he had been a frequent just-to-hear-your-voice telephoner, a daily, one-sentence e-mailer, a base-toucher, a checker-in. Once, he had stopped in the middle of his crack-of-dawn bike ride to call Pen and tell her he'd just seen a flock of birds flying in the whooshing, shoal-of-fish manner that she loved. Pen believed in her heart that anywhere her father was now, even in the most replete and splendid of all possible heavens, he would miss them.

But all that day, he never showed up. Not when Pen opened her parents' closet to hang up her mother's clothes and saw the leather aviator jacket he'd had since college, not when Augusta came clacking out of the garage with her sneakered feet stuffed into a pair of his old bike shoes, not even when Pen opened the door of his office and the great, polished, barren rectangle of his desktop (no computer, no overstuffed folders, no scarred globe, no road atlases, or years-deep stacks of *Science* and *Sports Illustrated*) rose up to break her heart.

Overall, it was a good day. Pen and Margaret cleaned and talked, sometimes shouting, impractically, over the sound of the vacuum cleaner, the way they had always done. ("Will was crazy enough to suggest that we all fly out to the Philippines to find Cat!" Pen hollered. "How crazy is that?" "Not crazy at all!" roared Margaret. "Do it!" "Listen to you!" shrieked Pen. "Globe-trotter! Jet-setter!" "Why are you shouting?" shouted Augusta. "Because they're insane! Total freaking nutjobs, and they're trying to drive us insane, too," yelled Jamie, unplugging the vacuum cleaner, and continuing to bellow into the quiet. "They must be stopped!" "Nutjobs, nutjobs, nutjobs!" sang Augusta at the top of her lungs. "Totally freaking out!")

Jamie got on the phone and had the mail, which had been forwarded to his apartment, unforwarded, restarted the newspaper delivery, telephone service, Internet service, and cable television, upgrading his mother to a premium package on this last one and having the bill sent to him, so horrified was he at her paucity of channels. In the afternoon, he shopped with Augusta, for whom a trip to the grocery store with Uncle Jamie was heaven on earth, and the two of them cooked dinner, noisily, drinking cranberry juice out of wineglasses (Augusta explaining to Pen solemnly and in an uncanny echo of Jamie's voice, "Because you gots to drink-a while you cook-a."). Augusta stood on a kitchen chair, wrapped like a burrito in Pen's father's barbecue apron, and sliced mushrooms with a butter knife, stopping only to literally dance with joy when Jamie did an extended impersonation of a hibachi chef, a performance that occasioned Pen to predict, "You will either chop off your hand at the wrist or drop dead from cultural insensitivity."

Later, after she had sat in the egg chair in her old room with Augusta and read aloud almost a whole chapter of *The Trumpet of the Swan* (after attempting to read a chapter of *Sideways Stories from Wayside School,* which had made Augusta laugh in an unbridled way that Pen feared would spell sleep-doom if it went on for long), and after lying down in the lower bunk with her and singing "Baby Mine" in her best Mrs. Jumbo voice, twice through, and after, in blatant defiance of every "help your kid learn to sleep" book she had ever read, staying with Augusta until she fell asleep, Pen went downstairs and out into the backyard and found her father.

She was headed, a Tupperware container of vegetable peelings in hand, for what had been her enthusiastic father's but was now her reluctant mother's compost tumbler. Like Jamie, Pen's dad was a gadget man, irresistibly drawn to peanut butter stirrers, bagel guillotines, and ergonomic snow shovels as Jamie was drawn to tiny bike handlebar GPS devices and anything with a lowercase "i" at the beginning of its name. A month before he died, Ben Calloway had come home with a contraption that he regarded as being "as pretty as any yard sculpture out there" but which Margaret thought looked like a giant blueberry with legs. The neighborhood association (and Pen, although she never said so) agreed with Margaret, so that the composter sat in the very back of the backyard, near the brick wall of the detached garage, half-hidden much of the year by a Texas beauty queen ball gown of a weeping cherry.

When Pen was about ten feet from the garage, the motion-activated floodlight attached to its roof came stunningly to life, and so as not to be blinded, Pen turned her face away and found herself staring at a creature of such astounding gorgeousness that it took her a few seconds to register what it was. It burned against the green grass, an impossible long, lean pour of orange (*neon paprika*, Pen thought afterward), with a glorious puffed tail as long as its whole body and nearly as big around. A fox.

Pen felt an instinctive jolt of fear, but then the fox turned its head and looked at her, and something happened that she found difficult to describe later, even to herself. It was nothing so simple as looking at the fox and seeing her father. The fox was altogether foxlike and other: precise black nose; extravagantly upright ears; white fur spilling down its front like milk. What regarded Pen through tilted amber eyes was not threatening or alarmed or even particularly wild, but it was surely not Ben Calloway.

However, as Pen and the fox stood with their eyes locked, Pen was suddenly rushed and lifted by the certainty that her father was with her, and this certainty came not only from the fox itself but from the ground under her shoes and the pulse of crickets and the stones of the garage wall behind her. The feeling effervesced delicately as fireflies in the rosebushes and slid with a startling *whomp* off the canted back roof of the house and into the yard, like sheets of snow. The air was alive with it. Not with it, with *him* just as Pen knew him: funniness, geekiness, bravery, a reserve that wasn't so much shyness as a deep sense of privacy, genuine interest, kindness like an ocean. She felt him prickle along her forearms and down the back of her neck. She felt him everywhere.

Joy was a high-pitched vertiginous singing in Pen's ears.

"Daddy," she said and dropped the Tupperware container.

The fox turned and walked into the trees, dragging its tail with the offhand elegance of a duchess dragging her train, and it was over. Pen stood, shaking, in the empty yard. When she could think enough to move, she leaned over, picked up the container, and stepped away from the garage so that the light snapped off and darkness dropped like a sheet over a birdcage. She sat down on the back steps, container on knees, fists on container, forehead on fists, and breathed.

"Are you sick or praying or just weird?"

Pen gave a convulsive start that sent the Tupperware container flying off her knees onto the walkway in front of her and looked up, a little wild-eyed. It was Jamie, back from his evening run.

"Whoa!" said Jamie, pulling the earbuds out of his ears. "Little jumpy tonight?"

"Stop sneaking up on people." Pen picked up the container and threw it at him. It bounced off his knee.

"Ow," said Jamie amiably. He sat down on the grass and pulled his T-shirt by the collar up over his face, wiping off sweat.

"That grass is probably full of mosquitoes," said Pen. "I hope they bite you to bits."

"Nah. They don't like me. You're the one they like."

This was true, and as soon as he said it, Pen felt one bite her upper arm. She slapped at it.

"See?" said Jamie. "What are you doing out here, anyway?"

Experiencing miracles, Pen thought about saying. Instead, she shrugged and said, "Taking the stuff from dinner to the composter."

"Really? Because it looked like you were sitting on the steps in the fetal position."

"Fetuses don't sit," said Pen. "Fetuses recline." She scratched her arm and eyed Jamie. "Can I ask you something?"

"Nope."

"Since Dad died, do you ever feel like he's—?"

"What?"

"I don't know. Around?"

"You mean like a ghost? Tapping on a tabletop, Ouija board kind of thing?"

Pen recognized Jamie's sarcasm for the wariness it was. Being at this house did it maybe, she thought, put Jamie on guard against sudden plunges into grief. She considered giving up and going inside, but who was there to talk to about this, apart from Jamie? Since her mother's return Pen hadn't really brought up her father much. As suspicious as she was of her mother's new, vibrant cheerfulness, she was afraid of its ending.

"Sort of. I mean do you ever feel him with you. With you, with you. Not just like a memory."

To Pen's surprise, Jamie didn't immediately shoot back a mocking response, but leaned back on his hands and appeared to be considering her question. It was something Jamie could do, take you seriously when you least expected it.

"His voice wakes me up sometimes," said Jamie at last. "It doesn't seem like a dream. And I can call it back up for hours, his voice saying whatever he said to me. Sometimes, after it happens, I can hear him all day."

Oh, Jamie. Pen felt, with a rush of urgency, that she needed to have another child and soon. For Augusta. There were some things with which no one should be left alone. Pen wished she could see Jamie's face, but it was too dark.

"What does he say?"

"Nothing profound," said Jamie, with a slight shift away from seriousness that Pen knew was deliberate. "No insights from the great beyond or anything. Mostly stuff he said to me when I was a kid."

"Tell me."

"Well, like once he said, 'Come look at this, Jamie: Fibonacci's sequence in an artichoke.'"

Pen smiled.

"He was here just now," she said tentatively. "It felt like that, anyway. There was a fox in the backyard, and it looked me right in the eye, and then Dad was just—here."

"Dad was a fox?"

"No, and I didn't see him or hear him, but I felt him all around me. That's never happened before."

She waited for him to make fun of her, but, after a moment, he just said, "Nice," and then, "Lucky."

She could see him nodding. With a groan, he got creakily to his feet. *You're a good brother,* thought Pen, *a good man.* She knew better than to tell him this.

"Looking a little stiff there, Grandpa," she said, standing up, too. A mosquito bit her other arm. "Ow," she said and slapped at it.

"Good mosquito," said Jamie.

PEN'S MOTHER HAD FOUND SOMEONE.

Owing to the fact that Pen was engrossed in watching *Foyle's War,* a show she adored, and to her mother's odd use of the word *found* (and also, possibly, to what Amelie would say was Pen's subconscious refusal to believe that her mother had found someone), Pen didn't immediately understand what she meant.

"Was someone lost?" asked Pen sleepily, rubbing her eyes. What had happened in the yard (she hadn't yet figured out what to call it— encounter? experience? visitation?) had sapped her.

"God, Pen," said Jamie.

When she looked over at him, he was glaring at her. Before Pen could make sense of the glare or of Jamie's tone of voice, he jumped up from the sofa where he and Pen sat, strode across the room, and switched off the television. It happened fast. The bright and everlasting calm of Foyle's blue eyes vanished.

"Hey!" said Pen.

Jamie threw open eyes and hands in a gesture that meant, *What the hell is wrong with you?*

Pen looked at Margaret, whose face was bright pink.

"Found someone?" said Pen, slowly. "You mean you—met someone?" Suddenly cold, she wrapped her arms around herself.

Margaret moved a stray curl off her cheek and tucked it behind her ear, a gesture that meant she was nervous.

"Yes," she said. "And no."

"What's that supposed to mean?" said Pen, mounting alarm turning her voice into a kind of bleat.

"Knock it off," said Jamie to Pen. He looked at his mother. "Hey, Mom. You want to sit down or something?"

"I will if you will," said Margaret with a bittersweet smile.

Jamie sat back on the couch, leaving his mother the armchair. She sighed and sat down. Margaret was short compared to Pen and Jamie, whose ranginess came from their father, but she had been a gymnast when she was younger and was still broad-shouldered and full of energy, even when she wasn't moving. But sitting there, on the edge of the chair, her hands clasped, her face full of worry, she looked fragile.

"This won't be easy for you two," she said, but she was looking at Pen. "And the last thing I want to do is hurt you."

"We just want you to be happy," said Jamie.

Under other circumstances, the grave sweetness in his voice would have touched Pen and made her proud of him, but she felt stony and resentful. *Oh, sure, the old good kid/bad kid routine,* she thought acidly. Her stomach was full of knots.

"Thank you," said Margaret quietly. "I didn't think I could ever be happy again. I didn't go looking for it, certainly."

"You didn't?" said Pen. "Why did you leave, then? You must have been looking for something." She would have liked for this to have come out sounding less childish and bitter, but she *felt* childish and bitter.

"What did you think it was?" Her mother sounded genuinely curious.

Pen gave a cranky shrug. "Tibet. India. Rome. What do people usually go looking for in those places? Spiritual enlightenment, I guess. The meaning of life. God."

Pen's mother's laugh was harsh. "God? I was looking for *God*?"

"Why is that funny?"

"Because I was furious with God, when I could bring myself to believe in him at all, which wasn't very often."

"Why did you choose those places, then?" asked Jamie. "You never told us."

His casual tone impressed Pen because the fact was that she hadn't just left out this one detail but had told them almost nothing. She had given them three days' notice that she was leaving (to be fair, this was no more notice than she'd given herself), had a friend drive her to the airport, and had only made phone calls—brief, static-riddled—every few weeks, facts that had hurt and baffled even Jamie.

Their mother's blue eyes were bright with tears. "Right before your dad died, we were talking all the time about traveling."

"And those were places you talked about going?" asked Pen.

Margaret wiped her eyes. "No. We talked about Wales, Brittany, bicycling through Scotland. The Galapagos, Brazil, Paris, Tanzania, Barcelona. So many more places. Your father and his maps."

Something softened in Pen, then, and she met her mother's eyes. *My father and his maps,* she thought. Her mother smiled at her. "What I did was choose places we had *never* talked about going. It wasn't easy."

"But why go at all?" said Pen.

"I was broken," said her mother. Her voice was steady and tender. "I had lost my capacity for anything but sadness. I don't mean to scare you, but I left because I thought I would die, and there was only one tiny part of me that cared, and every day that part got a little bit smaller."

"But it won in the end, right?" said Jamie quickly, still the kid who would read the end of the book before the beginning to make sure it ended happily. "The part that cared."

"It was like in *Horton Hears a Who!*," Margaret said with a sparkle in her eye. "Remember? The tiny part shouted at the top of its lungs for me to do something to save myself, and I almost didn't hear it, but then I did."

"It told you to leave?" asked Pen, narrowing her eyes.

"My girl," said Margaret, "for whom leaving is always the worst thing."

"Leaving *people*," said Pen impatiently.

"It told me to do *something*," said Margaret. "Leaving was the only thing I could think of. I had some money from your father's life insurance. To tell you the truth, I didn't think leaving was a very good idea, either, and I had almost no expectation that it would help, but I couldn't think of one other thing to do. Please try to understand."

The forlorn note in her mother's voice was like a fire blanket, putting out the anger that had begun to smolder inside Pen with one colossal whack. She looked at her mother and saw that since the conversation had started, some of the youthful, sun-streaked radiance she had been carrying in her face since she'd gotten home had faded, and, instantly, desperately, Pen wanted it back. She got off the couch to sit on the floor at Margaret's feet. She grabbed her hand, which was smaller than her own, and kissed it.

"I do understand," she said. "And, look, it did help: you came back happy."

Pen meant it. She did mean it, and she felt glad when she said it. Even so, when Jamie said teasingly, "All right, all right, cut the bonding crap and tell us about this international man of mystery," Pen couldn't help but give a sharp, internal flinch. As if her mother felt it, she rested her hand briefly, protectively on the top of Pen's head.

"I don't know quite where to start," she said, flustered.

"Then start with where," said Jamie.

"Bossy," said Pen. "As usual."

Margaret laughed a free, fluttering laugh. "In an airport in Mumbai. I was going to Vienna. He was going to Rome. Our flights were delayed and we got to talking, and I—I . . ." She broke off, blushing again. Margaret was a blusher, could go from zero to azalea pink in a matter of seconds. "I changed my flight."

"Mom!" said Pen, laughing. Pen was aware of sadness, out there and waiting, a big, foggy shape that would surely overtake her later. Just now, though, she let herself be carried by the current of her mother's happiness.

Jamie whistled. "Must've been some conversation."

"It was," said Margaret, "although it wasn't as though I had anything particular to do in Austria. I was just going to go. But, yes, it was a good conversation. And we actually did end up going to Vienna later." The "we" stung, but Pen closed her eyes and breathed past it.

"So you spent a lot of time together," said Pen.

"Yes. He travels for his job. I went with him."

Pen's impulse was to ask her mother how serious this relationship was, but she weighed the possible consequences of the question—her mother having a meaningless European fling versus her mother in love with a stranger—and held back.

"Okay," began Jamie. Pen saw the trace of uneasiness under his smile. *Oh, just don't,* she thought, but, of course, he did. "How serious is this?"

"Oh. Well." The way Margaret drew herself up and pressed the back of her hand against her mouth, she could have been holding tears or joy or both in check. Pen couldn't tell, but she knew it wasn't the gesture of a woman who was about to say, "Not serious at all." In a moment, she moved her hand away and said decisively, "Very."

"You're in love?" asked Pen. She found that she couldn't not ask it.

Margaret nodded, looking so demure with her lashes lowered and her hands folded in her lap that for a crazy moment, Pen imagined that the whole scene was ripped from a Jane Austen novel, with Pen and Jamie as the stern parents and their mother as the rose-fresh, marriageable daughter. *Gloves and a fan,* thought Pen, *that's all she needs.*

After a few seconds, Jamie sent these slightly hysterical fancies flying out the window by saying, "You know what? Dad would be glad."

Pen remembered the fox in the backyard, her father's kindness reverberating around her, not passive, but powerful, a force, and she had to admit that Jamie was right.

"I have never thought otherwise for one second," said Margaret.

"Not that what Dad would think should've stopped you." This was such a startling statement that, for a second, Pen wondered who could have made it, declared it, really, in that clear, certain voice.

"Holy cluck," said Jamie, staring at Pen. "Did you really just say that?"

"Yes," said Pen, trying to sound sure of herself. "Why? Do you think I'm wrong?"

"Oh, I think you're right," said Jamie. "I'm just not sure if you're you."

"What do you mean?"

"You know," said Jamie. "*You*. The never letting go of stuff. Ever. The insane loyalty."

At the mention of loyalty, Pen felt a little doubt inch in. "You think I'm being disloyal?"

"Of course, you're not being disloyal," said her mother.

"Jamie?" persisted Pen.

Jamie's face tensed, reflecting what was rare for him: an inner struggle. Pen thought he was on the verge of just agreeing with Margaret, but then he said, "I think you're being loyal to *Mom,* which is the way it should be because Dad's dead and Mom's alive. The living win, automatically. Especially if the living is Mom."

It hurt him to say this, Pen could tell, and she understood because she felt the same way: that just acknowledging that Dad was dead, relegating him to that state, lumping him in, however sorrowfully, with other dead people, constituted a kind of betrayal all by itself. Which made her blithe pronouncement that it didn't matter what her father would think about her mother's loving another man even more puzzling.

She considered Jamie's idea, that the living win, automatically. It wasn't exactly what she had been thinking when she'd said what she'd said, but it was such an elegantly simple statement, so translucent and true, while what she had been thinking had been so scattered and unformed (although nonetheless urgent)—more an impulse than a thought—and also so potentially embarrassing to piece together and articulate in the presence of Jamie that Pen just nodded and said, "Right."

WHEN PEN CALLED WILL LATER THAT NIGHT, WHEN SHE GOT TO THIS part of the story, she added, "I said 'right' because Jamie was right, but that's not really what I'd been thinking." It came out in a rush, unplanned. Pen closed her eyes. *Blurter,* she thought with exasperation. *Spiller.*

"Oh," said Will. "So what were you thinking?"

"Will you promise not to make fun of me?"

"Can't do it," said Will.

Pen sighed.

"How about if I promise not to make fun of you *immediately.*"

"Fine," said Pen. It was more than she would've gotten from Jamie. And because she felt suddenly overcome by shyness, she launched into a little conversation with herself inside of her head:

You want to say this thing, she said to herself.

Obviously. The question is why.

You have no idea why, but you want to say it. You need to hear yourself say it out loud.

But why now? And why to Will?

Because you just figured it out, and now is when you want to, and if you want to, why not to Will? He's as good at listening to the things you say as anyone, isn't he?

"Pen?" It was Will. "You still with me?"

"Yes," said Pen decisively.

From where she was sitting on the guest-room bed, she could see a ladybug creeping up the white lampshade on the dresser, and she remembered a story Amelie had told her about ladybugs infesting her aunt's house, how it became like something out of a horror movie, ladybugs everywhere, a scourge of tiny, lacquered bodies, a plague of cuteness. According to Amelie, they bit. Pen thought about telling this story to Will, along with Amelie's interesting assertion that *"anything in huge numbers becomes horrific,"* but she realized it was no time to dither. *Just say what you have to say as clearly as possible,* she instructed herself. *How hard is that?*

"What it comes down to is that I just don't see it as a choice. I mean, not really," she said.

"You don't?"

"Well, of course, technically, it's a choice. Free will and all that crap. Cartesian, right? Free will? Like the plane, I guess. René. It's a name a man can only pull off if he's French. But just because you get to choose doesn't mean there isn't one right choice. Right?"

"Descartes thought the pineal gland was the seat of the soul," said Will.

"That's disgusting."

"It's not what you think."

"Of course, there are situations in which it's the wrong choice," Pen went on, "for the same reason that anything is the wrong choice: you hurt people, you break promises. Although I suppose that not everyone would agree with that."

"Maybe not."

"But if you're not hurting anyone, then I think you have no choice but to, well, honor it."

"Honor? What do you mean honor?"

"Acknowledge it. Follow it. Chase it. Hold on to it. Whatever."

There was a silence on the other end of the line, during which Pen watched the ladybug fly, a black blur, from the lampshade to the curtain of the window next to the bed.

Will said, "All right, I give up."

"What?"

"I'm not getting it. Your pronoun reference."

"What are you talking about?"

"The 'it.' I need a real noun. The right choice, the thing you follow, hold on to, et cetera."

"Love," said Pen impatiently. "What else would I be talking about?" Another silence.

Finally, Will said, "So you're saying, 'Love wins, automatically.' "

"No. Well, maybe. Except that makes it sound easy when it's not. Or not most of the time. It's stringent. Exacting," said Pen. "I think love is an imperative. It obligates you."

"You think that because your mother fell in love with this man, she should be with him, even if your father would not have approved."

Pen recoiled from this, leaning back against the pillow propped against the headboard, but she said, "Yes. Even if it's hard. My mother. This man. Anyone. And I'm not just talking about being in love. I mean any kind of love. You don't mess around. You don't walk away. You can't."

"Can't. Can't is hard-core."

"It's what we're here for," explained Pen. "It's what we're *for*."

Pen realized that her face was burning, that the phone was pressed so hard between her ear and shoulder that she would probably have bruises, and that she was clenching the quilt that lay spread over the bed underneath her until her tendons popped out. Deliberately, she relaxed, released the quilt, cradled the phone in her hand, but as the silence between her and Will stretched on, she began to get anxious, fidgety.

"I think this is the good kind of ladybug," she said. "It's a true red. Like a Red Delicious apple. Or lipstick. Porsche-red. I'm pretty sure the infesting kind are more orange. And anyway, it's summer."

"Pen."

"They only go inside in groups in the cold weather. What's the word for that?"

"Hibernation?"

"Overwintering."

"You thought I would make fun of you?"

"Jamie would. Amelie would. Maybe even my mom would. They'd call me a romantic."

Will laughed. " 'Love is an imperative'? Not exactly hearts and roses stuff. You make it sound like joining the army."

"I guess."

"And, hey, look at that," said Will. "I was right."

"About what?"

"About what your mom had to tell you. Remember when I was on my way to see Sam and I was talking to you?"

"On your Bluetooth phone," said Pen quickly, "with both hands on the wheel."

"Even if that's not what she went looking for, it's what she brought back and gave you."

"What?" Then she said quietly, "Oh, I know. I remember."

"What?"

"The meaning of life." Pen looked up and caught her reflection in the full-length mirror on the back of the guest-room door. She was smiling. Not even the sight of her face, lit up and smiling into an empty room, made her stop smiling. Pen thought back to the conversation she had had with herself a few minutes earlier, when she'd said that if she had something to say, she might as well tell Will. As if she'd picked him at random. As if she could have told anyone else.

Time to tell the rest.

"You'd think that I would've gotten to enjoy it for a while," she said. "Knowing the meaning of life. You know, rest on my laurels."

"What happened?"

"It got put to the test. My meaning of life! Challenged! Tested! Can you believe that? After, what? Thirty seconds? How unfair is that?"

"What happened?" said Will again, and Pen knew that he wasn't fooled by her joking tone, as he should not have been. Even now, nothing about what had happened next in her conversation with Jamie and her mother struck her as funny.

She told him, then, how Jamie had said, "Do we get to meet him?" and how something in her mother's face after he asked it made Pen remember herself asking, "You met someone?" and her mother saying, "Yes. And no."

Before her mother could answer Jamie's question, Pen jumped in with, "What did you mean before: 'Yes. And no'? What did you mean when you said you 'found' someone? Why 'found'?"

Pen's mother smiled at Pen, the lines of her face holding affection and worry and something that looked like pleading. "You know why, don't you?" she said.

Pen was still sitting on the floor and she shifted, now, slightly away from her mother. "Why, but not who," she said bluntly.

Jamie looked from his mother to Pen and back, confused. "Did I miss something?"

"I was seventeen when I met your dad," said their mother. "It was my gift, my blessing to love him and no one else for forty years. If I had my way, that would have gone on forever."

"You don't even have to say those things, Mom," said Jamie, surprised.

"I want you to understand." She was looking at Pen.

"Okay," said Pen. She knew it wasn't enough, that the moment demanded more from her, but she felt so physically tense with waiting, her rib cage tightening and tightening, that it was hard to breathe. The name hovered around them. The air in the room was thick with it. She just needed it said.

"Who is he? Someone from high school? Someone you grew up with?" Pen asked, and she marveled at this for a moment, the possibility that someone you knew forty, fifty years ago could circle back into your life and make you fall in love with him.

Pen's mother slumped a little at this. She shook her head.

"Could you please just tell us?" said Pen.

"Mark Venverloh."

Pen stared at her mother. She opened her mouth, but no sound came out.

"Mr. V?" said Jamie in a choked voice. "You're in love with Mr. V?"

It seemed impossible, but of course, it wasn't. Pen didn't know why it hadn't occurred to her: that the man wasn't someone from her mother's distant past, that he was someone they all—even their father, their father *especially*—had known.

"Mr. Venverloh," said Pen, who had never called him "Mark" and was only vaguely aware that it was his name at all. Saying the name out loud failed to make her mother's loving him any more plausible.

To Will, Pen said, "Mr. *Ven*verloh. Can you believe that?"

"I can't if you say I can't," he said. "But I don't think I know who that is."

Pen considered this and realized it was true. Her dad hadn't started working for Mr. Venverloh until after Will and Cat had left. Unexpectedly, this realization filled Pen with sorrow, and for once in what seemed like forever, she wasn't sad on her own behalf. Cat and Will had had their reasons for leaving, but whatever they were (Pen still didn't understand them, only believed—still, eternally—that whatever they were, they weren't good enough), they had nothing to do with Ben Calloway, who had loved them unreservedly, just as they had loved him. And they had lost each other all the same. Incidental loss. Collateral damage. But permanent. Will and Cat had missed out on the last four years of Ben's life. Ben had spent the last four years of his life missing them. It was enough to break your heart.

"He loved you," said Pen. "He missed you." She hoped there was no reproach in her voice. She didn't feel reproachful, only sad.

Will didn't say, "Mr. Venverloh loved me?" He said, "I know. I wish I could see him again."

"You know my dad was an environmental engineer for the city for years, mainly in the water department, and he liked it a lot. It suited him: part environmentalist, part science geek. Then Mr. Venverloh started riding bikes with my dad's group about five years ago. He's rich, crazy rich actually, owns a big estate nearby."

"One of the baronets?" asked Will.

It was something she, Will, and Cat had always joked about, how little Wilmington, Delaware, birthplace of more than one gigantic corporation, was like something out of the nineteenth century or earlier, with a true landed gentry. "This place is more Middlemarchian than Middlemarch!" Cat had quipped.

"Yes," said Pen, "but he has a real job, too. Some finance thing. Anyway, he and my dad got to be friends, and when Mr. V's land manager retired, he asked my dad if he wanted the job."

"Land manager. That sounds so—"

"Feudal. I know. But my dad loved it: sustainable agriculture, native plants, eliminating invasive species, and he got to be outside. You know he grew up on a farm."

"I did know that."

"So that's my mom's new boyfriend. Mr. Venverloh. Mark. *Mark.* God."

"I can think of a lot of reasons why that might be tough for you," said Will.

"It's tough for Jamie, too. He didn't let on to my mom, of course, but later he told me that he wished it were someone who hadn't been in Mom and Dad's life. Jamie said that even though he knew it didn't really, he *felt* like it cast a shadow backward, memory-wise. He couldn't really explain that, but I think I sort of know what he means."

"Do you feel like that, too?"

"Not now, I don't think. I don't know. I think I like it that it's someone who cared about my father, who knew him. My dad liked him, too. He's nice, Mr. Venverloh. The thing that hurts—well, a lot of it hurts, to tell you the truth—but the thing that hurts right now—and I know this is probably stupid—is that, on paper, he—" It hurt even to say it.

Will bought her some time by saying, "Does he own a jet? That's all I really want to know."

Pen laughed. "My dad was the best man in the world, you know that, right?"

"Yep."

"But Mark Venverloh looks, to the untrained eye, like a—step up. Possibly even a gigantic one."

"Richer," said Will.

"And better dressed, which let's face it, isn't saying that much. And handsomer."

"Your dad was a good-looking man."

"He was, but he was regular-guy-handsome, not movie-star-handsome. I feel sort of sorry for my dad, and feeling sorry for him makes me feel terrible."

"I bet your mom doesn't think he's a step up."

"Of course not!"

"And I bet your dad could've handed him *and* his ten-thousand-dollar bike their asses in a mass start hill climb."

Pen smiled. *This is why I love Will Wadsworth,* she thought.

"On a platter," she said.

LATER THAT NIGHT, CLOSER TO MORNING REALLY, THE DOUBLE whammy of the fox and Mr. V having electrified Pen's usual insomnia so that the inside of her head was beehive-crowded, bristling with light, and a million miles away from sleep, Pen went downstairs to get herself some tea and was surprised to see lamplight coming from the family room. She looked in and saw Margaret tucked into one corner of the big sofa reading a book, and the sight of her made Pen catch her breath. She looked purely alone but content, as complex and self-contained as a Russian doll, inward and inward and inward. As Pen watched, her mother smiled a private smile at something in her book, and Pen thought she had never seen anything so incandescently lovely as her mother alone, until her mother glanced up and saw her and shut her book and became lovelier still, open-faced and alive.

Pen thought, *You are like me. You like your little pockets of solitude, but you're not made for being alone for long.* There were people who could live on their own and be happy, and then there were people like Pen and Margaret who needed the falling together, the daily work of giving and taking and talk and touch.

Even so, love? Commitment? Again? How much easier to just settle into a life of family and friends, of dating even, of traveling and reading and being at peace. She felt happy for her mother, but she felt scared for her, too.

"Come here, baby," said Margaret, and Pen sat down next to her and rested her head against her shoulder.

"I'm happy for you, Mom," said Pen. "I really am."

"I'm glad," said her mother. Then she added, "Mark wants us all to come to dinner at his house. He wants to know you and Jamie and Augusta, and for us to know his boys. He has three sons."

Agree, Pen told herself, *just suck it up and say yes.* But she pictured them, sitting around an enormous table, a chandelier sparkling overhead, casting its coins of light over them all, turning them into a family, and she could only think, *Oh, Daddy.*

She kissed her mother's shoulder. "Is it all right if I say 'Yes, but not quite yet'?"

"Can you say 'Soon'?"

Pen had to smile. Of all the things her mother was, she had never been a pushover.

"Yes," said Pen, closing her eyes. What else was there to do? "Soon."

CHAPTER FOURTEEN

THREE DAYS AFTER HIS LUNCH WITH SAM, WILL STILL HADN'T told Jason what he'd found out about Cat's whereabouts. He knew that he should. He knew that even Pen, who had, during more than one phone conversation, argued vehemently (and cantankerously) against telling him, knew that they should, even if she hated to admit it.

"We told him we would try to help him," Will had reminded her the night before. "We wouldn't have even known to call Sam if it weren't for him."

"We didn't *promise* that we'd tell him what she said," Pen had countered.

"The promise was implied."

"That's not how promises work," scoffed Pen. "They aren't implied. They're overt. There's a universally accepted method to them."

"And what's that?"

"You say, 'I promise.' Especially if the person asks you to promise, which Jason distinctly did not do."

"Maybe he didn't think he had to."

Will had waited, then, for Pen's innate sense of justice to come to the fore or, if not come to the fore, at least to start nagging her like an itch.

"It *might* be different if we actually knew where she was now," she had said finally, grudgingly. "We only know where she used to be: the name of a hotel, where she's probably not even staying anymore. We don't even know if she's still in the same city. When it comes right down to it, we don't even know if she's in the same country!"

"She told Sam fifty-nine days, which leaves her with about twenty-five to go."

"She's *allowed* to stay for fifty-nine. That doesn't mean she will. She's *Cat*, remember? She's whimsical. She might have changed her mind last week and headed to Australia to see a wallaby. She might be sailing around the world this minute on some guy's yacht."

"Don't you get the idea that this trip was serious for Cat, though? Not some wacky adventure?"

"Maybe. Yes." She made an exasperated cat-hiss noise. "Okay, but even so, she might not be where she was when she called Sam. It's a big country, right? I mean, not relative to this country, but relative to Cat, it's big. I googled it, and it has, like, seven thousand islands. She could be on any one of them."

"I googled it, too, and I'm pretty sure that a lot of those islands don't have people on them. They're basically just bumps in the ocean."

"Really? I didn't know that. What else did you find out?"

"Well, some people say that the number of islands changes, depending on the tide, although that could just be a myth."

"Hmm, I bet it's not a myth. What do you think?"

"I think you should hold it right there, Penelope."

"What?"

"You think I don't recognize a diversionary tactic when I hear one?"

"From what would I be trying to divert you?" asked Pen innocently.

"The fact that none of this really matters. The exact number of islands in the archipelago that is the Philippines doesn't matter."

"Maybe not to you, Yankee," interjected Pen, "but the Filipinos might care."

Will ignored this. "How whimsical or not whimsical Cat is doesn't matter, either. Neither does her exact location at this very second. We still have to tell Jason what we found out. It's only fair."

"What about what's fair to Cat?" snapped Pen. "She doesn't want him to find her. She doesn't like him."

Will had smiled. "Come on, she might *like* him."

In the turbulent silence that followed, Will had imagined that he could hear Pen struggling with her conscience the way he was struggling with his.

"Look, I know she doesn't want him to find her," Will had said finally. "Why do you think I didn't e-mail him right away?"

"No, you're right, you're right," said Pen grimly. "We'd be jerks not to tell him."

"We'll be jerks either way, when you think about it."

"Don't think about it," growled Pen. "Just send Jason the damn e-mail."

"At least if we tell him, we can be jerks taking the high road."

"Great," said Pen. "Very comforting."

However, that conversation had taken place the night before, and it was now almost noon, and Will was still treating his e-mail account as though it were radioactive. Not only his e-mail, but his entire computer, which meant that he was trying to write his novel (about a boy whose scientifically-doctored-with doghouse transports him into the mind of a twelve-year-old giant named Lulu) at the kitchen table with pencil on a pad of paper. This never worked for him before, and it didn't work now. He liked to see the words on the screen. He liked to delete words and have them be gone, extinguished, annihilated. When his pencil lead broke, he threw it across the room, aiming for the trash can, which was closed because it was always closed. It had a stainless-steel, spring-loaded lid, the kind that stays closed. Still, when the pencil bounced off the lid, fell on the floor, and rolled under the refrigerator, Will took it personally.

"Jesus. Fine," he hollered at the trash can.

There were seven messages from Jason in his inbox, their subject headings comprising a tidy narrative of Jason's frustration. The oldest one said "Hey man!"; the second newest, "WTF?" The most recent was the longest: "Once a dick . . . ," which struck Will as mildly funny by ordinary standards and mind-blowingly clever when you considered the source. He thought about opening that one to see if Jason had actually finished the sentence, but he deleted the e-mails without reading them and started a new one. At about the middle of the second paragraph, though, it hit him: Jason might never write back. What was there to stop him from grabbing the information and running? Will had to admit that, after waiting so long to fill Jason in, he probably deserved this, but it wouldn't work. He needed to witness Jason's reaction. He needed to know what he would do.

Will scratched his head, hissed "Shit," shot a malevolent look at his cell phone, and typed, I have some info about Cat. Give me a call, followed by his telephone number, which he stabbed in hard with one resentful but fatalistic finger. After he clicked Send, he got up to get himself a cup of coffee (actually, he jumped out of his chair like it was on fire), but the phone rang before he had even opened the cabinet where he kept the mugs. Cursing under his breath the whole way, he walked back to his office where he'd left his phone.

"Hello," he said and braced himself for a loud tirade, but Jason was surprisingly calm, even—disturbingly—friendly.

"Yo, dude," he said. "I thought you'd never call."

Will decided not to point out that Jason was the one who had called. He said, "Sorry, man. It's been a little crazy around here."

"No worries, no worries. Just glad you're not dead."

"Thanks."

"So . . ." Jason stretched the word out like gum and pronounced it "Sue."

Right there? That? Will told Jason inside his head. *That's why nobody likes you.*

Aloud, he said, "I saw Sam at that barbecue joint in Tennessee."

In an act of blatant procrastination, Will considered how he never used the word *joint* to mean "place," except when it came to barbecue. Or maybe gin. No, not gin. Who was he kidding? Burger? He looked out the window at the birdbath, which was empty, causing him to question, in a perfunctory manner, the hygiene of the local bird population. Jason breathed, audibly, into Will's ear. It still wasn't too late to hang up. Change his cell-phone number. Move.

"Hel-lo?" said Jason. "You saw Sam. What'd you think?"

"I liked her. I mean, she's a little, uh, theatrical, but she seems solid underneath all that. And funny. I can see how she and Cat would end up friends."

"Yeah, she hates me," said Jason casually and with a notable lack of malice. "Thinks I'm a pathetic idiot."

"Oh," said Will. "That's . . . too bad."

"Naw. No skin off my back. No problemo, you know what I mean?"

Neyeeeewww problemo. Will shut his eyes, overcome by nostalgia for the days when a phone receiver was substantial enough to effectively bang against your forehead.

"Anyway, we talked about Cat," he said.

"Take it with a grain of salt, that's all I have to say," said Jason. "Whatever Sam says requires a major grain. Not just grain, *grains.* Many a grain."

"Right," said Will and was busy making a mental record of "many a grain" for when he told Pen about the conversation later when it hit him that, in addition to mocking what Jason had just said, he could use it. "And that's exactly how I took everything she told me. She might know what she's talking about, but then again, she might not."

"She might be full of shit."

"Definitely possible." Will sent out a silent apology in what he estimated was Sam's direction.

"So, uh, what'd she say, anyway?"

Jason did not sound like a person who had begged abjectly for help in the moonlight or one who had shot off six e-mails in three days, jam-packed with escalating anger. His voice was nonchalant, bordering on breezy. It said, *Dude, since you happen to have gotten me on the phone and I have a sec, dude, you might as well, you know, tell me what you know:* the voice of an obsessed and desperate man desperately trying not to sound obsessed and desperate, maybe not the most pathetic sound Will had ever heard, but one of them. How could he tell this sad man where Cat was? How could he not? Will picked up a pen and wrote "Shit" three times on the back of an old envelope.

"She's in the Philippines," he said. "Cebu."

"Motherfucker!" The word slammed into Will's ear, more bark than yell, so venomous, so searingly vicious that Will jerked the phone away from his ear. Jason hung up.

For a dazed second, Will stared at the phone in his hand. Then, hurriedly, he began to flip through the possibilities. Was the expletive free-floating, an expression of frustration in general? At how far away Cat was? Will didn't think so. It sounded personal, directed, like that venom that snakes in Africa spit straight into the eyes of their enemies. But who was Jason spitting at? Will? Sam? Probably not, although Jason wasn't above being a "shoot the messenger" kind of guy. Cat's dad? Will remembered the conversation in the reunion tent, how Jason had said that Dr. Ocampo wasn't exactly a person who showed up for Cat. Pretty clearly, Jason hadn't been crazy about the man, had probably not liked him enough to be thrilled about Cat's going on a pilgrimage to his homeland, but he hadn't seemed to hate him, either, and that "motherfucker" had been all about hate.

Could he have meant it for Cat? Not Cat. Jason loved Cat. But who else was there?

"Shit," said Will again, this being a shit kind of morning, and he scrambled to call Jason back, dropping his phone in the process. As he picked it up, it rang.

"Sorry to hang up like that," said Jason with a hollow chuckle. "Guess what you said threw me off a little."

"Yeah, I guess so," said Will evenly.

"I just pictured my little Cat, all by herself in the tropics. And the traveling? The multiple plane changes and what have you? Forget about it. Cat gets lost on the way to the grocery store. I had this vision of her wandering around the Hong Kong airport like a lost kitten."

Will didn't buy it. Jason's "motherfucker" had been instantaneous, like a gun going off, with no time for him to picture much of anything. Anyway, the Cat Will had known had had as good a sense of direction as anyone. Pen was the one who got lost. Then there was Jason's tone of cheerful concern, which would've been creepily inappropriate, even if it hadn't been so obviously fake. Will knew a thing or two about rage, and he felt the rage seething under everything Jason said. Even as Jason fussed like a mother hen about his "little Cat," Will would've bet that he had just thrown something heavy across the room and watched it smash.

"It makes sense that you'd be worried," said Will neutrally.

"Plus, I thought she was over her dad. His death, I mean. Come to find out she's zipped off ten thousand miles to do what? Mourn at his birthplace? Get to know him? Discover her island roots?"

"Yeah, I guess she's not over it."

"Ya think?"

He's going to go after her, Will thought.

"What are you thinking?" he asked. "That you'll go look for her?"

There was a silence and then, with the good-guy tone turned up a notch, Jason said, "Nah. My wife wants some alone time. I can respect that. I'll just hang out, hold down the fort, as they say, until she's back."

It was exactly the right answer, and Will knew a lie when he heard it.

As soon as he hung up with Jason, Will called Pen.

"Hey, Will," she said. Her voice, hushed and quick, told him she was with someone, probably a client. "Call you back in an hour or two?"

"Sure," said Will. "Wait. Actually—" But Pen had already hung up.

Maybe it was better, Will thought, take a couple of hours, settle down, get some perspective. He could admit that, on its face, his reaction to Jason's reaction had been a little extreme, since all Jason had done was get mad, something Will had done plenty of times himself. A guy who had flat out attacked a whole slew of inanimate objects—and several animate ones—with his bare hands, whose temper had landed him (if not, by the grace of God, other people) in the emergency room more than once, should be able to cut Jason and his single outburst some slack. After all, the poor sap had just found out that his wife hadn't just walked out on him but had pretty much walked as far away from him as it was possible to go—and all without leaving so much as a note.

Still, Will couldn't shake the foreboding. It was as if that single, knee-jerk "motherfucker" had punched a hole in Jason's dopey-guy demeanor, and, through it, Will had glimpsed an interior that was uglier than he would've believed. Will's mother was always telling her kids to "listen to your inner voice," and Will's inner voice was practically shouting that Jason's heading off to find Cat with all of that ugliness churning just under his surface was a very bad idea.

Will looked at the clock: 12:45, about seven hours later than Will's preferred time for a run, especially in the summer, but he had a couple of hours to kill and there was no way he was getting any work done before he talked to Pen. He changed, zipped his cell phone into his pocket, gulped down a glass of water, and headed out. It was so muggy that his shirt was sticking to him before he'd gone a mile, but running had been a good idea. His worry unclenched, stretched and flattened like the hot ribbon of street, resolved itself into a flow of thought that was steady and more or less coherent.

Even though he knew it was the middle of the night where she was, he imagined Cat under the same high white sun that burned above him, making her way through a busy city. He had no trouble bringing Cat to life inside his head, he never did, her black hair and thin wrists and sandals, glamour-girl sunglasses covering half her face, a flowered dress. And even though he couldn't picture the city with any accuracy, had never even seen photos of it that he could remember, he sketched it in around her anyway: fruit stands, traffic, palm trees splayed against the sky, a goat tethered to a stake in somebody's yard. Cat was there, a girl on a mission, walking where her father had walked, looking for what?

Will came to the kind of hill that makes it impossible to think or do anything but force your body up it, but on the way down, inside his head but so clearly that he was tempted to look around to see who said it, Will heard a question being asked in a familiar voice: "How did your dad get to be your dad?" It took him only a second to realize the voice was Cat's.

The last day of sophomore year. Finals behind them and everywhere spring hitting its peak and toppling over into summer: humidity, old oak pollen balled like tumbleweed in the gutters, every kid on campus newly tan and as abundantly, showily happy as the trees were dense and green, except for Will who sprawled sullenly on the grass, the cast on his newly broken hand pissing him off with its whiteness, Cat next to him with her sunglasses on top of her head (she thought it was hideously rude to have a conversation with someone while wearing sunglasses) and her pink skirt tucked primly around her crossed legs.

His parents had swung through town the day before on their way to meet a bunch of other rich couples—friends of his father's—for a golf weekend at a southern mountain resort (the fact that his mother hated the resort, the couples, and golf evidently having no bearing on his father's decision to take her along or on her decision to go). Things went about the way they usually went between Will and his dad, except that this time, after the obligatory post-paternal-visit fistfight with something immovable and hard (in this instance, his car windshield), in addition to the usual breakage (spirit, dignity), Will had thrown in a few cracked metacarpals for good measure.

Cat and Will were drinking iced coffee and waiting for Pen, who was meeting with her nineteenth-century British lit professor to discuss a paper she'd written on images of women's hair in Victorian poetry, despite a horrified Cat's having pointed out to her that nobody, nobody, nobody in all of human history had ever made an appointment with a professor to discuss a paper she'd gotten an "A" on, especially on the last day of school before summer break. "He will be flabbergasted. Flummoxed," warned Cat. "He will almost definitely keel over and die right there in front of you." But Pen had gone anyway.

"How did your dad get to be your dad?" asked Cat suddenly. "Have you ever thought about that?"

"You mean how did he meet my mom?"

"No," said Cat impatiently. "I mean how did he get to be *your dad* in all his awful your dadness? How did he become the man he is?"

Will found that the question irritated him. "Does it matter?"

"Don't get testy with me, mister," said Cat, giving him what Pen called her "mad Persian cat face." "I'm not talking about an excuse because nothing gets him off the hook for being the rat bastard he is. I'm talking about an explanation. Where did he *come* from? How does someone *get* so mean?"

Oddly, Will had never really considered this question before, his father's meanness having always been one of the immutable bedrock facts of Will's life. With his family, Randall Wadsworth was either distant and indifferent or the coldest kind of cruel, and although there had always been moments when Will watched his father talk to other men and change into someone else, joking, backslapping, affable, the real man was still right there—Will could sense him—invulnerable and dangerous and enjoying his power.

"I don't think he *became*," said Will. "I think he was just born."

"Come on," said Cat. "He was a kid, right? He went to school. Drank chocolate milk. Wore pajamas."

"I don't think so."

"Even Hitler was, like, seven once, Will. There had to be a moment."

"A moment when he turned into a fucking, soulless monster?"

"No. A last chance that someone missed. A moment when he could've been saved."

The only evidence Will had that his father had ever been a child was a handful of memories of a visit to his father's mother's house. Will must have been about three or four, and he had stayed, alone, at his grandmother's for what had seemed like a long time, but was probably only a couple of days. The memories were more like fragments, tiny sensory scraps: a turquoise-and-white metal porch glider; the sound of the television going all day long in another room; crescent rolls that popped out of a cardboard cylinder and tasted like heaven; the silky edge of a scratchy blue acrylic blanket; and smoking, a lot of smoking: a cigarette perpetually balanced on the edge of a shell-shaped ashtray on the kitchen counter; his grandmother snapping beans on the porch with a cigarette somehow stuck between her fingers, sending the smell of smoke across the front yard to where Will dug in the mulch with a plastic trowel.

"She wasn't mean? Abusive?" asked Cat, when Will told her about this.

"Not to me."

"You liked her."

"I think so. Her house seemed—safe. Pretty soon after I went there, she died. I don't know how I know that, though. I can't remember going to a funeral or anything."

"What did your dad say about her, over the years?"

"Nothing."

"Nothing?"

"My dad isn't the storytelling type," said Will sardonically. "He doesn't spin yarns. When he does talk about growing up, it's like he's reading his résumé. The boarding school he got himself into in ninth grade, his whole thousand-mile-long record of achievement after that. His mother is nowhere, totally erased."

"What about his father?"

"No idea. Maybe he never had one."

"Maybe it was Satan," suggested Cat.

Will grinned. "That would explain things, wouldn't it?"

Cat's eyes grew serious. She touched her fingertips to Will's, the ones that emerged from the plaster of the cast. "Maybe you'll want to dig a little deeper one day," she said. "If you knew more about him, maybe he'd lose his power to hurt you." Even though Will didn't believe this, he heard the kindness in Cat's voice and felt the force of her friendship, her allegiance to him, and he thought, not for the first time, *You are my family, more than the rat bastard has ever been, you and Pen.*

Now, thinking about Cat searching for her father, Will realized that he had never searched for his, had never taken her advice. He'd had his mother back for years and had never asked her anything about who his father used to be, never even asked about the trip to his grandmother's house. Why had Will gone by himself? Where was that house, apart from inside Will's head, turning itself into myth? It was crazy: to visit a place once and spend your whole life missing it.

I might ask, he thought. *One of these days. Maybe after I come back from finding Cat.*

Which is when he knew that he would go. *Yeah, right.* He could almost hear Cat saying this. *Like there was ever any doubt.*

WHEN PEN CALLED, BEFORE WILL COULD SAY ANYTHING BESIDES, "Hey, Pen," she said, "Okay. I have a story and a question. In that order."

"Is it a long story?"

"What kind of question is that?"

"I have something to say, too, believe it or not," said Will, "which is why I called you."

"I called you."

"You're calling me back."

"Of course. You're right. Your story should take precedence, absolutely," said Pen. "But can I go first, anyway?"

"Okay."

"It is kind of a long story if you want to know the truth."

"Forget it, then."

"I just saw Patrick."

"Is that unusual?"

"I mean I sat across from him at a table at a café and had a conversation with him."

"Which is—unusual?"

"Highly. Ours is an Augusta-drop-off-pick-up relationship. That's about it."

"I see," said Will. "Hey, if I met Patrick, would I like him or would I want to slug him?"

"Yes," answered Pen emphatically, adding, "But I thought you were over the slugging thing."

"Over slugging, not over wanting to. I probably wouldn't want to slug Patrick, though, because I'm guessing Augusta wouldn't like it."

"Augusta," began Pen, and for a second, she sounded on the verge of tears.

"You okay?"

"Possibly. I'm not sure. I just left him about five minutes ago, so I haven't had much of a chance to sort things through."

Will was trying to stay neutral and open-minded, but he had to admit that he liked the sound of "left him."

"You want to talk about this later?" he asked.

"God, no. How will I ever sort it out if I don't talk to you about it?"

She'd been on her way to drop Augusta at day camp and run a couple of errands afterward when he called. When she looked at her cell phone and saw that it was Patrick, she let Augusta answer it.

"I am going to camp right now," Augusta announced in her cell-phone voice, painstakingly enunciated and somewhere between a shout and a bellow. "We are having baking today, but I won't be able to bring you any cookies because, generally, we eat them." *Generally* was her new word. "Iloveyoubyebye," she yelled and handed the phone to Pen.

"Let me call you back after I drop her off," said Pen. She cherished these mornings, walking through the city with Augusta, talking, feeling the delicate, stalwart bones of her daughter's hand inside hers, new light washing the sidewalks.

"Do you have any time today?" asked Patrick.

"For what?"

"To talk."

"You mean in person?"

Patrick gave a halfhearted laugh. "Why do you make it sound like such an outlandish idea? We talk in person all the time."

Pen ignored this. "I need to do a few things, stop in at the office, but I should be home around eleven. Okay if I call you then? I have to pick up a writer at five thirty, but I have some time in the middle of the day."

"Well, yeah. Don't want to put you out or anything." Pen could hear the pout in his voice. "Just call when you get home."

But when she got home, before she even got to her apartment building door, there he was, sitting at a sidewalk table at the café across the street, waving her over.

Will lay on his back on his front porch listening to this because Pen had called just as he was rounding the corner onto his street after his run, and he was too sweaty to lie anywhere else. The porch wasn't particularly comfortable, but Will was too engrossed in Pen's story to mind the porch boards grinding into his spine and shoulder blades. When a fly started buzzing around his head, he swatted at it absently, without fully registering what it was or even that it was there. In the old days, he and Pen had never really gotten the hang of phone conversations; they were together too much. Now, though, they had it down to a kind of art. With not a lot of effort, Will could close his eyes while Pen talked and have what she said come alive inside his head. At times, her descriptions were so vivid, it was almost like watching a movie, so that, in short flashes, he could even picture Patrick, whose face he'd never seen.

Patrick was sitting at the café table nursing a beer, a bad sign, Pen knew, since Patrick never drank in the daytime; it made him too sleepy.

After the waiter brought Pen an iced tea, she said, "All right, Patrick, what's up?"

"What's up is that Tanya got a job offer from this big-time health advocacy group, and she wants to move us to Boston."

Move us, thought Pen, as though Patrick and Lila were pieces of furniture, such a maddeningly apt choice of words that Pen didn't know whether to laugh or scream. She did neither, just sat there for a long, silent moment, feeling like a pond that Patrick had just dropped a rock into.

"What about," she said at last, in a flinty voice, "your daughter? Your other daughter, I mean." She felt the same jolt of anger she'd felt so many other times because she knew that the "other daughter" was who Augusta was and would always be, to Tanya but also—and there was no getting around this, no matter how much he loved her—to Patrick.

She waited for Patrick to defend Tanya, but he surprised her by getting angry instead, angry at Tanya. Patrick almost never got angry at anyone. Pen could never decide if it was due to inner peace or laziness or a kind of emotional ADD, but, whatever the reason, it just wasn't in his nature to get mad.

"It was almost comical," Pen told Will. "Like when one of those adorable, shaggy lap-doggy dogs with chocolate-drop eyes thinks he hears a burglar and starts barking? That was Patrick, except blue-eyed. An enraged Lhasa apso. A choleric cocker spaniel."

"Wow," said Will. "Could you do me a favor and never describe me? To anyone?"

"You want to know the sad thing, though? I liked it. I loved it. I found it so deeply satisfying—Patrick getting all husky-voiced and fiery-eyed and righteous on Augusta's behalf—that it was just this side of a turn-on. How pathetic is that? To be on the verge of throwing myself at a man because he shows, after so many years, a little fire, a little *fight* for his own child?"

"I'd say that if anyone in that scenario is pathetic, it isn't you." Right after Will said this, he wished he hadn't. Even though he was just being honest, bad-mouthing Patrick behind his back made Will feel like a sneak. "Still," he added, "good for him, right? What did he say?"

He had said, "Like I would just pick up and go hours and hours away from Augusta. Like, 'Oh sure, honey, I'll just rip up roots and trail after you like some stupid puppy.' Not to mention Lila, who has a life here, too, in case Tanya hasn't noticed."

Pen had been too thrown off by his anger to do more than nod.

"And here's the thing: this place has been asking her if she wants to work for them for years. She's had what amounts to a standing offer, and she's never said yes. But we've been squabbling lately. Not full-blown fighting, but pretty damn close."

Even though Pen knew Patrick was waiting for her to ask what they'd been fighting about, she didn't. She found herself to be peculiarly incurious, even slightly repelled at the idea of seeing into the cracks in Patrick and Tanya's marriage.

But Patrick went on as though she had asked. "Tanya's just so controlling. Case in point, she cut down my *tree*, if you can believe that." Pen wondered if he was speaking metaphorically, a thought that might have made her smile if her mind wasn't becoming increasingly bogged down with sadness at the thought that Augusta might lose her monthly weekends with her daddy.

"Your tree?" she asked.

"My Japanese maple. My buddy Vince was making some landscaping changes and came over one night with this tree he'd dug up from his yard. Prettiest, most petite thing you've ever seen, almost bonsai-sized, with leaves that turn the best color red in the world every fall. I planted it in our side yard and it was thriving, for God's sake, getting kind of shapely and lacy." He squeezed his face between his hands, like the guy in Munch's *Scream*. "It was a living organism! I put a little stone Buddha under it, you know, so that the tree was sheltering him, and one day, the tree was gone. She took a damn contract out on it and had it disappeared. And not gently, either. Turns out she had some ass-hole chop it down and dig up the roots. Obliterated it from the face of the earth. Because it didn't work with her *colors,* her fucking *plan.* It was too Asian. Can you imagine that? I found the Buddha just sitting there, exposed. A Buddha! It wasn't some damn garden gnome, you know? It was a religious icon."

Pen understood why this would upset Patrick, but it annoyed her anyway, the way he described it like it was the worst thing to ever happen, genocide and desecration rolled into one.

"Well, but it *was* decorative, right?" she couldn't resist saying. "I mean, you're not actually a Buddhist."

"Still," said Patrick, "a little respect. A Buddha's a Buddha. And a tree is a tree no matter how small."

Pen had to smile. Patrick, channeling Dr. Seuss. "You are the Lorax," she wanted to tell Patrick. "You speak for the trees."

Instead she hid her smile inside her glass of tea and then said, "I'm not sure I get it, though, how the, uh, squabbling has anything to do with her wanting to move you to Boston. I'm pretty sure people still bicker in Boston."

He looked surprised, as though he'd thought she would get it right away. "She's worried I'll go back to you."

Pen stared at him.

To Will, Pen fumed, "'Go back to you.' As if that's all it would take, his showing up on my doorstep."

Will couldn't think of anything to say to this that wouldn't qualify as maligning Patrick, so he didn't say anything.

"But then I thought about it," Pen went on. "How my life might look to Tanya or even to Patrick. I've dated here and there, but, honestly, not much, never anything serious. Nobody Augusta's even met, so Patrick probably doesn't even know, which means that unless Tanya's been having me followed—which is not outside the realm of possibility—she doesn't know, either. And, God, the idea of their thinking that I'm just waiting around for Patrick makes me insane."

On an impulse, Will asked, "What have you been waiting for?"

When Pen answered, her voice was solemn and sheepish. "How did you know? Because you're right. I am waiting. It hits me now and then: that I've been saving myself for something. A sign. A person." She gave an embarrassed laugh. "Mostly, though, I'm just busy."

When Patrick told her that Tanya was afraid he would go back to Pen, Pen said, "Well, that's a ridiculous thing to worry about."

All Patrick's bravado disappeared, and hurt filled his eyes. "*We* never bickered, did we?" he said.

Oh for God's sake, thought Pen.

So quickly that it made Pen's head spin, Patrick began to map out a plan: he would divorce Tanya at last, hire a cutthroat lawyer, file for custody of Lila; the four of them would be together, a family.

"It's what I should have done from the beginning," he told Pen.

There were so many things Pen could have said. "She would die before she let you have Lila." "You're mad at Tanya, but you won't stay that way." "You can't come back every time you get restless or angry or bored with your marriage." "It would be too confusing for Augusta, especially when you leave again, which you surely will."

"But I didn't say any of those things," Pen told Will.

"What did you say?"

"I said the thing that rendered all those other points, as true as they are, moot. I said it for the first time ever."

"What was that?" asked Will.

She had wanted to be gentle. Whether Patrick deserved it or not, Pen found herself wanting to be as kind as possible at that critical moment. She leaned across the table and took, not Patrick's hands, but his forearms, his skin warm inside her hands, and turned him directly toward her. She looked for a sign in his eyes that he knew what she was going to say, but they were hope-blue and as unsuspecting as a baby's.

"You can't come back to me, Patrick, because I don't love you," she said. "I care about you and I will thank you in my heart forever for helping me to have Augusta in my life, but I'm not in love with you. More importantly, I don't want you back, not at all, not anymore."

Will said, "Sounds rough."

"It was. Looking him in the eye and getting the words out was, but once it was over, I felt so good, like I'd been rained on by the cleanest rain in the world." She laughed. "A fat lot of good it did, though."

"Meaning what?"

"He didn't buy it."

"Uh-oh."

"He said, 'I know you're protecting yourself and Augusta. I get it. Why wouldn't you? You think I'll come back and then leave again, but I won't. I promise you that. We'll be so happy.'"

She had let go of his arms and told him, "I don't think you really believe that. I know I don't."

"You're hurt," Patrick said. "You're angry."

"No," said Pen. "I'm really not."

To Will, she said, "He said, 'Don't answer right now,' like I hadn't just answered."

"Did he tell you to sleep on it?"

"He did. He used those exact words. And then, *then* he started talking about how Tanya's moving them to Boston would really not have been that bad."

"Really?"

"Yes. He said, 'I'm glad I'm not going, *so* glad, even though Boston really probably wouldn't have been as bad as it sounds. It's not that far, when you think about it, and I could've kept my job, since I do most of it online and over the phone anyway. We have a lot of long-distance clients, in fact, maybe as much as forty percent of our business. I'd have to come here for meetings and such now and then, but that's it. But then there's Augusta, and, sure, when she gets a little older she could ride the train up by herself, under the care of the conductor or what-ever, or even fly, and I'd get down whenever I could, not monthly, but fairly often. But it wouldn't be the same. We'd have solid, quality time, I know that, but I'd miss things, concerts and school plays and . . .' He went on like that for quite some time."

"'Under the care of the conductor.' Sounds like he'd considered the idea pretty . . . thoroughly," said Will. Because this made Will feel weasly again, he added, "Which sort of makes sense."

"Oh, yeah," said Pen dryly. "It all makes a lot of sense. How some-one who had never had any intention of moving would consider every angle, in detail, except the one in which he stands up to Tanya and tells her that moving is a terrible idea for everyone."

"You think he'll go," said Will.

"Unless Tanya changes her mind or unless she's just been yanking his chain, which she might be doing, since she's an inveterate chain yanker, he'll go. Even if I said I'd take him back, he would go eventu-ally."

"Patrick being in Boston will be hard on Augusta, won't it?"

"It won't crush her, I don't think," said Pen. "But it will certainly hurt, and I could strangle him for that."

Will was quiet for a few seconds before he asked, "Are you sure about not taking him back?"

"Yes," said Pen. Will knew that he didn't have to tell Pen that she didn't sound sure. She groaned. "I'm sure for *me*," she said. "But how will I tell Augusta that her father wanted to come live with us and be a family and I said no?"

Will sat up stiffly, making the porch boards creak. He looked out across the grass, which needed cutting, and ran a hand through his hair.

"I don't know," he said.

"I don't, either."

"Patrick's still waiting for your answer?"

"I'll say what I said before," said Pen in a tired voice. "What else can I do? But I'm not looking forward to it, I'll tell you that. Which brings me to the question."

"What question?"

"I told you I had a story and a question, remember?"

"Now I do."

"Would it be terrible," Pen began carefully, "would it be a huge betrayal of Cat, if I had an ulterior motive—a very secondary ulterior motive, but still—for wanting to go find her?"

"I can't imagine you ever betraying Cat, hugely or unhugely," said Will. "But I don't really get what you mean."

"I wanted to go anyway, before all this. At this point, it's not even so much that I'm worried about her, although I am. We've just got this momentum, you know? I have never stopped missing her all these years, and, since the reunion, I've thought about her all the time. I want to see her more than ever. You know that, right?"

"Sure, I do."

"But when I found out how far away she went, well, the distance made going to find her seem crazy, even impossible. What is it? Ten thousand miles? More?"

"Something like that."

"But now, with my mom waiting for me to call and tell her I'm ready to get together with her new boyfriend and his entire family, which she wants to be my family, too, and with Patrick waiting for me to call and give his happily-ever-after plan the thumbs-up, which I can never do, no matter how happy it would make my child, well—"

"Ten thousand miles is suddenly sounding less crazy?" said Will.

"It's suddenly sounding kind of great."

"You're asking if it would be somehow unethical or insulting to Cat if you had more reason than just wanting to find Cat for going to find Cat?"

"Exactly."

For what wasn't the first time, Will imagined being with Pen in a faraway place, listening to her talk, her one and only voice shining against a backdrop of new sounds.

"I think Cat would think it was okay. I think she would call you a goody-goody for even worrying about it and then would remind you that wanting to get away from your problems for a while is only human."

He honestly believed this. What Cat would think of his own ulterior motive (he shut his eyes and caught a glimpse of Pen, face, hair, shoulders, the brown and gold gloss of her under a tropical sun) was another matter altogether.

"You want to go?" asked Will.

"I'll go if you go."

"I'll go if Augusta goes."

Pen laughed. "I promise to pay you back for the tickets, although it might take a while."

"I know where to find you," said Will.

As soon as they hung up, Will realized he had forgotten to tell her about his conversation with Jason and called her back. After he finished, she made him say "motherfucker" in the precise tone of voice in which Jason had said it. It took Will a few tries, but when he got it right, she let out a single, flat, doomed "Holy cluck" then went silent.

"Pen?"

"Thinking."

"Sorry."

Will watched a full thirty seconds tick by on his running watch before Pen said, "The question is: do we tell him or not tell him?"

"That we're going?"

"Yes."

"He'll go either way," said Will. "No way he's not going."

"Exactly!"

"You think he'll try to beat us there?"

"Do you think we should try to beat him there?" she countered.

Will's first impulse was to say yes, but after he considered the question for a few more seconds, he said, slowly, "We could, but just because we get there first doesn't mean we'll find her first. Or find her at all."

"You're right, it doesn't. And you know what I hate to think about?"

"I can make a pretty fair guess, but go ahead."

"Jason running like a madman around that island or all those seven thousand islands, give or take, by himself, looking for her and maybe finding her."

"If he's there, we want him where we can see him."

"Yes!"

"So—we should invite him to come with us?" asked Will, and even as he asked it, even though Jason fit nowhere in his being-alone-with-Pen-and-Augusta-in-a-distant-land ulterior motive, he understood that this was the only thing to do.

"I hate to say it, I *loathe* to say it," said Pen, "but yes."

Will hung up, called Jason, had a two-minute conversation, and called Pen back.

"He said no."

"No? Oh, no! Did he give a reason?"

"He said, 'Thanks but no thanks, bro. Like I said, I'm just keeping the home fires burning until Cat finds peace in her heart and makes her return.'"

"He couldn't possibly have said that. Nobody talks like that."

"Direct quote."

"Why didn't he jump at the chance to keep an eye on *us*?"

"If I had to guess, I would say that it hasn't occurred to him, yet, that keeping an eye on us makes more sense than trying to beat us to Cebu. He's not the kind of guy things occur to at the same pace that they occur to other people."

"You think he'll figure it out?"

"He might." Will hesitated for a few nervous seconds before he added, "I told him I'd e-mail him our itinerary, just in case he changes his mind. I don't know if that was the right thing to do, but I had to think fast."

Pen didn't answer immediately, and Will tried to gauge from the quality of her silence whether she was just thinking over what he'd said or was wordlessly cursing him for being a clucking moron and ruining all their plans.

"I could still not send it," he said, "and just say I forgot or something."

"No," said Pen decisively. "It's definitely worth a try. Either he'll figure out that it's a good idea to go with us and he'll call to say he's changed his mind or meet us at the hotel in Cebu or something. Or he won't figure it out and will try to get there first, which, as you said, doesn't mean that he'll find her first and really doesn't make anything worse than it would've been if we didn't tell him our plans."

"Okay," said Will, relieved. "I'll call the travel agent right now."

"Will?" said Pen.

"Yeah?"

"Thanks."

"For what?"

"For being—" she began and paused. The tremor in her voice was so slight that it might have been something or nothing, a phone reception glitch. Will couldn't be sure. "Back," she finished and added, "For everything."

"Anytime," Will told her.

In the end, it seemed easiest to meet in New York. Actually, technically speaking, coming from two different cities as they were, it wasn't very easy at all, not nearly as easy as meeting in Philadelphia and either driving to New York together or hopping on the same New York–bound plane at the Philly airport. But when they were discussing the various travel options, as soon as Pen proposed, shyly, meeting at JFK, they had both jumped on the idea. Will wasn't sure why. Maybe because Philadelphia was still the city in which they'd lost each other. Maybe because they didn't want to risk slowing down their momentum, which was sweeping them forward, into the future. They agreed to meet at the gate.

As soon as Will's plane landed at JFK, before they had even turned off the seat-belt sign or taxied to the gate, Will called Pen.

She answered the phone like this: "Where are you?"

"Just landed," said Will. "Where are you?"

"Still at home. We have almost three hours until our flight. Sorry you have to wait."

"No big deal," said Will. "Listen, I have to tell you something."

"You sound so serious. What's wrong?"

"I'm not a natural with kids. I just wanted to warn you. I'm not bad, but I'm definitely not a natural."

"Okay, forget it. The trip's off."

"Seriously, a lot of people expect me to be some kind of Pied Piper because of the books."

"Have you ever actually read that story? Because the Pied Piper might have played nice music, but, underneath the colorful outfit, he was a big fat brainwashing kidnapper."

"I didn't know that. I never wear colorful outfits."

"Of course, you don't," said Pen. "Look, thanks for the heads-up but don't sweat it. Augusta probably won't even notice. As long as you do whatever she says, she'll be happy as a clam."

"Good."

"See you soon."

As it turned out, he saw them before they saw him. In fact, he saw them coming from so far away that he was surprised he could recognize them. The distance obscured Pen's features, reduced her to nothing but shape and motion. She could have been anyone, any tall woman holding the hand of any little girl, but of course, she couldn't have been anyone but Pen, whom Will would've known anywhere: her uprightness, the delineation of her shoulders, the way her head didn't seem to just rest on her neck like most heads on most necks, but to balance, like an egg on the tip of a finger, if such a thing were possible. Mostly, he recognized the way she moved. Will shut his book and—registering every detail as though he might get quizzed on them later—watched Pen and Augusta come into focus.

Pen wore a white T-shirt, flat red shoes, and the kind of black pants that Audrey Hepburn wore in *Funny Face;* she had a gray sweater tied around her waist. She pulled a wheeled carry-on bag. Her hair was tucked behind her ears. Without making a big, self-conscious production out of it, she made walking through the airport look like ballet. Augusta's hair was bobbed and floating and almost black with a tiny, jeweled tiara riding on top. She wore a bright pink flowered party dress and neon yellow flip-flops decked out with floppy cloth flowers. She had a shiny red purse hooked over one forearm and bore a pink back-pack on her back that was big enough for her to climb inside.

When they were maybe thirty feet away, Will saw that the two of them were deep in conversation, Pen looking down, and Augusta looking up, so that even though they were close enough to see him, they didn't. It was a good thing, too, because Will found himself sud-denly choked up, which stunned him. He never cried, had just stopped one day when he was a kid (Ten years old? Eleven? Right around the time he'd started getting mad and hitting things) and had never started up again, but here he was with his eyes wet and his throat tightening at the sight of Pen with her daughter. He turned his face, ran his palms over his eyes; when he turned back, Pen looked up and saw him and smiled and became, like she always did, his old friend Pen, the clearest thing in the room.

Will walked up, hugged Pen, took her bag, and offered to take Augusta's, but Augusta wrinkled her nose, shrugged, and said, "I'm good."

"Thank you," prompted Pen.

"Thank you," said Augusta. She put one finger on his arm. "I know who you are."

Will crouched down so that he was eye to eye with her. "I'm Will."

"Will *Wads*worth," she corrected. "You knew my mom before I was born, and you write books."

"Yep."

"I can read." She narrowed her blue eyes at him. "*Books*. Signs. Anything." She raised both eyebrows. "Even bad words."

Will looked at Pen, who shrugged helplessly and said, "Graffiti."

Augusta tilted her head to the side and dimpled demurely, batting her long lashes. "It's a problem," she acknowledged and broke into a tinkling laugh.

Will stood up and stared at Pen. "Whoa," he said. "You know who she reminds me of?"

Pen laughed. "Of course, I do. It's freaky, isn't it?"

"How did that happen?"

Pen put up her hands in bafflement. "Cluck if I know. She just came that way."

"What way?" demanded Augusta.

Will looked back down at Augusta and grinned. "The cutest-little-fairy-princess-person-in-the-whole-world way."

After considering this for a moment, Augusta shrugged lightly and said, "I like that way," and after another eloquent glance from her mother, she added, "Thank you."

"OKAY," SAID PEN, SPREADING THEIR PRINTED ITINERARY OUT ON the table in front of them, "New York to Vancouver, don't get off the plane, then Vancouver to Hong Kong, get off the plane for a couple of hours, then Hong Kong to Cebu. Right?"

"Right," said Will.

Pen glanced quickly at Augusta, who was happily eating a pancake at the airport diner near their gate ("Breakfast for dinner is my favorite forever," she'd told Will) and said in a low voice, "That's a hell of a lot of plane time, isn't it?"

"Are you worried about Augusta?" asked Will.

"Oh, no," said Pen. "It's me. I have serious aviophobia."

"But birds are our friends, Pen."

"Ha ha. I never have actual external panic attacks, probably because of my acute fear of embarrassing myself, but I have multiple internal ones, even on short flights."

"What happens?"

"Sweating, sobbing, disorientation, vomiting, loud outbursts of profanity."

"All internal?"

"Yes."

"Ever try to wrestle open the exit door in midflight and jump out?"

"No, but I will now, thanks."

"What if I keep feeding you drinks, one drink every hour for twenty hours?"

"Could help," said Pen, smiling.

"Or you could just—" Will stopped. "Holy shit."

Augusta dropped her fork and covered her ears, laughing.

"Sorry," said Will.

"Nothing she hasn't heard before. She lives with Jamie, remember? And me. What's wrong?"

"I've read that itinerary. I had it stuck to my bulletin board for four days and I never put it together."

"You never put the itinerary together?" asked Pen. "What's that mean?"

"No. What Jason said, remember? How he hated the idea of his little Cat wandering around the Hong Kong airport. At the time, I thought he'd just chosen Hong Kong at random."

"This is Jason we're talking about. In all likelihood, he's lived his entire life without ever knowing Hong Kong existed." Her eyes widened as she absorbed what Will had said. "He knew. About the flight. Because he *checked* on the flight."

"Maybe. I mean, there have to be a lot of other routes. And he'd be flying out of Cincinnati, right? Or Kentucky. Wherever. Those flights might not go through Hong Kong at all. It's weird, though."

"And this was the conversation where you told him where Cat was, so if he already knew about changing planes in Hong Kong, then he already knew where she was."

"Or guessed."

"Why would he guess that? Cat flying to the Philippines on a pilgrimage to get to know her dead father better is a plausible idea to me," said Pen. "But I wouldn't have thought of it all on my own. And Jason, well, do you think he's capable of that kind of prescience?"

"No, but we don't really know him that well, and we can't forget that he's been married to Cat for six years."

"I wish I could. I tried."

"So did Cat, apparently," said Will. He and Pen exchanged wan smiles: it was a thing they preferred not to think about, that Jason knew Cat, had known her for all the years when the only thing Will and Pen could do was remember her, possibly—okay, definitely—knew things about her that they didn't.

"Whether he knew she was going or guessed, if he researched flights, it means we were right: he's planning to look for her," said Will.

"Maybe he already is," said Pen.

Will didn't know why he picked that moment to look over Pen's shoulder. They had chosen a table at the diner's outer edge, on a kind of pseudo-outdoor patio, so that they would be sure to hear the announcement that it was time to board. Walking toward them from the direction of their gate, across the flow of foot traffic, was Jason. He wore a cheesy grin, brown deck shoes, and a T-shirt emblazoned with an American flag and the words MADE IN AMERICA. *Like there could be any doubt,* thought Will. He shook his head. Whatever Jason's limitations, the guy had a flair for the dramatic.

"It's a good thing," murmured Will. "Just remember that. It's what we hoped would happen."

"What?" asked Pen, knitting her brows.

She turned to see what Will saw.

"Oh, for the love of God," she said, and Augusta put down her fork and covered her ears.

CHAPTER FIFTEEN

WHENEVER SHE FLEW, WHAT SENT PEN OVER THE EDGE AND flailing into an aviophobic abyss was an image so sharp and three-dimensional that next to it, every fact or figure she had ever learned (percentage of crashes with survivors; chances of dying in a plane crash; percentage by which your chances decrease by sitting in the tail versus the nose, blah blah blah) paled to insignificance. The image slunk around Pen's consciousness, waiting for its moment to dart in and terrify her. On every flight, she spent all of her energy warding it off in any way she could, reading, meditation, overeager conversation with co-travelers, prayer (if fervent and elaborate bargaining counted as prayer), but, every second, feeling, with her whole being, the image's dark presence, muscular and chillingly patient, like a lion waiting for the baby elephant to break from the herd. Then she would be in the middle of some ordinary, full-cruising-altitude task— reading or watching a terrible, nearly inaudible movie or ripping open a package of Twizzlers, her traditional flight comfort food—and there it was to stop her heart: the plane so flimsy and small, an aluminum gnat, surrounded on every side by an immense, freezing, howling, loveless nothingness.

And as she looked around at her fellow travelers, all of whom she believed were also secretly teetering on the brittle edge of being stark, screeching mad, her one (meager, selfish) comfort was that when the combination of hope and hubris holding them up gave out and they fell, at least they would all fall together.

She had thought it would be worse with Augusta there. It was not Augusta's first flight. Last year, she had gone to Paris with Tanya, Patrick, and Lila, a trip she did not (to Tanya's disgust) appreciate and from which she'd returned cranky, exhausted, with a marked lack of interest in French culture or art but crazy for pastries. However, this was the first flight she and Pen had taken together, and Pen braced herself, figuring that her usual fear would be multiplied by maternal love into something so gargantuan that its very weight might be enough to tug the plane into the ocean. Yet, here she sat, miles in the air, Augusta beside her, book closed, Twizzlers package intact, perfectly at peace.

She remembered, suddenly, the last time she had felt this way on an airplane. She was nine and flying to Florida with her family. It was not her first time on a plane, but at some point between her previous flight (to the Grand Canyon, where she'd fallen headlong into beauty without a single fear of falling into the giant hole) and this one, she had crossed from an age of unconsidered trust into one of watchfulness and worry (an age that turned out not to be an age at all, but a permanent condition, although, thankfully, she didn't know this at the time). When the plane hit a spot of turbulence, Pen found herself on the brink of hysteria, a state she recognized from her third-grade science class when her friend Minnie saw a photo of a real human brain and had to breathe into a paper bag.

It was Jamie who saved her. He sat across the aisle from her, his gray eyes starry in his tanned face (the result of not only baseball and swim team, Pen knew, but assiduous, if clandestine, sunbathing in the backyard), his shoulders inside his T-shirt already on their way to broad, chock-full of lanky grace, and way more beautiful than any thirteen-year-old kid had a right to be, a fact that was anything but lost on him. He flirted with the flight attendants. He swanned down the narrow aisle without touching the seats on either side, giving dropped-chin, faux-shy smiles to anyone female who looked at him. He listened to his Walkman in a way that made you want to hand over your entire savings account to be him for five minutes. Even as she loathed him, Pen understood, with resentment and relief, that no one that full of himself, that purely obnoxious could ever die in a plane crash.

Now, Augusta's presence worked a similar kind of magic on Pen. The child sat there and every single thing about her—the pitch of her voice and the points of her elbows, her messy hair, her radiant curiosity and knobby wrists—made crashing impossible. No harm could come to someone so wholly loved, so at home in her own skin—it was a simple fact.

Pen was so relaxed that, despite her considerable physical discomfort (the curse of the long-legged), her concern (unforeseen and exasperating but undeniable) about being slack-faced and open-mouthed in front of Will, and her long history of never, ever sleeping on planes (how would she get into the recommended crash position, let alone locate her inflatable life vest if she were anything but wide awake?), she spent most of the first leg of the trip asleep. As soon as Augusta, after one chattering, enchanted, snack-filled hour, curled up like a cat with her head in Pen's lap and drifted serenely off, as though she did it all the time, as though she were not the child who, at age five, still failed to sleep through the night in her own bed four nights out of seven, Pen turned to Will, said, "I think I'll just close my eyes for a minute or two," and was out for hours. When she woke up, briefly, the plane was fuzzily dark, pleasantly warm, and, for a moment, Pen was flooded with a sense of connection and comradeship: all those sleeping strangers together, shoulder to shoulder, suspended in a hush that was almost holy.

She woke up for good just before they began their descent into Vancouver. She didn't know what time it was, but inside the plane, it was still night. Sleepily, she turned her face and found the only scrap of illumination in the soft dark: Will, awake and writing in a notebook, head bent, face still, hand moving, entirely contained within his own small, private cone of light. The sight made her ache. *How can I not touch you?* she thought hopelessly, and then she was doing it, her fingers on his wrist. He didn't jump or even look at her, just stopped writing. Neither one of them moved, nothing moved, and the whole thing lasted three or four seconds at most, but when Pen took her hand away and started to breathe again, her chest hurt, as though she had been holding her breath for a very long time.

Will didn't give her a puzzled or dismayed or astonished glance. He didn't pull her face to his and kiss her, even though she could almost feel his hand on her cheek. He smiled his usual smile and said, "Hey," in a quieter version of his usual voice, as though nothing had changed. Pen was amazed. How could nothing have changed when everything had changed?

Maybe because you've touched him a thousand times before? she reminded herself derisively.

But this was a major touch, clearly a turning point touch, she shot back.

Not clear to Will. To Will it was a business-as-usual touch, a "Pen and Will being friends like always" touch. Except on an airplane.

On an airplane in the dark. *How could he not know it was different? How could he know it was different?*

If he wanted it to be different, she said to herself in the smallest of voices, *if he were waiting for it, he would know.*

She felt a lot of things at once, not primarily—not by a long shot—but including relief. No matter how you sliced it, Pen and Will being friends like always was a beautiful thing. In validation of this insight, the lights inside the plane came on, and it was morning.

Pen said to Will, "These seats are insane. I feel like a Poppin' Fresh roll, unpopped."

"I feel like a jack-in-the-box," said Will, "in the box."

"Jesus freaking Christ, please tell me this isn't the way you guys always talk." Jason, standing in the aisle next to Will: loud, looming, big as a barn, American flag T-shirt blazing. "Or I *might* have to change my mind about changing my seat, when the black dude in the sleep mask gets off at Vancouver."

As Will and Pen looked over at him, the black dude on the other side of Augusta lifted his sleep mask, took a long look at Jason, and told them, "Lucky you."

◆　◆　◆

A couple of hours into the flight from Vancouver to Hong Kong, an unlikely thing happened to Will, Pen, and Jason, more unlikely than the dissolution of Pen's aviophobia or the brief, half-asleep, flatly unacknowledged move she'd made on Will: they became a team.

When afterward Pen asked Will to give his best estimate as to where they were when this occurred, he guessed someplace over Russia, which wasn't what you'd call pinpoint-precise, not exactly a zeroing-in kind of guess, but even if it had been accurate, it wouldn't really have been accurate because while there was a single moment of clear-cut coalescence—Will's eyes meeting Pen's in agreement—the moment was more a culmination than a revelation. Their joining forces was a process that had begun back at the airport, not the second Jason had made his smirking appearance, but almost.

As Jason approached, Will had shot Pen a look that said, *Be as nice as you can,* so that by the time he stood by the table at a slightly backward-pitched angle, his hands in his shorts' pockets, thumbs sticking out, his head not so much nodding as bobbing like one of those red-and-white fishing things (later, Will would tell Pen they were called "bobbers") in a manner that made Pen want to grab a pancake off Augusta's plate and smack him with it, Will was standing to greet him, and Pen had turned her chair around enough to see him out of the corner of her eye.

"Well, look who's here," he'd said with a smile so sharky that Pen could tell it set even Will's knee-jerk good manners back on their heels because it took him almost a full five seconds to reach out to shake Jason's hand.

"We figured you'd show up," said Pen, with a cool, sidelong glance, and for a second or two, Jason's face collapsed into a look of injured disappointment that was downright toddler-like.

"Did *not,*" he said.

Listen to you, thought Pen, *you are straight out of the clucking sandbox.* It took her breath away a little, how Jason could, in the very same second, annoy the hell out of her and inspire a sympathy that was almost tender. Floundering in the face of these battling emotions, Pen took a prim sip of iced tea.

"Hey, man," said Will, "three heads are better than two, right?"

"I have a head," piped Augusta. "One head."

Before Augusta spoke, Jason hadn't noticed that she was there, and for a few seconds, he seemed confused. Then something happened so quickly that it would have seemed like a magic trick, if it hadn't been so obviously real: quite simply, before Pen's eyes, Jason became a different man. His shoulders relaxed, his chest unpuffed, all the defensiveness and wannabe thuggishness and petulance vanished.

"Really? Are you sure?" he said. "There's not maybe a teeny tiny one you've been hiding someplace?"

"No!" Augusta laughed. "And you know what else?"

"What?" asked Jason.

"Fifty stars and thirteen stripes." She said it like "firteen."

Jason looked up, down, all around, frantically searching. "Where?"

Augusta laughed again and pointed at his shirt. "Right there."

"Whoa," said Jason. "You are one wicked-fast counter."

"No, no, no," said Augusta, shaking her black-dandelion-fluff head. "No one counts that fast. Not even Mommy. Not even *Albert. Einstein.*" She pronounced "Albert" with three syllables: Alabert.

"Then how did you know?" asked Jason.

"I *learned*!" shrieked Augusta with joy. "From my teacher!"

"Learned? Come on. How could you have learned that already? You're only in—what? Fourth grade?"

More shrieking.

It had gone on like this, Jason becoming more starstruck, more unguarded, funnier, kinder, less and less of a horse's ass by the minute.

"Who is that guy?" Will had whispered to Pen, as the four of them lined up to board.

"If you didn't know him," Pen whispered to Will, "you might mistake him for someone who doesn't completely suck."

"Seeing him with her makes it kind of hard to hate him, doesn't it?"

"Don't go soft on me, Wadsworth," growled Pen, but it was Pen who was going soft. In her mind's filing cabinet, she maintained a list of things that she would've otherwise disdained but liked because they made Augusta happy, and she could feel Jason taking his place on it, muscling in with his big shoulders, until he was wedged into a spot well below hair glitter but several notches ahead of chicken fingers and stickers.

When Jason moved his seat in Vancouver, both he and Augusta were in hog heaven for hours. They played I-Spy. They watched the same cartoons and Disney movies on their individual seat-back screens, headphones on, commenting to each other on the action in voices booming enough to generate a flutter of smiling, gentle remonstrance from the ballerina-like Asian flight attendants. They colored in the coloring books Pen had purchased for the trip, Jason scrunching his large form into painful-looking positions in order to chase runaway crayons. They played seemingly endless rounds of Old Maid and tic-tac-toe, until Will offered to read to Augusta, and the four of them shifted seats, so that Will sat between Augusta and Pen and Pen sat next to Jason.

She recognized Will's offer as an act of mercy, one she herself would have appreciated, since her own tolerance for mindless and repetitive children's games topped out at around fifteen minutes, but which appeared to deflate Jason. Once Augusta was gone, he was visibly at loose ends, aimlessly channel surfing, flipping through the duty-free catalog, finally digging out a thick, daunting slab of a hardcover book, which Pen recognized with surprise as a recent, prizewinning presidential biography. When Jason said sarcastically, "Don't look so shocked. We graduated from the same college, remember? I do know how to read," Pen had the grace to be ashamed.

Still, ten minutes into the book, after a period of repeated head lolling and jerking awake, Jason was fast asleep. His left arm was inches from hers, his face maybe a foot away. She never got used to it, the forced intimacy of airplanes, and it took a while for her to look at Jason directly.

"Geez," she whispered to Will. "He looks so vulnerable, like an enormous baby chick."

"Don't do it," cautioned Will.

"Do what?"

"Put that little airplane pillow over his face. Augusta would be bummed." They both glanced down at Augusta, who was sleeping again, tucked under her blue blanket, her feet in Will's lap, and then looked back at Jason. "Plus, it might be too small. You might need something bigger."

"Seriously," whispered Pen, "it's weird to be this close to him."

"Better you than me, pal."

"Thanks a lot."

But she had to admit that Jason's face in repose held a kind of sweetness, smooth cheeks, dimpled chin, blond hair like a freshly mown lawn on top of his head. Seeing him like this, especially after seeing him with Augusta, it was slightly more possible to imagine why Cat married him. Maybe he had reservoirs of goodness under all that bluster. Maybe this face was his real face.

Maybe not, she told herself, sharply. He had lied and misled them multiple times; he had driven Cat away; he said "dude" frequently and without irony. Now was no time to get sappy.

Hours passed, who knew how many? Pen's inner clock had gone helter-skelter, befuddled by time zone switches, the plane's interior darkenings and illuminations, and the indeterminate meals, randomly served (she liked the fish congee, but was it dinner? breakfast? Pen had no idea). Time on the plane seemed to alternate between clotting to an immovable mass and thinning and dissipating, like air on a mountaintop. After that early gift of plane sleep, Pen couldn't even manage a catnap. She read; she watched several episodes of a crime show that made you desperate to be a forensic detective, if only for the sleek, glowing, is-it-a-lab-or-is-it-an-art-installation interiors and scuba-suit-tight pantsuits; she walked around and around the airplane like a panther in a cage; she ate every single thing the flight attendants put in front of her. Mostly, she talked to Will, talked and talked, like a thirsty person at a mountain spring, an enterprise that made time disappear altogether.

It was when she was giving up on her fourth nap attempt in an hour that it happened: Jason, still sleeping, shifted his knees and caused a minor earthquake in his seat, dumping an open bag of caramel corn onto the floor and sending the presidential biography tumbling over the armrest and onto Pen's lap. When she picked it up, it flopped open. Two photographs slid out and rested, facedown, on her knee. Even as her mother's voice told her to slip the photos back into the book without looking at them, she was switching on her reading light and turning them over in her hands.

The first was a wedding picture, Cat on Jason's lap, laughing, her whisper-delicate neck and shoulders rising from the bodice of an upside-down lily of a dress, her button nose pressed against Jason's cheek; Jason's face shining with beatific joy. The second was Cat by herself in leggings and a tiny T-shirt, turned sideways, her arms spread in a gesture that said *Ta-da!*

Because she was taking in Cat's lovely, devilish smile, her long hair (Cat had never had anything longer than a long bob in all the years Pen knew her), it took Pen a moment to understand the significance of the gesture, and then she saw it: an almost imperceptible rise above Cat's narrow hips, what would've just looked like ordinary stomach on anyone less waiflike. A baby bump.

As Pen stared and stared at the photo, her eyes burning with tears, she heard a small sound, the sound of a person clearing his throat deliberately: "Ahem." It came from the direction of Jason. Pen froze. People made a lot of noises in their sleep, but, in her experience, this wasn't one of them. Filling with dread, she braced herself and looked up.

Jason's eyes were on the photograph, and the expression on his face wasn't angry; in fact, it might have been the opposite of angry. Gently, he took the photos from Pen's hands.

"Twelve weeks," he said. "It's as far as we ever got. A couple of days after I took this picture, she started bleeding and, poof, our baby was gone." When he said "our baby," his voice was like the expression in his eyes: honest, bleak, rife with longing. Pen remembered what Sam had said, how Cat had told her that wanting a baby had nothing to do with her husband and everything to do with Cat's wanting to be a mother. Looking at Jason, Pen thought Cat had gotten it wrong. She wasn't the only one who had been stockpiling love.

"I'm so sorry," said Pen.

"She was at the grocery store when it happened," Jason went on.

"And then for, like, weeks afterward, she couldn't go back. Started ordering groceries from this online delivery service."

"Poor Cat. Poor both of you."

For the first time, Jason's eyes met hers. "You know, she didn't even tell me? I'd come home from work and the fridge would be full of food, and I didn't think twice about it. You know how I found out?"

"How?"

"I complained about the bananas." He squeezed his eyes shut for a second or two, as though trying to clear his head of something. "Can you believe that? They were too ripe, all those strings sticking to them when you peeled them. I hate that."

"So does Cat," said Pen, suddenly remembering this fact. "She liked them when they were so green you could barely peel them."

"Yeah, well, right about then, she wasn't eating much of anything, which also took me a while to notice." He shook his head in disgust. "My wife can't walk into a goddamn grocery store without having posttraumatic stress, and I'm complaining about bananas."

"Listen," said Pen with great seriousness, "if you didn't know, it was because she didn't want you to know. It wasn't your fault."

Jason looked at her for a few seconds before he said, with equal seriousness, "Thank you."

They sat in a prickly, awkward silence, until Pen couldn't stand it anymore. She turned to Will, who was facing the other direction, sleeping, and tapped lightly on the back of his head. He swatted at her hand for a few seconds and then turned around.

"Hey," he said reproachfully, glaring at her with half-closed eyes and running his hand across the top of his head, "I was asleep."

"I know and I'm sorry," said Pen. "But someone has to save us."

"Me and you?" asked Will. "From what?"

"Me and Jason," said Pen. "From ourselves."

Will peered across Pen at Jason. "You were fighting?"

"We were getting along," said Pen with a shudder.

"Yeah," snorted Jason, "Pen was *nice*. It was freaky."

"That is freaky," said Will.

Pen punched him in the arm.

"Ow!"

Rubbing his shoulder, Will narrowed his eyes into the Clint Eastwood squint and looked from one face to the other. Then he nodded. "Okay, fine," he said, "but if we're going to do this, we need to clear up a few things."

"Wait," said Jason, alarmed. "Do what?"

"Hey, you started it," said Will.

"We failed to treat each other like radioactive waste for a whole half a minute. So what?" said Pen.

"Yeah," said Jason, "don't get all one-giant-step-for-mankind on us, dude." But under the scorn, he sounded the way Pen felt: optimistic, goofy with relief.

"I'm going back to sleep," said Will, starting to turn away.

Pen tugged on his shirtsleeve. "Okay, okay, I'll tell you what's going on."

"What?" said Will and Jason at the same time.

"We being on the same side," she said.

No one made eye contact. Everyone fidgeted, each in her or his own way.

"Whatevs," said Jason finally. "I guess it only makes sense. We're all trying to find Cat, right?"

"Right!" said Pen. "Absolutely."

But Will was shaking his head. "Not so fast," he said.

"Fast?" said Jason. "Don't forget I hated you for, like, a decade."

Pen chuckled at this, and Will jabbed her with his elbow.

"What?" she protested. "It was funny!"

Being careful not to jostle Augusta's socked feet, which still rested in his lap, Will twisted in his seat to face Jason. "You need to explain something," he said.

"Oh, yeah?" said Jason with a brief flare of his old pugnacity. "And what might that be?"

" 'Motherfucker.' " Will didn't load the word with venom, as Jason had done on the phone, just divided it into two parts and impassively placed them in front of him: thunk, thunk.

Jason sat still, his forehead wrinkled, processing this. Pen watched him figure it out, every step written all over his face. Whatever the opposite of a poker face was, that's what Jason had. Finally, his brow cleared: he got it. But instead of answering, he pressed his lips together and rolled his eyes, hostile and bored at the same time. He looked like a teenager whose parents had just confronted him about the joint in his pocket.

"Come on, Jason," Pen said softly. "Just tell us."

He looked at her, then, and he didn't look like a teenager anymore. Pen saw something private and broken in his gaze. Will and Pen watched him take deep breaths, collect himself, get his emotions in check.

He breathed out. "There was a guy."

"Oh," said Pen. It wasn't what she had expected him to say, but as soon as he did, she realized that she wasn't surprised. Of course, of course, there was a guy.

"It wasn't her fault," Jason said quickly.

"Okay," said Will.

"We'd been doing the infertility thing for so long, her hormones were all screwed up. In addition, she was sad. Losing the baby at twelve weeks tore her up. Even when she was over it, she wasn't over it. She'd never talk about it, bite my head off if I even thought about bringing it up. A thing like that leaves its mark."

"I bet it does," said Pen.

"My point is she was vulnerable." He glared at Will and Pen, as if they might contradict him.

"Things can happen when a person's defenses are down," said Will carefully, "that wouldn't happen otherwise."

"You got that right," said Jason. "And then there was the Freudian shit on top of that."

This was unexpected. Pen and Will exchanged a glance.

"Go ahead," said Will to Jason.

"You know how Cat was about her dad, thought he hung the fucking moon. Dude forgets her birthday every single year, and I'm talking about not even a crappy Hallmark card, but she thinks he's Mr. Perfect. What's it called, the thing where the guy killed his father and then ripped his eyes out of their sockets. But for girls."

Pen winced. "I would hardly say she had an Electra complex."

Jason shrugged. "None of us are psychologists, right? Let's say that when it came to her dad, she was a little off."

Pen started to argue, but Will gave her elbow a surreptitious squeeze and she stopped.

"We all know she was crazy about her dad," said Will, "but what does that have to do with this guy?"

"Armando Cruz," spat Jason. "What kind of soap opera name is that?"

A nice name, Pen mused, like music: Armando Cruz and Catalina Ocampo—it sounded like a poem. As Pen considered the name, a light began to dawn. "Wait. He was Filipino? Like Dr. Ocampo? Is that what you meant by Electra?"

Jason turned the back of his hand to them and shot up a stubby index finger. "Filipino." He raised another finger. "From the same town as her dad." One more finger. "And he was a fucking doctor, to fucking boot. Tri-fucking-Electra-fecta."

A man's face appeared above the seat in front of Jason. "Do you mind?" he said. "I got a kid up here."

"My bad, bro," said Jason. The man disappeared. "Bottom line," Jason continued, "he took advantage of her."

"What do you mean," asked Pen, alarmed, "'took advantage of her'?"

"Not like that," said Jason. "I mean she was vulnerable—all those hormones bouncing around. He should have backed off, irregardless of her having a husband."

Regardless, Pen corrected inside her head. She wasn't about to challenge Jason's version of the story, but she wasn't convinced by the picture of Cat as a manipulated innocent.

"What did he look like?" she asked.

Jason shot her a look. "Why does that matter?"

"I just wondered if he looked like her dad."

"Oh." Jason's mouth worked itself into a hard line, and Pen could tell that he was picturing Armando Cruz next to Cat's short, squat, round-faced father, trying to find some common ground. "Not exactly."

I knew it, Pen thought. *He was beautiful.*

Jason blew out a short, painful laugh. "Put it this way: soap opera name, soap opera looks. The guy was cheesy: expensive haircut, ten million teeth, kind of dipshit who runs without a shirt. Honest truth is when I first met him, I thought he was gay."

"You met him?" asked Will.

"Dinner party some stupid neighbor threw. Out by the pool. Mr. Soap Opera was doing his fellowship or what have you at the hospital where her husband worked. Oh and listen to this," he said eagerly. "You guys are the type who will hate this."

"What?" said Pen.

"She invited him and Cat specifically to meet each other." Jason slapped his hand on the armrest.

"You mean that she set them up?" asked Will.

"Naw," said Jason. "I mean, she just assumed they would have shit in common because they were both Filipino."

"I see," said Pen. "How . . . presumptuous." But what she was really thinking was that Cat and Armando did have some pretty significant shit in common, at least eventually.

"Anyway," said Jason, "I saw him a few times after that. We kind of got to know him even." He scratched his head. "Well, some of us got to know him better than others, obviously."

Will said, "How did you know they had an affair?"

"I told you," said Jason angrily. "He took advantage. It wasn't your typical affair."

"All right," said Will. "But how did you know?"

"She told me," said Jason. The pride in his voice was enough to make you cry. "My wife couldn't stand to keep something like that from me, that's how close we are and that's how done with him she is.

After he left, she came clean, told me everything. They had sex, but never in our bed!" He said it as though forgoing sex in their bed was proof that Cat loved him, and who knew? Maybe it was. "It seemed like she expected me to kick her out, but I would never do that."

Pen turned and caught Will's eye, wondering if he was thinking what she was thinking: that there was a fine line between "expected me to" and "hoped I would." In answer, Will lifted one eyebrow, a fleeting, infinitesimal movement, and flicked his eyes back to Jason.

"Armando left?" he asked.

"His fellowship ended, and he went back to the homeland. Made it seem like it was this big noble thing, too. Who cares? Good riddance, asshole."

Pen waited for Will to ask what had to be asked, but she could sense that he was waiting for her to do it. It was an awful question, since it canceled out or at the very least called into deep question Jason's recent declaration that Cat was "close" to Jason and "done" with Armando, but, since they were on a plane to Cebu, there seemed to be no way not to ask it. When the pause in the conversation started to become unbearable, Will nudged Pen encouragingly. She ignored it. He nudged her again. She kicked him.

"So. Uh. Jason," said Will, "do you think she went to Cebu to be with Armando?"

"Oh, Will," Pen exclaimed, flinching. "'*Be* with him'? God. Could you not do better than that?"

"Hey, it's not like you were asking."

"Well, clearly, I should have."

"And you would've phrased it how?" demanded Will. "'Visit him'? 'Spend time with him'? Come on, we all know a euphemism when we hear it."

"All I'm saying is—" began Pen, but Jason raised his hand.

"Hello? I'm sitting right here," he said.

They both stared at him.

"Sorry," said Will. "I was just wondering if that's why you got mad on the phone that day when I told you Cat went to Cebu. Because you thought she'd gone to see Armando."

"Shit, yeah, that's why," said Jason. "Actually, though? Before you told me where she went, I didn't really believe she would follow him. I thought about it. I explored the possibility. I mean, I'm not completely stupid. But, in my heart, I trusted her." He shook his head. "So shit, maybe I am completely stupid."

Pen couldn't help but admire the grim candor with which he said this.

"Jason," she ventured nervously, "if Cat did that, if she did everything it's looking like she did, well—. It would seem to me that in doing those things, Cat did not have your best interests at heart."

"Ya think?" said Jason.

"I do," said Pen. "As much as I love Cat, I have to say that, if everything happened the way you say, then don't you think that maybe—and this is not rhetorical, I'm really asking—that maybe you should consider—" She broke off.

"What?" said Jason.

Pen sighed and said, as gently as she could, "Letting her go. Moving on."

Jason didn't look mad, just injured, like someone had punched him in the stomach. Injured and, suddenly, ten years older.

"I can't," he said raggedly. "Cat's my girl. She's everything to me." He swallowed and sat up straighter. "And, look, she was a wreck when her dad died, like I told you before. Superfragile. It's that Electra thing driving her: she's looking for her dad, really, not Armando. She doesn't need me to let her go. She needs me to help her."

Everyone should be loved like this, Pen thought. *Well, not exactly like this, but this much.*

Will said, "We'll look for him, then. Dr. Armando Cruz. Start looking as soon as we get there. It might take a while, but I bet we can find him."

Her eyes met Will's, and they both nodded, and, just like that, the three of them were a team. Co-conspirators. Partners in crime. God help them.

"I bet we can, too," said Pen staunchly.

"Oh, I bet we can, too," said Jason, a sly smile sliding onto his face, "especially since when Armando was bragging about how he was heading back to Cebu to work, guess what he told me?"

Pen thought for a second. Then her eyes lit up. "The name of the hospital."

"Bingo."

Jason winked at Pen and put out his fist so that she could bump it with her own, and even though she had never liked being winked at and, until very recently, had never liked Jason and still wasn't sure if *like* was the word to describe what she felt about him, she took a breath, winked back, and bumped.

Chapter Sixteen

EN NOTICED THE SMELL BEFORE SHE NOTICED THE HEAT, AL-
though, when she considered the smell later (and it may have
been the first smell ever that she had truly reflected upon), she realized that the two—smell and heat—were all of a piece, inextricably
entwined, born of, borne by each other. She smelled the smell before
she had even stepped foot outside the small, blessedly uncomplicated
airport. It wasn't a bad smell. In fact, she liked it. Charcoal fire and
wood smoke, exhaust and hot road and baking earth, with undertones
(or so Pen imagined) of leaves and fruit and the ocean. Even as she
smelled it for the first time, she knew that it would be one of those
smells that would haunt her, knew that she would be walking through
some future time and place, get blindsided by the smell, and think,
instantly: Cebu.

When they left the airport, after a few preliminary minutes when
stepping into the heat/smell was like hurling yourself full tilt into the
wall of a thickly padded cell, Pen found her body responding to it
differently from the way it responded to hot days at home. The heat
wasn't something she moved through; it didn't smother or beat down.
The Cebu heat was somehow more personal than other heat. It infil-
trated, became part of her, or almost. She wore it, like a dress.

As she, Will, Augusta, and Jason stood glazed over, baffled, and
reeling on the pavement outside of the airport's glass doors, she turned

to Will and said, "The heat, it's like being enfolded in one of those giant, pleated Issey Miyake dresses they have at the Met, isn't it?"

"Exactly what I was thinking," said Will, his voice the only dry thing in a world of humidity. Pen wondered if she looked as wrung out as he did, his face's topography even sharper than usual, his skin glowless in spite of his tan.

"Ixnay on the damn freak talk already," grumbled Jason. "At least until we're in the air-conditioning."

Augusta tugged on Pen's hand, raised her eyebrows, and pointed her finger at Jason. "Bad word," she said solemnly.

"It was a long trip, honeypot," explained Pen, leaning down to plant a kiss on top of her head. "I think we're all a little cranky."

"I'm not," said Augusta. But Pen recognized the signs that her girl was on the edge: smudgy eyes and a stretched-thin whine in her voice.

"Sorry, sis," Jason told Augusta, his eyes two pools of repentance.

"You're welcome," said Augusta absently. She looked very small, wispy, a spent, slumping point in the center of movement and crackling color, one finger twisting her hair. *Poor baby.* Just as Pen was about to pick her up and cuddle her, despite her own fatigue and the clinging heat, her face colored, came to life.

"Look, look, look, Mama, Mama, Mama!"

In an instant, she had yanked her hand out of Pen's and was flying toward the street, which was clogged with all manner of vehicles, most of them stopped and waiting for passengers, a fact that didn't prevent Pen's heart from leaping into her throat in the same instant that she leaped over Augusta's backpack and ran after her.

"Augusta!" she yelled. "Stop right there!"

Augusta stopped at the curb, possibly in response to Pen's command, but possibly not, since she had skidded to a halt inches away from the object of her desire, an arresting contraption consisting of a motorcycle and a tall, roofed, brilliant orange sidecar decked out in rows of lemon-drop-and-ruby-colored headlights and fiercely, eclectically painted: an ad for San Miguel beer, detailed renderings of both a gold-crowned Virgin Mary and Tweety Bird on his birdcage swing, and, in swirling script, what Pen thought was (but what couldn't possibly have been, could it?) a quote from a Journey song. A man in shorts, flip-flops, and a Baltimore Orioles cap stood next to the contraption (later, Pen would learn it was called a "tricycle"), eating pork rinds from a bag.

"Where would you like to go?" he asked Augusta, smiling.

"For a *ride*," she said, saucer-eyed and breathless.

"Ten pesos." He held up ten fingers. "Per person."

Augusta held her hands up, mirroring him, and turned to Pen, her eyes bright.

"Oh, no, thank you," said Pen to the man, smiling and taking Augusta's hand, which immediately began to twist inside hers like a tiny wild animal (*a gerbil* was Pen's weary, drifting thought). "There are four of us, plus luggage. We need something larger."

"No problem," said the man, hooking his thumb toward the tricycle. "Three on the motorcycle, one in the car with the luggage."

Pen looked at the vehicle dubiously. She had nearly fallen over with guilt and worry when they had checked in at the Philadelphia airport and the airline attendant had told her that Augusta couldn't use her booster seat on the plane because it wasn't FAA approved. But they had survived the flight—*flights*—without mishap, without so much as a spell of airsickness or a spilled drink. No way was she pushing her luck now.

"No, thank you," said Pen.

"Yes, thank you!" Augusta shrilled, her whine escalating incrementally in a way that might have been musical had it not been so piercing. "Yes, thank you!"

Uh-oh, thought Pen. She tried to turn Augusta around and lead her away, but Augusta wrenched her hand loose.

"I want to ride the *thing*!" she yelped. "You *said* I could.'

"Hey, you know what?" said Pen calmly. "Let's find a taxi. I bet they're fancy around here, too!"

At this, Augusta dropped to her bottom on the sidewalk with a thunk, her hands balled into fists, threw back her head, and detonated.

She burst into tears. Tears were the least of it. Wails. Shrieks. Chest-racking sobs. Violent back-and-forth headshaking. A small but potent amount of kicking.

Briefly, Pen observed Augusta with the detached horror and awe she felt when she watched a nature documentary: the shark heaving the gruesome gorgeousness of its body from the water, jagged tail lashing, sad, floppy seal snagged in its teeth, the roiling, roiling sea, the fathomless, stone-cold black eyes. She might have stood there until it was over, doing nothing, but there was Will, at her side, saying, "Can I help?" He had to raise his voice to be heard over Augusta's howls. Pen snapped out of her stupor and saw that the people on the sidewalk had pulled themselves into slightly tighter clusters and were looking discreetly away, for which Pen felt a pulse of gratitude.

"It's okay," Pen told Will, crouching down and wrestling Augusta, who had pinned herself to the ground with the special, deadweight gravity of an aggrieved child, into her arms. "Maybe just find a cab?"

"Stop! You're *hurting* me!" screamed Augusta, her voice louder than ever, bursting through the ambient sound like a wrecking ball. *Let the people not speak English,* Pen prayed, but she saw heads turning, maternal concern on every face, including those of the men, a girl who could not have been more than seven years old, and a miniature, soulful-eyed pug.

"Save me," whispered Pen hopelessly and to no one.

Salvation came in the form of a tiny minivan (a mini-minivan?) of a variety Pen had never seen. It had gray vinyl seats and smelled nauseatingly of air freshener. Jason presented the driver with the booster seat, but when the man examined it as though it were an artifact from another planet, Pen decided to forget about it. She was too defeated to feel guilty, although she knew she might later. Augusta had turned from fighting her to clinging to her like lichen, and the thought of prying her loose and belting her into a car seat was too much. Besides, unless they were somehow hidden, the van didn't appear to have seat belts. Once inside, tucked into one corner of the backseat on Pen's lap, Augusta quieted almost magically, bushwhacked by exhaustion, her sobs turning to hiccups. In a minute or so, before the driver had even finished loading their bags, she was asleep, her lips parted, her face angelically peaceful.

"I'm sorry," Pen told Will and Jason. "She doesn't usually behave that way."

"What, are you kidding? It was a relief. Totally got it out of my system," said Will with a smile that Pen could have put in her pocket and kept forever. Just like that: she felt better.

From the front passenger seat, Jason turned around to look at Pen. "Hell, yeah," he said, raising a solidarity fist. "Vicarious tantrums all the way."

Pen raised her fist back.

"'Vicarious,'" she said with a grin. "Impressive."

Joking. Joking with *Jason. How did I get here?* she asked herself and then took the question back. She knew how. Pen found that she felt happy, exuberant even, full of well-being, loose and free, and, somehow (ten thousand miles from home, with her carseat-less child in her lap and the traffic nudging in on either side, so close she could study the faces of the passengers in the van next to them) safe.

"More where that came from," said Jason. "I mean, not a lot more, but more."

For a few seconds they were all three smiling at one another, a triangle of grins, before Will said, "Okay, that's enough," and it was.

THE WARM FEELING LASTED UNTIL THEY WERE STANDING AT THE desk of the opulent hotel ("Marble," Pen had whispered to Will as they walked in. "Persian rugs. Flat screens." And he had whispered back, "Cat will be Cat will be Cat."), when the first thing Jason did after they checked in was to whip out a photo of Cat—one Pen hadn't seen before, a headshot—and ask the woman at the desk, in a voice straight out of a police procedural, if she were still a guest at the hotel.

The woman's doe eyes had startled in her cameo face, and she had said, with exquisite courtesy, "I'm so sorry I cannot help you, sir."

"Look," said Jason, jutting out his jaw. "She's my wife. I know she was a guest. All I want to know is if she's still here. Simple question."

"Jason," said Will, "come on."

"It is our policy not to give out information regarding our guests," said the woman, her voice as delicate as the rest of her.

A man in a suit and tie materialized at her side. "May I help you?" he asked.

"All's I want to know is," drawled Jason—('All's'? thought Pen. *Are you out of your mind?*)—"is my wife still a guest of this establishment. Period."

"I'm very sorry, sir," said the man behind the desk. "We must protect the privacy of our guests. We would do the same for you and your party, for anyone."

As Pen closed her eyes, vehemently wishing herself part of anyone else's party but Jason's, she heard Will say, "And we really appreciate that. We'll just go find our rooms now."

"And *I*," said Jason, "would really appreciate it if you would tell me if and when my wife checked out of this hotel." His tone grew seedy, conspiratorial. "Me and my friend Ulysses would be most appreciative."

My friend Ulysses and I, thought Pen, and then, *Oh, for the love of God, No. No, no, no*. But she opened her eyes and there he was, waving a fifty-dollar bill under the man's nose.

Simultaneously, the man and the woman took a step back, their faces shutting like boxes, their eyes impassive.

"Hey, man," said Will warningly. "Let it go." He was holding Augusta, her head on his shoulder, and as he said this, she stirred. Will rested his hand, lightly, on the side of her face and said, "Shhh."

If Jason heard Will, he didn't show it. He never took his eyes off the man and the woman behind the desk. From where she stood, Pen could see the back of his neck and his right ear turn scarlet. "Fine. You want to play hardball?" said Jason, banging the fist holding Ulysses on the counter. "She's my *wife*, and she's not well. So, fine, I'll double it. I'll *triple* it."

"If you pull out Ben Franklin," Pen said, her teeth gritted, "I swear to God I will deck you."

Jason dragged his gaze off the couple behind the desk and stared at Pen, bewildered. "What?"

"Do you *hear* yourself?" snapped Pen. "*Hardball? You* are the one who's not well."

Jason's bravado evaporated. He drooped and looked betrayed. "Fine," he said sullenly. "Great." He folded the money and stuffed it into his shorts' pocket, turning to glare at Pen and Will. "Way to have my back, guys. I appreciate it." And he stomped away.

Later, after Pen had unpacked, bathed Augusta, put her to bed, and then stood in the shower for a long time, the hot water pouring over her like hot water but also like divine, transfiguring bliss, there was a knock at the door. She opened it, and there was Will.

"Hey, I didn't wake you up, did I?" he asked.

"No," said Pen.

She saw that he was freshly shaven, his hair still wet. He wore a white polo shirt, open at the neck, and under the lights of the hotel hallway, his hazel eyes seemed to be ten different colors at once. As she looked at him, a drop of water ran from his ear to the V of his shirt, and Pen felt instantly shy, hyperaware of their mutual dampness.

Maybe Will felt the same way because when she asked him if he wanted to come in, he shook his head, glancing over her shoulder at Augusta asleep on one of the two twin beds.

"I'll stay out here," he said. "I'd hate to wake her up."

"I don't think a freight train could wake her up at this point. Jet lag, it's like a drug, isn't it?"

"Yeah," agreed Will, "a bad drug," but he stayed in the hallway.

"It felt a little weird putting on pajamas at three o'clock in the afternoon," said Pen, "but if I don't get some sleep, I think I might die."

It wasn't until she said "pajamas" that Pen remembered what she was wearing: baggy drawstring shorts that used to belong to Jamie and a white tank top. She flushed. *Please don't let him notice that I'm braless. Please don't let him think the shorts are Patrick's.* It took all of her self-control not to cross her arms over her chest and back away. Inside her head, she heard her mother's advice regarding embarrassing situations: *If you act like you don't notice, nobody else will notice.* She didn't believe it any more now than she had as a kid, but she fervently hoped it was true.

"I'll let you hit the hay," said Will. "But I wanted to tell you that Jason and I are taking a little trip to the hospital."

"What?" exclaimed Pen, imagining that Jason had done something ridiculous, cut off his ear while shaving, maybe. Then she remembered: Armando. "Oh. But why not wait until tomorrow? Get some rest? You guys must be as tired as I am, and it's not like a few hours will make a difference."

"Waiting makes sense," said Will. "So obviously Jason won't do it, and we can't let him go alone."

"Well, I guess we could," said Pen. A vision of Jason in the hospital came to her: bursting through operating room doors in his American flag shirt, ears blazing, waving money in front of nurses and surgeons and patients on gurneys. She groaned. "Of course, we can't. He'd get himself locked up for attempted bribery and unforgivable rudeness." She smiled at Will with sympathy. "Sorry you have to be alone with the big galoot. Will and Jason, playing detective together."

"Will and Jason and Jason's friend Ulysses," corrected Will.

Pen laughed. Then something occurred to her. "Hey, how do you know Armando will be there? What if he's off today?"

"Oh, Jason took care of that," said Will.

"Uh-oh. How?"

"He made an appointment. From Ohio. Under an assumed name."

Pen stared at him. "You can do that?"

"Only if you have tunnel vision and no discernible moral compass."

"He made up an ailment?" asked Pen.

"An ailment, a name, an entire medical history. He said he had to cancel his appointment with a doctor in Ohio because of an unexpected business trip to Cebu and didn't want to wait until he got home to get checked out."

"What kind of doctor is Armando, anyway?"

"A thoracic surgeon."

"So Jason said there was something wrong with his—what? Thorax? Do humans even have thoraxes? I thought insects were the ones with thoraxes."

"Well, that would explain why Jason has one," said Will.

It should have been a nothing moment, slightly funny but evanescent, a moment in a long stream of moments. Instead, for Pen at least, it separated itself, became self-contained and revelatory. Pen and Will looked at each other and smiled the kind of smiles people exchange when they have known each other for a very long time, and maybe it was the exhaustion or the fact of time's having been turned on its head, but Pen had the sensation that, right then, they were two bodies caught in perfect balance, the forces pulling them together precisely equal to the ones keeping them apart, Pen on one side of the doorway, Will on the other, and what she understood is that all the forces were love and that she was the opposite of lonely. This could be enough, she realized, this kind of being together. Friendship. In spite of all her longing (her fingers on his wrist), this could be enough.

"You'll have to come back," said Pen, taking a step backward into the room, "and tell me all about it."

"You know I will," said Will.

THE NEXT MORNING, WILL FOUND PEN AND AUGUSTA AT THE HOTEL pool. It was six thirty, which, for Pen, under normal circumstances and time zones, would have passed for the crack of dawn, but which felt remarkably late given the fact that she and Augusta had both been up for a grim, trapped, hungry, television-filled (thank God for the Disney channel) two and a half hours.

Augusta was in the baby pool cooing to the dolphin fountain, and Pen was feasting on warm, dense, cloven rolls called Elorde bread after a Cebuano boxing star (Pen had learned from the waiter that boxing was the most popular sport in the Philippines, with basketball and billiards close behind), sticky rice redolent with coconut milk, and mangoes, palm-sized, kidney-shaped, butter-yellow on the outside, with brilliant, silken, spoonable flesh of such acute deliciousness that, upon taking her first bite, Pen could have wept with joy.

"Was he cute?" had been Pen's first question.

"I wouldn't say 'cute,'" said Will.

"Because you never say 'cute' or because he wasn't?" asked Pen.

"Both," said Will.

"So what'd he look like?"

"The anti-Jason. Take Jason and substitute every single thing about him with its opposite, and you'll get Armando."

Pen considered this. "Jason has decent teeth. Are you saying Armando had bad teeth?"

"Every single thing about Jason except his teeth. I didn't pry open his mouth and go in with a flashlight, but I got the impression that his teeth are fine."

"What else about him is fine?"

"Pen."

Pen sighed. "I knew I should have had you take a picture. What was he like? Funny? Smart? Devastatingly handsome? Did he look great in his white coat? Did he even wear a white coat? Did he really seem like the kind of guy who would run without a shirt? Was he stunned to see Jason walk into his office?"

"Yes."

Pen narrowed her eyes at Will threateningly.

"Yes, he really did seem like the kind of guy who would run without a shirt," said Will.

"No!" yelped Pen, recoiling. "Wait, didn't you used to run without a shirt? I think you did. I seem to remember that."

"I never ran without a shirt. Occasionally, when it was unusually hot, I took my shirt off afterward, when I was cooling down. Totally different thing."

"Sure, Will. Sure, it is," said Pen, patting his arm. "Are you saying Armando was arrogant?"

"A little. Although it was kind of an awkward situation, so maybe he's not always like that."

"Tell me what happened."

"We didn't talk long. He walked into the examining room, where we were waiting—"

"Wait a minute. You went into the examining room with Jason? Didn't anyone find that odd?"

"He told the nurse we were brothers and that he had a tendency to panic in hospitals."

"You look like brothers," said Pen.

"So anyway, Armando walked in and we all shook hands, and Jason asked about Cat, and Armando said he preferred not to discuss it at work, and Jason said, 'I don't think you're getting how important this is,' and Armando said that, yes, he did, and then he invited us to his house, and then he said the thing that made Jason go apeshit, and Jason yelled, and before they could throw us out, we left."

"Hold on. You *shook hands*. Just like that? I mean, I know you; you'd shake hands with Attila the Hun right before he chopped off your head, but *Jason*? With Armando the motherclucker? Armando, his sworn enemy?"

"I was impressed, actually," said Will. "He was literally quaking—or at least kind of vibrating—with, I don't know, rage or a lust for vengeance or something, before Armando got there, but the second the guy walked in, he pulled himself together. He had that 'gotcha' look on his face he gave us when he showed up at the reunion, but he was strangely polite, even kind of dignified."

"But what about Armando?" Pen asked. "Wasn't he shocked?"

"No. He didn't miss a beat. It was crazy. Or at least, I thought it was crazy until the end, when he said the thing that made Jason go apeshit."

"Oh, boy."

"Right before we left, Jason said something like, 'BTW, way to play it cool, bro. It's like you were expecting me.'"

"He said 'BTW'? What is *wrong* with him? Nobody says that."

"A lot of things are wrong with him, remember?" said Will. "So then Armando gave him this arrogant smile and said, 'I *was* expecting you,' and Jason turned the color of Hawaiian punch the way he does and said, 'No, you weren't.'"

"He's such an infant," said Pen, sighing.

"And Armando said, 'First of all, you called from Ohio. Second of all, you called yourself "Clark Kent." ' "

Pen's eyes widened. "Jason really did that? Why?"

"Apparently, he's been a huge Superman fan his whole life."

Pen covered her face. "Oh no."

"Right. Then Jason said in this sneering voice, 'Why would that mean anything to you? You don't even *have* Superman here.' "

Her face still covered, Pen opened her fingers and peered out. "He is the ugliest American in the whole history of ugly Americans."

"Armando didn't refute the Superman thing, just gave Jason this sort of pitying look, and then said, 'I knew it was you because Catalina told me about your comic book predilection. She told me how embarrassing it was that you always made restaurant reservations under the name "Clark Kent." ' "

"Ai, yi, yi!" shrieked Pen.

"Ai, yi, yi!" echoed Augusta from the pool.

"That's when Jason turned purple and started yelling that Armando was full of shit and how he knew what 'predilection' meant and how Cat hated being called Catalina and loved it when he made reservations like that and how Cat called him 'her Superman' when they were alone." Will shuddered. "It was sad."

They sat and watched the lemon light pour through the coconut palms and skim across the serene blue pool, paying tribute to the sad, angry, devoted, appalling, lunkheaded hunk of humanity that was Jason with a moment of silence.

"I'm a mermaid, Will!" called Augusta.

"I can see that," said Will, smiling.

"So, hey," said Pen excitedly, "I'll meet him."

Will made a pained face. "You sure you want to be there? It could get ugly."

"Are you kidding? After you stopped by yesterday—or whenever it was—I got so jealous that you were meeting him and I wasn't that it took me thirty whole seconds to fall asleep."

It had taken her longer than that. She had lain for a long time, contemplating the familiar, easeful, uncluttered holiness of friendship and the memory of Will in the doorway with his damp hair and beautiful eyes, looking like all the Wills he had ever been. There was peace in it, in being the same old Pen who wanted, above all other things, for nothing to change, but still, her body had stayed awake, wired, her skin tingling, until sleep hit like a snowstorm, whiting out everything.

Will smiled. "Poor Pen."

"Pen's not poor!" corrected Augusta sternly, from the pool's edge. "Pen's rich!"

"True," said Pen.

"Armando's sending his car for us today at five," said Will.

"Fancy," commented Pen through a bite of mango. "I guess I'm not the only one who's rich." Then she sighed. "Poor Jason. Poor, poor, poor, poor Jason."

Augusta didn't say that Jason wasn't poor. She had left the world of adults. In joyous self-absorption, she leaned back like the bathing beauty she was, her toes pointed, her face to the sun; then she sat up and slid into the water like a seal.

THE INTERIOR OF ARMANDO'S CAR WAS ICE-COLD AND PRISTINELY, almost spookily clean, but it wasn't, to Jason's evident satisfaction, especially fancy, not a limousine certainly, which is what they'd all either dreaded or hoped for, not even a Mercedes, which seemed to be the luxury car of choice in Cebu, their slick, dignified shapes jostling incongruously through the city streets with tricycles, mopeds, and jeepneys (public conveyances of surpassing gorgeousness, flashing with chrome, dazzlingly painted, studded with hood ornaments, religious icons, proper names, and cryptic messages; Augusta declared that jeepneys were "the best things in the whole, wide world of shininess" and Pen had to agree). Instead, Armando's vehicle turned out to be a Japanese SUV, smallish and silver.

As they'd piled into it, Pen had heard Jason mutter to Will (or possibly to himself or to Armando or Cat, neither of whom were there),

"Not exactly a slammin' ride for Dr. Hot Shit," which had caused Pen to shoot a worried glance at the driver, whose imperturbable face reacted, if it reacted at all, by growing several degrees more imperturbable. When Will had introduced himself to the driver, the young man had identified himself as Ruben, emphasis (charmingly, Pen thought, and distinguishing him forever from her favorite sandwich) on the second syllable. Pen had winced when Jason, in what she knew he hoped was a blatant defiance of normal driver/rider protocol (although who could say for sure?), ignored the door Ruben held open and stuffed himself into the front passenger seat (it had been slid almost as far forward as it would go, presumably to accommodate passengers riding in the back where they belonged), but Ruben hadn't so much as fluttered an eyelash.

"So, uh, Ruben," said Jason, with a conspiratorial glance back at Will and Pen that made Pen want to strangle him, "you cart old Armando everywhere, do you? Where I come from grown men generally drive themselves, unless they're, like, extremely elderly or paralyzed or whatnot. It's a point of pride."

Pen had the urge to stick her fingers in her ears and sing "Mary Had a Little Lamb" at full volume. Instead, she stared pointedly out the window. They passed roadside fruit stands with their big, glorious, fanned bunches of bananas overhanging careful pyramids of red, green, and gold orbs. Sometimes, the traffic slowed enough for Pen to make out individual fruits, gorgeous and strange: giant green brains, strawberry-colored sea urchins, golden hedgehogs. She wanted to ask Ruben about them, but Jason was still talking. "No offense," he began, words to make your heart sink.

"No offense, but personally, you couldn't pay me to ride in the back while another dude drove. I'd feel like an I-don't-know-what. A toy poodle."

"Toy poodles ride in the backseat while another dude drives?" asked Augusta skeptically. "By themselves?"

"Of course not," said Pen. "Jason's just making stuff up."

Jason aimed a look of irritation at Pen and seemed about to start talking again, when Ruben said, "Dr. Cruz drives himself. I am the driver for the family."

Jason widened his eyes at this, his blond brows shooting up his forehead. "Dr. Cruz has a *family*?"

"Yes," said Ruben.

"This I did not know," said Jason, nodding, and adding in an inexplicable and heinous French accent (inspired by Hercule Poirot? Jacques Clouseau? Cousteau? Impossible to say), "Zee plot thickens!"

"Look at the kids, Mama," said Augusta, pointing. "All dressed the same."

They were schoolchildren, lovely in their uniforms, walking serenely along the dusty, busy street, some of them so young that Pen marveled at their being out alone, until she saw that they weren't alone. They walked in threes, fours, arms linked or loosely wrapped around each other's waists, each one connected to another, the little ones in between the bigger ones.

"Little kids in school uniforms," said Jason. "Doesn't get much cuter than that."

Pen caught Will's eye and telegraphed, *So clucking weird how he can do that, shrug off asinine-ness like an ugly jacket and get real and wistful.*

"All those kids," Jason went on. "You know something? It hit me last night that maybe that's the reason all this is happening."

Will looked at Pen, who shrugged.

"The kids?" asked Will.

"Yeah," said Jason. "One anyway. Hell, why not two or three? We've talked about it. Or I have. Cat wasn't ready to give up, I guess."

"You mean adoption," said Pen.

"It's a Catholic country. Highly Catholic," said Jason. "Some people are surprised by that, an Asian Catholic country."

"We know it's primarily a Catholic country," said Pen, hoping against all odds that he wasn't about to say something hideously insensitive in front of Ruben.

"So we're talking no birth control. Families with seven, ten kids. Cat and I could adopt some, take them home, give them everything they'd never get here."

Ruben didn't speak or shift his gaze from the road.

"What's birth control?" asked Augusta in a loud whisper, and Pen hushed her with a kiss.

"People say there's a reason for everything," Jason said. "And I'm thinking that maybe the reason for all this pain and upheaval is to give us the babies we've been wanting for so long. Because, as God is my witness, we would totally do right by them."

Jason was still staring out the window at the children. Pen didn't know what to say to him, but, looking at him, she could see that it didn't matter: he had forgotten they were there. The car kept nosing slowly forward, so full of burgeoning sorrow and longing, Pen thought the windows might blow out.

ARMANDO'S NEIGHBORHOOD WAS IN THE HILLS. PEN HAD NOT EVEN been aware of hills, until the car passed the guard stand at the neighborhood's entrance and began to wind up them. The houses weren't mansions but were bigger than any houses Pen had seen so far, a far, far cry from the plywood and aluminum shanties they'd seen on their way from the airport to the hotel. ("Squatters" the driver had explained; Pen hadn't known exactly what he meant by that and hadn't asked, but she hoped it had something to do with temporariness, hoped that those shanties were a stop on the road to someplace better, though she worried that they weren't.) As in the rest of Cebu, there were flowers in profusion, lopping over walls, bordering every doorway, banked against buildings, flaring along the roadsides: fiery pink bougainvillea, bushes thick with yellow bells, the white stars of sampaguita, which Ruben told Pen was the national flower. Here and there, bony dogs sprawled in scraps of shade.

"They look feral to me," said Jason. To Pen, they looked haggard and introspective.

Ruben stopped the SUV in front of an iron gate set in a long white wall and beeped the horn, and, after thirty seconds or so, the gate swung open and they drove through. When Pen turned around, she saw two small boys in flip-flops pushing the gate shut.

The house was the kind of house that instantly made Pen want to live in it, fine-boned, graceful, but solid and comfortable-looking, with pebbled steps leading down through a steep, tiered garden to a deep, shadow-pooled lawn. It glowed white as a shell in the mellowing sun.

Ruben opened the car door and lifted Augusta out and set her feet on the ground in a gentle, but matter-of-fact manner that led Pen to think he must be a father. Through the open door Pen saw a man standing on the salmon-colored tiles of the verandah, and even before he began to walk toward them, she knew he must be Armando. He was maybe five-foot-ten, compact and lean, with wavy black hair and the bearing of a prince. He wore stone-colored cargo shorts, leather fisherman sandals, and a loose, short-sleeved linen shirt in a periwinkle blue that offset his skin so impeccably that Pen suspected a woman (Cat?) had chosen it for him.

"Hi," he said with a smile. "Welcome."

He shook hands with everyone and was composed and convivial, as if he were greeting old friends, instead of the large, volatile, cuckolded husband of his former (or not former) lover and the cuckold's pals. As the five of them stood on the verandah, Pen saw the two boys who had closed the gate peeking their glossy heads around the corner of the house, and then a young woman, possibly a teenager, appeared with the boys in tow. They wore striped T-shirts and lovely, shy grins. The oldest could have been no more than eight; the smaller one a few years younger.

"Ask her," the woman said to the boys, her hands on their shoulders pushing them gently forward. "The way I told you."

Slowly, the boys approached Augusta, ducked their heads in miniature bows, and the older boy said, "My name is Paul, and this is my brother Nando. Would you like to play?"

After gaping at them with an expression of dewy-eyed enchantment, Augusta curtsied and said, "My name is Augusta," and looked up beseechingly at Pen, who nodded.

"Sure, as long as you stay in the yard."

"Yay!" she shrieked, breaking the spell, and the children bounded like terriers across the grass, the young woman following behind.

Pen smiled at Armando. "They're beautiful," she said. "Are they yours?"

"Beautiful maybe, but extremely loud," said Armando with a chuckle. "They're the sons of Lana, our cook."

"You have a cook?" blurted out Jason. Pen glanced quickly at him and her heart softened at the regret she saw on his face: he hadn't meant to sound so impressed.

"In the Philippines, a lot of middle-class households have helpers," explained Armando. "Nannies, cooks, drivers, housekeepers. Maybe it's because so many people are in need of employment. It's that way in many developing countries."

"Oh," said Jason grudgingly. "Makes sense, I guess. Must've been tough back in Ohio, huh? Fending for yourself and all."

At the mention of Ohio, everyone seemed to stiffen, social awkwardness setting in like rheumatism.

"Not so tough," said Armando finally, a slight chill in his voice, and for a second, Pen thought he was talking about Jason.

Will was looking down into the yard. "That's an amazing tree," he said.

They all looked, and Pen knew what tree he meant right away: some sort of palm, but not like any she had seen before, tall and flat and wide and shaped exactly like a showgirl's feathered fan.

"A traveler's palm," said Armando. "Although not a true palm tree, more closely related to a banana tree. Indigenous to Madagascar, so a non-native species."

Pen caught a glimpse of the arrogance Will had noticed at the hospital. Armando was a man who liked to know things and liked to tell people what he knew.

"I like it," said Pen defiantly. "Non-native or not."

Armando laughed. "I like it, too. I think it's cool."

Just like that, he was warm again. Maybe it wasn't real arrogance; maybe he resorted to didacticism in moments of social stress, the way she resorted to babbling and Jason to being a jerk (even though it could be argued—Pen had argued it herself, although she was less convinced of it than she once had been—that being a jerk was Jason's natural state). Armando walked to the front door and opened it, with a welcoming, if slightly officious sweep of his hand. "Why don't we go inside where we can talk?"

They all filed in, Pen and Will immediately, Jason after another leisurely look at the lawn in an act of rebellion for which Pen supposed he could not really be blamed. Still, it was embarrassingly transparent: Armando might have a cook, sculpted cheekbones, an affair with Jason's wife under his belt, and a fancy tree, but he couldn't make Jason go inside before Jason was good and ready. *You're not the boss of me.* Pen could almost hear him say the words, sandbox voice and all.

They walked into a smaller version of Patrick and Tanya's great room: kitchen, dining room, living room. It was nice, full of low, carved wood furniture, tall Chinese (at least, Pen assumed they were Chinese) jars, cushions in shades of gold, but it struck Pen as a little sterile, too tidy, as though most of the real living in the house took place elsewhere. Even the kitchen appeared pristine, unused. As she sat down on the sofa, she caught a glimpse of another room around the corner, kids, maybe teenagers watching television, its blue light washing over them, before one of the kids saw her looking and, with a smile, closed the door.

Armando called something in what Pen assumed was Cebuano, and a young woman—a different one from the one who had taken the children to play—appeared with a standing fan. She plugged it in and set it on rotate. When the stream of air hit Pen, she realized how hot she was. Pen smiled to herself, remembering how Cat used to say that if there were gods of fire and water and earth, there should be a god of air-conditioning because it was that elemental to human existence. She had joked about naming her firstborn child Freon.

"Can I offer you a drink? Coke? A beer?" asked Armando.

Pen would have loved a glass of water, but before she could ask for it, Jason said, "Let's cut to the chase. I know Cat's in Cebu, and it's crucial that I find her. If you know anything about her current location, you should tell me. ASAP. Time is of the essence."

Here we go, thought Pen. She wondered if Jason thought people really believed he was a detective when he talked like that.

For a moment, Armando's face grew contemplative. Finally, he said one word, calmly, like a person making his move in a chess game: "Why?"

Jason's face began to redden. "Why what?" he spluttered, and then said, "No, wait. Forget it. You don't get to ask questions. Just tell me what I need to know."

Coolly and as if he hadn't heard Jason take back the "Why what?" Armando said, "Why is it crucial that you find her? Why should I tell you where she is? Why is time of the essence?"

Jason rocked up out of the chair to his feet, one hand on his hip, the other pointing at Armando, and said, "Because she's my wife."

Pen was impressed by the simplicity of the answer, but she didn't like the wild look in Jason's eyes, which only grew more intense when Armando got up from his chair, too. He didn't move toward Jason, just stood there, but still managed to look quick, wary, and light-footed, like a boxer. Pen looked over at Will. He was still sitting, but Pen saw that he was full of coiled energy, his hands poised on the arms of his chair.

"I think you should sit down, Jason," said Will in a low voice.

"Fuck that," said Jason loudly, never taking his eyes off Armando. "What do you know about Cat?"

"Have you considered," said Armando coldly, "that if she wanted you to find her, she would not have left in secret, without telling you where she was going?"

"Shut up!" shouted Jason. "You don't know what the hell you're talking about."

Pen waited for it to dawn on him that he was wrong about this, that, clearly, Armando did know what he was talking about, and, sure enough, after staring into space for a few seconds, he jabbed his finger at Armando again. "You've talked to her. You wouldn't know that if you hadn't talked to her."

Armando seemed to consider his next move, before he raised his chin an inch or two and said, "Sure, I talked to her. We had dinner together the day after she arrived in Cebu."

At the same instant that Jason lunged across the coffee table toward

Armando, Will stood up as fast as a striking snake and grabbed him, his arm thrown across Jason's wide chest.

"No, Jason!" said Pen, but Jason was struggling to get himself free. He wasn't in shape, but he was a lot bigger than Will, and Pen knew it could be only a matter of seconds before he broke away. Without thinking, she lifted the delicate china bowl off the perilously positioned coffee table and cradled it in her lap.

"You son of a gun!" A great, loud bark of a voice, heavily accented.

All eyes turned in the direction of the voice. Standing in the entrance to the room was an elderly woman, very elderly, frail and tiny inside her loose batik housedress, but bristling with electricity. With her short gray hair puffed around her head like a nimbus, her ferocious black eyes, and her raised fist, she looked unreal, iconic, like a miniature goddess of vengeance.

"Coming into my house, yelling!" raged the woman, walking toward Jason with remarkably steady steps. "Throwing yourself around like an elephant!"

Jason had stopped struggling as soon as he had heard the woman's voice. Now, as the woman advanced upon him, he wilted inside Will's grasp, and Will let go.

"Sorry about that, ma'am," Jason said with hangdog politeness. "I-I didn't know this was your house. I didn't know you were here."

"Where else would I be?" scoffed the woman.

"Lola," said Armando softly, "it's okay."

He walked toward her and, with exquisite tenderness, took her hand in his. "I'm sorry we disturbed you."

"Ehhh!" said the woman. "You should be sorry!" And she reached up and cuffed Armando across his head, but Pen saw that her eyes had grown soft. "No more yelling!"

He smiled, kissed her cheek, and turned her around. "No more yelling, Lola. I promise."

"You, too, elephant!" said the woman, glaring at Jason over her shoulder.

"Me, too, ma'am," said Jason.

When the woman was gone, Armando turned back to them and said, "My grandmother."

"You live with your grandmother?" asked Jason. He didn't sound hostile, just dazed.

"My grandmother, my parents, my brother, Rey, who is in medical school, two of my younger sisters."

"Oh, so, they're the family Ruben meant," said Pen. "He said he was the driver for your family."

"That's right," said Armando.

"No wife?" asked Jason with a hint of snideness.

"Not yet," said Armando, chin up, eyes challenging.

"Jason and I are going out for a walk," said Will. "Get some air."

"I'm not leaving here until he tells me what he knows about Cat," said Jason in a blunt but thankfully unpetulant way.

"You guys go check on Augusta. I'll stay and talk to him," said Pen quickly, "if that's okay with you, Armando."

"No problem," said Armando amiably.

When they left, Armando slumped down onto the sofa, ran his hand through his hair, and gave a low whistle. Pen liked him for this open display of relief and vulnerability. A pattern seemed to be emerging: his aloofness and pomposity would push you away; his humor and humanness would pull you back—and just in the nick of time. Pen thought that she could only take this state of affairs for so long before it exhausted her, but she could imagine Cat's finding it exciting. She had always had a soft spot for thorny men with soft underbellies. Behind their backs, she and Pen used to call them echidnas.

"I think that went well, don't you?" said Pen.

"He's big, isn't he?" said Armando, widening his eyes. "You can forget how big and then he charges you like a bull and you remember."

"I've thought that before, that he's part bull," said Pen, smiling.

Armando sat up, gave her his out-of-the-blue, disarming white crescent of a smile, and said, "Thank you."

"For what? Showing up here with Jason so that he could disrupt your entire household?"

"For saving my mother's bowl."

Pen looked down at the bowl in her lap, which she'd forgotten she was holding, and laughed. "You're welcome."

"I should thank Will, too," said Armando. "Has he always had those ninja reflexes?"

Pen placed the bowl back on the table as she considered this. "I guess he has. He just used to use them for jumping on people instead of for jumping on the people who jump on people. But he reformed a while back."

"Lucky for me. I was surprised to find you and Will traveling with Jason. I didn't think you liked him."

"You know who we are?" asked Pen, startled.

"Of course. Cat and I talked a lot, and after I left, we e-mailed a lot. I've even seen pictures of you two. You're the friends."

"That's right. We're the friends. Jason's the husband. And you're the—?" She waited.

"I'm the guy who lives on the other side of the world," he said.

On impulse, Pen leaned forward with clasped hands and said, "I wish you would tell me about you and Cat."

She expected him to get supercilious and distant, to say it was none of her business, with which she really couldn't argue except to say that she loved Cat and missed her and that collecting what she could of Cat's story was her only means of feeling close to her. But instead, Armando's eyes lit up with eagerness, and for the first time since she'd met him, he looked young. Pen realized, with a start, that he was young.

"From the very first day, it was like we'd always known each other. We talked about our families, our pasts. It was easy. We both noticed that, how easy it was."

He was so boyish and warm and open-hearted. *Oh,* marveled Pen, *he loves her.* She hadn't expected him to love her.

"You were friends?" she asked cautiously.

"Yes, friends. Real friends." His tone took on a note of defiance, as he said, "It's true that we were both lonely. I was a long way from home, working all the time, and she was unhappy in her marriage, in her work, but that's not why we were together. We could have met under any circumstances and been—"

Pen watched him search for the word. His English was fluid, even formal, eloquent. It wasn't his command of the language that was failing him, she saw; it was that when it came to love, sometimes language just failed.

"I understand," said Pen.

"Thanks," said Armando.

"What job was she doing that she didn't like?" asked Pen.

"She was training to be a pharmaceutical rep. She thought it would be glamorous, the dinners, the parties. You must understand that she was much less happy than when you knew her. She found her life very drab." He said it as though he was apologizing for Cat's desire for glamour, as though glamour wasn't imprinted on Cat's DNA as firmly as her black hair, her tapered fingers.

"And it involved travel, of course," he continued. "She was always wanting to be someplace else, away."

"Away from Jason, you mean," said Pen.

"Of course!" Armando knit his straight black brows in disgust. "She didn't love him. How could she? He's ridiculous, unsophisticated, a—bonehead!"

Even as Pen suppressed a smile at the word *bonehead* coming out of Armando's mouth, and despite having known, for nearly a decade, the way she'd known that the sky was blue, that Jason was indeed a bonehead, she felt the unexpected urge to defend him, but she couldn't figure out how.

"He loves her," said Pen at last. It needed to be said.

"No, he doesn't. He wouldn't know how to love someone like Cat."

Pen would not be deterred. "I'm sure you're right that he doesn't love her the way she wants to be loved, but he loves her," she said. "Yes, he's a bonehead. Yes, I spend most of my time with him wanting to strangle him. But he loves Cat. She's the reason for everything he does."

"That's why you're here with him? You want him to find her because he loves her?"

Pen faltered. "I don't—know. I mean, no. We came because—" She made a frustrated sound. "It's a long story, but now Will and I are here for ourselves. We miss Cat. We've never stopped missing her all these years."

Armando's face softened. "And she never stopped missing you."

"But." Pen hesitated. Why not just leave it alone? Since when was she Jason's champion? Since never. Still. Pen sighed. "On this trip with Jason, I've come to realize that it matters that he loves her. I've tried to deny it, but I can't." Gently, she added, "And Cat did marry him, after all."

Armando shut his eyes. When he opened them, he looked young again, young, conflicted, and even regretful.

"We shouldn't have done it," he said quietly. "It was a mistake."

"Why?" asked Pen.

"Because, for one thing, I was never going to stay."

"Couldn't you have stayed? Did you try?"

"My city needs me," he said, with a touch of the old pomposity. "The Philippines needs me. There is a brain drain in my country; those with talent and skills leave as soon as they get the chance. The United States has plenty of good surgeons. Not so many here. I swore from the beginning that I would come back."

"I see," said Pen, feeling awkward. "Well, that was good of you."

"Also," said Armando with a grin, "I promised my mother that I would."

"Ah! If she's anything like Lola, I can see why you'd be afraid to break that promise."

"You got that right."

"What's the other reason?" said Pen. "You said 'for one thing.' Why else?"

Armando's head dropped for a second. "Because they were married, as you said. I believe in marriage, in taking vows. We made a mistake."

Pen felt suddenly annoyed at his ostentatious regret. "A mistake? You make it sound like an accident, like the two of you just tripped and—oops!—fell into bed. You must have discussed it. Even if you didn't, it was deliberate. I'm not saying it was wrong or that I haven't done things like that myself, because I have, sort of, but own up to it, for heaven's sake."

Armando stared at her. "What did you say?"

"Look, I didn't mean to sound judgmental. Or maybe I did mean to. But I shouldn't have. I'm sorry."

"Why do you think we fell into bed?"

"Because you just said so, for starters."

"We fell in love. That was our mistake. That's what I meant."

Pen felt flustered. "Wait. But you had an affair."

"No, not technically. Not the physical part."

"You mean, you didn't have—sex?" Sometimes, a thing needed to be spelled out.

Armando looked embarrassed. "No. I wouldn't." He corrected himself: "I mean, *we* decided not to."

We, thought Pen, *ha!* She knew her Cat better than that.

"You should not assume," said Armando, scolding.

"I didn't," snapped Pen, and then it hit her: Cat had lied to Jason. Women all over the world trying to hide affairs from their husbands, and Cat had gone and made one up and handed it to her husband, a mean lie dressed up as an act of humility and contrition, an act of trust.

"What do you mean?" asked Armando slowly.

"I mean that—" She tried to sort out exactly whom she would be betraying by telling Armando what Cat had done. Cat? Jason?

Armando watched her struggle with what to say and asked with bewilderment, "She told him that?"

Pen gave a resigned shrug. "That's what he said."

Armando looked like a kid trying to figure out a Rubik's cube, turning his thoughts this way, that way.

"If Cat isn't here with you, where is she?" ventured Pen, hoping to take advantage of his bemused state. "Can you tell me, please?"

"Will you tell Jason?"

Pen wanted to say no. "Yes. I have to. We're sort of in this together, now."

"In that case, why should I tell you? Why should I help him find her?"

"You would have every right not to," said Pen. "But Will and I love her and want to see her so much."

Armando folded his arms and looked at her. Her heart was pounding. They were so close; to lose Cat now, when they were so close, she would not be able to stand it.

"Also, you know that what she did wasn't really right," said Pen.

She may have said it in order to manipulate him into telling her, but as soon as she spoke the words, she realized that they were true. The more she spoke, the more she understood that she was speaking her own heart. "I hate to say that because I do love her, but it's true. I don't mean leaving him. That would've been all right. But leaving him the way she did. She tried to make him so angry that he would leave her or throw her out. When that didn't work, she sneaked away, just disappeared."

"Why would she do that?"

He asked it, but she could tell he knew the answer. She and Armando sat across from each other in his perfect house and in the same difficult spot, caught between loving Cat and admitting that she wasn't as good as they wanted her to be, that she had done a thing she should never have done.

"Because she chickened out," said Pen sadly. "She knew how he felt about her and she couldn't stand to see him fall apart when she told him she was leaving, so she ran away. She should have faced it, don't you think?"

"Yes." Armando turned his face in the direction of the fan, let the cool air flow across it. It seemed to help him decide his next move because, afterward, he looked Pen in the eye and said, "That's why she left the way she did," he said. "But she could have run anywhere. She came here for a reason."

"To see you, right?"

He shook his head. "I saw her. She had dinner here, at the house, with everyone. But I'm not why she came to Cebu."

"Then why?" asked Pen.

"Yes, why?" demanded a voice. It was Lola, stepping from the shadows into the room.

Armando shook his head and smiled. "She came to find her family."

Chapter Seventeen

MAYBE IT WAS THE FOOD OR THE MUTED LIGHT OR THE CEIL-ing fan's slow, hypnotic paddling of the air or maybe it was simply that every journey—and Pen had come to see herself as a person distinctly on a journey (in rare, solitary, un-ironic moments, "seeker" did not seem too strong a word, although what she was seeking, apart from Cat [and she was sure there was something else] she couldn't say)—has its land of the lotus eaters, its drowsy slowdown in momentum. There would be time to winnow out the reasons later, but as she sat in the living room of the house in which Cat's father had grown up, surrounded by someone else's family—Cat's family, the one she had flown across the world to find—with a plate of food on a tray in front of her, all Pen knew was that she wanted, with her heart, to become part of the place, to unpack her bags, hunker down, and stay.

Jason had wanted to call Dr. Ocampo's sisters right away, the same night they'd left Armando's house, right after Pen had recounted her conversation with Armando, giving Jason and Will a nutshell version (with a covert look at Will that meant she would tell him the rest later) that left out just about everything but Cat's real reason for coming to Cebu. As soon as she had told Jason that she had the sisters' phone number, he had stuck out his bear-sized paw, palm up, demanding it, and had gotten mad when she'd refused. Cat's aunts were elderly, she told him, it would be much more considerate to wait until morning, but the truth was she wasn't sure that Jason's making the call at all was a good idea, since having him talk to anyone about anything, especially Cat, was almost never a good idea, and she wanted time to discuss the matter with Will in private.

"Who died and made you queen of the world?" Jason had protested, loudly, in the hotel lobby. "You're not the boss. You don't get to say what we do!"

He had been so whiny and Pen so groggy and irritable, emotional exhaustion and jet lag's undertow pulling her down and down, that it was on the tip of her tongue to call him names, to say something low-down and cutting (*Your wife didn't jump in the sack with Armando after all, moron; she just wanted you to think she did!*—an incongruous put-down if Pen ever heard one), but before she could, a little, niggling, adult voice inside her head reminded her that, blowhard or not, the guy had already been hurt pretty wretchedly in ways he knew about and in ways he didn't and it would take an exceedingly mean-hearted person to hurt him more, at least right at that moment. Pen sat there trying to gauge whether she was mean-hearted enough and came down on the side of "No" but just barely. So all she said was, "Of course I'm not the boss, but I need to put Augusta to bed. Let's have breakfast by the pool tomorrow and make a plan. Okay?"

When Jason had begun to sputter at this, Will had said, "Take it easy, man, you're scaring Augusta," which of course were the magic words.

With a guilty glance at Augusta, who was sitting in a chair playing with her new favorite toy, a bunch of miniature bananas, each one no more than three inches long, a gift from Armando's Lola ("*You* are the tiniest!" "No, *you* are the tiniest!" "*You* are the tiniest and have three brown spots!"), and looking not the least bit scared, Jason mumbled, "My bad. See you in the morning."

In the end, it was Pen who called. She spoke to an aunt named Lita, a short conversation but one full of radical highs and lows—yes, Cat had been there; no, she was not there now; yes, she might be back; yes, they knew where she was; yes, they might be willing to tell Pen—and ending with an invitation.

"Come to the house tomorrow," said Lita, simultaneously bossy and kind. "As Catalina's friends and husband, you are welcome. Let us meet you and plan from there."

She hadn't said, "Let us meet you and judge your worthiness and sanity so that we can decide whether or not to entrust you with information regarding the whereabouts of our beloved Cat," but Pen had understood that this was what she meant.

Now, as she sat across from the three women, Lola Lita, Lola Fe, and Lola Graciela ("Lola" having turned out to be not a proper name, as Pen had assumed when she had met Armando's lola, but a word meaning something like "grandmother" or maybe "respected elderly female relative," since the three women could not [could they?] all be grandmothers to all of the people in the house—and there were lots of them—who called them "Lola"), their bright, dark eyes upon her, she knew she should have felt anxious, judged, but what she felt instead was intense contentment, a warmth that started someplace in the center of her body and radiated outward. As she bit into her second empanada, a golden half-moon stuffed with beef, raisins, potatoes, and heaven, she acknowledged that it was just possible that this central place was in the vicinity of her stomach.

The Lolas had thrown them a party. At least, Pen was fairly sure that this splendid profusion of food and people was a party, even though when she thanked Lola Lita for it, Lita waved her hand in the air, irritably, as though swatting away thanks along with the ridiculous notion that anyone had gone to any trouble, and scoffed, "It's nothing. Relatives and a little food. Lunch. Nothing special!"

But there was nothing "nothing special" about it: great piled tangles of noodles rife with bits of vegetables, meat, and shrimp; a concoction of eggplant, okra, green beans, squash, and bitter melon called *pinakbet;* banana blossom salad; whole fish, crispy and gleaming with sauce; thin eggrolls called *lumpia* that Pen could have eaten like popcorn; and, glory of glories, down the center of its own special table, a roasted suckling pig, burnt orange, glistening, dizzyingly fragrant. Pen had a momentary qualm at seeing it whole—snout, ears, tail, the small, poignant hooves ("even-toed ungulate" is the phrase that appeared, unbidden, in Pen's mind)—but once dismantled, the sublime combination of hard, crackly skin and nearly white, meltingly tender meat caused such rapture in her mouth that she gave hearty thanks to God that she was not a vegetarian.

Still, as astonishing as the food was, Pen knew that the source of her contentment was not solely, or even chiefly, gustatory, but had to do with her fellow partygoers. She would learn that nearly all of them lived there, if not in the main house, then in one of the two other houses that sat on the edges of the dusty backyard. Each tiny house was flanked by a riot of high-gloss green and flowers like little shouts of joy and faced a central space that bore a banana tree, a lanzone tree with cascading clusters of brown-yellow golf-ball-looking fruit, and, queening over everything, a green mango under which slept two black dogs. It was a compound, Pen supposed, although as un-Waco-like as it was un-Kennedy-like, surrounded by a high wall the top of which was spangled with broken bottles embedded in the cement. Despite this hint at a dangerous outside world, Pen felt that she had never been anyplace safer. Even the sharp shards of glass were pretty, glowing with mellow color under the sun.

Although she, Will, and Jason were introduced to each person individually, from the littlest, wobbly-legged toddler, to the skinny, pop-star-haired teenagers slouching in corners, to smiling adults, some chatty, some with shy lowered chins, Pen found that she could not keep straight how each was related to the others, how they all fit in. The titles (tito, tita, cousin, grandson, sister) blurred inside her head. But it seemed to her that specific relationships—who was married to whom, whose children were whose—mattered less here, in this household, than they would have at home.

What was clear was that they were a family, each person belonging to the other, held together by an intergenerational web of talking, teasing, scolding, feeding, pulling onto laps, shooing away, holding close. At the center of the web were the three Lolas. If Pen was initially impressed with their sameness—short gray hair; broad, brown, remarkably unlined faces; delicate hands; voluminous generosity; intelligent black eyes—she quickly began to see differences between them. Lola

Fe was jolly, effusive, the one the kids came to when they wanted someone to say yes. Lola Graciela was quiet but watchful; she seemed a little younger than the others. Lola Lita was the boss.

After dessert (Pen, Will, and Jason had slices of leche flan, wondrously eggy and bathed in caramelized sugar; Augusta dove headfirst into a bowl of deep violet-colored ube ice cream, which Pen later learned was made from a variety of yam, a fact that she did not share with Augusta), the party scattered, people going back to their usual Sunday afternoons. Except for the roaming pack of small children into which Augusta had been immediately and thoroughly absorbed, they were alone with the Lolas.

Lola Lita began. "We have been discussing the three of you, and we have a question."

"If you don't mind," added Lola Fe, giving her sister (if she was her sister; Pen wasn't sure) a look of good-humored remonstrance.

"Of course," conceded Lola Lita with a nod. "If you don't mind."

"We don't mind," said Pen.

"Sure," said Will.

"Fire away!" said Jason. His voice was jocular and too loud. Pen stole a glimpse and saw that he wasn't just stained red from collarbone to hairline; he was sweating and as antsy as a two-year-old. With reluctant but now familiar compassion washing over her, she thought that she had never seen him so nervous.

"Here is the question," Lola Lita said, her voice perfectly calm but her eyes burning like coals. "Do you think that Cat would want you to find her?"

The Lolas leaned back in their chairs and folded their hands. Pen and Will and Jason all looked at one another.

"Please," said Lola Fe quickly, sensing their uneasiness, "do not feel that one of you must answer for all. Maybe it would be best if you each spoke only for yourself."

Silence. The ceiling fan went slowly round and round. Pen saw a lizard, pale brown and no more than three inches long, dart up the wall. Then Will's voice, clear and easy: "I think she would. I don't know if Cat told you about us, about me and Pen—"

"She did," said Lola Lita with a droll look at the other Lolas. "She told us her life story. In some detail. You were included."

"Well, then maybe you know that when the three of us last saw each other, we were basically kids," said Will. "We meant well, but we were a little stupid."

"Hmm," sniffed Pen.

Will shot her a half-grin and continued, "Some of us were more stupid than others, but the thing is that each of us, in our own way, thought that if we couldn't keep being friends in *exactly* the way we'd always been friends, then everything would fall apart."

Did I think that? thought Pen. *I don't know if I thought that.*

You have always hated change, have resisted it with everything you're worth, she reminded herself, and she had to admit that this was true.

"I think we were wrong about that," said Will.

"You do?" said Pen, startled.

"Yeah," said Will, reddening. "I think we should've taken more risks, had more—faith, I guess. And now, I think we could use another chance."

"You think Catalina would agree?" asked Lola Lita.

Will nodded. "I do." He paused, smiling. "Plus, nobody loves surprises more than Cat."

Lola Fe laughed, a sweet, husky sound that filled the air inside the house.

"Thank you, Will," said Lola Lita.

Pen expected Jason to jump in then, but he just sat, staring at nothing, jiggling his knee, looking like he might cry or run out of the room, so Pen took a breath and stared into the faces of the Lolas. A trinity of Lolas. *The three Graces,* she thought, *the three Fates.*

"Cat would be as glad to see me as I would to see her," said Pen finally, and was mortified to hear the trembling in her voice. "She would. We were like sisters. We loved each other." She shook her head impatiently. "Not loved. Love."

"Love?" asked Lola Graciela, speaking for the first time. "Even after so many years?"

"Yes," said Pen staunchly. It was true. She felt the truth of it shine on her like a light. "Of course."

In unison, the Lolas rustled like a flock of doves, nodding and humming murmurs of assent and approval, at Pen, at one another, before settling down again, their eyes sparkling. Pen felt a rush of elation, as though she had passed a test.

Everyone turned to Jason. Pen braced herself, waiting for belligerence or bravado, an oversized, embarrassing burst of something, but Jason didn't say anything right away. He seemed to be willing himself not to fidget, with his knees pressed together, his hands gripping the sides of his chair seat. He opened his mouth and shut it again. Pen wasn't sure he was breathing.

Suddenly, Lola Graciela, who had been so quiet, came alive. She slapped her knee with one hand, and said, with an edge of anger in her voice, "The question is ridiculous for him! She is his wife, no matter what. Naturally, he must find her!"

The other two Lolas did not seem surprised at this outburst. They exchanged a knowing glance between them, and Lita reached out and put her hand over Graciela's.

"We know that you feel this way, Graci," said Lita kindly, and, at her touch, the tension seemed to leave Graciela. She lowered her lids and nodded.

Jason cleared his throat.

"Jason would like a chance to speak, I think," said Lola Lita.

Lola Fe gave him an encouraging thumbs-up with her tiny thumb.

"So, uh, contrary to popular belief," said Jason, "I'm not an idiot."

The Lolas shifted their gazes ever so slightly in the direction of Pen and Will who shrugged and nodded their apologies; then everyone turned back to Jason.

"I know how it looks, Cat leaving without telling me. And, hey, you probably even know about the Armando thing, too."

The Lolas nodded, as Pen squirmed inwardly, wondering which story Cat had told them, wondering what was worse, having a wife who cheated or one who lied in order to hurt you so much you'd throw her out, and wondering, too, not for the first time, whether she was obligated to tell Jason the truth. So much was getting fuzzy lately—Pen's loyalties, her obligations. She felt a jolt of anger at Cat for having lied, at Armando for having told the truth, at both of them—and she knew this wasn't really fair—for making her the keeper of a secret she did not want.

"I'm not gonna lie to you," Jason continued. "We've had our share of problems. The infertility stuff royally sucked, pardon my language, and, yeah, I know Cat wasn't happy with where we lived and whatnot. It's probably also the case that she wasn't always happy with me."

"No marriage is happy all the time," said Lola Graciela softly.

"She's too good for me." A bittersweet, affectionate smile appeared on Jason's face, flickered, and was gone. "I've always known that."

Pen thought, *Too smart, too funny, too sparkling and bewitching and quick, but maybe not too good,* and felt instantly ashamed, until she understood that she didn't mean that Cat wasn't good, but that, in some highly unexpected, mostly imperceptible, but fundamental way, Jason was.

"So I'd have to say it's possible she doesn't realize she wants me to find her. She might even, uh, actively think she does *not* want me to find her."

Pen had to admire his honesty. Maybe it was the Lolas, before whose clear and rock-steady gaze it was difficult to do anything but speak the truth. Maybe it was that Jason had nothing left to lose. Maybe, probably, it was that he was braver than Pen had given him credit for.

"But here's the deal." Jason's voice tensed. "When I find her, as soon as she sees me, she'll be glad I'm there. No lie."

"How do you know this?" asked Lola Lita sternly.

Jason's blue eyes brightened. "Because that's how it always happens. I mean, let's face it; Cat's thought about leaving me before. She even did it a few times, and there might even be times I don't know about. Probably there are. Anyway, she'd pack a bag and go to a friend's house or check into a hotel, or even just drive around aimlessly, with the bag sitting in the front seat." He lifted his weighty chin. "But she always came back, every time, and she'd see me in our house—I'd have, like, gotten her note or whatever and be just sitting there—and her heart would melt."

Oh, God, thought Pen.

"That's what she'd say. She'd say, 'I can't help it, little boy. No matter how mad I am, I see you and my heart melts.' She calls me 'little boy' which is hilarious when you consider how big I am compared to her."

If anyone found this hilarious, they didn't let on. Unexpectedly, Pen found herself thinking of Augusta. Augusta and her addled sleep habits, how on any one of thousands of nights her sobbing and shouts of "Mama!" would drag Pen out of sleep, two, three, even four times, how by the last wake-up, usually near dawn, Pen would be shaking with exhaustion and a resentment so acute it was almost rage. Her head throbbing and full of static, she would throw off sheets and comforter and stomp down the hallway to Augusta's room, muttering expletives, even threats (threats that, no matter how empty, would make her reel with shame in the light of day), but within seconds of arriving at her child's bedside, as soon as she saw the pale, wet face, the skinny shoulders, her anger would dissipate, lose itself in the warm, Augusta-scented air of the room. Her heart would melt. Pen would lie down next to Augusta and pull the small, baby animal bulk of the girl into the curve of her body, and give herself over to the business—her life's work—of loving this person who needed her.

Maybe Cat feels something like that; maybe that's why it was so hard to leave him, thought Pen, which should have been a nonsensical thought, since Jason was a full-grown (even, it could be argued, an overgrown) man, but Pen found that it made an absurd, sad, slightly unsavory kind of sense to her.

"Thank you," said Lola Lita, nodding elegantly, like an empress. "Thanks to all of you. Thanks and apologies; we do not usually interrogate our guests."

"That's okay," said Will and Pen.

"No prob," said Jason. "Totally understandable."

Pen wondered if the Lolas would retire someplace, perhaps to an inner fate-deciding sanctum, to discuss whether to tell them where Cat had gone, but they didn't budge, just set about wordlessly conversing through nods, raised eyebrows, almost imperceptible shrugs, and some of the mild dovecote sounds like the ones they'd made when Pen said that she and Cat still loved each other. Pen didn't feel impatient. She believed that she could sit and watch the three of them do that forever.

When the cooing and humming had concluded, Pen expected Lola Lita to speak first, but instead it was Lola Fe.

"Fine, but if we are telling them where Catalina is, I think we must also call her to let her know they are coming," she said.

"No!" said Jason, so loudly that Pen jumped.

The Lolas did not jump, just turned their heads in unison to gaze at him. He reached up and wiped the sweat from his brow. Seeing this, Lola Graciela leaned over to turn the electric fan in his direction.

"I mean, please," he said. "Could you—do you think you could just not tell her?"

The Lolas exchanged a complicated, lightning-quick set of looks.

"Why do you ask this?" said Lola Fe.

"Uh, like Will said," said Jason, forcing a grin, "Cat loves to be surprised."

Lola Fe did not react, except to keep her eyes trained on him, waiting for more.

"And, you know, like I said, she might think she doesn't want to see me. She might even leave if she knows I'm coming. Probably not, but it's possible. When I show up, though, she'll be very happy, rejoicing even. I swear to God."

Pen saw Lola Fe's eyebrows go up. She wondered if it was a good or bad idea to swear to God, here in this house that had an Augusta-sized Virgin Mary statue standing, wistful and blue-robed, in the yard and a crucifix—at least one—on nearly every wall.

"We should honor his wishes," exclaimed Lola Graciela with fervor. "He is her husband!"

Lola Fe stirred in her chair and seemed about to speak, maybe even speak loudly, but after a second, her face relaxed into cameo-blank inscrutability. Her eyes met Lola Lita's gaze and held it. Lola Lita closed her eyes and nodded, before turning to Will, Jason, and Pen with a smile.

"You must wait until tomorrow to go find Catalina, in any case," she said. None of them asked why this was so. The fact of her saying it was enough to make it indisputable. "We hope you will consider spending the night here, since you are Catalina's friends and family. I'm afraid our home isn't luxurious, but we would be most honored if you would stay."

"Oh, thank you! We'd love to," cried Pen, without so much as a questioning glance at Will or Jason and so hot on the heels of the invitation that Lola Lita laughed, a deep, buttery chuckle. Pen turned sheepishly to Will and Jason. "I mean, if it's okay with you guys."

Will smiled a smile that managed to be private, in spite of the other people in the room, and said, "You like it here. It's a Pen kind of place."

"I do," admitted Pen.

"We'd be honored to stay," said Jason.

"Good," said Lola Lita. "Now, why don't you go to pick up your things at the hotel? My nephew Everett will be glad to drive you."

"Great," said Will. "Thank you."

"Sounds good," agreed Jason.

Pen tried to imagine herself getting up and walking out of that house, even just for a short trip, and failed utterly. "Please," she said to the Lolas, "may Augusta and I stay here, while the boys go to the hotel? If I promise to stay out of your way?"

"Of course!" said Lola Lita. "If Will and Jason are willing."

"Would you mind?" she asked Will. "Our stuff is pretty much together. If you could just throw it all into my suitcase and Augusta's backpack?"

"Sure," said Will, shrugging. "But if I come back and you've polished off that pig? You're dead meat."

"Ha!" said Jason. "Pig. Dead meat. Get it?"

"Got it," said Pen, and all the Lolas nodded.

TUCKED AS SHE WAS INTO A SHADY CORNER OF THE BACKYARD, despite the children playing tag and screeching, despite the cold glass of calamansi juice in her hand, despite the tart perfection of the juice itself, Pen might have fallen asleep. Time changed in that yard. Minutes flowed by with rich, honeylike slowness. Pen's body felt more and more deliciously heavy. But before she could drift off, she opened her eyes to find Lola Lita sitting next to her, fanning herself with a large, woven palm-leaf fan, and regarding Pen with an amused affection that reminded Pen of her mother. Pen shook the sleepiness from her head and sat up.

"Sorry," she said, laughing. "I don't usually go falling asleep in people's yards, at least not people I've just met."

"Perhaps it means you feel at home here. I'm very glad."

"It's a marvelous place."

"Thank you," said Lola Lita, looking about her. "It isn't fancy. It's even a bit shabby, but it's home. My family moved here after the war, when we were all quite young. Manuel was no more than a baby."

"Manuel?" asked Pen. "Oh. Cat's father."

"Yes," said Lola Lita sadly. "My baby brother."

"I'm so sorry for your loss," said Pen and felt ashamed and surprised at herself for not having offered her condolences earlier, when they had first arrived. It wasn't that she had forgotten about Dr. Ocampo. It was just that this place seemed to Pen to be a world away from grief.

"Thank you," said Lola Lita again. She reached over and touched Pen's hand. "We have made a decision regarding your wish to find Catalina."

"You have?" Pen held her breath.

"We will tell you where she went," said Lola Lita.

Tears prickled Pen's eyes. She blinked. "Thank you. Thank you so much."

"She is visiting a resort island, quite enchanting as I have heard. We have secured tickets for you on the ferry for tomorrow morning, and we have made hotel reservations, as well. Our niece's friend from college is a travel agent, which made it possible for us to make the arrangements on a Sunday."

"Oh, that's wonderful! I can just imagine it, seeing her across the hotel lobby—" Pen broke off, overcome with gladness.

Uneasiness swept over Lola Lita's face and she gave Pen's hands a squeeze. "I am afraid that it won't be quite so simple."

"It won't?" asked Pen, worried. "Why?"

Lola Lita sighed. "We can be so stubborn. Fe, Graci, and I, we are usually in agreement, but when we're not, well, it can be—difficult."

"I can imagine," said Pen.

"The problem is that we have decided, after much discussion, to abide by Jason's wish that we not tell Catalina you are coming."

"I see," said Pen. "Well, it might be for the best. She might leave if she knows that Jason's coming."

Lola Lita's eyes glinted. "The best for Jason, maybe, and for you and Will. Possibly not the best for Cat."

"I guess you might be right," admitted Pen uncomfortably.

"But it also presents a problem for you because we know where she is but not precisely where."

"Oh."

"Bohol Province is composed of a large island and many smaller ones. We know that Catalina was planning to stay on Panglao Island. We also know which region of the island, but we don't know which resort. We're not even sure that she is still there, although I think she probably is."

Pen sipped her juice, then pressed her glass against her forehead.

"We have reserved rooms for the four of you at a resort on Panglao Island," Lola Lita continued, "but if we don't call Cat to say you are coming, we can't find out exactly where she is."

"Can't you call her to ask where she is, without mentioning us? Or call her travel agent and try to get the information from her?" Even as Pen said it, she realized how sneaky it sounded.

Lola Lita shook her head. "No. I'm sorry, but no. We can only tell you what we know about where she went, and even that feels—"

"Disloyal?"

Lola Lita smiled tenderly at Pen, "You must understand that this trip was very important to Cat. She wanted to be—undisturbed."

Pen's heart sank. "But we might not find her."

Lola Lita made soft hums of comfort and brushed a lock of hair away from Pen's cheek. "It is not a large beach, not even a kilometer long," she said. "And you can go to some of the Bohol tourist attractions that Cat will surely visit. I have heard that you do not want to miss snorkeling along the black coral reef."

Pen had her doubts about the snorkeling, fearing sharks and figuring that one sure way to decrease your chances of finding someone was to immerse yourself in the Pacific Ocean. She envisioned Cat swimming toward her, through shoals of brilliant fish, waving wildly, her hair floating like seaweed around her face. She smiled.

As if Lola Lita had read Pen's thoughts, she said, kind reproval in her voice, "I know you want to find Catalina, but who knows when you and your daughter will come back to the Philippines? So many people never get to go anywhere. Allow yourself to really be here. See what there is to see."

Pen nodded thoughtfully. Ever since she had arrived in the Philippines, Pen had been dazzled by a sense of improbability. *We were there*, she had thought, *and now we are here. How could it be true?* But it was true. The world was big and Pen was in it. The least she could do was pay attention.

"Okay," she agreed. "But can you tell me something?"

Lola Lita nodded her empress nod.

"Do *you* think we'll find her?" Pen held her breath, waiting.

Pensively, Lola Lita narrowed her eyes, sending sunbursts of wrinkles shooting from their corners. *No one can see the future*, thought Pen, breathlessly. *But if someone could, this is exactly how she would look.*

"Yes," said Lola Lita, "I do."

PEN DIDN'T KNOW WHAT WOKE HER, BUT SUDDENLY SHE WAS SITTING up, her senses prickling, her chest full of rising, undefined emotion. In near perfect darkness, in the bed next to hers, Augusta shifted, sighed, and drew herself into a tight ball, like an armadillo. Pen waited for her daughter's breathing to ease back into its cradle-rock rhythm and then noiselessly swung her legs over the side of the bed. They were in a tiny inner room, windowless and square. What light there was slid in over the tops of the room's walls, which did not quite reach the ceiling. Pen knew that Will was sleeping in the matching room next door. All around her, in every room, enfolded in the same heat, the same velvet silence, people slept.

Pen found the closed door, sliding her feet across the smooth tiles, and walked out into the narrow hallway that she knew would take her to the front of the house. Light from the front windows turned the darkness gray. Uncertainly, Pen rocked on the balls of her feet in the center of the living room, weighed down by what she now recognized as sadness. She knew that she needed to sit down, to be someplace solid and solitary when it overtook her completely, so she let herself out the front door onto the narrow, L-shaped porch. Her body felt separate from her, like a brittle, wounded thing; with care, she set it down on a wooden bench. Then she stepped off an edge and into the sadness and was lost.

After several minutes or thirty or an hour—it was impossible to say—Pen was called back to herself by the sound of the front door opening. Someone sat down next to her, someone put an arm around her shoulders, someone said, "Poor child." Pen wasn't sure who it was and for a moment, didn't think to ask or check. The person was pure kindness, consolation embodied, and Pen buried her face in the person's shoulder until she was calm. The shoulder was the most comforting spot Pen had ever been. It smelled like baby powder.

"I'm so sorry you are sad," said the person. Lola Fe.

Pen sat up and wiped her face but didn't pull away. "I'm sorry I woke you up."

"Don't be silly," admonished Lola Fe. "It is just what happens when you're my age. Your body forgets how to sleep."

"Does it also forget how to be tired?"

"No," said Lola Fe with a chuckle. "That it remembers very well."

They sat in companionable quiet, until a voice from the front yard, somewhere near the Virgin Mary statue, proclaimed, loudly, "Tuk-o!"

Pen looked at Lola Fe.

"Listen," said Lola Fe, pressing her finger to her lips.

"Tuk-o, tuk-o, tuk-o!" The voice began to slow, stretching the space between the syllables, like a toy running down; then it squawked and started over again, "Tuk-o!"

"Was the Virgin Mary doing that?" asked Pen. She hoped it wasn't a terrible joke to make.

Lola Fe laughed. "Not her. Her pet, our friend the tuko lizard."

"I like him," said Pen. "Or her." The sound of the lizard was like so many other things in this place, completely strange and, at the same time, completely natural, even inevitable. She hadn't felt the absence of the lizard before it began to sing, but as soon as it had sung, she understood that nothing would have been complete without it.

"My father died two years ago," said Pen, breathing the words out in a long stream into the quiet that was somehow different from the pre-lizard quiet, more resonant.

"I am very sorry," said Lola Fe. "You must miss him."

"I do," said Pen. "And this place, your home, makes me miss him more than I usually do. Even though he's never been here. Isn't that odd?"

"I don't know," said Lola Fe. "Maybe it's a place he would like."

"It is," said Pen. "He would love it, maybe for the same reason I do."

"The empanadas?" teased Lola Fe.

"Yes," Pen said, smiling, but her thoughts were solemn. It seemed important for her to articulate to Lola Fe what this place meant to her. "I just feel that the way things are here is the way things should be."

Lola Fe did not dispute this. She nodded and asked, "What do you mean?"

"A lot of things, but mostly I'm talking about the way everyone is together. Nobody leaving, nobody gone. Do you know what I mean?"

"I think so," said Lola Fe. She smiled at Pen. "You're wrong, of course. So many have left. Manuel and my sister Maria who died when she was just a girl and my parents and my cousin Gigi, who lives in New York, and my nephews and nieces who have gone to the States or to Canada or Dubai or Australia to live and work."

Lola Fe turned her smooth face to the dark yard, her eyes alert and tender as though she could see all of the missing standing out there among the shrubs and flowers. Then she looked back at Pen and said, "But you are right that nobody's gone."

Pen nodded, wanting her to go on.

"What is that saying? Gone but not—?" asked Lola Fe.

"Gone but not forgotten," said Pen.

"Yes, but it's more than that. Gone but not gone." Lola Fe laughed. "Gone but here. It must be why the house feels so small. We keep them all."

Gone but here, thought Pen. "How?" she asked.

"I don't know," said Lola Fe with a touch of crustiness. "How not? It's how things are. Just because someone happens not to be here doesn't mean he is lost." She said it as though the very idea of people being lost was ridiculous.

"Oh."

"You just make room for more. Always room for one more!" She laughed her wonderful, sandpapery laugh again.

"So you keep everyone?" asked Pen.

"Sure," said Lola Fe with an impatient shrug. "What else?"

CHAPTER EIGHTEEN

$\mathcal{I}$T WAS EVEN BEFORE SHE WAS ACTUALLY IN THE OCEAN, BEFORE she was surrounded on every side by streaming, swirling, darting, infinitely varicolored glory, while she was still riding in the snow-white water strider of a boat (delicate outriggers arching over the blue water) that took them from Alona Beach to Balicasag Island that Pen realized it: sometimes there is nothing to do but surrender yourself to wonder. You must stop searching for one small, dark-haired woman in a world of small, dark-haired women. You must stop missing your father. You must stop measuring—over and over—the line between loving and being in love. You must offer yourself, whole, to the cobalt starfish (and the orange one and the pale pink one and the biscuit-colored one with the raised, chocolate-brown art deco design) and to the clear, clear water and to the sweep of shining sky and to the silver scattershot of leaping fish (an entire school skipping across the ocean like a stone).

It's what they were all doing, Pen could tell. Will with his legs stretched out and his face to the wind. Augusta, who had, that morning, sobbed inconsolably upon learning that the naked children—hair bronze-streaked, skin mahogany from a lifetime of living outdoors ("*Badjao*," a woman next to Pen had whispered. "Sea gypsies!")— standing in small *banca* boats, hands outstretched, begging (there was no other word for it) the people boarding the ferry to Bohol for money or food were naked because they owned no clothes, was now consoled a thousand times over, her face singularly radiant, as she tilted it over the edge of the boat to look into the translucent ocean, searching for stars. Even Jason, who had grown brooding and taciturn since they'd left the Lolas' house, in spite of their being so close to finding Cat, or maybe because of it, was happy under the brim of his baseball cap, waving at passing boats with a broad, magisterial, welcoming smile, as though he owned it all: boat, sky, country, the sea and everything in it.

By the time they got to the coral reef off the edge of Balicasag ("coast" seemed too large a word to apply to Balicasag, which was tiny and, as their captain, Pedro, told them, "round like a *peso*" and boasting a single restaurant, owned by Pedro's cousin Nonoy), Pen had plunged so deeply into the beauty of the day that when it came time to plunge into the ocean (or at least to float on its turquoise surface), she found she had no room in her heart for fear. Even if she had been afraid, it wouldn't have mattered in the face of Augusta's cute but unconquerable desire to "snorgle with Mama."

There was no snorkel small enough for Augusta, so she held her breath and wore a pair of ordinary swim goggles, the kind she wore for the swim lessons she had been attending regularly, if sometimes wildly reluctantly, since before she turned three. Pen was grateful that Augusta was water-safe because it was clear that there was no keeping her out of that ocean. As soon as they landed at Balicasag, Pedro's friend Jing Jing appeared with a little paddle-powered *banca,* a pink peapod of a boat, to take them to the reef (it was a fish sanctuary; no motors allowed), and before the boat was even fully stopped, Augusta was lurching over its side, and Pen had to hold her back.

They snorkeled holding hands. The water was so salty that they almost didn't need to swim, just bobbed on its surface like corks, kicking slightly to propel themselves from one spot to another. The first time Pen put her face in the water and opened her eyes, her senses were so thoroughly and instantly overloaded that she emitted an involuntary yelp, which was a mistake, considering her snorkeled and undersea state. She lifted her head and coughed so long and hard that

Jing Jing leaned over the boat to give her a considerate, if ineffective, underwater clap on the back.

The second time, more prepared, she stayed long enough to understand that the coral reef off Balicasag Island packed more gorgeousness per square centimeter than any other place she had ever been. At the same time that it was exactly like something she had seen on a nature show, it was like nothing she had seen on a nature show because everything—from the imperious butterfly fish trailing their scarves to the brown undulating ribbons that Pen assumed were eels (but might not have been; it frustrated her not to know) to the neon blue coruscations, so penny-small and quick that they might have been tricks of light—each thing, every individual scrap of embodied beauty, was palpably, unmistakably *alive*.

So were Pen and Augusta, alive and in the thick of it. Pen had expected to look down and see fish, and she did, but when she looked to the side, there they were, too, suspended next to her face or flowing by in iridescent streams, and, when Will swam over to take Augusta to see an anemone clownfish and Pen dove downward, the fish were above her as well. She knew that she was an intruder, but she didn't feel like one. She felt like just another living creature, glowing and streamlined among the corals, corals like ferns and hair and platters and Queen Anne's lace. She stayed as still as she could and watched a parrotfish glide by, stippled, striped, and marbled with so many luminous pastels that it looked like a fish-shaped painting by Monet. *Showoff,* thought Pen and wanted to laugh with joy.

Later, Jing Jing paddled them into the deeper, darker waters beyond the steep drop-off in the coral reef wall, and, without warning, stopped. They all looked at him, and without actually understanding why, Pen was immediately, spine-tinglingly aware of vast movement under the water.

"Jackfish!" said Jing Jing excitedly. "Very good to eat!"

He pointed and they all looked down and saw them, under and around the boat, a great, circling body of bodies, lithe and flashing platinum, and, suddenly, the thought that had been skirting the edges of her consciousness since they'd boarded Pedro's boat at Alona

Beach—and probably before that, maybe as soon as they had arrived in the Philippines—hit Pen with the force of an epiphany, knocking the breath out of her. She turned to Will, who sat behind her. One glance at her face and he was pushing his sunglasses to the top of his head.

"What?" he said, resting his hand on her shoulder. "Are you okay?"

Pen nodded, struggling to put words to the thought.

"Hey," said Will, worried.

She shook her head and smiled to let him know she was all right.

"It's nothing," she said, but it wasn't nothing, although she realized it might sound that way. "It's just that—*all this time*. When we were home, driving our cars, drinking coffee."

Will leaned closer, trying to understand.

"This." Pen gestured toward the ocean around them. She meant the jackfish. She meant all of it. "All this time, every second: *this*."

Will stared down at the fish, then back at Pen. "It's not just when we're here. Is that what you mean? It's going on the whole time, at the same time as our lives."

"At the same time, in the same world," said Pen. "And I never knew."

She had never known, and, even now, she could just barely believe it. In a few weeks, Pen would describe what had happened to Amelie, and Amelie would nod and say, "That is *so* Soto Zen. 'All is one and all is different.' Or some people might call what you experienced the 'oceanic feeling.' Although not Freud, of course."

But there in the boat, Pen didn't call it anything. She licked the salt off her lips and wrapped her arms around herself, rocked by awe and the ocean, as the jackfish swirled beneath her like a typhoon or a galaxy or like a swirling school of silver fish.

THAT EVENING, AUGUSTA WANTED PIZZA. SHE DIDN'T JUST WANT IT; she was hell-bent on pizza, running in place on the porch of her and Pen's tiny "villa" and piling on the "pleases" to the rhythm of her feet in a way that Pen had seen before and knew spelled trouble. Under other circumstances, Pen might have given in. Augusta had been a remarkably good sport about eating unfamiliar foods on the trip, had even developed such a taste for the noodle dish *pancit,* shrimp and all, that Pen had vowed to learn how to cook it at home, even though it appeared to involve an awful lot of chopping. Plus, Augusta had been a trooper on the snorkeling outing. But this was Bohol; Bohol did not have pizza.

"We're going to walk down the beach," she told Augusta, "to one of those restaurants *right smack on the beach,* and we're going to buy some delicious fish, and eat it. *Outside!*"

Augusta stopped running in place. "Fish, like the ones we saw today at the reef?"

Uh-oh, thought Pen. "Well, not those exact fish. Those fish live in a sanctuary, where they stay safe and no one catches them. The fish we would eat would be different fish."

Augusta grew stony-faced. "They are still fish. They might have got lost and swum out of the sanctuary. Or they might be *relatives* of those fish." Pen could tell that, even in the throes of her pre-tantrum, Augusta was proud of the word *relatives.*

"*Relatives* is an awesome word," said Jason, who was standing nearby. He walked up to Augusta, crouched down, and lifted his hand. "High five on the vocab, baby girl."

Augusta gave his hand an obligatory pat, but then turned her face away. "I just want pizza, Mama. Pizza is the only thing I want in the whole world."

"I would give it to you, if I could," said Pen, cupping her daughter's pointy chin in her hand, "but there is no pizza in Bohol."

Will had slipped away as soon as the "pleases" had begun and slipped back maybe fifteen seconds later. Now, he stood behind Augusta and mouthed to Pen, "There is pizza in Bohol."

"Really?" said Pen. "Where?"

"According to the Americans sitting at the bar," said Will, gesturing in the direction of the resort's outdoor bar, "on the beach, about fifty yards from the beach entrance to the resort."

"Right smack on the beach," said Augusta with relish. "Right smack!"

It was good. Not chewy, as Augusta observed, but crisp and dotted with salty shavings of ham. After their long day on—and in—the water, they ate with gusto, washing down slice after slice with San Miguel beer, in the case of Jason and Will, or with mango shake, in the case of Augusta, or with bottled water, in the case of Pen, who thought she had never been so thirsty. It was a happy meal, although Pen could tell that, for Jason, the carefree feeling that had carried all of them through the long day was seeping away. As the meal waned, Pen observed him becoming increasingly fidgety and impatient. While Pen, Will, and Augusta watched the sunset, Jason watched, while pretending not to watch, the passersby on the darkening beach.

When they were getting ready to leave, Jason said, "So, hey, I was thinking I'd go take a look around for Cat, maybe inquire at some of the other resorts whether they've seen her."

He saw Will and Pen exchange concerned glances and lifted his hands, three fingers raised. "I'll be on my best behavior. Scout's honor."

"What about Ulysses and Ben?" asked Will.

"They stay in the old walleto," said Jason, patting the buttoned pocket on his cargo shorts.

"You were a Scout?" asked Pen.

Jason shrugged. "Briefly. Until the fake bear scat trail/pile of rocks incident." He waved his hand sheepishly. "That story's a little convoluted."

"I bet," said Pen.

"But high five on the vocab," said Will.

THEIR RESORT WAS ONE OF THE SMALLER ONES ON ALONA BEACH: AN open-air restaurant, a pool, and a wide crescent of one-bedroom/one-bath cottages, or villas, with nipa roofs and miniature covered porches. Pen and Augusta's villa was a twin, with Will on the other side of the wall, and after Pen put Augusta to bed, she came out onto the shared porch, where Will sat, drinking his second San Miguel.

"That was quick," said Will.

"Yeah," said Pen dryly. "It turns out that all Augusta needs to fall asleep at night is a coral reef. Maybe I should get one."

"She's slept like a pro the whole trip. Maybe you should get a Philippines, put it in your backyard," said Will. "Tonight, she conked out before I could even go to the bar and get you a drink."

"Here I am," observed Pen. She pointed across the pool. "And there's the bar."

The night seemed as hot as the nights in Cebu, but now and then, a breeze pleated the lit pool and stirred the bushes next to the porch. Voices and laughter drifted toward them from the restaurant. Someone seemed to be singing "Waltzing Matilda." ("This place is crawling with Aussies," Jason had observed earlier. "Apparently, they come for the diving," and Will had said, "Because they don't have any coral reefs back home.") Pen sipped her drink, icy calamansi juice spiked with Tanduay rum, and swore that it was the best drink she had ever had.

She told Will about her conversation with Lola Fe, including an only slightly edited version of her own crying jag.

"Do you think it works that way?" asked Pen. "Keeping everyone? Gone but not gone?"

"Hey, you won't catch me arguing with Lola Fe," said Will. "I might get hit by a thunderbolt."

Pen smiled. "The earth might open up and swallow you."

"Anyway, I kept *you* all those years, you and Cat. Even when I tried to shake you, you stuck."

"Like burrs," said Pen.

"Leeches," said Will.

"Oysters," said Pen. "Did you know that scientists are studying the way oysters adhere to each other in hopes of making better glues?"

"Oh yeah," said Will. "Who doesn't know that?"

Pen laughed, and maybe it was the drink or the heat or the thought of the Lolas or the jackfish epiphany or the sight of Will's face, which always looked most like his face when he was smiling at Pen the way he was doing right then, and which, paintbrushed with shadows and washed in the lunar light of the pool, made her heart leap, but, suddenly, Pen felt brave.

The bravery filled her and she said, "Can I tell you about what happened to my dad?"

She had never told anyone. Actually, she had told a lot of people, back when it first happened, but only because she had to, and even then, it wasn't her story that she had told. It was only facts, which belonged to no one. She had used as few words as she possibly could, and the words had been no one's, too.

"Sure," said Will quietly. "Of course. Whatever you want."

"We were visiting my parents in Wilmington, Augusta and I. We did that a lot back then. It was before we lived with Jamie, of course, and I think we were lonely." Pen smiled and corrected herself. "I was lonely. Augusta has never been lonely for a second of her life. She makes friends like that." Pen snapped her fingers. "With other kids, dogs, waiters, mean old ladies, police officers, Jason, the occasional schizophrenic in the park."

"Bananas," Will reminded her, and if Pen had had even the slightest doubt about telling him the story, it disappeared with this single word. Will knew what tone a situation called for; it was one of the things about him that she loved.

"Bananas," agreed Pen. "Very small ones. So we were at my parents' house and we'd just had dinner, and my mom had made a strawberry pie, and she realized she was out of ice cream."

"Breyers," said Will. "Vanilla bean."

"You remember," said Pen with gratitude.

"The no-apostrophe in the name drove you crazy, your whole family. But you loved it anyway."

"So my dad and I drove over to the Acme. You remember that Acme?"

"You called it the Soviet Acme because it was always running out of things."

"Like bread! And toilet paper. But that night, they had the Breyers, so we bought it, and on the way home, my dad says, 'I need to make a quick stop at the ATM, sweetheart.'" Pen's throat had gone dry, and she took a long sip of her drink. "I knew what he meant."

She looked up and met Will's eyes. "We were so broke. I was doing the author escort work with Amelie, but it had been slow, and rent and babysitting seemed to eat up everything that Patrick gave us. I probably should have asked him for more, but I was the one with custody of Augusta. I hated asking him."

"I can see how you would."

"My dad gave us money every time we visited or they visited us. He'd never say anything, just slip it into my bag or the kitchen drawer where I kept my car keys, and I would just hug him or something the next time I saw him. He knew what it meant."

Pen prepared herself for the next part of the story, and Will waited. Two buff-colored lizards, no longer than a finger, skittered around the edge of the villa and froze in the light.

"They eat insects. Mosquitoes," said Will, and Pen nodded and went on with her story.

"We went to the bank at the intersection across from that bar that's always changing its name. The one near the drugstore."

"I remember it," said Will.

"My dad parallel parked in front of the bar, like always, but he had to go a little way down the road because of all the cars. So I couldn't see him. I couldn't see the ATM from there. And he was taking a long time, but I wasn't really worried because sometimes there's a line at that ATM because of the bar, you know. It took longer and longer, though, so I called him on his cell phone, thinking maybe he'd run into someone he knew and started talking. He didn't answer, but even that didn't worry me all that much."

"He was the kind of guy who probably wouldn't answer his phone during a conversation," said Will.

"Yes," said Pen, smiling. "If he even remembered to bring it with him at all." She took a breath. "Finally, I got out of the car and went to find him."

Pen was crying now, quietly, and she wiped the tears off her face with both hands. "He was on the sidewalk in front of the bank behind one of those big potted plants that public buildings sometimes have. A hibiscus with white flowers, big as saucers. But he wasn't really hidden and the light from the streetlamp was shining right on him. I remember that, his face in the yellow light. He was lying on his side with his legs bent, like he was sleeping."

Pen closed her eyes and let herself see him. It was the first time that she had let herself see him without trying to chase the memory away.

"His face was his face," she said. "It looked peaceful, just the way it looked when he was sleeping, so it took me a few seconds to understand. Even when I did understand I didn't really because I thought he must have had a heart attack. But then I saw the blood on his shirt and pooling under his head, and I started talking to him and kissing his hands, begging him to be okay and to wake up. Telling him that I loved him. I was beside myself. I talked to him until the ambulance came."

She opened her eyes and stared out at the pool and at the moonlight resting on the peaked roofs of the villas. "He wasn't dead. He died almost as soon as the ambulance got him to the hospital, but when I was talking to him, he was alive. He didn't respond to me, his face never moved, but I don't know that that means he couldn't hear me. I think he could. I hope he could, even though it would have upset him to hear how distraught I was and to not be able to comfort me, but I hope that the last voice he heard was mine and not—"

"Pen," said Will.

When Pen looked at him, she saw that his face was full of sorrow and love and that he was crying. Even through her own sadness, she felt wonder at the sight of Will crying. He brushed his eyes, roughly, with the back of his wrist and then reached out and cradled her cheek with his hand.

"I'm sorry," he said. "I'm so sorry."

"Don't cry," said Pen. She turned her face to kiss his palm.

They sat like that for a little while, before Pen pulled carefully away and wiped her eyes.

"They caught him," said Pen. "The kid who did it. It wasn't hard. Between the video camera outside the bar and the one at the bank, they got the whole thing."

"A kid," said Will.

"Nineteen," said Pen. "A nineteen-year-old out of his mind on meth."

"He's in prison?"

"Yes. There wasn't a trial. They made a deal. He'll stay in for a long time, but not forever." Pen sighed. "I tried so hard to hate him. I wanted to hate him every day, every second of every day, for the rest of my life because of what he did."

"You couldn't?"

"His sister called me. After it was all over, months after."

"And she talked you out of hating him?"

"Sort of, but I was already giving it up, even though I tried so hard not to. I found out later that my dad told the kid, Joseph Cort, that he'd give him his wallet if he'd give my dad a minute to talk him out of it, out of ruining his life, which, as far as I can tell, was already a complete shambles. My dad was actually holding the wallet out, ready to hand it over, when the kid freaked and hit him. Joseph Cort killed my father with one of those little wooden bats they give away at baseball games. Every time I felt the hate slipping away, I would think about that bat. But even before I met with his sister, I knew I couldn't keep it up."

"You should not have had to meet her." Will sounded angry. "It wasn't fair of her to ask you."

"I know, but she needed it so much, for me to know who he used to be. Her little brother. Maybe I needed that, too." She gave a grim laugh. "I guess I'm not so good at hate."

"That's okay," said Will. "You're good at everything else."

"I've never told anyone that story, not since I told the police. I'm glad I told you, though. I feel better, clearer. Talking to you has always made me feel clearer."

Will nodded.

"You know, I wanted you, at my dad's funeral." Pen hadn't intended to say this, but once she started, she kept going. "I was so sad and sick and empty, and I wanted you and Cat so much, but mostly you." As soon as Pen said "mostly you," she realized that it was true. "I even thought you were there."

Will glanced quickly over at her. "What?"

"I mean, you weren't, but I thought that you were. I even looked for you."

Will looked stricken. "I wish I had known that you needed me."

"No, Will," said Pen soothingly. "How could you have known? Please don't look like that. I didn't mean that you let me down."

"I would have gone to find you if I'd known. I swear."

"You don't have to swear. I always knew that," said Pen. "But thank you."

"Don't thank me."

"I'll thank you if I want to thank you."

She nudged him with her elbow and smiled at him, and kept nudging and smiling until he smiled back.

She told him, "I e-mailed my mom this morning from the Lolas' computer."

"The Lolas have a computer?"

"They do. I e-mailed my mom from it and told her that when I got home, we should all have dinner: me, my mother, Augusta, Jamie, Mr. Venverloh and his sons, the whole gang. I told her to put it on the calendar."

Will gave her his sudden, lovely, open smile, all the regret from a moment before gone.

"So I guess you decided to keep everyone," he said.

Right at that second, as they sat there, somewhere in the dark ocean, and in Cebu, and in Wilmington, Delaware, all over the world, countless living bodies were living their countless, precious, mysterious lives.

"I guess I did," said Pen.

CHAPTER NINETEEN

THE FAMOUS CHOCOLATE HILLS OF BOHOL DID NOT LOOK PAR-
ticularly edible to Pen, as they bubbled up, brown and smooth,
out of their flat, green, ruffled surroundings, turning the landscape
into something out of Dr. Seuss, but her first thought upon seeing
them was that of all the people she could think of who would love
them (Jamie, Patrick, her mother), Cat Ocampo would love them the
most. She would complain every step of the way up the long, steep
flight of stairs to the overlook (Pen stopped counting at step 110), but
once she arrived at the top and beheld that crazily whimsical view,
she would squeal, jump for joy, and, almost definitely, grab the person
closest to her and kiss him (or her, but probably him).

After the snorkeling trip, they had spent two days searching for
Cat, splitting up, going to the other side of the island and into the city,
scouring beaches, restaurants, shopping malls. Nothing. Now, they
were doing as Lola Lita had suggested, hitting all the tourist stops,
beginning, at Augusta's request, with the Chocolate Hills.

Augusta had been exploring the overlook with Will, but now she
appeared, pink-cheeked, wild-haired, dressed in a rainbow of color.

"Can we do it, can we do it, can we do it?" she squealed. She was
jumping straight up and down with her arms pressed to her sides, a
specifically Augusta variety of overwrought jumping that Jamie called
"popcorning."

Pen smiled. "Maybe. Do what?"

"Check this out," said Will, and he took Pen by the wrist, leading her down some stairs toward a crowd of people, a camera on a tripod, and a large screen that turned out to be a giant, slightly washed-out photograph of the Chocolate Hills. Pen looked from the wan photograph of the view to the view itself, sunlit, rich with color under the blue sky, and unmistakably real.

"But . . . ?" she said.

"Wait," said Will.

As they watched, a college-aged couple stood in front of the backdrop and, at the photographer's cue, jumped into the air, arms raised in victory.

"Oh. My. Goodness," said Pen blankly.

"It makes a *picture* that looks like they're jumping over the hills!" cried Augusta with joy. "They print it out *right here,* and you can take it *home* with you!"

"Is that right?" muttered Pen.

"You can also use brooms," said Will, pointing to a couple of skinny, brown, witchy looking items leaning against the guardrail, "to make it look like you're flying."

"Fabulous," said Pen.

"Just exactly the kind of thing you like," said Will, deadpan except for his wicked eyes.

Taking this exchange as a yes, Augusta squealed, clapped her hands, skipped to the back of the line, and resumed popcorning.

Pen stared at the background, then said, slowly, "Not me, but I can think of someone who would love it."

Will nodded. "It's true. She never met a piece of kitsch she didn't love."

An idea lit up his face, and he pointed to an easel-propped bulletin board on the other side of the backdrop from where they stood. It was covered with photo samples.

"You don't think . . . ?" said Pen.

"Probably not," answered Will, but they were already on their way, squeezing behind the backdrop, mumbling "Excuse me" to the sight-seers in their path. When they got to the easel, Pen turned to look at Augusta, who waved and blew kisses, movie-star-fashion.

"Stay right there," mouthed Pen, pointing.

Augusta gave her a thumbs-up. Pen knew that Augusta wasn't going anywhere, wouldn't get out of that line for all the miniature bananas in the Philippines.

It was a big bulletin board. Some of the photos were faded and dog-eared, but some looked new.

"You start from the top," said Pen. "And I'll start from the bottom."

"Don't bother," said a dreary voice. Jason. "She's not there."

Jason looked even worse than he sounded, moist and slump-shouldered in his light blue golf shirt. In the merciless sunlight, Pen could see his scalp, shell-pink and vulnerable, through his pale hair, and when he took off his sunglasses, Pen saw that his eyes were blood-shot, watery, underslung with dark circles. They were the saddest things she had seen in a long time.

"I think I'm going crazy," he said hoarsely, squeezing his head be-tween his hands, hard.

Uncertain of what to do, Pen turned around to look at Will, who said, "You know what? I should probably go stand in line with Au-gusta."

"That's great, thanks," said Pen out loud. She narrowed her eyes and whispered, "Weasel!"

Ignoring her, Will clapped Jason on the arm, said, "Hang in there, man," and vanished behind the backdrop.

When Jason walked to the rail of the overlook and leaned against it, heavily, with both hands, the people around him discreetly moved away. Maybe they could sense his desperation or his need for breath-ing room. Maybe they noted his size and feared for the stability of the guardrail. In any case, the sight of him standing there, alone, was too much for Pen. She moved to his side and, after just a moment's hesitation, her arm hovering in the air behind him, she placed the arm around his shoulders, which were shaking.

"Hey, Jason," she said softly. "It'll be okay."

He shook his head. "I've been scanning faces for so long that it's literally making me sick. I feel like I might puke."

"Well, why don't you give it a rest for a while?" said Pen quickly, resisting the urge to take a step away. "Because you know what? If you're anywhere near her, she'll see you first anyway." She gave his shoulders a squeeze. "You don't exactly blend in, you know."

Jason mustered a feeble smile. "I'm like the Stay Puft Marshmallow Man walking around this place. You know, from *Ghostbusters*."

"Except he was mean, wasn't he? And you're nice."

Jason gave her a skeptical look. "You think I'm nice? Honestly?"

"Honestly?" Pen shrugged. "I think you're a lot of things, nice being one of them."

"Fair enough," said Jason. "So here's another question for you: do you really want me to find her?"

"Yes."

"Come on. Yes? Just like that?"

Pen took her arm away so that she could face him squarely.

"Yes, I want you to find her. I think you need—. I think you *deserve* a conversation, at the very least. You need a chance to be at peace, one way or another."

"Because I'm her husband, you mean."

"Because, as far as I can tell, you have loved her with a true and open heart for as long as you two have been together. And because no one should ever, ever leave without saying why."

To Pen's horror, Jason started to cry, to weep, his face crumpling, his body quaking, the tears pouring out from under his sunglasses, which he took off and handed to Pen, before pulling the collar of his shirt up and over his face, so that he was inside it, his fists clutching the blue fabric against his forehead. Jagged gasps and awful, puppylike whimpers came from inside the shirt. Pen looked around helplessly for Will and Augusta, but she couldn't see the photo line from where she stood. She thought about putting her arm around Jason again, but he was so pulled into himself that touching seemed like the wrong thing, so she stood there, gazing out at the rows and clusters of funny brown peaks because sometimes, she decided, all you could do for someone was stay.

After a little while, he slowed and sputtered to a stop, and Pen handed him his glasses, and he put them back on.

"Thanks," he said. "Sorry."

"Don't apologize."

"It's just that you were right. I have loved her to the best of my ability, and, fuck, do I hate that."

"Why?" said Pen, surprised.

"Because if I'd been an asshole, cheated or slacked off, well, there would be something for me to fix, right? There'd be hope." Quickly, he added, "Not that there's no hope. I totally believe that she loves me and that I can get her to come home. Okay?"

"Okay," said Pen. *Sure you do,* she thought.

"I'm just saying that if she *does* want to end us, well, then I got nothing. Zip. No leverage." He whacked his forehead with his fist, once, twice, three times, leaving a vaguely butterfly-shaped red mark on his forehead. "If she doesn't want me, then loving her to the best of my ability all those years was about the most stupid-ass thing I could have done."

"Stop it," snapped Pen, giving his shoulder a shove. "Right now."

Jason stared at her. "I just had a freaking nervous breakdown. You're not allowed to boss me around. Or *push* me."

"Too bad. Listen to me: you're wrong."

"Wrong, huh? Like you know."

"Everyone knows."

"Knows what?"

"That no matter what happens, loving someone to the best of your ability is exactly the right thing to do. It's the only thing to do."

Jason seemed about to dispute this, but then he shut his mouth and stayed quiet for a long time, staring at his hands on the railing instead of at the view. Finally, he said, "You really believe that bullshit?"

"Yep."

He let go of the rail and turned his hands over, empty, palms to the sky. "What will I do if she leaves me?"

The answer was so clear, so obvious that Pen had to fight to keep the impatience out of her voice.

"You'll love someone else."

AT THE BOTTOM OF THE HILL, WHILE THEY WERE WAITING FOR LUIS the tour driver to bring the SUV around, Augusta ate ice cream, and Pen, Will, and Jason came up with a plan.

"How about if we narrow our tour down to the places that Cat's most likely to go?" said Will, getting out the itinerary that the bar-tender/concierge back at the resort had made for them. "Then we can spend the rest of the time looking for her back at the beach."

"Good idea," said Pen.

"This is futile. We know that, right?" said Jason blandly. In the af-termath of his conversation with Pen, he seemed calmer, but whether this was because he felt better or because he was simply exhausted Pen couldn't tell. "The chances of running into her at one of these tourist attractions is, like, practically null and void. Even the beach is a shot in the dark. I checked at all the resorts I could find. No sign of Cat and not one damn person, no matter how much I sucked up to them, would tell me anything."

Will's eyes met Pen's, and she knew what he was thinking: that the whole trip to Bohol was a shot in the dark. It was a lot easier to believe in the hand of fate when you were sitting in the Lolas' house with the Lolas' sage, tranquil faces in front of you than when you were actually out in the world, searching.

"What should we do?" said Will to Jason. "If you want to go back to Cebu, we'll do it. Your call."

After staring up at the sky and frantically fiddling with the change in his shorts' pocket, Jason released a hard, drawn-out, sagging sigh and took the itinerary from Will.

" 'Church of San Pedro,' " he read. " 'Early seventeenth century. Spanish.' Blah blah blah. Boring. Forget it. 'Hanging Bridge.' Nope, she doesn't like heights. 'Loboc River Cruise and Floating Restaurant.' Cruise, restaurant? She'd be all over it. 'Tarsier sanctuary.'" He looked up. "What's a tarsier?"

"A monkey!" sang Augusta. "A weensy, teensy, a-dor-a-ble monkey!"

"We found it online, back at home when we were looking up the Philippines," explained Pen. "It's not a monkey, really, but it is a primate, almost the smallest in the world."

"How small?" asked Jason, squinting his eyes in concentration, as though the specific degree of smallness could make all the difference.

Pen held out her cupped hand. "Baby kitten-ish, give or take."

"Cute?" asked Jason.

"*Yes!*" shouted Augusta.

"Huge, round golden eyes; button nose; round head; long, grippy fingers; soft brown fur. And a smile," said Pen.

"Hell, that sounds like Cat," said Jason dryly.

"A smile?" said Will.

"In the pictures we saw, it was smiling. No lie," said Pen.

"Like this!" said Augusta, pressing her lips together and curling up just the corners so that her mouth was a prim, sideways "C."

"Beautiful," said Will.

"A tiny, big-eyed, smiling monkey," said Jason. "Are you kidding me? Wild horses couldn't keep her away."

THE RIDE TO THE TARSIER SANCTUARY WAS SO LONG THAT BOTH Augusta and Jason fell asleep, Augusta nestled into an ancient, threadbare booster seat (Pen had nearly kissed Luis when she saw it) in the SUV's third row and Jason in the front seat, snoring over the saccharine stream that poured, ceaselessly, out of Luis's radio. Bafflingly, the Philippines had turned out to be a bastion of old R&B and soft rock love songs ("Air Supply is all out of love everywhere but here," Will had noted, with grim awe, on the second day). Pen and Will sat in the second row, looking out of the thankfully untinted windows at the Bohol countryside: hardwood forests, houses on stilts, nipa huts, thickset palm groves, gas stations, stunningly green rice fields.

"Isn't it as though that rice field satisfies some little piece of your soul that's been waiting for that specific shade of green all your life, without your knowing it?" Pen said, solemnly and without stopping for breath, to Will, who laughed and said, "I was going to say that it's like the whole field is one of those glow sticks we used get at the beach when we were kids."

Children played in the yards of long, one-story school buildings, some of which had big, glassless windows, so that you could see straight through to the green on the other side. Slow, curved-horned water buffalo swung their bony hips along roadsides or through fields. Women hung laundry or cooked in the open air. Despite her efforts to not romanticize the place (none of the lives she glimpsed looked at all easy), Pen couldn't help feeling that a kind of peacefulness, a hazy, emerald quietude permeated everything she saw.

"It's beautiful here, isn't it?" she said.

"Yeah. It really is," said Will.

"Too bad Jason is missing it."

Will looked at the back of Jason's head and said in a low voice, "It's good, though. Poor guy needed a break."

"Wouldn't it be terrible," whispered Pen, "to love someone so much who didn't love you back?"

In the silence that followed her saying this, they drove past an entire rice field, one backed by hills and patchworked with bright quadrangles of water, more water winking like sequins between the dazzling shoots of rice.

"Will?" Pen said finally. "Are you there?"

"Sorry," said Will. "I was just thinking about what you said."

"Oh. So tell me."

"You're right: it would be terrible. But there are worse things."

"What do you mean?"

Will stopped looking out the window and looked at Pen instead. Against the lushness of Bohol, the clean-lined precision of his face was startling. It's what happened when beauty became familiar: you saw it and saw it and saw it without seeing it and then, suddenly, there it was to make your heart stand still inside your chest

"At least he did it," said Will. "Went all out. Gave her everything. He'll always know that about himself."

Flushing, Pen said, "I just told Jason almost that exact same thing, back at the Chocolate Hills, and I believe it. I always have. The really great thing is to love someone, no matter what." She smiled ruefully. "But I guess it's a lot easier to have philosophies than to put them into action because I look at him, and all I feel is sad, and all I want is for her to love him back. God, can't she just *do* that?" She stopped, feeling disloyal to Cat. "I mean, I want her to be happy, but I want the thing that makes her happy to be being with him."

Will nodded. Then he said, "And what about you? What's the thing that makes you happy?"

Look at him, Pen told herself.

She looked at him and thought: *Oh, just* look *at you.* The words flooded through her, but she didn't say them. How could she? That wasn't the language she and Will spoke to each other.

She said, "This trip. Augusta. Knowing you again."

"Well," he said after a few seconds, "that's good."

He smiled an unreadable half-smile at her, and the SUV kept moving and the two of them kept riding in it, and, through the windows, the green world kept offering them its extravagant loveliness, mile after mile after mile.

HAD THE MAN AT THE VISITORS CENTER NOT HAD PUPPIES, THINGS might have turned out differently, but there they were in a fenced-in square of yard just outside the tiny museum's open side door: black-and-white bundles, with fur so fuzzy it looked electrified. They were nothing like most of the dogs they had seen in Cebu, not bony and listless, but round-bellied and tumbling with a mild, watchful, well-fed mother nearby, whom Pen would've bet had more than a little border collie dog-paddling around in her gene pool. The second that Augusta spotted the puppies, everything else flew out of her head, displaced by rampant joy and utter besottedness. With one smiling nod from the visitors center man, whose name was Mr. P, she was in among them, sitting flat on her bottom on the grass, and she would not come out, not for love or money or even tarsiers.

"Mama, you said we can't touch tarsiers because they're dindangered," she explained. "But you can touch puppies! Touch and touch and touch!" Since her arms were full of them, it was hard to argue with this.

"How about just a quick look?" said Pen. "Mama wants to see the tarsiers."

Mr. P was as bright eyed and rotund as the pups and exuded grandfatherly kindness, but there was no way Pen was leaving Augusta with a man she had just met or even with Luis, who was leaning against the SUV, texting with fast, expert thumbs.

"I'll stay with her," said Jason.

As soon as they had pulled up to the sanctuary, it had been clear that they wouldn't find Cat there. Luis's SUV was one of three cars in the dirt lot, and the visitors center was tiny, one well-lit room full of tidy displays, photographs, informative signs, and an eerie and delicate little skeleton with enormous eye sockets. Unless you counted Mr. P and a young man sweeping the porch, they were the only visitors in sight. After noting this, Jason didn't get upset or seem eager to leave. He just shrugged and sat down on an outdoor bench near the puppy pen, looking like a man who had either achieved patience or had completely thrown in the towel.

"That's okay," Pen told him. "You should go see the tarsiers."

"Nah," said Jason, waving his hand dismissively. "You guys go on."

Mr. P nodded to the young man, who had stopped sweeping, and the man took off his straw hat, tucked it under his arm, and reached to shake Will's hand.

"I am Monching."

"Nice to meet you, Monching," said Will. "I'm Will, and this is my friend Pen."

They didn't have far to walk. Monching explained that the tarsiers lived wild throughout most of the sanctuary but that there were a few who had been rescued from captivity and were living in a small portion of the forest surrounded by a high fence. These were the tarsiers that they would see.

"It is not like a zoo," said Monching, perhaps anticipating disappointment. "The space is large, and they live as they do in the wild. But they are a little less shy than the ones out in the rest of the sanctuary."

"This is fine," said Pen.

Monching nodded and entered the dense forest. Will followed him for a few yards, then turned and held out his hand to Pen, and she didn't stop to wonder why or to consider the implications of taking it. She just took it, and this was how they walked down the narrow path, until Monching stopped, pointing.

"There," he whispered.

And there it was, just a few yards away, clinging to a low branch, its face turned away from them.

"And there." This one was closer and seemed to be sleeping.

"There will be more, if you are quiet," he said. "Please do not touch, but you can go close to them, take pictures."

Pen realized they had left the camera in the SUV, but it didn't matter. She was following the advice of Lola Lita: really being there, seeing what there was to see.

"I will wait," said Monching, pointing, "just there, beyond the edge," and noiselessly, he disappeared into the leaves.

Pen and Will looked at each other. Under the canopy of trees, it was shadowy and so hushed that it felt as though they stood in the very heart of the woods.

Will nodded toward the closest tarsier and whispered, "Go ahead. You first," which was exactly what Pen wanted.

Advancing slowly, placing her feet as silently as she could, Pen walked until her face was no more than a foot and a half away from the tarsier, close enough to look it in the eyes, if its eyes had not been closed. The creature was perfectly motionless and so exquisitely constructed, from the delicately wrinkled forehead to the flaring, rose-petal-shaped ears to the strong, knobby, shockingly human-looking hands. Pen stared and stared, happiness pouring through her, her heart beating so hard she could feel it in her wrists, and then the tarsier opened its tremendous eyes, and looked at her, giving her the gift of its wild gold regard, and she could have sworn that it wasn't just she, but the whole forest that caught its breath.

It wasn't cute. It had nothing to do with cute. It was strange and dignified, and Pen believed that she had never in her life felt so honored to be in anyone's company. She had come across the wide, tilted, spinning world and landed here to become one of two animals, looking at each other in a deep green wood. She was overcome. She longed for the moment to never end, but the ending was right there, waiting. *Stay,* she wanted to tell the tarsier, but it couldn't stay. *It's endangered,* she thought, and the thought broke her heart.

You are endangered, she thought with grief.

So are you, said a voice impatiently. *So is everything. But we're here now, aren't we?*

Then the tarsier turned its head, hopped from tree to tree to tree, and was gone.

Afterward, she would admit, readily, that no conversation had ever taken place. Tarsiers didn't talk, not even silently. She didn't need Amelie to tell her that the voice answering her own inside her head was also her own. It was a thing she did all the time: talking to herself. But she also knew that, at the time, in the brief, wide, fathomless moment that it happened, that wasn't how it felt at all.

She turned around and saw Will.

It would have been so easy for the two of them to simply fall together, to give in to gravity, but Pen wanted it to be clear, to be the very clearest thing they had ever done.

"I love you," she told him.

"I love you, too," he said, moving toward her.

She held up her hand. "I'm not talking about in a Will-and-Pen-business-as-usual kind of way."

He smiled. "Then how?"

But he was already reaching for her, and when she kissed him, the rest of the world didn't fade or fall away around them. It stayed, with Pen and Will firmly planted in its center, holding on to each other, all the Pens and Wills they had ever been but especially the ones they were now.

Before they left the forest for good, Pen said, "Listen, because of Augusta and Jason—God, especially Jason—we should probably, for now anyway—" She couldn't think of how to say it.

"Play it cool?" said Will, kissing her fingertips, her inner wrist, the palm of her hand.

"Yes," said Pen. "But I want you to know that if I ruled the world, I would never stop touching you."

"You don't rule the world?" said Will.

"Tell me that you love me," commanded Pen.

"I love you," said Will.

CHAPTER TWENTY

THEY WERE SITTING POOLSIDE AT THE RESORT EATING A DESSERT called halo-halo and listening to Celine Dion sing the theme song from *Titanic*. It was not, by a long shot, the first time they had heard the song since arriving in the Philippines, but it was certainly the loudest they had heard it, Celine's voice raining down upon them from the tree-mounted speakers, escalating from breathy to tremulous to so thoroughly full-throated and throbbing that Pen thought the ground might start to shake.

"Holy freaking hell," moaned Jason. "What's this song called, anyway?"

" 'My Heart Will Go On,' " said Will absently, eyeballing the contents of his raised spoon. "This has beans in it."

He looked up from the spoon to find Pen and Jason staring at him.

"What?" he said. "I like it. It's good. I'm just saying: it has beans in it. A dessert with beans in it. That's not something you see every day."

"How do you know that?" asked Pen.

"They're right here," said Will, holding up his spoon. "Beans."

"No. How do you know what this song is called?" asked Pen. "Nobody knows what this song is called."

Will looked from Pen to Jason.

"Sorry, dude," said Jason, "I have to go with Pen on this one. Everyone just calls it that *Titanic* song, if they even call it anything. Except, you know, *you*."

"So tell us," said Pen, raising an eyebrow. "How do you know?"

"I just know," said Will. "Come on, it's not like I *like* it."

"Man, you keep right on telling yourself that," said Jason, giving Will's shoulder a comforting pat.

Pen was happy to see that Jason was perking up a bit. Over the last twenty-four hours, the air of resignation he had adopted at the tarsier sanctuary had gradually deepened into a true, blue, dismal funk. Just a few hours earlier, on the floating restaurant cruise down the Loboc River, he had hit what appeared to be rock bottom, failing to go for even a second helping at the all-you-can-eat buffet and hardly noticing when, right in front of them, three little boys jumped what had to be thirty feet from the top of a coconut tree that leaned out over the river into the river itself and came up next to the boat, laughing.

Now, he seemed as close to lighthearted as he had since they'd arrived. Maybe it was the halo-halo, which was delicious. Maybe it was because they were leaving the next morning, going back to Cebu on the ferry, and Jason had resolved to return to the Lolas and ask them, one last time, to reunite him with Cat. ("I'm trying to think of the right approach," he'd told them, and Will had suggested, "Ritual supplication. Burnt offering. Maybe a small animal sacrifice.") In any case, with a playful gleam in his eye, Jason leaned over and tapped the shoulder of a man sitting with a group of people at the beer-bottle-covered table next to theirs. Pen recognized the man as one of the Australian divers.

"Sorry to interrupt," said Jason to the man. "We were just wondering if you knew the name of this song."

"Oh, wait, don't tell me," the man said, squeezing his eyes shut in concentration before guessing, " 'Total Bloody Shit'?"

"I think it's from the album *Songs That Make You Want to Rip Off Someone's Face*," sang out another man at the table.

After the Aussies had recovered from the hilarity into which these remarks had caused them to dissolve, the first man pointed to a woman across the table from him. "Addie here just presented us with the question of what we would listen to right now if we could listen to any song in the world," he said. "And now I am presenting it to you: What song would you listen to right now if you could listen to any song in the world? Please discuss." And he turned back to his friends.

Pen said, " 'Wild Honey' by U2."

Jason said, " 'The Climb' by Miley Cyrus," followed by, "What? It's inspiring!"

Will said, " 'Consecutive Seconds' by Thelonious Monk."

He said this partly because he loved the song, but mostly, Pen knew, so that she would make fun of him, which she did.

"Horrifyingly pretentious," she said. "Choose again."

"Oh, okay, sorry," said Will, abashed. After a moment's thought, he said, "Bach's Goldberg Variation Number 25 by Glenn Gould," which cracked Pen up, as he had known it would, and caused Jason to ask, "Do you want me to kick your ass? I mean, are you *asking* me to kick your ass?"

It amazed Pen, how they could sit there talking like they had always talked, as though the world had not been utterly transfigured, as though she and Will had not spent every waking hour of the last twenty-four driving themselves crazy trying to keep their hands off each other. Even as they sat, talking in the late afternoon sun, laughing, giving each other crap the way they always had, Pen was adding to the list inside her head of parts of him she wanted to taste: his sternum, the back of his neck, the skin beneath his left ear.

She loved him. She ached with loving him. He was her best and oldest friend and, also, he was a miracle to her. She looked at him and thought, *I would give you anything you wanted.* She wanted to tell him this, and then wondered if maybe, at some point, she already had because she realized that it had always been true. There was never a time, since the day she met him, when Pen hadn't loved Will. He was her clear-eyed conscience, her kind, wry, sharp, beautiful man. No one had ever come closer to reading her mind than Will. When she tried to examine, with a clinical eye, what had changed, she realized it boiled down to two things: she wanted to touch him as often as possible and in ways she had never wanted to touch him before; and she wanted to be with him every day, to live with him, in the same house, for the rest of her life.

◆ ◆ ◆

THAT EVENING, THEY WENT TO THE PLACE ON THE BEACH WHERE YOU could choose your own fish, the afternoon's catch displayed like necklaces (sapphires, rubies, diamonds) on a bed of crushed ice. Augusta took one look and chirped, " 'One fish, two fish, red fish, blue fish.' Pizza, please," and, under Pen's disapproving eye, Will had taken off down the beach to get her some and bring it back.

It was a good meal. The outdoor café was full of people and festive, with Christmas lights strung all over the bar and winding up the trunks of the palm trees like twinkling snakes. People strolled by on the beach, music played at a reasonable volume, and their waitress was so devastatingly pretty—the Filipina Lana Turner of waitresses—that Jason even made a couple of goofy but not totally unsuccessful attempts at flirting with her. They ate at a table not twenty yards from the water's edge with their feet in the sand and the ocean spread before them, the sun melting into it like a fat scoop of mango ice cream.

They didn't talk about Cat. They talked about Pen's newly formed and still mostly hazy plans to go back to teaching. They talked about Florida, where Jason had grown up, and about how when you read the news, every bad, crazy, unlikely thing to ever happen seemed to happen in Florida but how when you were there, it was wonderful. They talked about Will's books, and this part of the conversation gave way to a moment in which Jason said, "Dude, that sounds like a pretty awesome gig. Getting paid to sit around in your underwear, drinking coffee and making stuff up."

Will grinned and said, "Yeah. Plus, it's portable. In case anyone ever wants to, you know, transport me someplace."

Except to abruptly stop breathing, Pen didn't move a muscle, and Will didn't even glance in her direction. It was Jason who looked at her, at her, at Will, and back at her.

With his eyes on Pen's, he said, "I bet before long somebody will."

Jason, giving them his blessing. Pen didn't answer, just held his gaze, grateful, but after about three seconds of this, everything began to feel too serious, and Pen cast around for something to say, but nothing came to her, which left her with no choice but first to hum and then to sing the opening lines of the song Jason had said he would listen to if he could pick any song in the world.

"God, do I love this song," said Will, covering his ears.

"Aw, jeez," said Jason, laughing and leaning back in his chair, "I'm telling you, it's a great song!"

After a second, he joined in, then Augusta, and for a corny, beautiful minute, all three of them were singing the song (which Pen had to admit really was pretty inspiring), a song about how not the arrival but the journey is the point, until they were actually stopping traffic, people turning to give them amused and pitying glances, Will sinking lower and lower into his chair. Pen tapered off after a while, unsure of the words, but Jason and Augusta sang it through to the end. Jason's voice was unexpectedly good, deep and resonant, and when they were finished, the people at the neighboring tables applauded, with the Lana Turner waitress clapping hardest of all.

They walked on the beach, Augusta on Jason's shoulders waving, like the Queen of England, to passersby; Pen and Will walking several yards ahead of them, studiously not touching and thus whipping up around them such an atmosphere of buzzing, whirling sexual tension that Pen told him it was like walking inside a swarm of bees, a simile that made Will smile and shake his head and say, "Only you."

"See? How did you live without me for six years?" teased Pen.

"Poorly," said Will in a way that said he wasn't entirely kidding.

They came to a resort that was more glamorous than any of the others, subtly lit so that it seemed to glow from within, with a wide white stretch of palm-tree-dotted beach leading up to elegant, Japanese-style villas and one of those pools that was designed to appear endless when you were in it, as though it wasn't a swimming pool at all but an extension of the ocean itself.

"Look at that," said Pen in a low voice. "Now, who do we know who would stay in a place like that?"

Will looked and his eyes widened. "Should we say something? Go up and see if she's there?"

Pen shook her head. "He probably already checked there anyway."

"Yeah, but what if someone checked who wasn't acting like a seedy private eye and flashing cash?"

Pen took a quick glance back at Jason, who was talking up a storm and walking with a light step, in spite of the forty-pound child on his shoulders.

"You think we should leave it alone?" asked Will.

"He just looks so happy." She sighed. "Maybe on the way back."

The fancy resort marked the end of the strip, and, as they walked away from it, the beach grew darker. The moon had risen by now, though, and was nearly full—a big, silver, low-hanging plum—so there was still enough light to see by. Even so, Pen should not have been able to tell that it was Cat. Even with the moonlight above and its reflection on the water and the residual light from the strip behind them, it was too dim to make out much more than an outline—two small people, their arms linked—and still, without knowing how she knew (was it her walk? a fragment of barely heard conversation carried through the night air?), Pen knew.

"Will," she said, and she grabbed his arm and started walking faster.

"What are you doing?" asked Will.

"Hey, guys!" called Jason from behind them. "Yo! Slow up!"

"Cat," gasped Pen, pointing.

Will squinted into the dimness.

"Holy shit," he breathed, and together they broke into an almost-run.

Their approach was quiet, their hearts pounding more loudly, or so it seemed to them, than their footfalls, which were muffled by the sugary sand. Still, Cat must have heard them coming because before they got to her, before they could call her name, she stopped, let go of the arm of the person she had been walking with, and turned around, and even though Pen had pictured herself finding Cat and running straight into her arms, had pictured it over and over again, as soon as she saw her face, she slowed down, tugging Will to a stop, so that the first time Cat said her name it was across a distance. The space between them might have been six feet, a body length, but it felt wider than that, and Pen felt suddenly shaky, filled with doubt. From where Pen stood, Cat's face appeared completely impassive, chilly, registering nothing, not even bewilderment or curiosity. What if Pen had been wrong when she had told the Lolas that Cat would be happy to see her? Pen was still holding on to Will's arm, and, as she looked at Cat across that distance, she held on harder.

Then, in a very small voice, Cat said, "Pen. Will. Oh, how can this be?" and she covered her mouth with her hands and sank to her knees in the sand.

"We came to see you," explained Pen, but she found she couldn't move, so it was Will who walked over to Cat, held her gently by the shoulders, lifted her to her feet, grinned, and said, "Hey, sweetheart."

Cat came alive then, shouting, "Oh, my God," and throwing her arms around Will's neck, before dashing over to Pen, catching hold of both of her hands, and saying, "My sweet, sweet friend, my sweet, sweet, sweet, sweet friend," before pulling her into a hard hug.

It's okay, thought Pen, overcome with relief. *She loves me.*

Pen felt a tug on her skirt, and Augusta piped, "Mama, what's happening?"

Cat froze in Pen's embrace, and Pen extricated herself from the hug so that she could scoop Augusta into her arms.

"'Mama'?" whispered Cat. She stared at Augusta, and her face blossomed into awe.

"My little girl," said Pen, filled with awe herself, as sometimes happened at the sight of this glorious, full-fledged person who belonged to her but belonged mostly, and more and more, to herself, "Augusta."

Slowly, Cat lifted one of her pretty hands (the sight of that familiar, flower-delicate hand brought tears to Pen's eyes) and brushed the hair back from Augusta's face.

"She is breathtaking," said Cat, her eyes filling, too. "Imagine: Pen's little girl."

"Thank you very much," said Augusta, and she leaned forward and kissed Cat on the lips.

Cat touched her fingers to her own mouth, and then told Pen in her old irresistible, teasing way, "She receives compliments so gracefully. Guess she got that from her dad."

It was an old joke between the three of them, Pen's embarrassed ineptitude at handling praise. Once, back in college, when she was dressed to go out and Will told her she looked pretty, she had erupted into such a red-faced, stammering series of self-reproaches, disavowals, and disclaimers that Will said, "How about you just hit me in the head with a hammer and we'll call it even."

"Hold on one red-hot minute!" cried Cat, snapping her fingers, whirling around, and pointing at Will. "Augusta. She's not . . . ?"

"No," said Will. He shrugged. "I'd take her, though."

"You can *borrow* me," corrected Augusta.

Everyone laughed, and, afterward, a breathless, trembling silence swooped down upon Pen, Cat, and Will, as if each of them understood, in the same instant, that the three of them—Pen, Cat, and Will, *Pen, Cat, and Will*—were standing, in the year 2010, on a beach, in the Philippines, together. As they stood there, for the first time since she had seen her walking on the sand, arm in arm, with Cat, Pen became aware of the stranger. She stood a few feet away, a short, fine-boned woman, with long black hair and a bemused smile. Cat followed Pen's gaze, gave a little jump, said, "I'm so sorry!" and held out her hand to the woman, who took it.

"Does anyone have a drum?" asked Cat mischievously. "Because not to undercut the solemnity of the moment? But this would be a really good time for a drumroll."

"Nope," said Will, holding his arms out to demonstrate his drumless state.

"Sorry," said Pen.

"Um, Cat?" said Augusta. "We don't really *have* drums on vacation?"

Cat gave a theatrical sigh. "Oh, fine," she said. She let go of the stranger's hand, took a step to the side, and made a sweeping arc with her arm.

"This is Marisol Ocampo," she said, her face soft and starry-eyed, "my sister."

Marisol was nodding her head, princess-fashion, a slow, wide smile emerging on her face, when a voice boomed, "Your *sister?*"

There was Jason. Pen realized that he must have been there all along. Of course he had, hovering behind them in the shadows, watching, probably gathering his courage, keeping quiet, even though his heart must have either leaped up or cracked in two at the sight of his wife. Caught up in Cat, Pen and Will had forgotten all about him.

Jason took a few steps forward and stopped, his shoulders back, his feet spread apart like a gunfighter or a football coach. Pen couldn't bear to look at his face, but the sight of his hands alone was enough to make her heart hurt. They were clasped together in front of him, his fingers interlocked so tightly that, from where she stood, Pen could see the veins bulging in his arms. When she finally got up the nerve to look at his eyes, she saw that they were full of hope.

"I get it, now. You found out about her in your dad's will, didn't you? And you left home and came here to find her." His voice was husky with tenderness.

Cat stood as still as if she had been turned to stone.

Jason unclasped his hands and reclasped them on the top of his head. "Aw, babe, you could have told me that. I would have understood."

Cat did not tell him that her heart was melting at the mere sight of him, as he had predicted she would. With firm, deliberate steps, she walked until she was standing in front of him, and in a voice so cold that it didn't sound like Cat's at all, she said, "Jason, you don't understand a single thing. You never have. And you should not have, you should *never* have come here."

Pen wanted to tell Jason, "For God's sake, just let her go!" She wanted to tell Cat, "Be gentle with him!" She wanted to step between the two of them, but she couldn't be sure which person she wanted to shield from the other. In the end, she did none of these things because it was painfully clear to her that she shouldn't even be there; none of them—Pen, Will, Augusta, Marisol—should be there. If the world worked as it should, Cat and Jason would be alone, with their shared, messy, intensely private story, the years upon years of plans and disappointments, love and anger, the trying and the giving up. This was a scene that wanted no witnesses. Still, there they all were.

Pen thought, *She didn't call him "little boy,"* and when she looked at Jason's face, white under the white moon, she saw that he didn't look like a little boy at all, but like a man who had lost everything.

"ONE: I MARRIED THE WRONG MAN, BUT YOU KNEW THAT ALREADY. He's a good, decent man, just abundantly, inalterably wrong for me. Honestly, not to place blame, but what were the two of you thinking, letting me marry him? Two: When my father died, I felt like that guy in the David Bowie song, floating in space, cut off from everything, as lost as lost could ever be. Loster. Three: To make matters worse, I found out about Marisol and that my dad had had this other life, another life, another wife, before I was born and that he had *left* his *child*. God, here I had spent the last five years trying desperately to have a baby—and I know what you're thinking: why have a baby with a man I don't love? But I thought, well, I would do it and have it and then I would leave, and we would raise her (I always felt in my heart that it would be a girl) together but apart, the way so many other people do because even though Jason was all wrong as a husband, I knew he would be an excellent, no, a *stupendous* father—and all the while, my own father, whom I spent my life worshipping, had walked away from his daughter, left her thousands of miles away and kept her a secret, and I was so angry at him. I was sick with fury and disillusionment. Four: But one day, it suddenly came to me that I needed to come find her, that everything happens for a reason and here was the reason: I was meant to find my sister. And I found her, but not just her, although she would have been enough all by herself; I found my home, my true home and my true family, the one I had yearned for all my life."

It was the morning after they had found her. As they had planned before they had left her and Jason alone on the beach, they were having breakfast at Cat's resort. Marisol was sitting in the sun, reading, on the other side of the endless pool, in which Augusta swam, loping like a dolphin through the water, blissfully untouched by the adult drama that had unfolded around her. Before they had left to meet Cat, Pen had peered through the window of Jason's villa and had been relieved to see him there, sleeping.

After she told her story, Cat tilted her head thoughtfully and said, "I think that's it. The bare bones, I mean," and she scooped a forkful of sticky rice from her plate and popped it into her mouth.

Helplessly, dizzily, internally reeling with myriad, conflicting emotions, Pen looked at Will, who was smiling. She kicked him under the table.

"Ow!" said Will.

"What is the matter with you?" demanded Pen. "That was heart-wrenching!"

In truth, heart-wrenching was only one of the things Pen thought it was. Disturbingly cold-hearted (*husband as sperm donor?*) was another. Even as she thought this, though, she knew that it didn't change anything. Cat was flawed. So what? They were all flawed. Cat was a person Pen loved.

"I know!" said Will. "My heart's wrenched. It's just funny." The smile came back.

Cat was smiling, too, a smile, like Will's, full of barely contained laughter.

"What's funny about it?" asked Pen.

"Six years in four sentences. She really thinks that was four sentences."

Cat made a face at him, nose wrinkled, tongue out.

Pen gave them both a disapproving glare.

"Come on, Pen," said Will, "don't be mad." He started to reach for her, but stopped and set his hand down on the table.

"Oh, go ahead!" scoffed Cat. "Like I couldn't tell from the very first moment I saw you."

"You could?" asked Pen, too stunned to be embarrassed.

"Heck, yeah. I noticed, however, that you both left it out of your four-sentence biographies. It was all the more conspicuous for its absence, too. The unspoken fifth sentence: we are in love." She fluttered her lashes and sighed.

"All right, all right," grumbled Will.

"Cat. Be serious," said Pen. "Is it okay? With you, I mean?"

"That matters to you?" said Cat. "After all this time?"

Pen considered this. "Yes," she said, then added apologetically, "not that there's anything we can do about it, if you don't like it."

Cat smiled. "I do like it. There was a time, of course, when I would have hated it, when it would have seemed like the end of the world."

" 'Total friendship apocalypse,' " supplied Will.

"Exactly. But I knew that it would happen, once I left."

"Six years after," Will pointed out, "give or take."

"Slowpokes," said Cat, smiling. "Even so, I knew it would happen."

"No, you didn't!" said Pen, dismayed. "How could you have thought that?"

Cat turned her face to Pen, a face full of affection and entirely, exclusively Cat's.

"You never saw how things were," said Cat sweetly. "That's part of what made you so wonderful. You thought we all loved each other in the same way."

"We did," insisted Pen, suddenly near tears. "You make it sound like our friendship wasn't what it seemed to be."

"Our friendship was the best thing under the sun," avowed Cat. "I was wrong when I said that I had only just now found my family because you and Will were my family. You were the lights of my life."

"Oh," said Pen, wiping her eyes.

"But even in families, people have roles, spots that they fill. You and Will were the wonder twins. You were so in tune with each other, so connected." Cat linked her forefingers together, the forefingers that Pen had loved, as she had loved everything about Cat.

"We were *all* connected!" protested Pen. "I adored you."

"Of course, you did, both of you," said Cat. "I'm adorable! I was your darling, your angel, yours and Will's, which is precisely what I wanted to be. But you were the ones who belonged together. I was meant to leave, eventually, to go away and grow up. You two were the ones who were meant to go the distance. Will, back me up here."

Will said, "You don't need backup; you're doing fine."

"You think she's right?" asked Pen reproachfully.

"Why are you sad about this?" said Will. Under the table, he grabbed her hand. "I mean, I know why you're sad about this, but you don't have to be. It doesn't take anything away."

"Maybe not," said Pen doubtfully. "I need more time to think about it."

"I wish we had more time," said Cat sadly.

Pen blinked. "But we do. We can. We can change our ticket back to Cebu. Or you can come back with us."

Cat was shaking her head. "I need to be with Marisol, now. It wasn't easy for her to leave her job and her family to come here with me. We're heading off to a different island for a few more days. It might be the only time we have to get to know each other, alone, for a while."

"She has a family?" asked Will, then said, "Oh, the Lolas. Is that where she lives?"

Cat smiled. " 'The Lolas.' Aren't they magnificent? Jason told me that you were there."

"They're goddesses," said Pen.

"Exactly what I thought when I met them," said Cat. "Yes, Marisol and her husband and her little boy, my *nephew,* if you can believe it, live in the small house in back, the one painted yellow."

"You know, we might have met them," said Will. "We met a lot of people."

"You did meet her mother. Jason said so," said Cat. "Lola Graciela."

"So, wait a minute," said Pen, confused. "Your father was married to Lola Graciela? They lived at his family's house?"

"Briefly," said Cat. "That is, they were married briefly. But she's lived at his family's house for close to forty years."

"Wow, so even after he left, she stayed, she and Marisol," said Will. "That's pretty amazing."

"They don't find it amazing, I don't think," said Cat. "Marisol and her mom were part of the family by then. It's just how they do things here."

"You're lucky," said Pen a little wistfully, "to be part of that."

"I am straight-up blessed," said Cat with fervor.

She stood up and waved to Marisol, who began to gather her belongings, and Will stood, too. Pen knew he couldn't help it, that it was his dyed-in-the-wool courtliness kicking in, but she felt betrayed. There they both stood, as if standing up were fine, as if anyone could possibly be leaving.

"Wait!" said Pen, flustered. "Sit down! We need to make a plan. When will we see you? When are you coming back?"

"Oh," said Cat blankly, "I thought I told you. I'm not."

"You mean never?" said Will.

"Well, I don't know," said Cat slowly. "I'm extending my visit for as long as I can, and then, well, I'm thinking of applying for permanent residency."

She didn't meet their eyes but began rummaging through her tote bag. She took out a small, bright red leather case, out of which she pulled a card.

Reluctantly, Pen got to her feet. *She is not actually going to hand me a business card,* thought Pen, but that's just what Cat did. Pen stared down at it without really seeing it.

"It's my e-mail address," said Cat.

She walked around the table and hugged Pen.

"I loved seeing you," she said. "Be happy together—that's an order!"

Pen pulled back to look at Cat. "You're saying good-bye?"

That's when Pen saw it, a glimmer of impatience passing over Cat's vivid, black-eyed, smiling face. *She has moved on,* Pen understood with bewildered shock. *We are only part of who she used to be, not of who she is now.*

"I might have to come back to deal with the divorce or pack my things or something," said Cat. "In which case, I will definitely and absolutely call you."

Pen knew when she was being thrown a bone, but, still, she said, "But we only just found you!"

"I know," said Cat regretfully.

She put her arms around Will and kissed his cheek. Then she put her sunglasses on and gave them both a winsome, affectionate smile.

"And I will stay found. I promise," she told them. "But I also have to stay here."

Chapter Twenty-One

BECAUSE PEN AND AUGUSTA HAD A SIX-HOUR LAYOVER IN NEW York and, more significantly, because Pen and Will could not stand the thought of saying good-bye to each other, when their plane landed at JFK, they rented a car and drove to Philadelphia. It was just the three of them, Jason having decided to remain in the Philippines for "a few more days."

"I'm not staying because I think I can talk Cat into changing her mind," he had told them. "I know when I'm beat. I guess I just can't stand the thought of going home to our empty house, yet."

Will and Pen hadn't really believed him, but if they had learned anything about Jason, and they had learned a lot, it was that, once he had made up his mind to do something, there was no talking him out of it.

"He's steadfast," said Pen admiringly, "persevering."

"Delusional," added Will, "quixotic." But Pen could tell that Will admired him, too.

Jason had gone with them to the airport in Cebu, and before she had left him, after Augusta had cried and covered his face with kisses and Will had shaken his hand and told him to keep in touch, Pen had grabbed him by his enormous shoulders and said, "Listen to me: you keep the faith, all right? You will find someone who loves you the way you deserve to be loved. I know it," and he had given her a crooked smile and said, "Isn't it weird how you kind of like me, now?" and Pen had agreed that it was.

At a rest stop, Will called a hotel near Jamie's apartment and reserved a room.

"You could stay with us," Pen told him.

He had leaned in almost close enough to kiss her and, with a wicked gleam in his green, gold, orange eyes, said, "Or—you could stay with me."

When they were about half an hour away, Pen called Jamie on his cell phone to tell him they were coming.

"Did you find her?" he asked.

"We did," Pen told him, settling in. "It's kind of a long story, but basically, she went there to (a) leave her husband and (b) find her—"

"Yeah, yeah. Details later," said Jamie cutting her off. "Cut to the chase: Is Cat still smokin' hot or what?"

"You're a degenerate," said Pen.

"Just hurry up and bring my Gusty girl home, okay? I'll leave work early."

Pen smiled. "You miss the crushed goldfish crackers all over the floor, don't you?"

"And I'm getting way too much sleep," said Jamie. "It's completely out of hand."

As soon as Pen opened the door of the apartment, Augusta was a blur of hair and skinny legs and wild screeches, rushing Jamie like a miniature linebacker.

"Oof!" he said, staggering backward. "What were they feeding you in the Philippines?"

"Pizza!" shrieked Augusta. "And *pancit*! And the weensiest bananas you never saw!"

"You're right," said Jamie pulling her onto his lap and smiling at Pen through Augusta's tangled hair. "I never did."

For a moment, Pen just stood, watching them, until she noticed the flowers on the table, calla lilies, tall, white, posing like fashion models in a curvaceous vase.

"Jamie! You bought us flowers!"

Jamie gave the flowers a sidelong glance. "Uh, yeah, well, welcome home, right? Hey, where are the rest of your bags?"

"Oh," said Pen, with a wink at Augusta, "they'll be here shortly."

"Shhh," Augusta told Jamie. "It's a surprise."

When Jamie saw Will, he set Augusta on the ground and stood up. "Will Wadsworth, as I live and breathe. So good to see you, man."

"Good to see you, too, Jamie," said Will, grinning. "You got me flowers and everything."

"Come here, you little ray of sunshine," said Jamie, and he walked across the room and clenched Will in a hug that caused him to grimace and say, "I guess you started working out since I last saw you."

"Being famous must agree with you," said Jamie. "You look good, brother."

"Not 'brother,'" Pen said quickly. "Anything else but 'brother.'"

Jamie stared at Pen, and then a smile started in his eyes and spread across his face. "Well, maybe 'brother-in-law' would be a better choice?" he said, raising an eyebrow.

"Don't get ahead of yourself, big guy," said Pen.

"Smartest thing you've ever done. One of the only smart things you've ever done," said Jamie to Pen. "What happened over there? Did you get hit on the head with a coconut?"

"Anyway, I was thinking I'd move in here, too," said Will, sizing up the apartment. "You don't mind, do you?"

Pen knew he was joking, but for a few seconds, she was transported back to the Lolas' house, grandmothers, babies, nephews, sisters, everyone together, and she felt a pang of longing.

"Hey," said Jamie, opening his hands in welcome, "always room for one more."

LATER, PEN WOULD WONDER IF WILL HAD PLANNED TO TELL HER right away, as soon as she arrived at his hotel room, because when he opened the door, he wasn't smiling. His face was unusually serious, taut and focused and full of intention, but overcome by her own intentions, Pen didn't let him say anything, just stepped inside and pulled him into her, sliding her hands under his shirt, so that before the door was even closed, he was pressing her against it, lifting a fistful of hair to kiss her neck, her collarbone, and a minute went by filled with nothing but the ragged noise of their breathing, before he pulled away and said, "Wait."

"It's okay. I don't want to wait," Pen said, gasping, thinking he was worried about rushing her, his innate sense of chivalry compelling him to slow down, which turned out to be true, but not in the way she thought.

"Before we do this, there's something I have to tell you," he said, and despite his solemn tone, she wouldn't have been afraid, except that when she looked into his eyes, that's what she saw there: fear. He sat down on the edge of the bed.

"Can you sit for a second?" he asked. "And let me talk to you?"

"No," she said, her voice pleading, like a child's voice. "Please. Let's not talk right now."

"We have to. I'm sorry. I should have told you this before."

She shivered, took a breath, and instead of sitting on the bed next to him, she walked over to an ottoman a few feet away, sat on its very edge, and folded her hands in her lap. *Let him not be sick. Oh God, let him not be dying.*

"I was at your father's funeral," said Will.

This was so unexpected that it took Pen a few seconds to understand what he had said. She shook head. "No."

"I didn't follow Cat's rule, about not looking each other up. I read it online, first the newspaper report, then the obituary, and I came."

"So I was right. You were there." For a moment, all she could do was marvel at the fact that she had sensed him—and she had felt his presence in the church more acutely than she had felt anything all that long, numb day—and, lo and behold, she had been right. But as the awful implications of his having been there began to dawn on her, the wonder and satisfaction dissipated, and she demanded, "Why? What was the point of coming if you didn't even let me see you?"

"I came into the church before it got crowded, and I saw you right away, just the back of your head, but that was enough to know it was you. I saw your mom next to you, and I saw Augusta, sitting on your lap."

"Augusta." At the mention of Augusta, she slid back on the ottoman, farther away from him. "Did you know she was my daughter? Did you even know I had a daughter?"

"Not until I read the obituary."

"But if you knew about her before you came, why would that stop you from coming up to me?"

Will looked down at his lap and started to speak, but, like a slap, it struck her and she said, "Patrick."

"He was next to you. He had his arm around you."

Pen tried to remember. "I guess he did. I don't remember."

She looked at Will reproachfully. "But so what? Who cares if he was there? Why should that have mattered?"

"It mattered because I was in love with you." He shook his head in disbelief. "Didn't you know that? Maybe I always had been, but I only really knew it after Cat left."

Pen absorbed this information and realized that she wasn't shocked by it. For years, she had denied how Will felt about her to everyone, especially to herself, but all along, deep down, she had known.

"If you loved me, that was all the more reason for you to come be with me because whatever Patrick did, it didn't work. We were way past the point where he could even reach me. He helped with Augusta, but he didn't help *me*."

A wave of anger surged through Pen. "*You* could have, though. You are the one person who could have, on almost the worst day of my life, but you didn't. Why? Because you were *jealous*?" The word *jealous* came out as a contemptuous hiss. "I needed you!"

She had meant to hurt him, to make him feel guilty, and she could read in his eyes that it had worked.

"I didn't know that!" he said, a note of desperation in his voice. "You looked like a family. I didn't see any place for me there. Yeah, I was jealous. I can be a jerk like anyone else. But if I had known that you wanted me, if I thought I could have helped you in any way, I would have stayed."

Pen sat there, trembling with fury and staring at his face, the face that she loved, and she felt that his beauty was an affront, an indignity. He could have helped her. He could have *saved* her, and he had let her down. Then she thought of something that deepened her anger, turned it from hot to cold.

"Maybe I could have lived with all of this," she said icily. "But do you know what I can't live with?"

"Don't say that," he said. "I know what you're talking about, it's that I didn't tell you before, and I know I should have, but don't say you can't live with it."

Pen leaped to her feet.

"When I told you about Augusta, at the reunion, after our bike ride, you acted like you didn't already know. When I told you that my *father died*, you acted like you didn't know, and don't use the excuse that we were playing the four-sentence game and that you weren't supposed to comment on anything I said because that is such a cop-out." By the end of this, she was shouting.

Will watched her pace.

"And what about the night on the porch in Bohol? I had never told anyone that story who I didn't have to tell, but I told you. I trusted you! How could you not have told me that you already knew?"

He stood up and touched her, ran his hands along her arms, tried to look into her face, but she yanked herself away.

"Pen, I wanted to. I know how lame this sounds; I know it might sound like I'm making it up, but, listen, you were talking and I was with you. I wasn't thinking about the newspaper article. I was listening to you tell the story, and you were so sad, and I wasn't thinking about anything but how terrible it was that you had to go through what you went through. It wasn't until you said the thing about thinking I was at the funeral that it even occurred to me that I should tell you."

"But you didn't tell me, and not telling me is the same thing as lying."

"I'm telling you now."

"Why?"

Will looked startled. "What?"

"Why tell me at all? Why not just let it go?"

He gave her a confused look, as though her question didn't make any sense. "Because I want to be with you, and I don't mean a relationship. I mean a life. How fair would it be to start that with something already between us that I know about and you don't?"

Fair. What a Will thing to say. Pen felt herself soften at this, just a little, but somehow, that wasn't what she wanted. She wanted to stay mad. For reasons she could not explain, staying mad felt good, even hurting him felt good. Her bag was next to the door where she had dropped it. Deliberately, she walked over to it and picked it up.

"What are you doing?" asked Will.

"I can't do this. I have to go."

"Go?" Will sounded stunned. "Come on, you can't really believe that leaving is the right thing."

Pen turned on him, eyes blazing. "What the hell did you think would happen?"

"Do you think I didn't know it was a risk?" asked Will, exasperated, throwing out his hands. "But I thought you would forgive me. I still think so."

"God, do you know how arrogant that sounds?"

"We're supposed to be together. Believing that is not arrogance; neither is having faith in you."

"Faith in me? Like I'm supposed to fix this? You're the one who screwed it up!"

Will flared at this. "I did! I made a lot of mistakes. But what about you?"

"Me. *Me?* I didn't do anything."

"Exactly. You talk about how much you needed me, but I was only at the funeral in the first place because I decided to come. If you wanted me, you could have called me. You know I would have been there in a second."

"You can't be serious. My father was *dead.*" She threw the words at him.

"And I'm not just talking about the funeral. You say a lot about how much you missed me all those years we were apart, but you never called and told me that."

"You are the one who left!"

Will nodded, accepting this. "I know, and I shouldn't have. I wanted our friendship to turn into something else, and I thought maybe you wanted that, too, or that you would at least be open to it, but you had twisted the three of us into an *idea,* this pure, untouchable thing."

"We were." Pen began to cry. "We were special."

"We *were* special. It's not an exaggeration to say that you and Cat saved my life, more than once. But we were three people. We weren't a religion."

"Who knew you could be so mean?" she said. She felt stung, right on the edge of hating him.

Will didn't apologize or even react, just said in a quieter voice, "But I should have stayed, anyway. I should have been more like Jason."

Pen snapped her head up and said, mockingly, " 'Delusional'? 'Quixotic'?"

"Yeah, he carried it too far, but he *tried.* When he finally gives up, he'll know that he did everything he could. I should have fought for you, been less proud, more patient, made deals with the devil, whatever. I should never have left."

"Well, you did. I stayed and you left."

Will made a disgusted sound. "Don't you get sick of that? Feeling abandoned."

"I was abandoned!"

"And you didn't do one thing about it. All you had to do was call. I don't know what Cat would have done, but I would have been there so fast. Why don't you ask yourself why you never did?"

"Stop it," she said bitterly. "Shut up. Why are you doing this?"

Will sighed. "I love you. I've never hurt you on purpose in my life, but we need to say these things to each other."

She glared at him and said, "You shouldn't have told me you were at the funeral." She knew it didn't make sense, to go from being angry that he hadn't told her to angry that he had, but that's how she felt. "You ruined everything."

He said, "I knew you would be mad. I mean, I didn't think you'd be *this* mad." A glimmer of a smile. "The thing is," he said gently, "if you end things between us because of this, you would have ended them eventually anyway."

Pen didn't know how to answer this. She couldn't even process what it meant. She felt knotted and furious and wretched.

"But I don't think you will," said Will.

With two fingers, he touched her temple. He picked up a piece of her hair and kissed it. " 'Love is an imperative,' remember you said that? And this time, I'm not going anywhere."

Pen felt herself giving way, so she searched for a last reservoir of anger and found it, right in the middle of the memory of herself curled like a wounded animal on her childhood bed, a year after her dad had died.

"Fine," she said, "I'll save you the trouble."

She turned and tugged open the door.

"Hey, come on, this is Will. Could you please look at me?"

No way was she turning around. She braced herself for his touch, but it didn't come.

"Stay and get through this with me," he said.

"I feel like you trampled on my father's death, on our friendship, everything that is sacred to me. I'm going home," she said. "You should, too."

BY THE TIME SHE GOT TO THE APARTMENT, THROUGH SHEER FORCE of will, she had stopped crying. It was only seven o'clock. Despite the jet lag, Augusta might have been awake, and Pen couldn't let her see her like that. When she walked in, Jamie was watching television. He switched it off when he saw her face.

"Oh, crap, what happened?"

Pen shook her head. "I don't want to talk about it."

She went into her bedroom, grabbed an ancient duffel bag, and, indiscriminately began stuffing clothes into it. Jamie followed her and leaned against the door frame.

"You really think you're gonna need those long underwear?"

Pen sighed. "All my summer clothes are still in the suitcase."

"So—what? You guys had a fight?"

"Something like that. Can you stay with Augusta tonight?"

"Sure, where are you going? Back to Will's hotel?"

"That's over," said Pen, stomping into the bathroom for her toothbrush. "I want to see Mom."

"Hey! Crazy person!" In the bathroom mirror, she could see Jamie behind her, waving his hands in the air to get her attention. "You need to stay and work this out. People are allowed to have fights without the world ending, even you and Will."

Ignoring this, she brushed past Jamie and headed for the front door.

"Mom can't fix this for you," said Jamie, catching hold of her arm. "What are you thinking?"

Pen spun around to face him. "Could you mind your own business? Is that possible?"

Jamie's gray eyes grew flinty. "How many chances did you give Patrick?"

Pen turned her face away.

"So is that your policy?" asked Jamie. "Special deals for assholes and deadbeats. But for good guys, ones who might actually stick around and not suck, it's one strike and you're out."

"You don't know what you're talking about."

"Because that's brilliant, Pen. Really. That's genius. Way to go."

The phone rang, and even though the last thing she wanted to do was to have a phone conversation, she didn't want to talk to Jamie, either. She answered it.

"Hello."

"Hello." A woman's voice, unfamiliar, friendly. "Hey, this is Pen, isn't it?"

"It is." Pen rooted around in her handbag for her keys.

"Hi, Pen, welcome home. This is Susan, Susan Davis. Is Jamie there?"

"Oh, yeah, he's definitely here."

She turned around, and Jamie was standing there. He picked up her keys off the telephone table and tossed them to her, and by some miracle, she caught them in her free hand.

"Happy trails," he said.

"Don't tell him where I'm going," she said, and she thrust the phone at him and left.

THE ANGER CARRIED PEN ALL THE WAY OUT OF THE CITY, WHOOSHED her effortlessly past the billboard emblazoned with the ballerina's sculpted back, past the X-rated video store, through the narrow South Twenty-Sixth Street tunnel that she had always hated, past the DON'T FLY TO THE AIRPORT sign that she, Will, and Cat had always liked, past the oil refinery with its flames and towers and plumes of steam, and over the bridge, before dumping her onto I-95 and deserting her completely.

For several miles, she didn't think at all. She felt dazed, tingly, bruised, vaguely convalescent. What seeped in first was a baffled amazement: *How* had she gotten so angry? She wasn't an angry person in general, but she had given herself to it so willingly, even with a kind of relish, like a person swan-diving into a burning lake. What had Will said? That he had never hurt her on purpose in his life, but that's just what she had done to him. Hurt him and felt better for having done it. The thought filled her with so much shame that she almost scurried away from it, but at the last second, she gritted her teeth. *You have to understand this,* she insisted, and with deliberation, she began.

She had told Will that the part she couldn't live with was the lie: the way he kept the secret, even through her telling the story of her father's murder. He should have told her, that much was abundantly clear. He had chickened out, failed to step up, turned himself, in one fell swoop, from the most honest man she had ever known into a liar. No matter how you sliced it, he was wrong, ignoble, and she was justifiably aggrieved.

But when she considered the lie now, from within the small, safe space of the car (*hermit thrush*), with her hands on the wheel and the clear black sky overhead, she realized that it was something she could understand. She imagined his struggling with how to say it, how to edge it in, between her heartbroken story and his own grief (tears— *tears*—on his face, his hand against her cheek). If she were in Will's place, she might have wondered how telling would make anything better, how that particular truth could possibly set anyone free; she might have worried that telling would drive away the person she had loved for years. She might have let the moment for truth-telling slip right by.

No, the thing that had pushed her over the edge and into rage had not been the lie of omission, but the thing omitted: he had not been with her at her father's funeral.

Even this, she could understand. She remembered his stricken eyes, his voice telling her that if he had only known she needed him, he would have stayed. She had believed him then, and she believed him now. Still, that didn't change—nothing changed—the fact that Will hadn't helped her, he hadn't saved her from not only that hard, sorrowful day, but from the two hard, sorrowful years that followed it.

And there it was, the reason for her fury: she had made her suffering Will's fault.

It was *his fault!* a voice inside her cried, high and thready, like a child's voice.

But what could he have done? He could have put his arms around her. He could have told her he was sorry for her loss, and the words would have been different from other people's words and would have been in his voice, and they would have soothed her. He could have come back into her life and been her friend and e-mailed her and called her on the phone. He could have flown out for the first anniversary bike ride and the second and ridden beside her and made her feel less lost.

See all the things he could have done? wailed the angry child.

Yes, she answered, *and your father would still be dead.*

Pen had raged against Will with a child's rage because he hadn't fixed it, hadn't made it better, but Pen knew that losing someone you loved was like a virus, and people could make you soup and hold your hand and press cool washcloths against your face, and you might feel better for a moment, but the virus would still be there, on the other side of the moment, waiting, and all you could do was get through it—cough, fever, chills, body aches, crying jags, devouring loneliness, bursts of rage—step by painful step. Pen was getting through it. She was learning how to keep her father, as Lola Fe had said. But she wasn't there, yet, and that was no one's fault, not Will's, not even her own.

Oh, Will, my friend, forgive me.

MAYBE BECAUSE WHEN PEN WAS ALMOST TO HER MOTHER'S HOUSE, she remembered Jamie saying, "Mom can't fix this," or maybe because she suspected that her mother wouldn't validate her breaking up with Will, or because she suspected that she would, or because Pen just wanted to be alone for a little while more (and she knew that as soon as she pulled into the driveway, her mom would be running out the door to greet her), when Pen drove into her neighborhood, with her house still a half mile away, she pulled over, parked in front of someone else's house, got out of the car, slung the duffel bag over her shoulder, and began to walk.

The air rang with the high, heartbeat singing of cicadas. The trees stood tall next to the street. Pen passed house after familiar house. Her mind was loaded with things to figure out, but she was tired after all that concentrated thinking in the car, and for the duration of the walk, at least, she decided to let it wander. She thought about the tarsiers, and the snorkeling, about Jason's face when Cat told him he shouldn't have come. She thought about the Lolas and about the pride in Cat's voice when she said "My sister." She heard the voice in her head that was not the tarsier's saying, *"But we're here now, aren't we?"* She heard Will telling her to ask herself why she had missed him all those years but never called. She heard Will saying that he had wanted their friendship to change, saying, "We weren't a religion." She heard Jamie saying that she only gave second chances to the deadbeats, the ones who wouldn't stay.

The thoughts began to coalesce, to press forward more and more steadily, moving Pen toward a point she couldn't see, but before she got there, she was standing in front of her mother's house. With a touch of peevishness, she noted that she needn't have worried about pulling into the driveway because there was already a car in it, or not a car, but a truck, a dark, slightly battered, mud-spattered pickup that looked as though, unlike most of the pickups around there—and there weren't many—it might actually be used to pick things up. As Pen looked at the truck, a bell began to ring, faintly, someplace in the back of her mind.

Except for the porch light with its veil of bugs, the front of the house was dark, so Pen walked around to the back and saw that the kitchen lights were on, turning the windows to bright saffron squares. From where she stood, Pen didn't have a clear view of the kitchen, but she could sense movement, shadows on the yellow walls, and, without making a conscious decision to spy, she bent her knees, hunched her back, and padded, catlike, to the lowest window, staying close to the ground and close to the brick walls of the house so as to evade the sensors on the garage floodlights.

I love you, house, she thought, with her heart in her throat. *I love you, Daddy.* She stood on tiptoe and looked.

They were washing dishes. If they had been kissing or dancing or even cooking, Pen's reaction might have been different, but they stood there doing the dishes, Mark Venverloh at the sink, his back to Pen, her mother next to him, drying a pan (the old cast-iron skillet she used to make cornbread) with a dishtowel (one of the fish-print ones from the store in South Bethany that sold kitchenware, sandwiches, and the best seafood salad in the world), before holding it up and eyeing it to make sure it was clean. They weren't talking, just working, performing this comfortable, commonplace task in the kitchen in which Ben Calloway had made coffee for his wife every morning—for what had to have been thousands of mornings—since before Pen was born until the day he died. Pen wasn't resentful or jealous or hurt. She understood that she was looking at the bravest thing she had ever seen: her mother, after all she had lost, after she had broken apart and believed she would die, starting all over again, giving herself, plunging in, risking everything.

Pen crept away from the window. She walked back down the driveway, the sight of her mother and Mark still aglow inside her head, and sat down on the brick retaining wall at the edge of the yard. She looked out at the house across the street, at the particular darkness of neighborhoods, easeful, full of families that you couldn't see but knew were there, and, gingerly, took up the question of why she had, for six years, never called Will, who most surely would have come.

You know why, she told herself. *Because of that.*

Because of what?

Because you knew he would come.

Yes, he would have come. Of course, he would have.

He would have come and he would have been there, with you, the way he was with you at the summerhouse after Cat left, the way he was with you in the hotel room in Philadelphia, and you would have had to run away or make him leave.

Or I could have stayed.

And your life would have changed.

I would have had to love him.

You would have had to give him everything.

Jason, Cat, Will, her mother, the Lolas, everyone around her giving themselves away to the people they loved. Suddenly, she heard the unfamiliar voice from earlier that night: "This is Susan, Susan Davis. Is Jamie there?"

Jamie.

Even Jamie. Everyone and Jamie, too.

Pen reached into her bag and pulled out her phone.

CHAPTER TWENTY-TWO

As soon as his phone rang, Will knew who it was. He turned the music down.

"Pen."

"I'm sorry I kissed Damon Callas," said Pen.

Will smiled. "You mean just now?"

"I'm sorry I never called you, all those years, even though I missed you."

"You're calling me now, right?"

"Will, there are a lot of ways to run away from someone."

"Yes, I guess there are."

"Is that the Talking Heads?" she asked.

"Yes."

"Where are you?"

"In the car."

"You're driving?"

"Yes. I don't have a driver," said Will. "I'm not Armando, you know."

"So you're using the Bluetooth thing?"

"No. This isn't my car, remember?"

"You mean to tell me that you're driving and holding your phone and talking to me?"

Will laughed. *Pen.* "I love you."

"I know, but, come on, Will, hang up and find a rest stop."

"Uh, I don't think there's a rest stop anytime soon."

"Where are you?"

"Where are you?" he asked.

"Sitting on the wall outside my mom's house."

"In that case, I'm about two minutes away."

"From here?"

"One minute and fifty-six seconds. Fifty-five. Fifty-four."

"You mean you're not on your way home?" asked Pen. Will could hear the joy in her voice.

"Not unless you mean you," he told her. "I'm on my way to you."

CHAPTER TWENTY-THREE

ANOTHER MINUTE AND WILL WAS GETTING OUT OF THE CAR and walking toward her, the sight of him more astonishing than a blue starfish, than an entire coral reef. *I could watch you do that forever,* she thought, but already she was impatient, fairly leaping off the wall and into his arms.

"How did you ever find me?" she asked.

"Lola Lita arrived on a silver cloud from Mt. Olympus and told me where you were."

"Jamie," said Pen, "the little traitor."

"It wasn't his fault. I tortured him until he spilled."

"I'll bet."

Pen kissed Will's mouth, the skin beneath his left ear.

"Can we start over?" asked Pen.

"If you really want to, but I was thinking we should hang on to all of it, everything that brought us here."

Pen nodded. "You're right. That's what we'll do. Will, I want to say something."

"Uh-oh." He smiled. "Say anything you want."

"Lola Fe was right."

"Of course, she was. About what?"

"About keeping everyone."

"Gone but not gone," said Will.

"Gone but here. Like my dad, Cat, Lola Fe herself, all the Lolas, and you before you came back into my life," said Pen. "And 'gone but here' is a wonderful thing, a gift."

Will kissed Pen's forehead. Soon, the two of them would leave this spot and walk into the house together and see Pen's mother and the man she had found to love, walk into the house and into a whole changed world, but for now they would stay where they were.

"But if you can possibly swing it," Pen went on, "just plain here is better. Here is the best place anyone could ever be."

Will held her face between his hands and smiled in amazement. "And look," he said.

"I know," said Pen, looking with all of herself, with everything she had. "Here we are."

Acknowledgments

THANK YOU, THANK YOU, THANK YOU TO THE FOLLOWING people:

Jennifer Carlson, agent and precious friend, who does every single thing she does with uncanny insight and clear-eyed grace;

My lovely and gifted gift of an editor, Laurie Chittenden, and all the good people at William Morrow, including Liate Stehlik, Sharyn Rosenblum, Tavia Kowalchuk, Lynn Grady, Mike Brennan, Seale Ballenger, Shawn Nicholls, and Trish Daly.

My treasured early readers Kristina de los Santos, Dan Fertel, Susan Davis, Annie Pilson, Amanda Eyre Ward, and Sarah Davis Brandon (you are all so smart and kind);

Katie Martin for letting me steal *Middlemarchian,* Arturo de los Santos for answering my Cebu questions, John Willis for solving the mystery of the chapel window, and Annabel and Charles Teague for revealing that, in early childhood, both of them believed that the greatest jazz singer to ever live was named Elephants Gerald.

Anna Carapellotti, ballerina babysitter extraordinaire and all-around sweetheart;

My parents for loving me unreservedly and for cheering loudest of all;

Charles and Annabel Teague, brave, exuberant, and funny children among whom I am blessed to spend my days;

And David Teague, best writer, best reader, best friend, best everything.

This book is dedicated to my first family, but there have been so many families since, in Charlottesville and Houston and Philadelphia and Cebu and Wilmington and places in between. Some are gone but here. Some are just plain here.

I'm keeping all of you.